International Economics

International Economics

An Introduction to Theory and Policy

RAJAT ACHARYYA

Second Edition

OXFORD
UNIVERSITY PRESS

OXFORD
UNIVERSITY PRESS

Great Clarendon Street, Oxford, ox2 6dp,
United Kingdom

Oxford University Press is a department of the University of Oxford.
It furthers the University's objective of excellence in research, scholarship,
and education by publishing worldwide. Oxford is a registered trademark of
Oxford University Press in the UK and in certain other countries

First Edition published in 2014
Second Edition published in 2022

Published in the United States of America by Oxford University Press
198 Madison Avenue, New York, NY 10016, United States of America

British Library Cataloguing in Publication Data
Data available

Library of Congress Control Number: 2022939680

ISBN-13: 978-0-19-286514-4

DOI: 10.1093/oso/9780192865144.001.0001

Contents

Tables, Figures, and Boxes

Tables

Figures

Boxes

Preface

Over the last three decades, the nature of economic interdependence of countries has changed quite substantially as well as qualitatively due to their rapid integration through fragmentation, outsourcing of production processes, global value chains, and greater mobility of people. International capital flows and flexible exchange rate regimes in most countries have also linked their financial markets more significantly than ever before. At the same time, more complex dimensions of international exchange have emerged with the growing share of services in world trade. Development of ICT infrastructure has unlocked potentials for virtual and digital trade, which has emerged as a prominent feature of international economic exchange. Services in particular, which was earlier seen primarily as 'non-traded', have become globally traded aided by the ICT, such as financial services (like banking and insurance) and business services (like software development, call centres, consultancy services including medical advice, and the like). On the other hand, environmental issues now govern to a large extent promotion or restrictions on merchandise trade. The usual gains from trade thus need to be weighed against potential environmental degradation that freer international trade may cause for policy decisions regarding trade promotion or restrictions. Often national policies regarding environmental protection are unilaterally optimum but globally sub-optimum, and this calls for coordination of policies. Regional trading blocs and agreements provide scope for such policy coordination. On the other hand, due to alleged unfair trade practices by the developing countries by not implementing labour standards and TRIPS (or patent protection) strictly, the EU and the United States have been mandatorily linking these issues with their negotiations on free trade agreements with the developing countries.

Being a textbook meant for beginners, dealing with all the complexities and intricacies of international trade and payments in larger details is beyond its scope. Instead, the book aims to provide students the basic tools and foundations of principles underlying international exchange, trade policies, and exchange rate policies, which will enable them to analyse issues of a more complex nature at a later stage. The approach taken in this book is distinctly different from most of the existing textbooks on international economics in more than one way. Instead of model-specific discussions on international trade theory, this book begins with basic concepts like the basis, pattern, and gains from trade, characteristics of international equilibrium, and terms of trade, in the context of a general trading environment of open economies. Having developed the basic tools of international exchange and gains thereof, specific models of trade are introduced as alternative theoretical explanations for the basic principles of such exchanges.

WHAT IS NEW IN THIS EDITION

With rapid changes in the qualitative nature of global trade over the last one decade, in particular, inclusion of new contents and reorientation of some of the chapters have become highly relevant. International exchange has been taking place increasingly in intermediate and semi-finished products and in value chains along the vertical stages of production. This *vertical specialization* is in contrast to comparative advantage of nations in *different commodities*, or *the horizontal specialization*. With the advent of globalization on the one hand, and development of digital technology (ICT), on the other hand, virtual/digital trade has emerged as a prominent feature of service trade. After introducing these dimensions of international exchange and trade in Chapter 1, a detailed discussion of global value chains has been included in Chapter 16, and of virtual trade in intermediate services driven by time zone differences of countries in Chapter 17.

Welfare Property of International Equilibrium and revisiting the gains from trade theorem in light of that have been introduced in Chapter 4 on International Equilibrium and the Terms of Trade. The role of relative size of countries, or their respective workforces, is more precisely explained and exact conditions for post-trade complete specialization has been derived in Chapter 5 on Ricardian model of trade. Chapter 6 includes several new discussions. First, the price definition of factor abundance of a country is defined and a distinction of this definition from the physical definition is drawn (see Box 6.1). Second, additional explanations, insights, and implications of important theorems like output and price magnification effects and the Factor Price Equalization theorem have been discussed. In Chapter 8 on Theories of Intra Industry Trade, two theoretical discussions have been added. First is the factor endowment explanations for low-quality phenomenon of exports of developing countries, and the other is the firm heterogeneity model of Melitz (2003) that studies which firms in an industry export and which firms produce for the domestic market.

There are innumerable policies against the use of child labour like fines on employing firms, trade sanctions, boycotts of goods produced by child labour, and the like. None of these policies, however, have worked in reducing the incidence of child labour to any significant extent. It is important, therefore, to understand the supply side and demand side explanations for the prevalence of child labour in order to formulate effective policies to eliminate this menace. Box 18.5 in Chapter 18 summarizes these explanations.

Recent examples of interventions by the central banks of India and China to stabilize or defend pegged exchange rates of their respective currencies are added in Chapter 22 on International Currency Systems and Exchange Rate Regimes (see Box 22.4 and Box 22.5). An elaborate discussion on speculative attacks on domestic currency narrowing down its variations near the bands in a Target Zone is also presented. A new chapter (as Chapter 25, with the Chapter 25 of the First Edition being re-numbered as Chapter 26) has been added wherein financial crises in the developing world, and most significantly, occurring under overvalued pegged (or crawling peg) exchange rate regimes with or without capital and exchange controls have been discussed. Two major crises during the last two decades of the last century have been the focus in this context. First, the 1980 Debt Crisis in Latin America that led to a lost decade of development for these countries, and the policy issues involved in and management of the crises. Second, the dual financial crisis—balance-of-payments and banking crises—in Asia during 1997–98, that also spilled over to other parts of the globe, particularly in Latin America and East Europe.

Apart from these additional contents, data sets, tables, and charts have been updated throughout the book. New exercises are included in several chapters that will help the students comprehend the discussions in the chapters better.

ACKNOWLEDGEMENT

I have inherited intellectual debts over a long period of time spanning over almost 40 years, through repeated interactions on various issues in trade theory and policy with my teachers, co-authors, colleagues, and, of course, my students at different universities and institutes in India and abroad. It will be a rather long list to mention each of them, but I recollect and gratefully acknowledge contributions of all of them. It has been eight years since the First Edition of this textbook was published. During this long period I have gained new insights while teaching different aspects of international exchange and trade policy choices using the materials from the First Edition, and interacting with the students in the class. This Second Edition has been shaped much by these interactions, and also by informal discussions on many of the issues with Asis Banerjee, Dyuti S. Banerjee, Bill Ethier, Partha Pratim Ghosh, Kausik Gupta, Arye Hillman, Saibal Kar, Ngo Van Long, Surajit Mazumdar, Arup Mallik, Sugata Marjit, Biswajit Nag, Ranjanendra Nag, Pulin Nayak, Partha Ray, and C. Veeramani. Thanks also go to Shrimoyee Ganguly for providing valuable inputs and excellent research assistance on many of the new and additional materials of this Edition.

June 2022

Introduction

International economics is all about economic interactions between nations. Such interactions take many forms such as exchange of goods and services between economic agents of different countries, movement of labour and capital from one country to another, and competition and coordination among nations regarding economic policies to regulate exchange of goods and services and factor movements. Like the basic motive of an economic agent is to have a more desirable basket of resources in her possession, and thereby to increase her utility level, through exchange of goods with others, international trade in the eighteenth century was viewed by nations as a means of acquiring wealth for themselves through voluntary exchange of goods and services rather than through the exercise of military power. In the early history of such international trade, exchange was primitive and simple and was mostly confined to basic goods like cloth, consumables like wine, factors of production such as raw materials, and precious metals like gold and silver. But over centuries, international exchange has become more complex in nature, particularly with cross-country location of different stages of production processes and exchange of services of different kinds. It has also become more pervasive and important in the present era of globalization in which nations are increasingly integrated into the world economy. Nations are now more closely linked with each other than ever before. Business strategies of firms and economic policies of the government in a particular country must now take into account what firms and governments in other countries are doing. This has made the study of international economics and understanding the principles of international exchange all the more relevant and important.

WHAT DOES INTERNATIONAL ECONOMICS STUDY?

The subject matter of international economics can be divided into three broad categories—the theory of international trade and factor flows; analyses of unilateral, multilateral, and coordinated trade policies; and the theory of balance of payments and exchange rate. The theory of international trade and factor flows examines the basic principles of international exchange and analyses the consequences of international trade in goods, services, and factors of production. The consequences are usually evaluated in terms of national welfare, income redistribution, employment, and output growth. The theory of trade policy, on the other hand, is concerned with designing optimal national policies to regulate international trade in goods, services, and inputs and achieving more desirable outcomes than free trade. Finally, the theory of balance of payments and exchange rate analyses the monetary implications of the international exchange of goods and services and factor flows.

Three Basic Issues: Causes, Pattern, and Consequences of International Trade

There are three basic issues that the theory of international trade is primarily concerned with. First, when do countries engage in international trade in goods and services? What are the factors that drive goods and factors to flow from one country to the other? In the neoclassical theory of international trade in the tradition of David Ricardo, Eli Heckscher, Bertil Ohlin, and Paul Samuelson, the dissimilarities between countries in fundamentals like production technology, factor endowments, and tastes and preferences for goods and services provide the basis of trade. Such dissimilarities translate into differences in prices of goods (and services) across nations, or what is known as the *comparative advantage* of nations, and lead to cross-country arbitrage—buying cheap and selling dear—and hence international exchange or trade. Alternatives to this explanation of comparative advantage and arbitrage in international trade are based on economies of scale, product market imperfections, and product differentiation in the new trade theories that were developed in the late 1970s and early 1980s by Paul Krugman, James Brander, and Elhanan Helpman among others. For example, pricing above marginal cost under monopoly production of the same good in each country generates scope for national monopolists to dump their production in each other's markets and yet make profits. International trade in an identical good thus takes place through *reciprocal dumping* even when countries are similar, resulting in the same prices of similar goods everywhere and thereby leaving no scope for arbitrage.

The second issue involves two questions: Why do we observe certain patterns of trade between countries? Why do some countries export manufactured goods such as cotton textiles or leather goods and others export agricultural goods like rice? Even within the former group of countries, the pattern of trade varies widely according to the capital and skill content of manufacturing exports. In general, developed countries are observed to export more capital-intensive and more skill-intensive goods. Developing countries, on the other hand, are typically exporters of unskilled-labour-intensive commodities. At the same time, there are developing countries like Brazil, China, and India that export a sizeable volume of high-technology and skill-intensive goods and services like chemical products (including pharmaceutical products), scientific instruments, software, and office equipment, along with low-skill-intensive manufacturing goods like cotton textiles and leather manufactures. All these examples of diverse trade patterns of nations, in fact, reflect their dissimilarities; that is, the pattern of trade is also determined by the principles of comparative advantage. Heckscher and Ohlin, for example, postulated that countries that are relatively labour abundant will export relatively labour-intensive goods and import relatively capital-intensive goods from countries that are relatively capital abundant. This later came to be known as the *Heckscher–Ohlin theorem.*

In contrast to these positive questions concerning international trade, the third issue is the normative one of whether international exchange and trade are always gainful for trading nations. The *Gains from Trade* theorem postulates that under certain market and technological conditions, international exchange of goods and services by atomistic agents raises the national welfare of *all* trading nations if such exchanges follow the principles of comparative advantage. But in cases where prices fail to signal the true comparative advantage, such as when markets are imperfectly competitive or when externalities are present in production and consumption, international trade may not be welfare improving for all trading nations. More importantly perhaps, even when gains are ensured for all nations, international trade and exchange do not benefit *all* economic agents. It creates winners as well as losers within a trading nation.

What this means is that international exchange and trade redistributes incomes of economic agents within a country. This raises serious concern about who gains and who loses as a consequence of international trade. If unskilled workers lose, then with most of the poor being unskilled workers, international trade would make the poor poorer. In such a case, the Gains from Trade theorem, which means that international trade makes the country *as a whole* better off, makes little sense. Stolper and Samuelson were the first to provide a concrete answer to this question of the income distribution effect of international exchange in the 1940s. Though their original theoretical query was in the context of imposition of an import tariff, it can be reinterpreted in the context of opening up of international trade and exchange. Owners of factors of production that are relatively abundant in a country experience a rise in their *real* incomes, whereas owners of factors of production that are scarce experience a decline in their *real* incomes after the country opens up and engages in trade with the external world. This *Stolper–Samuelson theory* remained the cornerstone of international trade theory till it came in contradiction with empirical evidence regarding a rise in the wages of skilled workers relative to the wages of unskilled workers in most countries during the last two decades and a half. A new set of theories has since then emerged that generalizes the basic Heckscher–Ohlin–Samuelson (HOS) theory of trade to explain the observed wage inequality phenomenon.

International Trade and Output Growth

Achieving a high and sustained growth path constitutes a major economic target for countries since in public perception it is often the sole indicator of successful governance. Whether international trade augments or retards the growth process is thus another important issue in international trade theory and empirics. This issue has received much attention since the writings of Adam Smith in the late eighteenth century on the productivity gains that international trade may usher in by widening the scope of the market, thereby making greater division of labour possible. His productivity theory subsequently led to a theory of export-led growth as coined by Sir Denis Robertson in 1940. To David Ricardo, on the other hand, international trade was a way of delaying the stationary state for the fast-growing industrialized nations. Country experiences, however, do not always support the export-led growth hypothesis. More recent empirical studies by Dani Rodrik and others have refined this export-led growth hypothesis by emphasizing on the fact that *what* a country exports may matter more than *how much* it exports. High growth rate in many countries seems to have been driven more by exports of high-technology and skill-intensive goods rather than by low-skill-intensive and low-value addition goods than anything else. On the other hand, a diversified export basket, rather than a very specialized and concentrated export basket, seems to make the trade–growth relationship stronger at relatively lower stages of growth of countries. Specialization matters only after countries are already on a higher growth path.

At the same time serious concerns were raised by economists like Jagdish Bhagwati and Harry Johnson, among others, about welfare consequences of such export-led or export-biased growth. If growth caused by domestic factor accumulation augments the exports of a country, its terms of trade may move against it. This inflicts a secondary burden, which if large enough may outweigh the primary benefits of growth. Thus, growth in an open economy may be *immiserizing*. The other concern that arises and has been the subject of empirical study is the redistributive effect of growth that international trade causes. During the 1950s, Simon Kuznets argued about an inverted-U relationship between per capita income growth and income inequality. At the initial stages of growth, income inequality accentuates and beyond a threshold growth level it declines. This relationship, known as the Kuznets Curve, means that international trade may cause further income inequality through its growth impact, in addition to its short-run income redistribution effects. Growth may also be exclusive rather than inclusive as it may bypass the unskilled and the poor and benefit only the handful of rich. Faster output growth achieved by many countries in the present era of globalization and trade liberalization often has this inherent exclusiveness.

Free Trade versus Protection

Despite gains from trade, countries have often been observed, at least till the recent waves of globalization beginning in the 1980s, to restrict trade through import tariffs and non-tariff barriers. History of protectionism dates a long way back to the mercantilist idea in seventeenth- and eighteenth-century Europe that manufacturing exports should be encouraged and imports of the same should be discouraged. For raw materials, imports should be encouraged instead. The idea behind this selective trade restriction and promotion was that manufacturing production and exports are essential for development and growth and raw materials are an important component of the production for manufacturing. Later in the nineteenth century, Robert Torrens, John Stuart Mill, and Alfred Marshall argued that there exists scope for further improvement in a nation's welfare over and above the free trade level by restricting trade if the country is large enough to influence the terms of trade in its favour. This led to the theory of optimum tariff by Francis Edgeworth and Nicholas Kaldor.

The post–World War II development in the theory of international trade identified at least three more justifications for trade interventions. First, when externalities in production or consumption are present, which lead to incorrect patterns of production specialization and trade, trade intervention *might* be a better trade policy than free trade. This is, however, the theory of second best, since trade interventions cannot fully correct—and in some cases they may actually accentuate—these kind of *domestic* distortions. Second, a newly developed industry requires protection from foreign competition in its initial formative years when production and other operational costs are high. When the industry has grown sufficiently enough over time to attain its optimum scale of operation, average costs come down and it can then withstand foreign competition. The long-run gains to be had from protecting an infant industry must be thus weighed against the consumption and production losses in the short run. This is the *infant industry* argument for protection, which is essentially a dynamic argument.

Last but not least, the *strategic trade* theories provide a further justification for trade interventions. When national monopolies are large conglomerates and have market powers even in international markets for the goods that they produce, trade policies can be used by national governments to influence the international market share rivalry amongst these large monopolies to the national advantage.

However, in most of the cases discussed earlier, unilateral trade protection and promotion benefits a country at the cost of its trading partners. Thus, trading partners retaliate and this leads to multilateral trade protection, making everyone worse off. This, in turn, opens up the issue of *trade policy coordination and cooperation* by forming a regional trade bloc. Without such a binding agreement, multilateral trade liberalization within a region cannot be a self-enforcing proposition since all countries in that region will have unilateral incentives to impose tariffs on imports from others. Motivated primarily by this potential welfare gain through reciprocal market access, regional trading arrangements have proliferated since the 1990s. This has been a cause of concern as regional agreements have often overlapped and led to what Bhagwati calls the spaghetti bowl effect. Moreover, this regional approach has only slowed down the momentum in the multilateral approach to global free trade through GATT (General Agreement on Tariffs and Trade) and later WTO rounds of negotiations, and consequently raised the concern of whether the bilateral and regional approach to trade liberalization is a stepping stone or a stumbling block to multilateralism and global free trade.

Balance of Payments and Exchange Rate Regime

Values of exports and imports of goods and services and buying and selling of assets undertaken by economic agents according to principles of comparative advantage may not exactly match with each other. But a country cannot print foreign currency to meet the demand for these currencies by its importers of goods and services; that is, it will have to earn foreign currency by exporting goods and services or selling its domestic assets. So the issue that is of utmost importance is how to correct for payment imbalances when a country's receipts of foreign currency fall short of payments to be made for imports. This is linked to a country's choice of exchange rate regime. If a market-determined flexible exchange rate for its own currency vis-à-vis foreign currencies is chosen, then payment imbalances that actually mean excess demand for or excess supply of foreign currencies can be automatically corrected through changes in the exchange rate. But this comes with a cost as such exchange rate movements may cause inflation or trigger recession. A pegged exchange rate for its domestic currency, on the other hand, can insulate the real sectors of an economy from such adverse effects, but it calls for some policy interventions to correct for payment imbalances. Moreover, to meet the excess demand for foreign currency in cases of payment deficits, the monetary authority of the country must sell foreign currencies from its reserves. As we will learn from this book, this may potentially lead to a balance of payments crisis for the country in the long run when perpetual payment deficits run down reserves of foreign currencies. The country will then default on its international debt obligations as was almost the case for India in March 1991.

SCOPE AND ORGANIZATION OF THE BOOK

Given these perspectives, this textbook introduces students and researchers to the basic principles of international exchange and its causes and consequences, as expounded by David Hume in his international monetary analysis in the eighteenth century and David Ricrado in his principles of comparative advantage in the early nineteenth century, and further developed later by Eli Heckscher, Bertil Ohlin, and Paul Samuelson. More complex dimensions of trade and factor flows, intricacies of trade and exchange rate policies, international trade rules and standards, and open economy macroeconomic issues are also discussed in the later part of the book. Though this textbook is primarily meant for undergraduate students, some advanced topics are intended to take them beyond the standard undergraduate courses taught in universities and institutes around the globe. These topics can also be used as a primer for postgraduate courses on international trade theory and policy. In particular, Chapters 3, 12, 13, and 18 discuss such advanced topics, which may be skipped by for a basic undergraduate course without any loss of logical continuity. Similarly, there are a few sub-sections in some of the chapters marked as advanced topics, which may be optional segments in the basic undergraduate courses on international economics.

The prerequisite for this textbook is a basic understanding of intermediate-level microeconomics and macroeconomics, and high-school algebra. Basic concepts and issues of international economics are introduced through simple logical arguments followed by graphical illustrations. Algebra comes in only as a supplement to provide a structure to the argument, or where the issues at hand require quantification.

Part I of the book is devoted to providing answers to the three basic questions of international economics. Chapter 1 discusses the basic principles of international exchange and trade. It encompasses both the Smithian concept of absolute advantage and the Ricardian concept of comparative (cost) advantage. Public policies influencing a country's comparative advantage and pattern of trade are the added dimensions in the discussion on the basis of trade. Chapter 2 analyses when countries gain from trade and what such gains mean for different groups of economic agents within countries. Chapter 3 is meant for advanced readers who would like to know how the principles of comparative advantage can be estimated empirically. The determination of the terms of trade and properties of international equilibrium are discussed in Chapter 4.

Part II discusses alternative theories of comparative advantage and inter-industry trade whereas Part III focuses on the recent developments in the theory of intra-industry trade. The two basic models of trade that constitute the building blocks of international trade theory and policy—the Ricardian model and the HOS model—and their properties are discussed in Chapters 5 and 6, respectively. Chapter 7 discusses several digressions in the HOS model including higher dimensional issues. In contrast to these theories and models of inter-industry trade among dissimilar countries, Chapter 8 introduces alternative explanations for intra-industry trade among similar countries.

Part IV is devoted to unilateral and coordinated trade policy choices for countries. Chapters 9 and 10 examine implications of tariffs, subsidies, and non-tariff barriers to trade. Chapter 11 extends these analyses to cases of domestic and international monopolies. These market imperfections open up the possibility of a strategic use of trade policies as emphasized in more recent theories developed since the mid-1980s. Chapters 12 and 13 cover advanced topics. Political economy and endogeneity of trade policies are discussed in Chapter 12 whereas trade interventions in cases of distortions are discussed in Chapter 13. Chapter 14 examines costs and benefits of trade policy coordination among countries through regional trading arrangements. Evolution of the European Union is discussed as a case study in this context.

Part V discusses issues in input and services trade and trade–growth relationships. Different theoretical channels through which increased trade may augment output growth as well as the welfare implications of growth in an open economy are discussed in Chapter 15. An added dimension of the discussions on such a relationship is the current debate on whether growth is inclusive or exclusive. Chapter 16 studies the implications of international factor flows, foreign direct investment, and more topical issues like the fragmentation of the vertical chain of production, outsourcing and global value chain. Causes and consequences of services trade, which is growing in volume as well as in complexity, are discussed in Chapter 17. A new dimension that has been discussed in this context is virtual trade in intermediate services caused by time zone differences of countries. The emerging rules of international exchange and the role of the WTO are discussed in Part VI. Chapter 18 focuses on how product standards—labour and quality—and environmental regulations affect international exchange as new forms of non-tariff barriers. Chapter 19 introduces students to the role of the WTO and its rules in governing world trade.

Part VII is devoted to analyses of monetary issues and international currency systems. Chapter 20 studies the balance of payments account of a country, its different components, and the concepts of equilibrium and disequilibrium in the payments account. Determination of national income of an open economy and its relation to the balance of trade and current account are studied in Chapter 21. Chapter 22 narrates the evolution of international currency systems and different national exchange rate regimes. The origin of India's balance of payments crisis and the exchange rate policies introduced to manage the crisis are discussed as a case study. Chapter 23 discusses different balance of payment adjustment policies under a pegged exchange rate regime. The policy conflict that may arise in maintaining both internal and external balance is the focal point of analysis here. Monetarists view balance of payment imbalances as essentially reflections of monetary adjustments in an economy. In the long run, when such monetary adjustments are complete, the balance of payments is in equilibrium. This approach and its subsequent variations by Robert Mundell and J.M. Fleming are discussed in Chapter 24. In Chapter 25, a new chapter in this Second Edition, financial crises originating in the developing world, and occurring under overvalued pegged (or crawling peg) exchange rate regimes with or without capital and exchange controls have been discussed. Finally, Chapter 26 makes a comparison of flexible and pegged exchange rate regimes in light of the theories discussed in the earlier chapters. At the end of the book, a glossary of some of the important inter-governmental agencies is presented for ready reference.

PART I

Basis and Gains from Inter-industry Trade

1 Basis of Inter-industry Trade

International trade in commodities among countries can take a variety of forms. According to the nature of commodities being exported and imported, international trade can be classified into inter-industry and intra-industry trade. Trade is inter-industry in character if the commodities that are being exported and imported by a country belong to distinctly different industry groups. For example, when India exports rice, fruits and vegetables, and textiles, and imports wheat, sugar, and scientific instruments, such trade is inter-industry trade. But India, like many other countries, also exports and imports commodities that belong to the same industry group and are similar or may even be identical. These products are differentiated from each other either marginally or substantially. For example, software of different kinds and uses, or automobiles of different varieties and models, are exported as well as imported by India. This type of trade falls under the category of intra-industry trade.

A first-hand distinction between inter- and intra-industry trade can be made in the context of bilateral trade between China and India in 2004 as reported in Table 1.1. The top six export items for each country in terms of their shares in the respective total exports are shown in Table 1.1. Exports of iron and steel, plastics, cotton, and salt by India to China and exports of electrical machinery, nuclear reactors, silk, and mineral fuels by China to India are inter-industry in character. Both countries also export organic and inorganic chemicals to each other. In terms of this broad classification of industrial goods, this part of bilateral trade, which accounts for 11 and 18 per cent of the total bilateral exports from India and China respectively, is intra-industry in character.

Issues and explanations for these two types of trade are totally different. For example, in the context of inter-industry trade the relevant issue is what governs the pattern of trade between countries such as the one reported here between China and India. For intra-industry trade, on the other hand, it is important to know why both countries export similar industrial goods such as organic and inorganic chemicals in the above example, to each other. In this chapter we begin with the traditional explanations of inter-industry trade. Alternative explanations of intra-industry trade are discussed later in Chapter 8.

International Economics. Rajat Acharyya, Oxford University Press. © Oxford University Press 2022.
DOI: 10.1093/oso/9780192865144.003.0001

Table 1.1 Bilateral Trade between China and India in 2004

Share of Commodity in Total Exports from India to China	
Iron and Steel	20.42
Plastics and Articles thereof	9.03
Organic Chemicals	7.50
Cotton	3.64
Inorganic Chemicals	3.42
Salt, Sulphur, Stone, Lime, and Cement	3.05
Share of Commodity in Total Exports from China to India	
Electrical Machinery and Equipment	29.17
Organic Chemicals	15.89
Nuclear Reactors, Boilers	12.20
Silk	5.46
Mineral Fuels, Mineral Oils, and Mineral Waxes	5.46
Inorganic Chemicals	2.74

Source: WITS Commodity Trade Database, UNCTAD.

1.1 ARBITRAGE AND INTER-INDUSTRY TRADE

Arbitrage—*buying cheap and selling dear*—is the basic force behind most of the trade or exchange that takes place, whether spatial or across time. When arbitrage takes place across different geographical or national boundaries, it is known as international trade. Arbitrage (and hence trade) is possible only when price differences exist. It determines which of the goods produced in an economy are to be exported and which are to be imported. For example, if computers are sold at a lower price in the United States than they are in India, these will be bought cheap there and sold dearer in India. This will then constitute imports of computers by India from the United States. On the other hand, if cotton textiles are sold cheaper in India than in the United States or elsewhere, these goods will be bought cheap in India and sold dearer in the United States by Indian traders. This will then constitute exports of cotton textiles from India. Of course, the cost of transporting goods from India to the United States will also matter. If the cost of transporting goods to the United States is larger than the prevailing price difference, it will not pay to export cotton textiles there. Similarly, it will be profitable for traders to import computers from the United States only if even after paying for transport costs, the computers produced there can be sold at a lower price to Indian buyers than computers locally produced in India. Apart from transport costs, another important factor which determines the possibility of arbitrage and international trade is the price prevailing in countries that potentially compete with the country concerned. For example, for India to be able to export cotton textiles to the United States, it is not sufficient to know whether Indian cotton textiles are cheaper than American cotton textiles, but also whether they are cheaper than those produced in Bangladesh or China, or India's other major competitors in cotton textiles. Otherwise American traders will buy cotton textiles cheap from those countries, rather than from India, and will sell them dearer in the United States.

Note that cross-country price differences, net of transport costs, and consequent arbitrage become the only driving force of international trade if computers and cotton textiles, in our example, produced in India and elsewhere are of the same variety or quality. But, if these products are differentiated, and buyers prefer different varieties of the same good, international trade can take place in such differentiated varieties even if there is no cross-country price difference and hence no scope of arbitrage. We will return to this later in Chapter 8.

Thus, as long as we consider inter-industry trade in non-differentiated goods, arbitrage is the key force behind international trade, and for this there must exist cross-country differences in *pre-trade* prices. However, price differences are only a manifestation of the basis of trade. To understand the actual basis of trade, we need to know why prices may differ across countries for the *same* good that they produce. Suppose, India and the United States are the only two countries in our world and that computers and cotton textiles are the only two goods that they produce. Pre-trade or autarchic prices of these goods in the two countries depend on many factors. But in essence it is the relative scarcity or abundance that makes prices higher or lower in one country than in the other.

To exemplify and illustrate, suppose the relative demand for computers, which is the ratio of quantity demanded of computers per unit of quantity demanded of cotton textiles, $\left(d = \frac{D_C}{D_T}\right)$, is higher in India than in the United States. In other words, India has a relative *demand bias* in computers. In Figure 1.1, this pre-supposition implies that the relative demand for computers in India (I), labeled d_I, lies to the right of the relative demand for computers in the United States (U), labeled d_U. But suppose the domestic supplies of computers relative to that of cotton textiles, $\frac{S_C}{S_T}$, are the same in the two countries, as represented by the relative supply curve s. Computers would, therefore, be relatively scarce in India than they are in the United States resulting in a higher relative pre-trade price of computers that are locally produced: $p_I > p_U$. This difference in relative price will create scope for arbitrage and hence international trade. Note that in this example cotton textiles, on the other hand, are relatively abundant and hence their (relative) price is lower in India than it is in the United States. Thus, arbitrage will dictate international trade and its pattern: India will export cotton textiles to the United States and import computers from there. Of

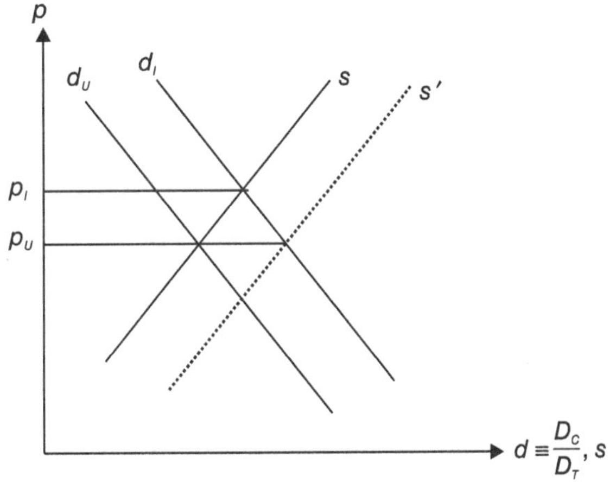

Figure 1.1 Cross-Country Pre-trade Relative Price Differential

course, as mentioned earlier, this pattern of trade will take place as long as transport costs do not erode the profits that the traders can realize through buying cheap and selling dear.

Alternatively, a similar pattern of trade will arise if the demand conditions prevailing in the two countries are the same, say as represented by the demand curve d_I, but relative production and supply of computers is larger in the United States than it is in India as represented by the relative supply curves s' and s respectively. Thus, in this case, the United States has a supply bias in computers. Once again, computers being relatively abundant in the United States, the pre-trade relative price of computers will be lower there. Thus computers will be imported by India from the United States.

In these illustrations, pre-trade price differences across nations and the consequent scope of arbitrage and international trade arise due to either a demand bias in India for computers or a supply bias in the United States for computers. Of course, a country may have both a demand bias and a supply bias in the same good relative to other countries. But in such a case, there may not be any cross-country price differences and hence any trade between the countries at all. For example, suppose India has both a demand bias and a supply bias in computers. Referring back to Figure 1.1, the relative supply curve for India is represented by s' and that for the United States is represented by s. But, as depicted, the demand and supply biases for India (relative to the United States) are such that in both the countries the prevailing pre-trade relative market price is p_U. There will thus be no scope for arbitrage and hence for international trade.

In general, trade will take place when a country has either a demand bias or a supply bias, or has both demand and supply biases but in *different* goods. A demand bias in computers makes it relatively dearer (and cotton textiles relatively cheaper) in that country, and these are imported from the other country. A supply bias in cotton textiles, in addition, makes them even cheaper and computers even dearer, thereby reinforcing the demand bias in computers. But when a country has a demand bias and a supply bias in the same good, that is, it has both a higher demand and higher local production than elsewhere, there are three possibilities. First, at any given relative price, the magnitude of the larger local production of the good relative to production elsewhere is larger than higher local demand for the good. This makes this good relatively abundant and hence its price lower than elsewhere (see Figure 1.2a). This good will then be *exported*. Second, at any given relative price, the magnitude of larger production and higher demand are the same so that the pre-trade local price is the same as elsewhere. In this case no trade takes place as illustrated in Figure 1.1. Finally, at any given relative price, the magnitude of larger local production of the good relative to its production elsewhere is smaller than higher local demand for the good. This makes this good relatively scarce and hence its price higher than elsewhere (see Figure 1.2b). This good will then be *imported*. For example, India can produce larger quantities of wheat than many other countries, and yet it may import wheat if the local demand for wheat is even larger.

What are the sources of these demand and supply biases? While all the factors that influence demand and supply are relevant here, the three fundamental sources are taste or preference, technology, and factor endowment. The traditional neo-classical trade theory emphasizes on cross-country differences in these fundamentals as determinants of trade. If tastes are homothetic in both the countries, the relative demand will depend only on the relative price

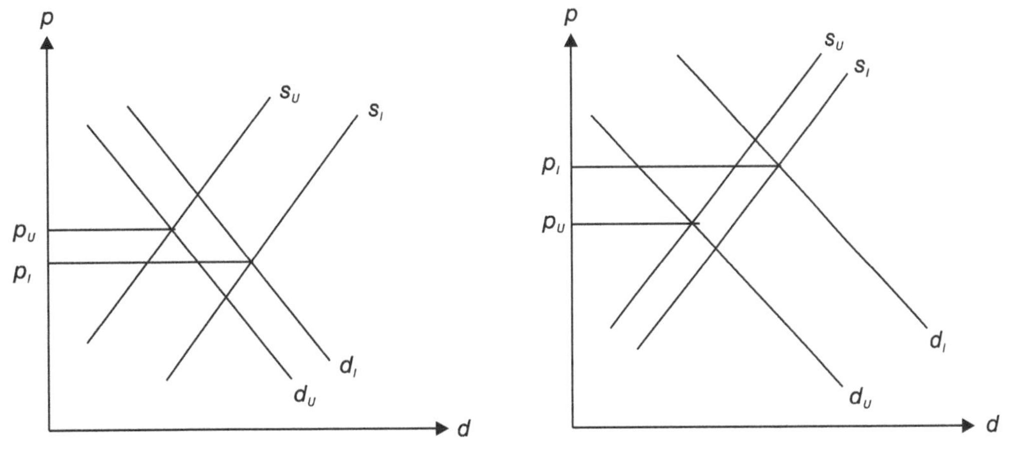

(a) A Larger Supply Bias and Export of Computers

(b) A Larger Demand Bias and Import of Computers

Figure 1.2 Demand and Supply Biases and Pattern of Trade

regardless of the per capita income levels of countries.[1] When tastes are identical as well, countries will demand the same relative units of computers. In contrast, the situations depicted in Figures 1.1 and 1.2 reflect India's *taste bias* in computers regardless of the per capita income levels in the two countries. On the other hand, if United States has superior technology in producing computers (or an inferior technology in producing cotton textiles) than India, it will have a supply bias as depicted in Figure 1.1. Thus, for example, if tastes are homothetic and identical, but production technologies are different across countries, a supply bias will arise that will result in differences in pre-trade (relative) market prices. In such a case, the actual basis of trade is cross-country differences in technology. This resembles the explanation given by David Ricardo (1971). As we will see later, a similar supply bias will arise for the United States if it is a relatively capital-abundant country and computers are relatively capital-intensive as compared to cotton textiles. Thus, with homothetic and identical tastes, the United States will export computers to and imports cotton textiles from India. This is the Heckscher-Ohlin explanation of trade between countries. We will have a more elaborate discussion on these explanations in Chapters 4 and 5.

What follows from these discussions is that the traditional trade theory emphasizes on *dissimilarity of countries as the basis of trade*. If both India and the United States had been identical or similar with respect to tastes, technology, and factor endowment, no arbitrage and trade could have been

[1] By homothetic tastes and preferences we mean that if a consumer prefers the consumption bundle (x_1, x_2) to (y_1, y_2) then she prefers the bundle (tx_1, tx_2) to (ty_1, ty_2) $\forall\, t > 0$. For such preferences, the income consumption curve is a straight line through the origin, meaning that a rich and a poor consumer (or a rich and a poor country) will buy the two goods in the same ratio if they face the same relative prices of the goods.

> **Box 1.1** Regulations on Arbitrage and Trade
>
> Often a large amount of a country's trade is regulated by the national government, prohibiting the scope of arbitrage and thus not allowing the pattern of trade that price differences and arbitrage would have resulted in. For example, exports and imports of food grains are often restricted on grounds of food security. Rice, wheat, onions, and sugar are some of the commodities that are not allowed to be traded freely by the Government of India according to price differences in India and in other countries. Apart from these specific instances related to food security, national governments may also limit the scope of arbitrage through tariffs on imports to protect domestic producers or to improve national welfare.

possible. Does this mean that similar countries do not trade among themselves? Yes, they do, and, in fact, they trade more among themselves than with dissimilar countries. As we will discuss later, a very large proportion of world trade is among similar countries. The new trade theories that are discussed in Chapter 8, explain such trade among similar countries in terms of economies of scale, strategic motives of firms and product differentiation.

1.2 COMPARATIVE ADVANTAGE

The cross-country differences in *pre-trade relative prices* that lead to arbitrage and trade essentially reflect the *comparative advantage* of the two countries. In our illustrations in Figures 1.1 and 1.2b, the United States has a comparative advantage in computers whereas India has a comparative advantage in cotton textiles. As it follows from the discussions in the earlier section, there are three fundamental sources of comparative advantage—technology asymmetry of countries, factor endowment differences across countries, and demand asymmetry or the taste bias of countries. Thus, comparative advantage reflects the relative strength of a country. Technological superiority of a country vis-à-vis the other, or abundance of a particular factor of production relative to other countries establishes its comparative advantage.

A nation's comparative advantage, however, is essentially determined through interactions of each of these fundamental sources. As exemplified earlier, favourable technological conditions in a nation in producing some goods will not lead to comparative advantage or lower relative pre-trade prices of these goods, if demand conditions and factor endowment conditions are not favourable as well.

An equally important element of a nation's comparative advantage is its government and public policies, which can improve or counter the comparative advantage based on fundamentals. In the next section we elaborate on this aspect.

1.2.1 Public Policy and Induced Comparative Advantage: Fundamental Sources

Public policies often generate externalities for the private sector. For example, public investment in infrastructure or social overheads such as transport, communication, power, and irrigation, generate positive externalities on the production of private consumption goods. Better roads lower the cost of transporting raw materials to factories. In cases of such positive externalities, public investments can offset inferiority of production technology and establish

Box 1.2 Doctrine of Comparative Cost Advantage

Comparative advantage as a determinant of pattern and gains from trade was first conceptualized by David Ricardo in his *Doctrine of Comparative Cost Advantage*. Ricardo argued that a country would have a comparative cost advantage in a good that it can produce at a lower cost due to its technological superiority relative to what other countries can do. Under the presumption of constant costs and perfectly competitive markets, this comparative cost advantage translates into comparative advantage (or relative price difference), which, as explained above, determines trade. But these assumptions do not always best approximate the real-world scenario. Price differentials may not always reflect cost differentials, particularly when marginal costs are increasing. Thus, it is quite possible that countries have a comparative advantage in goods in which they have comparative cost *dis*advantages in the Ricardian sense. Since trade is essentially an arbitrage activity that depends on the price differential, it is obvious that the pattern of trade will be dictated by the comparative advantage which may or may not reflect a comparative cost advantage.

a comparative advantage. Similarly, despite having better technology, a country may suffer from poor infrastructure. A typical example is the hardware industry. India performs many hardware assembly tasks for its domestic market with the components coming from East and Southeast Asia. This ability to organize this aspect of production could itself have been the basis for further development of India's hardware capabilities. Several East Asian countries also began mainly as assemblers of sophisticated components produced elsewhere and later gained comparative advantage in hardware products. But the development trajectory in India has not followed a similar path because the hardware industry requires high quality infrastructure which has not been there.

Even when the countries have no differences in their fundamentals—technology, factor endowment, and taste—differences in infrastructure facilities can create a supply bias and thus establish comparative advantage if positive externalities of public investment in the two sectors are asymmetric.[2] Another important example of public policy inducing comparative advantage is public investment in education and human capital formation. India's growing comparative advantage in information technology and software and in information technology enabled services (ITeS) over the last three decades is an example of this. Public investment in setting up Indian Institutes of Technology (IITs), together with English being the primary mode of instruction in a majority of the schools and institutions of higher education throughout India, has enabled it to enjoy a comparative advantage in these exports and services over China, Israel, and many other Asian and European rival countries. Unlike the hardware industry, poor infrastructure in India did not stand in the way of developing the software industry because

[2] There might also be an indirect demand effect of infrastructure development. To the extent to which infrastructure development raises national income we can expect relative demand to change and therefore differences in infrastructure facilities to generate a taste bias, if income elasticities are not unitary.

Box 1.3 Comparative versus Absolute Advantage

The significance of the doctrine of comparative advantage is that even a technologically backward country can do something *relatively* better than its advanced trading partner. This is in sharp contrast with Adam Smith's assertion that trade cannot take place between countries one of which is technologically superior than the other, or has *absolute advantage*, in all lines of production. Thus, for Smith trade can take place only if each country has absolute advantage in at least one good. Of course, such absolute advantage implies that the countries will also have comparative advantages in the goods in which they have absolute advantages. But by the doctrine of comparative advantage, trade can take place even between a technologically superior country such as the United States, and a technologically backward country such as Bangladesh, when the United States is *not equally superior* to Bangladesh in all lines of production. In such a case, it will have a comparative advantage in that line of production in which its technological superiority is the most, and a comparative *dis*advantage in the good in which its superiority is the least. Ricardo exemplified this case by his famous argument of a lawyer who can defend his client in a court of law as well as do all the related secretarial work better than his secretary. But his superiority being the greatest in the former, he can gain by specializing and devoting all his time in preparing himself for defending his client and appointing a secretary to do the job of typing and other related secretarial assistance.

relatively low infrastructure is required to use and create software. Of course, availability of cheap labour also helped.

Regulation of markets, particularly for goods that generate negative externalities, may similarly induce an altogether different comparative advantage than what the fundamentals could have established. Consider, for example, that our home economy produces iron and steel and cotton. Iron and steel being an industrial activity, its production generates pollution and degrades the environment. But cotton being an agricultural product does not pollute the environment. Suppose also that industrial ashes are deposited in the soil that erode its fertility. Consequently, cotton yield per unit of land declines.

This is a typical case of negative externality where industrial activity makes the marginal cost of agricultural production higher. Soil erosion, however, can be avoided by recycling industrial ashes through a cleaner technology for production of iron and steel. But such a technology involves higher costs for industrial activity (though lower costs for agricultural production) compared to the dirty technology. Accordingly, under the cleaner technology the country will produce relatively smaller units of iron and steel compared to what it produced under dirty technology. Such supply relationships are shown by curves s and s' respectively in Figure 1.3. The vertical distance between the two curves measures the (relative) pollution abatement cost incurred by industrial activity to correct for the negative externality that it generates.[3] Suppose India and the United States are similar countries and thus have no fundamental sources of comparative advantage. Thus, demand and supply relationships in the

[3] The curves s and s' actually reflect ratios of social marginal costs and private marginal costs respectively.

two countries are identical. But if the United States strictly enforces environmental standards requiring the cleaner technology to be used for the production of iron and steel, whereas India does not enforce any such regulation, the pre-trade relative price of iron and steel will be lower in India and higher in the United States. There emerges a comparative advantage for India, albeit perverse, in iron and steel because India under-values the environment.

This type of comparative advantage is different from the advantage derived from fundamental sources. The latter rests on the strength of an economy in a particular line of production, either in terms of relative labour productivity or in terms of the relative availability of a factor that is used more intensively in that line of production. These are cases of genuine comparative advantage. But the comparative advantage generated by environmental factors rests on the weakness rather than on the strength of the economy. *It is a perverse, rather than genuine, comparative advantage* because it is based on an under-estimation of (social) cost. International trade induces a country to specialize in production according to comparative advantage, but specialization dictated by a perverse comparative advantage only reinforces the weakness on which such an advantage rests.[4]

This is essentially known as *ecological dumping*—a comparative advantage in a *dirty* good arising due to lax environmental standards or taxes that allow it to be priced below the social marginal cost. This has become the bone of contention between the developed and developing countries, as the developed group of countries alleges that the developing countries are engaged in unfair trade by keeping their national environmental taxes and standards deliberately low.

1.2.2 Selective Factor Disadvantage, Innovations, and Shifting Comparative Advantage

Comparative advantage is not a static concept. In a dynamic world, comparative advantages of nations change rapidly causing rise or fall of countries as leading exporters of a particular commodity in global trade. Thus, a nation's comparative advantage in a commodity based on

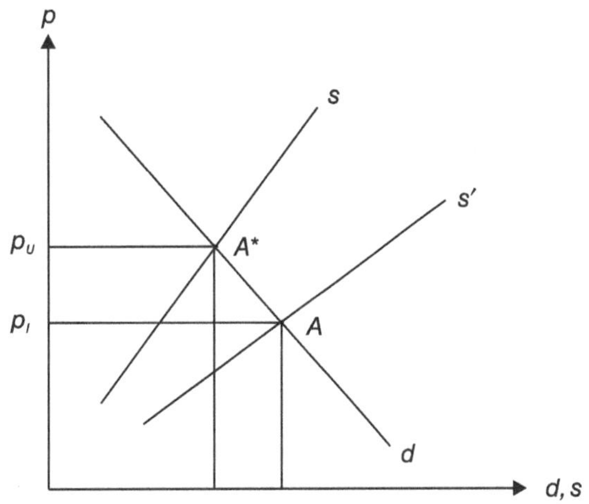

Figure 1.3 Environmental Standards and Comparative Advantage

[4] The use of child labour or the existence of very low safety standards may produce the same kind of perverse competitiveness by enabling a country to produce a good at a relatively lower cost.

one or two determinants may prove unsustainable in a globalized dynamic world. A narrow basis of comparative advantage often makes it easy for global competitors to circumvent it. But if a nation's comparative advantage is rooted in most of its determinants, the inter-play of advantages in such determinants makes it self-reinforcing in the long run and difficult for rival countries to replicate or leapfrog. In fact, comparative advantage may be a weakness rather than a strength in the long run as it may make a nation complacent with short-run benefits. Similarly, selective factor disadvantages force nations to overcome them and turn such disadvantages into advantages through changes in both public policies and technology brought about by firm-level innovations. Michael Porter (1990) was the first to argue and exemplify that innovations to offset selective disadvantages are more likely than innovations to exploit strengths. What may appear to be a weakness or disadvantage in the short run may become an advantage in the long run and in a dynamic competitive world.

Examples of comparative disadvantages being turned into comparative advantages abound. In many European markets, rigid labour laws brought in automation of production processes and improved production technologies. The automated production process in Japan replaced labour to a large extent, which reduced production costs and improved the quality of outputs to establish the country's comparative advantage in electronics. The cold and extreme weather conditions in the Netherlands are not conducive for horticulture. This disadvantage has been overcome by developing glasshouse growing techniques for its cut flower industry. Such techniques also allowed frequent upgrading as compared to traditional cultivation techniques. As a result, the Netherlands has been able to achieve continued differentiation in terms of freshness, quality, and variety of cut flowers and remain as the world leader in the cut flower industry for quite a long time.

For India, poor physical infrastructure prohibited its success in hardware development unlike China, Singapore, Korea, and Taiwan, and pushed skilled Indians to specialize in software development. Aided by adoption of information technology, language skills and low labour costs, India now commands most of the outsourcing activities in the world in software development and ITeS.

However, comparative disadvantage being a strength and a stimulant of innovation works in favour of a country only when the other determinants of comparative advantage are conducive. A significant pool of skilled personnel and a nation's progress in science and technology support innovation. Demand conditions, domestic or foreign, are also important. India's emerging strength and comparative advantage in software services and ITeS has been enabled by large pool of skilled labour and language proficiency. Its geographical location in a different time zone vis-à-vis the United States also makes it an important destination for outsourcing of ITeS for US companies.

Box 1.4 Innovation and Posner's Technology Gap Theory

In his technology gap theory, Michael V. Posner (1961) offered a dynamic version of technology asymmetry as a determinant and basis of trade. He argued that innovating countries can reap monopoly profits and gain from international trade as long as they can maintain their technological lead. But once imitation takes place, the traditional factors of production adjustment and specialization rule and determine trade flows. Subsequent development of this theme of the technology-gap approach to trade emphasizes inter-country differences in technical change as the basis of international trade flows. It is variations across countries in innovation capabilities within each sector which explain the pattern of trade. Countries with innovative capabilities will specialize in technology-intensive products. These countries continue to innovate and maintain their technological superiority in new products.

1.2.3: Comparative advantage in vertical stages of production: Global value chains

An important dimension of international trade that can be observed since 1990s is fragmentation of vertical stages of production with different countries producing and specializing in different stages of production. Now most of the manufacturing goods and, of course, services, are produced not in a single country. Different parts and components are produced in different countries before its final assembly or final production stage. That is, a single finished product often results from manufacturing and assembly in multiple countries, with each stage generating and adding value to the end product. This production processes, known also as the global value chains (GVCs), have led to phenomenal growth in trade in intermediate goods over the last three decades as outputs of lower stages are shipped from the countries specializing in such stages to the countries that specialize in higher stages, and from there to the country producing the final good. Such international fragmentation of production processes and GVCs have also led to a lot of capital inflows, foreign direct investment, and transfer of technical knowhow from the developed to the developing countries through outsourcing of different production stages or processes. We will have a more elaborate discussion on these dimensions in Chapter 16.

Such production specialization in 'stages of production' by nations is governed mostly by the comparative advantage of nations along the vertical stages of production. This *vertical specialization* is in contrast to comparative advantage of nations in different commodities, *the horizontal specialization*, as we have discussed earlier. However, the fundamental determinants of such comparative advantage in vertical stages of production are essentially the same: technology and factor endowment. The abundance of low skill labour in the developing countries establishes a comparative advantage for these countries in lower stages of production that are relatively low-skill and less capital intensive. But, as the successively higher stages of production become more and more skilled-labour intensive and/or capital intensive per unit of output in that stage, the developed countries endowed with relatively more of these factors have a comparative advantage in such stages. Thus, we can observe lower stages of production being organized usually in the developing countries whereas the higher stages of production including production of the final good are organized in the developed countries. For similar reasons, the product development stage, from research and development (R&D) to successful innovation of a product, its design and/or blue print, are done in the developed countries that not only have the skilled manpower but also invest significant proportions of the gross domestic products (or national incomes) on R&D. Much simpler tasks of assembly line production are outsourced to and organized in developing countries due to cheap labour there. Typical example is assembly line production in Mexico. The industry that has benefitted most from assembly in Mexico is the automobile industry as leading manufacturers like Ford, Toyota, Honda, BMW, Volkswagen have opened operations there. Assembly line productions of electronics, consumer products, and medical devices in Mexico are also expanding fast during the last decade. Of course, the notable exceptions in this hierarchy of innovations and product development are developing countries like China and India. Both countries have the skilled manpower, comparable to those in the developed countries. Despite spending only a negligible proportion of GDP on R&D, in sectors like pharmaceuticals, aerospace, and IT-enabled services India has established itself as a major player in the world. India's capability of producing generic drugs for deadly diseases like AIDS is saving millions of lives in poor countries so much so that India has been dubbed as the Pharmacy of the Third World.[5] On

[5] India is also one of the largest producers of vaccines innovated and patented by multinational firms belonging to advanced countries.

the other hand, technological capability, skill availability, and ability to organize large scale production of both medium and high technology intensive manufacturing have made China to emerge as the Factory of the World.

The international fragmentation of vertical stages of production, and location of different stages of production in different countries according to their respective comparative advantages, has been made possible largely by the advent of information technology. Locating production of different stages in different countries requires service links to be established to connect these production stages or *blocks*. Without the advent of information technology such service links would not have been cost-effective, and thus international fragmentation of vertical stages of production would not have been profitable. This also signifies that for developing countries to participate in the GVCs, they must invest in and develop information and communication technology (ICT) infrastructure.

1.3 DIGITAL AND VIRTUAL TRADE

Development of ICT infrastructure also unlocks potentials for e-trade/digital trade and services trade. In fact, since the turn of the present century, virtual/digital trade has emerged as a prominent feature of international economic exchange. Services in particular, which was earlier seen primarily as 'non-traded', have become globally traded aided by the ICT, such as financial services (like banking and insurance) and business services (like software development, call centres, consultancy services including medical advice, and the like). All these service activities have the inherent characteristics of non-requirement of physical transportation of product, and therefore have the scope of digitization. ICT and digital technology have made the direct interface of the service provider and service recipient and their simultaneous physical presence at the time of transaction redundant, and thereby facilitated even cross-border exchange of such services.

An interesting dimension of virtual trade, mainly in business processing services, is the time zone differences in countries engaged in such trade/exchange of services.[6] A lot of virtual trade in intermediate services has been taking place between India and the United States driven by their time zone differences. With these countries belonging to different and almost non-overlapping time zones, trade in services (or production processes) between them makes the production process to be completed virtually in 24 hours (or one-day time) and thus makes it cost-efficient. More generally, even if the fundamentals discussed earlier are the same, non-overlapping time zones can itself establish comparative advantage for nations and form the basis of trade between them. And, this force is stronger larger is the time difference, or, less overlapping the time zones of two trading nations are. Thus, geographical distance, which usually constrains international trade in goods by increasing cost of transporting goods from one country to the other, may actually promote virtual trade in intermediate services by placing countries in different and non-overlapping time zones. Marjit et al. (2020) call these time zone differences determining trade as the fourth dimension.

However, the tangible goods requiring physical shipment, and contact-based (or intensive) services like hair cut and the like, still remain outside the purview of virtual trade. Certain trading processes for 'tangible-goods trade' can of course be digitized, and thereby costs of delivery at least can be reduced significantly. One such case is replacing physical documents with electronic records.

[6] See Marjit, Mandal and Nakanishi (2020) for a detailed discussion.

Pandemics like the Covid-19 in 2020–21 make digital and virtual trade all the more important and urgent for maintaining livelihood of people. In fact, the Covid-19 pandemic has accelerated the adoption of digital technologies and services in many developing countries. Post-Covid we can expect this trend to continue. Virtual trade such as contactless trading on digital platforms will become more prominent. Many more services will become ICT-intensive reducing the interface between the service-provider and service-recipient. Glaring examples are that of health and education. Virtual medical advice and telemedicine have been increasingly relied upon by both doctors and patients. Education, on the other hand, has been virtually exchanged across locations including cross-border locations. Indian students attending online graduate classes of many US universities in Fall 2020 while still being in India is one among many such examples.

There are quite a few challenges that loom large, however. One such challenge is to prevent digital monopoly of a few countries. With the growth of digital and virtual trade, have and have-nots are likely to be determined more by the asymmetric development and access to ICT infrastructure and services across countries. There are also concerns about data privacy, ownership, and security, all of which adversely affect trust, which is a crucial pre-requisite of virtual/digital trade. A few countries have already turned to digital protectionism, which threatens to increase costs and reduce access to the digital services, and such interventions are expected to grow with the growth of the global digital trade.

1.4 ADVANCED TOPIC: REVEALED COMPARATIVE ADVANTAGE

Bela Balassa (1965, 1989) formulated the concept of Revealed Comparative Advantage (RCA) to estimate the comparative advantage of nations. But this estimate is not based on a bilateral comparison of pre-trade prices or labour costs. Rather this is an estimate based on actual exports and imports by countries.

By Balassa's measure, India's RCA in commodity *k* vis-à-vis other countries in the market in the United States can be calculated as:

$$RCA^k = \frac{\text{Share of India in total import of commodity-}k\text{ by the United States}}{\text{Share of the India in total import of all commodities by the United States}}$$

If the value of RCA^k is greater than one, India has a RCA in commodity *k*. Otherwise, export of commodity *k* does not reveal India's comparative advantage in that good. A greater than one value of RCA for a particular commodity means that exports of this commodity have a larger share in the total imports of that commodity by the United States than the share of exports of all commodities by India taken together in aggregate imports of the United States. That is, for the United States, India is a relatively better source of imports of commodity *k* than all other commodities taken together.

Table 1.2 reports India's RCA in selected commodities based on India's exports to the rest of the world. According to this estimate, India has *revealed* comparative advantage in the exports of labour-intensive agricultural goods, resource-based and manufactured goods like coffee, tea and mate, rice, fruits and nuts, cotton, jute, spices, iron ore and concentrates, textiles, clothing, leather and leather manufacture, travel bags, and footwear. While it has RCA in some skill-intensive exports as well, like organic chemicals, its exports of high-technology and capital-intensive products like

Table 1.2 India's Revealed Comparative Advantage in Merchandise Exports of Selected Products

	1995	2000	2005	2010	2015	2019
Fish, fresh, chilled or frozen	1.58	2.04	0.87	0.99	0.86	0.65
Wheat and meslin	1.01	0.04	1.01	0.00	0.25	0.08
Tea and mate	22.72	17.57	10.00	6.69	5.07	5.54
Spices	15.48	14.62	9.51	10.73	10.43	11.72
Jute	0.51	2.20	2.49	7.07	3.16	2.60
Iron ore and concentrates	9.60	5.71	15.17	3.97	0.19	1.11
Organic chemicals	2.22	5.14	7.52	5.06	3.79	4.36
Textile yarn	6.56	8.27	5.59	5.99	6.91	5.38
Fabrics, woven, of man-made fabrics	1.92	2.20	3.24	3.78	2.88	2.24
Automatic data processing machines	0.11	0.05	0.06	0.07	0.04	0.03
Telecommunication equipment	0.12	0.05	0.06	0.33	0.11	0.47
Motor vehicles for the transport of persons	0.13	0.05	0.20	0.56	0.50	0.54
Women's clothing, of textile	2.39	3.22	2.88	1.62	1.61	1.42
Footwear	2.03	2.01	1.62	1.18	1.30	1.09
Optical instruments & apparatus	0.04	0.04	0.02	0.02	0.02	0.02
Rice	29.68	14.48	16.77	7.68	17.14	16.67
Fruits and nuts	2.60	3.00	1.84	1.00	0.89	0.66
Sugar, molasses and honey	1.57	1.13	0.42	1.92	2.78	3.80
Coffee and coffee substitutes	4.68	3.51	2.21	1.28	1.34	1.25
Silk	0.68	3.17	2.13	1.38	1.95	1.37
Cotton	0.84	0.87	3.14	10.96	8.57	3.81
Inorganic chemical elements	0.48	0.77	0.70	0.84	0.49	0.62
Medicinal and pharmaceutical products	0.87	1.66	0.86	0.67	0.77	0.62
Leather	3.77	3.05	3.13	2.51	2.97	1.68
Leather manufacture	15.53	14.11	4.56	2.88	2.91	2.69
Cotton fabrics, woven	7.04	7.04	3.15	2.54	3.73	3.73
Pearls, precious & semi-precious stones	18.47	18.87	13.69	11.72	9.46	10.31
Electrical machinery & apparatus	0.22	0.31	0.30	0.34	0.30	0.42
Travel goods, handbags & similar containers	3.34	3.02	2.34	1.23	1.27	1.16

Source: Author's compilation from UNCTADStat 2020, UNCTAD.

automatic data processing machines, telecommunication equipment, transport equipment such as motor vehicles, optical instruments & apparatus, electrical machinery & apparatus, etc., do not reveal any comparative advantage. The other notable point is that India's revealed comparative advantages in traditional products like textiles, tea and mate, coffee, leather manufacture and travel good, have declined during the last two decades. Also, exports of fruits and nuts no longer reveal any comparative advantage after 2010.

However, note that RCA is an *ex post* estimate. Instead of explaining and predicting the pattern of trade, it estimates whether an observed pattern of exports reveals a country's comparative advantage. Moreover, as it appears from Balassa's measure, RCA indicates competitiveness of a country vis-à-vis its rival exporting countries at a particular export destination rather than whether the country has a comparative advantage vis-à-vis the importing country. Despite these limitations, this measure has the advantage that it does not depend on bilateral comparisons of pre-trade prices or relative labour costs, which are not always possible in a multi-commodity and multi-country world. It also shows that the actual pattern of trade of a country may not always follow its actual comparative advantage for various reasons, some of which are explained here.

SUMMARY POINTS

- Price differences across nations create scope for arbitrage, which is the basis of inter-industry trade. Price differences reflect dissimilarities in countries in terms of either supply bias or demand bias or both. Thus, inter-industry trade essentially takes place between dissimilar countries.
- Relative price difference indicates the comparative advantage. Comparative advantage as a determinant of pattern of trade was first conceptualized by David Ricardo in his *Doctrine of Comparative Cost Advantage*. Under the presumption of constant costs and perfectly competitive markets, this comparative cost advantage translates into comparative advantage (or relative price differences), which, as explained in this chapter, determines trade.
- The significance of the doctrine of comparative advantage has been that even a technologically backward country can do something *relatively* better than its advanced trading partner. This is in sharp contrast with Adam Smith's assertion that trade cannot take place between countries one of which is technologically superior than the other, or has *absolute advantage*, in all lines of production. But, Ricardo argued that a country may have absolute advantage in all lines of production, and yet may have comparative advantage in only a few commodities if its superiority is not uniform.
- There are three fundamental sources of comparative advantage—technology asymmetry of countries, factor endowment differences across countries, and demand asymmetry or taste bias of countries. Superior technology, small domestic demand, and abundance of the factor production which is used intensively in production of a commodity are the fundamental sources of comparative advantage of a nation in that particular commodity. A nation's comparative advantage is essentially determined though interactions of each of these fundamental sources.
- Public policies also establish comparative advantages for nations. Better quality infrastructure creates cost advantages for nations. Public investment in education and human capital formation can also establish or reinforce comparative advantage in skill-intensive commodities. On the other hand, lenient (or non-existent) public policies in cases of negative externalities such as environmental damage caused by industrial production, can lead to a perverse comparative advantage through under-valuation of the environment.
- Comparative advantage is not a static concept. In a dynamic world, comparative advantages of nations change rapidly. In such a context, the comparative advantage of a nation may be a weakness rather than a strength in the long run as it may make the nation complacent with short-run benefits. Selective factor disadvantages, on the other hand, may induce innovations and may become an advantage in the long run and in a dynamic competitive world.
- A single finished product often results from manufacturing and assembly in multiple countries, with each stage generating and adding value to the end product. This production process is known as the global value chain.

- Since the turn of the present century, virtual/digital trade has emerged as a prominent feature of international trade in financial services (like banking and insurance) and business services (like software development, call centres, consultancy services including medical advice, and the like). All these service activities have the inherent characteristics of non-requirement of physical transportation of product, and therefore have the scope of digitization. ICT and digital technology have made the direct interface of the service provider and service recipient and their simultaneous physical presence at the time of transaction redundant, and thereby have been facilitating even cross-border exchange of such services.
- A lot of virtual trade in intermediate and business process services has been driven by time zone differences. Even if the fundamentals like technology, factor endowment and tastes are the same, non-overlapping time zones can itself establish comparative advantage for nations and form the basis of trade between them. And, this force is stronger larger is the time difference, or, less overlapping the time zones of two trading nations are.
- Revealed Comparative Advantage as proposed by Bela Balassa is a measure of comparative advantage of nations based on actual exports and imports by countries, rather than on bilateral comparison of pre-trade prices or labour costs. It is an *ex post* estimate. Instead of explaining and predicting the pattern of trade, it estimates whether an observed pattern of exports reveals a country's comparative advantage.

KEYWORDS

- **Absolute advantage** reflects a country's ability to produce a good at a lower price (or at a lower cost) than its trading partner.
- **Arbitrage** is buying cheap and selling dear. Arbitrage across national borders constitutes international trade.
- **Comparative advantage** of a nation in any commodity reflects lower pre-trade relative price of that commodity than elsewhere.
- **Comparative cost advantage** reflects a country's ability to produce a good at a lower cost relative to other goods than its trading partner. Comparative cost advantage does not necessarily imply comparative advantage.
- **Ecological dumping** arises when lax environmental standards or taxes allow a good that degrades the environment to be priced below the social marginal cost, and thereby establishes a perverse comparative advantage in that good.
- **Inter-industry trade** is exports and imports of commodities belonging to distinctly different industry groups.
- **Intra-industry trade** is exports and imports of similar, though not necessarily identical, commodities.

EXERCISES

1. Consider India and Bangladesh producing and trading rice and cloth with each other. The countries are identical in every respect except for per capita income in India being higher than that in Bangladesh. If tastes are non-homothetic and cloth has income-inelastic demand, what will be the pattern of trade between these countries? (Normalize population size in each country to unity.)
2. In the context of two goods—computers and pharmaceuticals—and two countries—China and Germany—argue in which of the following cases trade will take place, and if trade takes place, determine the direction of trade.
   (a) China and Germany have identical tastes with Germany having higher per capita income and computers having unitary income elastic demand. All other characteristics are the same.
   (b) In addition to the above characteristics, Germany has a superior technology in producing computers.
3. China exports transport equipment to India and imports pharmaceutical products from India, though it can produce both these goods at costs lower than India. If costs are invariant with respect to output levels and markets in both countries are perfectly competitive, how will you explain this pattern of trade?
4. As in the preceding question, suppose China and India have identical technologies to produce transport equipment and pharmaceutical products. Russia, on the other hand, has better technology for producing transport equipment but an inferior technology in producing pharmaceutical products. Per capita income is the highest in Russia and the least in India. Tastes are non-homothetic. Normalize population size in each country to unity and assume everything else is identical in all these countries:
   (a) Will there by any bilateral trade between China and India?
   (b) Will there by any bilateral trade between China and Russia? If so, what will be the pattern of trade?
5. India (I) and Sri Lanka (S) both produce tea and rice. The relative demand and supply of tea in country-j , j = I, S, is:

   $$d_j = \alpha_j - \beta_j p_j,\ s_j = \delta_j p_j,\ \alpha_j, \beta_j, \delta_j > 0$$

   What restrictions on the parameters will you put to show:
   (a) that there will be trade between India and Sri Lanka?
   (b) that India will export rice to Sri Lanka?

   Explain what your restriction in each case implies.
6. Suppose the demand functions for textiles and computers in Bangladesh and United States are as follows:

   $$D_{Tj} = \frac{I_j}{p_j},\ D_{cj} = I_j p_j,\ j = \text{B, U}$$

   where, I_j = national income of country j, and p_j is the relative price of textiles.

   If $I_B = 2000$, $I_U = 10000$ and relative supply of textiles in Bangladesh and United States are $s_B = 100$ and $s_U = 64$ respectively, then which country will export textiles? What is the intuition behind your answer?
7. Suppose the demand and cost functions for coffee and tea are identical in the two countries, India and Brazil. But, whereas tea is produced by a monopoly firm and coffee by perfectly

competitive firms in India, coffee is produced by a monopoly firm and tea by perfectly competitive firms in Brazil. Per capita income and population sizes are the same in the two countries. Will there be any trade in such a context? If so, what would be the direction of trade?

8. Argentina (A) and Mexico (M) produce electrical machinery (E) and telecommunication apparatus (T). Cost functions for these goods in the two countries are: $C_{EA} = 20X_{EA}$, $C_{EM} = 20X_{EM}$, $C_{TA} = 10X_{TA}$, $C_{TM} = 8X_{TM}$. Argentina has a taste bias in electrical machinery. Given these data, answer the following:
   (a) If both the goods are produced by perfectly competitive firms in the two countries, then which good will be exported by Mexico to Argentina?
   (b) Telecommunication apparatus is produced by a single firm in Mexico, ceteris paribus. If the demand for it in Mexico is given by $P_{TM} = 20 - 5D_{TM}$, does the pattern of trade remain the same?
   (c) What happens when in addition to conditions stated in (b), electrical machinery is produced by a single firm in Argentina?
9. Public investment in telecom facility raises productivity of software engineers. If USA and Thailand produce rice and software, do you think a higher investment in telecommunication in USA relative to that in Thailand will enable USA to export software to Thailand? Explain your answer.
10. Suppose India is observed to export a dirty good and import a clean good from the United States. Can you conclude *from this observed pattern of trade* that environmental standards are lenient in India and strict in the United States? Explain your answer.
11. Can you think of a situation where a country with a higher pollution tax on production exports a dirty good? Explain.
12. The following table reports imports of selected commodities by Japan from India and from the world in 1990, 1992, and 1994. Calculate India's RCA in these commodities.

Commodity	India's Exports to Japan			Japan's Imports from the World		
	1990	1992	1994	1990	1992	1994
Shellfish	2,49,826	2,80,647.34	4,79,661.43	48,49,354	51,89,579	67,73,075
Fruits and Nuts	19,816	21,830.05	29,573.86	14,77,117	17,54,383	18,44,164
Tea and Mate	13,055	10,838.94	9,519.31	1,35,670	1,62,880	1,69,744
Spices	6,484	5,874.09	6,072.08	96,932	1,33,211	1,37,250
Iron Ore Concentrates	3,70,070	2,58,192.91	2,18,310.88	33,74,086	31,92,778	29,04,132
Medicines	3,863	6,891.57	1,811.31	15,83,543	20,13,601	2,17,1321
Leather	17,138	9,629.55	11,453.24	2,50,275	1,92,089	2,01,988
Textile Yarn	14,538	33,022.05	54,669.55	10,07,601	10,86,124	12,79,141
Cotton and Woven Fabric	8,893	6,815.51	10,609.49	4,95,390	4,38,676	5,57,948
Pearls and Precious Stones	5,33,549	4,63,628.25	5,61,507.23	33,78,660	24,38,764	30,58,062
Men's Wear	42,570	50,437.21	51,766.56	17,09,456	23,75,808	32,35,327
Footwear	5,733	5,043.84	4,924.44	13,63,977	18,26,330	23,73,233
Total	14,68,880	13,35,270	16,85,866	6,20,16,063	6,42,43,232	8,46,01,724

13. TRIPS allows poorer countries certain flexibilities in the implementation of patent protection in pharmaceutical products. Consequently, generic drug producers still continue to produce in countries like India and Brazil. How does this affect the prospect of exporting drugs by Indian generic drug producers and patent holder American multinationals to markets like Brazil?

SUGGESTED READING

Caves, R.E., J. Frankel, and R.W. Jones. (1995). *World Trade and Payments*, 5th Edition. New York: HarperCollins College Publishers.

Porter, M. (1990). *The Competitive Advantage of Nations*. New York: Free Press.

ADVANCED READING

Acharyya, R. (2013). *Trade and Environment*, Oxford India Short Introductions Series. New Delhi: Oxford University Press.

Balassa, B. (1965). 'Trade Liberalization and "Revealed" Comparative Advantage', *Manchester School*, 33: 99–123.

——— (1989). '"Revealed" Comparative Advantage Revisited', in B. Balassa (ed.), *Comparative Advantage, Trade Policy, and Economic Development*. New York: Oxford University Press, pp. 63–79.

Brulhart, M. (2009). 'An Account of Global Intra-industry Trade, 1962–2006', *World Economy*, 32 (3): 401–59.

Burange, L.G. and S. Chaddha. (2008). 'India's Revealed Comparative Advantage in Merchandise Trade', Working Paper No. UDE28/6/2008, University of Mumbai.

Posner, M.V. (1961). 'International Trade and Technical Change', *Oxford Economic Papers*, 13: 323–41.

2 Gains from Trade

In Chapter 1 we discussed the basis and direction of trade between countries. These are positive issues. Normative issues, on the other hand, are concerned with whether trade benefits countries or not. In this context, the essence of Ricardo's doctrine of comparative cost advantage is that trade is a positive-sum game; that is, free trade is beneficial for all the trading partners if each country exports the good in which it has a comparative (cost) advantage. This is known as the *Gains from Trade* theorem. The crucial underlying assumption, however, is that the market (price) correctly signals the trading partners' relative strengths in production patterns. There are two more caveats. First, trade creates both winners and losers in each country and as such the welfare argument of free trade is based on an implicit compensation principle. Second, post-trade relative price at which the goods are traded must strictly lie between the pre-trade relative prices in each country—that is, for each country, the terms of trade should strictly improve. In this chapter we discuss these issues and how trade according to comparative advantage leads to gains from free trade for all countries. Sufficient conditions and sources of such gains from trade are also discussed and illustrated.

2.1 TRADE, GAINS, AND REDISTRIBUTION

Consider a pair of countries, generalized as home country and foreign country, each producing the same set of goods, computers, and cotton textiles. Figure 2.1 depicts domestic markets for computers and cotton textiles in our home country. Domestic markets in the foreign country can similarly be depicted. Pre-trade, in each country all consumers together must buy computers and cotton textiles in quantities which are exactly what local producers in aggregate produce. Competitive conditions prevailing in the markets ensure that local demand and local supply must match. Otherwise, if aggregate local demand for textiles exceeds the aggregate local supply of textiles, the relative price rises and equilibrates the two in the process. On the other hand, if aggregate local supply of textiles exceeds the aggregate local demand for textiles, the relative price declines. Denoting the relative price of textiles by $p = \frac{P_T}{P_C}$, the pre-trade or autarchic *equilibrium* relative price at home and abroad, p_a and p_a^* thus must be such that:

International Economics. Rajat Acharyya, Oxford University Press. © Oxford University Press 2022.
DOI: 10.1093/oso/9780192865144.003.0002

$$D_j(p_a) = X_j(p_a), j = \text{C, T} \tag{2.1}$$

$$D_j^*(p_a^*) = X_j(p_a^*), j = \text{C, T} \tag{2.2}$$

where D_j denotes units of the j-th good demanded at home, X_j denotes units of the j-th good produced at home, and asterisk over a variable denotes the corresponding variable for the foreign country.

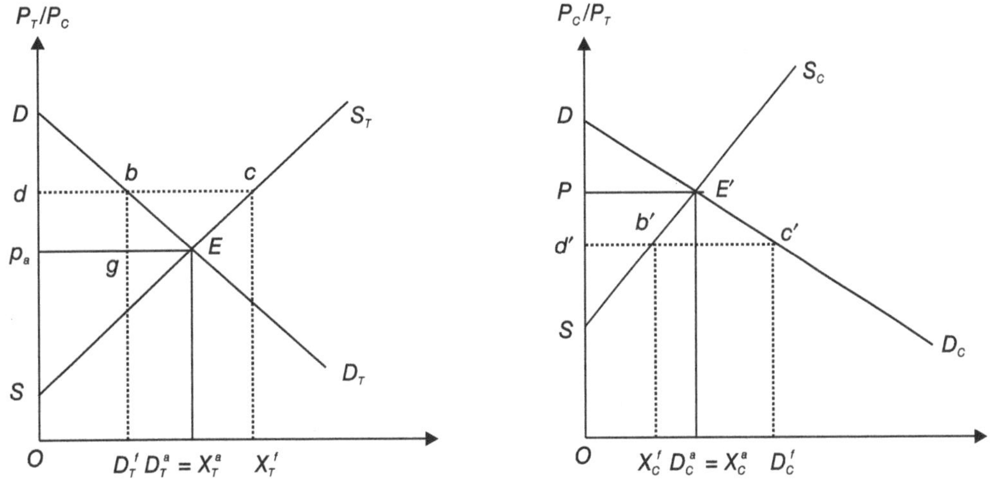

(a) Domestic Market for Textiles (b) Domestic Market for Computers

Figure 2.1 Pre-trade and Post-trade Equilibrium in the Home Country

However, if at a relative price p the aggregate demand for textiles at home exactly matches its aggregate production at home, the aggregate demand for computers should exactly match its aggregate production as well at the same relative price. Thus, essentially the pre-trade or autarchic equilibrium is described by only one condition each in equations (2.1) and (2.2). This is an important aspect of the competitive equilibrium for a many-commodity economy. The reason is simple. Note that the national budget constraint in each country must always be satisfied. This requires that the aggregate value of consumption of computers and cotton textiles in a country must equal the aggregate value of production of computers and cotton textiles in that country. The latter is in fact the produced national income of this country. For our home country, this national budget constraint means:

$$pX_T + X_C = pD_T + D_C \tag{2.3}$$

Rearranging terms and defining excess demand as $E_j = D_j - X_j$, equation (2.3) can be rewritten as:

$$pE_T + E_C = 0 \tag{2.4}$$

This is known as Walras' Law: The sum of the value of excess demand for all commodities produced and consumed in an economy is zero. This law holds for any relative price and regardless of whether markets are in equilibrium or in disequilibrium. By this Walras' Law, it is immediate that if the domestic market for textiles in the home country is in equilibrium (that is, $E_T = 0$) for a relative price p_a, then at the same relative price the domestic market for computers must also be in equilibrium (that is, $E_C = 0$).

Suppose, for any of the reasons spelled out in Chapter 1, our home country has a comparative advantage in textiles and the foreign country has a comparative advantage in computers. That is, $p_a < p_a^*$. Suppose there are no costs of transporting goods from one country to the other. Arbitrage will then lead to exports of textiles from the home country and imports of computers from the foreign country. This pattern of arbitrage and movement of the two goods will cause smaller units of textiles but larger units of computers available at home for local consumption at initial pre-trade prices. The emerging relative scarcity of textiles and abundance of computers will then raise the relative price of textiles at home above the pre-trade price p_a. Similar reasoning will imply a decline in the relative price of textiles abroad below the pre-trade price there p_a^*. Since arbitrage continues as long as cross-country price differences exist, relative price at home steadily rises and the price abroad steadily declines till these prices converge to a uniform level. No further scope of arbitrage will exist thereafter, and therefore, no further trade between these countries will take place. Of course, post-trade prices in each country will converge to a uniform level only if transport costs are zero. Let this uniform price level prevailing in both countries, or the terms of trade (TOT), be p_f. In general, we can expect that $p_a < p_f < p_a^*$, but it may be possible that $p_a = p_f$ or $p_f = p_a^*$ as is explained in Chapter 3.

International trade allows local consumption levels to vary from local production levels. More of a commodity can be consumed than locally produced by importing this good from abroad. Similarly, more of a commodity can be produced than locally demanded by exporting the excess production. Cross-country differences in pre-trade prices (or the comparative advantage of nations) and arbitrage govern which commodity can be imported and thus can be consumed in excess of the amount locally produced, and which commodity can be exported and thus can be produced in excess of the amount that is locally demanded. But the magnitude

Box 2.1 Walras' Law

Walras' Law is an important feature of a competitive general equilibrium system. It states that whereas there may be under-production or over-production in individual markets, there cannot be any under-production or over-production in the aggregate taking all markets together. That is, under-production (or excess demand) in some markets must be matched with corresponding over-production (or excess supply) of equal magnitude in other markets. On the other hand, in an n-market economy, if any $(n–1)$ markets are in equilibrium, so must be the remaining market. This law follows from simply summing up individual budget constraints for all individuals in an economy. However, Walras' Law holds even when some individuals borrow money provided of course the lenders belong to the same economy. Similarly, government's spending and taxes can also be accommodated.

of these excess demands, or the volume of imports, and excess production, or the volume of exports, are determined by national budget constraints (now evaluated at the post-trade uniform price or TOT) or Walras' Law. It follows from equation (2.4) that at the post-trade uniform relative price p_f, we must have:

$$E_C = -p_f E_T \tag{2.5}$$

Since, for our home country, $E_T < 0$ is the volume of exports of textiles and $E_C > 0$ is the volume of imports of computers, Walras' Law now requires that these trade volumes must be such that the value of imports exactly equals the value of exports. That is, international trade should be balanced for the home country. Similarly, trade should be balanced for the foreign country by Walras' Law.

To illustrate the gains for the home country from these exports and imports, refer back to Figure 2.1. Let *od* in panel-*a* be the post-trade relative price of textiles (that is, p_f). The excess supply of textiles of the magnitude $(X_T^f - D_T^f)$ constitutes the volume of exports by the home country and the area $bc\,X_T^f D_T^f$ constitutes the value of exports. It is easy to check that after trade, consumers' surplus falls by the area $dbEp_a$, whereas the producers' surplus increases by the *larger* area $dcEp_a$. Home consumers of textiles lose because arbitrage raises the local price of textiles whereas producers gain because trade creates an opportunity for them to sell textiles at a higher price both at home and abroad. The area $dbgp_a$ is the producers' surplus realized by selling textiles at a higher price to local consumers, and the area *bcEg* is the surplus realized by selling textiles abroad or by exporting textiles. Since the former and part of the area *bcEg* are a redistribution of surplus from local consumers to local producers, the area *bcE* constitutes the net gain from exports for our home economy.

Gains from imports can similarly be measured. In panel *b* of Figure 2.1, *od'* is the post-trade relative price of computers, $\frac{1}{P_f}$. Lower post-trade relative price raises the local demand for computers but lowers the local production. Excess demand of the magnitude $(D_T^f - X_T^f)$ is met through imports from the foreign country. Now home producers lose whereas consumers gain because of imports of cheaper computers. A part of the gains for consumers is a redistribution of surplus from local producers, which equals the area *PE'b'd'*. The area *E'b'c'* constitutes the net gain from imports for the home country.

From these discussions emerge two observations. First, gains from trade for the home country come from increased production and export of textiles in which it has a comparative advantage, and from increased consumption and import of computers in which it has a comparative disadvantage. Hence, these gains are called production gain and consumption gain respectively. Similar production and consumption gains arise for the foreign country in its respective comparative advantage and comparative disadvantage sectors. Second, arbitrage and trade redistribute surpluses among different economic agents. In the market for export goods, surplus is redistributed from consumers to producers and sellers, and hence the latter group gains at the cost of the former. In import-competing sectors, buyers gain at the cost of producers and sellers. However, gainers gain more than the losers lose so that each country gains in aggregate. Arbitrage and trade also redistribute the incomes of factor owners. As the production of computers declines and that of textiles increases in our home country, resources are reallocated across these sectors. Such reallocation, as we will spell out later, raises some factor returns while it lowers others. Hence, international trade creates both winners and losers within each country.

2.2 RESOURCE REALLOCATION AND GAINS FROM TRADE

The demand-supply approach discussed above is a convenient way of illustrating gains from exports and imports separately and the redistribution effect of trade in each sector. But the trade-off between production of export goods and import-competing goods, and implications of resource allocations across these sectors for gains from trade (henceforth, GFT) can be more clearly brought out in an alternative illustration using the production possibility frontier (PPF) and social or community indifference curves (CICs). This approach also enables us to put together the two gains *at balanced trade*.

PPF describes the technologically maximum (and efficient) output level of a commodity that the economy can produce for any given output of the other commodity exhausting all the resources of the economy. It is the upper boundary of the economy's feasible production set. Since pre-trade, a country can consume only what it produces domestically, PPF describes the limit on the consumption possibility of the economy.

The negative slope of PPF, as depicted in Figure 2.2, captures the trade-off between the two output levels. An expansion in the production of cotton textiles necessitates more resources or factors of production. With resources already being fully employed, additional resources required for a larger production of cotton textiles can be made available only by contracting the production of computers and releasing resources from there. Thus, the absolute slope captures the opportunity cost of producing an additional unit of cotton textiles in terms of the number of computer foregone. Alternatively, the absolute slope captures the marginal rate of transformation (MRT), that is, the rate at which computers are transformed into cotton textiles. The *change* in this opportunity cost or MRT is governed by both the diminishing marginal productivities and the returns to scale. As elaborated in Appendix A2, under non-increasing returns to scale along with diminishing marginal productivities, the opportunity cost or MRT increases with successive additional units of cotton textiles being produced. That is, PPF is strictly concave. Increasing returns to scale may also give rise to a concave PPF, provided it is not very strong.

Box 2.2 Gains from Trade and Pareto Improvement

Gains from trade do not mean that everyone in a country is better off. This only states that a country *as a whole* is better off after trade. What this means is that if the winners are forced to compensate the losers for their losses, they will still be better off than before. This is exactly what we have seen in our illustrations. But in reality such a compensation principle is hardly applied. Thus trade only *potentially* benefits *all* in a trading nation. That is, free trade is not a Pareto improvement over no-trade or autarchy, or gains from trade theorem is not a Pareto statement. A Pareto improvement requires that some agents are made strictly better off with others not being worse off. This once again necessitates a compensation principle for free trade to be a Pareto superior state to no-trade or autarchy.

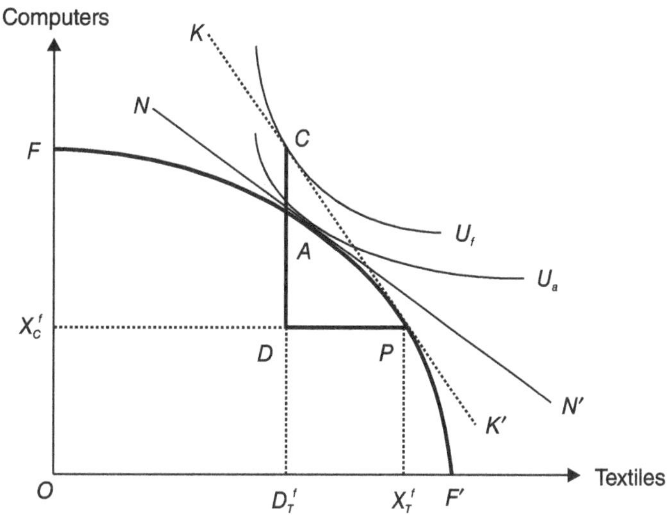

Figure 2.2 Gains from Trade for the Home Country

A CIC, on the other hand, is the locus of different bundles of consumption of computers and cotton textiles for which society or the country attains the same welfare level. A CIC has similar properties as an indifference curve—negatively sloped and strictly convex to the origin—except that despite all axioms of individual preferences being satisfied, any two community indifference curves can intersect each other. This makes ranking of community indifference curves in terms of the index of social welfare difficult. Such a problem can be avoided and a consistent social welfare ranking of commodity bundles can be, however, made in terms of the community indifference curves under identical and homothetic tastes of all individuals in a country.

Under perfectly competitive conditions with flexible factor prices, the pre-trade or autarchic equilibrium in a country, say home country, occurs at point *A* in Figure 2.2 where a CIC is tangent to the PPF. The reason is simple. In the absence of any externality in production and factor-price differential, the absolute slope of the PPF or the opportunity cost of producing textiles equals the ratio of private marginal costs of producing computers and cotton textiles,[1] $\frac{MC_T}{MC_C}$. Thus, for any production bundle on the PPF, the corresponding slope reflects the relative *supply price* of textiles because of the marginal-cost-pricing under perfectly competitive conditions. On the other hand, the absolute slope of a CIC gives us the common marginal rate of substitution in consumption across all individuals or the relative *demand price*, that is, the relative price that the consumers are willing to pay for textiles per unit of computers. Competitive equilibrium should therefore be at a point where these prices match, and this corresponds to the tangency point *A*. The absolute slope of the common tangent *NN′* reflects the autarchic relative price p_a in our home country. Thus, at autarchic equilibrium commodity bundle A:

$$MRS(A) = p_a = MRT(A) \tag{2.6}$$

Note that the national budget constraint in equation (2.3) is now represented by the common tangent NN' passing through bundle A. Thus both the autarchic production and consumption bundles being on the same budget line, the aggregate value of consumption for the home country is exactly equal to its aggregate value of production (or produced national income). At the same time, commodity bundle A being the bundle produced as well as consumed under autarchy, the equilibrium condition specified in equation (2.1) is satisfied as well.

Now allow international trade to take place, which for reasons spelled out in the earlier section, causes the post-trade relative price of textiles to rise to p_f under the assumption that home country has a comparative advantage in textiles. Increased relative price of textiles encourages its producers to expand production. On the other hand, lower relative price of computers lowers its production. Some resources are thereby released from this sector that move to the textiles sector to find employment, and thus make it possible to sustain increased production there. As long as the marginal cost of production in each sector is rising in respective output levels, such expansion in the production of textiles and contraction in the production of computers raises the ratio of marginal costs, $\frac{MC_T}{MC_C}$. The post-trade profit opportunities in the textiles sector thus decline and get completely exhausted once textile production expands to the level (and computer production contracts to a corresponding level) such that the corresponding $\frac{MC_T}{MC_C}$ equals the post-trade relative price p_f. No further production adjustment takes place thereafter. Referring to Figure 2.2, since under no production externality $\frac{MC_T}{MC_C}$ equals the opportunity cost of producing textiles or MRT, the post-trade equilibrium production bundle P must correspond to the tangency point between the national budget line (or the price line) KK' at the post-trade price and the PPF.

In the foreign country, production adjusts towards the computer sector because trade causes the relative price of computers to increase there. Thus, each country now specializes: the home country in the production of textiles and the foreign country in the production of computers. This is consistent with their respective comparative advantages as well. Thus, if prices correctly signal comparative advantage, post-trade production specialization takes place according to comparative advantage.

Note that due to strict concavity of the PPF we may have an interior production optimum, that is, incomplete specialization, even after international trade. If the PPF had been linear or strictly convex, then the margin $p_f - \frac{MC_T}{MC_C}$ at the autarchic production bundle would either remain the same or increase as the production of textiles was increased. This would result in a corner solution, that is, complete specialization in textiles.

On the other hand, given the post-trade higher relative price, consumption of textiles now falls whereas that of computers rises, with optimal consumption bundle C being the one for which $MRS(C) = p_f$. Note that international trade allows the consumption bundle to differ from the production bundle, meaning that condition (2.1) is no longer binding for optimal consumption decisions of home buyers. That is, PPF no longer constrains optimal aggregate consumption levels. However, the home country cannot spend on consumption of the two goods more than what it earns so that the national budget constraint at the post-trade relative price still needs to be satisfied. Thus, the optimal consumption bundle is now constrained by the post-trade price line *KK′*. MRS equals MRT even at the post-trade equilibrium but for different consumption and production bundles:

$$MRS(C) = p_f = MRT(P) \tag{2.7}$$

Thus, as illustrated in Figure 2.2, international trade according to the comparative advantage for the home country allows it to attain a CIC indexed by the social welfare level U_f. Under assumptions of identical and homothetic tastes, CICs do not intersect each other, so that a higher CIC represents strictly higher social welfare. Hence, trade raises the welfare of the home country from an autarchic social welfare level U_a to U_f. This is the social welfare measure of GFT. Essentially, international trade expands the feasible set of consumption by allowing a country to consume beyond its production possibility frontier and this creates scope for the welfare gain. Similar gains arise for the foreign country. Thus international trade makes *both* the countries better off.

This is an illustration of the so-called GFT theorem, which is the essence of the doctrine of comparative advantage. Pattern of trade consistent with comparative advantage makes all countries strictly better off in terms of social welfare. This strong result established by Ricardo, however, depends on a few restrictions on technology and market structure, as we will spell out later.

The GFT theorem has two implications. First, arbitrage by self-interested atomistic agents makes others and the country better off, which is in fact a reiteration of Adam Smith's invisible hand. Atomistic traders decide which goods to export and which goods to import according to the signals given by the market through price differences across countries and scope of arbitrage thereof. If these price differences correctly signal the comparative advantages of nations, such trading also creates opportunities for consumers to gain and ensures that the economy *as a whole* gains. The important underlying conditions for this, as we will see, are competitive markets with no externalities whatsoever.

The second implication of the GFT theorem is that trade according to comparative advantage makes *all* trading partners better off. That is, international trade is a positive-sum game: gains from trade for one country do not come at the cost of its trading partner. That is, a country need not exploit its trading partner to gain from trade. Of course, as we will see, free trade may not lead to *maximum* welfare for all countries. Some countries may, in fact, gain *further* by restricting their imports through tariffs or import quotas. But such gains will always be at the cost of their trading partners.[2] Only multilateral free trade makes *all* countries better off, and hence is globally Pareto optimal.

Once again to reiterate, not *all* economic agents at home (and abroad) necessarily gain from trade as explained in the earlier section. But as long as CICs are non-intersecting, the aggregate or social welfare is higher under free trade: $U_f > U_a$. This means that if a compensation principle is applied whereby the gainers are forced to compensate the losers, there will still be some gains left for them, so that the free-trade consumption bundle *C* is Pareto superior to the autarchic consumption bundle *A*. In the absence of any compensation principle, however, trade only *potentially* benefits *all* within a country. The GFT theorem thus should not be interpreted as a Pareto statement.

[2] In fact, as will be shown later, trade restrictions are in general negative-sum games.

Box 2.3 Trade Triangle

The triangle *CDP* in Figure 2.2 is called the trade triangle for the home country. Whereas the height *DC* measures the excess demand or volume of imports of computers from the foreign country, the base *DP* measures the excess supply or volume of exports of textiles to the foreign country. The slope of the hypotenuse *PC*, which is a segment of the national budget line for the home country, on the other hand, indicates the terms of trade p_f. Both the consumption bundle *C* and production bundle *P* being on the budget line, these volumes of exports and imports are consistent with balanced trade at the post-trade price p_f, satisfying the condition in equation (2.5).

2.3 DECOMPOSITION OF GFT: SPECIALIZATION AND EXCHANGE GAINS

The gains from trade illustrated in Figure 2.2 can be decomposed into two parts: gains due to specialization and due to exchange according to comparative advantage. To illustrate these two components isolated from each other, imagine what the home country could do at best if the production could not be adjusted to the post-trade relative price p_f. Of course, the economy could still consume beyond its PPF and exchange the autarchic production bundle *A* with the foreign country to reap the benefits of price differences. This is illustrated in Figure 2.3 by the movement of consumption point from *A* to *C'* along the post-trade price line *LL'* drawn through the autarchic production bundle *A*. The consequent gain indicated by the higher utility level *U'* would have been realized purely due to exchange of autarchic production bundles by the trading countries. This part of the GFT, therefore, is called the *exchange or consumption gain.*

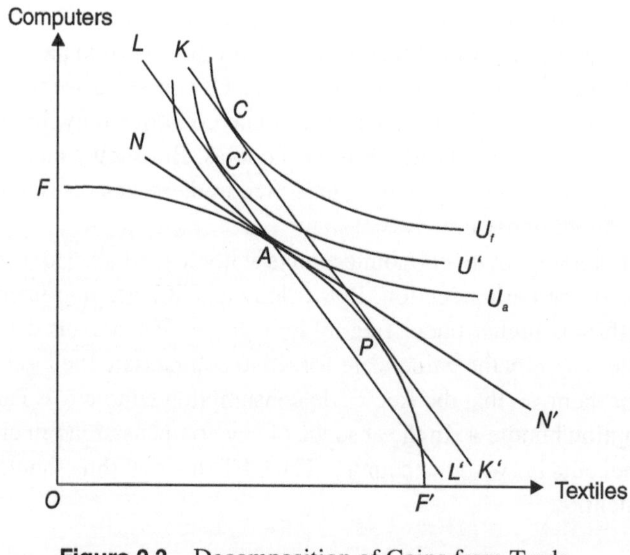

Figure 2.3 Decomposition of Gains from Trade

Now allow production to adjust to the post-trade price. Given the pattern of comparative advantage as signalled by the price difference, the economy now specializes in cotton textiles and this creates scope for further gain. The consumption point now can move further to the north-east since additional production of cotton textiles enables the country to get more of the cheaper computers from abroad in exchange for cotton textiles which are dearer abroad. Thus the additional gain over and above the exchange gain (indicated by the utility level U_f) is realized through production specialization and hence is called *the specialization or production gain.*

This specialization gain arises because resources can now be reallocated from the relatively inefficient production of computers towards the more efficient production of textiles. This was not possible under autarchy because local demand for computers had to be met through local production. International trade relaxes this constraint and makes it possible for an efficient reallocation of resources towards the comparative advantage good. This enables the country to raise its aggregate value of production and consequently increase its consumption possibility, as indicated by the higher budget line *KK'*. This is how the country gains over and above the exchange gain.

The magnitudes of these two components of GFT, however, depend on the substitution possibility in consumption and in production. We discuss the implications of such substitution possibilities below.

2.3.1 Substitution Possibility in Consumption and the Exchange Gain

The degree of substitutability of computers by cotton textiles in consumption and vice versa, determines the curvature property of CIC, or more precisely, its convexity. The less substitutable the two consumption goods are, more convex are CICs, and consequently less will be the magnitude of the exchange gain. At the extreme, suppose computers and textiles are consumed in a fixed proportion as indicated by the ray *OC* in Figure 2.4a. Thus, even if computers can be bought cheaper abroad, home consumers will not be able to substitute their consumption of cotton textiles by purchase of computers. Given this complementarity of the two goods, purchase of more computers will be beneficial only if textile consumption is increased proportionately as well. But without increased income, realized through larger production of textiles at home, this is not feasible. Consequently, there will be *no* exchange gain. Diagrammatically, CICs being L-shaped in this case, the consumption bundle cannot be shifted from point A without production adjustment, even if price differences exist. Consequently, the entire GFT consists only of specialization gain in this case.

2.3.2 Substitution Possibility in Production and Specialization Gain

Similarly, the specialization gain depends on the substitution possibility in production. For example, if factors of production are immobile across the two sectors, the production of either good cannot be increased from the autarchic level as given by the bundle *A*. Though production of computers (or that of cotton textiles) can be lowered, the laid off workers and excess capital cannot be moved to the production of textiles (or computers). Thus, PPF in Figure 2.4b will have a box-like shape. In such a case, there will be no specialization gain. However, as long as substitution possibilities in consumption exist, buyers can exchange the autarchic production

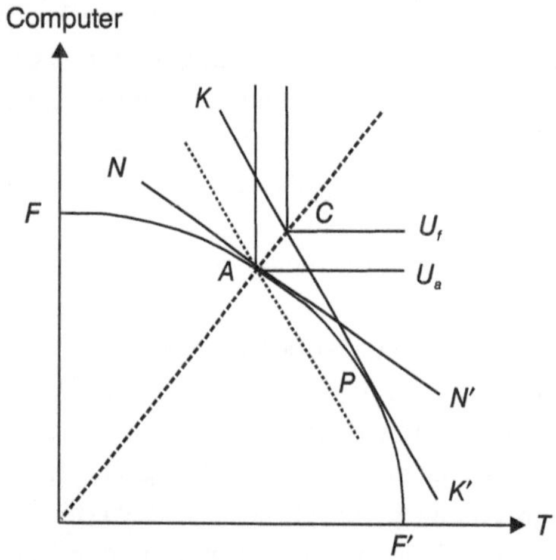

(a) No Exchange Gain When Two Goods Are Consumed in a Fixed Proportion

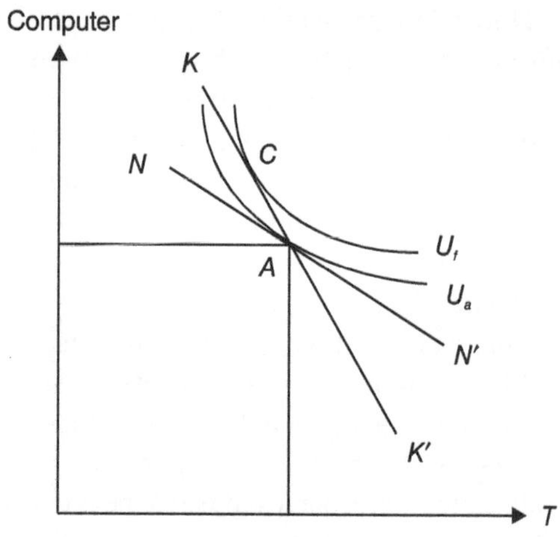

(b) No Specialization Gain When Resources Are Immobile across the Two Sectors

Figure 2.4 Substitution Possibilities and Magnitude of GFT

bundle and take advantage of the price differences across countries. Thus, now the entire GFT will be the exchange gain.

2.4 SUFFICIENT CONDITIONS FOR GFT[3]

We had mentioned earlier that GFT may not always be realized. It necessitates certain conditions to be satisfied. In general, for international trade to be welfare improving, the free trade price line *KK'* in Figure 2.2 must be a separating line. That is, the price line neither must cut PPF, nor any segment of it must lie within the PPF. To understand why we need these conditions, consider Figure 2.5. In panel *a*, the free trade price line *KK'* cuts PPF at the post-trade production bundle *P*. Suppose the home country has a comparative advantage in computers. Thus, it exports computers and imports textiles so that the consumption bundle *C* is now to the right of the production bundle *P*. If the autarchic production (and consumption) bundle had been anywhere in the segment *ab* along PPF, CIC passing through that bundle indicating the social welfare level attained under autarchy will be strictly above U_f. Thus, trade will be welfare reducing. This illustration suggests that the free trade price line must not cut PPF, that is, it must be tangent to it. This is what is called the *tangency condition.*

Does this mean that whenever the tangency condition holds, the country will gain from trade? The answer depends on the convexity of the production set. In panel *b*, a convex PPF is drawn so that the production set underneath the PPF is non-convex. Suppose now the free trade price line is tangent to it at point *P*. The economy consumes at point *C* and attains the welfare level U_f. But once again if the autarchic production (and consumption) bundle

[3] For an advanced reading, see Markusen and Melvin (1989).

Box 2.4 GFT in Commodity-Endowment and Factor-Endowment Models

A commodity endowment model (or an exchange economy) is the one where production levels are exogenously given. Since production does not take place, trade leads to welfare gain only through exchange. A factor endowment model (or a production economy), on the other hand, is one where the exogenously given endowments of resources are combined to produce goods. As long as all the factors of production are sectorally mobile, trade will lead to welfare gains through both exchange and specialization. Therefore, in general, we can expect GFT to be larger in a factor-endowment model than in a commodity-endowment model. But, if factors of production are sectorally immobile, the factor-endowment model essentially collapses to the commodity-endowment model and, *ceteris paribus*, gains are of the same magnitude.

had been anywhere in the segment *ab* along PPF, free trade would be welfare reducing. Here though the tangency condition holds, the free trade price line lies within the PPF. Hence, it does not constitute a separating line. Therefore, the production set must also be strictly convex (or PPF must be strictly concave) and this is what is known as the *convexity condition.*

Thus, for the GFT theorem to be valid, both the tangency and convexity conditions must hold. However, note that these are only *sufficient* conditions. In case of a concave PPF, referring back to panel *a* in Figure 2.5, if the country had comparative advantage in cotton textiles, the autarchic production bundle would have been to the left of *P*. That is, the home country would have then specialized in textiles, and as usual trade would have been welfare improving. We shall return to the non-convex production set being only a sufficient condition later.

The above tangency and convexity conditions require quite a few restrictions on the market structure and technology. For example, the tangency condition holds under the following circumstances—perfect competition or marginal-cost-pricing; no external economies or dis-

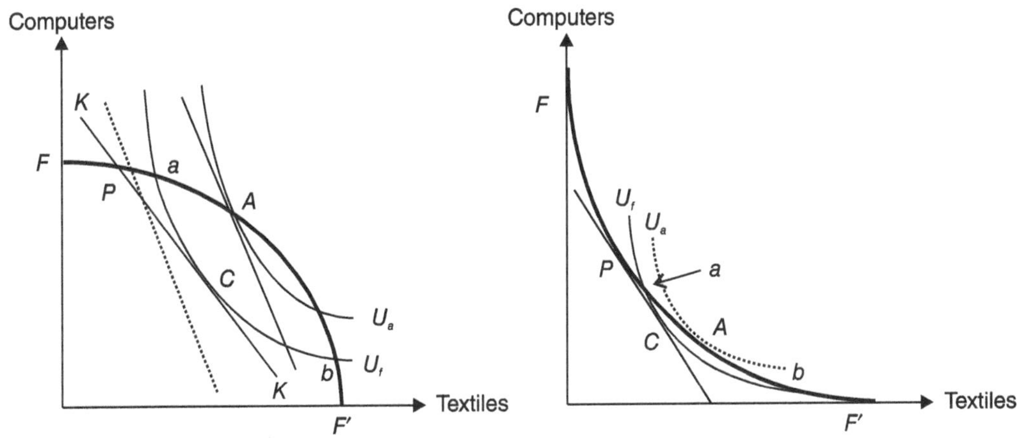

(a) Violation of Tangency Condition (b) Violation of Convexity Condition

Figure 2.5 Welfare Deteriorating Trade

economies of scale of production; and no internal economies of scale or increasing returns to scale. On the other hand, for the convexity condition we require non-increasing returns to scale with diminishing marginal productivity and distortion-free factor markets. Of course, we may have a convex production set even under increasing returns to scale (IRS), provided it is not so pronounced as explained in Appendix A2.

To exemplify how technologies exhibiting economies or diseconomies of scale violate the tangency condition, consider the case of negative externalities in production (or external diseconomies of scale). To draw from our earlier example in Chapter 1, suppose iron and steel (denoted by C) generate a negative externality in the sense that its larger production inflicts additional costs on textiles production. Production of iron and steel emits industrial ashes and thereby erodes soil fertility. This lowers cotton yield per acreage of cultivation. The consequent increase in the price of raw cotton feeds into a higher cost of production for the textiles industry. This additional cost, however, is not internalized by producers of iron and steel so that the private marginal cost of producing iron and steel is smaller than its social marginal cost. If textile production generates no externality whatsoever, its private and social marginal costs will be the same as usual. Hence, $\frac{MC_T}{MC_C} > \frac{SMC_T}{SMC_C}$. Thus, in an unregulated home country the marginal cost-pricing under perfectly competitive conditions will mean that the pre-trade relative price of cotton textiles will be higher than the opportunity cost or MRT. This is shown in Figure 2.5a as the pre-trade price line cuts PPF from above at the autarchic production bundle. Thus, the tangency condition is violated. Suppose the government in the foreign country forces iron and steel producers there to internalize the costs that they inflict upon cotton textile producers by imposing a production tax. Thus the pre-trade relative price of textiles there will be equal to the ratio of social marginal cost or MRT. Now if consumers in the two countries have homothetic and identical tastes, and $\frac{MC_T}{MC_C} > \frac{SMC_T^*}{SMC_C^*} > \frac{SMC_T}{SMC_C}$, the home country will have a comparative advantage in iron and steel. This is the situation depicted in Figure 2.5a by the pre-trade price line cutting PPF *from above* at production bundle *A*.

As trade opens up, the home country adjusts its production towards bundle *P*. Note that trade cannot restore the tangency condition because without government regulations, home-producers of iron and steel in the home country will not internalize the external costs that larger production inflicts upon society. Trade will then be welfare reducing for the home country. The reason is simple. If externalities are not regulated, market prices do not reflect actual or social marginal costs, which in this case are larger than private marginal costs. The cost of production is underestimated and this may generate a perverse comparative advantage causing the country to specialize in a commodity in which it may actually have a comparative disadvantage. International trade now reallocates resources towards the *in*efficient sector. Moreover, larger production of iron and steel under this perverse pattern of trade causes larger degradation of the environment and a corresponding higher external cost for the cotton textile sector. Thus, instead of a specialization gain, the home economy will now experience a specialization loss. There will, however, be the usual exchange gain because even under a perverse pattern of trade home buyers benefit from imports of cheaper cotton textiles from abroad. When the home economy specializes too much in iron and steel, the specialization loss is large enough to outweigh the exchange gain, and the economy experiences a welfare reduction under trade as illustrated above. But if specialization in the wrong commodity is not too much then there may still be GFT. This will be the case when the post-trade production bundle is not too far on the left from the autarchic production bundle. In Figure 2.5a, this possibility is shown by the broken pre-trade price line that cuts PPF.

2.5 POLLUTION: A TRADE-OFF BETWEEN GFT AND ENVIRONMENTAL DEGRADATION

The case of negative externality violating the tangency condition illustrates that international trade can make a country worse off relative to autarchy. On top of this violation of the tangency condition as a source of welfare loss under free trade, there can be direct utility losses compounding the problem. This is particularly important when commodities that an economy produces use up environment as a factor of production. Note that environmental degradation through pollution emissions by production of commodities can essentially be interpreted as the environment being used as a factor in the production process. In this interpretation, commodities can be ranked according to their pollution intensities, which is the pollution emitted per unit of output being produced. As we have explained earlier, international trade changes the composition of aggregate output through reallocation of resources from the lines of production in which the country has comparative disadvantages to the lines where it has comparative advantages. Thus, if a country has a comparative advantage in commodities with relatively higher pollution intensity—the dirtier goods—then we can expect the aggregate pollution level to rise by the *composition effect* of international trade.

There are two other effects of international trade on environmental degradation or the national pollution level. One is the *scale effect*. If resources were not fully employed initially, free trade will increase the scale of production of dirtier as well as cleaner goods. Once again the pollution level rises. The other is the *technique effect*. Free trade may induce producers to adopt cleaner production techniques by altering factor prices and the relative cost of pollution emission. The technique effect thus lowers the pollution level. Overall, the composition and scale effects dominate the technique effect so that free trade raises pollution levels in the country that has comparative advantage in dirtier goods and consequently exports these goods. Thus, when produced goods degrade the environment and inflict social losses, the welfare or real income gains from opening up of trade are to be weighed against these losses.

Two comments are warranted at this point. First, as we will elaborate in a latter chapter, these welfare losses through increased pollution do not necessarily call for restricting international trade. Trade prohibition is certainly not the optimal solution. Second, for many goods pollution is emitted while they are being consumed rather than while they are being produced. A typical example is emissions by cars. In case of such consumption externalities, effects of free trade on national pollution levels are exactly the opposite.

There is some evidence that the pollution content of India's trade basket had increased during 1990s, a period that coincided with her major economic reforms including exchange rate and trade liberalization. But empirical estimates of the overall effects of international trade on pollution levels are mixed, particularly because the effects vary from one indicator of pollution to the other. Frankel and Rose (2002), for example, observed in a cross-country study that for air pollution measures (SO_2, NO_2, and particulate matter), trade openness reduced pollution. But trade openness raised CO_2 emissions, which is a global pollutant.

2.6 INCREASING RETURNS TO SCALE (IRS) AND GFT

Under increasing returns to scale, the tangency condition is necessarily violated since the marginal cost-pricing does not hold. On the other hand, the production set may be non-convex (if IRS is strong) in which case the convexity condition is also violated. Does this mean that when a few (or all) goods are produced with IRS technology, there cannot be any GFT?

Note first of all, that the tangency and convexity conditions are only *sufficient* conditions. Second, under a strong IRS (leading to a non-convex production set), there may in fact be more potential gain. To illustrate we consider these two cases separately.

2.6.1 Case I: GFT under Weak IRS and Violation of Tangency Condition

As discussed in Appendix A2, unless IRS is strong to outweigh the cost reducing effect of diminishing marginal productivities when the composition of goods (or the production bundle) changes with full employment of resources, PPF will be strictly concave and the production set strictly convex as usual. But the tangency condition will no longer hold. Suppose production of computers exhibits IRS whereas cotton textiles are produced by constant-returns-to-scale (CRS) technology. Hence, for computers, we have average cost-pricing and since under IRS the average cost (AC) falls as the level of output is increased and is always larger than the marginal cost ($MC_C < AC_C$), so at the autarchic production bundle we must have $p_a < \dfrac{MC_T}{MC_C} = MRT$. This case is illustrated in Figure 2.6a. At the autarchic production (and consumption) bundle A, a CIC is tangent to the pre-trade price line that cuts the PPF *from below*. If the country has a comparative advantage in computers (which is an IRS-good), trade expands its production to point P and shifts the economy's consumption to point C thereby raising national welfare. But if the comparative advantage is in cotton textiles (which is a CRS-good), production shifts to the right of A and the economy *may* experience a loss in national welfare. Thus, a sufficient condition for GFT is that *trade should expand the production of IRS goods*. This is because a comparative advantage in an IRS good means that the economies of scale in the production of such a good can further be exploited through post-trade specialization. A comparative advantage in cotton textiles, on the other hand, will mean that post-trade specialization raises the *average* cost of producing computers. If this is not compensated by the exchange gain that arises due to the price difference, national welfare declines after trade.

2.6.2 Case II: GFT under Strong IRS and Non-convexity

Now consider the case of a strong IRS, which violates the convexity condition as well. Interestingly, this provides more scope for GFT. Since under autarchy both the goods must be produced domestically, in Figure 2.6b, the autarchic production bundle is shown at an interior point A. Note that the local demand for cotton textiles constrains exploiting IRS in computers to the fullest extent by completely specializing in its production under autarchy. But when the home country has a comparative advantage in computers, and as trade allows consumption of cotton textiles through imports, the economy will now be completely specialized in computers (an IRS-good) producing bundle F and realizing higher national welfare. However, the country would have gained through complete specialization in cotton textiles (a CRS-good) as well if it had a comparative advantage in textiles. In such a case, the post-trade relative price would have been higher than the pre-trade relative price of textiles and bundle F' would have been the post-trade production bundle. Thus, expansion of an IRS good under trade is no longer a necessary condition for GFT.

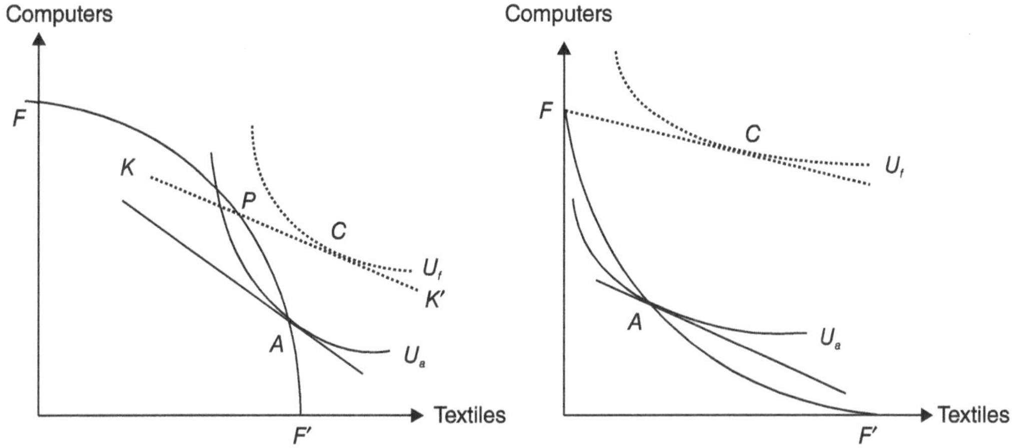

(a) Weak IRS and Violation of Tangency Condition

(b) Strong IRS and Violation of Both Tangency and Convexity Conditions

Figure 2.6 GFT under Weak and Strong IRS

The interesting point to note here is that even when the home country has a comparative *dis*advantage in producing computers, a complete specialization in this line of production *may* paradoxically raise welfare above the autarchic level. Thus, the home country may gain from trade by completely specializing in the IRS good regardless of whether it has a comparative advantage in the IRS good or not. Recollect that GFT through specialization in the good in which the country has a comparative disadvantage is not possible when both goods are produced by CRS technology. In case of IRS, this is possible because complete specialization in the IRS good enables the country to exploit the economies of scale (and consequently minimize the average cost of production) to the fullest possible extent and thus experience a specialization gain despite specializing in the good in which it has a comparative disadvantage. Since IRS is strong in this case (resulting in a convex PPF), the resulting specialization gain is large enough to outweigh the exchange loss that arises because the country being completely specialized in computers is forced to import textiles at a higher price from the foreign country.

APPENDIX A2

I. Returns to Scale and Convexity of the Production Set

Shape of PPF depends on how does the opportunity cost or MRT change when production of cotton textiles is increased and correspondingly the production of computers is decreased. If the opportunity cost or MRT increases, PPF is strictly concave. Opportunity cost is essentially the ratio of social marginal costs, and in absence of any production externality private and social marginal costs are the same. Thus a change in the ratio of private marginal costs, which is determined by both the returns to scale and the law of diminishing marginal productivities, governs the shape of PPF.

To explain, suppose at an initial relative price p_o, the economy was producing T_o units of textiles and C_o units of computers. Suppose also that at the initial wage–rental ratio, computers were produced by a relatively capital-intensive technique of production and textiles were produced by a relatively labour-intensive technique of production. Now consider an additional unit of production of textiles. With all resources initially fully employed, this requires a corresponding reduction in the production of computers. At the initial wage–rental ratio, producers of textiles will maintain the same technique of production while expanding their production. There will thus be a scale expansion in the textiles sector, that is, use of labour and additional capital will be increased proportionately. For similar reasons, a scale contraction will take place in the computer sector. Corresponding changes in marginal costs of production in the two sectors will therefore be governed by the returns to scale. If both the goods are produced under constant returns to scale (CRS) technology, the marginal cost of production, *at initial factor prices*, should remain constant in both the sectors. Hence, at initial factor prices, an expansion in the production of textiles and a corresponding contraction in the production of computers along PPF will not change the opportunity cost or MRT. If the goods are, however, produced under IRS, then the marginal cost of production should decline in the expanding textiles sector and should rise in the contracting computer sector. Note that IRS technology means that an additional unit of production of textiles requires less than one unit of additional labour and capital, and this is why average and marginal costs decline. Thus, under IRS, MRT declines at initial factor prices. Similarly, if the goods are produced by decreasing returns to scale technology, MRT at initial factor prices rises as textiles production expands.

But these are not the final effects because factor prices do not remain constant. Since producers of computers were using relatively capital-intensive techniques than producers of textiles at initial prices, they will release relatively more capital but less labour through scale contraction than what is needed in the textiles sector for its scale expansion. There will thus emerge an excess supply of capital and excess demand for labour. The wage–rental ratio should therefore rise, which will induce producers everywhere to adopt relatively capital-intensive techniques of production than before. Now the law of variable proportions comes into play. As long as marginal productivity of a factor is diminishing as it is used more intensively, the marginal cost in the expanding textiles sector now should rise and that in the contracting sector should fall. Thus with the change in factor prices and corresponding changes in the techniques of production, MRT should rise as long as marginal productivities are diminishing.

In sum, a movement downward along PPF implying an expansion of textiles production and corresponding contraction of computer production, causes a *scale effect* at initial factor prices and a *technique effect* as factor prices change subsequently. By the initial scale effect the opportunity cost or MRT increases if production technologies in both sectors are DRS, remains constant if CRS, and decline if IRS. The subsequent technique effect, on the other hand, raises the opportunity cost or MRT if marginal productivities are diminishing. Overall, for CRS and DRS technologies, along with diminishing marginal productivities, MRT increases. PPF thus will be strictly concave and the production set strictly convex. For IRS technology along with diminishing marginal productivities, the scale and technique effects influence the change in MRT in opposite directions. For a not so pronounced or weak IRS technology, technique effects dominate so that MRT increases and PPF is concave. But for a strong IRS, the scale effect dominates so that now PPF is convex as illustrated in Figure 2.6b.

SUMMARY POINTS

- Free trade is beneficial for all the trading partners if each country exports the good in which it has a comparative (cost) advantage. This is known as the Gains from Trade theorem. However, for this GFT to be realized, the market (price) must correctly signal the trading partners' relative strengths in production patterns, which requires, among other things, that technology does not exhibit external economies or diseconomies of scale.
- International trade expands the feasible set of consumption by allowing a country to consume beyond its production possibility frontier and this creates scope for the welfare gain.
- But international trade creates both winners and losers within each country. Domestic producers of the good exported gain whereas domestic consumers lose from a higher price. On the other hand, domestic consumers of the imported good gain whereas domestic producers lose from lower prices of the foreign good. Thus GFT does not mean that *all* agents in a trading nation are better off than before and accordingly it is not a Pareto statement. But if a compensation principle is applied whereby the winners are forced to compensate the losers for their losses, international trade is a Pareto improvement over autarchy. This is because GFT, which states that a country *as a whole* is better off after trade, ensures that the gainers will still be better off than before even after compensating the losers.
- GFT has two components: exchange gain and specialization gain. Gain realized purely due to exchange of autarchic production bundles by the trading nations is called *exchange or consumption gain*. The gain realized through production specialization and change in commodity composition according to the comparative advantages of nations is called *specialization or production gain.*
- These gains depend on the possibility of substitution in consumption and production. If the two goods are consumed in a fixed ratio, no substitution possibility in consumption exists. Accordingly, there will be no exchange gain. On the other hand, if all factors of production are immobile across sectors, no substitution possibility in production exists; accordingly there will be no specialization gain. The commodity endowment model is a special case where GFT, if at all, consists only of exchange gain.
- For GFT to be realized, the free trade price line must neither cut the PPF nor should any segment of it lie within the PPF. These are known as tangency condition and convexity condition respectively, which are, however, only sufficient conditions.
- In an unregulated economy, a good that pollutes the environment and thus generates negative externality, will be under-priced and thus may reflect a *perverse* comparative

(*contd*)

Summary Points (*contd*)

advantage. In such a case, the tangency condition will be violated and this economy will experience a specialization *loss* after trade opens up. If this loss is large enough, it may outweigh the exchange gain and make the nation as a whole worse off than before.

- In the above example, there can also be *direct* utility losses compounding the problem. Thus when produced goods degrade the environment and inflict social losses, welfare or real income gains from opening up of trade are to be weighed against these losses.
- In case of a good being produced under IRS technology, which is not strong so that only the tangency condition is violated, a sufficient condition for GFT is that *trade should expand production of the IRS good*. This is because a comparative advantage in the IRS good means that the economies of scale in the production of such a good can further be exploited through post-trade specialization. A comparative advantage in a CRS good, on the other hand, will mean that post-trade specialization raises the *average* cost of producing the IRS good. If this is not compensated by the exchange gain, national welfare declines after trade.
- In case of strong IRS, the convexity condition is also violated. But this creates further scope for GFT. Now the country may gain from trade by completely specializing in the IRS good regardless of whether it has a comparative advantage in this good or not.

KEYWORDS

- **Walras' Law** states that the sum of the values of excess demand for all commodities produced and consumed in an economy is zero. This law holds for any relative price and regardless of whether markets are in equilibrium or in disequilibrium.

  This law also requires that trade should be balanced for all trading partners.
- **Production possibility frontier (PPF)** is the locus of technologically maximum (and efficient) output levels of a commodity that the economy can produce for different levels of output of the other commodity by exhausting all the resources of the economy.
- **Pareto superior state/regime:** Regime A is Pareto superior to Regime B if some agents are made strictly better off with others not being worse off when the economy moves to Regime A from Regime B. Trade is not a Pareto improving state in the absence of a compensation principle because trade creates both winners and losers.
- **Opportunity cost** or the marginal rate of transformation in production (MRT) is the units of computers that the economy must forego to produce an additional unit of cotton textiles. This is the absolute slope of PPF and is in fact the ratio of social marginal costs for textiles to that for computers.
- **Community indifference curve** (CIC) is the locus of different bundles of consumption of computers and cotton textiles for which the society or the country attains the same welfare levels. Its absolute slope measures the common marginal rate of substitution in consumption across all consumers.

(*contd*)

Keywords (*contd*)

- **GFT theorem:** International trade according to comparative advantage makes all countries strictly better off in terms of social welfare. This is the essence of the doctrine of comparative advantage.
- **Exchange gain** is the improvement in social welfare through exchange of the autarchic production bundle at post-trade prices.
- **Specialization gain** is the improvement in social welfare through production specialization in the good in which the country has a comparative advantage. This specialization gain arises because resources can now be reallocated from relatively inefficient production of goods in which the country has a comparative disadvantage towards more efficient production lines.
- **A Commodity endowment model** (or an exchange economy) is one where production levels are exogenously given.

EXERCISES

1. Consider a two country world with n goods. Taking the n-th good as the numeraire, show that if for a set of relative prices $p = \{p_1, p_2, \ldots, p_{n-1}, 1\}$ trade is balanced for one country, so it must be for its trading partner.
2. Production possibility frontier (PPF) essentially reflects the resource constraint of an economy. Discuss.
3. On what factors does the shape of PPF depend? What does the strict concavity of PPC signify?
4. What can you infer about the shape of PPC in each of the following cases:

   (i) $X_1 = L_1^a K_1^{1-a}$, $X_2 = L_1^{0.4} K_1^{0.8}$

   (ii) $X_1 = L_1^{1.2} K_1^{1.4}$, $X_2 = L_1^{1.7} K_1^{1.7}$
5. Consider the following production functions for goods 1 and 2: $X_1 = AL_1^{\alpha} K_1^{\beta}$, $X_2 = AL_2^{\gamma} K_2^{\delta}$. For what range of values of α, β, γ, δ can you unconditionally say that PPF will be convex to the origin? Give reasons.
6. Suppose the marginal cost of producing jute bags (x) is 40 per unit, there is no fixed cost, the domestic demand for jute bags is $p^d = 60 - x$, and the world price of jute bags is 30 per unit. If jute bags in the domestic economy are produced by a perfectly competitive industry, should jute bags be imported or exported? Calculate the gains from imports or exports as the case may be. Does your answer depend on the domestic market structure?
7. Before trade was allowed, a single firm in Japan was producing data processing equipments at a total cost of $10x + \frac{x^2}{2}$, where x is the level of output. The domestic demand for data processing equipments is $p_d = 100 - 2x$. If the world price of

(*contd*)

Exercises (*contd*)

data processing equipments is 30 per unit, how much the firm should produce when trade is allowed? What will be volume of imports or exports, as the case may be?

8. In the above example, suppose the monopolist's cost function is given by $250+10x+\frac{x^2}{2}$, where 250 is the sunk cost. Should the monopolist produce any data processing equipments when trade is allowed?

9. Show that if soccer balls are produced by perfectly competitive firms whereas digital cameras by a monopolist in a country, then the tangency condition is violated. If both the goods are produced by constant returns to scale technology and the country has a comparative advantage in soccer balls, should it gain from trade? Explain.

10. Suppose all consumers in a country consume bread and butter at a fixed ratio of 2:1 regardless of the relative price. Suppose the opportunity cost of producing bread (or butter) is constant. 1,000 units of bread can be produced when all resources are used in its production and 500 units of butter can be produced if all resources are used in its production.
    (a) Illustrate the pre-trade equilibrium.
    (b) What will be the pre-trade relative price of bread?
    (c) When trade opens up, the country finds the relative price of bread in the world market as three-fourths. Which good will it export?
    (d) Calculate the country's volume of exports.
    (e) Will the country gain from trade? If so, what is the source of its gains from trade?

11. (a) Consider the following equation of India's production possibility curve (PPC):
$$600=10X_T+20X_C+X_TX_C$$
where T stands for textiles and C for computers. Is the opportunity cost for producing textiles increasing or decreasing?
    (b) If textiles and computers are consumed in a fixed ratio of 2:1, then find out the autarkic relative price of textiles, and illustrate the autarkic equilibrium in a diagram.
    (c) If the world relative price of textiles is 2, which good should India export when trade is allowed and why?
    (d) What can you say about the post-trade production of textiles and computers in India?

12. Suppose both Home and Foreign Countries have the same production possibility frontier (PPF) given by $5000 = 2X_1 + X_2$. The tastes of consumers are represented by downward sloping and strictly convex community indifference curves.
    (a) If the Home country has a taste bias in good 1, will it import this good from the Foreign country?
    (b) If the Foreign country's PPF is given by $5000 = X_1 + X_2$, whereas the Home country's PPF is as given above, then how will your answer change?
    (c) Check your answer in both the cases by comparing autarchic relative prices.
    (d) Illustrate the post-trade equilibrium and gains from trade for both the countries in the case stated in (b).

(*contd*)

Exercises (*contd*)

13. Suppose India produces only software and footwear, each of which requires specific types of skilled labour, along with the same type of capital. If capital and both types of labour are fully mobile, will there be any gain from trade for India when it exports software in which it has a comparative advantage? If so, what would be the source of such gains?

14. Consider the following PPF of a country:

$$1000 = \begin{cases} x_1 \ \forall x_2 \leq 1000 \\ x_2 \ \forall x_1 \leq 1000 \\ 0 \ \ elsewhere \end{cases}$$

Draw the production set. When can such a PPF occur? If the community indifference curves are strictly convex and downward sloping, and the country has a comparative advantage in good 1, will it gain from trade with the rest of the world?

SUGGESTED READING

Caves, R.E., J. Frankel, and R.W. Jones. (1995). *World Trade and Payments*. New York: HarperCollins College Publishers.

Krugman, P.R. and M. Obstfeld. (2000). *International Economics: Theory and Policy*, Fifth Edition (chapter 5). New Delhi: Pearson Education.

ADVANCED READING

Frankel, J.A. and A.K. Rose. (2002). 'Is Trade Good or Bad for the Environment? Sorting out the Causality', mimeo, Harvard University.

Markusen, J.R. and J.R. Melvin. (1989). 'The Gains-from-Trade Theorem with Increasing Returns to Scale', in H. Kierzkowski (ed.), *Monopolistic Competition and International Trade*. Oxford: Clarendon Press, pp. 10–33.

3 Test of Comparative Advantage and Measuring GFT

In this chapter we discuss some of the measurement issuers and empirical testing of the doctrine of comparative advantage and gains from trade. Some of the concepts use the duality approach to consumer behaviour in microeconomic theory. These concepts and measurement issues can be treated as advanced topics intended for advanced undergraduate students.

3.1 MEASURING THE WELFARE CHANGE: COMPENSATING AND EQUIVALENT VARIATIONS

Gains from trade (GFT) is a theorem regarding pre- and post-trade welfare levels. But social welfare is not always measurable, particularly because of its ordinal utility dimension. The duality approach, however, provides us a more convenient way of measuring GFT in terms of the expenditure function. The expenditure function, which indicates the minimum expenditure to attain a particular level of welfare or utility, can be used to measure change in welfare or utility in monetary units. Two concepts are particularly relevant here. One is the compensating variation (CV) and the other is the equivalent variation (EV).

Compensating variation (CV) requires the amount of money that is to be given to a consumer to fully offset her for the loss from a price rise, that is, to allow her to remain on the same indifference curve as before the price rise. Equivalent variation (EV), on the other hand, considers what fall in money income would hurt a buyer as much as the price increase does. Figure 3.1 illustrates these two measures for a typical consumer's choice problem. The representative buyer allocates her given money income M_o on two goods—X and Y—and does not save. Her preference ordering satisfies all the standard axioms and assumptions, which can be represented by smooth, downward sloping, and a strictly convex set of indifference curves, with successively higher indifference curves indicating successively higher utility indices. Given a budget set $\{M_o, P_X^o, P_Y^o\}$, the consumer's most preferred bundle is indicated by C_0 on the budget line AB_0. An increase in price of good X, *ceteris paribus*, rotates her budget line to AB_1, and changes the most preferred bundle to C_1. Her utility falls to U_1.

International Economics. Rajat Acharyya, Oxford University Press. © Oxford University Press 2022.
DOI: 10.1093/oso/9780192865144.003.0003

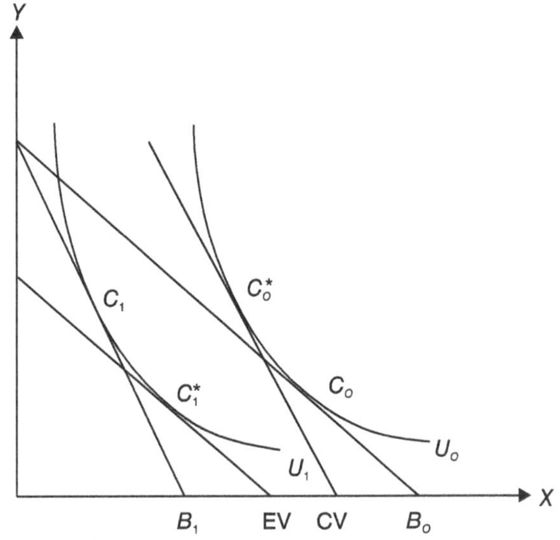

Figure 3.1 Compensating and Equivalent Measures of Welfare Change

Under compensating variation, the consumer must be given a money income that pushes her budget line to the one labeled CV to allow her to consume the bundle C_O^* on the earlier higher indifference curve U_0. Let $e\ (p_1,\ U_0)$ and $e\ (p_1,\ U_1)$ denote respectively minimum expenditures required to attain utility level U_0 and U_1 at the new price $p_1 = \{P_X^1,\ P_Y^o\}$. Hence, the CV measure of welfare change of this price increase is the difference $[e\ (p_1,\ U_0) - e\ (p_1,\ U_1)]$.

On the other hand, for measuring the welfare change by EV, we allow the consumer to buy goods at the initial prices but hypothetically tax the consumer so that her budget line shifts down to the one labeled EV to enable her to purchase the bundle C_1^*. This amount of money income that is *taxed away*, $[e\ (p_0,\ U_0) - e\ (p_0,\ U_1)]$, is the EV measure of the change in welfare following the price rise.

In the next two sections, we use these alternative monetary measures of welfare change to measure or estimate GFT.

3.2 GFT BY CV MEASURE

As we have discussed in the earlier chapter, countries gain from trade if:

$$U_f^h > U_a^h \ \forall \ h \tag{3.1}$$

where h denotes countries, and f and a denote respectively free trade and autarchy. Let, $e\ (p_f,\ U_f)$ denote the minimum expenditure to attain the post-trade welfare level and $e\ (p_f,\ U_a)$ denote the minimum expenditure to attain the pre-trade welfare level at equilibrium terms of trade p_f. These are indicated by parallel lines *LL* and *KK'* in Figure 3.2. Therefore, by CV the gains from trade can be restated as:

$$e(p_f, U_f) > e(p_f, U_a) \tag{3.2}$$

Hence, the CV measure of GFT is $[e(p_f, U_f) - e(p_f, U_a)]$.

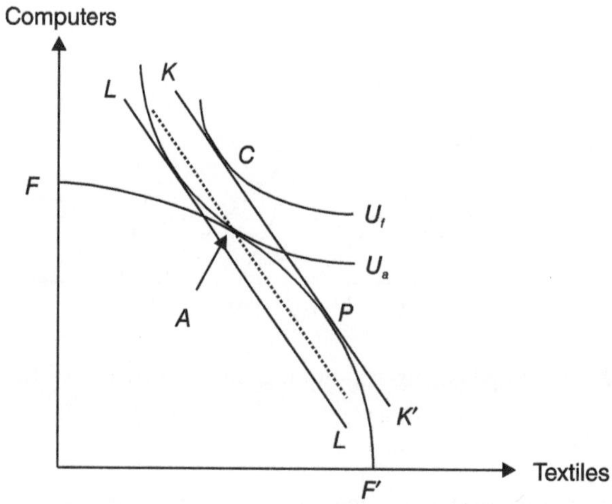

Figure 3.2 Measuring the GFT by CV

Further, it is clear from Figure 3.2 that if there is GFT then the value of the autarchic consumption bundle (at point *A*) evaluated at the international price p_f, as indicated by the line parallel to the post-trade price line *KK'* and drawn through bundle *A*, is less than the value of the post-trade consumption bundle:

$$\Sigma P_i^f D_i^f > \Sigma P_i^f D_i^a$$

where D_i denotes consumption level of good-*i*. But by the autarchic condition, $D_i^a = X_i^a$, and the post-trade budget constraint, $\Sigma P_i^f D_i^a = \Sigma P_i^f X_i^f$, this boils down to:

$$\Sigma P_i^f X_i^f > \Sigma P_i^f X_i^a \tag{3.3}$$

Therefore, the countries gain whenever the value of the free trade production bundle at free trade prices is greater than the value of the autarchic production bundle.

A generalization of this condition was first formulated by Ohyama (1972).

3.3 EQUIVALENT VARIATION AND GFT

The EV measure of GFT is illustrated in Figure 3.3. Estimates of GFT by the computable general equilibrium models, as developed by Alan Deardorff and Nicholas Stern of Michigan School, are based on this EV measure.

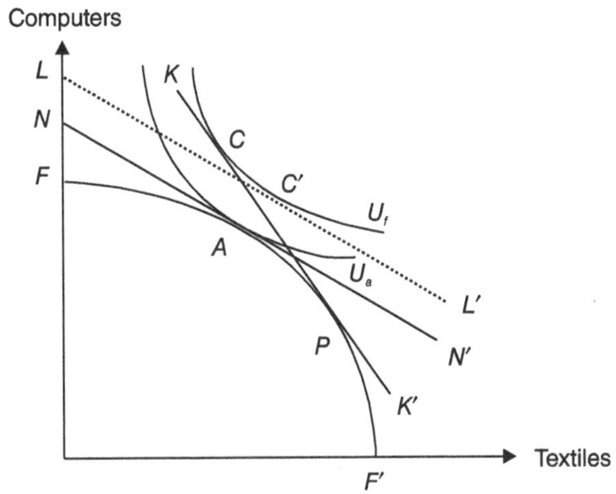

Figure 3.3 Measuring the GFT by EV

The EV measure is based on income or expenditure adjustment to enable the economy to reach the new welfare level at autarchic prices. Thus, we draw a line *LL′* parallel to *NN′* to capture such equivalent expenditure change. Accordingly, the EV measure of GFT is the gain in income (or expenditure) by the amount $[e(p_a, U_f) - e(p_a, U_a)]$.

The EV measure constitutes the basic underlying approach in computable general equilibrium (CGE) estimation of welfare effects of trade policies. For example, Chadha et al. (1998) used a CGE model for India to estimate gains from its liberalization policies during the 1990s that we will discuss in Chapter 9. The problem with measuring GFT, however, is that it necessitates a comparison between pre-trade and post-trade prices. But apart from Japan in the nineteenth century as the only exception, it is hard to find any country being completely de-linked from the external world in trade relations and then suddenly (or gradually) opening up its economy. What we can observe is relatively more or less open economies in terms of the magnitude and coverage of their respective trade protection instruments. Even the most 'closed' economies or those that had raised their trade barriers in the immediate post–World War II period, have had some trade with the rest of the world. In recent times, countries have lowered their trade barriers either unilaterally or under a regional reciprocation approach. These policy changes provide case studies for examining the gains from trade protection and trade liberalization, which are, however, fundamentally different from the GFT argument (gains from opening up of trade from a state of autarchy) as we will see later when we discuss trade restrictions and their implications.[1] Thus, estimates of gains from say tariff reductions or elimination of import quotas cannot be used as measures of GFT.

[1] For economies that are small buyers of their imports and small sellers of their exports in the world market, gains from trade liberalization and GFT may be similar. But as we will show later in Chapter 9, for larger economies, welfare change following tariff reductions is non-monotonic. Thus, though there may be welfare gains from moving from a state of autarchy to a state of free trade, welfare of these economies may actually fall when they move from a state of non-prohibitive tariff-restricted trade to the state of free trade.

3.4 A TEST OF COMPARATIVE ADVANTAGE: THE CASE OF JAPAN

The GFT theorem of international trade, as explained in Chapter 2, rests on the premise that the trade pattern of countries follows their pattern of comparative advantage. However, apart from externality related problems, the comparative advantage doctrine does not extend to the many commodity cases. Hence, it is of interest to examine whether the actual trade pattern conforms with the pattern of comparative advantage or whether there is any systematic divergence between the two. In this context, the correlation version of the law of comparative advantage developed by Alan Deardorff (1980) is quite useful. Deardorff's analysis asserts that an economy's net export vector evaluated at autarchy prices is negative. In a two-commodity world this is equivalent to the proposition that the economy will export the good in which it has a comparative advantage measured in terms of relative opportunity cost. Referring to Figure 3.3, note that the country under consideration has a comparative advantage in good X because the opportunity cost of producing its autarchic output level as indicated by the bundle *A* is assumed to be lower than the opportunity cost of producing good X abroad. This country thus exports good X and imports good Y. It is then straightforward to check the following inequalities:

$$\Sigma P_i^a D_i^f > \Sigma P_i^a X_i^a > \Sigma P_i^a X_i^f \tag{3.4}$$

Now, define volume of trade $T_i = X_i^f - D_i^f$. $T_i > 0$ if *i* is exported and $T_i < 0$ if *i* is imported. Hence, by equation (3.4):

$$\Sigma P_i^a T_i = \Sigma P_i^a (X_i^f - D_i^f) < 0 \tag{3.5}$$

Hence, if a country's trade pattern is consistent with its pattern of comparative advantage, the country's net export vector evaluated at autarchic prices, $\Sigma P_i^a P_i$, is negative. Generalizing to the case of more than two goods, the theory asserts that, *on average*, a country will import what is dear and export what is cheap when evaluated at autarchy prices.

There is, however, another problem in estimating GFT by the above mentioned measures and in examining the empirical validity of the doctrine of comparative advantage underlying the GFT theorem. This is concerned with the data problem. As Deardorff (1984: 470) himself notes '[a]lmost all countries have engaged in trade throughout history, so that there is no experience with autarchy from which to draw data.' The only notable exception in economic history is Japan. As a well-developed market economy, it experienced the state of autarchy over two centuries and thus generated a rich record of price data. Then it was forced by Western powers to move abruptly to a free trade trading regime in 1859. The shift from autarchy to free trade was rapid and complete. Good communication, well developed commercial networks, and national markets in many commodities prompted a substantial penetration of Japanese markets (Howe 1996; Nakamura 1990). As Bernhofen and Brown (2004) note, by 1873, Japan's imports per capita were three times the imports by China. Thus, Japan offers a natural experiment uniquely suited to test the core proposition of the theory of comparative advantage.

Using such historical data for Japan opening up its economy to external trade in 1860, Bernhofen and Brown (2004) offer a test of the above mentioned correlation version of the law of comparative advantage as an explanation for Japan's observed pattern of trade. In conducting their test, they applied the insight of Helpman and Krugman (1985: 39) that, 'To the extent that a static trade model is used as a proxy for a dynamic world.... The question is not where you are after trade compared with where you were before, but where you are after trade compared with where you *would have been* without trade'. Thus they make a comparison between the observed free trade regime in the 1870s and an autarchy regime at the same time period that would have prevailed had Japan not opened its doors to world markets.

Using detailed product-specific data on autarchy prices and trade flows, Bernhofen and Brown (2004) find that the autarchy-price value of Japan's trade is negative for each year of the period 1868–75. This confirms the prediction of the correlation version of the law of comparative advantage. The historical narrative demonstrates that the Japanese economy during the time period of their investigation was compatible with the assumptions of the underlying theory.

SUMMARY POINTS

- The duality approach in microeconomic theory provides us a convenient way of measuring GFT in terms of the expenditure function. Two concepts are particularly relevant here. One is the compensating variation (CV) and the other is the equivalent variation (EV).
- By the CV measure, countries gain whenever the value of free trade production bundle at free trade prices is greater than the value of the autarchic production bundle.
- The EV measure constitutes the basic underlying approach in computable general equilibrium (CGE) estimation of welfare effects of trade policies as developed by Alan Deardorff and Nicholas Stern of the Michigan School.
- The correlation version of the law of comparative advantage developed by Alan Deardorff (1980) asserts that an economy's net export vector evaluated at autarchy prices is negative. In a two-commodity world this is equivalent to the proposition that the economy will export the good in which it has a comparative advantage measured in terms of relative opportunity cost. Generalizing to the case of more than two goods, the theory asserts that, *on average*, a country will import what is dear and export what is cheap when evaluated at autarchic prices.
- Using historical data for Japan's opening up its economy to external trade in 1860, Bernhofen and Brown (2004) test the correlation version of the law of comparative advantage as an explanation for Japan's observed pattern of trade. They find that the autarchy-price value of Japan's trade is negative for each year of the period 1868–75, and thus confirm the prediction of the correlation version of the law of comparative advantage.

KEYWORDS

- **Expenditure function** indicates the minimum expenditure to attain a particular level of welfare or utility. This can be used to measure change in welfare or utility in monetary units.
- **Compensating variation** requires the amount of money that is to be given to a consumer to fully offset her for the loss from a price rise, that is, to allow her to remain on the same indifference curve as before the price rise.
- **Equivalent variation** considers what fall in money income would hurt a buyer as much as the price increase does.

EXERCISES

1. Distinguish between the equivalent variation and compensating variation measures of GFT.
2. If the tangency condition is violated then:
   (a) Show that it may be possible that $\sum P_i^f X_i^f < \sum P_i^f X_i^a$.
   (b) $\sum P_i^f X_i^f > \sum P_i^f X_i^a$ still implies that the country gains from trade.
3. By the CV measure, how can GFT be restated in terms of values of pre- and post-trade production bundles when the convexity condition is violated?
4. What does the correlation version of the law of comparative advantage mean? How does this measure follow from the EV measure of GFT? What difficulty will you encounter in examining the empirical validity of this correlation version of the law of comparative advantage?

SUGGESTED READING

Bernhofen, Daniel M. and John C. Brown. (2004). 'A Direct Test of the Theory of Comparative Advantage: The Case of Japan', *Journal of Political Economy*, 112: 48–67.

Chadha, R., S. Pohit, A.V. Deardorff, and R.M. Stern. (1998). 'Analysis of India's Policy Reforms', *World Economy*, 21 (2): 235–59.

Deardorff, Alan V. (1980). 'The General Validity of the Law of Comparative Advantage', *Journal of Political Economy*, 88: 941–57.

——— (1984). 'Testing Trade Theories and Predicting Trade Flows', in Ronald W. Jones and Peter B. Kenen (eds), *Handbook of International Economics*, volume 1, Amsterdam: North Holland, pp. 467–517.

Helpman, Elhanan and Paul R. Krugman. (1985). *Market Structure and Foreign Trade*. Cambridge, Mass.: MIT Press.

Howe, Christopher. (1996). *The Origins of Japanese Trade Supremacy*. London: Hurst and Company.

Nakamura, Satoru. (1990). 'The Development of Rural Industry', in Chie Nakane and Shinzaburō Ōishi (eds), *Tokugawa Japan: The Social and Economic Antecedents of Modern Japan.* Tokyo: University of Tokyo Press.

Ohyama, M. (1972). 'Trade and Welfare in General Equilibrium', *Keio Economic Studies*, 9: 37–73.

4 International Equilibrium and the Terms of Trade

The discussion of the GFT theorem in the previous chapter suggests that improvement in terms of trade (TOT) is a necessary condition for trading nations to gain from trade. This chapter discusses how TOT is being determined and the conditions underlying improvements in TOT after trade opens up.

It may be obvious that TOT being the price of exports relative to the price of imports, the volume of exports and imports of countries should matter in its determination. For a given TOT, the volume of exports of a good by the home country is the supply of that good in the world market whereas the volume of imports of this good by the foreign country is its demand. The equilibrium TOT will thus be the one for which these export and import volumes are the same. Note that by the Walras' Law discussed earlier, for the other good, the volume of imports by the home country and the volume of exports by the foreign country will be the same as well at that TOT. Thus, the international equilibrium can be described by *either* of the following world market clearing conditions:

$$X = M^* \tag{4.1}$$

$$M = X^* \tag{4.2}$$

where X and M denote respectively the volume of exports and the volume of imports by the home country, and variables with asterisks denote those for the foreign country.

The same can be alternatively stated in terms of trade balance conditions. Recall from the discussion in the earlier chapters that international trade should be balanced for each country for trade volumes satisfying national budget constraints. Thus, the equilibrium TOT should alternatively be such that trade is balanced for both countries in our two-country world. Let p^w denote the world relative price of computers which is imported by the home country and $P^w \equiv \frac{1}{p^w}$ denote the relative world price of cotton textiles which is exported by the home country. Then p_e^w will be equilibrium TOT, if:

$$p_e^w M = X \tag{4.3}$$

International Economics. Rajat Acharyya, Oxford University Press. © Oxford University Press 2022.
DOI: 10.1093/oso/9780192865144.003.0004

$$p_e^w X^* = M^* \tag{4.4}$$

Note that when trade is balanced for both countries simultaneously, combing equalities in (4.3) and (4.4) we get back to the world-maket clearing conditions. However, instead of describing the international equilibrium by both these trade balance conditions we can use the following equilibrium condition:

$$p_e^w M = M^* \tag{4.5}$$

This condition is derived by substituting the world-market clearing condition (4.1) in the home country's trade balance condition (4.3). Note that by the other world-market clearing condition (4.2), the equality in (4.5) also implies that the foreign country's trade is balanced. That is, by the market clearing conditions (4.1) and (4.2), trade is balanced for both countries when the equality in (4.5) holds. Hence, international equilibrium can be described, alternative to the market clearing conditions or trade balance conditions, by the equality stated in (4.5). That is, an equilibrium TOT is the one for which the value of imports by the foreign country is exactly equal to the value of imports of the home country.

The combinations of import and export volumes of a country, or its excess demand and excess supply quantities respectively, constitute its *offer* to its trading partner. The locus of such combinations or offers, called *offer curves*, provides us a convenient and useful graphical representation for determining TOT. In the following section, we discuss how these curves are constructed and used to represent international trade equilibrium.

4.1 OFFER CURVE OF THE HOME COUNTRY

An offer curve of the home country is defined as the locus of pairs of its export offer and import demand at different TOT that maintain balanced trade. Consider Figure 4.1 where trade triangles indicating such balanced trade pairs of export offers and import demand are illustrated for two different TOT. For the world relative price of home exports, P_0^w, the home country offers to export *ab* units of cotton textiles in exchange for *ac* units of import of computers. For a higher relative price P_1^w, a larger export offer of *a'b'* units of cotton textiles is made in exchange for a larger import demand of *a'c'* units of computers.

When these balanced trade pairs of export offer and import demand are plotted in the (X, M) space, the locus connecting such trade pairs or bundles including the bundle (0, 0) representing the autarchic situation gives us the offer curve for the home country. This is shown in Figure 4.2. Essentially the triangles *Oab* and *Oa'b'* in Figure 4.2 correspond to the trade triangles *abc* and *a' b' c'* respectively in Figure 4.1. Note that by construction, at any point on the offer curve, trade is balanced for the home country. Thus, the home offer curve is essentially a locus of its trade balance condition: $p^w M = X$.

The slope of the home country's offer curve *OH* at the origin is the autarchic relative price of textiles. On the other hand, the slope of the ray connecting any point along the offer curve *OH* and the origin gives us the corresponding post-trade relative price or TOT. Note that as the slope of any ray through the origin in the (X, M) space is the ratio $\frac{M}{X}$, so a

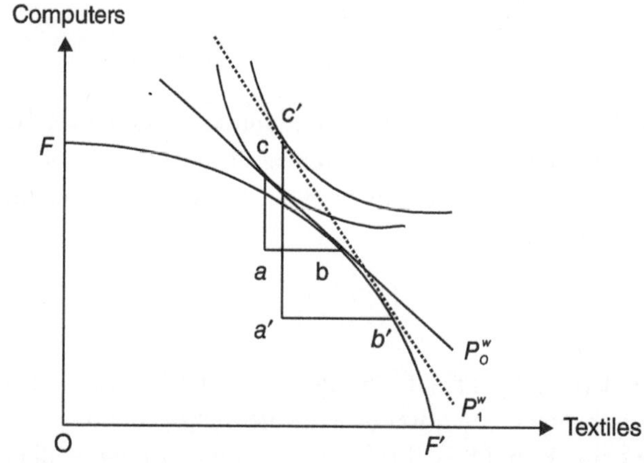

Figure 4.1 Export Offer and Import Demand by the Home Country

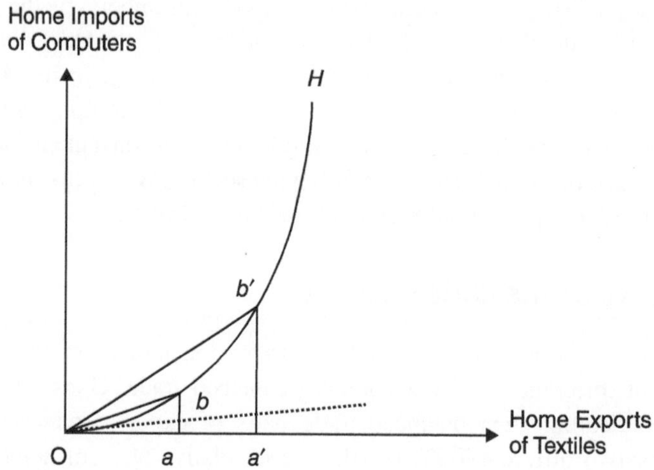

Figure 4.2 Home Offer Curve

steeper TOT line means that the home country can exchange a larger amount of imports for the same amount of exports. That is, the world relative price of home exports is now higher. Alternatively, the world relative price of home imports is now lower. TOT thus improves for the home country (and worsens for the foreign country). Similarly, a flatter TOT line indicates a TOT deterioration for the home country (and improvement for the foreign country).

The upward slope of the offer curve *OH* reflects that a larger volume of import demand requires a larger export offer by the home country to finance it. On the other hand, the convex downwards (or more specifically, convex to the home export axis) shape of the home offer curve as depicted in Figure 4.2 reflects two things. First, a larger volume of exports is offered only at a higher relative price of exports, that is, only when TOT improves. The reason is simple. The home country can offer a larger volume of textiles exports when either the domestic production of textiles expands or domestic consumption of textiles declines or both. If the opportunity cost of producing textiles is increasing (meaning that PPF is strictly concave as explained in Chapter 2), production expansion necessitates a higher relative price of textiles. On the other hand, by the law of demand, lower domestic consumption of textiles also necessitates a higher relative price of textiles. A TOT improvement induces domestic consumers to substitute their consumption of textiles by computers as computers are now relatively cheaper than textiles. This allows the home country to offer more exports. Thus, the convexity of the offer curve is a reflection of the increasing opportunity cost (or MRT) and law of demand. Later we will discuss how the shape of the offer curve changes when opportunity cost is constant (or PPF is linear).

The second implication of the convexity of the offer curve is that successively smaller additional units of exports are sufficient to finance successively larger additional units of import demand. This follows from the fact that as the relative price of exports rises (or the relative price of imports falls) as we move up along the convex offer curve, a less than proportionate additional export offer is sufficient to finance additional import demand. This can be easily verified from log differentiating the trade balance condition for the home country:

$$\hat{X} = \hat{M} + \hat{p}^w \tag{4.6}$$

where 'hat' over a variable denotes its proportional change, that is, $\hat{p}^w = \dfrac{dp^w}{p^w}$.

Since $\hat{p}^w < 0$, as we move up along the convex home offer curve, so a 1 per cent increase in import demand can be financed through a less than 1 per cent increase in export supply. Interestingly, if along the offer curve, the decline in the world price of home imports is more than the increase in its imports demand, the export supply need not be raised to finance the import bill. In fact, it will be *lowered* to maintain balanced trade. This interesting case is discussed below.

4.2 BACKWARD BENDING OFFER CURVE

In the case mentioned above where TOT improvement along the offer curve is more than proportionate to the change in import demand so that the additional import demand may be financed by even smaller export volumes being offered, the offer curve is backward bending towards the import-axis after a certain high level of import demand. Figure 4.3 depicts such a backward-bending home offer curve.

What appears from equation (4.6) and the above discussion is that the upward slope and backward bend of the offer curve can be related to the value of import demand elasticity measured along the offer curve. The price elasticity of the home import demand, denoted by ε, is the percentage change in home import demand for computers for a 1 per cent change in the (relative) price of computers in the world market:

$$\varepsilon \equiv -\frac{\hat{M}}{\hat{p}^w}$$

Note that ε is the absolute measure of import demand elasticity.

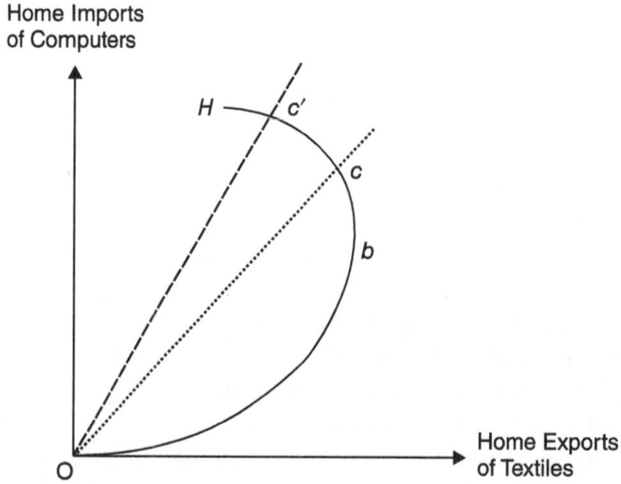

Figure 4.3 Backward Bending Home Offer Curve

For a movement up along the rising part of the offer curve, O*b*, from one point to another, the volume as well as value of the export offer increases. The volume of imports, on the other hand, rises as well whereas TOT improves, that is, p^w declines. The import bill may thus go up or down. But since the value of exports rises along this rising part of the offer curve, the import bill or value of imports by the home country must rise proportionately to maintain trade balance. This can happen only when the import demand is price-elastic ($\varepsilon > 1$), that is, increase in import demand is more than proportionate to the decline in p^w at the margin.

Along the backward bending part *bH*, on the other hand, value of exports declines necessitating a decline in the import bill as well. This means the import demand should now rise by less than proportionately to the decline in the import price. Hence, along the backward bending part of the offer curve, import demand must be price-inelastic ($\varepsilon < 1$). Putting this discussion upside down, we can say that when home import demand is price-elastic, an improvement in TOT raises the import demand more than proportionately and thereby raises the import bill. This must be financed through a larger volume of exports. Hence, the offer curve slopes upward. But when the home import demand is price inelastic, an improvement in TOT raises the import demand less than proportionately. The import bill thus falls and now the home country can lower the offer of exports. Hence, the offer curve now bends backward.

An example of an offer curve being backward bending for a high level of trade volume is when the underlying import demand function is linear in the (relative) import price. Note that along a linear import demand curve, the (absolute) value of price elasticity of imports falls from infinity to zero as we *move down*. That is, smaller is the import price and hence larger is the import demand, the smaller is the value of ε. Thus, initially as TOT improves (or import price declines) from the autarchic (relative) price, the value of ε declines but being greater than one, the offer curve slopes upward. But when the value of ε declines below one for a high volume of import demand, the offer curve bends backward.

Box 4.1 Other Elasticities Measured along an Offer Curve

Two other elasticities can be measured along an offer curve. One is the price elasticity of export supply, which is denoted by η and defined as the percentage change in export supply by the home country for one percentage change in the relative price of exports:

$$\eta = \frac{\hat{X}}{\hat{P}^w}$$

The other elasticity is the elasticity of the offer curve, denoted by φ and defined by the percentage change in the export offer by the home country for one percentage change in its import demand:

$$\varphi = \frac{\hat{X}}{\hat{M}}$$

The values of both η and φ are positive as long as the offer curve slopes upward.

4.3 OFFER CURVE UNDER CONSTANT OPPORTUNITY COST

When the opportunity cost of producing textiles is constant, the offer curve has a linear segment as illustrated in Figure 4.4. Note that PPF (drawn in the left hand panel) in this case is a straight line implying that resources can be shifted from one sector to the other at the same (relative) marginal cost till the economy specializes completely in one of the goods. Recalling the discussion in Section 4.1, the home country in this case can offer higher exports by expanding production *at a constant cost*. That is, higher export offers can be made even at a constant TOT. This, however, is possible as long as resources can be shifted out of the industry producing computers and employed in the textiles industry. But once the economy reaches the point of complete specialization (as at point *F'* in left hand panel of Figure 4.4), the production of textiles cannot be raised any further since all the resources of the economy at this point have been fully exhausted. The only way the export offer can be raised from this point onwards is through lowering domestic consumption of textiles. But this requires the (world) relative price of textiles to rise, that is, TOT to improve. Hence, beyond point *K*, the home offer curve is non-linear and convex downwards. Point *K* along the home offer curve corresponds to the complete specialization point *F'*, and the larger is the maximum possible volume of production of textiles (that is, larger is the horizontal intercept of the linear PPF), the more elongated is the linear segment *OK* of the offer curve. As we will see later, this has a far-reaching implication for post-trade TOT movement and Ricardo's analysis of GFT.

4.4 FOREIGN OFFER CURVE AND THE INTERNATIONAL EQUILIBRIUM

The foreign country's offer curve can similarly be constructed and depicted with the same properties as the home country's offer curve. The foreign country's offer curve slopes upward as long as foreign import demand is price elastic ($\varepsilon^* > 1$) but bends backward when it is price inelastic. Note, however, that since the home country's export good (textiles) is the foreign

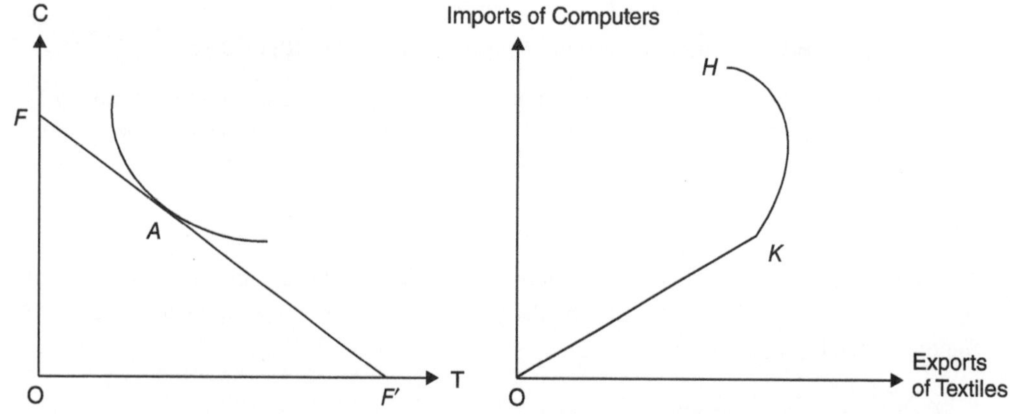

Figure 4.4 Offer Curve under Constant Opportunity Cost

country's import good and vice versa, the foreign country's offer curve should be drawn concave to the home export axis as shown in Figure 4.5 by the curve *OF*.

With help of these two offer curves, we can now illustrate the equilibrium TOT. Recalling the world-market clearing conditions in equations (4.1) and (4.2), the equilibrium TOT (or world relative price of textiles which are exported by the home country) will be the ones for which the offer of exports of textiles by the home country exactly matches with the import demand for textiles by the foreign country. Of course, as argued earlier, this should also mean by respective trade balance conditions that the offer of exports of computers by the foreign country exactly matches with the import demand for computers by the home country. Referring to Figure 4.5, such an equilibrium TOT is given by the ray from the origin *OE* that passes through the point of intersection of the two offer curves, *OH* and *OF*. In this illustration, this is

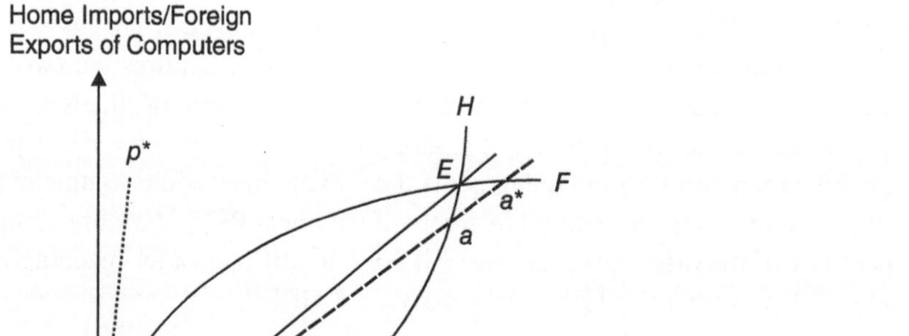

Figure 4.5 Equilibrium TOT

the unique equilibrium TOT as well. For no other TOT, the export offer of one country matches with the import demand by the other country. Consider, for example, TOT indicated by the broken line flatter than *OE*. For such a TOT, or a lower world price of textiles, the offers of the home and foreign countries are indicated by trade bundles *a* and *a** respectively. The home country offers smaller exports of textiles than the foreign country prefers to import. Thus, the world market for textiles does not clear. A similar argument shows that any TOT other than *OE* cannot be the equilibrium TOT, since we will have either excess demand for textiles (and correspondingly excess supply of computers) in the world market or excess supply of textiles (and correspondingly excess demand for computers).

It is pretty straightforward to check that the equilibrium depicted in Figure 4.5 is Walrasian stable. As explained above, for a lower relative world price of textiles (as indicated by the flatter broken TOT line), an excess demand for textiles arises. Hence, competitive forces will raise the relative price of textiles and TOT will accordingly adjust towards *OE*. Similarly, for any steeper TOT line than *OE* indicating a higher relative world price of textiles, an excess supply of textiles arises. Competitive forces will drive down the relative world price of textiles and TOT will again adjust towards *OE*. Therefore, the equilibrium is stable. As derived in Appendix A4, the algebraic condition for Walrasian stability of international equilibrium in our two-country world requires that the sum of absolute values of the home and foreign import demand elasticities must exceed one:

$$\varepsilon + \varepsilon^* > 1 \tag{4.7}$$

This is known as the Marshall-Lerner condition.[1] Note that, as we have explained above, since at the equilibrium point *E* both the offer curves slope upward, so both the home and foreign import demands are price elastic. Hence, at *E*, the Marshall-Lerner condition of Walrasian stability is satisfied.

But the international equilibrium is not necessarily unique, and in cases of multiple equilibria, not all of them are Walrasian stable. Consider the famous shoelace diagram in Figure 4.6. Both the offer curves bend backward and cross each other more than once. Offers match for three trade bundles *a*, *b*, and *c*, of which only *a* and *c* are stable equilibria. That the international equilibrium with trade bundle *b* is unstable is easy to check. Consider a deviation of TOT to *OL*, that is, a fall in the world relative price of textiles. For such a TOT, the home country's offer of exports of textiles exceeds the import demand of textiles by the foreign country. The consequent excess supply of textiles in the world market lowers its relative price further. That is, TOT deviates from the equilibrium TOT further. Hence, this equilibrium is unstable. Similar reasoning shows that the other two equilibria are stable.

Comparing these stable equilibria and the one depicted in Figure 4.5 with the unstable equilibrium for trade bundle *b*, it is evident that an international equilibrium is stable if the two

[1] This condition was first discussed in the context of whether a nominal devaluation of the home country's currency vis-à-vis the foreign country's currency improves the trade balance of the home country.

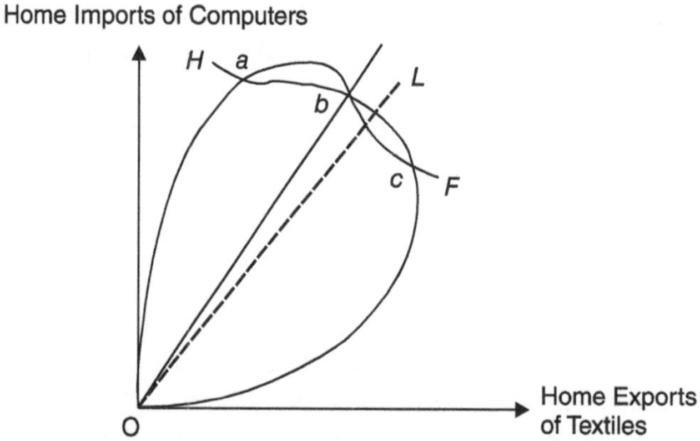

Figure 4.6 Multiple Equilibria and Instability

offer curves cross each other *from below* and unstable if they cross each other from above. For trade bundle *b*, both the offer curves bend backward meaning that both the import elasticities are less than one in value, and at the same time their sum is less than one as well. That is, the Marshall-Lerner condition is not satisfied and the equilibrium is unstable.

4.5 WELFARE PROPERTIES OF THE INTERNATIONAL EQUILIBRIUM

Welfare property of the international equilibrium can be discussed in terms of a set of trade indifference curves (TICs). A TIC for a country is the locus of different combinations of her export supply and import demand that yield the same level of her national welfare. As explained in the appendix, a TIC is positively sloped in the offer space. It has similar properties as the CIC. The most relevant in the present context is that a higher TIC (that is a TIC away from the country's export axis) represents higher national welfare. That is, while national welfare realized from a trade bundle is indicated by the TIC on which that trade bundle lie, a higher welfare is realized from a trade bundle on a higher TIC than from a trade bundle on a lower TIC. Thus, at free-trade equilibrium E in Figure 4.7, the home country attains the welfare level as indicated by TIC_f and the foreign country attains the welfare level as indicated by TIC_f^*. Moreover, from the alternative derivation of offer curves as suggested by James Meade, and discussed in the appendix to this chapter, it follows that the pair of TICs of the home and foreign country passing through free trade bundle E will be tangent to the terms of trade line OE, and consequently will be tangent to each other. This tangency property of the free trade bundle makes it a globally Pareto optimal bundle. We will return to this dimension of the free trade bundle after revisiting the gains from trade.

4.5.1 Gains from trade revisited

Figure 4.7 provides an alternative illustration of the gains from trade (GFT). Since a higher TIC represents higher welfare so the better set to the free trade bundle for the home country is the region above TIC_f and the worse set is the region below it. Similarly, for the foreign

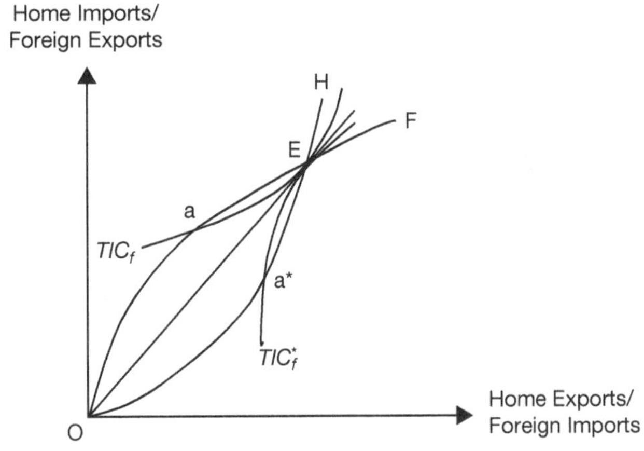

Figure 4.7 Welfare levels at free trade equilibrium

country, the region above (or to the right of) represents the better set to the free trade bundle and the region below it (or to the left of it) TIC_f^* represents the worse set. The autarkic bundle (0, 0) lies in the worse set to the equilibrium trade bundle E for both the countries. Hence, both countries gain as they open up trade between them.

However, though free trade raises welfare for both the countries, it does not maximize their welfare levels. The home country can gain further by offering any trade bundle along the segment aE of the foreign curve since all such trade bundles lie in the better set to the free trade bundle. By similar reasoning, the foreign country can gain further by offering any trade bundle along the segment a*E of the home offer curve. Therefore, the gains from trade do not mean that welfares of the trading nations are maximized under free trade. It simply states that free trade will make trading nations better off relative to no-trade or autarchy. What follows from this is that each country will have unilateral incentive to deviate from the offer of the free trade bundle E. As we will see in Chapter 9, each country can achieve these preferred bundles by trade restrictive policies like tariff (or import tax) and import quota. Of course, the size of the countries, or their importance in world trade, will matter as we will learn later. For countries that are *large enough* in world trade to influence the terms of trade by altering their export offers (or import demand), free trade does not maximize their respective national welfare levels, even though it raises welfare above the autarchic level. This forms the basis for welfare motive for restricting trade, rather than pursuing free trade, for such countries.

4.5.2 Global Pareto optimality of free trade bundle

Free trade bundle, despite being sub-optimal for each *large* country in the case specified and illustrated above, is globally Pareto optimal. A Pareto optimal bundle is the one such that if we deviate from this bundle then at least one of the countries will be worse off. This can be verified from Figure 4.7. All the bundles along the aE segment of the foreign offer curve lie in the better set to the free trade bundle for the home country, but in the worse set to the free trade bundle for the foreign country. Thus, for all such trade bundles, achieved by the home country through a trade restriction policy, the home country will be better off but the foreign country will be worse off. Similarly, for all trade bundles along a*E segment of the home offer curve, achieved by the foreign country through a trade restriction policy, the foreign country will be better off but the home country will be worse off. On the other hand, for any trade bundle that lie below TIC_f below TIC_f^* and—such as bundles along the Oa segment of the home offer curve and along the Oa* segment of the foreign offer curve—both countries are worse off relative to free trade.

Note that, free trade bundle emerges as the globally Pareto optimal bundle because of the fact that a pair of TICs of both the countries are tangent to each other for this bundle. If the TICs would have crossed each other at the free trade bundle, then some other trade bundles would have existed for which either both countries would have been better off; or one of them would have been better off with the other country being indifferent, that is, having the same welfare as for the free trade bundle.

This global Pareto optimality property of the free trade bundle has some far-reaching implications for trade wars, and for formation of regional trading blocs, as we will learn later.

APPENDIX A4

I. Geometric Measurement of the Import Demand Elasticity along Offer Curve

Recall the expression for the absolute home import demand elasticity:

$$\varepsilon \equiv -\frac{\hat{M}}{\hat{p}^w}$$

Using the percentage change form of the trade balance condition in (4.3), $\hat{X} = \hat{M} + \hat{p}^w$, this boils down to:

$$\varepsilon = -\frac{\hat{M}}{\hat{X} - \hat{M}} = \frac{1}{1 - \dfrac{dX}{dM}\dfrac{M}{X}} \tag{A4.1}$$

In Figure A4.1, at point R, the slope of the home offer curve $\dfrac{dM}{dX}$ is the slope of the tangent RS, which is the measure $\dfrac{RT}{ST}$. On the other hand, at point R, the ratio of imports to exports equals $\dfrac{RT}{OT}$. Hence, import demand elasticity at point R along the home offer curve equals:

$$\varepsilon = \frac{1}{1 - \dfrac{ST}{RT}\cdot\dfrac{RT}{OT}} = \frac{OT}{OS} \tag{A4.2}$$

That is, the import demand elasticity at any point of the home offer curve is the ratio of the distance between the origin and the foot of the perpendicular drawn from that point to the distance between the origin and the foot of the tangent at that point. This ratio is larger than one in value at any point along the upward sloping segment of the home offer curve. Hence, home import demand is price elastic ($\varepsilon > 1$). At the point of inflexion b, the perpendicular drawn

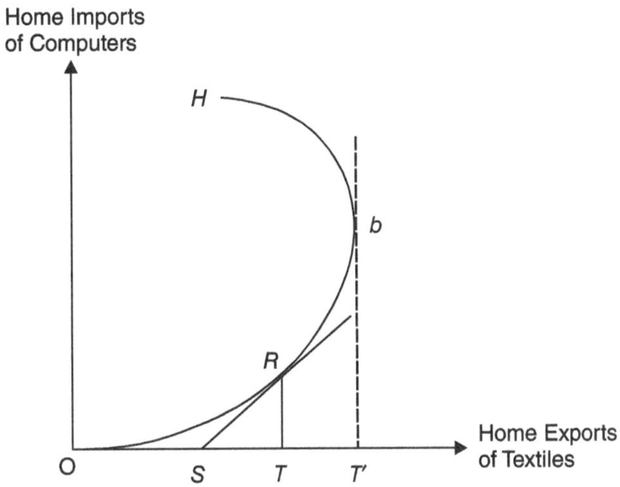

Figure A4.1 Backward Bending Home Offer Curve

from that point being tangent to the offer curve as well, the ratio is equal to one and hence at that point the home import demand is unitary price elastic ($\varepsilon = 1$). By similar logic, it is easy to check that at any point along the backward bending segment of the home offer curve, the home import demand is price inelastic ($\varepsilon < 1$).

II. Existence, Uniqueness, and Stability of International Equilibrium

Existence of international equilibrium depicted in Figure 4.5 requires that the two offer curves must cross each for a trade bundle containing strictly positive volumes of export offer and import demand. The assumption of non-decreasing opportunity costs and corresponding convexity of offer curves though help in this regard, but they may not be sufficient. Assuming that the offer curves are continuous, a sufficient condition for existence of international equilibrium is that at least one offer curve must be backward bending. However, though this might ensure existence, it may lead to multiple equilibria. This is evident from Figure 4.6.

Algebraically, the conditions of existence, uniqueness, and stability can be derived using the excess demand function approach. Consider the world market for the good imported by the home country and exported by the foreign country (that is, the world market for computers). Referring back to equation (4.2), define excess demand function $E(p^w)$ as:

$$E(p^w) = M(p^w) - X^*(p^w) \tag{A4.3}$$

By the world-clearing condition (4.1) in the text, the (world) equilibrium price p_e^w is such that, $E(p_e^w) = 0$. Then, if this excess demand function is continuous in p^w, the following conditions ensure that $p_e^w > 0$ (that is, an equilibrium price exists):

(a) There exists a price $p_0^w > 0$ such that $E(p_0^w) > 0$
(b) There exists a price $p_1^w > 0$ such that $E(p_1^w) < 0$

Figure A4.2 under the assumption that $p_0^w < p_1^w$ illustrates this. However, note that the above set of conditions do not mean that $p_e^w > 0$ will be unique. This is illustrated in Figure A4.2b. As it appears, the uniqueness is ensured by a monotonic excess demand function.

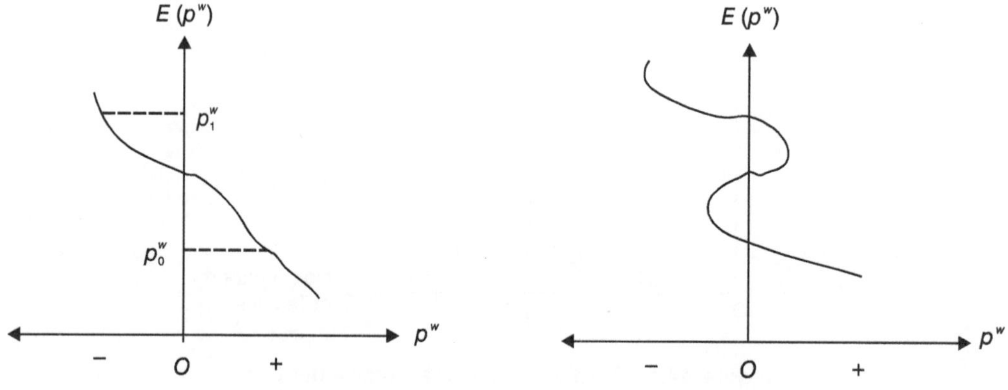

(a) (b)

Figure A4.2 Unique and Multiple Equilibria

The Walrasian stability of international equilibrium, on the other hand, requires that the excess demand function be negatively sloped:

$$\frac{dE(p^w)}{dp^w} < 0$$

Using equation (A4.1), this condition can be rewritten as:

$$\frac{dM}{dp^w} < \frac{dX^*}{dp^w}$$

Dividing both sides by $\frac{M}{p}$ and using the initial equilibrium condition in equation (4.2) and the home country's trade balance condition in equation (4.3) in the text, this boils down to:

$$\frac{dM / M}{dp^w / p^w} < \frac{d(M^* / p^w)/(M^* / p^w)}{dp^w / p^w}$$

$$\Rightarrow \frac{\hat{M}}{\hat{p}^w} < \frac{\hat{M}^* - \hat{p}^w}{\hat{p}^w}$$

$$\Rightarrow -\varepsilon < \varepsilon^* - 1$$

Rearranging sides, we arrive at the Marshall-Lerner condition for Walrasian stability:

$$\varepsilon + \varepsilon^* > 1$$

III. Trade Indifference Curves and Alternative Derivation of Offer Curves

Trade indifference curves (TICs) are a useful tool in discussing the welfare properties of free or restricted trade equilibrium. James Meade used TICs to propose an alternative way of deriving offer curves. A TIC for a country is the locus of different combinations of its export supply and import demand that yield the same national welfare for the country. Accordingly, the country is indifferent among all such combinations. In the export-import space, each TIC is positively sloped. The reason is as follows. An increase in export supply by the country means lesser units of the export good are now available for domestic consumption. This lowers the welfare of the country. Thus, to compensate and keep the national welfare at the same level, the other good (which is imported by the country) must be available for domestic consumption in greater quantity. Hence, along a TIC, an increase in export supply must be accompanied by an increase in import demand.

The other properties of TICs are similar to that of CICs, since TICs by definition replicate CICs in the excess-demand (or offer) space. That is, each TIC is convex to the export-axis and a higher TIC, which is further away from the country's export-axis, represents a higher national welfare. That a higher (non-intersecting) TIC represents a higher national welfare is easily comprehensible, and is left as an exercise. It is also assumed that taste patterns are such that TICs do not intersect each other so that, like the CICs, we can attach a unique utility or welfare index to each TIC and the export-import combinations on different TICs can be Pareto ranked in the sense discussed earlier. The TIC map for the home country is illustrated in Figure A4.3.

Actual offer of exports in exchange for import demand by the home country, however, should be consistent with its budget constraints at the post-trade prices. The budget constraints for different TOT are shown by TOT lines through the origin. Thus facing the TOT indicated by the ray Oa_1, the home country makes an offer of the combination b_1 that maximizes its welfare. An improved TOT enables the country to improve its welfare by offering b_2, and so on. Note that each of these offers is consistent with balanced trade. The locus connecting this

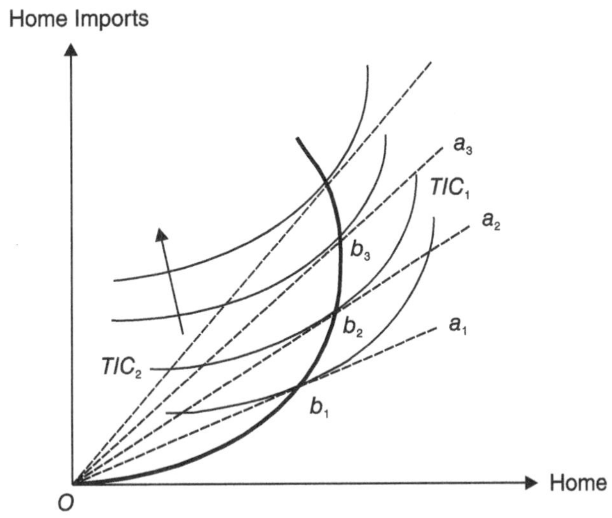

Figure A4.3 Trade Indifference Curves and Offer Curve

welfare-maximizing and balanced trade offers traces out the offer curve for the home country. From this alternative derivation of a country's offer curve emerges the welfare property of offers made by it for different TOT. Any point on the offer curve represents an offer of export supply and import demand for which trade is balanced and welfare is maximized for the corresponding TOT.

Note that by construction, at the free trade international equilibrium point E in Figure 4.5, the trade indifference curves of the two countries are tangent to the TOT line OE and hence are mutually tangent to each other.

IV. Measurement and Trends in Barter TOT

A country may export and import thousands of commodities, and thus it only makes sense to measure a country's TOT by the export price index relative to the import price index. Often these price indices are measured by the unit value indices for exports and imports. These unit value indices are constructed from data on exports and imports—both value and volume—reported by countries. The unit value of exports, as a proxy for the export price index, is simply the index of value of exports divided by the index of volume of exports. The unit value of imports is similarly calculated. Finally, the ratio of the unit value index of exports to the unit value index of imports gives us the *net barter terms of trade* of a country.

Figure A4.4 illustrates movements in net barter TOT for four developed countries—Canada, Japan, UK, and USA–during 2000–19 with 2000 as the base year, as reported in UNCTAD Trade Statistics 2020. Both UK and the United States have stable and almost unchanged net barter TOT during this period. Canada experienced steady improvement in its net barter TOT till 2008 before it worsened. But, the net barter TOT for Japan deteriorated sharply before

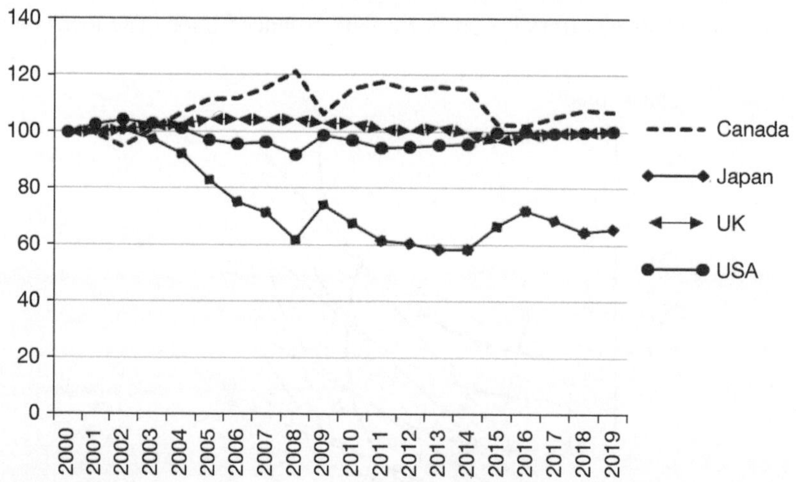

Figure A4.4 Net Barter TOT Index for Selected Developed Countries (Base Year 2000 = 100)

Source: Compiled from UNCTAD Trade Statistics (2010).

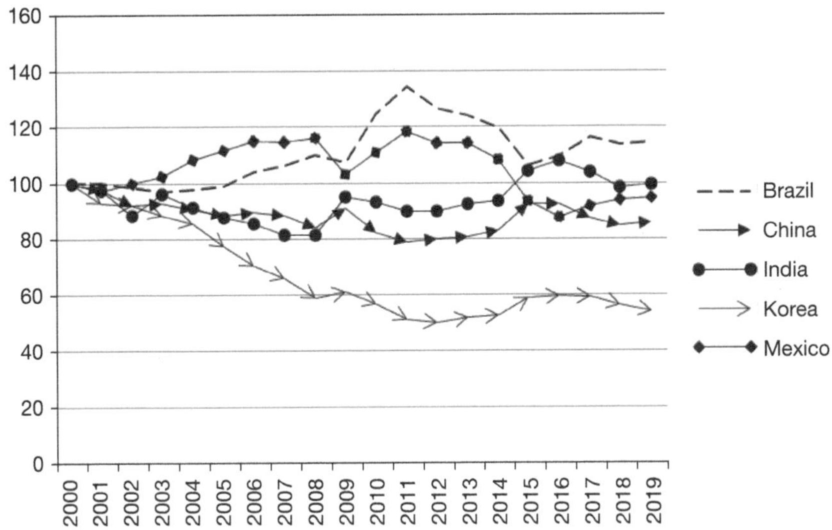

Figure A4.5 Barter TOT Index for Selected Developing Countries

(Base Year 2000 = 100)

Source: Compiled from UNCTAD Trade Statistics (2020).

improving marginally after 2016. Figure A4.5, on the other hand, illustrates movements in net barter TOT for the developing countries like Brazil, China, India, Korea, and Mexico during the same period. Similar to Japan, Korea experienced continuous worsening of its net barter TOT till it stabilized to some extent after 2015. The most interesting observation that can be made is movements in TOT of the other four countries. TOT of China and India, on the one hand, and of Brazil and Mexico, on the other hand, moved in tandem though almost exactly in the opposite directions. That is, while China and India experienced worsening of their respective TOTs during 2000–12, Brazil and Mexico enjoyed improving TOT. Subsequently, after 2015 in particular, the trends reversed for these countries.

There are many plausible explanations for such wide variations in TOT movement both across time and across countries as we will learn in later chapters.

SUMMARY POINTS

- In a two-commodity world, international equilibrium is obtained when world markets for any one good clear. By the Walras' Law the world market for the other good should also clear. Alternatively, trade must be balanced for both countries at equilibrium. Accordingly the equilibrium TOT should be the one that makes trade between countries balanced. The offer curve technique provides us a convenient and useful graphical representation for the determination of TOT.
- The offer curve of a country represents pairs of its balanced-trade export offer and import demand at different TOT. That is, an offer curve of a country is essentially a locus of its trade balance condition.
- The offer curve slopes upward as long as import demand elasticity is greater than one in value, but bends backward for very high volumes of import demand for which import demand elasticity is less than one in value.
- The offer curve is usually convex downwards, which reflects the increasing opportunity cost (or MRT) of producing a good. That is, a larger volume of exports is offered only at a higher relative price of exports, that is, only when TOT improves. The second implication of the convexity of the offer curve, as long as it slopes upward, is that successively smaller additional units of exports are sufficient to finance successively larger additional units of import demand.
- If the opportunity cost (or MRT) of producing a good is constant, as represented by a linear PPF, the offer curve will have a linear segment up to the level of the export offer for which the country completely specializes in its export good, and will be convex downwards (and possibly bending backward) thereafter.
- International equilibrium is not necessarily unique and in cases of multiple equilibria, not all of them are Walrasian stable. An international equilibrium in our two-country world is Walrasian stable if the sum of absolute values of the home and foreign import demand elasticities exceed one. This is known as the Marshall-Lerner condition. Graphically, an international equilibrium is stable if the two offer curves cross each other *from below* and unstable if they cross each other *from above*.

KEYWORDS

- **Offer curve** of a country is the locus of pairs of its export offer and import demand at different TOT that maintain balanced trade.
- **TOT** improves for the home country (and worsens for the foreign country) when the world relative price of the home export good rises.
- **Price elasticity of import demand** is the percentage change in import demand for a good for a 1 per cent change in its (relative) price in the world market.
- An equilibrium is **Walrasian stable** if any deviation in the price from the equilibrium value creates a state of excess demand that will in turn induce competitive forces to cause the price to return to the initial equilibrium value. Since, in a state of positive excess demand, competition among buyers bids up the price and in a state of negative excess demand, competition among sellers lowers the price, so Walrasian stability requires that a price decline must lead to an excess demand situation and a price rise must lead to an excess supply situation.

EXERCISES

1. Draw a country's offer curve when its import demand is infinitely elastic. What will be the value of the elasticity of the offer curve in this case?
2. Show that along a country's offer curve the sum of export supply elasticity and (absolute) import demand elasticity is one.
3. What does it mean for the shape of the offer curves when the home country is small in the sense that it cannot influence its TOT by changing its offer of exports or demand for imports?
4. If the import demand function of a country is $M_d = 60–5p^W$, then find out the world price below which the corresponding offer curve is backward bending.
5. Given the following home import demand function and foreign export supply function, determine the equilibrium TOT and check whether the equilibrium is stable or not:

   $M = M_o - p^W, X^* = X_o + 2p^W$
6. In a two-country world, find out the equilibrium terms of trade given the import demand functions of the home and the foreign country as $M = 60–5p^W$ and $M^* = 25 + 50p^W$. Is the equilibrium stable? Illustrate the free trade equilibrium in terms of offer curves.
7. Show that:
   (a) If the opportunity cost of producing textiles and computers is increasing in both countries, then the equilibrium TOT will lie strictly between the pre-trade price ratios.
   (b) If the opportunity cost of producing textiles and computers is constant in both countries, then the equilibrium TOT may not lie strictly between the pre-trade price ratios.

(contd)

Exercises (*contd*)

8. Should all countries gain necessarily when the opportunity costs of producing textiles and computers are constant?
9. After a new medical invention reporting that consumption of tea is good for health, Britons increase their demand for tea imported from India.
   (a) How does this affect UK's TOT vis-à-vis India? Illustrate your answer using offer curves.
   (b) If health improvements are negligible, does UK gain in the process?
   (c) How would you modify your answers if India could produce tea at a constant opportunity cost?
10. In 2001, India abolished its import duties or taxes on almost all import goods of final consumption. This lowered the prices of imports that the Indian consumers had to pay. Assuming computers as the only good being imported from the rest of the world (ROW), and rice being the only good exported by India to ROW, how do you think that the trade liberalization policy may have affected India's TOT?
11. Intuitively explain that a higher (non-intersecting) TIC represents higher national welfare.

SUGGESTED READING

Bhagwati, J.N., A. Panagariya, and T.N. Srinivasan. (1998). *Lectures on International Trade*, Second Edition. Massachusetts: MIT Press.

Meade, J.E. (1952). *A Geometry of International Trade*. London: Allen and Unwin.

PART II

Theories of Comparative Advantage and Pattern of Trade

5 Technology and Trade

In his *Principles of Political Economy and Taxation*, David Ricardo (1817) argued that the pattern of trade will be determined by the methods of production available in the trading nations, and that trade will increase the 'mass of commodities and, therefore, the sum of enjoyments'.[1] Though technology asymmetry across countries as a basis of trade was emphasized in Adam Smith's doctrine of *absolute* advantage, Ricardo offered a more general explanation in his doctrine of *comparative cost advantage*. More important, however, was his construction that all trading nations gain mutually through trade according to their respective comparative advantages, unless nations have very asymmetric sizes. In this chapter, we present these arguments in terms of what is known as the textbook version of the Ricardian model.

While quite a significant part of world trade may be technology-driven, there can also be a reverse causality between technology and international trade. International trade may influence innovation choices at the firm level and push the barriers of technology. In the latter part of this chapter we discuss this reverse causality.

5.1 CONSTANT OPPORTUNITY COST, TECHNOLOGY, AND TRADE

Consider a home country producing two goods, computers and cotton textiles, using only labour with a fixed coefficient technology. Suppose labour is homogeneous and can move around freely without any cost. Production of computers does not require any specific skills so that the same workers can do both the jobs. All this means that workers earn the same money wage, W, everywhere in the home country. The production technology, however, differs across the two sectors, which is reflected in different labour–output ratios in computers and textiles production. More precisely, suppose a_{LC} units of labour are required to produce one computer and a_{LT} units of labour are required to produce one unit of textiles. These labour coefficients depend on the technology available in the home country. A technological improvement in

[1] Another important conclusion by Ricardo was that international trade will increase the rate of profits in a country if the imported commodities enter the real wage basket.

International Economics. Rajat Acharyya, Oxford University Press. © Oxford University Press 2022.
DOI: 10.1093/oso/9780192865144.003.0005

the computer sector, for example, means a smaller number of workers can produce one unit of computers. Given these labour requirements, if L_C number of workers are employed in computer production and L_T number of workers in textiles production, the output levels are:

$$X_C = \frac{L_C}{a_{LC}} \quad (5.1)$$

$$X_T = \frac{L_T}{a_{LT}} \quad (5.2)$$

Note that under the assumption of fixed coefficient production technology, a_{LC} (and a_{LT}) reflect reciprocal of both average and marginal productivities.

Zero profit conditions under perfectly competitive market conditions everywhere mean that computers and textiles in our home country are produced up to the level for which price equals average (and marginal) cost:

$$P_C = a_{LC} W \quad (5.3)$$

$$P_T = a_{LT} W \quad (5.4)$$

Combining (5.3) and (5.4) we get the relative supply price for computers as the ratio of per unit labour requirements:

$$\frac{P_C}{P_T} = \frac{a_{LC}}{a_{LT}} \quad (5.5)$$

Note, under constant costs, the pre-trade equilibrium relative price of computers at home equals this relative supply price of computers. Since per unit labour requirements are fixed by technology and are invariant with respect to the output levels, so the relative supply price for computers is constant and the relative supply curve for computers is horizontal to the output axis as shown in Figure 5.1. Thus, the autarchic equilibrium relative price of computers is technology or cost-determined, independent of the domestic demand conditions. Domestic demands for goods determine only the output levels.

To reiterate, horizontal (or flat) relative supply curve is reflection of constant costs under fixed coefficient production technology so that the relative supply price is invariant with the output level. Accordingly, the equilibrium autarchic relative price equals the relative supply price, and is also technology (and cost) determined as specified in (5.5) above.

The above expression captures the essence of the *labour theory of value*: the relative price of commodities reflects the ratio of labour embodied in these commodities. The other notable observation is that the pre-trade price ratio is independent of domestic demand conditions. This follows from the assumption of *constant costs*. The fixed coefficient production function implies that the marginal cost of production is invariant with the increase in the scale of

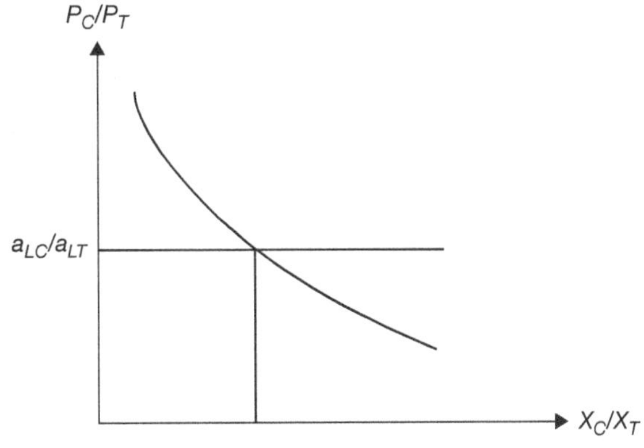

Figure 5.1 Autarchic Equilibrium

production, and thus the cost-price under perfectly competitive conditions is constant for any given money wage. Hence, variations in domestic demand bring in only changes in the amount of production without any change in the price ratio.

It is straightforward to check that trade between our home country and a foreign country will be determined entirely by the technology asymmetry across these countries. Assuming that similar production conditions prevail in a foreign country, the pre-trade relative price ratios there will be:

$$\frac{P_C^*}{P_T^*} = \frac{a_{LC}^*}{a_{LT}^*} \tag{5.6}$$

Suppose, the foreign country has a relatively superior technology in the production of computers in the following sense:

$$\frac{a_{LC}}{a_{LT}} > \frac{a_{LC}^*}{a_{LT}^*} \tag{5.7}$$

That is, the foreign country has a comparative *cost* advantage in producing computers whereas the home country has a comparative *cost* advantage in producing textiles. Since under constant costs prices are cost-determined, so these comparative cost advantages translate into comparative advantages whereby the pre-trade relative price of computers is lower in the foreign country. Thus, through arbitrage, the home country exports textiles and imports computers.

A higher relative price of textiles in the foreign country encourages producers to expand textile production in the home country whereas cheaper imports of computers from abroad lowers production of computers there. Workers thus move out of the computers sector and into the textiles sector. Initial price differences are wiped out through arbitrage and consequent movements of goods across these countries. As long as country sizes are not too asymmetric in the sense defined later, the relative prices converge to a level strictly between the pre-trade price ratios. Due to constant costs, on the other hand, expansion in the production of textiles (and contraction in the production of computers) does not erode the price-cost margin. Thus, expansion in the production of textiles in the home country continues till all labour resources are exhausted and the home country is completely specialized in textiles. Through similar production expansion, the foreign country specializes completely in the production of computers.

The pre-trade and post-trade equilibria are shown in Figure 5.2. The straight lines MN and M^*N^* are the production possibility frontiers (PPF) in the home and foreign countries respectively. Note that these are essentially the full employment loci with constant slopes equal to the labour ratios specified in equations (5.5) and (5.6):

$$\bar{L} = a_{LC}X_C + a_{LT}X_T \tag{5.8}$$

$$\bar{L}^* = a^*_{LC}X^*_C + a^*_{LT}X^*_T \tag{5.9}$$

$\bar{L}$ and $\bar{L}^*$ are the total labour force in the two countries and reflect the size of the two countries. The PPFs are drawn on the basis of the assumption in equation (5.7). Note that a larger labour force in the home country shifts out its PPF, as the economy will now be able to produce larger quantities of both goods. Assume identical tastes for consumers in both countries, which are captured through the same set of community indifference curves. The pre-trade production points are A and A^* respectively for the home and foreign countries. The post-trade uniform relative price is shown by (the absolute slope of) the broken line M^*N. Production in the home country shifts to N with complete specialization in textiles and in the foreign country to M^* with complete specialization in computers. The post-trade consumption shifts to E, with the home country exporting BN units of textiles in exchange for B^*M^* (= BE) units of computers. Both the countries thus gain from trade.

For this post-trade equilibrium with complete specialization in different goods by the home and foreign countries, the relevant zero profit conditions in the two countries imply the following equality:

$$\frac{P^W_T}{P^W_C} = \frac{a_{LT}}{a^*_{LC}} \times \frac{w}{w^*}$$

where $\frac{P^W_T}{P^W_C}$ is the world relative price of textiles or the commodity terms of trade (TOT).

Thus, the home wage relative to the foreign wage, known as the *double factoral* TOT, is determined by the production technologies for the goods in which they completely specialize and by the commodity TOT:

$$\frac{w}{w^*} = \frac{a^*_{LC}}{a_{LT}} \frac{P^W_T}{P^W_C} \tag{5.10}$$

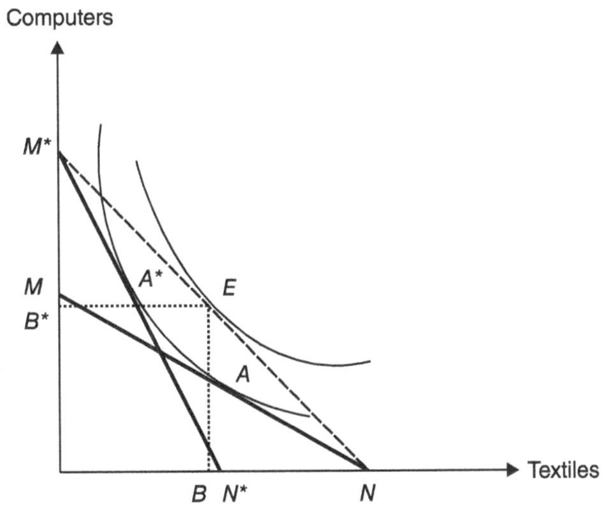

Figure 5.2 Complete Specialization and GFT in Ricardian Model

The complete specialization by countries after trade follows from the assumption of constant opportunity cost as reflected in the linear PPF depicted in Figure 5.2. Note that, as explained in Chapter 2, the opportunity cost of producing goods may be constant even with many factors of production instead of labour as the only factor of production as is assumed here. At the same time, as we will see later, the demand conditions in relation to supply conditions (which in a sense are related to the size of the countries) are also important for this complete specialization result. The home country can completely specialize in the production of textiles only if it can meet its consumption of computers through imports. But if its domestic demand for computers is too large compared to what the foreign country can supply after meeting its own consumption requirements, then it is not possible for the home country to not produce any computers domestically. In such a case, the home country will be incompletely specialized, or produce both textiles and computers, even if the pattern of comparative cost advantage indicates that producing only textiles is gainful.

What appears from this argument is that though under the assumption of constant (opportunity) cost, the demand for computers and textiles has practically no role to play in determining trade and its direction, it does determine post-trade production specialization and consequently the volume of trade. What is even more important, the demand for commodities in relation to the supply of commodities also determines the distribution of real income gains from trade across the two countries. Gains from trade (GFT), as discussed earlier in Chapter 2, follows from countries specializing according to their comparative advantages, and consequently gaining from favourable terms of trade. But under constant costs, as we will see in the following sections, the demand conditions largely determine the deviation of prices from pre-trade levels and hence gains from trade thereof.

5.2 ROLE OF RELATIVE SIZE OF TRADING NATIONS AND DISTRIBUTION OF GFT

For open economies, excess demand or trade volumes reflect their sizes. A country may be consuming and producing a lot of commodities and in very large quantities, yet it may be small in the world market if there is very little over-production to be exported or very little excess demand to be imported. Ricardo argued that all the gains from trade will accrue to such a small country when it trades with nations that export and import relatively larger volumes. The explanation is that the larger country in this sense cannot specialize completely, because if it does, then its demand for the other good cannot be met by imports from a smaller trading partner. Consequently, it will not experience any improvements in the terms of trade after trade and therefore will not gain. His argument can be illustrated in terms of Figure 5.3, where the post-trade international equilibrium in a Ricardian set up is shown in terms of offer curves. Recall from Chapter 4 that offer curves will have linear segments under constant opportunity costs. The length of the linear segment depends on the maximum possible production of export goods. In the Ricardian set up with labour as the only factor production, this in turn depends on the size of the labour force in each country. This can be verified from (5.2) in the case of our home country.

In Figure 5.3, given labour coefficients, if the home and foreign countries do not have significantly different sizes of their respective labour forces, they will not differ much in their maximum production capacities for textiles and computers respectively. This case is illustrated by the foreign offer curve being OK_0^*F. The terms of trade, the slope of the line connecting the origin and the intersection of the offer curves *OKH* and OK_0^*F, lies strictly between the pre-trade price ratios in the two countries as reflected by the absolute slope of line segments *OK* and OK_0^*.

The offer curve OK_1^*F' represents a larger sized foreign country. The international equilibrium now occurs at point *E* along the linear segment of the foreign offer curve so that the terms of trade is the same as the pre-trade price ratio. There is thus no improvement in the terms of trade for the foreign country after trade, and hence no gains from trade. Note that the foreign country is incompletely specialized, producing textiles along with computers. As mentioned earlier, if it had been completely specialized, neither its volume of exports of computers could

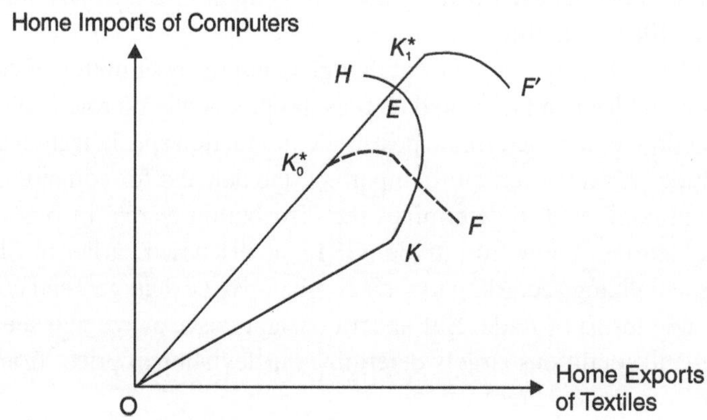

Figure 5.3 Country Size and Terms of Trade

be fully demanded, nor its larger import demand for textiles could be fully supplied by the smaller home country. Thus, the foreign country is forced to be incompletely specialized and fails to take advantage of the cross-country price differences that exist. The smaller home country, on the other hand, is completely specialized as its corresponding export supply and import demand can be realized and it thus takes away all the gains from trade.

To sum up, similar sized countries in the sense defined above will mutually gain from opening up of trade among them provided the pattern of trade follows a comparative advantage. But when relatively asymmetric sized countries engage in trade among them, all the gains from trade accrue to the country that is small in international trade.

Box 5.1 Relative Demand and Supply curves, Size of Countries and the Post Trade equilibrium

Relation between size of countries or their workforces and the nature of post-trade equilibrium in the Ricardian model can be alternatively illustrated with the help of world relative demand and world relative supply curves. The world relative supply curve is a step-like curve shown in Figure 5.4 below. To explain, note that, from Figure 5.2 it follows that if the world relative price of textiles equals $\frac{a_{LT}}{a_{LC}}$ then the home country is incompletely specialized producing any amount of textiles between zero and $\frac{L}{a_{LT}}$. But for such a world relative price of textiles, the foreign country is completely specialized in computers producing $\frac{L^*}{a^*_{LC}}$ units. Thus, the world relative supply of textiles is anything between zero and $\frac{L}{L^*}\frac{a^*_{LC}}{a_{LT}}$. This is represented by the lower step in the world relative supply curve. By similar reasoning, for the world relative price of textiles equal to $\frac{a^*_{LT}}{a^*_{LC}}$, the Foreign country is incompletely specialized, that is, produces any amount of textiles from zero to $\frac{L^*}{a^*_{LT}}$ and correspondingly produces any amount of computers ranging from $\frac{L^*}{a^*_{LC}}$ to zero. But, the home country will be completely specialized in textiles producing $\frac{L}{a_{LT}}$ units. Thus, the world relative supply of textiles for $p^W = \frac{a^*_{LT}}{a^*_{LC}}$ will be at least $\frac{L}{L^*}\frac{a^*_{LC}}{a_{LT}}$. Note that, larger is the units of textiles and correspondingly smaller are the units of computers produced by the foreign country, larger will be the relative world supply of textiles. This is represented by the upper step in the world relative supply curve. For all world prices between these two extremes—which are the autarchic relative prices of textiles in the two countries—the two countries are completely specialized with home producing $\frac{L}{a_{LT}}$ units of textiles and foreign producing $\frac{L^*}{a^*_{LC}}$ units of computers. Thus, for all such intermediate prices the relative world supply of textiles remains the same at $\frac{L}{L^*}\frac{a^*_{LC}}{a_{LT}}$.

This is represented by the vertical segment of the world relative supply curve. On the other hand, given that textiles and computers are substitutes in consumption, the world relative supply curve is downward sloping. The countries will be completely specialized at the world relative price p^W if $d(p^W) = \frac{L}{L^*}\frac{a^*_{LC}}{a_{LT}}$ as shown in Figure 5.4. Since, after trade the two countries will be completely specialized if $\frac{a_{LT}}{a_{LC}} < p^W < \frac{a^*_{LT}}{a^*_{LC}}$, so we can derive the range of relative size of countries (or their workforces) for which the countries will be completely specialized as: $\frac{a_{LT}}{a_{LC}} < d^{-1}\left(\frac{L}{L^*}\frac{a^*_{LC}}{a_{LT}}\right) < \frac{a^*_{LT}}{a^*_{LC}}$. Given the demand parameters, the larger is the size of L (for any given L^*), smaller is the world relative price. At the extreme, the relative price of textiles coincides with $\frac{a_{LT}}{a_{LC}}$ in which case the home country incompletely specializes. See Exercise 9 for the specific condition for a Cobb-Douglas utility function. Alternatively, for any given sizes, a strong taste bias in computers makes the relative demand for textiles small for all p^W so that the relative demand curve intersects the relative supply curve along its lower step. Again, the home country incompletely specializes.

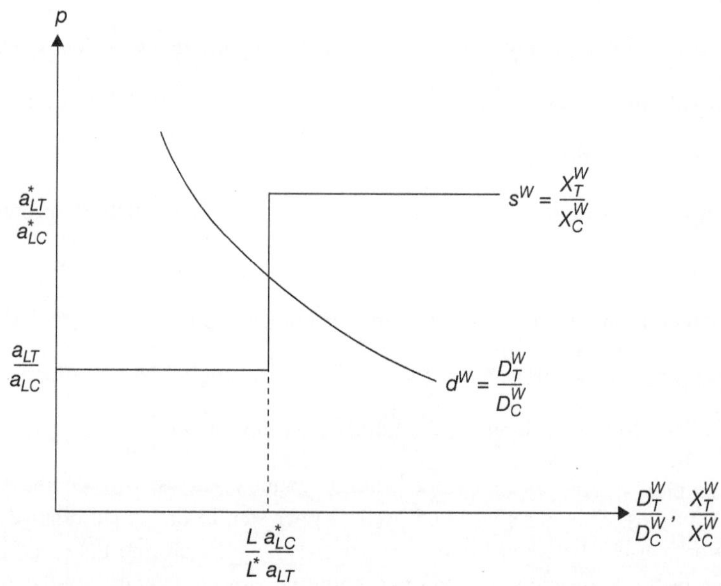

Figure 5.4 Post-trade World Equilibrium

5.3 ADVANCED TOPICS

5.3.1 Many Commodity Extension

When the home and foreign countries produce many goods, the pattern of trade between them is still determined by the relative labour ratios but now in relation to the ratio of wages of the two countries. Suppose pre-trade each country produces the same set of n number of goods. These goods are indexed in a way that labour requirement at home relative to that in the foreign country is larger for successively higher indexed good:

$$\frac{a_{L1}}{a_{L1}^{*}} < \frac{a_{L2}}{a_{L2}^{*}} < \ldots\ldots < \frac{a_{Ln}}{a_{Ln}^{*}} \tag{5.11}$$

Note that for any pair of goods the home country has a comparative cost advantage in a relatively lower ranked good:

$$\frac{a_{Li}}{a_{Li}^{*}} < \frac{a_{Lj}}{a_{Lj}^{*}} \Rightarrow \frac{a_{Li}}{a_{Lj}} < \frac{a_{Li}^{*}}{a_{Lj}^{*}} \quad \forall i < j \tag{5.12}$$

Thus, in equation (5.11) goods are indexed according to a diminishing home country comparative cost advantage. Now suppose the ratio of the pre-trade foreign wage to the pre-trade home country wage is such that:

$$\frac{a_{L1}}{a_{L1}^{*}} < \frac{a_{L2}}{a_{L2}^{*}} < \ldots \frac{a_{Li}}{a_{Li}^{*}} \leq \frac{w^{*}}{w} < \frac{a_{Lj}}{a_{Lj}^{*}} . < .. < \frac{a_{Ln}}{a_{Ln}^{*}} \tag{5.13}$$

In case of weak inequality, the home country can produce the i-th good at the same or lower cost than the foreign country:

$$a_{Li} w \leq a_{Li}^{*} w^{*} \tag{5.14}$$

Thus, given the diminishing home country comparative cost advantage pattern defined in equation (5.11) or in equation (5.13), through competitive forces and arbitrage all goods indexed lower than i will be produced only in the home country and all goods indexed higher than i will be produced only in the foreign country. In case of *strict* inequality in equation (5.14) and in equation (5.13), good i will also be produced only in the home country. In such a case, all goods 1, 2, … i will be exported by the home country, and goods j, …, n will be exported by the foreign country. Thus, the Ricardian post-trade complete specialization result holds. But if good i is equally costly in both the countries, this good will be produced by both and the countries will be incompletely specialized. The domestic demand patterns will then determine which country will export this good i.

The demand conditions are also relevant for determining the post-trade relative wage, or the double factoral TOT, that holds the key in determining the pattern of specialization of the countries in the many commodity case. In a continuum of good case, Dornbusch et al. (1977) spell out the mechanism through which demand conditions along with comparative advantage of countries in the sense defined in equation (5.11) determine the pattern of specialization and

Box 5.2 Many Goods and Chain of Comparative Advantage

In a world with many commodities and many countries, bilateral comparisons of prices may fail to predict the pattern of trade. Under constant costs, as shown above, Ricardo's doctrine of comparative cost advantage determining the pattern of trade can be extended to the world of many commodities but two countries using bilateral comparisons in a chain of relative labour costs. In a many country world, such generalizations become less obvious. Yet, as shown by McKenzie (1954) and Jones (1961), *an* efficient pattern of trade must satisfy bilateral comparisons of relative labour costs for all possible pairings of commodities and countries. But other (inefficient) pattern of trade may also exist. For example, as Drabicki and Takayama (1979) show, in a three-commodity world a country may export a commodity which is relatively more expensive and import the least expensive commodity.

trade. To elaborate, consider continuum of goods indexed by Z over the unit interval [0, 1]. Let $a(Z)$ and $a^*(Z)$ denote the unit labour requirements in the home and foreign country respectively to produce good Z. As in equation (5.11), goods are indexed according to diminishing home country comparative cost advantage, which in this continuum of goods case means that the relative unit labour requirement $A(Z)$ is increasing in Z:

$$A(Z) = \frac{a(Z)}{a^*(Z)}, \quad A'(Z) > 0 \tag{5.15}$$

Denoting foreign wage relative to home wage by $\omega^* \equiv \frac{w^*}{w}$, any commodity Z will be produced at home if:

$$A(Z) \leq \omega^* \tag{5.16}$$

Strict equality defines a commodity $\bar{Z}$ such that:

$$\bar{Z} = A^{-1}(\omega^*) \tag{5.17}$$

Given the assumption in equation (5.15), it then follows that for any given relative foreign wage, the home country efficiently produces the range of commodities $[0, \bar{Z}]$ and the foreign country produces the range of commodities $[\bar{Z}, 1]$.

The relative wage is determined by demand for commodities and corresponding trade balance conditions. Under the assumption of homothetic and identical taste, a constant share of national income $b(Z)$ is spent on each good in each country such that $\int_0^1 b(Z) = 1$. Let $\phi(\bar{Z}) = \int_0^{\bar{Z}} b(Z)$ denote the share of the home country's national income spent on all goods produced domestically. Thus, $[1 - \phi(\bar{Z})]wL$ is spent by the home country on imports from foreign country. On the other hand, since the foreign country imports all good $Z \in [0, \bar{Z}]$, so its total import expenditure is $\phi(\bar{Z})]w^*L^*$. Thus the trade balance condition can be written as:

$$[1-\phi(\overline{Z})]wL = \phi(\overline{Z})w^*L^* \Rightarrow \omega = \frac{\phi(\overline{Z})}{[1-\phi(\overline{Z})]}\frac{L^*}{L} \tag{5.18}$$

This can be rewritten in an implicit form as:

$$\omega = B(\overline{Z}, \frac{L^*}{L}), \frac{\partial\omega}{\partial\overline{\overline{Z}}} > 0 \tag{5.18a}$$

The positive sign of the change in the relative wage when the home country produces a larger set of goods can be easily checked from equation (5.18) using the property of the $\phi(\overline{Z})$ function. Intuitively, we can explain this sign as follows. For any given relative endowment of labour, $\frac{L^*}{L}$, the relative home wage depends on the value of $\overline{Z}$. An increase in $\overline{Z}$ means a larger set of commodities is produced at home and a smaller set in the foreign country. Thus the derived demand for labour is now larger at home and smaller in the foreign country. Hence, the relative home wage rises.

The conditions in equations (5.17) and (5.18) together determine the pattern of comparative advantage and the relative wage as shown in Figure 5.5. Thus, at the equilibrium, the home country specializes in all commodities $Z \in \left[0, \overline{\overline{Z}}\right]$ and the foreign country in all commodities $Z \in \left[\overline{\overline{Z}}, 1\right]$. Countries are thus incompletely specialized.

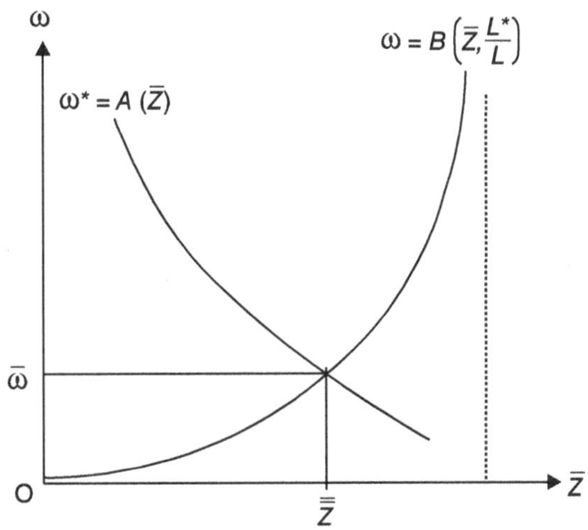

Figure 5.5 Pattern of Specialization with Continuum of Goods

5.3.2 World Production Possibility Frontier and Many Countries Extension

Like the many commodities but two countries model, the Ricardian conclusions mostly carry over to the case of many countries but two commodities. A convenient way to discuss how the Ricardian conclusion generalizes to the case of trade among many countries is through the construction of the world production possibility frontier (PPF). To simplify matters, begin with the construction of world PPF in the case of two countries and two commodities. Consider the pattern of comparative cost advantage depicted in Figure 5.2. For given labour endowments and production technologies for the home and foreign countries, the maximum world production of textiles equals $ON_w = ON + ON^*$. Such a maximum potential level of world textile production is attained for all relative prices of textiles that are larger than pre-trade prices in both countries so that both completely specialize in textiles. In Figure 5.6, this will be the case for all post-trade price lines steeper than M^*N^*. For a lower world relative price of textiles that equals the pre-trade price ratio in the foreign country, but is still larger than that in the home country, the home country is still completely specialized in textiles producing ON amount, but for the foreign country the production of textiles can be any amount over the range $[0, N^*]$ depending on its domestic demand condition. Thus, for such a TOT, the world production of textiles can at the most be ON_w and at the least be ON when the foreign country specializes in computers. This gives us the linear stretch RN_w of the world PPF.

For the world relative price of textiles smaller than the pre-trade price ratio in the foreign country but larger than that in the home country, as reflected by all price lines flatter than M^*N^* but steeper than MN, the home country remains completely specialized in textiles whereas the foreign country now completely specializes in computers. The world production combination is thus R, which is known as the Ricardo point. For an even lower relative price equal to the pre-trade price ratio in the home country, the foreign country produces only computers but the

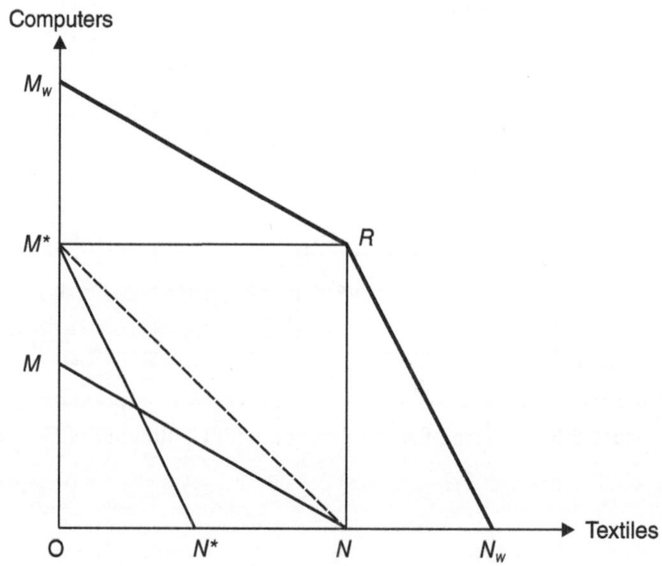

Figure 5.6 World Production Possibility Frontier

home country may produce any combination of computers and textiles leading to the RM_W linear stretch of the world PPF. Finally, for all world relative prices smaller than the pre-trade price ratio at home, both the countries completely specialize in computers and the world as a whole produces the maximum feasible units of computers, $OM_W = OM + OM^*$. Thus the two-country world PPF is given by the kinked curve $M_W RN_W$.

Extending this logic, world PPF for four countries *A*, *B*, *C*, and *D* is drawn in Figure 5.6. Suppose the countries are indexed in order of diminishing comparative advantage in textiles:

$$\frac{a_{LT}^A}{a_{LC}^A} < \frac{a_{LT}^B}{a_{LC}^B} < \frac{a_{LT}^C}{a_{LC}^C} < \frac{a_{LT}^D}{a_{LC}^D} \tag{5.19}$$

The world PPF now has four linear stretches with the absolute slope of each reflecting the pre-trade price ratio or the labour ratio in the corresponding country. For example, the absolute slope of $M_W R_A$ reflects the labour ratio in country *A* as specified in equation (5.19). Suppose U_W represents a world indifference curve, that is, a locus of the consumption of textiles and computers for which the world as a whole is indifferent to. In Figure 5.7, this world indifference curve is tangent to world PPF at point *E* along the linear stretch $R_A R_B$. Thus, the post-trade relative price of textiles that is given by the absolute slope of this world indifference curve at point *E* equals the pre-trade relative price of textiles prevailing in country *B*. Therefore, country *A* will be completely specialized in textiles whereas countries *C* and *D* will be completely specialized in computers. But country *B* will be incompletely specialized, producing both computers and textiles. The total world demand for textiles *GE* will be supplied by countries *A* and *B*, and the total demand for computers *EH* will be supplied by countries *B*, *C*, and *D*.

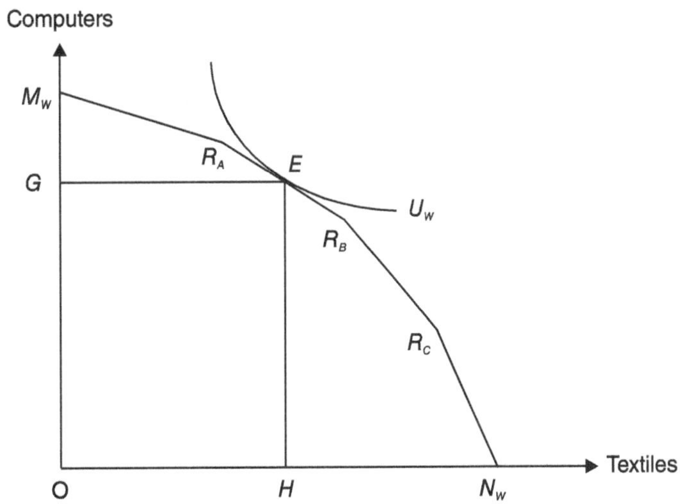

Figure 5.7 A Four-Country Example

In the above example, country B is thus a *large country*, which does not gain from trade as it experiences no improvement in its terms of trade. All the gains from trade among these countries will accrue to the smaller countries A, C, and D. Thus, once again the demand condition determines whether all countries will be completely specialized and will gain from trade.

5.3.3 Technology for Sale

Mutual gains from trade for all trading nations through commodity trade as discussed in the earlier chapters and formalized above, can further be augmented through trade in productive factors if free commodity trade leaves scope for such trading. We will discuss this in a later chapter on factor mobility. Beladi et al. (1997) discuss further scope of augmenting aggregate gains from trade through transfer or sale of improved technology that a nation possesses to its trading partner. Of course, the technical knowledge that is traded must not be embedded in the productive factors and hence cannot be transferred between countries through movement of productive factors. Otherwise, the gains from factor movement may not be augmented further through transfer or sale of technical knowledge. Note that the labour coefficients defined above capture several dimensions of technology and technical knowledge—blueprint, labour skills, and even climatic conditions that make labour productivity differ. Labour skills are, of course, embedded in labour and thus can be transferred between countries through migration of labour. In fact, the Ricardian idea of different technologies and consequent labour productivity differences across trading nations is rooted in the climatic and blueprint dimensions of technological knowledge rather than in labour skills that are intrinsic to labour. Beladi et al. (1997) argue that if it is the blueprint that differentiates the two countries in terms of production technology and consequent labour productivities, then a transfer or sale of such technical knowledge will raise total gains further above the gains from commodity trade. They offer several cases in support of their argument, of which we consider the simplest one below to exemplify their argument.

Suppose the home country has absolute advantage in producing both computers and textiles but has a comparative *dis*advantage in computers that it imports from the foreign country. Thus, though $a_{LC} < a_{LC}^*$ and $a_{LT} < a_{LT}^*$, the productivity differences are asymmetric in the two lines of production such that equation (5.7) holds. When the home country transfers its superior technology of producing computers (in which it has a comparative *dis*advantage) to the foreign country, the unit labour requirements for producing computers in both countries will be the same, which is, a_{LC}.

Thus, the labour coefficient ratio in the foreign country will now be $\frac{a_{LC}}{a_{LT}^*}$. The comparative disadvantage of the home country in computers will be more pronounced now: $\frac{a_{LC}}{a_{LT}} > \frac{a_{LC}^*}{a_{LT}^*} > \frac{a_{LC}}{a_{LT}^*}$.

The World PPF in Figure 5.8 which was $M_W R N_W$ before the transfer, becomes $M'_W R' N_W$ after the transfer. Note that the transfer of superior technology for producing computers to the foreign country enables it to produce more computers for any given production of textiles and hence labour available for computer production. Hence, world PPF shifts out, though non-uniformly. Consequently, the world as a whole gains from this technology sale or transfer. Setting aside the transfer fee, the distribution of this additional gain (over and above what the

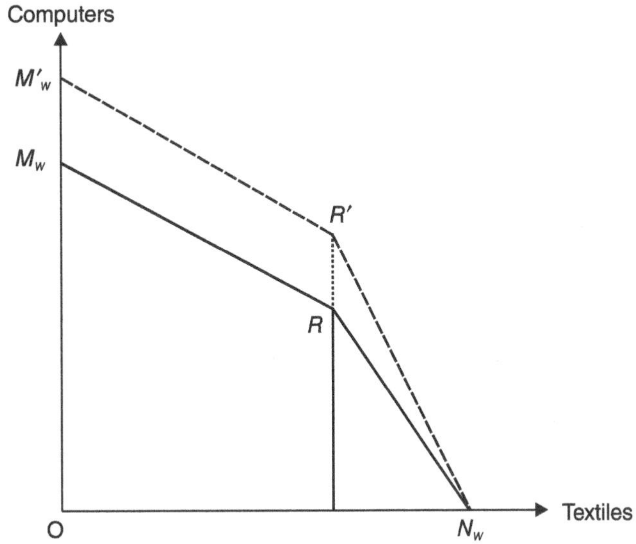

Figure 5.8 World PPF after Technology Transfer

world as a whole could get through commodity trade), however, is uncertain and depends on the relative price movement as a consequence of change in the world supplies of commodities that technology transfer results in.

As an example, suppose that before the transfer the countries were completely specialized at *R*. Technology transfer thus enables the foreign country to produce more of its exports ($X_C^{*\prime} = \frac{L^*}{a_{LC}} > \frac{L^*}{a_{LC}^*} = X_C^*$). TOT thus moves in favour of the home country, which then unambiguously gains. For the foreign country, deterioration in TOT brings in a welfare loss, which if large enough can outweigh the gains from the technology transfer and the expanded production set. There is thus an immiserizing possibility for the foreign country that was first noted by Bhagwati (1958) in the context of the welfare effect of growth for a trading nation that we will discuss in Chapter 15.

5.4 INTERNATIONAL TRADE AND TECHNOLOGY CHOICE

What is now clear from the discussion so far is that production technologies available to countries determine the pattern of their respective comparative advantage and consequently the pattern of trade. However, as discussed in the earlier chapters, countries can upgrade production technologies and develop new goods or newer varieties through research and development (R&D) undertaken by firms. International trade by itself can create the environment and provide incentives to undertake such R&D activities and lead to technological changes. Comparative advantage itself thus can be strengthened or even reversed. This was the essence of Adam Smith's dynamic productivity gains from trade and Michael Porter's argument of selective factor disadvantage. A similar argument also holds centre-stage in literature on trade and endogenous growth that will be discussed in a later chapter.

In a recent case study of Korean information and communication technology (ICT) sector, Onodera and Kim (2008) observe that more open trade and investment increased incentives for innovation through greater competition. A host of factors contributed towards this favourable effect. Tariffs in the ICT sector that still exceeded 10 per cent in the early 1990s, were cut rapidly, the import diversification programme that protected the Korean industry from Japanese competitors in the domestic market was progressively phased out, and foreign direct investment (FDI) was increasingly opened up. These open trade and investment policies provided stronger incentives for Korean companies to innovate and seek out international markets while also improving access to a wider range of foreign technology. The introduction of international standards and the deregulation of telecommunication services were also extremely important for innovations in the telecom equipment industry. This policy resulted in Korea emerging as one of the early developers of the CDMA technology in mobile telephone services. The R&D policy and the intellectual property rights policy supported the transformation of the ICT industry. Increased protection of intellectual property rights had a positive impact as the average number of patents granted in the United States to Korean firms increased five-fold from about 200 per annum during 1987–91 to about 1,000 per annum during 1992–96, and to over 3,000 per annum during 1997–2001.

However, the favourable impact of international trade on R&D and technological upgrading is neither a self-enforcing proposition theoretically nor are country experiences in this regard unambiguous and conclusive. The idea behind trade having a favourable impact on technology is that competition from cheaper imports from abroad induces local firms to invest in cost-reducing and product-quality enhancing R&D. On the flip side is the argument based on the Schumpeterian hypothesis that competition is not necessarily conducive to innovation. Too much competition lowers profits of firms and thus lowers the incentives for firms to undertake R&D that is uncertain and involves huge sunk costs. We will learn more about this later.

Box 5.3 Trade-Related Intellectual Property Rights (TRIPS) and Innovation

The Schumpeterian idea is the main motivation for implementing patent protection and trade related intellectual property rights (TRIPS) across the globe. The basic argument is that an innovator must be allowed to extract rent from buyers to recover the huge amount of R&D costs for its innovation. Otherwise, a potential innovator will not undertake R&D and this will mean a smaller number of innovations. While this seems obvious and justified, there are several caveats to this argument. First, to what extent and how long the innovator should extract rent to recover its R&D costs? Second, is there any evidence that TRIPS has accelerated the rate of innovation? Third, how far can the above argument be extended to the market for healthcare and drugs for diseases like AIDS, malaria, and tuberculosis?

Whatever little evidence is available from country studies does not suggest that TRIPS will have any significant positive impact on innovations in the developing world, particularly in the pharmaceutical sector. This is because not only investments in basic R&D and costs of the full development of a commercial drug are very high, but also most of the developing countries, with notable exceptions like India, lack the technological capability and skill to undertake basic R&D (Lall 2003). The monopoly power that patent protection confers upon the patent holder firm, on the other hand, has resulted in quite high prices for essential drugs for AIDS in the developing and poor countries. The cost of individual AIDS-combination therapy in India a few years ago was prohibitively high for a vast majority of the Indian population. A similar situation prevailed in Pakistan, Indonesia, and other low-income countries. Given that more than 95 per cent of all HIV-infected live in developing countries, patent protection for medicines and drugs simply implies denying these patients access to available drugs and consequently their right to live.

SUMMARY POINTS

- Ricardo offered a more general explanation of technology asymmetry across countries as a basis of trade in his doctrine of *comparative* cost advantage.
- Under the assumption of constant costs, prices are cost-determined and so comparative cost advantages of nations arising out of their technology asymmetry translate into comparative advantages whereby the pre-trade relative price of computers is lower in the foreign country.
- The post-trade pattern of specialization and gains from trade depends on domestic demand conditions, relative supply conditions, or the relative sizes of trading partners.
- If the trading partners are not too asymmetric in their labour endowments and thus in productive capacities, all countries specialize completely in their respective comparative advantage goods and unambiguously gain from trade.

(*contd*)

Summary Points (*contd*)

- But when relatively asymmetric sized countries engage in trade among themselves, the larger partner will be incompletely specialized since its consumption requirements cannot fully be met through imports from the smaller partner. The larger country thus experiences no TOT improvement after trade opens up and all the gains from trade then accrue to the smaller trading partner.
- Ricardo's conclusions mostly hold in cases of many commodities but two countries and many countries but two commodities.
- If it is the blueprint that differentiates the two countries in terms of production technology and consequent labour productivities, then a transfer or sale of such technical knowledge will raise total gains further above the gains from commodity trade.
- International trade by itself can create the environment and provide incentives to undertake R&D activities and lead to technological changes. The Ricardian comparative (cost) advantage thus can be strengthened or even reversed.
- But the favourable impact of international trade on R&D and technological upgrading is neither a self-enforcing proposition theoretically nor are country experiences in this regard unambiguous and conclusive.

KEYWORDS

- **Fixed coefficient production technology** is one that allows only one combination of inputs to produce an output. For labour as the only input required to produce an output, such a production technology means a fixed amount of labour required to produce one unit of the output.
- **Labour theory of value** states that the exchange value of a commodity is essentially the value of labour embodied in the commodity.
- **Double factoral TOT** is the ratio of wages in the two trading nations after trade.

EXERCISES

1. Discuss the logical basis of Ricardo's assertion that similar sized countries will be completely specialized after trade.
2. The marginal productivity of Italian workers in making bread is 0.4 units and that of making mobile phones is 0.2 units. If Swedish workers' marginal productivity in making bread and mobile phones is respectively 0.4 units and 0.6 units, what will be the pattern of trade between these two countries?
3. Consider the following production functions in H and F countries for Textiles (T) and Computers (C):

   $$T = 2L_T, C = 3L_C\,,\; T^* = L_T^*\,,\; C^* = \frac{3}{2}L_C^*$$

   (a) If $W = W^* = 5$, what is the pattern of absolute advantages of the two countries? Will there be any trade between H and F?

   (b) Suppose there is a technological innovation in textiles sector in F which improves productivity of workers there by 40 per cent. Will your answers in (a) change? Explain.
4. Why cannot a country gain from trade with a smaller trading partner?
5. Indian producers require 5 units and 4 units of labour respectively to produce wheat and tea, whereas American workers require 3 and 7 units of labour respectively. There are 2,000 workers in India and 2,100 workers in the United States:
   (a) What will be the pattern of trade between India and the US?
   (b) Draw the world PPF assuming that these are the only two countries in the world.
   (c) If consumers everywhere consume wheat and tea at a fixed ratio of 4:5, determine the TOT.
   (d) Will both countries be completely specialized after trade? How much of wheat and tea will India and the US produce after trade?
6. In the above exercise, find out the volume of trade for each country. Will both countries gain from trade?
7. Two goods 1 and 2 are produced by competitive producers in the two countries, Home (H) and Foreign (F), using only labour under fixed coefficient technologies such that $L = a_{L1}X_1 + 5X_2$ and $L^* = 2X_1^* + X_2^*$. H has a taste bias in good 1 and F in good 2.

   (a) Will there be any trade between H and F? If so, who will export which of the two goods?

   (b) Suppose, $a_{L1} = 20$, $L = 100$ and $L^* = 100$. When trade opens up, the world relative price of good 1 settles at 3 per unit. How much of the two goods will be produced by H and F? Illustrate that both the countries gain from trade.

Exercises (*contd*)

8. India produces one unit of mango (M) by using one unit of labour and one unit of Rice (R) using two units of labour. If total number of workers is 500, draw the PPF. Rice is produced by competitive farmers at a constant marginal cost $MC_R = \frac{1}{2}$, whereas mango is produced by a monopolist who charges Rs. $\frac{1}{6}$ at the pre-trade equilibrium. Illustrate the pre-trade equilibrium assuming mango and rice are substitutable in consumption. If the world relative price of rice is $\frac{1}{3}$, will there be GFT? Explain and illustrate your answer. If there is GFT, decompose it into two components.
9. Suppose the aggregate utility function of all consumers in the home and foreign countries taken together (for consuming two goods 1 and 2) is given by $U = C_1^{\alpha} C_2^{\beta}$. If the home country has a comparative advantage in good 2, derive the restrictions on relative size of its workforce for which both countries will be completely specialized.
10. In the above example, suppose sizes of workforce of the two countries are the same. Will the countries be completely specialized if countries are equally efficient in production of good 1 whereas the foreign country is more efficient in production of good 2?
11. Suppose there is a sudden change in tastes across the globe towards use of computers, which raises its price relative to that of textiles. Assuming that the countries continue to specialize completely in their respective comparative advantage goods, how does this change in taste redistribute per capita wage incomes across countries?
12. If the use of computers rises across the globe so much that both trading nations in a two-country world produce only computers, how is Adam Smith's absolute advantage relevant for the double factoral TOT?
13. [Advanced] Consider the following pattern of comparative (cost) advantage for Bangladesh (B), India (I), and the United States (U) in producing textiles (T) and computers (C): $\frac{a_{LT}^{B}}{a_{LC}^{B}} < \frac{a_{LT}^{I}}{a_{LC}^{I}} < \frac{a_{LT}^{U}}{a_{LC}^{U}}$. If trade opens up amongst these countries, what will be the pattern of trade? Should all countries necessarily gain?
14. [Advanced] In the context of the above pattern of comparative advantage, suppose United States has absolute advantage over Bangladesh in both textiles and computers, but absolute advantage over India in only computer production. Draw the world PPF. If the United States transfers both its technologies to Bangladesh for free, how does the world PPF change?

Exercises (*contd*)

15. [Advanced] Production functions for Bread (B), Cheese (C), Potato (P) and Milk (M) in a Home and a Foreign Country are as follows:

$$B = 2L_B, C = \frac{2}{3}L_C, P = \frac{1}{4}L_P, M = 5L_M \text{ and } B^* = 2L_B^*, C^* = \frac{1}{3}L_C^*, P^* = \frac{3}{4}L_P^*, M^* = 3L_M^*$$

   (a) How would you determine the pattern of comparative advantage, pattern of production and pattern of trade?
   (b) Can $W = 1$ and $W^* = 4$ constitute equilibrium wages in the post-trade situation?
   (c) Suppose, $\frac{W}{W^*} = \frac{10}{15}$ for which trade takes place between these two countries. Then, what will be the pattern of production specialization and trade?

16. [Advanced] In the continuum of the Ricardian model, suppose the unit labour requirements for producing any good $Z \in [0, 1]$ are $a(Z) = Z$ and $a^*(Z) = Z^3$ respectively in the home and foreign countries. If consumers in both the countries spend $b(Z) = Z$ fraction of their incomes on good Z, find out the set of goods produced and exported by each country.

SUGGESTED READING

Caves, R.E., J. Frankel, and R.W. Jones. (1995). *World Trade and Payments*. Fifth Edition. New York: HarperCollins College Publishers.

Krugman, P.R. and M. Obstfeld. (2010). *International Economics: Theory and Policy*. Fifth Edition, (chapter 5). New Delhi: Pearson Education.

Ricardo, David. (1971) [1817]. *The Principles of Political Economy and Taxation*. New York: Penguin.

ADVANCED READING

Beladi, H., R.W. Jones, and S. Marjit. (1997). 'Technology for Sale', *Pacific Economic Review*, 2(3): 187–96.

Bhagwati, J.N. (1958). 'Immiserizing Growth: A Geometric Note', *Review of Economic Studies*, 25: 201–5.

Dornbusch, R., S. Fisher, and P. Samuelson. (1977). 'Comparative Advantage, Trade and Payments in a Ricardian Model with Continuum of Goods', *American Economic Review*, 47: 823–39.

Drabicki, J.Z. and A. Takayama. (1979). 'An Antinomy in the Theory of Comparative Advantage', *Journal of International Economics*, 9: 211–23.

Jones, R.W. (1961). 'Comparative Advantage and Theory of Tariffs: A Multi-country, Multi-commodity Model', *Review of Economic Studies*, 28: 161–75.

Lall, S. (2003). 'Indicators of Relative Importance of IPRs in Developing Countries', *Research Policy*, 32: 1657–80.

McKenzie, L. (1954). 'Specialization and Efficiency in World Production', *Review of Economic Studies*, 21: 165–80.

Onodera, O. and H. Kim. (2008). 'Trade and Innovation in the Korean Information and Communication Technology Sector: Trade and Innovation Project—Case Study No. 5', OECD Trade Policy Working Papers, No. 77, OECD Publishing.

Steedman, I. and J.S. Metcalfe. (1979) [1973]. 'On Foreign Trade', *Economia Internazionale*. Reprinted in I. Steedman (ed.), *Fundamental Issues in Trade Theory*. London: Macmillan.

6 Factor Endowment and Trade

An alternative source of comparative advantage of nations and explanation of the basis of trade was offered by Eli Heckscher (1949) and Bertil Ohlin (1933). Their analyses that related pattern of trade of a country with its relative factor endowment abundance has come to be known as the Heckscher–Ohlin theory.[1] This positive aspect of explaining the *pattern of trade* has been the primary focus of the Heckscher–Ohlin theory in contrast to Ricardo's focus on the normative aspect of explaining how countries mutually gain through trade according to their pattern of comparative advantages. Subsequently, Samuelson (1948) and Stolper and Samuelson (1941) established two more important theories in the similar factor endowment model used by Heckscher and Ohlin. One is the *Factor Price Equalization* theorem, which postulated the convergence of factor prices across countries after international trade equalizes commodity prices. The other is the Stolper–Samuelson theorem, which postulated the asymmetric movement of *real* returns to the scarce and the abundant factors within a country when it restricts trade by imposing an import tariff. In a broad sense, these two theorems specify how trade redistributes income across and within trading nations. The Heckscher–Ohlin (HO) theorem, the Factor Price Equalization (FPE) theorem, and the Stolper–Samuelson (SS) theorem together constitute what is, loosely speaking, known as the Heckscher–Ohlin–Samuelson (HOS) model. In this chapter we discuss the factor endowment explanation of the pattern of trade and the basic properties of the HOS model.

6.1 ASSUMPTIONS AND THE STRUCTURE OF THE HOS MODEL

The basic HOS model has a 2×2×2 structure: two countries, the home country and the foreign country, produce two goods, computers and cotton textiles, using two factors of production, labour (L) and physical capital (K). There are certain assumptions of the model that apply equally for both the countries, and there are others that differentiate the two countries. Among the first set comes the assumption that each factor of production is homogeneous everywhere

[1] As we will see later, factor abundance of a country, which determines its pattern of trade, is defined in terms of factor proportions and hence this theory or explanation of pattern of trade is also known as the Factor Proportions theory.

International Economics. Rajat Acharyya, Oxford University Press. © Oxford University Press 2022.
DOI: 10.1093/oso/9780192865144.003.0006

(in all lines of production and in both countries) and can move freely and without any cost from one sector to another within each country. That is, both computers and textiles use the same type of labour and physical capital. The homogeneity and free mobility of labour and capital together imply that each factor earns the same return everywhere within each country. But factors cannot move from one country to the other, and thus labour (and capital) may earn different wages in the two countries. The second assumption is that all markets are perfectly competitive. Perfect competition in commodity markets implies that producers earn no super-normal profit at the long-run equilibrium. On the other hand, competition in factor markets along with fully flexible factor prices ensure that the labour force is fully employed and all physical capital is fully exhausted in production in both the countries. However, maintaining full employment is more of a concern under autarchy because production of commodities (and consequently derived demand for labour and capital) cannot exceed domestic demand. But when trade opens up, if the output produced by fully utilizing all domestic resources exceeds domestic demand, the excess output can be exported and thereby full employment of all domestic resources can be maintained.

Third, the production technology for each good follows constant returns to scale with diminishing returns to the variable factor. Fourth, unlike Ricardo, Heckscher and Ohlin assumed that each good is produced by the same technology in both the countries and thereby ruled out technology asymmetry as an explanation of trade amongst nations. But the production technologies for these goods differ from each other in each country. That is, both labour and capital are needed to produce these two goods, but the combination in which these factors are used differs in the two lines of production. More important, there should not be any factor intensity reversals meaning that for all possible factor price ratios, one good must be relatively capital-intensive and the other good must be relatively labour-intensive. In other words, the two goods must be uniquely ranked in terms of their relative factor intensities. Cases of factor intensity reversals, whereby the same good is relatively capital-intensive for some smaller values of factor price ratios and relatively labour-intensive for some larger values of factor price ratios, are ruled out by assumption because these may invalidate both the HO and the FPE theorems as we will see later.

The factor intensity ranking of the two goods depends on production technology and the corresponding least-cost choices of input combinations or production *techniques* by the producers of the two goods. Figure 6.1 illustrates these choices and the factor intensity ranking of the two goods in terms of the *unit value isoquants*. A unit value isoquant for computers is the locus of different combinations of labour and capital that produce units of computers worth revenue earning of one rupee.[2] That is, if P_C is the price per unit of computers in domestic currency, then the unit value isoquant will have an output index of $\frac{1}{P_C}$. Similarly, the unit value isoquant for textiles will have an output index of $\frac{1}{P_T}$. Let us assume that the production technology for computers requires more intensive use of capital whereas the production technology for textiles requires more intensive use of labour. This means that the unit value isoquants for computers will be more inclined towards the capital axis and that for textiles towards the labour axis. Thus as long as the producers everywhere face the same *W/r* ratio (so that the iso-cost lines will have the same slope in every line of production), the least-cost choice of production techniques will be more capital-intensive for computer production and less capital-intensive (or more labour-intensive) for textiles production. These different least-cost choices of techniques are shown by the k_C and k_T rays in Figure 6.1. Note that the unit value isoquants need not be tangent on the same iso-cost line. Even if the unit value isoquant for textiles, for example, was higher up, by the assumption of constant returns to scale technology, textiles producers would have chosen the same technique of production.

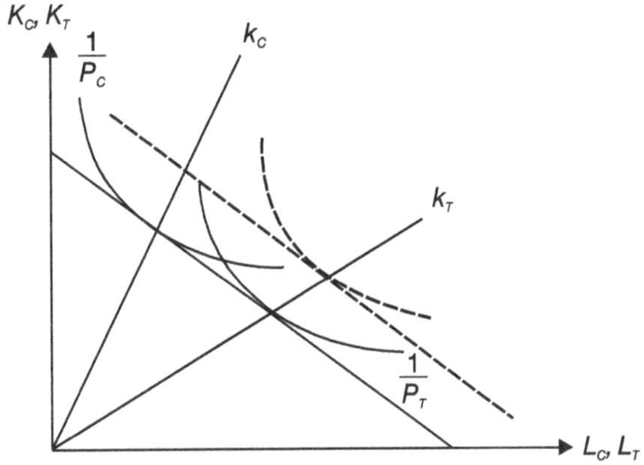

Figure 6.1 CRS Production Function and Least-Cost Choice of Techniques

In Figure 6.1 the two isoquants intersect each other only *once* and this rules out any possibility of *factor intensity reversals*. That is, *for any and all* factor price ratios (*W/r*), the least-cost choice of the capital–labour ratio will be larger in computer production than that in textiles production:

$$k_C > k_T \ \forall \ W/r \tag{6.1}$$

But if the two isoquants cross each other more than once or are tangent to each other, factor intensity reversals will arise. Thus, for example, computers are relatively capital-intensive for some smaller values of relative wages but relatively capital-intensive for some higher values of relative wages:

$$k_C > k_T \ \forall \ 0 < W/r < (W/r)' \tag{6.1a}$$

$$k_C < k_T \ \forall \ W/r > (W/r)' \tag{6.1b}$$

The next important assumption of the HOS model is regarding the demand for goods: consumers everywhere have identical and homothetic tastes. As discussed earlier, this assumption rules out taste bias as a source of comparative advantage. An interesting further implication of homothetic taste is that the per capita incomes of countries do not influence relative prices and hence the trade patterns either.[3] Both the assumptions of identical and homothetic tastes and identical technology for the same good across countries are intended to establish cross-country differences in factor endowments as the source of supply bias and consequently comparative advantage of nations. Of course, countries may differ with respect to their technological advancements and taste patterns. However, for countries not having very wide variations in these dimensions, most of the properties of the HOS model remain valid.

[3] When tastes are homothetic, the relative demand for goods defined in Chapter 1 will depend only on the relative price but not on the income levels of the countries.

Finally, the assumption that differentiates the two countries is that their relative endowments of capital and labour differ. In particular assume that the foreign country is endowed with relatively more capital than labour compared to the home country:

$$k^* > k \tag{6.2a}$$

where k and k^* denote the ratio of the stock of physical capital to the total labour force, or the capital-labour endowment ratio, in the home country and in the foreign country respectively. Note that, (6.2a) can be rewritten as,

$$l > l^* \tag{6.2b}$$

where, l and l^* denote the labour–capital endowment ratio in the home country and in the foreign country respectively. Essentially, by the *physical definition of factor abundance*, (6.2a) or equivalently (6.2b) states that the foreign country is relatively capital abundant (or labour scarce) and the home country is relatively labour-abundant (or capital scarce). Thus, factor abundance of countries is defined by the ratio of their exogenously given capital stock and workforce.

Given these set of assumptions, the 2x2x2 HOS model can be specified by the following set of equations and equilibrium conditions for the home country:

Box 6.1 Price Definition of Factor Abundance

Factor abundance of a country can also be defined in terms of relative factor prices. Under the price definition, the home country is said to be relatively abundant in labour and the foreign country relatively abundant in capital, if the wage-rental ratio is lower in the home country than in the foreign country: $\frac{W}{r} < \frac{W^*}{r^*}$. This price definition takes into account both the relative supply and relative demand of a factor, unlike the physical definition that takes into account *only* the relative supply of a factor. If the demands for factors are the same in the two countries, then of course abundance of a factor in a country by physical definition will also mean its abundance in that country by the price definition. But, if factor demands are not identical, then the two definitions will not mean the same thing. For example, if the demand for labour is very high (relative to capital) in the home country than in the foreign country, then even if the home country has a relatively larger labour force than the foreign country ($l > l^*$), the relative wage may be higher in the home country. Hence, by price definition, *home country will be said to be scarce in labour and abundant in capital contrary to what the physical definition would indicate*. Since, factor demand is essentially a derived demand, so this contradiction between price and physical definition may arise when a country having a relatively larger workforce has a strong taste bias in relatively labour intensive goods (like textiles, leather manufacture, etc.). Similarly, a country endowed with relatively larger stock of capital may said to be labour abundant by price definition if it has a strong taste bias in relatively capital intensive goods (like computers, scientific instruments, etc.) resulting in a relatively higher demand for capital and consequently a higher relative return to capital (or lower wage-rental ratio).

$$P_C = a_{LC}W + a_{KC}r \tag{6.3}$$

$$P_T = a_{LT}W + a_{KT}r \tag{6.4}$$

$$a_{ij} = a_{ij}(W/r),\ i = L, K;\ j = C, T \tag{6.5}$$

$$L = a_{LC}X_C + a_{LT}X_T \tag{6.6}$$

$$K = a_{KC}X_C + a_{KT}X_T \tag{6.7}$$

where W and r are the wage to labour and return to capital respectively in the home country; P_C is the price of computers and P_T is the price of textiles in the home country; X_C and X_T are output levels of computers and textiles respectively produced in the home country; and a_{ij} denotes per unit requirement of the i-th factor in j-th production.

Equation system (6.3)–(6.7) describe the supply side of the HOS model. With all markets perfectly competitive, competitive forces drive down profits to zero in the long run in each final good sector. Thus, commodity market equilibrium is described by the equalities of price and average cost in equations (6.3) and (6.4). Per unit input requirements or the input-output ratios a_{ij} reflect the least-cost choices of input levels as illustrated in Figure 6.1. Note that, $a_{Lj} \equiv \dfrac{L_j}{X_j}$ and $a_{Kj} \equiv \dfrac{K_j}{X_j}, j = C, T$. Hence, the ratio $\dfrac{a_{Kj}}{a_{Lj}}$ denotes the least-cost production technique in sector j. The assumption of constant returns to scale (CRS) technology, as mentioned above, means that these input choices do not depend on the level of output produced. Finally, equations (6.6) and (6.7) specify the full employment or market clearing conditions for labour and capital in the home country. The right hand side in each of these conditions gives us the total demand for the factor concerned whereas the left hand side variable is its total endowment, which is exogenously given.

The demand side, on the other hand, is specified by the following set of relations and conditions:

$$D_j = D_j(p_j, y),\ j = C, T \tag{6.8}$$

$$y = p_C X_C + X_T \tag{6.9}$$

where y is the real income measured in terms of textiles and p_C is the relative price of computers.

The domestic demand functions for the two goods are specified in equation (6.8) and the produced real income is specified in equation (6.9). Domestic demand for good j depends on own relative price p_j and real income y.

Finally, we have the Walras' Law as explained earlier:

$$p_C E_C + E_T = 0 \tag{6.10}$$

and the market clearing conditions for the final goods, that are, however, relevant only under autarchy (and that too *any one* of the following):

$$D_j = X_j,\ j = C, T \tag{6.11}$$

The structure of the foreign country can be specified by the same set of conditions except that the factor endowments are different in the sense defined in equation (6.2a) or (6.2b). Of course, as we show below, at pre-trade equilibrium, relative commodity price, p_C^*, and consequently the returns to labour and capital, W^* and r^* respectively, will differ in the foreign country. This, in turn, will mean a different set of choice of production techniques though by the identical technology assumption the same functional relationship specified in equation (6.5) will hold:

$$a_{ij} = a_{ij}(W^*/r^*),\ i = L, K;\ j = C, T \tag{6.12}$$

Had the technology been different in the two countries for producing the same good, as in Ricardo, different techniques of production would have been chosen by producers in the two countries even when they would have faced the same factor price ratio. This has a far-reaching implication for the FPE theorem as we will see below.

6.2 AUTARCHIC EQUILIBRIUM AND THE PATTERN OF TRADE

The HO theorem states that if trade opens up between these two countries, the relatively labour-abundant home country will export the relatively labour-intensive cotton textiles and the relatively capital-abundant foreign country will export the relatively capital-intensive computers. As explained earlier in Chapter 1, for this pattern of trade to emerge the pre-trade relative price of computers must be higher in the home country than in the foreign country: $p_C > p_C^*$. Alternatively, textiles must be cheaper at home than abroad. Thus, to explain the HO theorem and check its validity, we need to determine pre-trade prices in the two countries.

Referring back to the set of conditions specified above, first of all note that for any given set of commodity prices, the factor prices and corresponding input choices are determined by the conditions in equations (6.3)–(6.5). Finally, given these input coefficients, full employment conditions determine output levels. Any change in the relative commodity price affects these outputs through changes in input choices consequent upon induced factor price changes. The emerging supply relationship is the one shown in Figure 6.3. The algebraic derivation of the relative supply curve in the home country is set out in Appendix A6. Note that regardless of the factor intensity ranking of the two goods, the relative supply of computers rises with the increase in its relative price. An alternative derivation of the relative supply curve is as follows.

As explained earlier in Chapter 1, the production possibility frontier (PPF) is the locus of combinations of output levels of computers and textiles that maintain full employment. Given the above mentioned assumption of CRS technology with diminishing returns to the variable factor, PPF will be bowed out (or concave downwards) as illustrated in Figure 6.2. At the competitive equilibrium, the output combinations will be such as to satisfy the condition $MRT = p_T$, for any given relative price of textiles p_T. That is, the equilibrium output combination will correspond to the tangency point between the price line and the PPF. For a very low relative price of textiles, as labeled by p_{min}, the home country will produce only computers. That is, the price of textiles relative to that of computers is so low that it makes sense to put all the resource of the economy in the production of computers. A higher relative price of textiles (or a lower

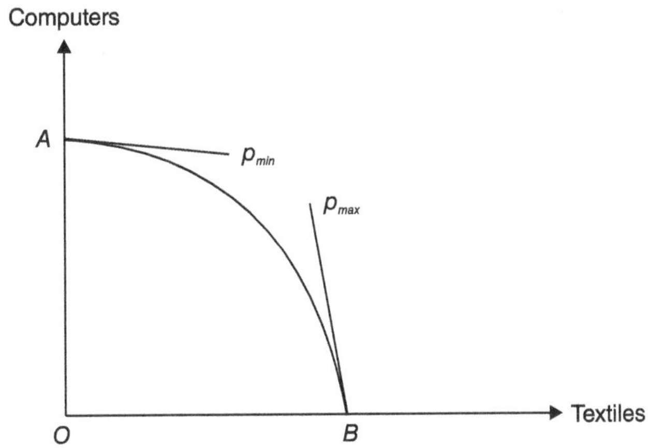

Figure 6.2 PPC in the HOS Model

relative price of computers) makes the production of textiles profitable. The home country then starts producing textiles along with computers. For successively higher relative price of textiles more and more units of textiles and less and less units of computer are being produced so that the relative supply of textiles, $s = \frac{X_T}{X_C}$ rises. Note that the trade-off in production comes from the full employment of factors. At the other extreme, a very high relative price of textiles p_{max} chokes off production of computers and all resources are put in the production of textiles. Thus as we approach this p_{max}, the relative supply of textiles becomes asymptotic as shown in Figure 6.3.

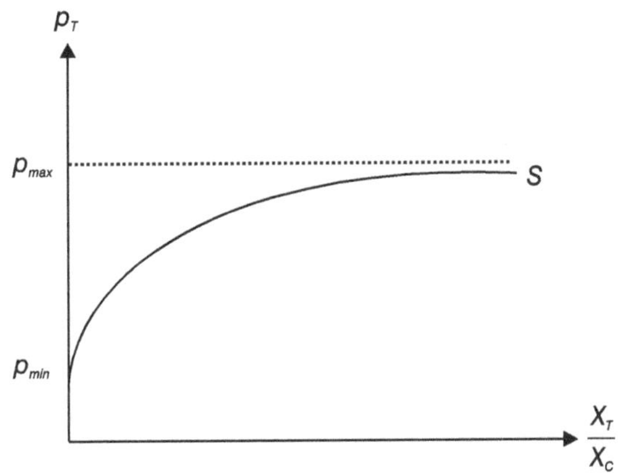

Figure 6.3 Relative Supply Curve for Textiles in Home Country

For the foreign country, we can similarly derive the relative supply curve for textiles. But the assumed capital abundance of the foreign country means that it will be producing relatively larger units of computers and smaller units of textiles compared to the home country for the *same* relative price of computers prevailing in the two countries. Hence, the foreign relative supply curve for textiles will be to the left of the home relative supply curve.

To see why this is so, consider Figure 6.4. For any given relative price of computers and corresponding factor prices and input choices, the full employment conditions in equations (6.6) and (6.7) are drawn as LL' and KK' lines respectively. Note that these full employment loci slope downward that reflects the trade-off between the production of the two goods. The absolute slope of the LL' line is $\frac{a_{LC}}{a_{KT}}$ and that of the KK' line is $\frac{a_{KC}}{a_{KT}}$. Thus by our assumed factor intensity ranking, the LL' is drawn flatter than the KK' line.

The output combination P ensures full employment of both labour and capital in the home country. The corresponding supply of textiles relative to that of computers is shown by the ray connecting the origin and the full employment output bundle P. Now consider the simplest possible sub-case for our factor abundance assumption in equation (6.2a): the foreign country is endowed with the same number of workers as the home country, but with a larger stock of capital. That is, $L = L^*$ and $K < K^*$. Consider the same relative price of computers prevailing in the foreign country as in the home country. Thus, corresponding factor prices and input choices will be the same as well since both the countries have access to the same production technology. Given these assumptions, the full employment condition for labour in the foreign country is represented by the same LL' line. But the line representing full employment for capital in the foreign country will lie to the right of the KK' line as shown by the broken $K^*K^{*\prime}$ line. This follows from the fact that a larger endowment of capital enables the foreign country to produce larger units of computers for any given units of production of textiles. Therefore, commodity bundle P^* ensures full employment of both the factors in the foreign country and the corresponding relative supply of textiles is given by the ray from the origin through this bundle. What emerges from these discussions is that for any given (and the same) relative price of textiles prevailing in the two countries, the relative supply of textiles will be larger in the labour-abundant home country as compared to that in the capital-abundant foreign country. Since the choice of the initial relative price of textiles was arbitrary, so this inequality in

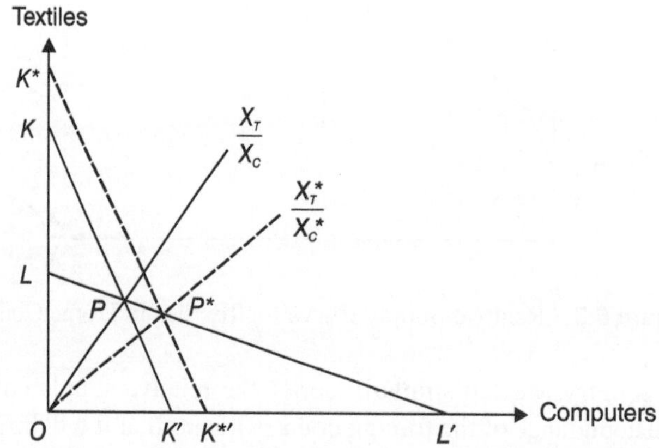

Figure 6.4 Endowment Difference and Relative Production

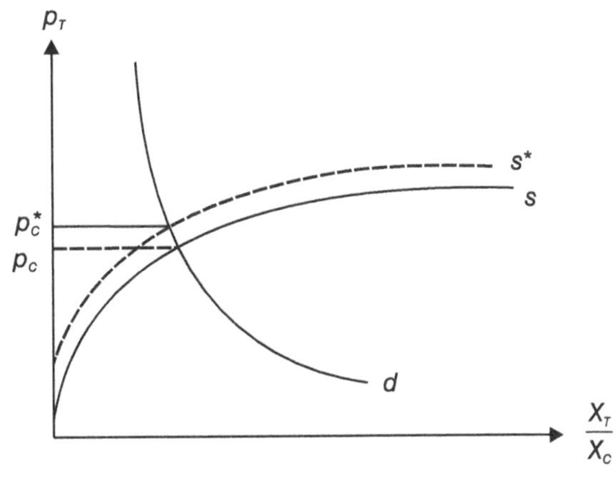

Figure 6.5 Supply Bias and Pattern of Trade

relative production of textiles in the two countries will hold for *all* possible relative prices of textiles. This is illustrated in Figure 6.5 by the s and s^* curves.

The final step in establishing the HO theorem is to bring in demand. By the assumption of identical and homothetic tastes in the two countries, we draw the same relative demand curve for both countries. The pre-trade price of textiles is, therefore, lower in the home country and higher in the foreign country. This reflects the supply bias for the home country arising from its labour abundance as explained above. Hence, as stated by the HO theorem, the relatively labour-abundant home country exports relatively labour-intensive textiles to the capital-abundant foreign country and imports the relatively capital-intensive computers from it.

Recalling the discussions on the sources of comparative advantage in Chapter 1, if diversity in tastes across countries are allowed, and the foreign country has a very strong taste bias in computers (or alternatively, the home country has a very strong taste bias in textiles), the capital-abundant foreign country *may* export labour-intensive textiles and import capital-intensive computers. Thus, a stronger taste bias in the relatively labour (capital) intensive good in the relatively labour (capital) abundant country is a source of invalidation of the HO theorem. We will discuss more about this in the next chapter where we will discuss the empirical test of the HO theorem by Leontief (1954) and its subsequent refinements.

6.3 TWO PROPERTIES OF THE MODEL: OUTPUT AND PRICE MAGNIFICATION EFFECTS

There are two important properties of the HOS model that are essentially comparative static results with respect to an exogenous change in factor endowment and an exogenous shock to the traded commodity prices.

6.3.1 Endowment Shock and Output Changes

As mentioned earlier, factor endowments of countries are exogenously given in the HOS model. Rybczynski (1955) studied how exogenous changes in the factor endowment of a country, *ceteris paribus*, change the full-employment output composition of the country *at constant commodity prices*. He established the result, which is known as the Rybczynski theorem (and more generally as the output magnification effect), that if there is a more than proportionate exogenous growth in capital compared to the growth in labour force, then the production of the capital-intensive good will increase more than the growth in capital, whereas increase in the production of the labour-intensive good, *if at all*, will be less than proportionate to the growth in labour force. Algebraically stated, *given our assumption that computers are relatively capital-intensive*, if $\hat{K} > \hat{L} > 0$ then output changes will be such as:

$$\hat{X}_C > \hat{K} > \hat{L} > \hat{X}_T \tag{6.13}$$

But if the labour force grows faster than capital accumulation, both caused by exogenous factors, then production of textiles expands fastest and that of computers expands, *if at all*, the least:

$$\hat{X}_T > \hat{L} > \hat{K} > \hat{X}_C \tag{6.14}$$

Essentially, the Rybczynski theorem provides us the direction in which the relative supply curve of a country *shifts*. Since the above effects on output levels are derived at any set of constant commodity prices, so it means that the relative supply curve s for computers in the home country in Figure 6.3 shifts to the right if $\hat{K} > \hat{L} > 0$, and to the left otherwise. Of course, the relative price will change as a *consequence*, but the direction of the price change will be governed by the nature of the supply shift.

The above result, however, tells us more than just this compositional effect (an increase or decrease in $\frac{X_C}{X_T}$) or the nature of the supply shift. It tells us that output changes will be a *magnified proportion* of factor endowment changes. Hence, the results stated in equations (6.13) and (6.14) are also known as output magnification effects (see Jones 1965). Put simply, if capital grows by 20 per cent and the labour force by 15 per cent, the difference in growth rates being 5 per cent, then production of computers will grow at more than 20 per cent and that of textiles (if at all) by less than 15 per cent so that the difference in output growths will be *larger* than 5 per cent.

The output magnification effect stated in (6.13) and (6.14) also displays excluded-middle phenomenon, by which the two output changes do not lie between the changes in the factor endowments. Either textiles grow more and computers grow less than the growth in both capital and labour—as in (6.14)—or textiles grow less and computers grow more than the growth in both capital and labour—as in (6.13)—depending on which factor endowment is growing faster and, of course, the relative factor intensity of textiles and computers. When such a property holds, as in (6.13) and (6.14), then it means that *both* the factors have *symmetric effects* on the two sectors: Either they favour a sector by causing its expansion, or hurt the sector by causing its contraction. If, however, an output change had been trapped between the factor endowment changes, that is when the excluded-middle phenomenon is lost for a particular sector or output, then factor growths would have asymmetric effects on production of that good. In the next chapter, we will see under what circumstances this can happen.

The algebraic proof of the output magnification effect is given in Appendix A6. We provide here an intuitive argument for this. To begin with, consider only an accumulation of capital with no growth in the labour force. Referring back to equation (6.13), the production of textiles in this case unambiguously *declines*. The reason is simple. Since initially all workers were employed, without any growth in the labour force, additional labour required for an expansion in computer production will be available only through a reduction in the production of textiles and consequent release of labour from there. This is also evident from Figure 6.4 once we reinterpret $K^*K^{*\prime}$ line as representing the capital constraint corresponding to the larger capital stock in the home country. Growth in capital, *ceteris paribus*, relaxes the capital constraint to some extent and thereby enables an expansion in the production of computers, but still the trade-off between the productions of the two goods exists due to the constraining effect of labour. Thus, the production of textiles declines. But in the process the production of computers expands more than proportionately to the growth of capital because the contracting textiles sector also releases capital along with labour.

When the labour force also grows (though less than proportionately to the growth in capital), the trade-off between the production of the two goods *may not* arise. That is, the production of textiles need not necessarily decline to release labour from this sector for realization of the expansion of the production of computers. That would still be a necessity only if the labour force grows too little compared to the growth of capital. Thus depending on the relative growth in factor endowments, the production of textiles *may rise or fall*. But even when it rises, the expansion will be less than proportionate to the growth in labour force.

Could it be possible to have an expansion in textiles, instead of computers, more than proportionate to the growth of capital? Certainly not, because textiles being relatively labour-intensive, capital cannot be fully employed when it grows faster than the labour force. This will be possible only when the labour force grows faster than the growth in the capital stock as in equation (6.14).

Box 6.2 Output magnification effect and the HO theorem

The output magnification effect provides an alternative proof of the HO theorem. As explained above, it indicates the direction of the shift in the relative supply curve. For example, (6.13) suggests that if the home country's capital stock grows by more than proportionate to the growth in its labour force, then the relative supply of capital-intensive computers will increase there. Alternatively, we can say that if the home country has a higher *relative* endowment of capital than the foreign country, so that it is a relatively capital-rich country by the physical definition, then it will produce relatively more computers and lesser units of textiles than the foreign country. That is, the capital-rich home country will have a supply bias in the relatively capital-intensive good. Under homothetic and identical tastes, this means that the relative price of computers will be lower in the home country (and conversely, the relative price of textiles will be lower in the foreign country). Accordingly, the home country will export computers and the foreign country textiles, so that the pattern of trade will follow Heckscher-Ohlin.

6.3.2 Price Magnification Effect

Consider an exogenous shock that causes the relative price of computers to rise. How do the factor prices change as a consequence? As established in Jones (1965), if the price of computers rises more than proportionate to the price of textiles in the home country, the real return to capital will unambiguously rise whereas the real wage will unambiguously fall given that computers are relatively more capital-intensive than textiles. That is, if $\hat{P}_C > \hat{P}_T > 0$ then:

$$\hat{r} > \hat{P}_C > \hat{P}_T > \hat{W} \tag{6.15}$$

This strong statement regarding how the changes in commodity prices affect real wages of the two factors of production follows from the excluded-middle phenomenon displayed by (6.15). Due to this property, in (6.15) capital owners' real incomes rise whereas workers' real incomes fall regardless of how we measure their real incomes. Since, for economic agents who are free of money illusion, real income is the indicator of their well-being, so in situations like the one stated in (6.15) we can say that an increase in the relative price of computers makes the capital owners unambiguously better off and the workers worse off. Such a strong statement could not be made if the excluded-middle phenomenon did not hold. For example, if the rate of return to capital had been trapped between the two price changes, then the change in real income and welfare of the capital owners would depend on the shares of their incomes spent on computers and textiles. If they spend a larger proportion of their incomes on computers then they would have been worse off by the increase in the relative price of computers. Otherwise, they would have been better off. In the next chapter, we will see when situations like this can arise where the excluded-middle phenomenon is lost and real income changes are ambiguous.

In general, the real return to capital unambiguously rises and the real wage unambiguously declines when the *relative* price of the good that uses capital intensively rises. Otherwise, the real wage unambiguously rises. Note that a decline in the real wage as in (6.15) does not mean that money wage falls too. What equation (6.15) indicates is that even when the money wage rises it cannot be more than proportionate to the least rising commodity price (in this case, price of textiles). Once again, we have a magnification effect: the rate of increase in the return to capital relative to the wage rate, $\hat{r} - \hat{W}$, is a magnification of the rate of increase in the relative price of computers, $\hat{P}_C - \hat{P}_T$. Stolper and Samuelson (1941) derived this result in the context of a small open economy imposing a tariff. They argued that the real wage of the abundant factor will fall and the real wage of the scarce factor will rise as a consequence of imposition of an import tariff. By the HO theorem, a country exports the good which is intensive in its abundant factor and imports the good which is intensive in its scarce factor. An import tariff raises the domestic relative price of the import-competing good and, therefore, the real wage of the scarce factor that is intensively used in that good. The price magnification effect, however, is a generalized statement in the sense that it does not relate factor price changes to the scarcity or abundance of factors in a country.

Algebraic proof of this price magnification effect is given in Appendix A6. Intuitively, suppose only the price of computers rises, that is, $\hat{P}_C > 0 = \hat{P}_T$. This raises profitability of computer production and consequently changes the composition of output towards this sector. Resources are thus reallocated away from the textiles sector which now contracts and to the expanding computer sector. But since computers are relatively capital-intensive, the contracting textiles sector will release more labour and less capital than are required for the expansion in computers production. Thus, an excess supply of labour and excess demand for capital emerge as the economy adjusts its composition of aggregate output to the rising relative price of computers. As a consequence, the wage rate will decline and the rate of return to capital will rise. Figure 6.6 illustrates this in terms of factor price frontiers. A factor price frontier for the computer sector, say, is the locus of the combinations of minimum factor prices consistent with zero profit in that sector, given its price. The factor price frontiers P_C and P_T essentially represent the zero profit conditions (6.3) and (6.4) for any given set of commodity prices with absolute slopes equal to $\frac{a_{LC}}{a_{KC}}$ and $\frac{a_{LT}}{a_{KT}}$ respectively. The former is flatter than the latter because computers are relatively capital-intensive as compared to textiles. Initial equilibrium factor prices were those corresponding to point *a* that satisfies both the zero profit conditions. Increase in only the price of computers shifts up the P_C-frontier and the equilibrium factor price bundle changes to *c*, with a rise in the rate of return to capital and a decline in the wage rate. When both prices rise, both these factor price frontiers shift up with the P_C-frontier shifting up more under the assumption that the relative price of computers rises. The rate of return to capital still rises (though now less than when only the price of computers rises) whereas the wage *may rise or fall*. In the particular case that is illustrated here, money wage falls.

Note that the above price magnification effect suggests how the opening up of trade with the external world will change factor prices in the home country. For example, if the trade pattern of the home country, which is labour-abundant by assumption, follows the Heckscher-Ohlin pattern, it will export textiles and import computers. As explained earlier, arbitrage will raise the price of textiles and lower the price of computers at home. Reversing the argument above, real wage should then rise and both the money and the real return to capital should fall:

$$\hat{W} > \hat{P}_T > 0 > \hat{P}_C > \hat{r} \tag{6.16}$$

Thus international trade should benefit workers and harm capitalists in a labour-abundant country as long as the trade pattern conforms with the HO theorem. As we will see later, actual country experience is at odds with this conclusion.

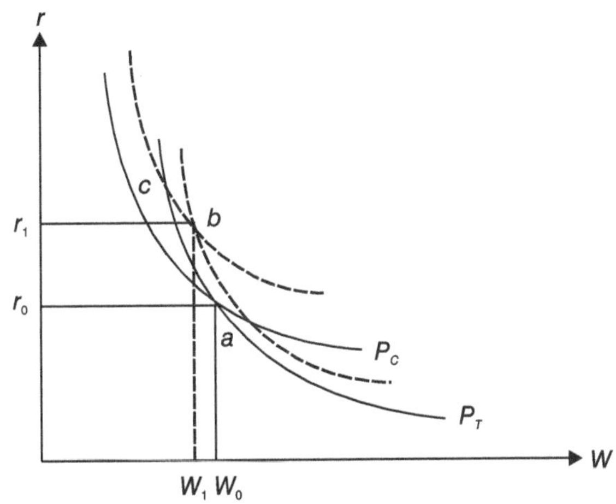

Figure 6.6 Factor Price Frontiers and Price Magnification Effect

6.4 FACTOR PRICES AT THE POST-TRADE EQUILIBRIUM

Post-trade, there are some significant changes in the properties of the HOS model that deserve attention. The most important change compared to the situation under autarchy is that now the prices of the traded commodities are no longer determined in the local economy but in the world market in the way spelled out in Chapter 4. Thus, prices P_C and P_T are now exogenous to the equation system (6.3)–(6.11). The local market equilibrium condition (6.11) is also no longer relevant because local demand and supply need not and should not match when trade opens up, as long as both computers and textiles can be traded. Thus local supplies and hence aggregate employment are no longer constrained by local demand.

There are two important implications of commodity prices being determined from 'outside' and exogenously given to the equation system. First, is that local demand and supply conditions affect commodity and factor prices only *indirectly*, if at all. Consider, for example, an exogenous change in consumers' taste away from textiles in the home country. This will increase both the excess supply of textiles and the excess demand for computers. The home country's offer of exports of textiles and import demand for computers thus rise. If the home country trades only an infinitesimally small proportion of the world trade volume, these increases will only have a very negligible effect on world demand. Hence, there will be no change in the relative price of its traded goods or the TOT that it faces. The home country in this case, being an insignificant buyer and seller, is a *price taker* in the world market. Like a perfectly competitive firm, it cannot influence world prices by changing its own trade volumes however large the change may be. That is, the demand conditions are irrelevant for a small open economy except for determining its trade volumes. If on the other hand, the home country is a large or significant buyer and seller in the world market, changes in the taste pattern and consequent change in its volume of trade will affect its TOT. TOT will deteriorate, that is, the relative price of its exports will fall in the world market in this instance. Such a price change will then affect factor prices. Thus, for a large home country changes in local demand conditions only *indirectly* affect commodity prices and factor prices in local markets. These cases contrast with the pre-trade situation where changes in local demand conditions affect prices *directly*. It is in this sense that the HOS model is a supply side model in the post-trade situation.

The second implication is the irrelevance of factor endowment and changes thereof for local factor prices in the home country. Referring back to the supply side equation system (6.3)–(6.7), it is immediate that once the traded commodity prices are determined in the world market, the price sub-system comprising of equations (6.3)–(6.5) are dichotomized from the physical sub-system comprising of equations (6.6)–(6.7). What this means is that factor prices, wage rate and the rate of return to capital, are determined *solely* by commodity prices, regardless of factor market conditions. Once again the *factor endowment conditions matter only indirectly*. For example, consider a *ceteris paribus* increase in the capital stock in the home country. By the output magnification effect explained earlier, this will raise the production of computers and lower that of textiles at initial commodity and factor prices. Given the local demand for the two goods, both the excess supply of textiles and excess demand for computers will fall. Consequently the home country will offer less exports and demand less imports. If it is a small open economy, these changes will not affect its TOT and hence factor prices. Otherwise, TOT will change and so will the factor prices. Thus what emerges from this discussion is that a change in factor endowment can affect factor prices in the local market *only* through its impact on commodity prices in the world market.

This irrelevance of factor endowment conditions and the correspondence between commodity prices and factor prices are the key factors behind the Factor Price Equalization theorem mentioned earlier. To understand the precise nature of this correspondence, recall the argument for the price magnification effect discussed above. An increase in the relative price of textiles raises the wage rate relative to the rate of return to capital as long as textiles are relatively labour-intensive. This relationship is shown in Figure 6.7a. Two comments are warranted at this point. First, by the price magnification effect, the upward sloping curve showing the one-to-one correspondence between the commodity price ratio and the factor price ratio is flatter than any ray through the origin. Second, the one-to-one correspondence that implies that factor prices are *uniquely* determined by commodity prices, presumes no factor intensity reversals. Recalling the case of factor intensity reversals, if textiles had been relatively labour-intensive for some lower values of factor prices but relatively capital-intensive for some higher values, the relationship between commodity prices and factor prices would have been hump shaped as illustrated in Figure 6.7b. For relative price of textiles p_o, the factor price ratio may be either ρ_o or ρ_1. Thus no longer are the factor prices uniquely determined by commodity prices. The one-to-one correspondence breaks down in case of factor intensity reversals.

To sum up, when trade opens up, factor prices in the local market are *solely* determined by commodity prices that free and costless trading equalizes across the trading nations. Other factors like local demand or factor endowment conditions are relevant in determining factor prices only to the extent to which they affect world prices, which in turn depends on the country's ability to influence world prices or TOT through change in its actions. There are quite a few sources of disruption to this aspect as we will learn through the next chapters such as the number of traded goods being less than the number of domestic factors of production, immobility of factors across sectors within an economy, and the like. The one-to-one correspondence or factor prices being *uniquely* determined by commodity prices, on the other hand, depends on no factor intensity reversals, that is, on technological conditions that prohibit isoquants for the two goods to cross each other twice or to be tangent to each other.

Having this one-to-one correspondence between commodity and factor prices in trading nations, it is easy to establish the Factor Price Equalization (FPE) theorem. The FPE theorem states that free commodity trade between countries will equalize the factor prices across these countries. Thus even without any international migration of labour and movement of capital, workers will earn the same wages and capital will earn the same returns everywhere. The important point to note here is that the factor prices are equalized across countries despite one country being labour-abundant and the other being capital-abundant. This interesting possibility arises because of the irrelevance of factor endowment conditions and the fact that factor prices are solely and uniquely determined by commodity prices. Thus, free commodity movement acts as a substitute for international factor movements. The intuition behind this interesting result is that by exporting labour-intensive products, a labour-abundant country essentially exports labour embodied or contained in those goods to a labour scarce country. By exporting goods, a country exports both labour and capital embodied in those goods. Similarly, by importing goods it essentially imports labour and capital embodied in such goods. Since by the HO theorem, the relatively labour rich country exports relatively labour intensive goods and imports relatively capital intensive goods, so it exports more labour than it imports. On the other hand, it imports more capital than it exports. That is, by the HO theorem, *the relatively labour rich country is essentially a net exporter of labour and net importer of capital.* By

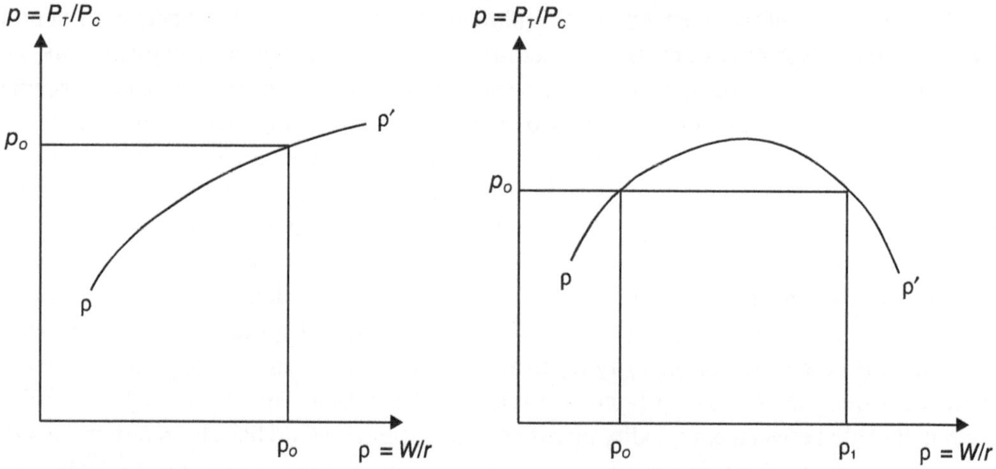

a: One-to-One Correspondence   b: Non-unique Relationship

Figure 6.7 Correspondence between Commodity and Factor Prices

similar logic, *the relatively capital rich country is a net exporter of capital and net importer of labour*. Thus *as if* the supplies of the scarce factors rise and supplies of abundant factors fall in both countries, which bring in convergence of the factor prices in these countries.

Proof of the FPE theorem is simple. Consider Figure 6.8. By our assumed factor abundance of the countries and the HO pattern of comparative advantage, the pre-trade relative price of textiles is lower in the home country and higher in the foreign country. The corresponding relative wages are ρ_a and ρ_a^* respectively. After opening up of trade, arbitrage and free movement of commodities equalize the relative prices and the post-trade relative price settles between autarchic prices (as explained in Chapter 4) at, say, p'. Correspondingly the relative wages equalize as well at ρ'. Hence, the FPE result.

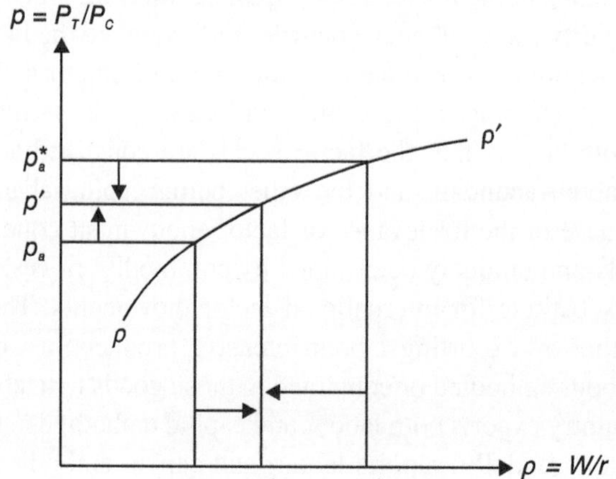

Figure 6.8 FPE Theorem

As it appears from this simple proof, the one-to-one correspondence holds the key. Intuitively, so long as factor prices are solely and uniquely determined by commodity prices, regardless of factor endowment differences of countries, commodity price equalization through free trade should equalize factor prices. Two sources of disruption of the one-to-one correspondence and thus invalidation of the FPE theorem are worth discussing here. First, if countries completely specialize after trade, as in the Ricardian model, and second, if technologies exhibit factor intensity reversals. On both occasions, the one-to-one correspondence may break down and thus FPE *may* not hold. These two cases can be explained with the help of Figure 6.9. The two upward sloping curves represent capital intensities in the computers and textiles sectors. An increase in the relative wage (*W/r*) induces producers everywhere to employ more capital-intensive techniques of production by substituting labour by capital to the extent needed to minimize costs at the increased relative wage. These capital intensity curves are drawn non-intersecting implying that there is no factor intensity reversal. The horizontal *k*-line, on the other hand, represents the relative capital endowment of the home country. Given this endowment, the equilibrium factor price range compatible with full employment is given by $[\rho_0, \rho_1]$. For any relative wage lying strictly within this range, the economy will produce both the goods, whereas for $\rho = \rho_0$ the economy will be completely specialized in computers and for $\rho = \rho_1$ the economy will be completely specialized in textiles.

To see why, note that for any given relative wage, the aggregate relative demand for capital k_d is the weighted average of sectoral capital intensities. By definition, $k_d = \dfrac{K_C + K_T}{L_C + L_T}$, which after little manipulation boils down to:

$$k_d = \frac{L_C}{L} k_C + \frac{L_T}{L} k_T = \lambda_{LC} k_C + \lambda_{LT} k_T \tag{6.17}$$

where λ_{LC} and λ_{LT} are the proportion of labour employed in the computers and textiles sectors respectively. When, for example, the country is completely specialized in textiles, $\lambda_{LC} = 0$ and $\lambda_{LT} = 1$. Hence, by the property of the weighted average with weights adding up to unity, $k_c > k_d > k_T$.

Now consider any relative wage lower than ρ_0 such as ρ'. For such a low relative wage, producers everywhere choose highly labour-intensive production techniques. The relative demand for capital, measured by the corresponding heights of the capital intensity lines, is thus much less than the relative endowment of capital even when the economy produces only computers, which is the most capital-intensive good. The excess supply of capital and corresponding excess demand for labour pushes up the relative wage towards ρ_0. By similar logic, for any relative wage higher than ρ_1 such as ρ'', there would be excess demand for capital and excess supply of labour even when the economy produces only the least capital-intensive (or most labour-intensive) textiles. Competition then lowers the relative wage towards ρ_1. Hence, as long as factor prices are flexible, these prices will adjust through competitive forces in the factor markets towards the specified range.

Given that the factor price ratio will always settle in the range $[\rho_0, \rho_1]$, we can now explain why the pattern of production specialization will vary over this equilibrium factor price range as mentioned above. When $\rho = \rho_0$, if the economy produces both the goods, full employment

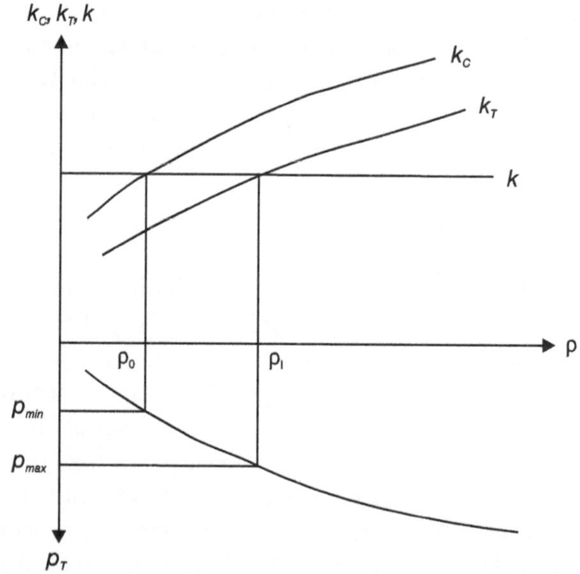

Figure 6.9 Factor Endowment and Equilibrium Factor Prices

cannot be maintained by equation (6.17) and the property of weighted average $k_d < k$. But if the economy produces only computers, all factors will be fully employed since for this relative wage computer producers choose a production technique that exactly matches with the country's endowment of capital and labour: $k_C(\rho_0) = k$. Similar logic explains why the home country should be completely specialized in textiles for $\rho = \rho_1$. For any relative wage that is strictly greater than ρ_0 but less than ρ_1, both goods can be produced. For such a relative wage, the overall capital–labour ratio of the economy lies between the capital intensities in the two sectors and thus makes it possible to match with the aggregate relative demand for capital when both goods are produced. Further, as the relative wage rises from ρ_0 towards ρ_1, successively higher units of textiles are produced and smaller units of computers are produced. Hence, the relative supply of textiles rises over this range of equilibrium factor prices. Note that this merely reinstates that the relative supply curve is upward sloping. This is immediate from the one-to-one correspondence relationship drawn in the lower panel. The minimum and maximum relative wages actually corresponds to the relative price of textiles p_{min} and p_{max} respectively (refer back to Figure 6.2). Now as the relative price of textiles rises from p_{min} towards p_{max}, the relative wage rises for reasons spelled out above and consequently changes the composition of the full employment production bundle towards textiles.

In Figure 6.10, we bring in the relative capital endowment of the foreign country, k^*, to show the equilibrium factor price range there. Since the foreign country is assumed to be capital-abundant relative to the home country, $k^* > k$, its relative capital endowment line lies above that of the home country's. If the endowments of the two countries are not too different, the equilibrium factor price ranges for the two countries will have an overlap, indicated by the range $[\rho_0^*, \rho_1]$ with a corresponding overlap of the commodity price range, $[a^*, b]$. If the post-trade relative price settles in this range, the relative wages in the two countries correspondingly get equalized. But if the foreign country is much more capital-abundant, as shown by its relative capital endowment line $k^{*\prime}$, there will be no overlapping factor price range and hence no scope for the FPE result to hold. To exemplify, suppose the post-trade relative price of textiles equals *Ob*. The home country is then completely specialized in textiles and the relative wage there is ρ_1. But this cannot be the post-trade equilibrium relative wage in the foreign country because for such a relative wage its relative capital endowment $k^{*\prime}$ would be in excess of its relative capital demand regardless of whether it produces both goods or only any one of them. The relative wage there will thus adjust upwards and settle at ρ^* with the foreign country completely specializing in computers.

To sum up, as long as the factor endowments of countries are not too different in the sense that the range of equilibrium factor prices in the two countries overlap, FPE may hold. Both countries will then be incompletely specialized, that is, they will be producing both the goods. Note that even in that case, if the post-trade relative price of textiles is such that $a < p_C^w < a^*$, FPE will not hold as $\rho < \rho_o^* = \rho^*$. The home country will then be producing both the goods whereas the foreign country will be producing only computers. On the other hand, if endowments are too different to allow for any overlap in their equilibrium factor price range (and hence range of incomplete specialization), FPE will *never* hold. *At least one country will then be completely specialized.* What follows from these discussions is that if the post-trade relative price of textiles is such that both the countries continue to produce both the goods, FPE holds. The intuition for this is that factor prices are then solely determined by commodity prices independent of factor endowment conditions, that is, the one-to-one correspondence holds, and accordingly equalization of the commodity price ratio through trade equalizes the factor price ratio.

Does it mean that FPE will not hold when production technology is such that factor intensity reversal exists for which one-to-one correspondence breaks down as shown earlier?

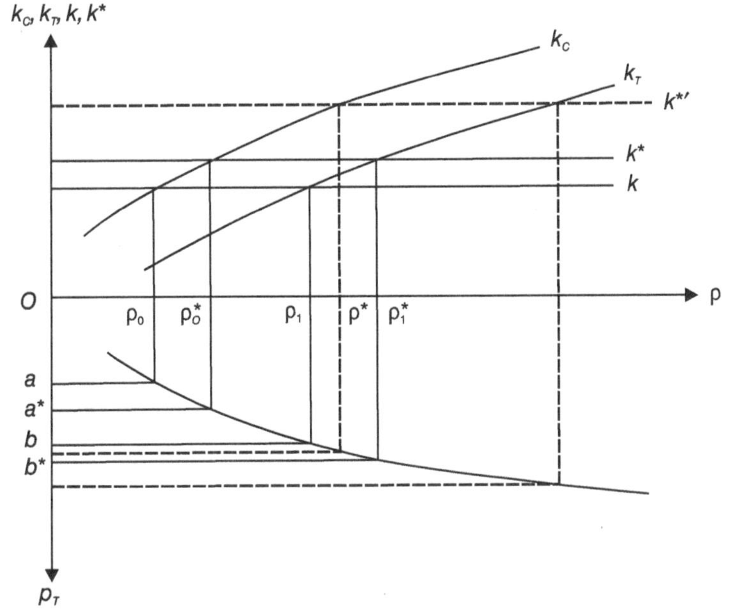

Figure 6.10 Factor Endowment, Incomplete Specialization, and FPE

The unambiguous answer is that *factor intensity reversal per se does not invalidate the FPE theorem.* Once again what matters is whether factor endowments are too different to allow incomplete specialization by both countries after trade opens up. Figure 6.11 illustrates this point.

The capital intensity lines cross each other for relative wage $\bar{\rho}$ indicating factor intensity reversal. Textiles are labour-intensive relative to computers for relative wages lower than $\bar{\rho}$ but are relatively capital-intensive for higher relative wages than $\bar{\rho}$. The relationship between the relative price of textiles and the relative wage shown in the lower panel is thus non-monotonic. If relative capital endowments of the two countries are k and k^* so that the equilibrium factor price ranges are on the same side of the cross-over, the one-to-one correspondence still holds for all relevant *equilibrium* factor prices. In this instance, the upward sloping segment *ab* of the price correspondence will be the relevant one. Given this, a post-trade TOT like p' will lead to FPE with corresponding factor price ratios in the two countries converging at ρ'.

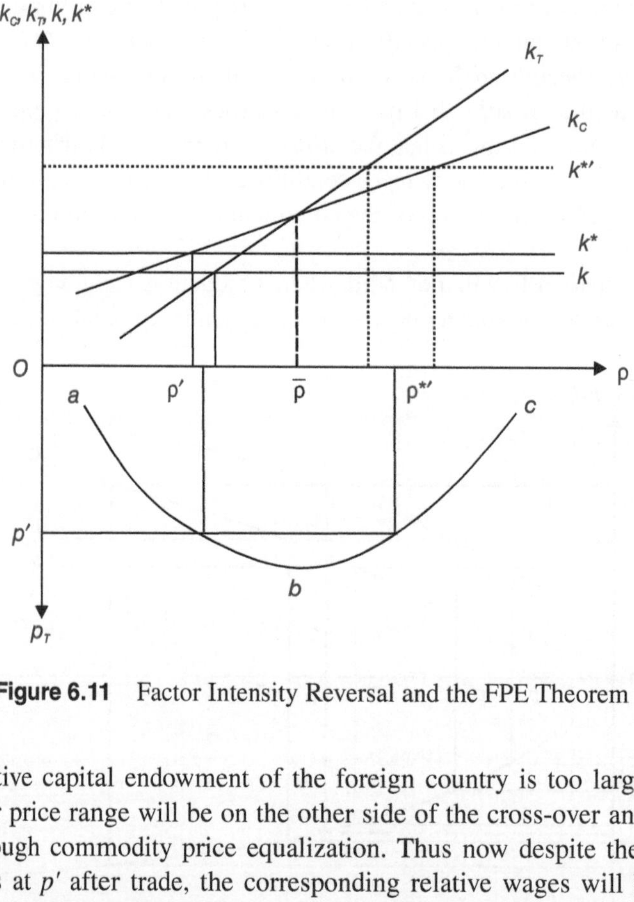

Figure 6.11 Factor Intensity Reversal and the FPE Theorem

But if the relative capital endowment of the foreign country is too large such as $k^{*\prime}$, its equilibrium factor price range will be on the other side of the cross-over and, therefore, will rule out FPE through commodity price equalization. Thus now despite the convergence of commodity prices at p' after trade, the corresponding relative wages will be ρ' and $\rho^{*\prime}$ respectively. Note that even though the one-to-one correspondence holds for *each* country, the relationship between the relative price of textiles and relative wage are opposite of each other in the two countries. Thus in a sense one-to-one correspondence breaks down *across* countries, and thereby invalidates the FPE theorem.

To sum up, as mentioned earlier factor intensity reversals per se do not invalidate the FPE theorem. Like the earlier cases, if endowment differences are not too large so that there is scope for incomplete specialization by *both* the countries for the *same* set of values of relative wages, FPE *may* hold. Factor intensity reversal does not matter as the one-to-one correspondence will still hold for the relevant *equilibrium relative wages*. But if the endowment difference is too large so that the range of equilibrium factor prices for the two countries are on the two sides of the cross-over (thereby ruling out any overlap of the equilibrium factor price ranges), FPE is ruled out. Note the difference between this case and the one illustrated in Figure 6.10. Here both the countries may still be incompletely specialized unlike the previous case, but FPE does not hold because it is not possible for both the countries to be incompletely specialized for the *same* set of equilibrium factor prices. This case suggests that both countries being incompletely specialized and thus factor prices being solely and uniquely determined by commodity prices *within* each country is not a sufficient condition for FPE after commodity trade. This brings out the importance of the factor intensity reversal.

APPENDIX A6[4]

I. Full Employment Output Levels and Conditions for Incomplete Specialization

Recall the full employment conditions in equations (6.6) and (6.7) that are reproduced below in matrix notation:

$$\begin{bmatrix} a_{LT} & a_{LC} \\ a_{KT} & a_{KC} \end{bmatrix} \begin{bmatrix} X_T \\ X_C \end{bmatrix} = \begin{bmatrix} L \\ K \end{bmatrix} \tag{A6.1}$$

The coefficient matrix, known as the technology matrix, has the following property:

$$|A| = a_{LT}a_{KC} - a_{KT}a_{LC}$$

Thus, $|A| > 0$ if textiles are relatively labour-intensive:

$$\frac{a_{LT}}{a_{KT}} > \frac{a_{LC}}{a_{KC}} \Rightarrow l_T > l_C \Rightarrow k_T < k_C \tag{A6.2}$$

Solving for the two output levels by Cramer's Rule we obtain:

$$X_T = \frac{a_{KC}L - a_{LC}K}{a_{LT}a_{KC} - a_{KT}a_{LC}} \tag{A6.3}$$

$$X_C = \frac{a_{LT}K - a_{KT}L}{a_{LT}a_{KC} - a_{KT}a_{LC}} \tag{A6.4}$$

[4] The appendix is based on the simple algebraic formulation of the HOS model developed in Jones (1965).

These are the expressions for full employment combinations of textile and computer production levels. These can be further expressed in terms of capital labour ratios as follows. Consider equation A6.3 which can be written as:

$$X_T = \frac{a_{LC}L\left(\dfrac{a_{KC}}{a_{LC}} - \dfrac{K}{L}\right)}{a_{LT}a_{LC}\left(\dfrac{a_{KC}}{a_{LC}} - \dfrac{a_{KT}}{a_{LT}}\right)} = \frac{L(k_C - k)}{a_{LT}(k_C - k_T)} \tag{A6.3a}$$

Similarly:

$$X_C = \frac{L(k - k_T)}{a_{LC}(k_C - k_T)} \tag{A6.4a}$$

Now, $X_C = 0$ if $k_T = k$, and $X_T = 0$ if $k_C = k$. These are the cases discussed in the text and illustrated in Figure 6.9. On the other hand, given (A6.2), both the output levels will be strictly positive, that is, the country will be incompletely specialized if:

$$k_C > k > k_T \tag{A6.5}$$

That is, for any factor price ratio, as long as the capital–labour endowment ratio is less than the capital-intensity in computer production but larger than that in textile production, the economy will be incompletely specialized at that factor price ratio.

II. Price Magnification Effect

To derive the price magnification effect, totally differentiate the zero profit condition in equation (6.3) to obtain:

$$dP_T = a_{LT}dW + a_{KT}dr + (Wda_{LT} + rda_{KT})$$

Thus, change in the price of textiles is brought about by changes in factor prices and/or in technique of production. It is, however, convenient to express the price change in the proportional form as:

$$\frac{dP_T}{P_T} = \frac{a_{LT}W}{P_T}\frac{dW}{W} + \frac{a_{KT}r}{P_T}\frac{dr}{r} + \left(\frac{a_{LT}W}{P_T}\frac{da_{Lt}}{a_{LT}} + \frac{a_{KT}r}{P_T}\frac{da_{KT}}{a_{KT}}\right)$$

$$\Rightarrow \hat{P}_T = \theta_{LT}\hat{W} + \theta_{KT}\hat{r} + (\theta_{LT}\hat{a}_{LT} + \theta_{KT}\hat{a}_{KT})$$

Similarly, total differentiation of the zero profit condition in computer production as specified in equation (6.4) yields:

$$\hat{P}_C = \theta_{LC}\hat{W} + \theta_{KC}\hat{r} + (\theta_{LC}\hat{a}_{LC} + \theta_{KC}\hat{a}_{KC})$$

where $\theta_{LC} = \frac{a_{LC}W}{P_j}, j = T, C,$ is the labour-cost share in unit production of good j and $\theta_{Kj} = \frac{a_{Kj}r}{P_j}, j = T, C,$ is the capital-cost share in unit production of good j. But, cost minimization means that the change in the technique of production be such that:

$$\theta_{LT}\hat{a}_{LT} + \theta_{KT}\hat{a}_{KT} = 0$$

$$\theta_{LC}\hat{a}_{LC} + \theta_{KC}\hat{a}_{KC} = 0$$

Note that these equalities essentially reflect the tangency condition between the isoquant and iso-cost line, that is, MRTS = W/r conditions, in each sector. To see why, note that:

$$\theta_{LT}\hat{a}_{LT} + \theta_{KT}\hat{a}_{KT} = 0 \Rightarrow \frac{a_{LT}W}{P_T}\frac{da_{LT}}{a_{LT}} = -\frac{a_{KT}r}{P_T}\frac{da_{KT}}{a_{KT}} \Rightarrow \frac{W}{r} = -\frac{da_{KT}}{da_{LT}}$$

Thus, using these cost minimization conditions, the price changes can be rewritten as:

$$\hat{P}_T = \theta_{LT}\hat{W} + \theta_{KT}\hat{r} \tag{A6.6}$$

$$\hat{P}_C = \theta_{LC}\hat{W} + \theta_{KC}\hat{r} \tag{A6.7}$$

The matrix formed by the coefficients of the price changes in these two equations is known as the cost-share matrix:

$$\left[\theta_{ij}\right] = \begin{bmatrix} \theta_{LT} & \theta_{KT} \\ \theta_{KC} & \theta_{KC} \end{bmatrix}$$

with the following properties:

$$\theta_{Lj} + \theta_{Kj} = 1,\ j = T, C \tag{A6.8}$$

$$|\theta| = \theta_{LT}\theta_{KC} - \theta_{KT}\theta_{LC} \tag{A6.9}$$

It is easy to check that $|\theta| > 0$ if $\frac{\theta_{LT}}{\theta_{KT}} > \frac{\theta_{LC}}{\theta_{KC}} \Rightarrow \frac{a_{LT}}{a_{KT}} > \frac{a_{LC}}{a_{KC}}$. Furthermore, using equation (A6.8), $|\theta|$ can alternatively be expressed as:

$$|\theta| = \theta_{LT} - \theta_{LC} \tag{A6.10a}$$

$$= \theta_{KC} - \theta_{KT} \tag{A6.10b}$$

Now, given these properties, subtracting equation (A6.7) from equation (A6.6) we obtain:

$$\hat{P}_T - \hat{P}_C = (\theta_{LT} - \theta_{LC})\hat{W} + (\theta_{KT} - \theta_{KC})\hat{r}$$
$$= |\theta|(\hat{W} - \hat{r})$$

Hence:

$$\hat{W} - \hat{r} = \frac{\hat{P}_T - \hat{P}_C}{|\theta|} \tag{A6.11}$$

Thus, an increase in the relative price of textiles, $\hat{P}_T > \hat{P}_C > 0$, raises the relative wage, that is, $\hat{W} > \hat{r}$, if textiles are relatively labour-intensive, $|\theta| > 0$. On the other hand, since the absolute value of $|\theta|$ is less than one by equation (A6.10a) or equation (A6.10b), so equation (A6.11) implies the price magnification effect:

$$\hat{W} - \hat{r} > \hat{P}_T - \hat{P}_C > 0 \Rightarrow \hat{W} > \hat{P}_T > \hat{P}_C > \hat{r}$$

Similar logic shows that if $|\theta| < 0$, that is, if textiles are relative capital-intensive, then:

$$\hat{r} > \hat{P}_T > \hat{P}_C > \hat{W}$$

III. Algebraic Derivation of the Relative Supply Curve

To derive the slope as well as shift of the relative supply curve of textiles in the home country, we consider changes in commodity prices as well as endowments. Note that a relative supply curve is a relationship between the relative price of textiles and the units of production of textiles relative to that of computers.

Total differentiation of the full employment conditions for labour and capital, equations (6.6) and (6.7), yield the following expressions:

$$dL = a_{LT}dX_T + a_{LC}X_C + (X_T da_{LT} + X_C da_{LC}) \tag{A6.12}$$

$$dK = a_{KT}dX_T + a_{KC}X_C + (X_T da_{KT} + X_C da_{KC}) \tag{A6.13}$$

Dividing equation (A6.12) throughout by L and little manipulations yield:

$$\frac{dL}{L} = \frac{a_{LT}X_T}{L}\frac{dX_T}{X_T} + \frac{a_{LC}X_C}{X_C}\frac{dX_C}{X_C} + \frac{a_{LT}X_T}{L}\frac{da_{LT}}{a_{LT}} + \frac{a_{LC}X_C}{L}\frac{da_{LC}}{a_{LC}}$$

$$\Rightarrow \hat{L} = \lambda_{LT}(\hat{X}_T + \hat{a}_{LT}) + \lambda_{LC}(\hat{X}_C + \hat{a}_{LC}) \tag{A6.14}$$

where $\lambda_{Lj} \equiv \dfrac{a_{Lj}X_j}{L}$, $j = T, C$, is the share of sector *j* in total labour employment. Proceeding similarly, equation (A6.13) boils down to:

$$\hat{K} = \lambda_{KT}(\hat{X}_T + \hat{a}_{KT}) + \lambda_{KC}(\hat{X}_C + \hat{a}_{KC}) \tag{A6.15}$$

where $\lambda_{Kj} \equiv \dfrac{a_{Kj}X_j}{K}$, $j = T, C$, is the share of sector *j* in total capital employment.

Before proceeding further, consider the properties of the employment share matrix formed by the coefficients of the output changes in equations (A6.14) and (A6.15):

$$\left[\lambda_{ij}\right] = \begin{bmatrix} \lambda_{LT} & \lambda_{LC} \\ \lambda_{KT} & \lambda_{KC} \end{bmatrix}$$

First of all, each row sum is equ al to unity by definition:

$$\lambda_{LT} + \lambda_{LC} = 1 \tag{A6.16a}$$

$$\lambda_{KT} + \lambda_{KC} = 1 \tag{A6.16b}$$

Second, the sign of the determinant depends on the factor intensity ranking of the two goods:

$$|\lambda| = \lambda_{LT}\lambda_{KC} - \lambda_{KT}\lambda_{LC} \tag{A6.17a}$$

Thus, $|\lambda| > 0$ if:

$$\lambda_{LT}\lambda_{KC} > \lambda_{KT}\lambda_{LC} \Rightarrow \frac{a_{LT}}{a_{KT}} > \frac{a_{LC}}{a_{KC}} \tag{A6.17b}$$

Recalling the condition for $|A| > 0$, it is immediate that $|A| > 0 \Rightarrow |\lambda| > 0$. That is, $|\lambda| > 0$ is positive if textiles are labour-intensive relative to computers.

Using equations (A6.16a) and (A6.16b), the expression in equation (A6.17) can be rewritten as:

$$|\lambda| = \lambda_{LT} - \lambda_{KT} \tag{A6.18}$$

$$= \lambda_{KC} - \lambda_{LC} \tag{A6.19}$$

Subtracting equation (A6.14) from (A6.15) and using (A6.18) and (A6.19) we obtain:

$$\hat{K} - \hat{L} = (\lambda_{KT} - \lambda_{LT})\hat{X}_T + (\lambda_{KC} - \lambda_{LC})\hat{X}_C + \lambda_{KT}\hat{a}_{KT} + \lambda_{KC}\hat{a}_{KC} - \lambda_{LT}\hat{a}_{LT} - \lambda_{LC}\hat{a}_{LC}$$

$$= |\lambda|(\hat{X}_C - \hat{X}_T) + \lambda_{KT}\hat{a}_{KT} + \lambda_{KC}\hat{a}_{KC} - \lambda_{LT}\hat{a}_{LT} - \lambda_{LC}\hat{a}_{LC} \tag{A6.20}$$

Now define factor substitution elasticity along an isoquant in sector j as a ratio of the percentage change in marginal rate of technical substitution between labour and capital (MRTS) to a percentage change in the capital–labour ratio. Since, at the least cost choice $\text{MRTS}_j = W/r$, and by definition, $\frac{a_{Kj}X_j}{a_{Lj}} \equiv \frac{K_j}{L}$, so denoting the absolute value of the factor substitution elasticity as σ_j, we can write:

$$\sigma_j = \frac{\hat{a}_{Kj} - \hat{a}_{Lj}}{\hat{W} - \hat{r}},\ j = T, C \tag{A6.21}$$

Using the cost minimization conditions and equation (A6.21), changes in least-cost input-output ratios in equation (A6.12) can be expressed as:

$$\hat{a}_{LT} = \hat{a}_{LT} - \theta_{LT}\hat{a}_{LT} - \theta_{KT}\hat{a}_{KT} = \theta_{KT}(\hat{a}_{LT} - \hat{a}_{KT}) = -\sigma_T\theta_{KT}(\hat{W} - \hat{r}) \tag{A6.22a}$$

$$\hat{a}_{KT} = \hat{a}_{KT} - \theta_{LT}\hat{a}_{LT} - \theta_{KT}\hat{a}_{KT} = \theta_{LT}(\hat{a}_{KT} - \hat{a}_{LT}) = \sigma_T\theta_{LT}(\hat{W} - \hat{r}) \tag{A6.22b}$$

$$\hat{a}_{LC} = \hat{a}_{LC} - \theta_{LC}\hat{a}_{LC} - \theta_{KC}\hat{a}_{KC} = \theta_{KC}(\hat{a}_{LC} - \hat{a}_{KC}) = -\sigma_C\theta_{KC}(\hat{W} - \hat{r}) \tag{A6.22c}$$

$$\hat{a}_{KC} = \hat{a}_{KC} - \theta_{LC}\hat{a}_{LC} - \theta_{KC}\hat{a}_{KC} = \theta_{LC}(\hat{a}_{KC} - \hat{a}_{LC}) = \sigma_C\theta_{LC}(\hat{W} - \hat{r}) \tag{A6.22d}$$

Substitution of (A6.22a)–(A6.22d) in (A6.20) yields:

$$\hat{K} - \hat{L} = |\lambda|(\hat{X}_C - \hat{X}_T) + \left(\lambda_{KT}\sigma_T\theta_{LT} + \lambda_{KC}\sigma_C\theta_{LC} + \lambda_{LT}\sigma_T\theta_{KT} + \lambda_{LC}\sigma_C\theta_{KC}\right)(\hat{W} - \hat{r})$$

Hence, using (A6.11) and rearranging we obtain:

$$(\hat{X}_C - \hat{X}_T) = \frac{\hat{K} - \hat{L}}{|\lambda|} + \frac{\delta}{|\lambda||\theta|}\left(\hat{P}_C - \hat{P}_T\right) \tag{A6.23}$$

where

$$\delta = \left(\lambda_{KT}\sigma_T\theta_{LT} + \lambda_{KC}\sigma_C\theta_{LC} + \lambda_{LT}\sigma_T\theta_{KT} + \lambda_{LC}\sigma_C\theta_{KC}\right) > 0.$$

Therefore, change in the relative supply is governed by a change in the relative factor endowment and a change in the relative commodity price. The supply relationship is obtained from a *ceteris paribus* change in relative prices, that is, from equation (A6.23) by letting $\hat{K} = \hat{L} = 0$:

$$(\hat{X}_C - \hat{X}_T) = \frac{\delta}{|\lambda||\theta|}\left(\hat{P}_C - \hat{P}_T\right) \tag{A6.24}$$

Note that regardless of the factor intensity ranking, the product $|\lambda||\theta|$ is positive, because as we have shown earlier, $|\lambda|$ and $|\theta|$ will always have the same sign. Hence, given $\delta > 0$, equation (A6.24) implies that relative supply of computers is an increasing function of its relative price. Alternatively, the relative supply of textiles rises with the relative price of textiles as shown in the text.

Moreover, this also implies that PPF is bowed out or concave downwards. Note that a positive supply relationship is consistent with only a concave downwards PPF. The reason is that such a PPF means the opportunity cost of producing an additional unit of textiles rises, and hence the (relative) supply-price for textiles must rise. By similar reasoning, a convex downwards PPF means the corresponding (relative) supply price for textiles must fall, that is, the relative supply curve for textiles is downward sloping.

IV. Output Magnification Effect or the Rybczynski Theorem

Recall that the underlying condition for the output magnification effect is constant commodity prices. Hence, letting $\hat{P}_C = \hat{P}_T = 0$ in equation (A6.24) we obtain:

$$(\hat{X}_C - \hat{X}_T) = \frac{\hat{K} - \hat{L}}{|\lambda|} \tag{A6.25}$$

Thus, an increase in the relative endowment of capital, $\hat{K} > \hat{L} > 0$, raises the relative supply of computers, that is, $\hat{X}_C > \hat{X}_T$, if computers are relatively capital-intensive (or textiles are relatively labour-intensive), $|\lambda| > 0$.

On the other hand, since the absolute value of $|\lambda|$ is less than one by equation (A6.18) or (A6.19), so (A6.25) implies the output magnification effect:

$$\hat{X}_C - \hat{X}_T > \hat{K} - \hat{L} \Rightarrow \hat{X}_C > \hat{K} > \hat{L} > \hat{X}_T$$

Similar logic shows that if $|\lambda| < 0$, that is, if computers are relatively labour-intensive, then:

$$\hat{X}_T > \hat{K} > \hat{L} > \hat{X}_C$$

V. A Fixed Coefficient HOS Model

An alternative to the production technology that allows for a menu of techniques of production as indicated by the smooth isoquants shown in Figure 6.1 is the Leontief production technology. Such a technology allows for only one production technique (for each good) and is known as the *fixed-coefficient production technology*. Thus, the a_{ij}s are no longer a choice variable as specified in equation (6.5), but are exogenously given. Changes in factor prices brought about by changes in commodity prices no longer affect the production technique in the two sectors. As a result, full employment of both factors of production cannot be maintained at all feasible commodity prices.

The core propositions, however, remain unchanged. For example, the output magnification effect will be precisely the same because it presumes constant commodity prices, which essentially fix factor prices and hence techniques of production. So it does not really matter whether production technology allows for only one or more than one technique of production. Moreover, this output magnification effect relates the supply bias of a country with its endowment bias, and accordingly the HO theorem remains valid. On the other hand, since the one-to-one

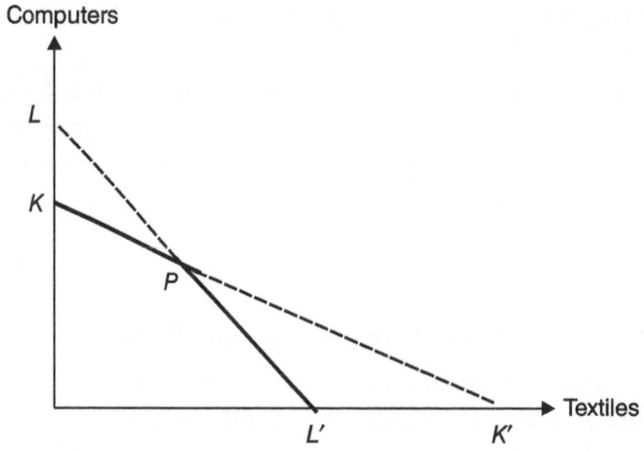

Figure A6.1 PPF with Fixed Coefficient Production Technology

correspondence depends on something else rather than a flexible coefficient production technology, the FPE theorem holds as well as long as these other conditions are satisfied as spelled out above.

The only change with a fixed coefficient production technology will be the shape of PPF and correspondingly the shape of the relative supply curve. Of course, as mentioned earlier, full employment of both labour and capital will not necessarily be characterizing the pre-trade equilibrium as well. To see this, consider Figure A6.1 where the full employment constraints are drawn. With a fixed coefficient production technology, these constraints will not change their positions when commodity prices and consequently factor prices change. PPF is generated by the lower envelope *KPL′* of these two constraints. This is because to the left of point *P* the capital constraint is binding whereas to the right the labour constraint is binding. For any relative price of textiles that equals $\frac{a_{LT}}{a_{LC}}$, the economy can produce any combination of the two goods along the *PL′* segment. Thus, except for the bundle *P* and the complete specialization bundle *L′*, only labour will be fully employed and capital will be in excess supply.

Note that unlike the case of a flexible coefficient, this excess supply of capital cannot be wiped out through a fall in the rate of return to capital. For all relative prices of textiles higher than this, the economy will be completely specialized in textiles. Thus, the price $\frac{a_{LT}}{a_{LC}}$ is analogous to the price p_{max} in Figure 6.2. On the other hand, for all relative prices of textiles smaller than $\frac{a_{KT}}{a_{KC}}$, the economy will be completely specialized in computers, whereas for price exactly equal to $\frac{a_{KT}}{a_{KC}}$, the production combination is once again indeterminate as it can be any combination along the *KP* segment of PPF. Now, except for the complete specialization point *K* and the vertex bundle *P*, for all other output bundles only capital stock will be fully exhausted with some workers remaining unemployed.

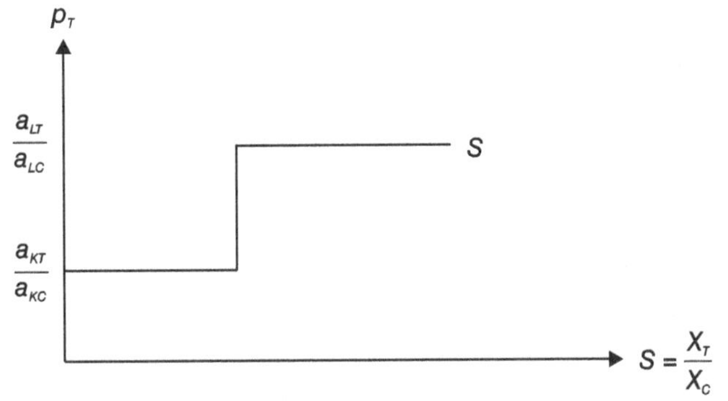

Figure A6.2 Relative Supply of Textiles under Fixed Coefficient

Finally, for all $\frac{a_{KT}}{a_{KC}} < p_T < \frac{a_{LT}}{a_{LC}}$, the economy will be producing bundle *P* with both labour and capital being fully employed. The corresponding relative supply curve for textiles is thus a step-like curve as illustrated in Figure A6.2.

SUMMARY POINTS

- Eli Heckscher (1949) and Bertil Ohlin (1933) demonstrated that the comparative advantage of nations and their patterns of trade are related to their exogenously given factor endowments. Their theory, known as the Heckscher–Ohlin theory, states that the relatively labour-abundant country will export the relatively labour-intensive commodity and the relatively capital-abundant country will export the relatively capital-intensive commodity. Their analytical structure was further enriched by Paul Samuelson, among others, and is thus known as the Heckscher–Ohlin–Samuelson (HOS) model.
- A country is said to be abundant in labour relative to another country if it is endowed with more labour and less capital than the other. The other country is thus capital-abundant. These are *physical definitions* of factor abundance and are applicable when there are two factors of production.
- This factor endowment difference or supply bias explanation of the pattern of trade is based on the assumption of identical and homothetic tastes of consumers. When tastes are neither identical nor homothetic, the HO theory may still be valid if the taste biases and supply biases of countries are in different goods.
- There are three other important propositions or properties of the HOS model: the Rybczynski theorem or output magnification effect, the price magnification effect, and the factor price equalization (FPE) theory.

(*contd*)

Summary Points (*contd*)

- The Rybczynski theorem or the output magnification effect states that if there is a more than proportionate exogenous growth in capital compared to the growth in labour force, then the production of the capital-intensive good will increase more than the growth in capital, whereas increase in the production of the labour-intensive good, *if at all*, will be less than proportionate to the growth in the labour force.
- The price magnification effect, which is the generalization of the Stolper–Samuelson theory by Ronald Jones (1965), if the price of the capital-intensive commodity rises more than proportionate to the price of the labour-intensive commodity in a country, then the real return to capital will unambiguously rise whereas the real wage will unambiguously fall.
- The FPE theorem states that free commodity trade between countries will equalize the factor prices across these countries. Thus even without any international migration of labour and movement of capital, workers will earn the same wages and capital will earn the same returns everywhere. That is, free commodity trade acts as a substitute for factor trade.
- This interesting possibility arises because of the irrelevance of both demand and factor endowment conditions in determining factor prices. The domestic demand for goods and factor endowment conditions can affect factor prices only through their effects on commodity prices in the world market, which in turn depends on whether the country is small or large as a buyer (or importer) and seller (or exporter) in the world market. Thus post-trade factor prices are solely and uniquely determined by the prices of the traded goods, which are determined in the world market. This one-to-one correspondence between commodity and factor prices means that once prices of traded goods are equalized across countries through arbitrage and trade, so are the factor prices, despite countries having different endowments of the factors of production.
- There are two possible sources of disruption of the one-to-one correspondence and thus invalidation of the FPE theorem: if countries are completely specialized after trade, and if technologies exhibit factor intensity reversals. On both occasions, the one-to-one correspondence breaks down and thus FPE *may* not hold.
- Incomplete specialization and absence of factor intensity reversals, by themselves, are neither necessary nor sufficient conditions for the FPE theory to hold. What is important is that the endowment differences should not be too large so that there is scope for incomplete specialization by *both* the countries for the *same* set of values of relative wages.

KEYWORDS

- **Unit value isoquant** is the unit of that good that fetch the producer-cum-seller a revenue worth of one unit of the domestic currency.
- **Factor intensity reversal** is said to exist when the production technologies of the two goods are such that the same good is capital-intensive relative to the other for some factor price ratios, but labour-intensive for some other factor price ratios.
- **The HO theorem** states that a relatively labour-abundant country will export relatively labour-intensive goods and import relatively capital-intensive goods from a capital-abundant country.
- **Factor price frontier** for a good is the locus of the combination of minimum factor prices consistent with zero profit for producing that good, given its price.
- **One-to-one correspondence** between commodity and factor prices means that factor prices are solely and uniquely determined by commodity prices, regardless of the factor endowment conditions of a country.
- **Small country** is the one that is an insignificant buyer and seller and hence is a *price taker* in the world market, like a perfectly competitive firm. It cannot influence world prices by changing its own trade volumes however large these may be for itself.
- **Large country** is a significant buyer and seller in the world market and can influence its TOT by changing its action.

EXERCISES

1. What will be the implications of both textiles and computers being produced by an identical CRS technology?
2. Prove that if good 1 is relatively labour-intensive, its share in total employment of labour is greater than its share in the total employment of capital.
3. Can the goods be ranked unambiguously according to their factor intensities when technology exhibits factor intensity reversal?
4. Least-cost techniques of production for textiles and computers are given as

   $$k_T = 5 + 3\rho \text{ and } k_C = 10 + 2\rho.$$

   (i) Which good is relatively labour intensive?
   (ii) If the economy's endowment ratio k is 15, how does your answer in (i) change?

   Determine the pattern of production for $\rho = \frac{10}{3}$.
5. Suppose good 1 is produced by one unit of labour and one unit of capital, whereas good 2 is produced by one unit of labour and two units of capital. If the economy has 30 units of capital and 40 workers, answer the following questions:
   (a) Draw the production set.

(contd)

Exercises (*contd*)

(b) Is it possible to employ both capital and labour fully?

(c) What level of output will generate the maximum employment level? What is the level of the maximum employment?

6. Suppose salt is produced by five units of labour and one unit of capital, and pepper by one unit each of labour and capital. The economy has 110 workers and 50 units of capital.
   (a) What output levels will ensure full employment of both capital and labour?
   (b) If consumers like to consume salt and pepper in a fixed ratio 1:2, what output levels should the economy produce? Illustrate your answer.
   (c) What will be the pre-trade equilibrium price ratio?
7. Home and foreign countries produce leather bags (B) and corn (C) using labour (L) and land (T). Technologies in the two countries are identical and are summarized in the following set of fixed input coefficients: $a_{LB}=5, a_{LC}=3, a_{TB}=10, a_{TC}=9$. The home country is endowed with 1000 workers and 1200 acres of land, whereas the foreign country with 600 workers and 1800 acres of land.
   (a) Find out the autarchic relative price of leather bags in the two countries and comments on their comparative advantages.
   (b) Is the pattern of comparative advantage and pattern of trade (between them) are consistent with the HO theorem? Explain.
   (c) How many leather bags and how much of corn will each country produce after trade?
8. Consider the following full employment conditions in the United States and India:

   $L_j = 5X_T + 2X_C$, $K_j = 2X_T + 4X_C$, $j =$ USA, India.

   Suppose, $L_{\text{USA}} = 1{,}000$, $L_{\text{India}} = 800$, $K_{\text{USA}} = 800$, and $K_{\text{India}} = 400$. Consumers in both the countries have identical tastes and consume the two goods at a fixed ratio: $\dfrac{D_C}{D_T} = \dfrac{1}{2}$.
   (a) Do you think both labour and capital will be fully employed in the pre-trade situation?
   (b) What are the pre-trade price ratios in the two countries?
   (c) When trade opens up between the US and India, what will be the pattern of trade? Is this consistent with the factor abundance of the countries?
9. Suppose tastes are homothetic but not identical. India, being a labour-abundant country, has a taste bias for textiles which is relatively labour-intensive. Will India export textiles to the United States and import computers from there?
10. Suppose tastes are identical across countries but non-homothetic. If the demand for computers is income elastic and per capita income in the United States is higher than that in India, will the HO theorem be valid?
11. An alternative to the physical definition of factor abundance of a country is the price definition. It states that the home country is relatively labour-abundant if relative wage is cheaper there than in the foreign country: $\rho < \rho^*$. Using price definition of factor abundance as specified in Box 6.1, prove the HO theorem.

(*contd*)

Exercises (*contd*)

12. Show that one-to-one correspondence breaks down in the country that is completely specialized after trade and hence prove that FPE dose not hold.
13. Consider an economy with a 2x2 HOS production structure and homothetic tastes for leather bags and computers. If in the pre-trade situation, the government imposes a production tax on leather bags, does it hurt the workers?
14. Given the structure of the economy as in the preceding question, if the economy is small, how does a production tax imposed on leather bags in the post-trade situation affect workers?
15. Suppose per unit requirements of producing bread (B) and corn (C) in the home country are: $a_{LB} = 4, a_{LC} = 5, a_{TB} = 6, a_{TC} = 2$. Find out the wage rate and the rate of return to capital in the home country if P_B = Rs100 and P_C = Rs 80. When trade opens up with the rest of the world, the country exports leather bags. Does it hurt workers? Explain logically and then check your answer if the world prices are Rs. 110 and Rs. 75 for bread and corn per unit respectively.

SUGGESTED READING

Bhagwati, J.N., A. Panagariya, and T.N. Srinivasan. (1998). *Lectures on International Trade.* Cambridge, MA: MIT Press.

Caves, R.E., J. Frankel, and R.W. Jones. (1995). *World Trade and Payments.* New York: HarperCollins College Publishers.

Jones, R.W. (1965). 'The Structure of Simple General Equilibrium', *Journal of Political Economy*, 73: 557–72.

ADVANCED READING

Heckscher, E. (1949). 'The Effect of Foreign Trade on the Distribution of Income', in H.S. Ellis and L.A. Metzler (eds), *Readings in the Theory of International Trade.* Philadelphia: Blackiston, pp. 272–300.

Leontief, W.W. (1954). 'Domestic Production and Foreign Trade: The American Capital Position Re-examined', *Economia Internazionale*, 7: 3–32.

Ohlin, B. (1933). *Interregional and International Trade.* Cambridge: Harvard University Press.

Rybczynski, T.N. (1955). 'Factor Endowment and Relative Commodity Prices', *Economica*, 12: 336–41.

Samuelson, P.A. (1948). 'International Trade and Equalization of Factor Prices', *Economic Journal*, 58: 181–97.

Stolper, W. and P.A. Samuelson. (1941). 'Protection and Real Wages', *Review of Economic Studies*, 9: 58–73.

7 Digressions on Factor Endowment Theory and Trade Empirics

The Heckscher–Ohlin–Samuelson (HOS) model and its core propositions had raised considerable interest among trade theorists and empiricists to put it under empirical tests as well as under robustness checks. Not always have such tests and robustness checks yielded results consistent with the predictions of the model. Recent empirical observations regarding wage movements also run counter to the predictions of the price magnification effect and the Factor Price Equalization (FPE) theorem. Yet, the HOS model has remained the workhorse of international trade theory and observations at odds with the basic model have often been explained by relaxing some of the underlying assumptions of the model and by extending its scope.

In this chapter we will discuss some of the empirical issues and extensions of the basic model to reconcile theoretical predictions and empirical observations. These issues and extensions are discussed in two particular contexts. First is the empirical test of the Heckscher–Ohlin (HO) theorem by Leontief who found the predicted and actual pattern of trade being at odds with each other, and subsequent refinements of the test in terms of a generalized theorem known as the Heckscher–Ohlin–Vanek (HOV) theorem. Plausible theoretical explanations are discussed briefly. Second, we discuss the two variations of the HOS model in terms of non-traded goods and immobility of factors across sectors (or sector specificity of factors) and their implications for the one-to-one correspondence and related price magnification effect and the FPE theorem. These cases have far-reaching implications for the observed global rise in wage inequality since the mid-1980s which is in sharp contrast to the prediction of the HOS model. Finally, higher dimension issues in the HOS model such as implications of many goods and many factors of production in an economy for the core propositions of the HOS model are discussed as an advanced topic.

7.1 EMPIRICAL TESTS OF THE HO THEOREM: LEONTIEF PARADOX

The foremost empirical test of the HO theorem was done by Leontief (1954). Using the data for exports and imports of the United States after World War II, he observed that it was exporting relatively labour-intensive goods to the rest of the world. But the United States was by far

International Economics. Rajat Acharyya, Oxford University Press. © Oxford University Press 2022.
DOI: 10.1093/oso/9780192865144.003.0007

the most capital-abundant country in the world. Given the export composition of the United States in 1947, Leontief estimated labour and capital requirements for producing a bundle of export goods to be worth USD 1 million. On the other hand, observing the import composition of its imports, he estimated labour and capital required to produce USD 1 million worth of imports if these were produced in the United States instead of being imported. His estimates showed that domestic production of the imported goods would have required 30 per cent more capital per worker than what the production of export goods required. He repeated his tests for 1951 and observed a similar pattern of trade though the relative capital intensity of import replacement was substantially less than what it was in 1947. Hence, he concluded that the United States was importing relatively capital-intensive goods. This observation, known as the Leontief Paradox, raised considerable interest among trade theorists to reconcile it with the HO theorem that a capital abundant country should export relatively capital intensive goods. Further tests for 1962 data supported the paradox, but for 1972, Stern and Maskus (1981) observed the paradox to vanish for the United States. Leontief's test, when applied to other countries' trade data, yielded similar paradoxical results. Pattern of trade in more recent times for China and India, for example, also provide indirect evidence that a country's trade pattern may not be fully consistent with its endowment pattern. Despite these countries being unskilled labour-abundant countries, their basket of exports even to the skilled-labour-abundant countries contains a large proportion of high-technology and skill-intensive commodities.

A theoretical reconciliation of the Leontief Paradox with the HO theorem was offered primarily in terms of a stronger taste bias, factor intensity reversal, and cross-country technology differences. As explained in the earlier chapters, if consumers in a labour-abundant country have a very strong taste bias in labour-intensive commodities, the country may end up exporting capital-intensive commodities. In case of factor intensity reversal, on the other hand, referring back to Figure 6.10, when the endowment differences of the countries are too large, relative wages in the two countries differ in a way that textiles are produced with relatively labour-intensive techniques in the home country but by relatively capital-intensive techniques in the foreign country. Thus, if the capital and labour required to produce import replacements in the foreign country are measured, as Leontief did, it will appear that the foreign country being relatively capital abundant imports relatively capital-intensive textiles.

Leontief's own position regarding the paradox, however, was that the United States was technologically quite advanced and its workers were more productive compared to most of the countries. This led to a pattern of comparative advantage for the United States that was not consistent with its endowment pattern. His position, which was later supported empirically by Trefler (1993) in a generalized test as explained below, is illustrated in Figure 7.1. As assumed earlier in Chapter 6, the foreign country (the United States in Leontief's test) has a larger stock of physical capital than the home country but the same endowment of labour. But suppose foreign workers are more productive in all lines of production than the home workers. Thus, in productivity or efficiency units, the foreign country has a larger endowment of labour and can produce more of both goods than the home country. This is shown by the higher broken labour constraint line for the foreign country. If the labour productivity difference is too large, the foreign country appears to be relatively labour-abundant when measured in efficiency units and thus produces larger units of textiles relative to computers than the home country. This is illustrated in Figure 7.1 by the production bundle P^* and this supply bias in textiles causes its

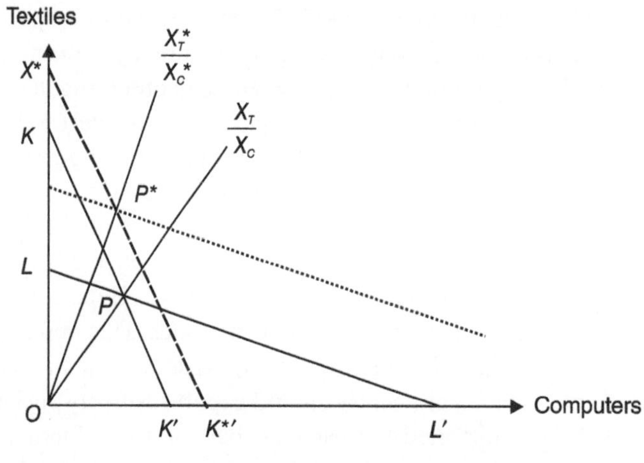

Figure 7.1 Labour Productivity and the Leontief Paradox

pre-trade relative price to be smaller than the price in the home country. Hence, the foreign country exports textiles, which seems to be at odds with the HO theorem when its factor abundance is measured in physical units, but is consistent with the theory when its factor abundance is measured in efficiency units (or in productivity-augmented units).

7.2 FACTOR CONTENT AND THE HOV THEOREM

The HO theory was generalized by Jaroslav Vanek (1968) into a theory of *factor content of trade* known as the Heckscher–Ohlin–Vanek (HOV) theory. The HOV theory or the theory of *factor content of trade* provides the theoretical basis for the empirical tests of the HO theorem by Leamer (1984), Brown et al. (1987), Trefler (1993), Davis and Weinstein (2001), and others. Factor content of trade is a measure of how much of a factor is embodied in a traded good.

Let there be $c = 1, 2, \ldots..C$ number of countries, and $j = 1, 2, \ldots..J$ number of final traded goods produced with $i = 1, 2, \ldots.I$ number of factors of production. Let V_i^C denote the endowment of the i-th factor in country c, and X_j^C be the production level of the j-th good in country c. Full employment of all factors in country c means:

$$\begin{bmatrix} V_1^c \\ V_2^c \\ \\ \\ V_I^c \end{bmatrix} = \begin{bmatrix} a_{11}^c \; a_{12}^c \ldots\ldots a_{1J}^c \\ a_{21}^c \; a_{22}^c \ldots\ldots a_{2J}^c \\ \\ \\ a_{I1}^c \; a_{I2}^c \ldots\ldots a_{IJ}^c \end{bmatrix} \begin{bmatrix} X_1^c \\ X_2^c \\ . \\ . \\ X_J^c \end{bmatrix} \tag{7.1}$$

$$\Rightarrow V^c = A^c X^c$$

$$\Rightarrow X^c = \left[A^c\right]^{-1} V^c \tag{7.2}$$

Let preferences be homothetic and identical across countries, which implies that the demand vector will be proportional to the world output (or income) vector:

$$D^c = s^c X^W \tag{7.3}$$

where, s^c is the country c's share of the world income:

$$s^c = \frac{Y^c}{Y^W} \tag{7.4}$$

Since, $X^W = \sum_{c=1}^{C} \left[A^c\right]^{-1} V^c$, so:

$$D^c = s^c \sum_{c=1}^{C} \left[A^c\right]^{-1} V^c \tag{7.5}$$

Let $T^c = X^c - D^c$ denote the vector of net exports of good j. Note, $T_j^c > 0$ if good j is exported and $T_j^c < 0$ otherwise. Content of each factor i in the vector of good j is the corresponding element of the vector FC^c:

$$FC^c = A^c T^c = A^c X^c - A^c D^c$$

$$= V^c - A^c s^c \sum_{c=1}^{C} \left[A^c\right]^{-1} V^c \qquad \text{[by (7.5)]}$$

But by the HO assumption, all countries share the same technology so the above boils down to:

$$\begin{aligned} FC^c &= V^c - A^c s^c \left[A^c\right]^{-1} \sum_{c=1}^{C} V^c \\ &= V^c - s^c V^W \end{aligned} \tag{7.6}$$

A typical element i is:

$$FC_i^c = V_i^c - s^c V_i^W \tag{7.6a}$$

which is a number that measures the 'net' content of factor i in all goods traded by country c. Now the measured content of factor i in trade $FC_i^c > 0$ if it is more intensively used in exports since by definition:

$$FC_i^c = \sum_{j=1}^{J} a_{ij}^c T_j^c$$

Thus, what the factor content equation $FC_i^c = V_i^c - s^c V_i^W$ tells us is that if country c is abundant in factor i in the sense that it has a larger share of world stock of factor-i:

$$\frac{V_i^c}{V_i^W} > s^c \equiv \frac{Y^C}{Y^W} \tag{7.7}$$

then, from equation (7.6a), $FC_i^c > 0$, which implies that factor i will tend to be used more intensively in exports than in imports. Thus, a labour-abundant country implicitly exports labour. This is the HOV theorem.

Using the HOV theorem and the factor content approach, Leamer (1984) re-specified Leontief's test and found support for the HOV theorem that a country endowed with a relatively larger share of the world's stock of a factor of production will largely make net exports of goods that are intensive in that factor. Brown et al. (1987), on the other hand, estimated endowments of 12 factors of production for 27 countries and found that the United States was not very capital-abundant. But for most of the factors of production, the association between the share of the United States in the world's stock of that factor and the net exports being intensive in that factor is not statistically significant.

Subsequent modifications and refinements of the HOV model display better consistency with actual trade data. These refinements mainly focused on cross-country productivity differences, home country bias in consumption, trade costs and distances, trade in intermediate inputs, and non-traded final goods. Trefler (1993), for example, modified the factor content equation by taking into account productivity differences to test Leontief's own explanation of the paradox. Let π_L^c denote the marginal product of labour. Thus, he augmented labour endowment of country c measured in physical units by labour productivity:

$$fe_L^c = \pi_L^c V_L^c \tag{7.8}$$

Proceeding as before, the factor content equation augmented by the productivity parameter boils down to:

$$fc_L^c = \pi_L^c V_L^c - s^c \sum_{c=1}^{C} \pi_L^c V_L^c \tag{7.9}$$

Assigning a value of $\pi_L^{US} = 1$, Trefler (1993) then estimated the value of labour productivity in UK as $\pi_L^{UK} = 0.66$. That is, after the World War II period, British workers were a third less productive than American workers. Thus, he concluded that Leontief was right.

7.3 PRICE MAGNIFICATION EFFECT AND FPE REVISITED

The one-to-one correspondence and the price magnification effects discussed earlier may fail to hold in at least two extensions of the HOS model. First is when some factors of production are not mobile across sectors or are specific to some sectors, and second is when an economy produces non-traded goods along with traded goods. In the following two sub-sections we discuss these dimensions.

7.3.1 Factor Immobility and Specific Factors

Recall that one of the assumptions of the HOS model is that all factors move freely and instantaneously from one sector to another within a country that offers a higher rate of return. But this may not be the case always. Some factors are less mobile than others. For example, in the very short run, we can expect that physical capital is completely immobile. It is only in the medium or long run that physical capital employed or installed in one sector can be transferred to the other sector. The immediate implication of this immobility of physical capital within a country is that if initially there had been any difference in the rate of return to capital in the two sectors, that difference will persist in the short run, though it will evaporate in the long run when capital can move to the high-return sector.[1] This case of immobility of some factors significantly alters almost all the core propositions of the HOS model.

Alternatively, all factors may be mobile even in the short run, but different sectors may require different skill levels and/or different types of capital. For example, production of computers requires the skills of hardware engineers, which is not of much use in textile production. Production of textiles requires altogether different types of skilled workers. Similarly, capital required to produce computers may be of a different type than the capital required to produce textiles. Thus, factors may have sector-specific use. This specific factor case in essence is the same as the case of factor immobility in the sense that the rate of return for specific types of capital or skills will differ across sectors. The difference between the two cases, however, is that the differential rates of return will persist even in the long run in the specific factor case. Once again, the core propositions are altered in the same fashion as in the case of factor immobility. To illustrate, we follow the Specific Factor (henceforth, SF) model developed by Ronald W. Jones (1971). This model essentially extends the 2×2 HOS model into a two-commodity-three-factor model. Thus, what this SF model indicates is that some of the core propositions or the properties of the 2×2 HOS model do not extend to higher dimensions.

Suppose K_C and K_T are the two types of capital required to produce computers and textiles respectively. To keep things simple we assume that the same type of skill can be combined with sector-specific capitals to produce the two goods. Let r_C and r_T denote the rate of returns to these sector-specific capitals. The supply side of the SF model can be described by the following set of zero-profit conditions, least cost input choices, and full employment conditions:

$$P_C = a_{LC}W + a_{KC}r_C \tag{7.10}$$

$$P_T = a_{LT}W + a_{KT}r_T \tag{7.11}$$

$$a_{ij} = a_{ij}(W/r_j),\ i = L, K;\ j = C, T \tag{7.12}$$

$$L = a_{LC}X_C + a_{LT}X_T \tag{7.13}$$

$$K_C = a_{KC}X_C \tag{7.14}$$

$$K_T = a_{KT}X_T \tag{7.15}$$

Before proceeding further, a few comments are warranted. First, since each sector-specific capital has no *alternative* use, its transfer earning is zero and hence its entire return, r_CK_C (or

[1] Due to this time dimension, the HOS model with immobile factors is often referred to as the short-run HOS model. Michael Mussa (1974) analysed the implications of this immobility for the price magnification effect.

$r_T K_T$) is essentially the scarcity rent. Second, full employment of all factors can be maintained only when input coefficients are flexible. The fixed coefficient or Leontief production function (discussed in earlier chapters) and full employment of all factors of production is incompatible in the SF model. To illustrate, consider Figure 7.2 where given the initial set of factor prices, corresponding three factor constraints indicated by the bold lines are in positions such that the feasible production set is the rectangular area enclosed by the two capital constraint lines. Thus, the labour constraint is non-binding and all workers cannot be employed wherever within this set the economy's initial production is. Suppose the economy was initially producing bundle *a*.

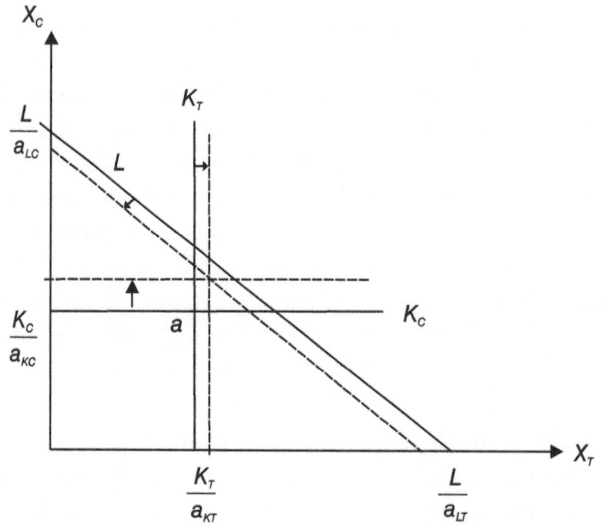

Figure 7.2 Full Employment in the SF Model

Starting from this initial output bundle, competition among the unemployed workers offering to work at lower wages will drive down the market wage rate. For fixed coefficient production functions, this fall in wage rate will have no change in the technique of production. With the specific factors already fully employed, any output expansion will not have been feasible either. Hence, despite the fall in wage, the unemployment of labour will persist. But, for flexible coefficient production functions, the decline in wage will induce producers everywhere to employ relatively labour-intensive techniques, thereby raising the demand for labour and lowering unemployment. On the other hand, at initial output levels, less capital-intensive techniques of production will free some capital in both the sectors that can then be used to expand production levels. This scale expansion in the both sectors will raise the demand for labour further. These adjustments in technique and scale of production through declining wages will continue till all workers are fully employed in the two sectors together. In Figure 7.2, these adjustments are shown by movements of labour and capital constraint lines in the directions specified till the three broken lines pass through the same production bundle so that all factors of production are fully employed. Note that a more labour-intensive technique means a higher value of a_{Lj} and a lower value of a_{Kj}, which shifts the constraints in the specified direction.

Does the pattern of trade for trading nations with a specific-factor production structure relate to the endowment pattern of countries? Note that with three factors of production, the factor abundance of a country cannot be defined by its relative factor proportion. However, in the spirit of the HOV theorem, suppose the home country has a larger share of world stock of capital specific to the textile sector than the foreign country, everything else being the same: $K_T > K_T^*$. Since this capital is specific to the production of textiles, for any given set of commodity prices, the home country will produce a larger quantity of textiles than the foreign country, and the trade-off along the labour constraint implies that it will produce a smaller number of computers. That is, the relative supply of textiles will be larger in the home country having a larger share of the world stock of capital that is specific to this sector. Hence, the pre-trade relative price of textiles will be lower in the home country enabling it to export textiles and import computers from the foreign country. A similar trade pattern would arise if the foreign country has a larger share of the world stock of capital that is specific to the production of computers. Thus, the pattern of trade does relate to the relative endowment of specific factors of the countries. However, such a relationship is less unambiguous when countries differ in respect of their shares in the world's labour endowments as the output magnification effect worked out in Appendix A7 shows.

Let us now turn to the other two propositions—the FPE theorem and the price magnification effect. Referring back to conditions (7.10)–(7.15), it is immediate that the prices of the two traded commodities determined in the world market and thus exogenous to this system of equations, are no longer sufficient to determine three factor prices. Hence, unlike the HOS model, the independence of the price sub-system, comprising of zero profit conditions and least-cost input choices specified in (7.10)–(7.13), from the physical sub-system does not hold. That is, factor endowment conditions, along with world commodity prices, now determine factor prices. Factor prices are no longer *solely* determined by commodity prices. Consequently, commodity price equalization through free commodity trade will not lead to factor price equalization across the trading nations.

However, will there be any *tendency* for factor prices in the two trading nations to converge, or they will diverge away from each other further through commodity trade and consequent commodity price equalization? This issue can be addressed through the price magnification effect. As worked out in Appendix A7, an increase in the price of textiles, *ceteris paribus*, *unambiguously* raises the return to capital specific to this sector more than proportionately and *unambiguously* lowers the return to the capital specific to the computer sector. More significantly, the change in the wage rate is trapped between commodity price changes:

$$\hat{r}_T > \hat{P}_T > \hat{W} > \hat{P}_C = 0 > \hat{r}_C \tag{7.16}$$

The important point to note is that factor intensity conditions are no longer relevant as in the case of the price magnification effect in the HOS model. It is obvious that as textile production expands in face of its rising price relative to that of computers, return to capital specific to its production will rise because additional capital cannot be made available through contracting production elsewhere. As the rate of return to capital specific to textile production rises, producers there use less capital-intensive techniques, whereby some units of capital used earlier in the production become excess and thus can be used to expand the scale of production. The wage rate, however, cannot rise to the same extent since increased demand for labour in the expanding textile sector is mitigated to some extent by release of some workers from the contracting computer sector. On the other hand, the rate of return to capital specific to computer production should unambiguously fall since it has no alternative use. The excess capital due to contraction of output must be absorbed in that sector itself by inducing producers to choose a more capital-intensive technique to produce computers.

Thus, the price magnification effect in equation (7.16) differs from that in a HOS model without sector specificity (or immobility) of factors in one important respect. The change in *real* wage is now ambiguous. Of course, workers lose in our example of computers and textiles if computers are not consumed by them. In a more general situation when both commodities are consumed by the workers, such as rice and textiles, and both the prices increase but at a differential rate, then whether workers gain or lose depends on the share of income spent on the two goods. If, for example, more of their income is spent on rice, and the price of rice has risen less than proportionate to the price of textiles, then it is more likely that the workers' real wage will rise. There is no such ambiguity regarding changes in the real wage in the 2×2 HOS model as discussed in Chapter 6. In the SF model, as equation (7.16) indicates, unambiguous statements regarding change in real returns can be made only for the specific factors without requiring any additional information regarding the nature of goods and their expenditure shares. Moreover, the factor intensity ranking of the two goods is not relevant either. These changes in real returns to the factors have some far-reaching and interesting implications for the political economy of government policies that are in sharp contrast with the same in the HOS model. The interests of workers and capitalists for a policy change that brings about asymmetric movements in commodity prices may no longer be conflicting. For example, when a tariff on import of computers by the home country government raises their local (or tariff-inclusive) prices in the home country, changes in real returns to the three factors can be obtained from the corresponding price magnification effect:

$$\hat{r}_C > \hat{P}_C > \hat{W} > \hat{P}_T = 0 > \hat{r}_T \tag{7.16a}$$

Thus, owners of capital specific to the computer sector unambiguously gain whereas other capitalists unambiguously lose. If computers are not consumed by the workers, they also gain unambiguously. Hence, both workers and owners of capital specific to the computer sector will support a protectionist policy. Note that if the same capital could have been used everywhere as in the HOS model, the interests of the workers and the capitalists would have always been in conflict with each other. For example, recalling the price magnification effect spelled out in Chapter 6, a tariff on imports of computers would have raised the real return to capital and lowered the real wage since computers are relatively capital-intensive:

$$\hat{r} > \hat{P}_C > \hat{P}_T = 0 > \hat{W} \tag{7.16b}$$

Thus, capitalists everywhere would have supported a protectionist policy whereas the workers would have opposed it.

Let us now see how these price magnification effects help us say about (less than full) convergence or divergence of factor prices across the trading nations. Consider Figure 7.3 where the value of marginal product of labour (VMP_L) curves in the two sectors are drawn for the two countries that determine the allocation of labour across the two sectors and the corresponding wage rate for any given set of commodity prices. Suppose at the pre-trade equilibrium the wage rate in the foreign country was W^* and labour employed in textile production was a^*, corresponding to the equality between VMP_{LT} and VMP_{LC}. Now to keep things as simple as possible, suppose the home country has a larger stock of capital specific to textile production, *ceteris paribus*: $K_T > K_T^*$. Larger capital to work with will make home workers in the textile sector more productive and this is shown by the broken VMP_{LT} curve on the extreme right. (Though the VMP_L curves are drawn parallel, they need not be so.) At the same time, higher stock of capital specific to textile production will lower pre-trade textile prices in the home country so that the VMP_{LT} curve shifts down a bit. This is shown by the thicker broken curve.

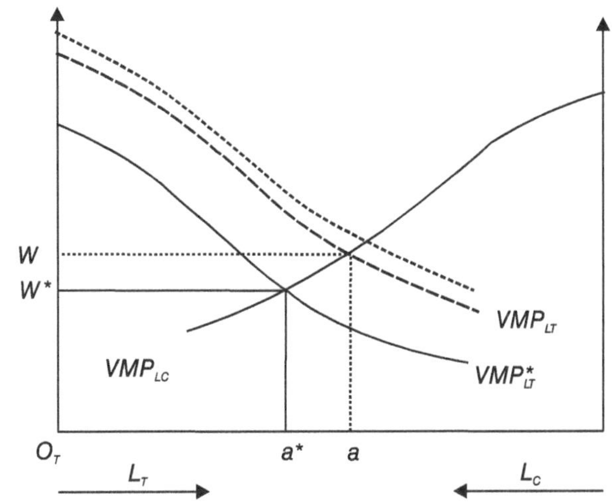

Figure 7.3 Labour Allocation and Wages

A larger proportion of the labour force will thus be employed in the textile sector with a higher wage rate in the home country than in the foreign country. Note that the higher pre-trade price of computers in the home country will shift up the VMP_{LC} curve and raise the wage there further. The rate of return to K_T in the home country should be lower. This is because for any given rate of return to K_T, a larger capital stock enables the home country to produce a larger quantity of textiles which makes their prices lower there. Then by the price magnification effect, the rate return to capital specific to this sector must be lower in the home country by more than proportionate to the price difference across the home and the foreign country. The rate of return to K_C must be lower as well in the home country because the computer sector there will be smaller in size and hence the demand for this type of capital will be smaller. Thus, given that the home country has a larger stock of K_T, everything else being the same in the two countries, we can expect $W > W^*$, $r_C < r_C^*$ and $r_T < r_T^*$. After opening up of trade, arbitrage and free commodity movement raise textile prices in the home country and lower the same in the foreign country. The price of computers, on the other hand, declines in the home country and rises in the foreign country. Hence, by the price magnification effect, r_T should rise and

r_C should fall in the home country, whereas r_T^* should fall and r_C^* should rise in the foreign country. That is, the rates of returns to capital specific to the computer sector should diverge after trade rather than converging as the FPE theorem tells us.

Following the above argument, we can readily verify whether the output magnification holds or not in this SF production structure. Referring back to Figure 7.3, a *ceteris paribus* increase in K_T raises the wage by raising the marginal product of labour in the textile sector. Recall the underlying assumption of output magnification effect, namely, effect of endowment changes on output levels at constant commodity prices. Thus, the VMP_L curve in Figure 7.3 will not be shifting down in the middle position through a decline in prices. The increase in the wage rate, at constant prices, will lower the rate of return to capital in the textile sector. Consequently, a more capital intensive-technique of production will be chosen, that is, $\hat{a}_{KT} > 0$. Hence, given $\hat{K}_T = \hat{X}_T + \hat{a}_{KT}$, it is immediate that the expansion of the textile production will be less than proportional:

$$\hat{K}_T > \hat{X}_T > 0$$

Therefore, given that the computer sector contracts as some labour moves out of this sector in response to the higher wage in the textile sector, we have the following relation between endowment change and output changes:

$$\hat{K}_T > \hat{X}_T > 0 = \hat{K}_C = \hat{L} > \hat{X}_C \tag{7.17}$$

By similar logic, for a *ceteris paribus* increase in K_C we have:

$$\hat{K}_C > \hat{X}_C > 0 = \hat{K}_T = \hat{L} > \hat{X}_T \tag{7.18}$$

Thus, the output magnification effects do not hold as not all output changes are more than proportional to changes in factor endowment.

From the above discussions it follows that the relative supply of the good increases if the supply of capital specific to its production increases. But change in the relative supply of goods is not unambiguous when there is an exogenous increase in labour supply. As shown in Appendix A7:

$$\hat{X}_T - \hat{X}_C = \frac{1}{\gamma}\left[\sigma_T \frac{\theta_{LT}}{\theta_{KT}} - \sigma_C \frac{\theta_{LC}}{\theta_{KC}}\right]$$

Thus, an exogenous increase in labour supply raises the relative supply of textiles if:

$$\sigma_T > \frac{\theta_{KT}\theta_{LC}}{\theta_{LT}\theta_{KC}}\sigma_C$$

Suppose, $\theta_{LC} > \theta_{LT}$, which in turn means $\theta_{KC} > \theta_{KT}$. Then the above condition requires that $\sigma_T > \sigma_C$. The intuition for this condition is as follows. Increase in labour supply lowers the wage–rental ratio in both the sectors and induces producers everywhere to use less capital-intensive production techniques. If $\sigma_T > \sigma_C$, at the margin, capital is substituted by labour relatively more in textile production than in computer production. Thus, a larger amount of capital will now be released for scale expansion in the textile sector than in the computer sector. Therefore, textile production rises more than computer production.

7.3.2 Non-traded Goods

Some goods cannot be traded due to their very nature. For example, many services are actually location-specific and cannot be dissociated from service providers. Thus, trade in those services essentially depends on the movement of the service provider from one country to the other. But in such cases, these are not service trade but factor movements. Of course, with improvements in telecommunications, many services can be provided without the service provider moving from one location to the other. A typical example is core banking systems whereby customers can operate their accounts and get related banking services even without having to be physically present in the branch that they have their accounts in. At the other extreme is a hair cut, the service for which the provider and the customer must have physical contact.

For goods, tradability depends on both transport costs and their perishable nature. The higher the cost of transportation and the shorter the self life, the less tradable a good is. Freshly prepared food (not the packaged, frozen, or ready-to-eat variety), for example, is not generally a tradable good. It will be sold in the location that it is prepared in.

The most important implication of a non-traded good is that arbitrage is not possible and hence cross-country (or cross-location) price differences will persist. Thus, cost of a hair cut will differ in the United States and in India (when denominated in the same currency). Similarly, freshly prepared food in one city or country does not directly compete with the same elsewhere. The law of one price thus does not hold for non-traded goods. Their prices are *locally* determined, and their output levels are constrained by local demand conditions. Unlike traded goods, the economy cannot produce these goods in excess of what their demand is locally. As a consequence, the independence of factor prices from domestic demand conditions does not hold even for a small country as discussed earlier. Second, one-to-one correspondence may also break down as the local factor market conditions become important too, thus creating scope for factor prices to differ across trading nations. A simple check for both these is whether the number of traded goods is *at least* equal to the number of internationally immobile domestic factors of production.

To explain, consider the two-commodity, two-factor HOS model but with the following change. Suppose, besides the two traded goods, textiles and computers, the home country also produces a non-traded good (*N*). If this non-traded good is produced by the same labour and capital as used in the production of the two traded goods, one-to-one correspondence will still hold (that is, factor prices will still be solely and uniquely determined by the world prices of the traded goods), assuming away any factor intensity reversal. The factor prices corresponding to the *given* set of world prices for textiles and computers for our small home country will peg the technique of production in non-traded production and consequently the average cost of producing it. This is immediate from the zero profit condition in the non-traded sector:

$$P_N = a_{LN}W + a_{KN}r \tag{7.19}$$

Thus, in this type of a production structure, the price of the non-traded good is cost determined, and is invariant with respect to changes in the demand for the non-traded good. The non-traded sector behaves like a constant cost industry in this small open economy. Note that any expansion of the non-traded sector means a corresponding contraction of the traded sectors as it draws labour and capital from the same pool. There will thus be changes in the volume of trade. But as long as the home country is small, this will have no impact on world prices of textiles and computers, and accordingly on factor prices in the home country. The cost of production thus does not change with the output of the non-traded good. The supply curve in Figure 7.4 is thus horizontal to the output axis till output expansion exhausts all the labour force squeezing out the traded sectors. Output of the non-traded good is, however, constrained by its local demand:

$$X_N = D_N(p, y) \tag{7.20}$$

where $p \equiv \frac{P_T}{P_N}$ is the relative price of the composite traded good or the *real exchange rate*.

That is, in this production structure, the demand for the non-traded good is relevant only in determining its output. Note that the local market clearing condition for the non-traded good in equation (7.20) means that trade is balanced. This is because, by Walras' Law, when the local market for the non-traded good clears as indicated by equation (7.20), the sum of excess demand for the two traded goods must be zero. But this means that trade is balanced.

What follows from the above discussion is that for this type of production structure, the non-traded good does not essentially change the core propositions of the HOS model including the FPE theorem.

But the non-traded good does make a difference if, instead, the economy is completely specialized in its export good, or if in the incomplete specialization case (as specified above)

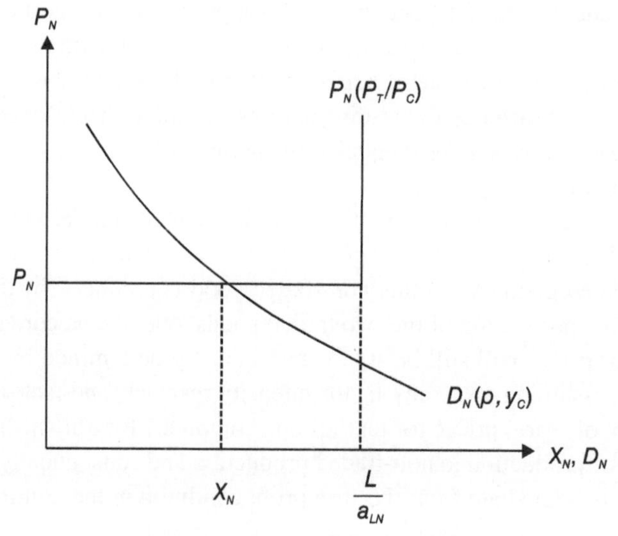

Figure 7.4 Non-traded Market

the non-traded good is produced by a specific factor, say, land (V), along with labour. In this specific factor case, the zero profit condition in equation (7.19) is now rewritten as:

$$P_N = a_{LN}W + a_{VN}R \tag{7.19a}$$

where R is the rate of return to land.

Now, factor prices cannot be solely determined by the prices of the traded commodities. This is understandable from the discussion of the specific factor model. What is more, and herein comes the role of the non-traded good, along with factor endowment, local demand conditions also influence factor prices. The essential difference between this case and the one where the production of the non-traded good requires the same factors of production as used in production of the traded commodities, is that the price of the non-traded good is no longer cost determined. With factor prices no longer being tied down by the world prices of textiles and computers, diminishing returns in land use raise the marginal cost of expanding the production of the non-traded good. The supply curve for the non-traded good is thus upward sloping so that changes in the demand for the non-traded good bring in changes in both its supply and its price. Consequently, all factor prices change even without any change in world prices of traded goods.

To exemplify, consider an exogenous change in consumers' taste away from textiles and computers towards the non-traded good. At the initial price P_N, this creates an excess demand and thus serves to raise the price of the non-traded good. With the corresponding demand for both labour and land increasing, the wage and the rate of return to land both should rise. In fact, similar to the price magnification effect discussed above in the context of the specific factor model, the rate of return to land will rise more than the wage increase, and this makes expanding the production of the non-traded good feasible through a less land intensive technique of production being used now. On the other hand, as the wage cost rises in both the traded sectors, given the world prices, these sectors contract, which in turn lowers the demand for capital and, therefore, its rate of return. Note that since capital is not used in the production of the non-traded good in this structure, it must find its employment in the traded sector. The fall in the rate of return to capital ensures this by inducing the producers to employ more capital-intensive techniques of production. Of course, the consequent release of some labour earlier employed in the traded sector will offset the initial wage increase to some extent, but not fully. Hence, an exogenous increase in the demand for the non-traded good *directly* affects factor prices in the home country.

The role of local demand for the non-traded good in determining factor prices and the break down of the one-to-one correspondence can be more clearly brought out, delineating it from the role of specific factors, in a two-by-two production structure of a composite traded good and a non-traded good model developed by Jones (1979). The idea is that since the home country is assumed to be small in the sense defined earlier and thus faces a set of prices of its traded commodities given exogenously, we can lump the two traded goods into a composite traded good (*T*). With this change, even if we assume that both the composite traded and the non-traded good are produced by the same set of factors—labour and capital—we still have a lesser number of traded goods than the domestic factors of production, and thus the factor prices can no longer be determined solely by the world prices of the traded goods. To fix the

Box 7.1 The Dutch Disease

During the 1980s, rapid development of sectors producing natural gas in the Netherlands caused the other traditional export sectors in the Dutch economy to contract significantly. A similar phenomenon occurred in UK and Norway. The non-traded sectors were less affected though. This Dutch Disease can be explained by using the SF production structure and the price magnification effect that it leads to. Suppose the world prices of computers rise, *ceteris paribus*, which raises the return to the capital specific to this sector. More importantly, referring back to equation (7.16a), money wage increases. This raises the wage cost in all the sectors and thereby squeezes out the other export sectors, the prices of which have not changed in the world market. The non-traded sectors will not be affected to the same extent because their prices are determined locally and thus can be adjusted to absorb part of the wage shock through rise in prices and passing it on to local consumers. Moreover, real income increase consequent upon the export sector boom may raise the local demand for the non-traded good to account for the rise in cost.

idea, consider the following set of conditions to specify this composite traded good, non-traded good framework:

$$P_T = a_{LT}W + a_{KT}r \tag{7.21}$$

$$P_N = a_{LN}W + a_{KN}r \tag{7.22}$$

$$a_{ij} = a_{ij}(W/r_j),\ i = L, K;\ j = T, N \tag{7.23}$$

$$L = a_{LT}X_T + a_{LN}X_N \tag{7.24}$$

$$K = a_{KT}X_T + a_{KN}X_N \tag{7.25}$$

$$D_N = D_{LN}(p, y) \tag{7.26}$$

$$y = pX_T + X_N \tag{7.27}$$

It is immediate now that the exogenously given world price of the traded good is not sufficient to determine two-factor returns. The price of the non-traded good depends on the its local demand condition and factor supplies or endowment, the latter coming into play both by determining the supply of the non-traded good and the produced real income, *y*. This is illustrated in Figure 7.5.

Now, a change in taste away from the traded good towards the non-traded good shifts the demand curve in Figure 7.5 to the right and raises the price of the non-traded good. This in turn changes factor prices similar to what has been discussed above. On the other hand, to see how changes in the factor endowment affect factor prices, suppose there is an exogenous increase in the economy's labour endowment. At initial prices, by the output magnification effect, this

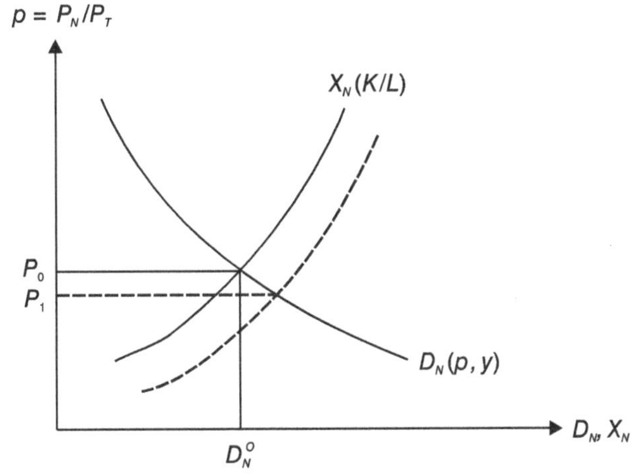

Figure 7.5 Local Market for the Non-traded Good

will raise the supply of the non-traded good if it is relatively labour intensive. This is shown by the rightward shift of the supply curve in Figure 7.5. Accordingly, the price of the non-traded good and hence the real exchange rate, given P_T, falls.

The consequent factor price changes can be worked as follows. Taking percentage changes of equations (7.21) and (7.22) following the steps elaborated in Appendix A6 with Chapter 6, the expressions below can be obtained:

$$\hat{P}_T = 0 = \theta_{LT}\hat{W} + \theta_{KT}\hat{r} \tag{7.28}$$

$$\hat{P}_N = \theta_{LN}\hat{W} + \theta_{KN}\hat{r} \tag{7.29}$$

Solving for changes in the factor prices yield:

$$\hat{W} = -\frac{\theta_{KT}}{|\theta|}\hat{P}_N,\ \hat{r} = \frac{\theta_{LT}}{|\theta|}\hat{P}_N \tag{7.30}$$

where $|\theta| = \theta_{LT}\theta_{KN} - \theta_{LN}\theta_{KT} < 0$ if the non-traded good is relatively labour-intensive, which is mostly the case because usually services are non-traded goods.

Referring back to our examples, an exogenous increase in the demand for the non-traded good raises the money wage and lowers the rate of return to capital by raising the price of the non-traded good. On the other hand, an exogenous increase in labour endowment lowers the money wage and raises the rate of return to capital by lowering the price of the non-traded good.

Hence, the factor prices are no longer independent of domestic demand and factor endowment conditions. Accordingly, the one-to-one correspondence breaks down, and with it goes away the FPE theorem. In fact, the comparative static result discussed above suggests why factor prices will not be equalized across countries through commodity trade. The change in relative wage obtained from equation (7.30) clarifies this point:

$$\hat{W}-\hat{r}=-\frac{(\theta_{KT}+\theta_{LT})}{|\theta|}\hat{P}_N=-\frac{1}{|\theta|}\hat{P}_N \tag{7.31}$$

Clearly, if the non-traded good is relatively labour-intensive, its price will be lower in the relatively labour-abundant country. Consequently, the relative wage should also be lower there compared to that in the foreign country. Thus, even though free commodity trade equalizes the price of the composite traded good everywhere, the FPE theorem fails to hold because the endowment differences of the countries will lead to different prices of the non-traded good and consequently different factor prices in different countries.

Note that the price magnification result still holds. This is immediate from equation (7.31). If the price of the non-traded good declines (as in case of growth in labour force) then money wage declines more than proportionately:

$$\hat{r}>\hat{P}_T=0>\hat{P}_N>\hat{W} \tag{7.32}$$

Thus, the real wage falls and the real return to capital rises.

7.3.3 Advanced Topic: FPE in Higher Dimensions

The above cases of a specific factor production structure and a non-traded good suggests a simple rule for the validity of the FPE theorem in higher dimensions with respect to the number of goods produced in an economy and the number of factors of production it is endowed with. Suppose there are m number of goods that are produced even after trade by n number of domestic factors of production, and among these goods t number of goods are being traded. Of course, $t \leq m$. With all other assumptions of the HOS model being satisfied, commodity trade will equalize factor prices across the trading nations if $m > t \geq n$. That is, the number of traded goods being produced is at least equal to the number of factors of production. The reason is simple. As demonstrated by Samuelson (1953), for $m > t = n$, given the prices of the traded goods, the t number of zero profit conditions for the traded goods and tn number of least-cost input choice condition specified below provides us a perfectly determinate system of $t + tn$ number of independent equations to solve for n number of factor prices and tn number of least-cost input choices:

$$P_j = a_{1j}W_1 + a_{2j}W_2 + \dots\dots\dots + a_{nj}W_n,\quad j = 1, 2, \dots t \tag{7.33}$$

$$a_{ij} = a_{ij}(W),\quad i = 1, 2, \dots, n; j = 1, 2, \dots t \tag{7.34}$$

where, W_i is the wage or return to the factor i, and W is the wage vector. Thus, factor prices get determined *solely* by the prices of the traded commodities in this instance, which is the basis for the FPE theorem. The factor prices being so determined, the zero profit conditions for the non-traded good along with conditions for the input choices in these sectors, on the other hand, determine the price of the non-traded good:

$$P_j = a_{1j}W_1 + a_{2j}W_2 + \cdots\cdots + a_{nj}W_n, \quad j = t+1, t+2, \ldots m \tag{7.35}$$

$$a_{ij} = a_{ij}(W), \quad i = 1, 2, \ldots, n; j = t+1, t+2, \ldots m \tag{7.36}$$

Thus, prices of non-traded goods are cost-determined here as discussed earlier. Note that for $m = t$, the equation system (7.35) and (7.36) drops out and we have an extension of the HOS model in $t \times n$ (or $m \times n$) dimension.

When $t > n$, the system of equations in (7.29) and (7.30) may seem to be *over determinate* as we have more equations to solve for the factor prices and the least-cost input combinations. But that is not the case because only n number of traded goods will be domestically produced with the rest $(t - n)$ traded goods being entirely imported. The reason is simple. Once the n number of factor prices get determined (along with the least-cost input choices) from *any n* number of zero profit conditions, given the price of these traded goods, the cost of production for the rest $(t - n)$ of the traded goods are tied down accordingly. The production costs for these $(t - n)$ traded goods thus determined by the prices of the *other* traded goods will most likely not match with their prices that are, in turn, determined in the respective world markets. If all these production costs exceed the prices, these goods will not be produced at all. If some of these production costs, on the other hand, are lower than the given prices, producers will shift resources from other sectors to reap the profit opportunities in these sectors. Factor prices will, therefore, change raising production costs in some of the n traded goods sectors causing them to shut down. Thus, at equilibrium, the economy will produce *at most* the n number of traded goods. The system is once again determinate meaning that the one-to-one correspondence and consequently the FPE theorem still hold good.

Finally consider the case in which the economy produces less traded goods than the factors of production it is endowed with. If there are no non-traded goods, this $m = t < n$ case essentially resembles the SF model. The price system is then indeterminate and factor prices are no longer determined solely by the prices of traded goods independent of the factor endowment conditions. Hence, the one-to-one correspondence breaks down and the FPE does not hold.

7.4 ADVANCED TOPIC: EVIDENCE ON WITHIN COUNTRY WAGE MOVEMENTS AND THE WAGE GAP DEBATE

The price magnification effects in the HOS model and its variants suggest that the return to the factor that is intensively used in or specific to the export good of a country must increase and the return to the factor used intensively in or specific to the import-competing good must decline as international trade opens up or is liberalized. The movement of factor prices should be in the opposite direction in its trading partner. This is because opening up of trade raises the relative price of textiles in one country and lowers it in its trading partner. Thus, *asymmetric relative price changes in trading nations lead to asymmetric wage movements in the two countries*. Empirical evidence regarding changes in factor prices during the last two decades and a half that mostly coincide with the era of globalization and trade liberalization is, however, at odds with this theoretical prediction. The wage inequality between skilled and unskilled workers has almost universally risen, except for a few East Asian countries. Different country studies and the findings by different researchers are summarized in Marjit and Acharyya (2003). Table 7.1 provides a snapshot version of this wage inequality or wage-gap phenomenon.

Table 7.1 Wage Inequality in Different Regions

	Skill Premium		Studies
	Widened	Narrowed	
Latin America	Chile, Mexico, Uruguay, Costa Rica		Robbins (1995a); Beyer et al. (1999); Pederson (1998)
Asia	China, HK, India, Sri Lanka	Korea, Taiwan, Singapore, Malaysia	Wood (1997); Robbins (1995b); Rodrigo (1988); Shariff and Gumber (1999)
Europe	Belgium, Denmark, Germany, UK		Lawrence (1994); Katz et al. (1992)
Other Regions	Australia, Canada, Japan, USA		Leamer (2000); Freeman and Katz (1994)

Source: Marjit and Acharyya (2003).

Thus, whereas the theory predicts *asymmetric wage movements* across countries, empirical observations suggest almost symmetric wage movements.[2] This has posed a serious theoretical challenge to the Stolper–Samuelson (SS) theorem or the price magnification effect to provide analytical explanations for two aspects of the observed phenomena: first, how does trade liberalization increase intra-country wage inequality in the developing countries given that they in general import skilled labour-intensive goods, and second, how does it increase intra-country wage inequality in *both* the developing and the developed countries alike. Since the turn of the millennium, there have emerged some notable theoretical analyses to explain these observations. One set of analyses that attempts to explain the first aspect, is based on the extension, generalization, and modification of the Stolper-Samuelson result by looking beyond the 2×2×2 HOS models and even beyond the competitive framework (Dogan 2008; Marjit and Acharyya 2003; Ruffin 2003; and Xu 2003). These analyses consider, separately or in combination, the production of non-traded goods, segmented domestic labour markets in developing countries, and a diverse trade pattern of some of the relatively advanced developing countries (like China and other East Asian countries, and India) that generates a complementarity between exports with different skill-intensity for such countries.

[2] Empirical observation regarding symmetric or global rise in wage inequality that is at odd with the predictions of HOS and the SS theorem has triggered a debate over its cause: trade versus technology. Different dogmatic positions taken by Alan Deardorff, Paul Krugman, Edward Leamer, and Arvind Panagariya among others in the debate over trade versus technology are summarized in Marjit and Acharyya (2003). See also Jones and Engerman (1996).

Box 7.2 Asymmetric Changes in Relative Wages across Different Skills

In Chile, India, and the US, relative wages for different skill or education levels have changed asymmetrically. In the US, relative to the wages of college graduates, wages of workers with some college education had *improved* whereas that of high school graduates had *declined* during 1985–94. In Chile, during the 1980s, in the age group 25–35 years, wage gap between university graduates and primary level educated workers increased but between secondary level and primary level educated workers *declined*. In India, compared to 1987–88, the relative wages of graduates in 1993–94 in a few manufacturing sectors declined relative to secondary level educated workers but improved relative to non-literates.

The specific factor model discussed above, suitably modified, can potentially offer a framework of analysis for such a phenomenon. On the other hand, Marjit and Acharyya (2003) provide an altogether different analytical explanation for the asymmetric changes in the wages of skilled workers vis-à-vis moderately-skilled and low-skilled workers.

There have been some explanations for the two-sided growing wage gap as well. Acharyya (2010) uses the same 2x2 HOS model as discussed in Chapter 6 but allows for a paradoxical change in the domestic relative price of imports when import tariffs are lowered successively. It is shown that the wage inequality may grow in both trading partners at later stages of trade liberalization. We will return to this explanation in a latter chapter. However, the major explanation comes from countries commonly producing 'middle' goods, in a multi-commodity setting of the HOS model, for which the local and global skill-intensity ranking differs (Davis 1996; Feenstra and Hanson 1996; Marjit and Acharyya 2003, 2006; Zhu and Trefler 2005). In Feenstra and Hanson (1996) and Zhu and Trefler (2005), the two countries specialize along the vertical production chain of a final good. Thus, the middle good is an intermediate stage of production. To explain, consider Figure 7.6 where a continuum of different stages of producing a final good is defined over the unit interval [0, 1] with increasing skilled–unskilled labour ratio as we consider successively higher stages of production in the vertical chain. That is, a higher order production stage, or the intermediate good that is produced at that stage, is more intensive in skilled labour relative to the immediate preceding stage of production. Suppose

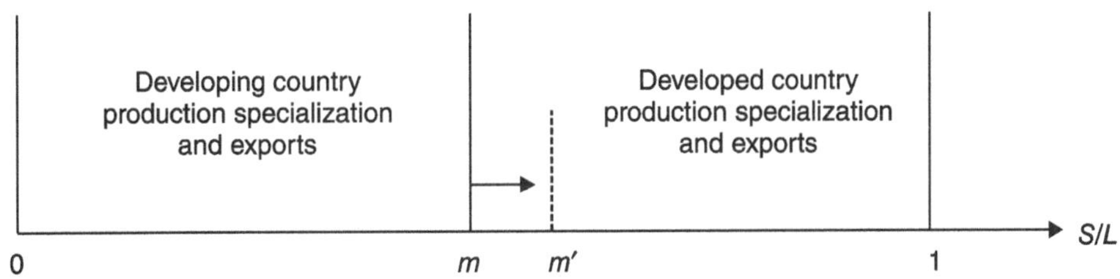

Figure 7.6 Local and Global Factor Intensity and Wage Inequality

pre-trade skilled and unskilled wages were such that all lower stages of production up to stage *m* were cost efficient in the developing country whereas all production stages higher than stage *m* including the final production stage were cost efficient in the developed country. Thus, the post-trade production specialization will be as indicated in Figure 7.6. Note that, similar to the Ricardian continuum good case, the intermediate good *m* will be produced by both the countries. However, the intermediate good required to produce the intermediate good at stage *m* (as well as the intermediate good *m* itself) will be imported by the developed country from the developing country, and the final good produced at the end of the production stages will be exported to the developing country. Note that the intermediate good *m* is the most skilled labour-intensive good that the developing country produces but the least skilled labour-intensive good that the developed country produces. That is, the *local factor intensity* of this commonly produced good differs in the two countries.

Now consider a capital inflow from or foreign direct investment (FDI) by the developed country that relocates production stage *m* and some other higher stages of production from the developed to the developing country. In Figure 7.1, this is shown by the production specialization in the developing country in a larger set of production stages over the interval $[0, m']$. These additional stages, defined by the upper sub-subset $[m, m']$, being successively more and more skill-intensive compared to the stages of production lower than stage *m*, the relative demand for skilled labour will increase in the developing country. The wage inequality thus will rise there. In the developed country, on the other hand, the relative demand for unskilled workers will decline because the stages of production that are now relocated in the developing country were the least skill-intensive or most unskilled labour-intensive stages of production in the developed country. Hence, wage inequality should rise in the developed country as well.

In contrast, Davis (1996) and Marjit and Acharyya (2003) couch their analyses in multi-country and multi-commodity settings respectively with trade and specialization in only *final goods* in a generalized HOS setting. Consider three goods *X*, *Y*, *Z* indexed according to the decreasing order of the skill-intensity for any given relative wage. That is, good *X* is the most skill-intensive and good *Z* is the least skill-intensive as shown by the rays through the origin in Figure 7.7. First of all, note that any country will produce only two of these three goods for reasons spelled out in the above section. Which pair of goods a country will produce, on the other hand, depends on its endowment of skilled labour relative to unskilled labour. The three rays through the origin indicating the relative skill-intensity ranking of the three goods produce two cones of diversification, $l_X O l_Y$ and $l_Y O l_Z$. These are called cones of diversification because if a country's relative endowment of skilled labour lies, say, in the cone $l_X O l_Y$ then the country will diversify by producing both the goods *X* and *Y*. Recall from our discussion in Chapter 6 that the condition for diversification (or incomplete specialization) is that the relative endowment of skilled labour must not be larger than (or smaller than) the skill-intensity of both the goods. If so, then the country will be completely specialized in the most (or least) skill-intensive good.

Now suppose that the factor endowments of the United States and India are so different that these endowment bundles lie in different cones of diversification as shown in Figure 7.7. Thus, whereas India produces the pair of goods (*Y*, *Z*), the United States produces the pair of

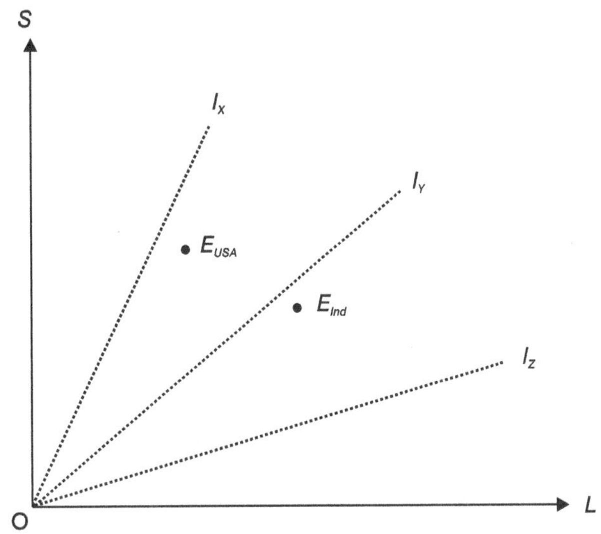

Figure 7.7 Cone of Diversification and Production Specialization

goods (X, *Y*).[3] Note that good *Y*, produced by both the countries, is the middle good in the global intensity ranking but is the least skill-intensive in the United States and most skill-intensive in India. Thus, similar to the continuum of production stages in Feenstra and Hanson (1996), the global and local intensity of the commonly produced good differs. Suppose, good *Y* is exported to the United States along with good *Z* and good *X* is imported from the United States by India. If the United States had earlier imposed a tariff on the import of good *Y*, which it now lowers or abolishes, increased import demand in the United States will raise the world price of good *Y* but lower the domestic price of it there. Note that though the increase in the world price of good *Y* will raise the local price of imports in the United States, this will in general be less than proportionate to the initial fall in the domestic price as a consequence of tariff reduction.[4] Since good *Y* is the least skill-intensive good there, by the price magnification effect skilled wage will increase and the unskilled wage will fall. Hence, the wage inequality will rise in the United States. On the other hand, the domestic price of good *Y* in India will rise proportionately with the rise in the world price of good *Y*. Good *Y* being the most skill-intensive in India, this price increase will raise wage inequality there by the price magnification effect. Thus, once again, the wage inequality rises in *both* the countries.

APPENDIX A7

I. Price Magnification Effect in the SF Model

Differentiating the full employment conditions in (7.13)–(7.15) and expressing in proportional change forms we obtain:

$$\hat{L} = \lambda_{LT}(\hat{X}_T + \hat{a}_{LT}) + \lambda_{LC}(\hat{X}_C + \hat{a}_{LC}) \tag{A7.1}$$

$$\hat{K}_T = \hat{X}_T + \hat{a}_{KT} \tag{A7.2}$$

$$\hat{K}_C = \hat{X}_C + \hat{a}_{KC} \tag{A.7.3}$$

Substitution of (A7.2) and (A7.3) in (A7.1) yields, using $\sigma_j = \dfrac{\hat{a}_{Kj} - \hat{a}_{Lj}}{\hat{W} - \hat{r}_j}$:

$$\begin{aligned}\hat{L} - \lambda_{LT}\hat{K}_T - \lambda_{KC}\hat{K}_C &= \lambda_{LT}(\hat{a}_{LT} - \hat{a}_{KT}) + \lambda_{LC}(\hat{a}_{LC} - \hat{a}_{KC})\\ &= -\lambda_{LT}\sigma_T(\hat{W} - \hat{r}_T) - \lambda_{LC}\sigma_C(\hat{W} - \hat{r}_C)\end{aligned} \tag{A7.4}$$

On the other hand, from the zero profit conditions we obtain:

$$\hat{P}_T = \theta_{LT}\hat{W} + \theta_{KT}\hat{r}_T \tag{A7.5}$$

$$\hat{P}_C = \theta_{LC}\hat{W} + \theta_{KC}\hat{r}_C \tag{A.7.6}$$

Solving for the rates of return for sector-specific capitals and substituting the values in A7.4, we obtain:

$$\begin{aligned}\hat{L} - \lambda_{LT}\hat{K}_T - \lambda_{KC}\hat{K}_C &= -\lambda_{LT}\sigma_T\left[\hat{W} - \frac{1}{\theta_{KT}}\hat{P}_T + \frac{\theta_{LT}}{\theta_{KT}}\hat{W}\right] - \lambda_{LC}\sigma_C\left[\hat{W} - \frac{1}{\theta_{KC}}\hat{P}_C + \frac{\theta_{LC}}{\theta_{KC}}\hat{W}\right]\\ &= -\left(\frac{\lambda_{LT}}{\theta_{KT}}\sigma_T + \frac{\lambda_{LC}}{\theta_{KC}}\sigma_C\right)\hat{W} + \frac{\lambda_{LT}}{\theta_{KT}}\sigma_T\hat{P}_T + \frac{\lambda_{LC}}{\theta_{KC}}\sigma_C\hat{P}_C\end{aligned}$$

$$\Rightarrow \gamma\hat{W} = \gamma_T\hat{P}_T + \gamma_C\hat{P}_C - \left[\hat{L} - \lambda_{LT}\hat{K}_T - \lambda_{KC}\hat{K}_C\right] \tag{A7.7}$$

where $\gamma = \left(\dfrac{\lambda_{LT}}{\theta_{KT}}\sigma_T + \dfrac{\lambda_{LC}}{\theta_{KC}}\sigma_C\right)$, $\gamma_T = \dfrac{\lambda_{LT}}{\theta_{KT}}\sigma_T$, $\gamma_C = \dfrac{\lambda_{LC}}{\theta_{KC}}\sigma_C$

Thus, for no changes in endowment, a proportional change in money wage is weighted average of the proportional changes in commodity prices, so that if the relative price of textiles rises more than proportionately then:

$$\hat{P}_T > \hat{W} > \hat{P}_C$$

This combined with (A7.5) and (A7.6) yields the price magnification effect:

$$\hat{r}_T > \hat{P}_T > \hat{W} > \hat{P}_C > \hat{r}_C \qquad \text{(A7.8)}$$

II. Growth in Labour Force and Relative Supply

From (A7.2) and (A7.3) the change in relative supply, for $\hat{K}_T = \hat{K}_C = 0$, can be obtained as:

$$\hat{X}_T - \hat{X}_C = -\hat{a}_{KT} + \hat{a}_{KC} \qquad \text{(A7.9)}$$

As derived in Appendix A6 (with Chapter 6), from the cost-minimization condition:

$$\hat{a}_{KT} = \hat{a}_{KT} - \theta_{LT}\hat{a}_{LT} - \theta_{KT}\hat{a}_{KT} = \theta_{LT}(\hat{a}_{KT} - \hat{a}_{LT}) = \sigma_T\theta_{LT}(\hat{W} - \hat{r}_T)$$

$$\hat{a}_{KC} = \hat{a}_{KC} - \theta_{LC}\hat{a}_{LC} - \theta_{KC}\hat{a}_{KC} = \theta_{LC}(\hat{a}_{KC} - \hat{a}_{LC}) = \sigma_C\theta_{LC}(\hat{W} - \hat{r}_C)$$

Substitution of these values in (A7.9) yields:

$$\hat{X}_T - \hat{X}_C = -\sigma_T\theta_{LT}(\hat{W} - \hat{r}_T) + \sigma_C\theta_{LC}(\hat{W} - \hat{r}_C) \qquad \text{(A7.10)}$$

From (A7.5) and (A7.6), solving for factor price changes for no change in commodity prices as:

$$\hat{r}_T = -\frac{\theta_{LT}}{\theta_{KT}}\hat{W} \text{ and } \hat{r}_C = -\frac{\theta_{LC}}{\theta_{KC}}\hat{W}$$

Substitution of these values along with $\gamma\hat{W} = \hat{L}$ from (A7.7) in (A7.10) yields the expression in the text:

$$\hat{X}_T - \hat{X}_C = \frac{1}{\gamma}\left[\sigma_T\frac{\theta_{LT}}{\theta_{KT}} - \sigma_C\frac{\theta_{LC}}{\theta_{KC}}\right]\hat{L} \qquad \text{(A7.11)}$$

SUMMARY POINTS

- In an empirical test of the HO theorem, Leontief (1954) observed that in 1947 and 1951 the United States was exporting relatively labour-intensive goods to the rest of the world, though it was by far the most capital-abundant country in the world. Further tests for the 1962 data supported this finding, known as the Leontief Paradox.
- Theoretical explanations of the Leontief Paradox include a stronger taste bias, factor intensity reversal, and cross-country technology differences. Leontief's own position was that the United States was technologically quite advanced and its workers were more productive compared to most of the countries.
- The HOV theory or the theory of *factor content of trade,* a generalization of the HO theorem by Jaroslav Vanek (1968), provides the theoretical basis for empirical tests of the HO theorem in more recent periods.

(contd)

Summary Points (*contd*)

- By the measure of factor content of trade—how much of a factor is embodied in a traded good—the HOV theorem tells us that factor i will tend to be used more intensively in exports than in imports by a country which has a larger share of world stock of factor i.
- Factors of production may have sector-specific use, or they may be immobile across sectors. In such cases, the factor prices are no longer *solely* determined by commodity prices, regardless of factor endowment conditions. Consequently, commodity price equalization through free commodity trade will not lead to factor price equalization across the trading nations. The price and the output magnification effects do not hold either.
- Many services are actually location-specific and cannot be dissociated from the service providers. Such services are non-traded services. For goods, tradability depends on both transport costs and their perishable nature.
- The law of one price does not hold for non-traded goods because arbitrage is not possible. Their prices are *locally* determined, and their output levels are constrained by local demand conditions.
- Domestic demand conditions, along with factor endowment conditions, now influence factor prices; this may invalidate the FPE theorem.
- Whereas theory predicts *asymmetric wage movements* across countries, empirical observations suggest almost symmetric wage movements. The major explanation comes from countries commonly producing a 'middle' good, in a multi-commodity or continuum of stages of production setting, for which the local and global skill-intensity rankings differ.

KEYWORDS

- **Leontief paradox** refers to the paradoxical findings of W.W. Leontief that the United States of America exported relatively labour-intensive goods and imported relatively capital-intensive goods from the rest of the world in the immediate post–World War II period so that its trade pattern was not consistent with its capital abundance.
- **Factor content of trade** is a measure of how much of a factor is embodied in the traded goods taken together for a country.
- **Heckscher–Ohlin–Vanek (HOV) theorem** states that if a country has a larger share of the world stock of a factor than its share in world income, then this factor will be used more intensively in its exports than in its imports.
- **Non-traded goods** are those which due to their very high transport costs or perishable nature can neither be exported nor imported. Their markets are essentially local. Freshly prepared food is a typical example. Many services, like hair cuts, are also non-tradable.
- **Real exchange rate** is the price of traded goods relative to the price of non-traded goods.

EXERCISES

1. Suppose China has superior technology in producing textiles that requires less workers and smaller units of capital per unit of output than capital and labour required to produce per unit of textiles in Bangladesh. The technology in producing leather manufacture is the same in the two countries. Bangladesh has more workers than China but the same endowment of physical capital, and leather manufacture is relatively more capital-intensive everywhere. Should the pattern of trade between Bangladesh and China follow the HO pattern of trade? Assume that tastes are identical and homothetic.
2. Three goods are produced in India by labour, capital, and land. The technology matrix (the numbers in first row indicate per unit labour requirements in the three sectors and those in the second row indicate per unit capital requirements in the three sectors), and trade vectors are given as:

$$\left[a_{ij}\right] = \begin{bmatrix} 1 & 2 & 3 \\ 2 & 3 & 1 \\ 3 & 2 & 1 \end{bmatrix}, T = \begin{bmatrix} 10 \\ -20 \\ 12 \end{bmatrix}$$

   Find out the factor content of trade for each factor and identify in which factor(s) India's exports are intensive.
3. In the above example, suppose $Y_i = 500$, $Y_W = 50{,}000$, $L_i = 100$, $L_W = 20{,}000$, $T_i = 300$, $T_W = 25{,}000$. Check whether the HOV theorem holds for India's trade with the rest of the world (W).
4. Draw the PPF in a fixed coefficient 2×3 SF model with capital and land being specific factors in the industry and agriculture and labour the mobile factor when:
   (a) Only capital and land constraints are binding.
   (b) All three constraints are binding for different combinations of industrial and agricultural output levels.

   In the second case, depict an autarchic equilibrium with only labour being fully employed.
5. Explain that unemployment in the SF model is technology driven.
6. A country produces office equipments (O) and garments (G) using skilled and unskilled labour respectively in combination with capital.
   (a) Algebraically prove that a *ceteris paribus* exogenous increase in the endowment of skilled workers will raise the production of office equipment less than proportionately.
   (b) How does your answer change when a fixed proportion of the unskilled workers gets trained and instantaneously acquires the skill required to produce office equipment?
7. In the above context, show that if endowments of both types of labour increase exogenously, the relative supply of office equipment will increase ($\hat{X}_O - \hat{X}_G > 0$) if

$$\frac{\sigma_O}{\sigma_G} = \frac{\theta_{SO}\theta_{KG}}{\theta_{LG}\theta_{KO}}.$$

8. [Advanced] Consider an economy producing an agricultural good, rice, and a manufacturing good, textiles, using the same type of labour and same type of capital. Let L_R number of workers be initially living in rural areas and engaged in rice cultivation. In

(contd)

Exercises (*contd*)

the urban areas live L_U number of workers who work in textile factories. Workers cannot migrate from either region in the short run, but capital can be shifted from one production to the other. The country trades both these goods with the rest of the world and is a large country. In such a context, how does an exogenous growth in capital stock change the TOT of the country if it exports the agricultural good?

9. In an SF model, the workers, who are used in the production of both the goods, spend 20 per cent of their wage income on good *X* and rest on good *Y*. *Ceteris paribus*, in the year 2012 the world prices of good *X* and good *Y* increased by 15 and 10 per cent respectively over their prices in the previous year. Recalling from equation (A7.7) that $\hat{W} = \frac{\gamma_X}{\gamma}\hat{P}_X + \frac{\gamma_Y}{\gamma}\hat{P}_Y$, check whether the real wage will increase or decrease if $\gamma_X = 2$ and $\gamma_Y = 3$.
10. In the above exercise, if the prices rise as a consequence of globalization and the policy of integration of the Indian economy with the world economy, how do the different factor owners react to such a policy? If the Government of India, being a democratic government, pursues a policy only if it is supported by a majority of the factor owners, should this policy be pursued? How does your answer change when the workers do not consume good *Y*?
11. Consider a small open economy producing a composite traded good and a non-traded good with two factors of production, labour and capital. Assume homothetic taste such that $\frac{D_T}{D_N} = f(p)$, where *p* is the real exchange rate. Show that an exogenous increase in the world price of the composite traded good leaves the real exchange rate unchanged. [Hint: Define the absolute value of relative demand elasticity as $\varepsilon = -\frac{\hat{D}_T - \hat{D}_N}{\hat{P}_T - \hat{P}_N}$. Then use the market clearing condition $\hat{D}_T - \hat{D}_N = \hat{X}_T - \hat{X}_N$ and the supply relationship similar to the one derived in Chapter 6, to show that $\hat{P}_N = \hat{P}_T$.]
12. In the above exercise, how do factor prices change? What does your finding signify?
13. With a fixed money wage, how does an exogenous increase in the world price of the composite good change the real exchange rate?
14. [Advanced] In the same framework as in Exercise 11, suppose the government pegs the money wage at a level higher than the money wage that ensures full employment of all factors for any given P_T. Work out the effect of this rigid-wage policy on: (i) price of the non-traded good and (ii) aggregate employment.
15. [Advanced] Suppose India produces software, leather manufacture, and rice. Rice is produced by unskilled labour and land, leather manufacture by unskilled labour and capital, and software by skilled labour and capital. India exports both rice and software, and imports leather manufacture from the rest of the world. If there is a *ceteris paribus* increase in the world price of rice, how does unskilled wage change? Does the wage inequality between skilled and unskilled workers in India decline as a result?

(*contd*)

Exercises (*contd*)

16. [Advanced] Suppose three goods *X*, *Y*, and *Z* can be produced using skilled and unskilled workers in fixed proportions such that good *Z* is the most skill-intensive and good *X* is the least skill-intensive. When does the local and global intensity ranking of good *Y* differ in China and Japan? Using such a scenario where local and global factor intensity rankings differ from each other, construct a case where trade liberalization by either China or Japan lowers wage inequality in both the countries.

SUGGESTED READING

Caves, R.E., J. Frankel, and R.W. Jones (1995). *World Trade and Payments*. New York: HarperCollins College Publishers.

Leamer, E.E. (1984). *Sources of International Comparative Advantage: Theory and Evidence*. Cambridge, MA: MIT Press.

Marjit, S. and R. Acharyya (2003). *International Trade, Wage Inequality and the Developing Countries: A General Equilibrium Approach*. Heidelberg: Physica/Springer Verlag.

Rivera Batiz, L.A. and M.A. Oliva (2003). *International Trade: Theory, Strategies and Evidence*. Oxford: Oxford University Press.

Trefler, D. (1993). 'International Factor Price Differences: Leontief was Right!', *Journal of Political Economy*, 101: 961–87.

ADVANCED READING

Acharyya, R. (2010). 'Successive Trade Liberalization and Wage Inequality', *Keio Economic Studies*, 46: 29–42.

Beyer, H., P. Rojas, and R. Vergara (1999). 'Trade Liberalization and Wage Inequality', *Journal of Development Economics*, 59: 103–23.

Brown, H.P., E.E. Leamer, and L. Sveikauskas (1987). 'Multicountry, Multifactor Test of the Factor Abundance Theory', *American Economic Review*, 77: 791–809.

Davis, D. (1996). 'Trade Liberalization and Income Distribution', NBER Working Paper No. 5693.

Davis, D.R. and D.E. Weinstein (2001). 'An Account of Global Factor Trade', *American Economic Review*, 91(5): 1423–53.

Dogan, C. (2008). 'Three Essays on Trade, Distribution, and Tariffs', PhD dissertation, The University of Houston.

Feenstra, R. and G. Hanson (1996). 'Foreign Investment, Outsourcing and Relative Wages', in R. Feenstra, G. Grossman, and D. Irwin (eds), *Political Economy of Trade Policies. Essays in Honour of J.N. Bhagwati*. Cambridge, MA: MIT Press.

——— (2001). 'Global Production Sharing and Rising Inequality: A Survey of Trade and Wages', NBER Working Paper No. 8372.

Freeman, R., and L. Katz (1994). 'Rising Wage Inequality: The United States vs. Other Advanced Countries', in R. Freeman (ed.), *Working Under Different Rules*. New York: Russell Sage Foundation, pp. 29–62.

Jones, R.W. (1971). 'A Three Factor Model in Trade, Theory and History', in J.N. Bhagwati, R.W. Jones, R.A. Mundell, and J. Vanek (eds), *Trade, Balance of Payments and Growth: Essays in Honor of C.P. Kindleberger.* Amsterdam: North-Holland.

——— (1979). *International Trade: Essays in Theory*. Amsterdam: North-Holland,

Jones, R.W. and S.L. Engerman (1996). 'Trade, Technology and Wages. A Tale of Two Countries', *American Economic Review*, 86: 35–40.

Katz, L., G.W. Loveman, and D.G. Blanchflower. (1992). 'A Comparison of Changes in the Structure of Wages in Four OECD Countries', NBER Working Paper No. 4297.

Lawrence, R.Z. (1994). 'Trade, Multinationals and Labour', NBER Working Paper No. 4836.

Leamer, E. (2000). 'What's the Use of Factor Contents?', *Journal of International Economics*, 50: 51–71.

Leontief, W.W. (1954). 'Domestic Production and Foreign Trade: The American Capital Position Re-examined', *Economia Internazionale*, 7: 3–32.

Marjit, S. and R. Acharyya. (2006). 'Trade Liberalization, Skill-Linked Intermediate and Two-Sided Wage-Gap', *Journal of Policy Reform*, 9(3): 303–17.

Mussa, M. (1974). 'Tariffs and the Distribution of Income. The Importance of Factor Specificity, Substitutability and Intensity in the Short and Long Run', *Journal of Political Economy*, 82: 1191–1204.

Pedersen, K. (1998). 'Comment on Trade and Employment in Latin America', in O. Memedovic, A. Kuyvnhoven, and W. Molleet (eds), *Globalization of Labour Markets. Challenges, Adjustments and Policy Response in the European Union and Less Developed Countries*. USA: Kluwer Academic Publishers.

Robbins, D. (1995a). 'Earnings Dispersion in Chile after Trade Liberalization', Harvard Institute for International Development, Working Paper.

——— (1995b). 'Trade, Trade Liberalization and Inequality in Latin America and East Asia. Synthesis of Seven Country Studies', Harvard Institute of International Development, Working Paper.

Rodrigo, C. (1988). *Employment, Wages and Income Distribution in Sri Lanka*. New Delhi: ILO/ARTEP.

Ruffin, R.J. (2003). 'Oligopoly and Trade: What, How Much, and For Whom?', *Journal of International Economics*, 60: 315–35.

Samuelson, P.A. (1953). 'Prices of Factors and Goods in General Equilibrium', *Review of Economic Studies*, 21(1):1–20.

Shariff, A. and A. Gumber (1999). 'Employment and Wages in India: Pre and Post Reforms', *Indian Journal of Labour Economics*, 42: 195–216.

Stern, R.M and K.E. Maskus. (1981). 'Determinants of the Structure of U.S. Foreign Trade, 1958–1976', *Journal of International Economics*, 11: 207–24.

Vanek, J. (1968). 'The Factor Proportions Theory: N-Factor Case', *Kyklos*, 21(4): 749–56.

Wood, A. (1997). 'Openness and Wage Inequality in Developing Countries: The Latin American Challenge to East Asian Conventional Wisdom', *World Bank Research Observer*, 11(1): 33–57.

Xu, B. (2003). 'Trade Liberalization, Wage Inequality and Endogenously determined Nontraded Goods', *Journal of International Economics*, 60(2): 417–43.

Zhu, S. and D. Trefler. (2005). 'Trade and Inequality in Developing Countries: A General Equilibrium Analysis', *Journal of International Economics*, 65(1): 21–48.

PART III

Basis and Gains from Intra-industry Trade

8 Theories of Intra-industry Trade

In a now well-known book *Intra-industry Trade: The Theory and Measurement of International Trade in Differentiated Products* (1975), Grubel and Lloyd noted that a majority of the world trade has two important characters that are not well explained by the standard trade theories discussed so far. First, that trade among similar countries—amongst advanced industrialized nations in particular, or North–North trade—is much larger in magnitude and proportion of the world trade than trade among dissimilar countries, that is, between rich and the poor countries or North–South trade. Arbitrage thus does not seem to be a major driver of world trade since its scope is rather limited among similar or Northern countries. Second, a large proportion of world trade is in *similar* products, that is, intra-industry rather than inter-industry in character.

Table 8.1 documents the pattern and growth of intra-industry trade during more recent periods. As it appears, there are wide variations in the share of intra-industry trade in manufacture, ranging from 77.5 per cent for France to 29.8 per cent for Australia during 1996–2000. For countries like Austria, Canada, France, Germany, the Netherlands, Spain, Switzerland, and UK, the share of intra-industry trade (IIT) in total manufacturing trade is more than 70 per cent. Shares of IIT in *total* trade, however, are much lower than these numbers. For all countries taken together, 27 per cent of the world trade was intra-industry in 2006.

Grubel and Lloyd's observations laid the foundation for the development of new trade theories beginning in the late 1970s with Paul Krugman's explanation of IIT under monopolistic competition and James Brander's theorization of IIT under oligopolistic competition, which later came to be known as the strategic trade theory. These pioneering works and their subsequent generalizations and extensions offer explanations of trade in similar products among similar countries in terms of economies of scale, imperfect competition, and product differentiation. Figure 8.1 depicts the taxonomy of alternative theories and explanations of intra-industry trade.

In all these different categories of IIT theory, the common underlying assumption is that the trading partners are identical with respect to their endowments, technology, and taste patterns. This is to purposely rule out the scope for arbitrage and the basis of trade arising out of the dissimilarity of countries, and to instead locate the basis of IIT solely in market imperfection and economies of scale.

International Economics. Rajat Acharyya, Oxford University Press. © Oxford University Press 2022.
DOI: 10.1093/oso/9780192865144.003.0008

Table 8.1 Intra-industry Trade

Country	Manufacturing IIT as Percentage of Total Manufacturing Trade		
	1988–91	1992–95	1996–2000
Australia	28.6	29.8	29.8
Austria	71.8	74.3	74.2
Canada	73.5	74.7	76.2
Denmark	61.6	63.4	64.8
Finland	53.8	53.2	53.9
France	75.9	77.6	77.5
Germany	67.1	72.0	72.0
Greece	42.8	39.5	36.9
Italy	61.6	64.0	64.7
Japan	37.6	40.8	47.6
Korea	41.4	50.6	57.5
Mexico	62.5	74.4	73.4
Netherlands	69.2	70.4	68.9
New Zealand	37.2	38.4	40.6
Portugal	52.4	56.3	61.3
Spain	68.2	72.1	71.2
Sweden	64.2	64.6	66.6
Switzerland	69.8	71.8	72.0
Turkey	36.7	36.2	40.0
United Kingdom	70.1	73.1	73.7
United States	63.5	65.3	68.5

Source: OECD International Trade Statistics.

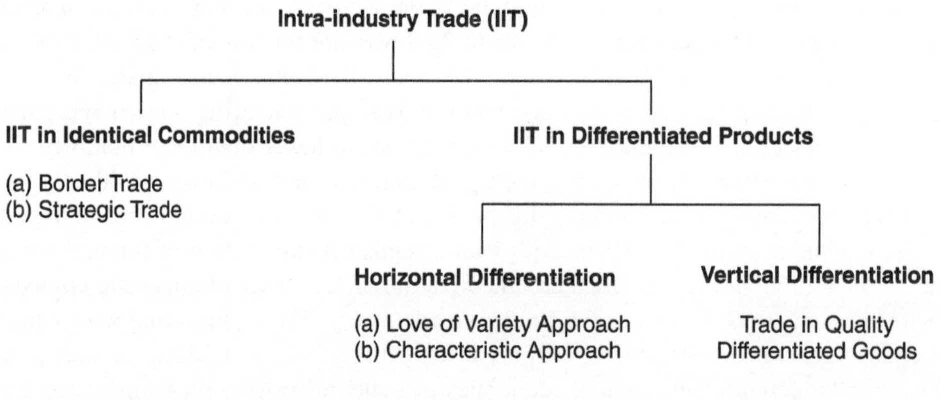

Figure 8.1 Types of Intra-industry Trade and Alternative Theories

8.1 IIT IN IDENTICAL PRODUCTS

IIT in identical products may arise for two reasons. The first and the simplest reason lies in transport costs. Consider two large neighbouring countries Canada and the US. When transport costs increase with the distance that a good is transported then it is cost minimizing for a trader to buy a good from a production location nearest to his selling location. If transport costs are the same regardless of the destination, being within the same or across political boundaries, and there is free movement of goods across countries, then the nearest production location may well be across the border. For example, it may be cost saving for an American seller in the Buffalo county region to import a good from border-states in Canada rather than transporting the same good from production units in California or Arizona in the United States.

Similar incentives may exist for a Canadian seller in British Columbia for importing the same good from the border-states of the United States such as Alaska or Washington DC, to save on transport cost. Thus, transport costs may explain this type of *border trade* in identical goods. However, note that this explanation holds only for trading nations that have a large common border and are themselves large geographically so that transporting a good from a production location within the country is costlier than transporting the same good from a production location in the other country.

The second reason why IIT in identical products can arise is rooted in the motive for reciprocal dumping under market imperfections. This explanation does not require trading partners to have common borders or be geographically large themselves. James Brander (1981) was the first to offer this explanation for IIT in identical goods among similar countries, which was subsequently refined and extended by James Brander and Paul Krugman (1983). A voluminous body of literature grew thereafter with different underlying assumptions regarding the market structure and the strategic interaction not only among firms but also among national governments in terms of their trade policy instruments. For these defining characteristics of strategic interaction, this body of IIT literature is also known as the *strategic trade theory*.

Suppose computers of an identical variety are being produced in India and the United States by monopoly firms in each country. The production technology is the same everywhere and exhibits constant returns to scale. Setting aside other goods that are being produced under perfectly competitive conditions in India, the domestic market for computers is depicted in Figure 8.2. Suppose the local demand for computers varies linearly with its price, and the marginal cost of production is constant with no fixed costs of production whatsoever. The pre-trade price for computers in India will be the monopoly price charged by the sole Indian

Box 8.1 Linder Hypothesis: Demand Similarity

Much before the development of new trade theories motivated by Grubel and Lloyd's observations, Staffan Burenstam Linder (1961) emphasized the similarity of demand as a determinant of trade. In addition to emphasizing on similarity, he proposed a demand based theory of trade in contrast to the usual supply based theories involving technology and factor endowment asymmetries. Linder hypothesized that nations with *similar demands* would develop *similar industries* and would trade with each other in similar, but differentiated goods. His idea was that countries have similar demands for manufacturing with others that have similar per capita income levels. This is particularly important when new products are introduced by a country. Thus, the trade patterns in manufacturing are dependent on the similarity of preference among nations.

producer for which its marginal revenue and marginal cost are equal. If the American monopoly producer has an identical production technology and faces the same local demand conditions in the United States for computers, it will charge the same monopoly price there under no trade. If the local demand and cost conditions for the other goods produced under perfectly competitive conditions are identical in both the countries as well, then the pre-trade relative prices will be the same and there will be no scope for arbitrage. This is what is known as the *market symmetry* property as assumed by Brander (1981) and, in fact, in almost all these classes of models, to rule out comparative (price) advantage as an explanation of trade between countries. The constant marginal cost of production, on the other hand, causes the markets to be *segmented* from the production aspect in the sense that output decisions in one market do not depend on output decisions in other markets. We will return to this *market segmentation* property and its implication later.

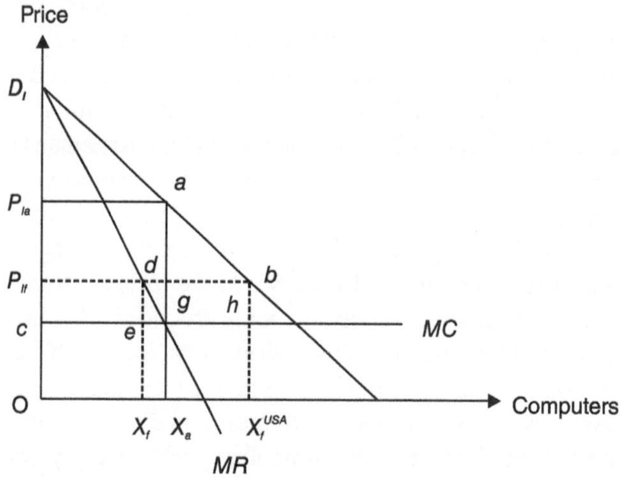

Figure 8.2 Market in India, Reciprocal Dumping, and IIT

But despite the market symmetry property and consequently even without the scope of arbitrage, trade between India and the United States will take place. The reason is simple. When all trade barriers are removed and firms are allowed to sell in each other's markets, the Indian firm realizes that profit opportunity exists in the US market as the price there is higher than the marginal cost of production. By dumping part of its production in the US market it can gain a market share there as this will raise supply, bring down prices, and thereby induce American consumers to buy its computers. Similar incentive for dumping its produce in the Indian market exists for the American producer.

Thus, trade takes place in an identical variety of computers through reciprocal dumping, despite the pre-trade price of computers being the same in both the countries thus leaving no scope for arbitrage. *The source or basis of trade here is the market power of firms.* Note that if the good was produced under perfectly competitive conditions in both the countries, the pre-trade price of computers would equal the marginal cost. Hence, there would have been no profit opportunity for either firm to export (or dump) goods in the other's market. This is because the price would then fall below the marginal cost so that the firm would incur a loss by exporting the good.

Post trade, in each country market there will be duopolistic competition between the domestic and the foreign firm. Brander (1981) characterized such competition as the Cournot type so that each firm chooses its profit maximizing output level, but not the price, given the other's output level. The post-trade price in both the countries, once again being identical by market symmetry property, will therefore be strictly above the marginal cost. Hence, pre-trade profit opportunities of reciprocal dumping (and exports) are actually realized after trade.

That countries gain through this reciprocal dumping and consequent IIT in identical products is easy to check. Consumers everywhere will gain from the lower price of computers through the pro-competitive effect. Of course, the local producer's profit declines due to competition from the foreign firm, but this is partly compensated by its profit from exports. Overall, each country gains from IIT. In Figure 8.2, if the post-trade price is P_{If} in India, the consumers' surplus increases from the area aD_IP_{Ia} to bD_IP_{If}. The Indian firm's profit changes from $aP_{Ia}cg$ to $dP_{If}ce$ from local sales and *dehb* from exports. Note that since Indian and the American firms are identical, they have equal shares in their respective local and export markets. The profits will thus be equal in each market. Hence, the area $dP_{If}ce$ that actually measures the profit for the American firm from selling computers in the Indian market, will also measure the Indian firm's profit from exports of computers to the US market under the market symmetry assumption. Given this market symmetry and consequent *profit symmetry*—profit from exports being the same for both the firms—the net *increase* in total surplus for India is measured by the area *abgh*. Under the market symmetry property, the United States gain by the exact magnitude.

Note that the above arguments for reciprocal dumping and consequently IIT in the same variety of computers would prevail if instead of monopoly producers in India and the United States, there had been identical oligopoly producers who compete among themselves in the Cournot fashion. The only difference in that case would have been that by the pro-competitive effect, the pre-trade price in each country would have been lower than the monopoly price (but still strictly above the marginal cost). The post-trade price would have been lower as well than the one with post-trade duopoly.

The cost of transporting goods to another location from the point of production, which is pivotal in the argument for border trade, can also be incorporated into the analysis. Following Samuelson's iceberg model of transport cost, Brander (1981) assumed that a fraction of output is lost or damaged in transit while exporting the good. For example, if 100 computers are exported to the United States, only 90 computers are delivered in good condition. Thus, whereas the production cost is incurred on exports of 100 computers, revenues for only 90 computers are earned by the Indian producer. The profit from exports is thus less than the area *dehb*. A higher transport cost means more computers are damaged in transit, and hence even smaller profit from exports. On the other hand, though consumers gain from the pro-competitive effect and larger production and consumption (by the magnitude $X_fX_f^{USA}$ in Figure 8.2), the production diversion (by the magnitude of X_fX_a in Figure 8.2) from the low cost domestic producer to the high cost US firm entails a loss. Note the transport cost effectively makes the US firm a high-cost firm in the Indian market. Similar loss is borne by the United States. For small enough transport costs, the countries still gain from IIT. But for larger transport costs, the profit from exports for a firm may be too small to compensate for its losses due to foreign competition in its own market. The cost of production diversion to the foreign supplier is larger too. Hence, the country may lose overall. In Appendix A8, the algebraic presentation of Brander's (1981) analysis derives the range of transport costs for which countries gain from IIT in identical products.

8.2 IIT IN HORIZONTALLY DIFFERENTIATED PRODUCTS

Economies of scale, or increasing returns to scale technology, which itself gives rise to market power for firms, is a main explanation for IIT in *differentiated* products. The theoretical explanations for this category of IIT are couched in terms of a monopolistically competitive market environment under the assumptions of economies of scale and different varieties of the same good that are distinct and yet close substitutes of each other. Economies of scale do not allow a particular variety to be produced by more than two firms. Thus, each firm has monopoly power over the variety it produces. At the same time, the varieties are assumed to be close substitutes to each other in consumption and hence to compete with each other. The market power of firms is thus limited. Given such a monopolistically competitive market environment, two distinct theoretical explanations have emerged that differ with respect to the characterization of consumers' preferences and the nature of the differentiated varieties. One is Paul Krugman's (1979) analysis based on Dixit and Stiglitz's (1977) 'love for variety' approach and the other is Helpman's (1981) analysis based on the 'characteristics' approach developed by Lancaster (1979).

8.2.1 Love for Variety Approach, Monopolistic Competition, and IIT

Paul Krugman in his seminal works in 1979 and 1980, used the Chamberlinian monopolistic competition and the Dixit-Stiglitz type consumer preference for a love for variety to offer his explanation of IIT in differentiated products. By the love for variety specification, a typical consumer prefers variety and thus buys *all* the varieties that are available in the market. Her utility improves not only from the number of units of each variety that she consumes, but more importantly from the number of varieties that she can consume. Thus, if n varieties are available in the market, then the simplest way to capture her preference is through the following additively separable utility function:

$$U = v(c_1) + v(c_2) + v(c_3) + \ldots\ldots + v(c_n),\ v'(c_i) > 0,\ v''(c_i) < 0 \tag{8.1}$$

where c_i is the unit of the i-th variety purchased and consumed. Note that all varieties enter her utility function in the same way, meaning that a particular variety per se does not matter. What matters to her is the number of varieties that she consumes. This is not something which is unusual because in the Chamberlinian product variety concept, varieties are superficially differentiated from each other. On the other hand, examples of love for variety are not hard to find. The typical example is that of dress material. When we buy more than one shirt, it is highly unlikely that we will buy two shirts of the same colour. We may have a preference for a particular colour, green or blue or grey, but here this is immaterial. Despite our preference for a particular colour, we do mix our wardrobes with shirts of different colours because we love variety. Similar love for variety is evident in purchase of neck-ties, shoes, contact lenses, ear-rings, ice-creams of different flavours, and the like.

Now, consider two countries Germany and France, each having n number of firms, that produce the same differentiated good with increasing returns to scale (IRS) technology. Since under IRS, no single variety can be produced by more than one firm, there will be exactly n number of varieties of the good produced in each country at the pre-trade equilibrium. Note that under IRS, the long-run average cost curve is downward sloping. Thus, any one firm can expand its output to serve the entire market and hence compete out all other producers of the same variety. Now consider opening up of trade between Germany and France. Even if the varieties produced in Germany in the pre-trade situation are the same as those produced in France, once trade opens up and German and the French markets are integrated, by the same argument the German firms and the French firms will produce distinct varieties under the IRS technology. Though the number of varieties in each country will shrink, *in aggregate the total number varieties for consumption will increase*. Note that since buyers everywhere prefer 'more' varieties to less, each firm can sell its variety in its own native country as well as abroad (which is exports) even if the prices of all the varieties are the same everywhere leaving no scope for arbitrage. That is, the demand for the variety produced by each firm (in each country) will rise, and so will be the output per variety. Thus, in each country, the given endowment of labour can now enable production of a smaller number of varieties. However, since in the global economy the total number of varieties will increase, so there will be gains for all consumers everywhere, and hence for each country in aggregate, at the extensive margin.

The pattern of trade is, however, indeterminate in the sense that it is not possible to identify whether all German firms will continue to produce the same varieties that they were producing under autarchy and all French firms will switch to the production of newer varieties or the reverse. It is even possible that only some of the German and French firms can continue producing the earlier varieties with others switching to newer varieties. This indeterminacy in the pattern of trade leaves very little scope for trade policy. But there is no ambiguity in both the countries gaining from this IIT in differentiated products. There are two sources of gains. First, consumers everywhere will gain from this trade as they can buy newer varieties. This is evident from the additively separable utility function in equation (8.1) displaying love for variety. Each variety is consumed in less quantity now but, as Krugman shows, this is over-compensated by the availability of newer varieties. Second, real wage increases in both the countries. With labour as the only factor of production, there are thus real income gains for each country. The reason for the real wage increase after trade is simple. A larger integrated market allows each firm to expand its production and thus lower the average cost of production. Since under monopolistic competition with free entry, firms cannot charge more than their average cost of production, the price of each variety falls. On the other hand, increased output demands more labour, which given the labour supply, raises the money wage in each country.

As regards firms, they neither gain nor lose because free entry drives down the profit to zero for each monopolistically competitive producer in both pre-trade and post-trade situations.

8.2.2 Characteristic Approach

Though people have love for variety, budget constraints often do not allow them to purchase all the varieties of a good that are available in the market. Expenditure on durables like home appliances, automobiles, computers, music stations, home theatres, and the like constitutes a large proportion of a buyer's income. Thus, more often consumers buy only one unit or only one variety of the good. Even the richest buyers buy only a limited number of varieties or models of automobiles, for example. For IIT in differentiated products of these categories, we need an altogether different approach. The characteristic approach to consumers' preference developed by Lancaster (1979) provides such an alternative explanation.

In the characteristics approach, every consumer views a product as a bundle of characteristics or attributes. For example, a car has many characteristics like its size, elegance, interior design, fuel efficiency, and engine power. A particular model or brand of car is differentiated from the other models or brands with respect to any one or all of these attributes or characteristics. Thus, cars produced by BMW, Chevrolet, Fiat, General Motors, Hyundai, Nissan, Suzuki, and Volkswagen, for example, are essentially different bundles of characteristics. Similarly differentiated with respect to the bundle of characteristics are different models of cars of the same company like the models Alto, Estilo, Ritz, Maruti Esteem, SX4, and WagonR produced by Maruti Suzuki in India. Computers, to consider another example, are bundles of characteristics like chipset, RAM speed, cache memory, hard disk space, monitor type, and screen size. Different models of computers differ from each other with respect to specifications of each or a combination of these characteristics. Laptops offered by Lenovo, Dell, Sony, and Compaq, on the other hand, are differentiated in the bundle of characteristics like screen size, weight, design, and battery durability. This idea of goods or products being a bundle of characteristics is one building block of the characteristic approach to the explanation of IIT in differentiated products.

The other building block is consumers' preferences. Each buyer has her own *ideal* product or bundle of characteristics. Preferences are heterogeneous and thus an ideal product varies across different consumers. If a buyer gets her ideal product in the market, her satisfaction is maximized and she buys that product. If a buyer does not get her ideal product, she buys the *best approximate* available in the market.

Now consider two countries Germany and the United States producing different models of cars under IRS technology. In each country, heterogeneous consumers are spread along the circumference of a unit circle according to their preference pattern or ideal product. That is, each point along the circumference denotes a group of consumers (who are identical among themselves) with a particular ideal product.[1]

To begin with, suppose Germany produces only four models (or bundle of characteristics) labeled m_1, m_2, m_3, and m_4. These models are the ideal products for consumer groups c_1, c_2, c_3, and c_4 respectively and thus they buy these models. But consumers located elsewhere according to their preference for ideal products, buy only the best approximates from amongst these four available models because their ideal products are not produced at home (Figure 8.3).

Best approximates are identified as products in the closest proximity to their respective locations or ideal product. For example, consumers located at the mid-point m between m_1 and m_2 are indifferent between these two products since both products are equally different from their most ideal product (which is m but is not available under our presumption). But for all the consumers to the left of point m, the best approximate would be the product m_2 rather than the product m_1. Similarly, for all the consumers to the left of point m', the best approximate would

[1] This idea of capturing preference heterogeneity of buyers through different locations of buyers in the preference space dates back to Hotelling, and thus this approach is also known as the neo-Hotelling approach to IIT.

be the product m_2 rather than the product m_3. Therefore, the total demand for the home product equals the number of consumers located in the interval (m, m'). This way, the pre-trade demand for other available varieties can be determined. Note that by this circular city approach, models equi-distant from an ideal product on both sides of it are equally ranked by the concerned consumers.

Suppose the United States is identical in every respect with Germany except that it produces four *different* varieties of the product. For convenience of exposition, let these varieties be m, m', m'', and m'''. When trade opens up, these products will be available to German buyers. Immediately, all consumers located at m will switch to the car of variety m imported from the United States as this is their ideal product. Others located between point m and the mid-point between m and m_2 will switch from the German variety m_2 to the imported US variety m as well because the imported variety is now a better approximate. Similar demand for other imported varieties will be made by consumers located elsewhere in Germany.

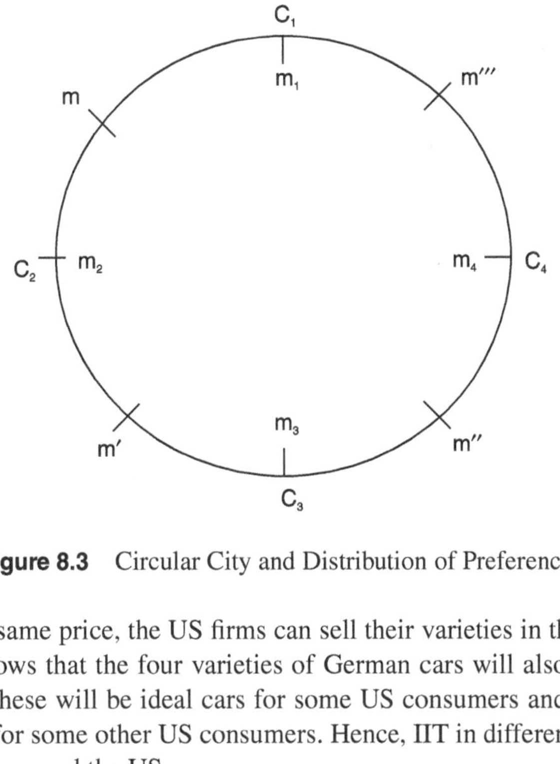

Figure 8.3 Circular City and Distribution of Preferences

Thus, even at the same price, the US firms can sell their varieties in the German market. A similar reasoning shows that the four varieties of German cars will also have demand in the United States since these will be ideal cars for some US consumers and better approximates than the US models for some other US consumers. Hence, IIT in differentiated products takes place between Germany and the US.

Note that under the presumption that pre-trade models produced in the two countries are distinctly different, we can easily determine the pattern of trade. But, like the Krugman model, if identical models of cars were initially produced in both the countries, the pattern of trade will be indeterminate. In such a case, given the increasing returns to scale technology, competition among German and US firms producing an identical model before trade, will force one of them to produce a different model. But whether it will be the German or the US firm which switches to a new model remains ambiguous and so does the pattern of trade.

The countries, however, gain from IIT unambiguously. The source of gain is utility gains for consumers who get their ideal product and who can buy better approximates than they could under no trade. The set of consumers who could buy their ideal models under no trade, such as consumers c_1, c_2, c_3, and c_4 located at m_1, m_2, m_3, and m_4 respectively, do not participate in trade and do not experience any utility gain or loss. On the other hand, for a sufficiently large number of firms (and a corresponding large number of models of cars) and free entry, super-normal profits are always driven down to zero. Thus, countries gain unambiguously.

8.3 PRODUCT DEVELOPMENT AND IIT IN VERTICALLY DIFFERENTIATED PRODUCTS

In the above explanations of IIT, products are assumed to be horizontally differentiated from each other in the sense that differences are not real or significant. But products are often qualitatively differentiated from each other in any one or all of their characteristics. Quality differentiation may range from pure and adulterated milk sold in many developing countries, original and pirated software, to Pentium and Celeron processors for personal computers, efficiency of innovated and imitated goods, texture of dress material, budget hotels and five-star hotels, service in a bank, and business and economy class travel in airplanes. Goods may also be of higher and lower *environmental quality* according to the level of environmental damage that they cause while being produced or being consumed. For example, automobiles and air conditioning machines that cause lower levels of air pollution can be regarded to be of higher environmental quality. Thus, the same good of different qualities coexists in the market and is often traded internationally.

The primary reason for the coexistence of both low and high qualities is the income disparity among consumers both within and across countries. Higher quality varieties are costlier which the poor buyers may not be able to afford. Alternatively, richer buyers may have a higher marginal willingness to pay for a higher quality variety than poorer buyers. This creates scope for producers to *quality discriminate* among buyers. Similar reasons may explain trading high and low quality varieties by countries. Generally speaking, developing and poor countries are observed to be producers of low quality goods whereas the advanced richer countries produce high quality goods. Average per capita income being lower in a developing country discourages producers there both in terms of the willingness-to-pay and the ability-to-pay to provide better quality of a good compared to what is being provided in a richer nation.

Technological disadvantages in developing countries is another plausible explanation why poor countries are typically low quality producers. Such technological constraints may arise in two ways. First, the marginal cost of quality is higher resulting in a lower quality being chosen by domestic producers. Second, firms in a developing country may be equally cost efficient, but the technology available to them may just allow them to produce a range of qualities that is only a *lower sub-set* of the qualities that firms in richer nations can produce. Investments in R&D or innovation can relax these technological constraints. However, expenditure on R&D itself is quite low in developing countries as available evidence regarding this suggests. An oft-quoted explanation of such low R&D expenditure and innovation levels in developing countries is that the protective trade policies eliminate foreign competition and thereby lower the incentive for innovations whatsoever (Lall 2000; Marjit and Raychaudhuri 1997). This argument is based on Kenneth Arrow's (1962) hypothesis that competition is conducive to innovation as mentioned in Chapter 5.

An alternative explanation of the low-quality phenomena in developing countries is that most of the markets in developing countries resemble the features of *contestable markets*: many small producers with no sunk cost and free and easy entry and exit. The incumbents are vulnerable to hit-and-run entry should they ever try to exert their potential market power by raising prices above marginal costs. In such cases, there will be little scope and incentive for the incumbents to build their reputations by offering higher quality goods. Potential entrants, on the other hand, being transient in nature, entering the market whenever there is any profit opportunity and leaving once some profits are reaped, care little about how consumers regard quality.

Whatever be the reasons for the low-quality phenomenon in developing or poor nations, income disparities within poor and rich countries create scope for these countries to export the same good of different qualities to each other. Richer buyers in poor countries can gain from imports of higher quality from richer nations whereas relatively poorer buyers in rich nations can gain from imports of lower quality varieties from poor countries.

There can also be the usual factor endowment basis for comparative advantage and trade in vertically differentiated products. Higher quality products are typically intensive in capital and/or skilled labour. Thus, the production of higher quality goods in the advanced rich countries may reflect relative abundance of capital there or the higher skills of their workforce relative to developing countries. Schott's (2004) finding lends some support to this as well. First that export unit values, which are often used as proxy for quality of exports, increase systematically with per capita income and relative endowments of physical and human capital of the exporting countries. Second, higher unit values of imports of the United States come from capital- and skill-abundant countries. This factor endowment story can be captured

Box 8.2 Innovation, Imitation, and the Product Life-Cycle Theory

Raymond Vernon (1966) extended Posner (1961) and Linder's (1961) ideas by developing a product life-cycle model in which innovation is first created in the most advanced countries, and it subsequently diffuses to lesser and lesser advanced countries. A new innovated product goes through four stages of its life: introduction, growth, maturity, and decline. The production location shifts from one country to the other according to its life-cycle stage. Initially, new products are introduced to meet national needs, and are exported to similar countries, that is, countries with similar needs, preferences, and incomes. In the second stage, a copy (or imitated) product is developed in other countries. In the third stage, production shifts to a country that is a low cost producer of the good. The global industry thus contracts and concentrates in that country. Now the usual comparative cost advantage reasons determine trade flows. The technologically advanced innovating countries become net importers of the product. In the final stage, due to the development of new substitute products in technologically advanced countries, global demand for this outdated good declines and the poor countries constitute the only markets for the product. Therefore, by this theory, almost all declining products are produced in the least developed countries (LDCs).

through a simple extension of the basic Heckscher-Ohlin-Samuelson model, or the non-traded good model described in Chapter 7. Acharyya and Jones (2001) developed a variant of the latter to exemplify the role of factor endowment, and corresponding factor prices, for quality of exports. Consider a small open economy producing a quality-differentiated export good Z, with its quality indexed by $Q \in [0,1]$ that is observable to all, along with a composite traded good (T) and a non-traded good (N). Whereas the composite traded and non-traded goods are produced by homogeneous and sectorally mobile capital and unskilled labour, good Z is produced by capital and skilled labour. That is, skilled labour is specific to the production of the quality-differentiated good. The small open economy thus displays a diversified trade pattern: It exports both a quality differentiated skill-based good and a good produced by unskilled labour.[2] This type of diversified export pattern is not at odd with the export baskets of some of the relatively better endowed and technologically advanced developing countries like Brazil, China, India, Korea, Mexico, and Vietnam. Due to availability of specific types of skill, and technical capability, these countries produce a wide range of export goods and services from low-skill agricultural products and manufacturing like textiles, leather manufacture, and the like, to high skill, capital and technology intensive products like chemicals, software, office equipment, transport equipment, and scientific instruments, financial services, and IT-enabled services. As a simplification, Acharyya and Jones (2001) assumed that all the goods are produced by fixed coefficient technology so that per unit input requirements are constant. But, higher qualities of good Z require more intensive use of capital per unit of output. The rate at which larger units of capital are required to produce a higher quality variety of good Z is, however, technologically determined as reflected in the capital-output ratio:

$$a_{KZ} = a_{KZ}(Q), a'_{KZ}(Q) > 0, a''_{KZ}(Q) > 0 \ \forall \ Q \in [0,1] \tag{8.2}$$

Two comments are warranted at this point. First, the assumption of the same number of skilled workers per unit of output even for higher quality varieties of good Z helps Acharyya and Jones (2001) avoid the trade-off between quality and quantity of the export good Z. Since skilled labour is specific to this sector, so if higher qualities also require larger number of skilled labour per unit then an increase in quality of good Z will necessarily lower the output of good Z.[3] Second, the average (and marginal) cost of producing good Z increases with its quality at an increasing rate due to the technological requirement of successively larger units of capital for successively higher qualities, which reflects diminishing returns for capital:

$$C_Z(w_S, r, Q) = a_{SZ} w_S + a_{KZ}(Q) r \quad \frac{\partial C_Z}{\partial Q} = a'_{KZ}(Q) r \ \forall \ Q \in [0,1] \tag{8.3}$$

On the other hand, since the foreign buyers are willing to pay a higher price for a higher quality variety, so the world price of good Z that this small open faces increase with its quality. For, simplicity assume that the rate of increase is constant. More precisely,

$$P_Z^W = P_Z^W(Q), P_Z^W(0) > 0, P_Z^{W'}(Q) > 0, P_Z^{W''}(Q) = 0 \ \forall \ Q \in [0,1] \tag{8.4}$$

Good Z is produced by perfectly competitive firms so that for any given Q, each firm earns zero profit:

$$P_Z^W(Q) = a_{SZ} w_S + a_{KZ}(Q) r \tag{8.5}$$

[2] This is essentially a variant of the model used by Gruen and Corden (1970) to study that a tariff may worsen the terms of trade.

[3] Ganguly and Acharyya (2021) have considered such a generalized case.

On the other hand, each firm chooses quality of good Z for which the marginal revenue from quality equals the marginal cost of quality:

$$P_Z^{W'}(Q_0) = a'_{KZ}(Q_0)r \tag{8.6}$$

For any given skilled wage and the rate of return to capital, (w_S^0, r^0), selection of export quality is illustrated in Figure 8.4. Note that at the tangency point E_0, both the zero profit condition (8.5) and the marginal condition (8.6) are satisfied. It is easy to check that a ceteris paribus increase in the rate of return to capital raises the marginal cost at the initial level of quality, and thus induces producers to downgrade the quality of good Z. Referring back to Figure 8.4, a steeper C_z curve will now be tangent to the $P_Z^W(Q)$ locus on the left of E_0. This inverse relationship capturing all combinations of the rate of return to capital and profit-maximizing quality is shown in Figure 8.5 by the downward sloping *QQ* curve.

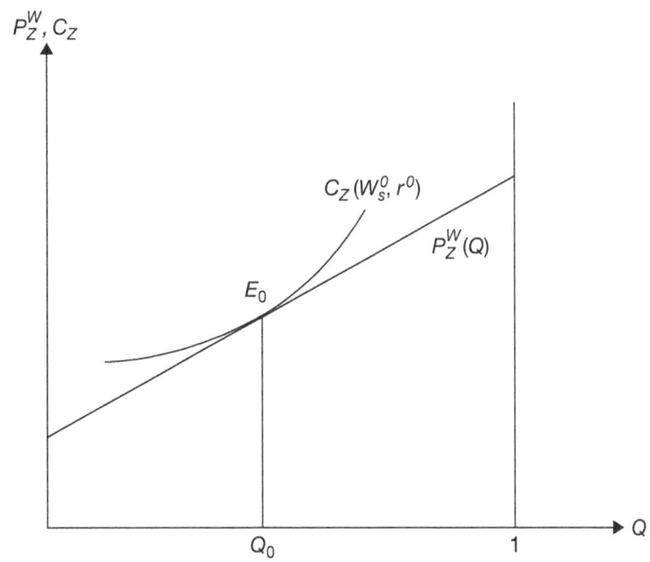

Figure 8.4 Profit-maximizing Selection of Quality

The market clearing condition for the non-traded good along with the full employment conditions, on the other hand, gives another relationship between the rate of return to capital and quality of export good Z with the causality running in the opposite direction. Writing down the other relevant conditions will help understand this:

$$P_T^W = a_{LT}w + a_{KT}r \tag{8.7}$$

$$P_N = a_{LN}w + a_{KN}r \tag{8.8}$$

$$\frac{D_N}{D_T} = f(p) = \frac{X_N}{X_T} \tag{8.9}$$

$$\overline{K} - a_{KZ}(Q)X_Z = \tilde{K}(Q) = a_{KT}X_T + a_{KN}X_N \quad (8.10)$$

$$\overline{S} = a_{SZ}X_Z \quad (8.11)$$

$$\overline{L} = a_{LT}X_T + a_{LN}X_N \quad (8.12)$$

Once the output of good Z is fixed by the full employment condition for skilled labour in (8.11), from the capital constraint condition (8.10) it appears that a ceteris paribus increase in quality of good Z will lower the availability of capital for the (*T, N*) sub-system. This will trigger an output-magnification like effect whereby the output of the non-traded good will rise and that of the composite traded good will fall if the former is relatively unskilled labour intensive. Such an excess supply of non-traded good will lower its (relative) price, which in turn will trigger a price-magnification like effect whereby the unskilled wage will fall and the rate of return to capital will rise. Thus, we now have a positive relationship between the quality of the export good Z and the rate of return to capital as depicted in Figure 8.5 by the *rr* curve. Note that the same positive relationship can be obtained if the non-traded good would have been relatively capital intensive.

The equilibrium quality and the rate of return to capital are thus determined simultaneously corresponding to the point of intersection of the *QQ* and the *rr* curve.

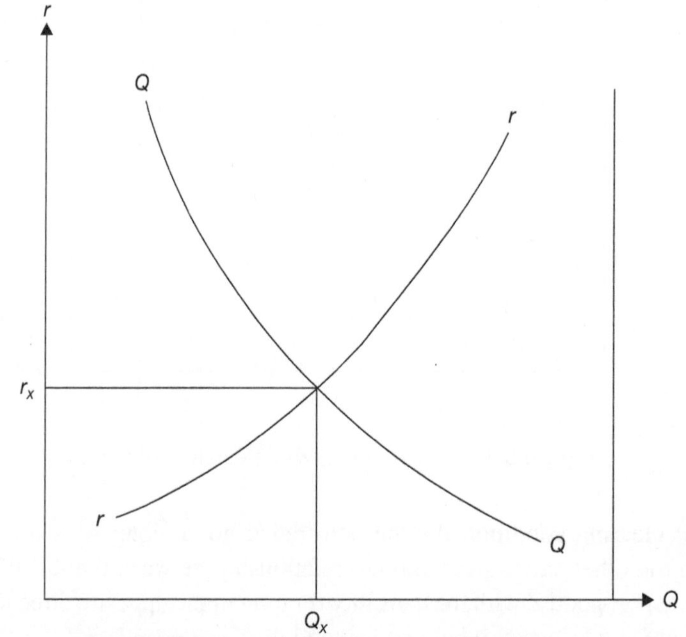

Figure 8.5 Equilibrium Export Quality

Now, it can be easily checked that a growth in unskilled labour will raise the output of the non-traded good through the output-magnification effect. Consequent fall in the price of the non-traded good will lower the unskilled wage and raise the rate of return to capital by the price-magnification effect. Hence, the marginal cost of quality will rise and producers of the export good Z will downgrade the quality. Similar reasoning shows that a growth in capital will lead to an upgrading of export quality. Thus, a relatively unskilled labour abundant country, typically the developing countries, will be producers of low-quality export good(s), whereas a relatively capital-abundant country, typically the developed countries, will be producers of high-quality export good(s).

In a more generalized case where higher qualities require more of both skilled labour and capital per unit of output though at different proportions, as considered in Ganguly and Acharyya (2021), a country having a larger endowment of skilled workers, ceteris paribus, will be producing higher qualities of good Z than countries with relatively lesser number of skilled workers *if higher qualities are relatively skill intensive*. Otherwise, if higher qualities are relatively capital intensive then the endowment of capital, ceteris paribus, will matter as in the specific case of Acharyya and Jones (2001) discussed above.

8.4 FIRM HETEROGENEITY AND EXPORT DECISION

In a pioneer work, Melitz (2003) introduced firm heterogeneity in the Krugman model of monopolistic competition and international trade to study which firms in an industry export and which firms produce for the domestic market. His theoretical work was motivated largely by the observations of Bernard, Eaton, Jensen, and Kortum (2003). In 1992, only 21 per cent of firms in the United States reported exporting their production and approximately 75 per cent of exporting firms sold less than 10 per cent of their output abroad. Firms were also heterogeneous in terms of their labour productivities, averaging 33 per cent more than the non-exporting firms. These observations seem to suggest that the most productive firms self-select into export markets.

To capture these observations, Melitz (2003) extended the Krugman model with heterogeneous firms and the fixed cost of entry in the export market(s). While the fixed cost of production is the same across all firms in an industry, the variable labour costs decrease with the firm-specific productivity. To enter an industry and produce, firms must first invest in a fixed entry cost and thereafter get to know their respective labour productivities. Conditional on such productivity, a firm decides about whether to stay and produce or to exit and not produce. Free entry and the consequent zero profit condition defines a cut off level of productivity. Firms with realized labour productivity less than that cut off level exit.

If there are no trade costs, then after trade the autarchic equilibrium is replicated as the outcome of the integrated world equilibrium. Just like the Krugman (1979) model, it is equivalent to a growth in a country's labour force, and welfare increases because of the variety effect. Trade costs, however, change the outcome significantly. Melitz (2003) considered both variable and fixed costs of trade. Fixed costs are paid after the realization of productivity, so that while deciding about whether to export or not firms know their respective productivity levels. The variable or per unit trade cost is modelled as iceberg one: More than one unit of goods must be shipped for one unit to arrive at the destination. All countries are assumed to be identical so that wages everywhere are the same. This assumption allows him to abstract from firm selection and aggregate productivity driven by relative wage differences. Again, there will be a cut off productivity level, higher for domestic market entry than the one under autarchy, and an even higher level for entry to the export market. Thus, firms with very low labour productivity will no longer survive and exit after trade, i.e., do not enter the domestic market; firms with moderately high productivity will sell only in the domestic market; highly productive firms will operate in the domestic market as well as will export. The reason for trade forcing least productive firms to exit is simple. Trade provides new profit opportunities for most productive firms who can afford to pay the entry cost of exporting. These higher potential profits increase entry and consequently raise the demand for labour. The highly productive incumbent firms also increase their demand for labour as they expand their scale of production for exporting. All these increase the real wage and accordingly force the least productive firms to exit. Hence, in addition to the variety gain, trade raises the average productivity of the economy.

8.5 ADVANCED TOPIC: INTRA-INDUSTRY TRADE INDICES

There are several measures of intra-industry trade that exist in literature. The most commonly used is the Grubel–Lloyd (GL) index proposed by Grubel and Lloyd (1975). There are also refinements of this index offered by Balassa (1979), Bergstrand (1983), and Greenaway and Milner (1984) among others. We start with the GL index in the following sub-section and then discuss the refinements and alternative measures in a subsequent sub-section.

8.5.1 The Grubel–Lloyd (GL) Index of Intra-industry Trade

For any particular product class *i*, the GL index of *bilateral* intra-industry trade in the product class *i* between countries *A* and *B* is given by the following ratio:

$$GL^i_{AB} = \left[1 - \frac{\left|X^i_{AB} - M^i_{AB}\right|}{X^i_{AB} + M^i_{AB}}\right] \times 100 \tag{8.13}$$

where X^i_{AB} is the value of exports of product class *i* by country *A* to country *B*, and M^i_{AB} is the value of imports of product class *i* by country *A* from country *B*.

The value of this index lies between 0 and 100, inclusive of both the extreme values. The minimum value of 0 implies that there are no products in the same product class that are both imported and exported. When all trade in the product category is intra-industry so that export and import values are equal, the index takes the maximum value of 100.

Three further aggregations based on equation (8.13) are relevant. First, bilateral indices of IIT between country *A* and country *B* for *all* manufacturing product classes are obtained as the weighted average of the indexes in equation (8.13) for all product classes *i*. The weights are given by the share of total manufacturing trade of product class *i*:

$$GL_{AB} = \sum_i \left[1 - \frac{\left|X^i_{AB} - M^i_{AB}\right|}{X^i_{AB} + M^i_{AB}}\right]\left[\frac{X^i_{AB} + M^i_{AB}}{\sum_i \left(X^i_{AB} + M^i_{AB}\right)}\right] \times 100 \tag{8.14}$$

Second, the bilateral indices of intra-industry trade in the product class *i* between country *A* and *all* its trading partners are obtained as a weighted average of the bilateral indices in equation (8.13) for each partner country. Denoting the partner country by j (instead of B in equation [8.13]), and using the share of partner country j in the total trade of A in the product class i as weight, such a *bilateral* GL index for *all* trading partners is measured by:

$$GL_A^i = \sum_j \left[1 - \frac{\left| X_{Aj}^i - M_{Aj}^i \right|}{X_{Aj}^i + M_{Aj}^i} \right] \left[\frac{X_{Aj}^i + M_{Aj}^i}{\sum_j \left(X_{Aj}^i + M_{Aj}^i \right)} \right] \times 100 \tag{8.15}$$

Note that $j \neq A$.

Finally, a bilateral GL index of *total* IIT for country A can be obtained by taking weighted average of GL_{AB} (or GL_{Aj}) for all trade partners:

$$GL_A = \sum_j \left[\frac{X_{Aj} + M_{Aj}}{\sum_j \left(X_{Aj} + M_{Aj} \right)} \right] GL_{Aj} \tag{8.16}$$

These indices, however, are sensitive to the level of disaggregation of a product class. The industry classification under different systems like the Standard International Trade Classification (SITC) and Harmonized Systems (HS) ranges from 2-digit codes to 8-digit codes. At the 2-digit codes the industries are most broadly categorized, such as cereals (SITC code 10), pharmaceutical products (SITC code 30), fertilizers (31), rubber and rubber products (40), silk (50), iron and steel (72), electrical machinery and equipment (85), aircraft and spacecraft (88), and the like. Successively more disaggregate sub-divisions under the 2-digit codes or broad industry groups are labeled by successively higher digit codes. Table 8.2 illustrates the sub-classification and disaggregation at the 4-digit SITC level under the three 2-digit groups inorganic chemicals, cotton, and articles of not-knitted apparels.

If one measures IIT using the 2-digit or 3-digit industry classification, it is more likely that trade in not so similar products will also be treated as IIT as these products will be included in the same aggregate product group. Thus, the index of IIT will be an overestimation of the actual. On the other hand, a more disaggregate industrial classification such as product groups at 6-digit or 8-digit levels will be better approximates because these disaggregate groups will include products that are more similar. For example, Brulhart (2009) measures the IIT for 2006–7 to be 27 per cent of global trade at the 5-digit level of disaggregation, and 44 per cent at a 3-digit level of aggregation. The problem, however, is that higher digit industry classification codes mean successively a larger number of product categories to be dealt with in measuring the IIT index. In Brulhart's estimation of IIT, at the SITC 5-digit level, trade is categorized into 1,161 different sectors, whereas at the SITC 3-digit level, trade is categorized into 177 sectors.

Table 8.3 documents the pattern and growth of intra-industry trade measured by the GL index, both for the manufacturing sector and across total traded commodities and illustrates the bias in its measurement in the broader industry classification. The first column reports the OECD measure of the GL index for manufacturing product groups at the 2-digit aggregation level, reproduced from Table 8.1. The second and third columns, on the other hand, report Brulhart's estimate of the bilateral GL index specified in equation (8.16) for all trade partners and product groups at the 3-digit and 5-digit level disaggregation respectively for 2006. Clearly the extent of IIT is much less when measured by the 5-digit product classification than when measured by the 3-digit product classification. As it appears from Table 8.3, there are wide variations of the share of intra-industry trade in manufacture both across countries and across the level of aggregation of the product categories. The share of intra-industry trade in total trade by the GL index for India, for example, is 31.8 per cent at the 3-digit classification and 12.7 per cent at the 5-digit classification.

Table 8.2 SITC Classification of Products at Two-Digit and Four-Digit Levels

Code	Product
28 Inorganic Chemicals	
2801	Fluorine, chlorine, bromine and iodine
2803	Carbon
2804	Hydrogen, rare gases, and other non-metals
2807	Sulphuric acid; oleum
2811	Other inorganic acids and other inorganic oxygen compounds of non-metals
2812	Halides and halide oxides of non-metals
2818	Artificial corundum; aluminium oxide; aluminium hydroxide
2821	Iron oxides and hydroxides
2827	Chlorides, chloride oxides, and chloride hydroxides; bromides and bromide oxides; iodides and iodide oxides
2831	Dithionites and sulphoxylates
2832	Sulphites; thiosulphates
2833	Sulphates; alums; peroxosulphates
2836	Carbonates; peroxocarbonates
52 Cotton	
5201	Cotton, not carded or combed
5203	Cotton, carded or combed
5204	Cotton sewing thread, whether or not put up for retail sale
5205	Cotton yarn (other than sewing thread), containing 85% or more by weight of cotton, not put up for retail sale
5207	Cotton yarn (other than sewing thread) put up for retail sale
5208	Woven fabrics of cotton, containing 85% or more by weight of cotton, weighing not more than 200 g/m^2
5209	Woven fabrics of cotton, containing 85% or more by weight of cotton, weighing more than 200 g/m^2
5210	Woven fabrics of cotton, containing less than 85% by weight of cotton, mixed mainly or solely with man-made fabrics, weighing not more than 200 g/m^2
5211	Woven fabrics of cotton, containing less than 85% by weight of cotton, mixed mainly or solely with man-made fabrics, weighing more than 200 g/m^2
5212	Other woven fabrics of cotton
62 Articles of Apparel and Clothing Accessories, Not Knitted or Crocheted	
6203	Men's or boys' suits, ensembles, jackets, blazers, trousers, bib and brace overalls, breeches, and shorts (other than swimwear)
6204	Women's or girls' suits, ensembles, jackets, blazers, dresses, skirts, divided skirts, trousers, bib and brace overalls, breeches, and shorts
6205	Men's or boys' shirts
6206	Women's or girls' blouses, shirts, and shirt-blouses
6214	Shawls, scarves, mufflers, mantillas, veils, and the like

Source: *UNCTAD Trade Statistics*, www.unctad.org

Table 8.3 GL Index of Intra-industry Trade

Country	OECD Estimate of Manufacturing IIT as Percentage of Total Manufacturing Trade (3-digit)	Brulhart's Estimates of Total IIT in 2006	
	1996–2000	3-digit	5-digit
Australia	29.8	19.8	9.0
Austria	74.2	60.0	42.1
Canada	76.2	59.9	42.1
Denmark	64.8	51.0	32.0
Finland	53.9	40.3	22.5
France	77.5	60.0	42.4
Germany	72.0	57.0	41.9
Greece	36.9	21.0	13.1
India		31.8	12.7
Italy	64.7	49.7	34.4
Japan	47.6	39.8	23.8
Korea	57.5	41.2	24.0
Mexico	73.4	47.8	33.4
Netherlands	68.9	51.6	34.1
New Zealand	40.6	29.8	13.3
Portugal	61.3	48.5	29.2
Spain	71.2	50.3	33.8
Sweden	66.6	51.1	33.0
Switzerland	72.0	56.1	39.6
Turkey	40.0	21.7	13.0
United Kingdom	73.7	52.5	36.2
United States	68.5	50.3	31.7

Source: Compiled from *OECD International Trade Statistics* and Brulhart (2009).

The GL index of intra-industry trade does not allow the causes of intra-industry trade to be identified. However, using the information on unit values and defining trade in vertically differentiated products as being the ones where import and export unit values differ by more than 15 per cent, Fontagné and Freudenberg (2002) could provide some estimates of IIT in these products. They found that most of the increase in intra-industry trade in Europe over the last two decades of the twentieth century had been trade in vertically differentiated products rather than horizontally differentiated products.

8.5.2 Other Measures and Refinements of the GL Index of Intra-industry Trade

Balassa (1979) proposed a measure of intra-industry trade by taking the sum of the ratios of trade balance to total trade for each product group and then dividing by the number of product groups:

$$BL_{AB} = \frac{1 - \sum_i \left| \tilde{X}^i_{AB} + \tilde{M}^i_{AB} \right|}{\sum_i \left| \tilde{X}^i_{AB} + \tilde{M}^i_{AB} \right|} \tag{8.17}$$

where $\tilde{X}^i_{AB} = \frac{X^i_{AB}\left[X_{AB} + M_{AB}\right]}{2X_{AB}}, \tilde{M}^i_{AB} = \frac{M^i_{AB}\left[X_{AB} + M_{AB}\right]}{2M_{AB}}$, X_{AB} are the total exports by country A to country B and M_{AB} are the total imports by country A from country B.

According to Balassa, when the share of intra-industry trade increases, BL_{AB} declines from one to zero.

A critique of the GL index is that it fails to correct for an imbalance in a country's overall trade and thus underestimates the true extent of intra-industry specialization. Thus, the GL indeed needs to be adjusted for trade imbalances. For this purpose, Bergstrand (1983) proposed that the intra-industry trade should be measured as a proportion of a country's trade with each of her trading partners. His bilateral intra-industry trade index adjusted for each country's multilateral trade imbalance is given as:

$$BG_{AB} = 1 - \frac{\left|\tilde{X}^i_{AB} - X^i_{BA}\right|}{\tilde{X}^i_{AB} + X^i_{BA}} \tag{8.18}$$

where $\tilde{X}^i_{AB} = \frac{1}{2}\left[\frac{X_A + M_A}{2X_A} + \frac{X_B + M_B}{2M_B}\right]X^i_{AB}$ and $\tilde{X}^i_{BA} = \frac{1}{2}\left[\frac{X_A + M_A}{2M_A} + \frac{X_B + M_B}{2X_B}\right]X^i_{BA}$.

On the other hand, Greenaway et al. (1994) break down total intra-industry trade (IIT) into horizontal intra-industry trade (HIIT) and vertical intra-industry trade (VIIT). Their approach assumes that quality is reflected in price and price can be proxied by unit values. Reconsider the GL index in equation (8.13). Greenaway et al. (1994) define their index IIT in product class i at the 3-digit level of classification as

$$IIT^i_{AB} = 1 - \frac{\sum_k \left|X^{ik}_{AB} - M^{ik}_{AB}\right|}{\sum_k \left[X^{ik}_{AB} + M^{ik}_{AB}\right]} \tag{8.19}$$

where X^i_{AB} is the export of product k at the 5-digit level in product class i at the 3-digit level by country A to country B, and M^i_{AB} is the import of product k at the 5-digit level in product class i at the 3-digit level by country A from country B. By definition:

$$IIT^i_{AB} = HIIT^i_{AB} + VIIT^i_{AB} \tag{8.20}$$

$HIIT^i_{AB}$ is given by equation (8.19) for those products k in product class i for which the unit values of imports UVM_{ik} and unit value of exports UVX_{ik} satisfy the following condition:

$$1 - \alpha \leq \frac{UVX_{ik}}{UVM_{ik}} \leq 1 + \alpha \tag{8.21}$$

where α is an exogenously given dispersion factor.

On the other hand, the $VIIT^{i}_{AB}$ is given by equation (8.19) for those products k in product class i for which:

$$\frac{UVX_{ik}}{UVM_{ik}} < 1-\alpha \text{ or } \frac{UVX_{ik}}{UVM_{ik}} > 1+\alpha \tag{8.22}$$

Greenaway et al. (1994) calculate HIIT and VIIT for UK using both $\alpha = 0.15$ and $\alpha = 0.25$. Using the narrower spread of 15 per cent, VIIT turns out to be the most important form of IIT in UK trade. For a larger spread of 25 per cent, VIIT remains as important as HIIT.

To sum up, there are broadly two refinements of the GL index, one of which is aimed at providing a more meaningful basis for the analysis of adjustment needed due to trade imbalances, and the other is targeted at disentangling vertical and horizontal IIT.

APPENDIX A8

I. Algebra of Brander (1981) Model with Transport Cost: Linear Market Example

Consider identical linear inverse demand functions in the two countries, labeled as home and foreign:

$$P = a - (x_h + gx_h^*) \tag{A8.1}$$

$$P^* = a - (gx_f + x_f^*) \tag{A8.2}$$

where P and P^* are the prices of the good in the home and foreign country respectively; x_j and $x_f^*, j = h, f$, are the home firm's and the foreign firm's production for market j respectively and $g \in [0, 1]$ is the fraction of output lost in transit that captures transport costs. Thus, the actual supply (or exports) by the home firm to the foreign country and by the foreign firm to the home country are gx_f and gx_h^* respectively. Higher the value of g, lower are the transport costs.

Suppose firms have identical and constant marginal costs of production, c. Thus, the profit functions of the firms can be written as:

$$\pi = Px_h + P^*\left[gx_f\right] - c\left[x_h + x_f\right] = ax_h - x_h^2 - gx_hx_h^* + agx_f - g^2x_f^2 - gx_fx_f^* - c\left[x_h + x_f\right] \tag{A8.3}$$

$$\pi^* = agx_h^* - g^2x_h^{*2} - gx_hx_h^* + ax_f^* - x_f^{*2} - gx_fx_f^* - c\left[x_h^* + x_f^*\right] \tag{A8.4}$$

First order conditions for profit maximization yields:

$$\frac{\partial \pi}{\partial x_h} = 0 \Rightarrow a - 2x_h - gx_h^* - c = 0 \tag{A8.5}$$

$$\frac{\partial \pi}{\partial x_f} = 0 \Rightarrow ag - 2g^2x_f - gx_f^* - c = 0 \tag{A8.6}$$

$$\frac{\partial \pi^*}{\partial x_h^*} = 0 \Rightarrow ag - 2g^2x_h^* - gx_h - c = 0 \tag{A8.7}$$

$$\frac{\partial \pi^*}{\partial x_f^*} = 0 \Rightarrow a - 2x_f^* - gx_f - c = 0 \tag{A8.8}$$

Looking at these conditions it is immediate that the pair of first order conditions in equations (A8.5) and (A8.7) relevant for the home market are independent of the pair of first order conditions in equations (A8.6) and (A8.8) relevant for the foreign market. This reflects the *market segmentation property* due to the assumption of constant marginal cost of production. Moreover, these pairs of first order conditions are symmetric. Hence, the output pair for the home market (x_h, x_h^*) will be the same as the output pair for the foreign market, (x_f, x_f^*). This reflects the *market symmetry property* due to the assumption of identical demand and cost conditions.

By this market symmetry property, it is sufficient to solve for domestic supply and foreign supply (or imports) in the home country market. Solving the first order conditions (A8.5) and (A8.7), the output levels can be obtained as:

$$x_h = \frac{1}{3g}[ag + c - 2cg] \tag{A8.9}$$

$$x_h^* = \frac{1}{3g^2}[ag - 2c + gc] \tag{A8.10}$$

From equation (A8.10) we can derive the condition for invasion in the home country market by the foreign firm and hence its exports as:

$$g > \bar{g} = \frac{2c}{a+c} \tag{A8.11}$$

Note that $\frac{2c}{a+c} < 1$. Otherwise $a < c$ and the home firm's production will not be viable under autarchy. So equation (A8.11) implies that as long as the transport costs are not too high in the sense that $g \in \left[\frac{2c}{a+c}, 1\right]$, it is profitable for the foreign firm to invade and dump its production in the home country market. By the market symmetry property, the same condition implies that it is profitable for the home firm to invade the foreign country's market. Therefore, equation (A8.11) provides us the condition for reciprocal dumping and IIT in identical products. Note that this condition includes no transport cost ($g = 1$) as discussed in the text.

To check GFT, note that the national welfare in this partial equilibrium framework comprises of consumers' surplus and domestic firm's profits. Once again, by the market symmetry property, it is sufficient to check GFT for the home country. Given the linear inverse demand function, the consumers' surplus equals $\frac{1}{2}(a - P)(x_h + gx_h^*)$. From equations (A8.1), (A8.9), and (A8.10) it is easy to check the following:

$$X_h = x_h + gx_h^* = \frac{1}{3g}[2ag - c - cg] \tag{A8.12}$$

$$P = \frac{1}{3g}\left[ag + c + cg\right] \tag{A8.13}$$

Hence, consumers' surplus (CS) in the home country after trade equals:

$$CS = \frac{1}{18g^2}\left[2ag - c - cg\right]^2 = \frac{1}{2}\left(X_h\right)^2 \tag{A8.14}$$

The home firm's profit from domestic sales and exports, on the other hand, equals:

$$\pi = P[x_h + gx_f] - c[x_h + x_f]$$

$$= \frac{(ag + c + cg)(2ag - c - cg)}{9g^2} - c\left[\frac{ag + c - 2cg}{3g} + \frac{ag - 2c + gc}{3g^2}\right] \tag{A8.15}$$

Adding equations (A8.14) and (A8.15) and simplifying we obtain the home country's post-trade national welfare by the surplus measure as:

$$W = \frac{8a^2g^2 - 8acg^2 - 8acg - 14c^2g + 11c^2g^2 + 11c^2}{18g^2} \tag{A8.16}$$

On the other hand, pre-trade, the home country's national welfare is the sum of monopoly profit and consumers surplus at the monopoly price $(a + c)/2$:

$$W_a = \frac{3}{8}(a - c)^2 \tag{A8.17}$$

Subtracting equation (A8.17) from (A8.16) yields:

$$W - W_a = \frac{5a^2g^2 + 22acg^2 - 32acg - 56c^2g + 17c^2g^2 + 44c^2}{18g^2}$$

Now, $W{=}W_a$ if $g = g' = \dfrac{22ac + 22c^2}{5a^2 + 22ac + 17c^2}$ and $g = g'' = \dfrac{34ac + 10c^2}{5a^2 + 22ac + 17c^2}$.

On the other hand, $\dfrac{\partial(W - W_a)}{\partial g} > 0$ for all $g > \tilde{g} = \dfrac{88c^2}{32ac + 56c^2}$. It is easy to check the following relationship among these critical values of the transport cost:

$$g'' < \bar{g} < \tilde{g} < g' < 1$$

Given this ranking, Figure A8.1 illustrates the welfare change.

Hence, IIT lowers the home country's welfare for $g \in [\bar{g}, g']$ and raises it for $g \in [g', 1]$. That is, IIT in an identical product with positive transport costs is not always beneficial for reasons spelled out in the text.

II. Monopolistic Competition and IIT in Differentiated Goods: Krugman (1979)

Consider a home country. Given the Dixit-Stiglitz preference function defined in Equation (8.1) that displays love for variety, Krugman (1979) assumed that labour is the only factor of production. He specified the production relation as:

$$l_i = \alpha + \beta x_i \tag{A8.18}$$

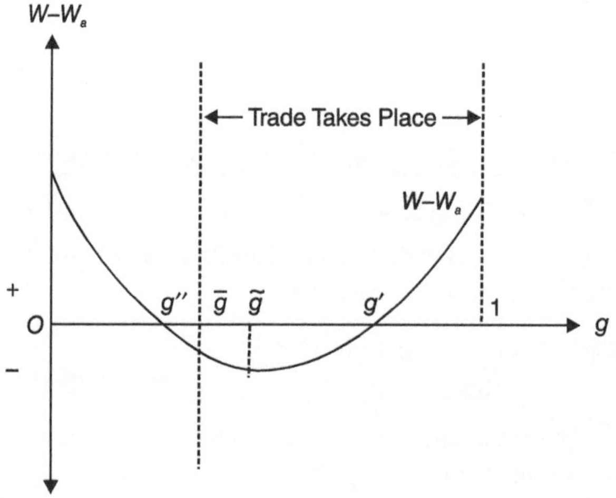

Figure A8.1 Transport Cost and Gains from Intra-industry Trade

wherework x_i is the output of the i-th variety, and $\sum_i l_i = L$. Thus, production functions for all varieties are the same. Note that L is the total number of workers as well as the total number of consumers in the home country. Hence, the market equilibrium under autarchy for each variety requires:

$$x_i = c_i L \tag{A8.19}$$

Under monopolistic competition, each firm having monopoly power over the variety that it produces, equates marginal revenue (MR) with marginal cost (MC). If ε_i denotes the absolute price elasticity of demand for the i-th variety, MR equals $p_i\left(1-\frac{1}{\varepsilon_i}\right)$. On the other hand, given that workers everywhere in the home country earn the same wage, W, since they are homogeneous and sectorally mobile, from equation (A8.18) it follows that the MC equals βW. Hence:

$$\beta W = p_i\left(1-\frac{1}{\varepsilon_i}\right) \Rightarrow \frac{p_i}{W} = \frac{\varepsilon_i}{\varepsilon_i - 1}\beta \tag{A8.20}$$

Free entry of firms, on the other hand, drives down super-normal profits for all firms to zero implying that the price of each variety equals its average cost (AC):

$$p_i = \left(\frac{\alpha}{x_i} + \beta\right)W \Rightarrow \frac{p_i}{W} = \left(\frac{\alpha}{x} + \beta\right) \tag{A8.21}$$

Equations (A8.20) and (A8.21) together solve for the real wage and the output level of the i-th variety. This is shown in Figure A8.2. Note that since production and demand functions are the same for all varieties, so will be their prices and output levels. Now assuming that ε (which is identical as well) varies inversely with the number of units consumed (which is the case, for example, for a linear demand function), the combinations of $\frac{p}{W}$ and c for which MR = MC is a positively sloped locus. On the other hand, the combinations of $\frac{p}{W}$ and c for which p = AC is a negatively sloped locus. The pre-trade real wage and the consumption of any variety are thus given by $\left(\frac{p}{W}\right)_a$ and c_a in Figure A8.2. Hence, the number of varieties produced under autarchy in the home country equals:

$$n_a = \frac{L}{l} = \frac{L}{\alpha + \beta x_a} \tag{A8.22}$$

In an identical foreign country, the real wage, the output levels, and the number of varieties are similarly determined and will be the same as in the home country. Now consider opening up of trade between these identical home and foreign countries.

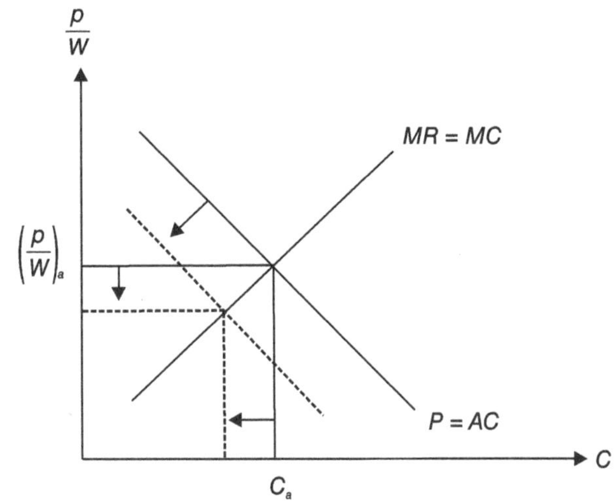

Figure A8.2 Effect of Trade on Real Wage and Consumption

Market integration increases the number of consumers for each variety. This is, in fact, equivalent to a growth in the labour force in a country. At initial consumption levels, an increase in the number of consumers (or growth in L), raises the output of each variety in the home country (as well as in the foreign country), and thus lowers AC. The price must then fall by free entry. Thus, the p = AC curve in Figure A8.2 shifts down. The equilibrium real wage rises and the consumption of each variety thus falls.

It immediately follows then that the number of varieties will increase in the global economy. Note, trade and market integration has the same effect on the *total* number of varieties as a growth in labour force has on the number of varieties produced by a country. For the integrated world economy, $(L + L^*)$ represents both a larger number of consumers and a larger workforce to produce the total number of varieties. So, algebraically, we can work out the effect of trade on the total number of varieties, $n + n^*$, by a growth in L on the number of varieties n. Algebraically, from equation (A8.18) we have,

$$(\alpha + \beta x)dn + n\beta dx = dL$$

$$\Rightarrow \hat{n} + \frac{\beta x}{\alpha + \beta x}\hat{x} = \hat{L}$$

$$\Rightarrow \hat{n} = \hat{L} - \frac{\beta x}{\alpha + \beta x}\hat{x} \tag{A8.23}$$

Since, for the reasons spelled out above, consumption of each variety will fall (see Figure A8.2), so the output of each variety will decline to some extent. Thus, at the final equilibrium the percentage increase in the output levels of each variety will be less than proportional to the percentage increase in the labour force (and the number of consumers):

$$\hat{x} = \hat{L} + \hat{c} < \hat{L} \ \text{[since } \hat{c} < 0\text{]} \tag{A8.24}$$

Since $\frac{\beta x}{\alpha + \beta x} < 1$, so by (A8.24), $\hat{n} > 0$.

Thus, trade and market integration raise both the real wage in each country and the total number of varieties. The countries thus unambiguously gain from IIT.

SUMMARY POINTS

- Grubel and Lloyd (1975) observed that a large proportion of world trade is among similar countries and in similar products. Such trade, which emphasizes trade among dissimilar countries, needs a different explanation than arbitrage and comparative advantage.
- The new trade theories that emerged in the late 1970s and in the 1980s offer explanations of intra-industry trade (IIT) in similar products among similar countries in terms of transport costs, economies of scale, imperfect competition, and product differentiation.
- IIT in identical products can arise due to market imperfection and the motive for *reciprocal dumping* by firms. The post-trade oligopolistic market structure creates scope for strategic interaction among firms as well as among national governments. As such this body of IIT literature is also known as the *strategic trade theory*.

(*contd*)

Summary Points (*contd*)

- Economies of scale, or increasing returns to scale technology, which itself give rise to market power for firms, is a main explanation for IIT in *differentiated* products. There are two distinct theoretical explanations, one is based on Dixit and Stiglitz's 'love for variety' approach and the other on the 'characteristics' approach developed by Lancaster.
- Income disparity within poor and rich countries creates scope for these countries to export the same good of different qualities to each other. Thus, income disparity is a major explanation for IIT in vertically (or quality) differentiated products. There can also be the usual factor endowment basis for comparative advantage and trade in vertically differentiated products.
- The most commonly used measure of intra-industry trade is the Grubel–Lloyd (GL) index. There are broadly two refinements of the GL index. One is aimed at providing a more meaningful basis for the analysis of adjustment needed due to trade imbalances, and the other is targeted at disentangling vertical and horizontal IIT.

KEYWORDS

- **Intra-industry trade** is export and import of identical or similar products. Similar products may be products of different varieties or of different qualities.
- **Dumping**, in the context of international trade law, is defined as the export of a product at a price that is either below the price charged in the domestic market or a substantial increase in supply of a good in the export market.
- **Love for variety** preference suggests if utility improves with the number of varieties that a consumer can consume, then she will buy all the available varieties if her income permits.
- **Characteristics approach** suggests that every consumer views a product as a bundle of characteristics or attributes.

EXERCISES

1. Why cannot comparative advantage and arbitrage be a plausible explanation for trade between similar countries?
2. When and how is IIT in identical products possible?
3. Suppose Sony and Kodak produce an identical variety of digital camera at an identical and constant cost of 20 per unit. They face the following identical linear demand for their products in their respective native countries, $P = 100 - X$, where X is the total supply of digital cameras.
   (a) Find out the pre-trade prices and output levels in each country.
   (b) When trade opens up between Japan and the United States, at what price should each digital camera be sold in the two countries? Assume that Sony and Kodak choose their respective output levels in a Cournot fashion.
   (c) Do the countries gain from trade?
4. Suppose exporting digital cameras involves transport costs, which are identical for Sony and Kodak and are given by $T = \frac{1}{2}(x_{ij})^2$, where x_{ij} is the export of the i-th firm (Sony or Kodak) in the j-th country (Japan or the United States) market. Given the demand and cost functions specified in the above problem, should there be any trade in digital cameras? If so, will there be gains from such trade?
5. How does your answer to the above problem change, if at all, if the transport costs are iceberg type as specified in the text with $g = \frac{1}{4}$?
6. How are the economies of scale relevant in explaining IIT in differentiated products?
7. Why is the pattern of trade indeterminate in the 'love for variety' approach to IIT in horizontally differentiated products?
8. In the characteristic approach to IIT in horizontally differentiated products, if all consumers everywhere have identical preferences, should IIT take place?
9. Suppose there are only two groups of consumers C_1 and C_2 with their ideal bundle of characteristics (or product) being M_1 and M_2 respectively in each of the two countries, say, Germany and Italy. Pre-trade neither of these ideal products was available in the two countries. Is two-way trade possible between Germany and Italy?
10. In the set up discussed in Section 8.3 in the text, explain how the following policies will affect the selection of quality by the producers of good Z:
    (a) a small capital inflow
    (b) a minimum unskilled money wage set by the local government above the market clearing rate.
11. [Advanced] Suppose chemicals are produced in India by skilled labour and capital. Its quality is indexed by $Q \in [0, \overline{Q}]$ and is observable to all. Per unit requirement of each factor is fixed for any given quality of it though increases with higher quality. Suppose, 1 per cent increase in quality requires more than 1 per cent increase in skilled labour but less than 1 per cent increase in capital per unit of output. Show that any exogenous shock that increases the rate of return to capital will raise the quality of chemicals produced.

(contd)

Exercises (*contd*)

12. [Advanced] In the table below data on bilateral trade between China and India is reported for select product categories at the 3-digit and 4-digit levels of disaggregation for the years 2000, 2002, and 2004.
    (a) Comment on the nature of trade in cotton yarn (not put up for retail sale) during these years.
    (b) Calculate the bilateral IIT using the GL index defined in section 8.3 for 3-digit and 4-digit product classes. Assume that India and China trade with each other only in these products.

Table Bilateral Trade between China and India (Values in '000 USD)

Product Class/Category	HS	India's Exports to China			China's Exports to India		
	Code	2000	2002	2004	2000	2002	2004
Cotton, not carded or combed	5,201	0	120	17,120	19,179	5,130	490
Cotton Yarn, not put up for retail sale	5,205	36,395	38,320	31,290	473	140	200
Cotton Yarn, put up for retail sale	5,207	19,909	17,550	23,620	0	0	0
Woven Fabrics of Cotton, weighing not more than 200 g/m^2	5,208	6,026	2,210	2,630	7,214	13,110	42,140
Woven Fabrics of Cotton, weighing more than 200 g/m^2	5,209	4,835	4,320	4,060	1,351	10,070	20,450
Cotton Yarn and Fabrics, (3-digit)	**520**	**67,165**	**62,520**	**78,720**	**28,217**	**28,450**	**63,280**
Woven Fabrics of Cotton, mixed, weighing not more than 200 g/m^2	5,210	318	150	20	736	2,380	4,970
Woven Fabrics of Cotton, mixed, weighing more than 200 g/m^2	5,211	0	0	970	266	750	5,720
Other Woven Fabrics of Cotton	5,212	124	50	240	182	240	10
Cotton Fabrics, Mixed (3-digit)	**521**	**442**	**200**	**1,230**	**1,184**	**3,370**	**10,700**
Synthetic Filament Yarn	5,402	255	330	1,640	1,673	6,320	60,920
Artificial Filament Yarn	5,403	0	370	70	131	21,440	17,230
Woven Fabrics of Synthetic Filament Yarn	5,407	417	790	210	2,812	36,060	75,760
Filament Yarn (3-digit)	**540**	**672**	**1,490**	**1,920**	**4,616**	**63,820**	**1,53,910**
Synthetic Staple Fibres	5,503	627	1,260	13,070	12	920	3,240
Artificial Staple Fibres	5,504	61	220	330	0	0	110
Yarn of Synthetic Staple Fibres	5,509	226	550	260	273	540	1,600
Staple Fibres (3-digit)	**550**	**914**	**2,030**	**13,660**	**285**	**1,460**	**4,950**
Yarn of Artificial Staple Fibres	5,510	393	1,150	80	471	1,330	4,260
Other Woven Fabrics of Synthetic Staple Fibres	5,515	1,089	1,550	1,580	3,133	630	2,990
Woven Fabrics of Artificial Staple Fibres	5,516	228	70	0	873	1,210	5,870
Other Yarn and Fabrics of Staple Fibres	**551**	**1,710**	**2,770**	**1,660**	**4,477**	**3,170**	**13,120**

SUGGESTED READING

Acharyya, R. and R. W. Jones. (2001). 'Export Quality and Income Distribution in a Small Dependent Economy'. International Review of Economics and Finance 10, 337–51.

Bhagwati, J.N., A. Panagariya, and T.N. Srinivasan. (1998). *Lectures on International Trade*. Cambridge, MA: MIT Press.

Brander, James A. (1981). 'Intra-industry Trade in Identical Commodities', *Journal of International Economics*, 11: 1–14.

Brander, J. and P. Krugman. (1983). 'A Reciprocal Dumping Model of International Trade', *Journal of International Economics*, 15: 313–21.

Krugman, P.R. (1979). 'Increasing Returns, Monopolistic Competition and International Trade', *Journal of International Economics*, 9(4): 469–79.

Lancaster, K. (1979). *Variety, Equity, and Efficiency*. New York: Columbia University Press.

Melitz, M. J. (2003). 'The Impact of Trade on Intra-industry Reallocations and Aggregate Industry Productivity'. Econometrica, 71(6): 1695–725.

ADVANCED READING

Arrow, K. (1962). 'Economic Welfare and the Allocation of Resources for Invention', in R. Nelson (ed.), *The Rate and Direction of Inventive Activity*. New Jersey: Princeton University Press, pp. 609–25.

Balassa, B. (1979). 'Intra-industry Trade and the Integration of Developing Countries in the World Economy', in H. Glersch (ed.), *On the Economics of Intra-industry Trade*. Tubingen, Germany: J.C.B. Mohr, pp. 245–70.

Bergstrand, J.H. (1983). 'Measurement and Determinants of Intra-industry International Trade', in P.K. Mathew Tharakan (ed.), *Intra-industry Trade— Empirical and Methodological Aspects*. North Holland: Amsterdam, pp. 201–53.

Bernard, A. B., J. Eaton, J.B. Jensen and S. Kortum. (2003). 'Plants and Productivity in International Trade'. American Economic Review, 93(4): 1268–90.

Brulhart, M. (2009). 'An Account of Global Intra-industry Trade, 1962–2006', *World Economy*, 32 (3): 401–45.

Dixit, A. and J. Stiglitz (1977). 'Monopolistic Competition and Optimum Product Diversity', *American Economic Review* 67(3): 297–308.

Fontagné, L. and M. Freudenberg (2002). 'Long-Term Trends in Intra-industry Trade', in H. Grubel and H.H. Lee (eds), *Frontiers of Research on Intra-Industry Trade*, chapter 8. London: Palgrave.

Ganguly, S., and R. Acharyya. (2021). 'Emigration, Tax on Remittances and Export Quality'. *South Asian Journal of Macroeconomics and Public Finance*, Online First. DOI: 10.1177/2277978720980236.

Greenaway, D., R. Hine, and C. Milner. (1994). 'Country-Specific Factors and the Pattern of Horizontal and Vertical Intra-industry Trade in the UK', *Weltwirtschaftliches Archiv*, 130: 77–100.

Greenaway, D. and C.R. Milner. (1984). 'A Cross-Section Analysis of Intra-industry Trade in the UK', *European Economic Review*, 25: 319–44.

Grubel, H.G. and P.J. Lloyd. (1975). *Intra-industry Trade: The Theory and Measurement of International Trade in Differentiated Products*. New York: Wiley.

Gruen, F.H. and M.W. Corden. (1970). 'A Tariff That Worsens the Terms of Trade'. In: I.A. McDougall and R.H. Snape (eds.), *Studies in International Economics*. North Holland, Amsterdam.

Helpman, E. (1981). 'International Trade in Presence of Product Differentiation, Economies of Scale and Monopolistic Competition: A Chamberlin-Heckscher-Ohlin Approach', *Journal of International Economics*, 11: 305–340.

Lall, S. (2000). 'The Technological Structure and Performance of Developing Country Manufactured Exports, 1985–1998', *Oxford Development Studies*, 28(3): 337–69.

Linder, S.B. (1961). *An Essay in Trade and Transformation*. New York: Wiley, pp. 337–70.

Marjit, S. and A. Raychaudhuri. (1997). *India's Exports: An Analytical Study*. New Delhi: Oxford University Press.

Posner, M.V. (1961). 'International Trade and Technical Change', *Oxford Economic Papers*, 13: 323–41.

Schott, P. K. (2004). 'Across-Product versus Within-Product Specialization in International Trade'. *The Quarterly Journal of Economics*, 119(2): 647–78.

Vernon, R. (1966). 'International Investment and International Trade in the Product Cycle', *Quarterly Journal of Economics*, 80: 90–207.

PART IV

Trade Intervention and Coordination

9 Import Tariff and Export Subsidies

International trade among countries has hardly been unrestricted and free in the past as well as at present. Countries, developing and developed alike, adopt different types of trade policies to influence the free flow of commodity trade. Some countries are more *inward-looking* and adopt import restriction policies. Others are more *outward-oriented* and thus adopt export promotion policies. The modes of trade restrictions and promotion also vary widely across countries. There are varieties of reasons for such trade interventions and restrictions. This chapter and the next discuss the different modes and rationale for trade restrictions and promotion.

The different types of trade interventions can be categorized and distinguished from each other in broadly two ways. The first distinction is between trade policies that restrict trade and those that promote trade. Trade restriction policies include import tariffs, import quotas, export tax, and voluntary export restraints. Trade promotion policies, on the other hand, include export and import subsidies. The second distinction is between trade interventions that regulate or affect the *prices* of traded goods and trade interventions that regulate the *volume* of imports or exports. The former are price interventions (such as tariffs, export tax, subsidies, and pollution content tariffs) and the latter quantitative restrictions (QRs) or non-tariff barriers (NTBs) to trade (such as import quotas, voluntary export restraints, and environmental standards). In some cases, price interventions or policies are equivalent to the corresponding QR or NTB in their economic effects, and in some cases they are not, as we will see later.

In this chapter we discuss price interventions like import tariffs and export subsidies. QRs or NTBs and the equivalence with relevant price interventions are discussed in the next chapter. We begin with the economic effects of an import tariff and the dead-weight loss that it introduces in the market for the import good under consideration. Effects on the rest of the economy and the global economy are considered thereafter; this also enables us to focus on the consequent change in the terms of trade (TOT) and the corresponding change in the national welfare level.

International Economics. Rajat Acharyya, Oxford University Press. © Oxford University Press 2022.
DOI: 10.1093/oso/9780192865144.003.0009

9.1 ECONOMIC EFFECTS OF AN IMPORT TARIFF: A PARTIAL EQUILIBRIUM ANALYSIS

Consider the domestic market for an import-competing good in the home country, say locally produced computers, as illustrated in Figure 9.1. Suppose, imported computers and the locally produced ones are identical or perfect substitutes for each other. In Figure 9.1a, given the domestic demand and the supply curves for computers, the pre-trade (relative) price of computers is Op_a. In Figure 9.1b, which depicts import demand (or the domestic excess demand for computers) and the import supply curves, the import demand corresponding to this pre-trade price is zero. If the free trade price ratio p^W is Oa, the country imports $be = M_f$ units of computers, which is the excess demand in the home country market at that price.

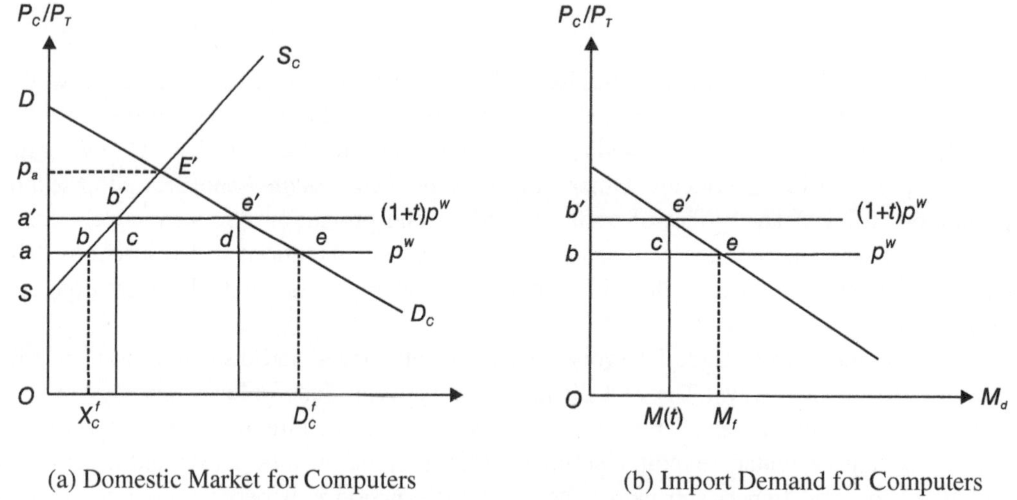

Figure 9.1 Economic Effects of an Import Tariff

Now suppose an ad-valorem tariff at the rate $t < 1$ is imposed by the home country on the import of computers. This raises the domestic import price of computers to $(1 + t)\ p^W$, at the initial p^W. Of course, the world price may change as we will discuss later, but in this partial equilibrium analysis, under the *ceteris paribus* assumption, we hold it fixed. The higher domestic price of computers raises local production and lowers local demand for computers. As a consequence, the import volume falls to $b'e' = M(t)$. There are several implications of this import tariff and consequent rise in the domestic relative price of computers. First of all, the import tariff generates protection for local computer producers. Competition from efficient foreign producers is now restricted by the tariff, and this enables them to produce more computers locally. As a consequence, local producers gain in terms of local market share as well as producers' surplus. The *increase* in the producers' surplus, by the surplus measure discussed in Chapter 2, is the area *aa'b'b*. Second, the domestic consumers now pay a higher price for both imported and locally produced computers. They buy less now, and suffer utility losses as measured by the decline in the consumers' surplus by the area *aa'e'e*. Third, the domestic government earns a tariff revenue, $tp^WM(t)$, as measured by the area *b'cde'*.

Does the economy gain or lose from imposition of this import tariff? Referring back to Figure 9.1a, the total surplus declines by the area *bb'c* and the area *de'e*. Thus, by the surplus measure in this partial equilibrium analysis, *the economy loses at the initial TOT*. Note that, of the total loss in the consumers' surplus (the area *aa'e'e*), the area *aa'b'b* is redistributed among domestic producers of computers as increase in their surplus and the area *b'cde'* goes to the domestic government as tariff revenue. Thus, the area *bb'c* and area *de'e* constitute the net loss or *dead-weight loss* (DWL) from the imposition of an ad-valorem import tariff, at the initial TOT. The corresponding loss in the total surplus or DWL in Figure 9.1b is the area *ce'e*.

These two components of DWL (in Figure 9.1a) are production and the consumption losses respectively. Production losses arise because an import tariff replaces in part the low-cost and efficient foreign supply by the high-cost and inefficient local production of computers. Consumption losses, on the other hand, arise because of the reduction in the consumption of computers due to the higher tariff-inclusive price of computers. The magnitudes of these DWL depend on three things: the rate of tariff, the price elasticity of demand for computers, and the price elasticity of the supply of computers. It is immediate that the larger the tariff rate, *ceteris paribus*, larger will be production and consumption losses. This is because a higher tariff taxes the consumers more and thereby lowers the consumption of computers by a greater magnitude. Thus, the consumption loss will be larger. On the other hand, a higher tariff generates more protection for cost-inefficient local producers and replaces the cost-inefficient foreign supply by a greater margin. Hence, the production loss will be larger as well. Similar effects are achieved when the demand and supply curves are *more elastic*. A more elastic demand curve means a 10 per cent tariff and corresponding proportionate increase in the tariff-inclusive

Box 9.1 Trade Protection and Dead-Weight Losses in the Indian Manufacturing Sector

During the 1970s and 1980s domestic industries in India were highly protective with tariff protection being more than 100 per cent in many lines of production. QRs were also widespread. From 1985 onwards the trade liberalization processes began, but more drastic policy changes were implemented only after the balance of payments crisis in 1991. In March-April 1991, India had foreign exchange reserves that could barely finance its import bills for two weeks. This forced policymakers to restructure and rationalize both its trade and exchange rate policies. By April 2001 almost the entire contingent of importable commodities was brought under the open general license (OGL) category. Subsequently, peak tariff rates have been lowered considerably.

Satya P. Das (2004) measured changes in DWL following such tariff reductions during 1993–98 in eight manufacturing sectors using the surplus measure as discussed above. The estimated DWL was quite high in sectors like iron and steel and inorganic chemicals, because tariff rates were still quite high on the import of these goods. On the other hand, DWL declined significantly in the machinery sector from Rs 1,433.45 crore in 1995–96 to Rs 180.30 crore in 1997–98 and in the pearls, precious, and semi-precious stones sector from Rs 478.84 crore in 1995–96 to Rs 78.41 crore in 1997–98. In these sectors, tariff reductions amounted to more than 80 per cent.

domestic relative price will cause the demand for computers to decline by a larger magnitude than when the demand curve is less elastic. On the other hand, local production and supply increases more when the supply is more elastic than when it is less elastic.

Thus, it seems that trade restrictions through an import tariff are not good for the economy *as a whole* at the initial TOT. These benefit local producers of computers and also bring revenue for the national exchequer, which by themselves may be important for governments in poor countries. But they adversely affect consumers, and by the surplus measure this loss far outweighs the gains for the producers and for the exchequer. Overall, the economy loses. Reversing the argument, it appears that import liberalization through a tariff reduction should benefit consumers more than it hurts local producers and the national exchequer as long as TOT does not change. Thus, the economy gains overall from such a policy of import liberalization through tariff reduction.

Two comments deserve attention. First, tariff protection (or conversely, tariff reduction) generates a conflict of interest among the relevant economic agents and accordingly the political support for such a policy change is divided. The conflict of interest also means that a tariff policy is not Pareto superior to unrestricted imports, without a compensation for the losers. Second, there seems to be a conflict between the objectives of the local government as well. The revenue motive for imposing an import tariff comes with a welfare cost. On the other hand, tariff reduction lowers DWL and thus raises social welfare, but at the same time it *may* mean a loss of tariff revenue.

The above protective and welfare effects may, however, be different when the effects of an import tariff on the rest of the economy and the world are considered in a general equilibrium setting. This is because TOT may change, which in turn affects the domestic relative price of the imported and locally produced computers. Moreover, the partial equilibrium analysis above takes into account only the volume of import effect. There would be an impact on the volume of exports as well. The overall welfare effect of a tariff imposition (or tariff reduction) thus will be different when we take into account the *volume of trade* and the TOT effects as we explain in Section 9.3.

9.2 REVENUE MOTIVE AND REVENUE MAXIMIZING TARIFF

As we have mentioned, international trade in many developing and poor countries is an important source of tax revenue for the governments. Box 9.2 and Figure 9.2 illustrate this. This is one reason, apart from protecting domestic industries, particularly infant industries (to which we will return later), why countries often impose tariffs on the import of *consumer goods*. However, even the revenue motive does not necessarily justify very high tariff rates being imposed on many imported goods. Figure 9.3 explains this. The hump-shaped curve is the tariff revenue curve plotted against tariff rates. The tariff revenue curve starts from the origin because zero tariff (or free trade) does not generate any revenue. On the other hand, as is evident from Figure 9.1, a very high tariff chokes off or prohibits all imports of computers so that no revenue is earned either. This tariff rate is the prohibitive tariff rate (t_p) such that $(1+t_p)p^W = p_a$. For positive tariff rates less than this prohibitive rate, tariff revenue is a strictly concave function: it first increases with the tariff rate and beyond a critical rate t_R declines with further increase in the tariff rate.

Box 9.2 Trade Taxes as a Source of Government Revenue

For many countries, particularly for the poorer countries, trade taxes have been a major source of revenue. As illustrated in Figure 9.2, low and lower middle-income countries collected approximately between 6 and 8 per cent of their total tax revenues from trade taxes during 2008–18, despite significant reductions of tariff rates and other trade taxes by most of these countries after 2000. The interesting point to note is that the share of trade taxes in total revenue is somewhat inversely related to the income level of countries. Whereas for middle-income countries, trade taxes have contributed approximately 5 per cent of their total tax revenue, for upper middle-income countries the share has been even lower. India, given its legacy of long years of protectionism, has been one of the very few developing countries that have been collecting large amounts of revenues from trade taxes. Whereas the share of traded taxes was almost one-third in 1980s and 1990s, it has still been quite high, hovering around 12–14 per cent during 2008–16.

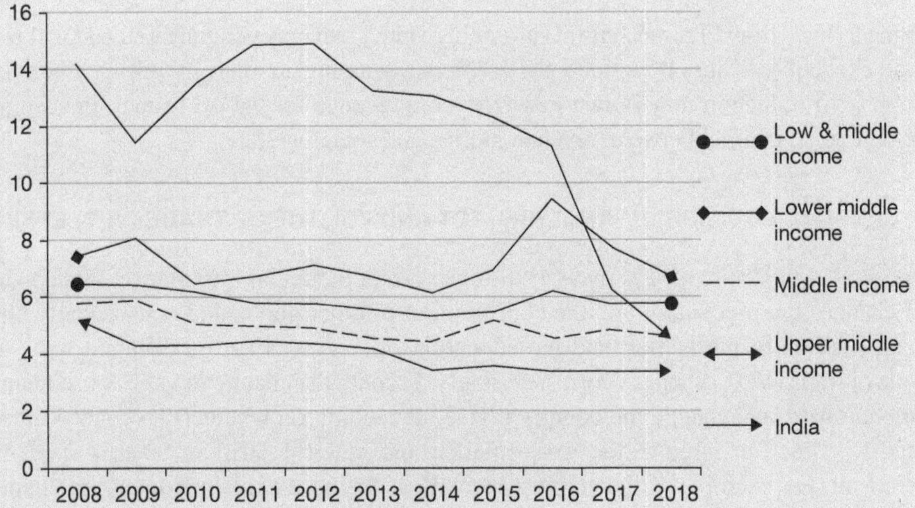

Figure 9.2 Taxes on International Trade (Per cent of Tax Revenue)

Source: Compiled from World Development Indicators, World Bank.

The reason for this is simple. An increase in tariff raises the domestic price of imported computers proportionately for a given TOT, and consequently lowers the import volume. Total revenue increases if this fall in import volume is less than proportionate to the price increase (or the rate of increase in the tariff rate), that is, if import demand is inelastic. Otherwise, when import demand is elastic, tariff revenue declines with an increase in the tariff rate. For a low tariff rate, the corresponding tariff-inclusive domestic price of imported computers is low as well. For the linear import demand curve in Figure 9.1b then, the import demand is inelastic for low price and corresponding high volume of imports. Thus, starting from a low tariff, if the tariff rate is raised, the import demand being inelastic, tariff revenue rises.

But when tariff rates are high (and so are the tariff-inclusive prices), the elasticity value becomes large to lower tariff revenue. Appendix A9 provides the algebraic derivation of this condition and expression for the revenue maximizing tariff rate t_R.

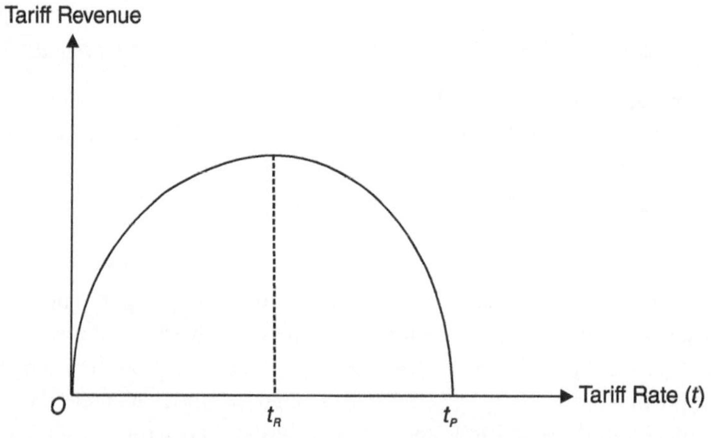

Figure 9.3 Revenue Maximizing Tariff Rate

What follows from Figure 9.3 is that a very high tariff rate may generate a small tariff revenue for the exchequer. Thus, if initially the tariff rate was higher than t_R, import liberalization through tariff reduction may in fact generate more revenue for the exchequer. In such a case, there will be no conflict between revenue motive and social welfare.

9.3 GENERAL EQUILIBRIUM ANALYSIS: TOT AND VOLUME OF TRADE (VOT) EFFECTS

In a general equilibrium set-up, two sets of issues are of particular importance. First, an import tariff changes the production and the consumption of other goods and consequently changes the composition of production and the allocation of resources across different sectors. The volume of trade (VOT) changes correspondingly. Second, the change in VOT consequent upon an import tariff may change the country's TOT, depending on whether the country imposing the tariff is small or large in the world market and how the tariff revenue is spent by the government. For example, if the country is small, as we have explained in earlier chapters, it cannot influence its TOT. It is a price taker in the world market. Its TOT will thus not change however large the tariff may be and regardless of whether the tariff is raised or reduced. It is only for a large country that an imposition of a tariff (or a change in its rate, raised or lowered) will have any impact on its TOT. The direction of the change in TOT, however, will depend on how the tariff revenue collected is being used by the government. Before elaborating on these issues, we examine the change in the composition of output and the consequent resource allocation for a small country. The small country case allows us to separate out these effects and the consequent VOT change from the change in TOT.

9.3.1 Change in Output, Consumption, and Volume of Trade for a Small Economy

Consider a small open economy producing two commodities—computers (being imported) and cotton textiles (being exported). For a given TOT, a 10 per cent ad-valorem tariff on the import of computers raises its domestic tariff inclusive relative price by the same percentage points. As we have explained above, this higher relative price of computers will encourage domestic production of computers. But, if initially all resources were fully employed in the production of these two goods, expansion in the production of computers must draw resources from the textile sector, thereby causing a contraction of this sector. Thus, an import tariff expands the domestic import-competing sector and contracts the export sector. On the other hand, higher domestic relative price of computers shifts consumption away from computers to textiles. Consequently, both the excess demand for computers (or the volume of imports) and the excess supply of textiles (or the volume of exports) *decline*. That is, an import tariff *lowers the volume of trade*.

As a consequence, the economy unambiguously loses. The welfare loss arises on two counts. First, a tariff now reallocates resources towards the production of the import-competing good in which the country has a comparative *dis*advantage. There is thus a specialization loss. Second, domestic consumers are forced to pay a higher price for computers and thus change their desired consumption pattern. These output, consumption, and welfare changes for any given TOT (or for a small open economy) are illustrated in Figure 9.4.

Under the assumptions of CRS technology and diminishing marginal productivities, PPF is drawn strictly concave downwards. Initially, under free trade, the domestic and world relative prices of computers were the same and this is reciprocal of the absolute slope of the price line p^W. Free trade production and consumption were thus at points P and C respectively. An import tariff raises the domestic relative price above the world price and this is measured by the reciprocal of the absolute slope of the price line p_d. Production thus shifts to P_t where this price line is tangent to PPF, thereby satisfying the marginal condition $1/p_d = MRT$. Thus, resources are reallocated towards the import-competing sector. The consumption bundle, on the other hand, must now satisfy the condition $1/p_d = MRS$, because domestic consumers now pay p_d rather than p^W for computer imports. At the same time, since the economy pays p^W to the rest of the world for its imports, the value of the consumption bundle must equal the value of production bundle P_t at world price p^W. That is, the consumption bundle C_t must lie on the broken line through production bundle P_t which is parallel to the p^W-line, and be such that the CIC that contains this bundle is tangent to the line which is parallel to the p_d-line reflecting the tariff-inclusive relative price of computers. Thus, the consumption of computers declines. The volume of imports now equals KC_t and the volume of exports equals KP_t, both smaller than the free trade levels.

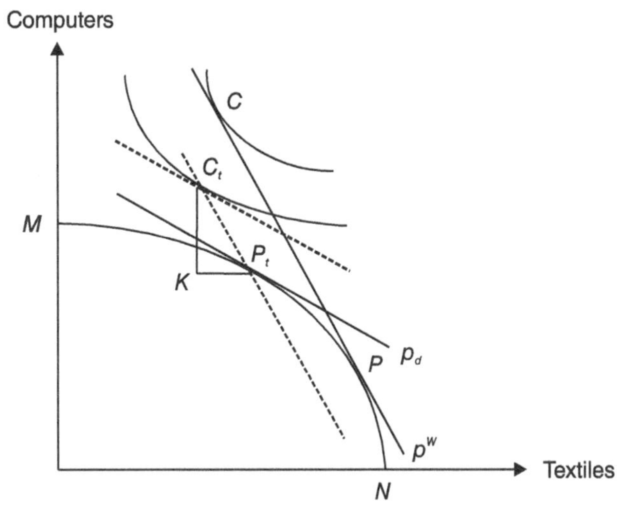

Figure 9.4 Effect of Tariff on Production and Consumption

It is also immediate that tariff lowers welfare, at the given TOT. Thus, for a small open economy, tariff is unambiguously welfare reducing. Moreover, higher the tariff rate, the smaller is the volume of trade and hence lower is its national welfare. That is, the welfare of a small country *monotonically decreases* as the tariff rate is raised successively. Figure 9.4a below illustrates this. Welfare or real income (W) falls till the prohibitive tariff rate t_p chokes off and prohibits all trade. The real income remains invariant at the autarchic level W_A beyond this rate. Alternatively, trade liberalization through successive reduction of tariff rates monotonically raises the welfare of a small open economy. Thus, free trade is its best policy as far as the national welfare of the economy is concerned.

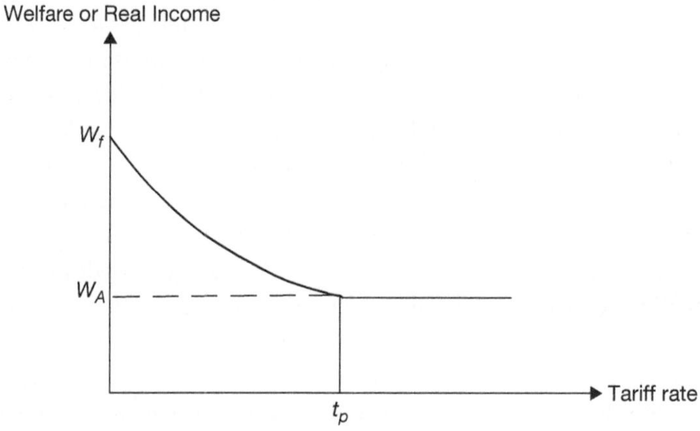

Figure 9.4a Tariff and Welfare of a Small Country

9.3.2 TOT Effect, Welfare Change, and the Optimum Tariff for a Large Country

For a large tariff-imposing country, a tariff changes its TOT along with its VOT. The direction of change in TOT, however, is related to how the tariff revenue is used by the government. The implicit assumption used in the standard trade theory and in the discussion above is that the tariff revenue is redistributed among domestic consumers in a lump-sum manner. Abba P. Lerner (1936) considered an alternative case where the government itself spends the tariff revenue on computers and textiles. His case is discussed in Appendix A9.

The implication of the assumption of redistribution of tariff revenue is as follows. A tariff raises the domestic price and lowers the import demand by the absolute value of the import demand elasticity (ε) *at the margin*. On the other hand, since the redistribution of tariff revenue raises the income of consumers, they *raise* their import demand by the value of marginal propensity to consume *at the margin*. Thus, a tariff changes the demand for imports by the magnitude ($m - \varepsilon$) *at the margin*. But, as shown in Appendix A9, the import demand elasticity has three components: the compensated price elasticity of demand for the import good ($\bar{e}$) that captures the pure substitution effect of a change in the domestic relative price; the marginal propensity to import or to consume the imported good (m) that captures the (real) income effect of the price change; and the price elasticity of the supply of the import-competing good (e_S). Therefore, when tariff revenue is redistributed among domestic consumers, the income effect that it triggers is washed out by the income effect of the change in the domestic relative price. Consequently a tariff unambiguously lowers the import demand *at initial TOT* by the pure substitution effect in demand and the substitution effect in supply (or the decline in the supply of the import-competing good).

It is then immediate that a tariff imposed by a large country on its import of computers will improve TOT in its favour. This is because as the tariff lowers its import demand, it generates an excess supply of computers in the world market at the initial TOT. The country being large, a fall in its import demand and consequent excess supply is significant enough to lower the world relative price of computers. Figure 9.5 depicting the offer curves in a two-country world illustrates this. An import tariff shifts the home country's offer curve to the left since at the initial TOT a lower volume of exports can finance its smaller import demand. That is, the tariff-imposing home country's offer of exports falls when it imposes an import tariff. Larger the tariff rate, the smaller is its import demand necessitating an even smaller export offer to finance the import bill. Hence, larger is the leftward shift (or rotation) of its offer curve. The global market equilibrium under an import tariff imposed by the home country now shifts to E_t and TOT improves for the home country as indicated by the absolute slope of the steeper line segment OE_t.

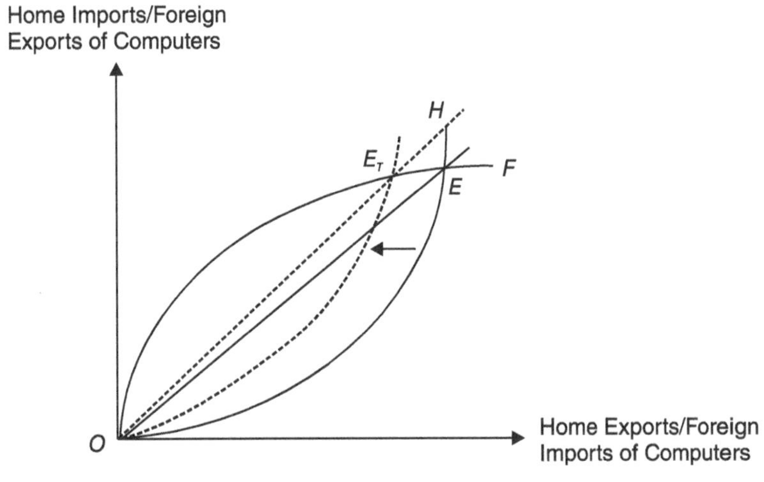

Figure 9.5 Import Tariff and TOT

TOT improvement for the large tariff-imposing country (under the assumption that the tariff revenue is redistributed among domestic consumers in a lump-sum way) brings a real income gain or welfare improvement. The reason, as explained in Chapter 4, is that the country can now buy its imports cheaper and sell its exports dearer. This welfare improvement due to TOT improvement counters the welfare loss due to a decline in VOT as explained above. Note that in Figure 9.5, both the volume of imports and the volume of exports fall. Thus, the change in welfare following a tariff imposition (or increase in its rate) depends on these favourable TOT and adverse VOT effects. For small tariff rates, the decline in volume of trade is small and consequently the welfare of the home country improves through a stronger TOT effect. But as the tariff rate is raised successively, VOT declines by greater magnitudes and consequently the welfare loss on this account becomes successively larger. Beyond a critical rate of tariff, the

VOT effect dominates the TOT effect and the country's welfare starts declining. The critical rate of tariff for which the TOT and the VOT effects are equal at the margin, and the tariff-imposing home country's welfare is maximum, is the optimum tariff rate, t_{opt}.

Recall from the analysis in Chapter 4 that a country's welfare from trade can be measured by its trade indifference curve (*TIC*). Referring back to Figure 9.5, the welfare of the home country corresponding to the tariff equilibrium could be indicated by *TIC* (not drawn) passing through the point E_t (but not tangent to the post-tariff TOT line OE_t).[1] Compared to the *TIC* tangent to the free trade TOT line OE, this *TIC* will be higher and thus indicate a higher national welfare. Thus, using the concept of *TIC* and its properties, we can rank different tariff rates in terms of the corresponding national welfare levels that they yield for the tariff-imposing country. Figure 9.6 illustrates such welfare ranking of tariff rates.

Note that *TICs* are assumed to be non-intersecting with each other (for the same reason as CICs are assumed to be non-intersecting with each other). It is then immediate from Figure 9.6 that for any tariff rate that displaces the home offer curve along the *EE′* segment of the foreign offer curve *OF*, the corresponding *TIC* will be strictly higher than the TIC_f that corresponds to free trade. That is, all such tariff rates raise the home country's welfare above the free trade level. But for tariff rates even larger, VOT declines so much that welfare dips below the free trade level. Among the tariff rates for which the welfare is higher than the free trade level, the optimum tariff rate is the one for which the country attains the highest possible *TIC* and thus realizes the maximum possible welfare, *given the foreign offer curve*. This is the tariff which displaces the home offer curve to OH_{opt} that passes through the point E_{opt} where the home TIC_{opt} is tangent to the foreign offer curve.

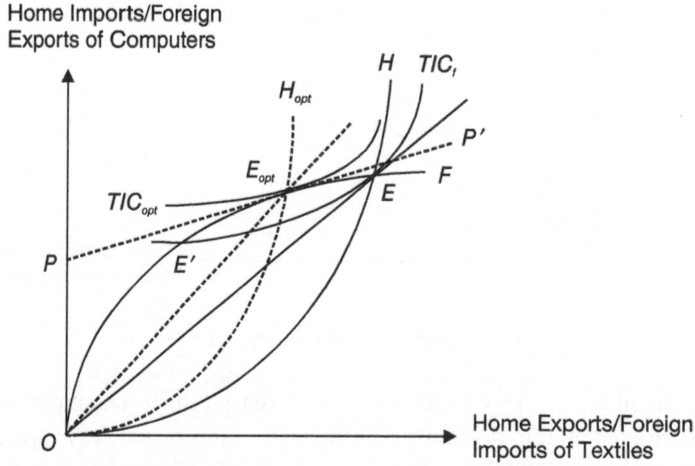

Figure 9.6 Optimum Import Tariff

Corresponding to this optimum tariff rate, TOT or the world relative price of imports is the reciprocal of the slope of the line segment OE_{opt}, and the optimum tariff-inclusive relative price

[1] Under an import tariff, $MRS = 1/p_d = 1/(1 + t)\, p^W$. Hence the home TIC will *not* be tangent to the post-tariff TOT line.

of imports (of computers) in the home country is the reciprocal of the slope of the line segment *PP'*. Since *PP'* is flatter than the line segment OE_{opt}, so the optimum tariff-inclusive relative price of imports (of computers) in the home country is larger than the world relative price at the optimum tariff equilibrium.

As derived in Appendix A9, the value of the optimum tariff for the home country is related to the foreign import demand elasticity in the following way:

$$t_{opt} = \frac{1}{\varepsilon^* - 1} \tag{9.1}$$

The optimum tariff is positive since for such a tariff the foreign import demand must be elastic ($\varepsilon^* > 1$). The reason is analogous to a monopolist charging its profit maximizing price along the elastic segment of the demand curve that she faces. Suppose that at some small tariff rate $\varepsilon^* < 1$, that is, the foreign offer curve is backward bending. It is easy to check that an increase in the tariff rate that shifts the home offer curve along the inelastic import demand (or backward bending) segment of the foreign offer curve, raises the import volume. TOT improves, on the other hand, regardless of the foreign import demand elasticity. Thus, as long as the home tariff shifts its offer curve along the inelastic import demand segment of the foreign offer curve, a successive increase in the tariff rate *monotonically raises* home welfare. But when a tariff shifts the home offer curve to the elastic import demand segment of the foreign offer curve, a further increase in the tariff rate lowers volume trade. Home welfare can still improve because of the TOT effect. But when tariff is raised too high (and correspondingly the VOT decline is too large) welfare will fall. Thus, the large home country will stop raising its tariff rate to maximize its welfare at some point along the elastic import demand segment of the foreign offer curve.

The non-monotonic relation between the welfare of a large country and its tariff rate, is illustrated in Figure 9.7. The free trade (or no tariff) welfare is denoted by W_f and the pre-trade welfare level by W_a. The tariff initially raises the welfare above the free trade level monotonically (but at a decreasing rate) up to the optimum tariff rate. The welfare gain from an improvement in TOT is larger than the welfare loss from a decline in VOT for all these tariff rates. For tariff rates higher than the optimum rate, VOT loss is larger than TOT improvement

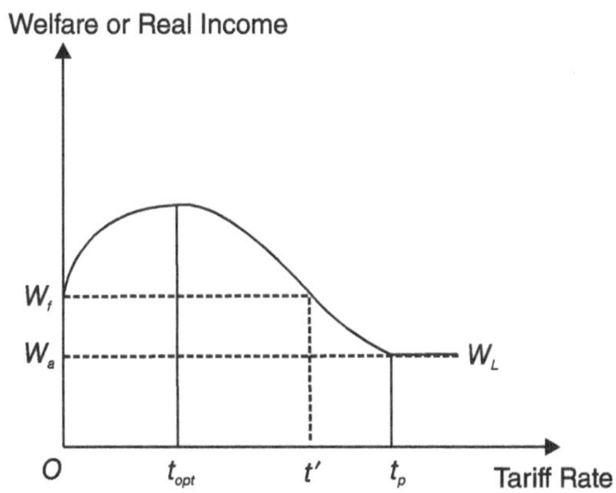

Figure 9.7 Tariff and Change in Welfare of a Large Country

Box 9.3 Optimum Tariff for a Small Country

The offer curve analysis can be used to show that for a small country, which cannot influence its TOT, the optimum tariff is zero. Since a small country is an insignificant buyer in the world market, so even if a tariff lowers its import demand, the world relative price of its imports will not change as a consequence. In terms of the above offer curve analysis, a small country *perceives* that it faces a linear foreign offer curve along which the foreign import demand that it faces is perfectly elastic ($\varepsilon^* = \infty$). However, note that the foreign offer curve is not actually a linear one. The logic here is that the *home country perceives it to be linear because it is so small that it can export and import any volume at a given TOT*. This is analogous to a perfectly competitive firm perceiving the demand for its product being perfectly elastic, despite the industry demand curve actually being downward sloping. It is immediate then that under this perception of $\varepsilon^* = \infty$, $t_{opt} = 0$ by the formula in (9.1). In Figure 9.8 below, when the small Home country imposes a tariff on imports from the foreign country, its offer curve shifts to the left—under the same conditions as for the large Home country—along the *perceived* linear offer curve of the (large) foreign country. The volume trade falls and the new trade bundle E_t lies in the worse set to the free trade bundle *E*. Tariff thus unambiguously lower its welfare. That is, free trade maximizes welfare, or equivalently, the optimum tariff is zero for a small country.

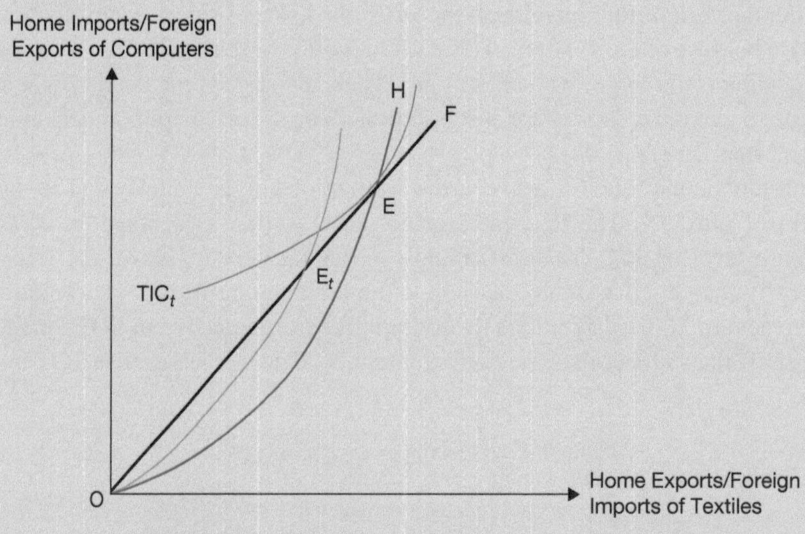

Figure 9.8 Optimum Tariff for a Small Country

and the welfare falls monotonically. The tariff-imposing large country's welfare is still above the free trade level up to the rate t', but thereafter it falls below the free trade level and attains the pre-trade welfare level at the prohibitive tariff rate, t_p.

9.3.3 Tariff Retaliation and Trade War among Countries

In the above welfare argument for an import tariff for a large home country, we have assumed that its trade partner, the foreign country, does not impose a tariff on its own imports of textiles from the home country. But this need not be the case. As long as the foreign country is also a large country, it will have a similar incentive to impose an import tariff to maximize its own welfare just as the home country does.

In fact, the incentive for the foreign country for imposing a tariff on its imports of textiles will be even larger when the home country imposes a tariff on import of computers from the foreign country. The reason is simple. When the home country alone imposes a tariff, TOT moves in its favour and *against the foreign country*. This TOT deterioration for the foreign country reinforces its welfare loss from a decline in VOT. Thus, *the foreign country is unambiguously hurt by an import tariff imposed by the home country*. It should then not remain passive, but retaliate by imposing a tariff. This is because a tariff imposed on its imports of textiles from the home country will move TOT in its favour and compensate partly for the welfare loss inflicted upon it by home country's tariff. Once the foreign country retaliates by imposing a tariff and thus improves its TOT, the corresponding welfare loss will induce the home country to retaliate by raising its tariff rate even higher. Thus, large countries, guided purely by the welfare maximization motive, are expected to engage in a tariff war.

Scitovsky (1942) argued that such tariff retaliation through successive increase of respective tariff rates will result in all trade between countries being terminated at the end. Thus, countries return to a no-trade or autarchic state, which is certainly bad for both the countries. The important policy implication that emerged from this argument is that free trade is the best option for even a large country. However, this poses a Prisoners' Dilemma kind of problem, though Scitovsky himself was not explicit on this. Each country understands that it is better not to impose any tariffs on imports from the other country because otherwise the trading partner will retaliate and the ensuing tariff war will dwindle away all trade between them. Yet, free trade (or no tariff) is not a Nash equilibrium strategy for either country. To explain why, suppose that the countries agree to trade goods without any restrictions. But such an agreement is not binding in the sense that there is no punishment scheme if a country deviates from the agreement. Then by the optimum tariff argument, each will have an incentive to unilaterally deviate from this free trade agreement by imposing a tariff on imports from the other. Thus, both countries imposing tariffs will be the Nash equilibrium.

But this does not necessarily mean that the prohibitive tariff rates that terminate all trade between them will be the only Nash equilibrium of the bilateral tariff war. Harry G. Johnson (1953) qualified the Scitovskian argument and characterized the post-retaliation global equilibrium using the best-response or the welfare-reaction functions similar to the output-reaction functions of Cournot oligopoly firms. He arrived at two important conclusions. First, some trade between the countries may still be left at the post-retaliation equilibrium (that is, at the Nash equilibrium choices of tariffs). In other words, there may exist a pair of Nash equilibrium *non*-prohibitive tariff rates for the home and foreign countries. Second, at the post-retaliation equilibrium, *one* country (though not both) *may* still gain compared to its free trade policy. His argument is illustrated in Figure 9.9. The welfare reaction functions of the home and foreign curves are shown by the curves ORR_H and ORR_F respectively. These curves represent the loci of best-response (or welfare maximizing) tariff-restricted trade bundles for a country given the tariff imposed by the other country. The graphical derivation of these curves is shown in Appendix A9. The tariff-retaliation Nash equilibrium is where the best-response tariff-restricted trade bundles match, that is, the two welfare-reaction functions intersect each other. Two possible equilibria are shown in Figure 9.9. One is the point *O* where all trade between the countries terminates. This is the Scitovskian equilibrium. The other is point *R* where countries still trade with each other. This is the Johnson equilibrium. At this equilibrium, as illustrated in Figure 9.9, both the countries lose since point *R* is below the *TIC*s corresponding to the free trade equilibrium point *E* for both the countries. TOT, as given by the absolute slope of the line segment *OR*, worsens for the foreign country relative to the free trade TOT. Thus, the foreign country unambiguously loses after tariff retaliation. For the home country, at the tariff-retaliation equilibrium TOT improves, but the consequent welfare gain is not large enough to compensate for the welfare loss due to a decline in VOT.

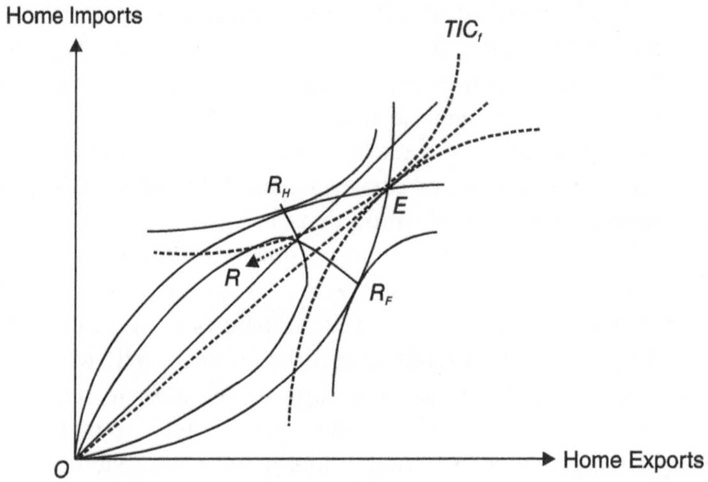

Figure 9.9 Tariff Retaliation and National Welfare

But if, for example, the two reaction functions intersect each other above the home country's TIC_f, then even after tariff-retaliation, the home country gains. However, the foreign country still loses. Thus, it is possible that one country may still gain after tariff retaliation.

9.4 TARIFFS AND PROTECTION OF DOMESTIC INDUSTRIES

Tariffs and quantitative restrictions are usually imposed on the import of foreign goods to protect the domestic import-competing industries from foreign competition. This protective effect is evident from Figure 9.1. A tariff, by raising the domestic price of imports, encourages domestic computer producers to expand production. For the small country, however, protection for domestic industries comes with a welfare cost as explained earlier. Despite such costs, an oft-quoted argument for protection is that of an infant industry. In more recent times, tariff is also used to protect the national environment from the import of polluting or dirty goods. This is known as green protectionism. We turn to the infant industry motive for tariff protection below. Green protectionism is discussed in Chapter 17.

9.4.1 Infant Industry Argument for Protection

Infant industry protection is essentially a dynamic argument. It rests on the premise that a newly developed industry requires protection from foreign competition in its initial formative years when production and other operational costs are high. As the industry grows over time and attains its optimum scale of operations, average costs come down and it can then face foreign competition. Thus, there are long-run gains to be had from protecting an infant industry that must be weighed against consumption and production costs in the short run.

The counter argument is that an infant industry being protected by a tariff (or an import quota) and thus having a sizeable share of the domestic market will never have the urge to grow and become efficient. Thus, long-run efficiency gains will hardly be realized. Moreover, in a dynamic world with a fast changing technology frontier, firms survive by innovation and continuous upgrading of their production technologies that lower the costs of production or improve the product quality. In many instances infant industries become complacent by their assured profits in the protected domestic markets and do not invest in technological innovations. Thus, even when they grow and attain their optimum scale of production, they hardly emerge as internationally competitive.

9.4.2 Imported Input and Effective Rate of Protection

International trade among countries is not just confined to final consumption goods as we have assumed so far. Input or intermediate goods like petroleum, raw cotton, fertilizers, iron and steel, and organic and inorganic chemicals, are also traded in rather large volumes by the countries. Input trade is subject to trade restrictions just like trade in final commodities, and a similar motive of protecting domestic input or intermediate goods producers' works behind these trade restrictions. Tariff duties on imported inputs, however, have far-reaching implications for protection generated by an import tariff for the domestic final good producers who uses those imported inputs. In particular, the actual or the effective rate of protection (ERP) may be larger than the nominal rate of protection for the final good. Of course, when input trade is free or when no imported input is used in domestic import-competing production, the nominal rate of protection and the effective rate of protection are the same. Referring back to our discussion in Section 9.1, a 10 per cent ad-valorem tariff raises the domestic relative price of the imported and the import-competing final goods by the same percentage points for a small country. The nominal rate of protection is thus 10 per cent.

Now suppose this import-competing final good under consideration uses an imported input that is subject to an ad-valorem tariff at the rate 5 per cent. Since, the domestic production of the import-competing final good is essentially adding value to the imported input (by transforming it to a final consumption good using labour), so what matters now is how this value added by the domestic producers is affected by the 10 per cent nominal tariff on the import of the final good. This measure is called the effective rate of protection (ERP) for the producers of the import-competing final good. More precisely, ERP measures the percentage by which the value added in the production of an import-competing final good changes due to tariffs on the import of the final good and on the import of the input that it uses.

To fix ideas, let p_j^w be the world relative price of the final imported good, p_i^w be the world relative price of the imported input, and t_j and t_i be the ad-valorem nominal tariff rates on, or nominal rates of protection (NRP) for the imported final good and the imported input

Box 9.4 Infant Industry Protection in History

Many countries have successfully industrialized behind tariff barriers. UK was the first country to successfully use the infant industry promotion strategy. The protection of woolen textile industry in fifteenth century enabled UK to emerge as a major woolen manufacturing nation from being a raw-wool exporter. The eighteenth century industrial development in UK was also aided by infant industry protection. Similar infant industry argument was the motivating force behind high tariff barriers on trade by the US during the eighteenth and nineteenth centuries. In the post–World War II period, almost all the newly industrialized countries in Asia adopted some form of infant industry promotion strategy when they were in catching-up positions.

Despite this, infant industry protection is controversial as a policy recommendation. The typical example of how infant industries may never grow up is that during the 1980s Brazil enforced strict controls on the import of foreign computers in an effort to nurture its infant computer industry. But this industry never matured. The technological gap between Brazil and the rest of the world actually widened. Krueger and Tuncer (1982), on the other hand, ran an empirical test of the infant industry argument on Turkish data. They did not find any evidence that the more protected industries in Turkey experienced a higher rate of cost decline as compared to the less protected industries.

respectively. Now if the imported input (or its domestic variety) is the only input used besides local labour, then the value added by the production of good *j* (denoted by VA_j) is the value of production less the cost of the (imported) input. In *per unit* terms, the value added (va_j) equals $P_j^w - a_{ij}P_i^w$ under free trade and $(1+t_j)P_j^w - a_{ij}(1+t_i)P_i^w$ under tariff. Therefore, ERP is defined as:

$$ERP_j = \frac{va_j^t - va_j}{va_j} = \frac{t_j - \theta_{ij}t_i}{1-\theta_{ij}} \tag{9.2}$$

where $\theta_{ij} < 1$ is the cost-share of the imported input (or its domestic variety).

This gives us a relation between ERP and NRP for the final good. If NRP for the domestically produced import-competing final good and the import-competing input are the same, that is, $t_j = t_i$, then $ERP_j = NRP_j$. But, otherwise, ERP and NRP for the final goods producers' differ. That is, though a 10 per cent ad-valorem tariff on the final good raises the tariff-inclusive domestic price of the final good proportionately, it does not necessarily generate effective protection for the domestic final goods' producers to the same extent. To see this, we rewrite equation (9.2) as:

$$t_j = (1-\theta_{ij})ERP_j + \theta_{ij}t_i \tag{9.3}$$

This tells us that NRP for the final good is the weighted average of ERP for the final good and NRP for the input. For weights adding up to one, by the weighted average rule then $ERP_j > t_j$ if $t_j > t_i$. But if $t_j < t_i$, then $ERP_j < t_j$. Thus, when the imported inputs are subject to tariff duties, the nominal rate of protection or the rate of ad-valorem tariff is not a true indicator of the actual protection generated for the domestic final goods' producers.

Table 9.1 illustrates the differences in NRP and ERP for Brazil and Vietnam in 1997 and 2009 respectively for some selected commodities. Except for non-metal mineral products and transport and motor vehicles for Vietnam, in every other instance ERP is higher than NRP. ERP exceeded NRP by the highest margin in Vietnam in 2009 for tobacco products.

Table 9.1 Nominal and Effective Rates of Protection

Product	Vietnam (2009)		Brazil (1997)	
	NRP	ERP	NRP	ERP
Non-metal Mineral Products	1.07	0.52	7.3	14.5
Paper and Paper Products	3.87	8.02	11.9	12.6
Pharmaceuticals	4.8	8.48	10	9.9
Textiles	7.2	31.87	15.8	21.5
Tobacco	51	268.56	9	10.8
Transport and Motor Vehicles	86.22	25.54	16.7	33.8

Source: Compiled from Trinh (2010), and Ferreira and Rossi (2003).

Many production activities have several stages of production and each stage of production may require inputs which are traded in the international markets as well. A simple example is threads are produced from raw cotton, which in turn is used to produce cloth or cotton textiles. Finally, garments are made from cloth. All these intermediate goods—raw cotton, threads, cotton textiles—can also be imported. In such a case of a vertical chain of production structure, we can calculate ERP for the (intermediate) goods produced at each stage by equation (9.2), when the import of the intermediate good in the preceding stage is subject to an import tariff. What is interesting to note is the following. If nominal rates of protection at every stage of production are 10 per cent, then all ERPs will also be 10 per cent. But if the import tariff on raw material at the base, raw cotton in our example of producing garments, is zero or less than 10 per cent then ERPs vary along the vertical chain of production. Alternatively, if a national government wishes to obtain vertical uniformity in 10 per cent ERP at all stages of production or processing, then the nominal rates of production must be *escalated* successively at successively higher stages of production or processing.

To illustrate, suppose there are n stages of production with successively higher stages labeled by a larger number: 0, 1, 2, 3, …, n. Let $t_0 = 0$, and the government wishes to maintain an ERP of τ at each stage. Then by equation (9.3):

$$t_1 = (1-\theta_{01})\tau,$$

$$t_2 = (1-\theta_{12})\tau + \theta_{12}t_1,\quad t_3 = (1-\theta_{23})\tau + \theta_{23}t_2, \ldots\ldots, t_n = (1-\theta_{n-1,n})\tau + \theta_{n-1,n}t_{n-1}$$

It is then immediate that, $t_1 < t_2 < t_3 < \ldots\ldots < t_n < \tau$. This is known as *tariff escalation.*

Table 9.2 reports tariff escalation in selected developing and developed countries in different years during 1994–2000 in agricultural and industrial production activities. The tariff rates reported are the simple averages of the tariff rates imposed on all goods produced at the three stages. With the exception of the countries in the European Union, Japan, and the United States, the average tariff rates on industrial imports are raised successively in all the other countries for successively higher processing activities. But, for these three countries, the tariff rates were the highest on the imports of semi-processed goods. On the other hand, for agricultural processing activities, there is evidence of tariff escalation for countries with larger agriculture like India, Brazil, Colombia, Australia, Canada, the European Union, and Japan. For the rest, again nominal tariff rates were the highest at the semi-processed stage. This means, these countries had differential ERPs at different processing stages.

Table 9.2 Tariff Escalation in Developing and Industrial Countries, 1994–2000 (unweighted average in %)

		Agricultural Product			Industrial Product		
Country	Year	1st Stage	Semi Processed	Fully Processed	1st Stage	Semi-processed	Fully Processed
China	1997	19.3	34.3	29.2	7.4	13.3	19.3
Korea	1999	49.9	93.2	31.8	3.4	7.8	8.0
India	1997	25.4	29.9	42.8	23.6	35.4	36.4
Brazil	2000	9.5	13.2	15.6	8.9	11.9	15.8
Colombia	1998	12.8	17.7	18.6	6.9	9.6	12.2
Mexico	1998	15.1	14.9	30.5	8.2	10.2	14.2
Australia	1998	0.3	0.7	2.3	0.7	5.6	6.5
Canada	1999	1.7	3.6	7.0	0.7	4.2	5.1
European Union	1999	7.3	12.0	13.1	0.6	4.9	4.0
Japan	1999	4.5	14.3	15.5	0.6	4.5	3.5
United States	1999	7.1	4.5	10.3	0.6	5.0	4.1

Source: WTO CD-ROM (2000) and *WTO Trade Policy Review*, various issues (1995–2000).

9.4.3 Tariff Protection in a Large Country: The Metzler Paradox

For a large country, there arises an even more basic issue. Does an import tariff always protect domestic industries? This issue arises because for a large country a tariff lowers the world price of imports and thus makes foreign goods more competitive. If the world price falls too much, the tariff inclusive domestic relative price of imports *may* decline as well. This will cause the domestic import-competing industries to contract. A tariff in such a situation cannot protect domestic industries. Recalling that $p_d = (1 + t)\, p^W$, changes in the domestic relative price, the world relative price and the tariff rate are related in the following way:

$$\hat{p}_d = \gamma\, \hat{t} + \hat{p}^W \tag{9.4}$$

where $\gamma \equiv \dfrac{t}{1+t}$. As discussed above, as long as tariff revenue is redistributed among consumers, a tariff unambiguously lowers p^W, that is, $\hat{p}^W < 0$. Thus, if a 10 per cent ad-valorem tariff imposed at the initial free trade equilibrium (so that $\gamma\, \hat{t} = dt = t$) lowers the world relative price by more than 10 per cent, the domestic relative price declines and domestic industries contract. Lloyd Metzler first pointed out this possibility and accordingly this paradoxical case of an import tariff failing to provide protection to domestic industries is known as the *Metzler Paradox*.

When can this happen? To find out, suppose, p^w declines proportionately to the tariff rate thereby leaving the domestic relative price in the home country and hence its import demand for computers unchanged. Thus, with no change in the volume of import of computers, the home country's real income increases proportionately with the improvement in the TOT. Let us now check the state of excess demand in the world market for the home export good (that is, textiles) under this pre-supposition. The increase in the home country's real income raises its domestic demand for textiles and hence lowers its supply of textiles to the world market by the marginal propensity to consume textiles (or the export good), k. On the other hand, if the foreign country had not imposed any tariff on its import of textiles from the home country, its domestic relative price of textiles will move in tandem with the world relative price. As the home tariff lowers the world relative price of its imports, or equivalently raises the world relative price of textiles, foreign import demand for textiles falls, first through a substitution of consumption of textiles by computers, second through an increase in the production of textiles (and corresponding decline in the production of computers), and third through a real income effect as TOT deterioration lowers the real income of the foreign country. Whereas the first two effects are captured through the compensated price elasticity of demand (or the substitution effect) and the price elasticity of the supply of textiles (or an import-competing good) respectively, the real income effect is captured by the marginal propensity to consume imports. As shown in Appendix A9, foreign import demand elasticity (ε^*) combines all these three effects. That is to say, a tariff imposed by the home country that worsens the TOT for the foreign country causes its import demand for textiles to fall by the value of ε^* at the margin. Hence, at the pre-supposed lower level of TOT (that left the domestic price in the home country unchanged), both the home export supply of textiles and the foreign import demand for textiles decline at the rates k and ε^* respectively at the margin. An excess demand for textiles arises if $\varepsilon^* < k$. If so, the world relative price of textiles rises, or equivalently the world relative price of computers (p^w) declines *further* below the pre-supposed level. Hence, if $\varepsilon^* < k$, the world relative price of home imports (that is, computers) declines more than the ad-valorem tariff rate. Consequently, the domestic relative price of imports fall and the Metzler Paradox arises. Conversely, if $\varepsilon^* > k$, an import tariff protects domestic industries however small the tariff rate is.

A few observations are in order. First, in this two-commodity world, since the marginal propensity to consume the imported good, denoted by m for the home country, and the marginal propensity to consume the export good, denoted by k, add up to one, so the above condition for the Metzler Paradox can be restated as $\varepsilon^* < (1 - m)$. Second, since $(1 - m) < 1$, the foreign import demand elasticity must not only be inelastic but *sufficiently inelastic* for the Metzler Paradox to arise. The point is that the Metzler Paradox can never occur if the initial equilibrium was along the upward rising part of the foreign offer curve. At the same time, it *does not necessarily mean* that a tariff will fail to protect domestic industries if the initial equilibrium was at the backward bending part of the foreign offer curve. We need foreign import demand not just inelastic but sufficiently inelastic in the sense defined above. Note that a leftward shift of the home offer curve (caused by the tariff) along the backward bending part of the foreign offer curve does increase the volume of imports by the home country. But this does not mean that such an increased import volume necessarily displaces local production of computers. The reason is that a tariff by improving TOT raises the real income of the home country and this real income improvement *shifts* the demand curve for computers to the right. Hence, import demand can rise even with increase in the domestic production of computers. That is why inelastic foreign import demand and a corresponding increase in thc volume of imports does not necessarily mean that the domestic import-competing industry contracts.

Third, the Metzler Paradox is ruled out for a small tariff-imposing country simply because the TOT for such a country does not change. Thus, a tariff raises the domestic relative price of imports proportionately for such a country and its import-competing industry is always protected by an import tariff.

9.5 TARIFF AND INCOME DISTRIBUTION

An import tariff redistributes factor incomes within countries and the direction of such changes are determined by two factors: First, how does an import tariff change the domestic relative price, and second is the nature of the price magnification effect, as discussed in the earlier chapter. For example, for a small tariff-imposing country, an import tariff raises the domestic relative price of its imports and the import-competing good. In the standard two-commodity, two-factor world, when all factors of production are fully mobile across sectors within countries, by the price magnification effect the real wage will decline and the real return to capital will rise if the country imports the relatively capital-intensive good. The pioneer work in this regard was that of Stolper and Samuelson (1941) who demonstrated that protection raises the real wage of the scarce factor. However, their assertion is based on the HO theorem discussed earlier. By the HO theorem, a country imports the good that is intensive in its relatively scarce factor. A tariff, by raising the domestic relative price of imports, thus raises the real wage of the scarce factor by the price magnification effect. In general, we can say that tariff protection will raise the real return to the factor that is used intensively in the production of the import-competing good.

But if capital is immobile or sector specific, then owners of capital specific to the production of the import-competing good will gain in real terms but the owners of capital specific to the export sector will lose. Workers will experience an increase in their money wage, but *may* still lose in real terms as discussed in Chapter 7.

When a small country imposes a tariff on its imports, there will be no redistribution effect generated in its trading partners because TOT remains unchanged. But, for a large tariff-imposing country, TOT worsens for its trading partner, thereby causing changes in factor incomes there as well. In the standard HOS framework, changes in factor incomes will be asymmetric in the two countries, which though may be at odds with the observed changes in the context of wage inequality as noted in Chapter 7. However, the Metzler Paradox discussed above offers an alternative explanation for observed symmetric changes in factor prices (or wage inequality). Under the condition $\varepsilon^* < (1 - m)$, an import tariff lowers the domestic relative price of imports in the tariff-imposing country, say the home country. If it imports a relatively capital-intensive good, such as computers, the return to capital will now decline and wage will rise in the home country. For its trading partner, a deterioration in TOT and a corresponding rise in the relative price of its imports, textiles, will raise the wage there and lower the rate of return to capital. Thus, in both countries, income is redistributed in favour of the workers. In the context of wage inequality, this result means that an import tariff imposed by a country that imports a relatively unskilled-labour-intensive good, the wage inequality will rise there as well as in its trading partner country. Thus, the Metzler Paradox offers an explanation for a symmetric rise in wage inequality in trading nations.

There is an important point to be noted in this context. Referring back to equation (9.4) that relates changes in domestic and the world prices with a change in the tariff rate, it is evident that the initial tariff rate is an important determinant of the domestic price change as well. An increase in the rate of tariff from an initial positive rate and an increase from an initial zero tariff or free trade situation may have altogether different implications. In the context of trade liberalization through tariff reductions, these initial conditions give another twist to the wage inequality result. As demonstrated by Acharyya (2010), when a country reduces its tariff rates sequentially from a very high level, wage inequality may grow in only one country in the initial stages of tariff reduction, but may grow in both countries at later stages.

9.6 EXPORT SUBSIDY, TOT DETERIORATION, AND WELFARE LOSS

Governments often provide subsidies to their exporters to encourage exports. This is a payment made to an exporter, for its sales abroad, over and above the price she gets in a foreign country. Such a payment may be for per unit of exports, called *specific or unit* export subsidy, or may be for per unit value of exports, called the *ad-valorem* export subsidy. In either case, the exporter exports up to the volume for which the domestic price exceeds the price abroad by the per unit amount of the subsidy. The reason for a rise in domestic prices is simple. An export subsidy makes sales abroad more profitable than sales in the domestic market. A larger proportion of production is thus now exported. This creates an excess demand in the domestic market at the initial domestic relative price (which was the same as the world relative price of exports). Competition among buyers then raises the domestic price of the export good and consequently lowers the domestic demand for the export good. The price increase also encourages producers to produce more. The magnitude of excess supply thus rises above the magnitude corresponding to the pre-subsidy domestic (and world) relative price of the export good. This actually makes it possible for producers to export a larger volume.

For a small home country with a given TOT, the rise in the domestic price for an ad-valorem export subsidy and its economic effects are illustrated in Figure 9.10. At the world relative price of textiles *Oa*, the home country was exporting *cd* units of textiles. An ad-valorem export subsidy at the rate *s*, which is a payment to textile producers over and above this world price, raises the domestic relative price of textiles to *Oh*. Note that $\frac{P_T}{P_C} = \frac{(1+s)P_T^W}{P_C^W} = \frac{(1+s)}{P^W}$. Domestic production rises to *hf* and domestic demand for textiles falls to *hg*. The amount of export subsidy given by the government to the producers (and exporters) of textiles is the rectangular area *befg*. By a similar surplus measure as we had done in the case of an import tariff, it is easy to check that the net welfare loss for this small country is measured by the areas *bcg* and *edf*. Note that the consumers' surplus declines by the area *acgh*, which is in fact redistributed among the producers of textiles as their surplus increases by the area *adfh*. But, the subsidy given is a loss to the economy. Of the total subsidy given, the part measured by the area *gcdf* is actually the part of the increase in surplus for textile producers and thus is redistribution rather than a loss to the economy. But, the other parts of the subsidy measured by the area *bcg* and area *edf* do not constitute gains for someone else in the economy, and hence are dead-weight losses.[2] These are consumption and production losses respectively and are similar to those under tariff. Therefore, just like an import tariff, an export subsidy inflicts a welfare loss on a *small* open economy.

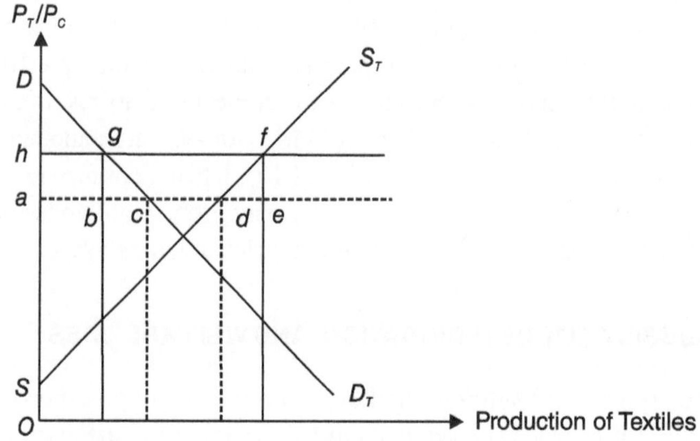

Figure 9.10 Ad-valorem Subsidy on Textile Exports

For a large country providing an export subsidy, there will be a TOT effect. But in contrast to an import tariff, an export subsidy unambiguously *worsens* the country's TOT. The reason is simple. An export subsidy raises the export offer of the country. At the initial TOT, this creates an excess supply in the world market for textiles, and consequently lowers its relative price, or worsens its TOT. This TOT deterioration reinforces the welfare losses discussed above. That is, *an export subsidy lowers the welfare of a country regardless of whether it is small or large in the world market*. The decline in welfare for the large home country is illustrated in Figure 9.11 below. An export subsidy increases the volume of exports of textiles at the initial TOT and consequently at the initial level of imports of computers. The home country's offer curve thus shifts to the right as shown by the broken curve. The post export subsidy equilibrium shifts to $E_{subsidy}$ where the new offer curve of the home country cuts the foreign offer curve OF. This subsidy-ridden trade bundle lies in the worse set to the free trade bundle E, implying a welfare loss. Note that, for the reasons spelled out above, the TOT now worsens for the subsidy-giving large home country as shown by the flatter (and broken) TOT line. Despite an increase in the volume of trade, as higher exports now finance higher level of imports, this adverse TOT effect is stronger to reduce the welfare of the home country. Thus, unlike an import tariff, there is no TOT or welfare motive for governments to provide export subsidies to their domestic export firms in a world with perfect competition.

[2] The area *bcg* is actually part of the loss of consumers' surplus, part of the gain in producers' surplus, and part of the export subsidy.

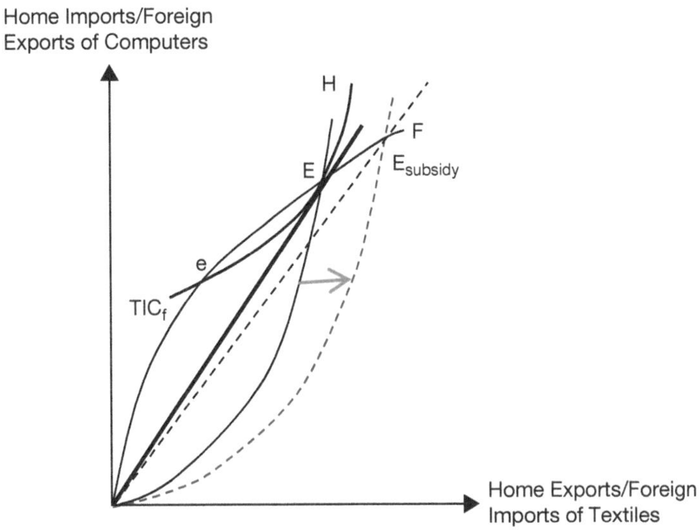

Figure 9.11 Export Subsidy and Welfare

Box 9.5 Export Subsidies

Generally, agricultural and dairy products are provided export subsidies by most of the countries. In eighteenth century UK, export subsidies or *bounties* were provided to new export items like silk products and gunpowder and to traditional products like sailcloth and refined sugar. Export subsidy programmes in the United States, called the Export Enhancement Programme (EEP), cover products like wheat, wheat flour, semolina, rice, frozen poultry, frozen pork, barley, barley malt, table eggs, and vegetable oil. In recent years the US government has made annual outlays of over USD 1 billion in its agricultural EEP and its Dairy Export Incentive Programme (DEIP). In Europe, the Common Agricultural Policy (CAP) has evolved into a large export subsidy programme and the EU usually spends over USD 4 billion annually to encourage export of its agricultural and dairy products. East Asian countries, on the other hand, provide most of the export subsidies on cotton.

In many countries, there are indirect export subsidy schemes. One such scheme is the duty drawback on imported raw material and inputs for export production that was in place in eighteenth century UK and during 1970s and 1980s in India.

However, as we will see in Chapter 11, in an oligopolistic market environment, there may be strategic incentives for national governments to provide export subsidies to their export firms. This might provide some justification for why export subsidies are prevalent in many parts of the globe, particularly in the developed countries.

APPENDIX A9

I. Import Demand Elasticity and Its Decomposition

Recall that the home import demand elasticity is the percentage change in the home import demand for computers following a 1 per cent change in its relative price. Thus, denoting the absolute value of the import demand elasticity as ε, and given $M = D_C - X_C$, we have:

$$\varepsilon = -\frac{p^W}{M}\frac{dM}{dp^W} = -\frac{p^W}{M}\left(\frac{dD_C}{dp^W} - \frac{dX_C}{dp^W}\right) \tag{A9.1}$$

The first term on the right hand side is the change in domestic demand for computers when its relative price changes. This can be decomposed by the Slutsky method into pure substitution effect, $\frac{\partial D_C}{\partial p^W}$, and an income effect, $-(D_C - X_C)\frac{\partial D_C}{\partial y}$, where ∂y denotes the change in real income measured in terms of the export good (textiles). Defining the marginal propensity to imports (or consume computers) as $p^W \frac{\partial D_C}{\partial y}$, the income effect thus equals $(-\frac{M}{p^W}m)$. On the other hand, define absolute value of the pure substitution elasticity for demand for import-competing good (or computer) as:

$$e = -\frac{p^W}{M}\frac{\partial D_C}{\partial p^W} \tag{A9.2}$$

Thus, using the Slutsky decomposition, the first term in the parenthesis on the right hand side in equation (A9.1) can be expressed as:

$$\frac{dD_C}{dp^W} = -\frac{M}{p^W}(e+m) \tag{A9.3}$$

Finally, define the elasticity of supply of import-competing production (that is, production of computers) as:

$$e_S = \frac{p^W}{M}\frac{\partial X_C}{\partial p^W} \tag{A9.4}$$

Substitution of equation (A9.3) and (A9.4) in equation (A9.1) yields:

$$\varepsilon = e + m + e_S \tag{A9.5}$$

II. Change in Real Income and the Optimum Tariff

For an open economy, national welfare may increase for two reasons. First, for an improvement in its TOT, and second, for a growth in the factors of production (or technical progress), which shifts the PPF of the country outward. To see this, define the social welfare function for the home country as:

$$U = U(D_T, D_C) \tag{A9.6}$$

where D_T and D_C are the total consumption of textiles and computers respectively by home consumers. Total differentiation of equation (A9.6) yields:

$$dU = \frac{\partial U}{\partial D_T} dD_T + \frac{\partial U}{\partial D_C} dD_C$$

$$\Rightarrow \frac{dU}{\partial U / \partial D_T} = dD_T + \frac{\partial U / \partial D_C}{\partial U / \partial D_T} dD_C \tag{A9.7}$$

The left hand side expression in equation (A9.7) can be interpreted as the change in welfare measured in terms of the export good (textiles), or the change in the *real income* for the home country, denoted by *dy*. Now, with p_d being the relative price of computers that the home consumers face, utility maximization means, $\frac{\partial U / \partial D_C}{\partial U / \partial D_T} = p_d$. Note that under free trade $p_d = p^W$. But, p_d is greater than or less than p^W when trade is restricted through an import tariff. Thus, equation (A9.7) boils down to:

$$dy = dD_T + p_d dD_C \tag{A9.8}$$

But, any change in welfare or real income (thus measured in terms of the export good) must be consistent with the balanced trade for the country evaluated at the equilibrium TOT or the equilibrium relative price of home imports:

$$p^W M = X$$

Note that, as discussed earlier, the above trade balance condition essentially means that the national budget constraint evaluated at the equilibrium TOT is satisfied: $p^W D_C + D_T = p^W X_C + X_T$.

Total differentiation of the balanced trade condition yields:

$$p^W dM + M dp^W = dX \tag{A9.9}$$

Using $M = D_C - X_C$ and $X = X_T - D_T$, this boils down to:

$$dD_T + p^W dD_C = -M dp^W + (dX_T + p^W dX_C)$$

Under free trade, since $p_d = p^W$, so:

$$\Rightarrow dy = -M dp^W + (dX_T + p^W dX_C) \tag{A9.10}$$

The first term on the right hand side captures the TOT effect. An improvement in TOT, $dp^W < 0$, raises the real income of the home country. The second term captures the growth effect—the increase in the aggregate value of production evaluated at the world relative price or TOT—which also raises real income.

Under tariff, however, we have a volume of trade effect as well. To see this, rewrite equation (A9.9) as:

$$(p^W - p_d)dM + Mdp^W = dX - p_d dM$$

Again using $M = D_C - X_C$ and $X = X_T - D_T$, this boils down to:

$$dD_T + p_d dD_C = -Mdp^W + (p_d - p^W)dM + (dX_T + p_d dX_C)$$

$$\Rightarrow dy = -Mdp^W + (p_d - p^W)dM + (dX_T + p_d dX_C) \quad \text{(A9.11)}$$

For a *ceteris paribus* change in the home country's import tariff rate, and assuming away the Metzler Paradox, the corresponding change in the home country's real income can be expressed as:

$$dy = -Mdp^W + tp^W dM \quad \text{(A9.12)}$$

Note that a *ceteris paribus* change in the tariff rate means, corresponding change in the domestic relative price changes *only* the composition of the aggregate value of production along the PPF. So, the last term in equation (A9.11) is zero. Thus, an import tariff generates two effects: A TOT effect, $-Mdp^W$, which improves welfare or the real income, and a VOT effect, $tp^W dM$, which lowers real income. For small tariffs, the VOT effect is very small in magnitude but the corresponding volume of imports being large, the TOT effect is quite large. Thus, for small tariffs, $dy > 0$. The optimum tariff rate now can be derived from equation (A9.12) by setting $dy = 0$ since it is the tariff that maximizes the home country's real income (or welfare):

$$t_{opt} = \frac{M}{dM}\frac{dp^W}{p^W} = \frac{\hat{p}^W}{\hat{M}}$$

But from the global equilibrium condition $p^W M = M^*$, we can write $\hat{p}^W + \hat{M} = \hat{M}^*$. Using this, the expression for the home country's optimum tariff boils down to:

$$t_{opt} = \frac{\hat{p}^W}{\hat{M}^* - \hat{p}^W} = \frac{1}{\dfrac{\hat{M}^*}{\hat{p}^W} - 1} = \frac{1}{\varepsilon^* - 1} \quad \text{(A9.13)}$$

III. Revenue Maximizing and Optimum Tariffs

Recall that the tariff revenue generated by an ad-valorem tariff imposed by the home country equals:

$$R = tp^W M(p_d) \tag{A9.14}$$

By log differentiating and using hat notations, the proportional change in tariff revenue is a simple sum of proportional changes in the tariff rate, the world relative price of home imports, and home import demand:

$$\hat{R} = \hat{t} + \hat{p}^W + \hat{M} \tag{A9.15}$$

It is easy to check that:

$$\hat{M} = -\varepsilon \hat{p}_d \tag{A9.16}$$

which, using $\hat{p}_d = \gamma\, \hat{t} + \hat{p}^W$, boils down to,

$$\hat{M} = -\varepsilon\gamma\, \hat{t} - \varepsilon \hat{p}^W \tag{A9.17}$$

where $\gamma \equiv \dfrac{t}{1+t} < 1$ captures the initial level of protection.

Substitution of equation (A9.17) in equation (A9.15) yields:

$$\hat{R} = (1-\varepsilon\gamma)\, \hat{t} + (1-\varepsilon)\hat{p}^W \tag{A9.18}$$

For a small country, TOT remains unchanged so that the change in tariff revenue boils down to:

$$\hat{R} = (1-\varepsilon\gamma)\, \hat{t}$$

$$\Rightarrow \frac{dR}{dt} = p^W M[1-\varepsilon\gamma] \tag{A9.19}$$

Note that the value of import demand elasticity itself varies inversely with the domestic relative price and hence with the tariff rate for a large class of import demand functions including a linear demand function. When the tariff rate is raised from a very low level of tariff the values of both ε and γ are small so that the tariff revenue increases. But as the tariff rate is raised successively, ε and γ rise and so beyond a critical tariff rate the tariff revenue declines with the increase in the tariff rate. Thus, the tariff revenue curve is hump-shaped as illustrated in Figure 9.3. Note that the revenue maximizing tariff rate (t_R) is such that:

$$1 = \varepsilon(t_R)\frac{t_R}{1+t_R} \tag{A9.20}$$

For a large country, however, the tariff lowers p^W. The tariff revenue thus falls at the initial level of import demand. But, price decline raises import demand by ε at the margin, which in turn raises tariff revenue. Thus, the tariff revenue changes by $(1-\varepsilon)\hat{p}^W$ when TOT changes, as shown by the last term on the right hand side in equation (A9.18). To compare the revenue maximizing tariff rates for a large and a small country, rewrite equation (A9.18) as:

$$\frac{dR_L}{dt} = p^W M[1-\varepsilon\gamma] + tM(1-\varepsilon)\frac{dp^W}{dt} \qquad \text{(A9.18a)}$$

When this change in tariff revenue is evaluated at the revenue maximizing tariff rate for the small country, by equations (A9.19) or (A9.20), the first term in equation (A9.18a) vanishes so that:

$$\left.\frac{dR_L}{dt}\right|_{t_R} = tM(1-\varepsilon)\frac{dp^W}{dt}$$

But at t_R, $\varepsilon = \frac{1}{\gamma} > 1$. Hence, $\left.\frac{dR_L}{dt}\right|_{t_R} > 0$ given that $\frac{dp^W}{dt} < 0$. This implies, $t_R > t_{RL}$. That is, the tariff revenue maximizing rate is larger for a large country than that for a small country.

To see now the relationship between the revenue maximizing tariff rate and the optimum (or welfare maximizing) tariff rate, consider the national budget constraint:

$$p^W D_C + D_T = p^W X_C + X_T$$

Subtracting $p_d D_C$ and $p_d X_C$ from both sides this can be rewritten as:

$$(p^W - p_d)D_C + D_T - p_d X_C = (p^W - p_d)X_C + X_T - p_d D_C$$

$$\Rightarrow p_d D_C + D_T = p_d X_C + X_T + tp^W M \qquad \text{(A9.21)}$$

Total differentiation of equation (A9.21) yields the expression for the home country's real income change following a *ceteris paribus* change in the tariff rate as:

$$dy = -Mdp_d + d(tp^W M) \qquad \text{(A9.22)}$$

Since at the revenue maximizing tariff (t_{RL}), $d(tp^W M) = 0$, so $dy = -Mdp_d < 0$. This implies that the real income is maximum at a rate smaller than t_{RL}. That is, the optimum tariff is *smaller* than the revenue maximizing tariff.

Alternatively, (A9.22) can be rewritten as,

$$dR_L = dy + Mdp_d$$

Since at the optimum tariff dy = 0 and Metzler paradox is ruled out, so

$$\left.dR_L\right|_{t=t_{opt}} = Mdp_d > 0$$

$$\Rightarrow t_{RL} > t_{opt}.$$

IV. Welfare Reaction Curves

A welfare reaction curve for the home country is the locus of tariff-equilibria that maximizes its welfare for any given tariff imposed by the foreign country. In Figure A9.1, *OH* and *OF* are the home and foreign offer curves respectively when neither country imposes tariffs on imports from the other country. Given zero foreign tariff, the home country's welfare is maximized at the trade bundle R_H for which its *TIC* is tangent to *OF*. This is achieved by the home country through the optimum tariff that shifts its offer curve to a position to intersect the foreign offer curve *OF* at point R_H. When the foreign country imposes a tariff at the rate t_1^* on imports from the home country, its offer curve rotates inward to $OF(t_1^*)$. Given this foreign tariff, the maximum welfare attained by the home country is indicated by the *TIC* that is tangent to $OF(t_1^*)$ at point *a*. This welfare maximizing trade bundle is again achieved by an optimum tariff, which is the tariff rate that maximizes the home welfare given t_1^*. This way, for each foreign tariff rate, we identify the maximum home welfare level along the corresponding tariff-ridden foreign offer curve, which is attained through a corresponding home optimum tariff rate. For a higher foreign tariff t_2^*, such a maximum welfare point (or trade bundle) is *a'*. When we join the home welfare maximizing trade bundles along the different tariff-ridden foreign offer curves for all possible foreign tariffs (including zero tariff) like R_H, *a*, and *a'*, we get the welfare reaction curve OR_H for the home country. It starts from the origin because when the foreign country imposes a prohibitive tariff, the maximum welfare that the home country can achieve (regardless of the level of tariff that it imposes) is autarkic welfare. By construction, the point O indicates the welfare maximizing position for the home country.

The foreign welfare reaction function shown in Figure 9.8 can be similarly derived. It is the locus of tariff-equilibria that maximizes its welfare for any given tariffs imposed by the home country.

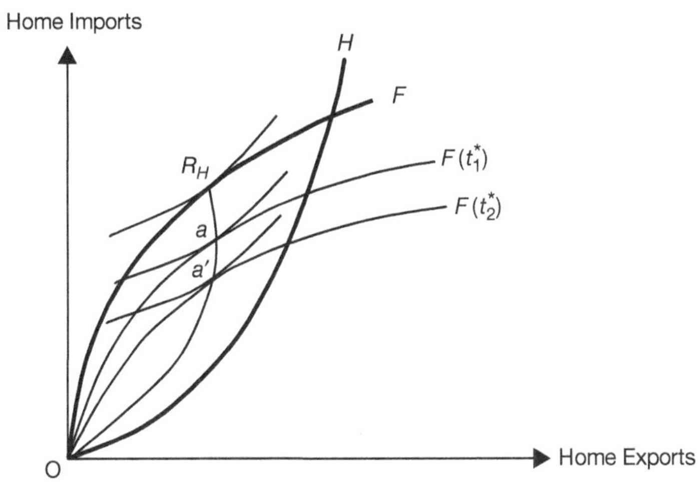

Figure A9.1 Home Welfare Reaction Curve

V. Lerner's Symmetry Result

Abba P. Lerner (1936) demonstrated that an import tariff and an export tax are similar or symmetric in their economic effects. To illustrate, consider a 10 per cent ad-valorem export tax imposed by the home government on its exporters. An export tax creates a wedge between the price that foreign buyers pay (and the home exporters receive) in the world market for buying the home country's export good and the price that the home exporters can *retain* with them. When the home country is small and hence its exporters have no market power, the burden of the export tax is borne entirely by them. That is, if the world market price of the good that the home country exports (which in our example is textiles) is USD 50 per unit of exports, the exporters effectively get USD 45 and pay USD 5 per unit of exports to the national exchequer. With no tariff on imports, *an export tax thus lowers the domestic relative price of exports in the home country*. Equivalently, it raises the domestic relative price of imports in the home country, just like an import tariff does. In algebraic notations, if τ denotes the ad-valorem export tax and $p_d(\tau)$ is the domestic relative price of imports in the home country, then:

$$p_d(\tau) = \frac{1}{(1-\tau)} p^W > p^W$$

Thus, the production of the export good (textiles) contracts and resources are reallocated towards the import-competing sector (computers). That is to say, an export tax expands the production of the import-competing sector and thereby indirectly protects this sector. With full employment of all factors of production, an import tariff does the same. By raising the domestic relative price of computers, and encouraging an expansion of this sector it causes a contraction of the export sector.

The TOT effect will also be similar. An export tax discourages home exporters to export textiles. The supply of textiles in the world market thus declines creating an excess demand for textiles at the initial TOT. This excess demand raises the world relative price of textiles, which means a TOT improvement for the home country just like an import tariff.

Similarly, an export subsidy and an import subsidy are symmetric. To illustrate, it is sufficient to note that an import subsidy lowers the price paid by home consumers for the foreign imported computers that they buy. This forces local producers to lower the price of computers that they produce. Hence, an import subsidy lowers the relative price of imports or raises the relative price of exports, just like an export subsidy. Once again, under the condition of full employment, an import subsidy and an export subsidy will have similar resource allocation and production effects.

VI. Lerner's Case: Government Spending and TOT Deterioration

The optimum tariff argument for a large country and the tariff war that the welfare improving effect of tariff may cause is based on import tariffs improving TOT for the tariff-imposing country. But Lerner (1936) demonstrated that when the government itself spends the tariff revenue on the two traded goods, an import tariff may *worsen* the country's TOT. To explain, suppose, the home country government spends λ proportion of the tariff revenue earned (or income in general) on computers and $(1 - \lambda)$ proportion on textiles. Thus, when the government increases its tariff rate, and tariff revenue increases, its demand for computers rises by λ *at the margin.* This increase in the demand for computers now is to be weighed against the fall in import demand by consumers by the magnitude λ *at the margin* to determine the direction in which the country's total import demand changes. In general, we can expect that the marginal propensity to consume for the government and for an individual consumer will be different, that is, $\lambda \neq m$. Thus, we cannot say a priori that $(\lambda - \varepsilon) < 0$ unlike the case when the tariff revenue is redistributed among consumers in a lump-sum way as discussed earlier. If $\lambda > \varepsilon$, then an increase in the rate of tariff actually raises the country's total import demand. The higher import bill consequent upon this increased import demand for computers at the initial TOT necessitates a higher export offer of textiles as well. Thus, the country being large, there arises an excess demand for computers and an excess supply of textiles in the world market, which raises the world relative price of computers (or lowers the world relative price of textiles). The home offer curves in Figures 9.5 and 9.6 shift to the *right* with the corresponding TOT line at the tariff equilibrium (now to the right of the free trade equilibrium point E on the foreign offer curve) being flatter. TOT thus worsens for the tariff-imposing home country. Even though VOT rises, overall welfare of the tariff-imposing country falls.

However, though this case seems interesting and may be relevant as consumption spending of governments is indeed large in many countries, developing and developed alike, the condition for TOT deterioration is very restrictive. Since λ *is a fraction by definition,* so the condition $\lambda > \varepsilon$ implies that for Lerner's Case to hold the tariff-imposing country's import demand must be *inelastic*, that is, the tariff-imposing country's offer curve must be backward bending in the neighbourhood of initial equilibrium. But if at the pre-tariff equilibrium the tariff-imposing country's import demand is elastic, a tariff (or an increase in its rate) will lower the import demand despite the government's demand for the imported good rising. The export offer will then decline, the offer curve will shift to the *left,* and TOT for the tariff-imposing country will improve as usual.

VII. Symmetry of Lerner's Case and the Metzler Paradox

It is obvious that Lerner's Case and the Metzler Paradox are mutually exclusive for the same country. This is because a large improvement in TOT underlies the Metzler Paradox, whereas in the Lerner's Case an import tariff worsens the TOT of the tariff-imposing country. But the interesting case that Tsai (1989) had demonstrated is that when both the home and foreign countries impose tariffs on their respective imports, the Metzler Paradox in one country *may* imply the Lerner's Case in the other. That such symmetry is plausible is evident from a closer inspection of the conditions underlying these two paradoxes. Suppose, a tariff imposition by the foreign country worsens its TOT when its government spends a part of the tariff revenue on its import good (textiles). Recall from the discussion above that this happens when foreign import demand is sufficiently inelastic in the sense that $\varepsilon^* < \lambda^*$. Now when the home country imposes a tariff on its import of computers from the foreign country, the foreign import demand being inelastic it is plausible that the condition for the Metzler Paradox for the home country is satisfied, that is, $\varepsilon^* < (1-m)$. Tsai (1989) demonstrated that when both the governments spend their tariff revenues by themselves instead of redistributing them among their respective consumers, the symmetry perfectly holds if the governments spend the *same fraction* of tariff revenues on the same good, that is, either on textiles or on computers.

SUMMARY POINTS

- In a small economy, an import tariff imposes a dead-weight loss in the domestic market for the import-competing good due to substitution of efficient foreign supply of imports by inefficient domestic production of the import-competing good (production loss) and due to the higher price paid by consumers for imports (consumption loss). In a general equilibrium setting, this welfare loss is measured through a loss in VOT.
- In a large economy, an import tariff lowers VOT but improves TOT, provided the tariff revenue is redistributed among domestic citizens. For smaller rates of tariff, the TOT effect is larger than the VOT effect so that the country's welfare rises. But beyond a high rate of tariff, the VOT effect becomes larger, which causes the country's welfare to fall.
- The rate of tariff at which TOT and VOT effects are equal in magnitude at the margin, and the country's welfare is maximum, is called the optimum tariff. This optimum tariff varies inversely with the (absolute) value of the foreign country's import demand elasticity.
- If the government itself spends the tariff revenue on export and import-competing goods, instead of redistributing it among domestic citizens, and the government's marginal propensity to consume the import good is larger in magnitude than the value of the import demand elasticity, TOT worsens. This is known as the Lerner's Case.
- The optimum tariff argument does not hold when the trading partner retaliates to the tariff imposition by imposing a tariff. According to Scitovsky, such retaliation or tariff war will end with termination of trade between the countries. Johnson, on the other hand, established that some trade may still exist at the post tariff-retaliation equilibrium, and that one country may still gain compared to free trade.
- When imported inputs are subject to tariffs, the nominal rate of tariff protection and the actual or effective rate of tariff protection for the final good may be different. Thus, even for a small country, a 10 per cent tariff on final imports may not mean that the effective rate of tariff protection is 10 per cent.
- For a large country, an import tariff may actually cause the tariff inclusive domestic relative price of imports to decline and thus cause the domestic import-competing industries to contract. Import tariff then fails to protect the domestic import-competing industries. This paradoxical case, known as the Metzler Paradox, may arise if the import tariff lowers the world price of imports more than proportionate to the rate of tariff itself.
- Lerner's case and the Metzler Paradox are mutually exclusive for the same country, but may simultaneously hold in both the countries.
- An export subsidy lowers the welfare of a country regardless of whether it is small or large in the world market. Unlike an import tariff, there is no TOT or welfare motive for governments to provide export subsidies to their domestic export firms in a world with perfect competition.
- In a full employment model of trade, like the HOS model, an import tax and an export tax are symmetric in their economic effects. Similarly, an import subsidy and an export subsidy are symmetric. These are known as Lerner's Symmetry.

KEYWORDS

- **Optimum tariff** rate is the one that maximizes a country's welfare given the tariff rate of its trading partner. For such an optimum tariff rate, TOT gain and VOT loss are equal at the margin.
- **Prohibitive tariff rate** is the rate of tariff for which the volume of imports is zero.
- **Domestic import-competing industry** is protected when it raises the tariff-inclusive price above the pre-tariff price level and thus enables the domestic industry to expand its production, regardless of whether the volume of imports rises or falls.
- **Infant industry protection** concerns protection of an industry in its early development stages when it is small in size and the firms in the industry are small in their scale of operation to attain the economies of scale.
- **Effective rate of protection** (ERP) measures the percentage by which the value added in the production of an import-competing final good changes due to tariffs on the import of the final good and on the import of the input that it uses.
- **Metzler paradox** is a situation when an import tariff lowers the tariff-inclusive price below the pre-tariff level and consequently fails to protect the domestic import-competing industry.
- **Welfare reaction curve** for a country is the locus of tariff-equilibria that maximizes its welfare for any given tariff set by its trading partner.
- **Lerner case** occurs when a tariff worsens the TOT of the tariff-imposing country as the government spends the tariff revenue itself.

EXERCISES

1. Show that an import tariff is essentially a combination of a tax on consumption of computers and a production subsidy to the local producers of computers.
2. A specific or unit import tariff is a tariff imposed on per unit of import volume. If t is the ad valorem import tariff rate, what will be the equivalent specific tariff rate τ that raises the domestic price above the (given) world price by the same extent?
3. Consider the following domestic demand and supply functions for transport equipment in India:

   $D_i = 170 - p_i, S_i = 20 + 2p_i$

   (a) If $p^W = 30$, does India import or export transport equipment?
   (b) Find out the volume of import or exports as the case may be.
4. In the above context, suppose India imports transport equipment from the rest of the world when $p^W = 20$. If the Government of India imposes a 50 per cent ad-valorem tariff on imports, measure the production cost, the consumption cost, and the dead-weight loss, assuming that p^W does not change.
5. How does your answer to the above question change, if at all, when p^W falls by 20 per cent?

(contd)

Exercises (*contd*)

6. Suppose the import demand function is $M = 100 - 10p_d$. Find out the tariff revenue maximizing tariff rate if the country is small.
7. Find out the exact expression for change in the tariff revenue for a large country when it changes its tariff rate.
8. Using the offer curve diagram explain that if at the initial free trade equilibrium, foreign import demand is inelastic, a tariff imposed by the home country raises its import demand.
9. In the context of trade between two large countries, show that each will have unilateral incentives to deviate from free trade by imposing a tariff when at the free trade equilibrium the import demands are elastic.
10. If at the free trade equilibrium the home import demand is inelastic, will the home country have a unilateral incentive to deviate from free trade?
11. [Advanced] Show that a unilateral optimum tariff is globally Pareto sub-optimal and hence argue that there will be no scope for compensation or side payments by the tariff-imposing country to its trading partner to avoid retaliation.
12. Referring back to Figure 9.6, what is the geometric measure of the optimum tariff imposed by the home country?

    [Hints: Extend the PP' line segment towards the horizontal axis and then use the geometric measure of the slopes of line segments OE_{opt} and PP'.]
13. Suppose the foreign import demand function is $M^* = 20 - \frac{15}{p^W}$, where p^W is the world relative price of the good imported by the home country. Calculate the home country's optimum tariff rate if its tariff lowers p^W by 50 per cent. Assume that initially $p^W = 2$.
14. Is the Lerner's Case consistent with the stability of international equilibrium?
15. [Advanced] Suppose import demand in each country is perfectly income inelastic. Then work out the proportional change in p^W when the home country raises its initial tariff rate. Hence show that:
    (a) If the world market is stable, the increase in the tariff rate improves the home country's TOT.
    (b) The extent to which TOT improves depends on the initial tariff rate.
    [Hints: Totally differentiate the balanced trade condition $p^W M(p_d) = M^*(p^W)$ and use the definitions of the import demand elasticities.]
16. [Advanced] Ignoring income effects on import demand (as in the above question), find out the condition for a tariff increase failing to protect the domestic import-competing industry.
17. Why does a tariff on import that worsens the TOT of a large country protect its import-competing sector?
18. Calculate the ERP for the final good when it uses n number of imported inputs, all subject to ad-valorem tariff.

(contd)

Exercises (*contd*)

19. How does the ERP on the local production of computers change in the following situations:
    (a) A production subsidy to producers of computers.
    (b) A consumption tax on domestic consumers of computers.
20. Consider four production stages to produce garments, in each stage the intermediate good used as input is also imported. The input requirements increase at the rate of 10 per cent at each stage over the previous stage of processing such that $a_{12} = 1.1a_{01}$, $a_{23} = 1.1a_{12}$, $a_{34} = 1.1a_{23}$. If $a_{01} = 0.5$, and $P_i = P_j = 1$ then:
    (i) Calculate the ERP at each stage (except stage 0) if a vertically uniform ad-valorem tariff rate of 20 per cent is imposed on imported inputs at each stage.
    (ii) Calculate the rates of tariffs to be imposed on imports of inputs at each stage to achieve a vertically uniform ERP of 20 per cent if $t_0 = 0$.
21. Consider the following domestic demand and supply functions for textiles in the home country:

$$p_T^d = 220 - 2Q_T,\ p_T^s = 100 + Q_T$$

    (a) If the world price of textiles is Rs 150, find out the volume of exports.
    (b) What will be the volume of exports when the home government provides a 20 per cent export subsidy to its exporters?
    (c) Calculate DWL if the home country is small.

Suggested Reading

Bhagwati, J.N., A. Panagariya, and T.N. Srinivasan (1998). *Lectures on International Trade*. Cambridge, MA: MIT Press.

Caves, R.E., J. Frankel, and R.W. Jones. (1995). *World Trade and Payments*. New York: HarperCollins College Publishers.

ADVANCED READING

Acharyya, R. (2010). 'Successive Trade Liberalization and Wage Inequality', *Keio Economic Studies*, 46: 29–42.

Das, S.P. (2004). 'Welfare Costs of Import Protection: Some Selected Estimates', *Economic and Political Weekly*, 39(20): 2055–60.

Ferreira P.C. and J.L. Rossi (2003). 'New Evidence from Brazil Trade Liberalization and Productivity Growth', *International Economic Review*, 44(4): 1383–1405.

Johnson, H.G. (1953). 'Optimum Tariffs and Retaliation', *Review of Economic Studies*, 21: 142–53.

Krueger, A.O. and B. Tuncer. (1982). 'An Empirical Test of the Infant Industry Argument', *American Economic Review*, 72: 1142–52.

Lerner, A.P. (1936). 'The Symmetry between Import and Export Taxes', *Economica*, 3(11): 306–13.

Metzler, L. (1949). 'Tariffs, the Terms of Trade, and the Distribution of National Income', *Journal of Political Economy*, 57(1): 1–29.

Scitovsky, T. (1942). 'A Reconsideration of the Theory of Tariffs', *The Review of Economic Studies*, 9: 89–110.

Stolper, W. and P.A. Samuelson. (1941). 'Protection and Real Wages', *Review of Economic Studies*, 9: 58–73.

Trinh, B. (2010). 'Measuring the Effective Rate of Protection in Vietnam's Economy with Emphasis on the Manufacturing Industry: An Input-Output Approach', DEPOCEN Working Paper Series No. 2010/12 (available at http://www.depocenwp.org).

Tsai, Pan-Long. (1989). 'A Note on the Symmetry between Lerner's Case and Metzler's Paradox', *Journal of International Economics*, 27: 373–79.

10 Quantitative Restrictions, Non-tariff Barriers, and Equivalence

Besides the price interventions to trade as discussed in the previous chapter, quantitative restrictions (QRs) on trade and non-tariff barriers (NTBs) are also highly prevalent in many countries. These QRs and NTBs take many forms like import quotas, export quotas, or voluntary export restraint (VER), content protection scheme, and product standards. This chapter discusses these alternative modes of trade interventions and restrictions, except product standards, under the assumption of perfectly competitive markets and later compares these QRs with corresponding price restrictions. Product standards as non-tariff barriers are discussed in detail in Chapter 18.

10.1 IMPORT QUOTA, IMPLICIT TARIFF, AND SCARCITY RENT

An import quota puts a physical restriction on the volume of imports by a country. Under perfectly competitive conditions, it generates similar effects like an import tariff. There is, however, an important difference. An import tariff is like a tax, which allows any amount to be imported at the tariff-inclusive price. Under an import quota, on the other hand, domestic consumers cannot buy foreign goods more than what is permitted by the quota regardless of how large the price they pay. Figure 10.1 illustrates the economic effects of an import quota in domestic markets for import of computers. Suppose the government imposes an import quota by which it allows up to $\overline{M}$ volume of imports. This import quota is administered through issuing import licenses to importers and restricting the volume of imports permissible under each license to a stipulated amount. The aggregate volume of imports permissible under all licenses taken together equals $\overline{M}$. Of course, this import quota will be *binding* on importers as long as $\overline{M}$ is less than the free trade level of imports at a particular TOT as illustrated in Figure 10.1. Otherwise, importers will not import up to the volume that is permissible under the import license, and the import quota will *not* have any effect whatsoever.

Such a binding import quota generates a scarcity of the import good as the supply of imported computers is now restricted to $\overline{M}$. This scarcity raises the relative price of imported computers (and correspondingly the price of locally produced computers) in the home country

International Economics. Rajat Acharyya, Oxford University Press. © Oxford University Press 2022.
DOI: 10.1093/oso/9780192865144.003.0010

above the world price. In Figure 10.1, this domestic price level $\tilde{p}$ is the one for which the home country's import demand equals the import quota level, which is now the *effective import supply*. Thus, an import quota implicitly taxes domestic consumers and the implicit tax or tariff rate is the rate by which the domestic (relative) price exceeds the world price:

$$t_q = \frac{\tilde{p} - p^W}{p^W} \tag{10.1}$$

This implicit tax or tariff on the import of computers and the corresponding proportionate increase in the price of locally produced computers lowers the total home demand for computers and raises the local production of computers. Thus, the economic effects are similar to an import tariff. There is, however, one difference. Instead of a tariff revenue accruing to the national exchequer under an import tariff, there arises a scarcity rent under an import quota as measured by the rectangular area $p^W \tilde{p} e' d$.

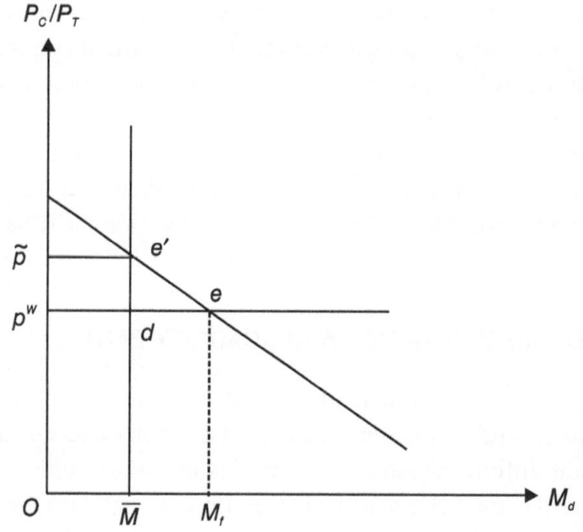

Figure 10.1 Quota on Import of Computers

Importers buy computers in the world market at the price p^W but sell them at the higher price $\tilde{p}$ in the home country taking advantage of the scarcity of (or excess demand for) computers that the import quota generates at the world price p^W. Thus, import licenses generate a scarcity rent of $(\tilde{p}-p^W)$ for each unit of imports. If the home country government auctions off import licenses, it can extract all these rents from importers at an auction price of $(\tilde{p}-p^W)$ per unit of imports. In such a case, the scarcity rent under the import quota will accrue to the national exchequer. Otherwise, when the licenses are given away on a first-cum-first-serve basis or through a lottery among all the applicants, the scarcity rent accrues to importers who obtain import licenses. Of course, a part of the scarcity rent can still accrue to the government if a license fee is to be paid by the importers.

Box 10.1 Import Restrictions through Licenses in India

In India import licensing till the mid-1990s was pervasive and was observed for almost all the imported goods. Goods were divided into banned, restricted, limited permissible, and subject to open general licensing (OGL). The OGL category was the most liberal. In 1976, the OGL list had only 79 items on it. In 1987–88, OGL covered only 30 per cent of the imports. In 2001, as part of the import liberalization policy, 414 items were removed from the restricted list allowing these to be imported against a Special Import License (SIL). These goods can be procured in the market by importers at a small premium. Fruits like oranges and pomegranates, and soft drink concentrates were placed in the SIL category whereas a range of marine food products, vegetables, assorted fruits and juices, spices, edible oils, jams, and jellies were brought under OGL.

Box 10.2 Binding Import quota and Domestic Price

For any given world relative price of the import good of the home country, p^W, an import quota $\overline{M}$ will be binding if $\overline{M} < M_d(p^W)$. If $\tilde{p}$ denotes the domestic price under a binding quota, then it will be such that $\overline{M} = M_d(\tilde{p})$.

Example: Let the import demand function be $M_d = 100 - 10p$, the world relative price be $p^W = 5$ and the import quota be $\overline{M} = 20$. First of all, since $M_d(p^W = 5) = 50$, so the import quota is binding. The domestic price $\tilde{p}$ will then be such that $20 = 100 - 10\tilde{p}$. Hence, $\tilde{p} = 8$.

The economic costs or DWL of the import quota are also similar to those of an import tariff. There are production losses as an import quota encourages the inefficient domestic producers to produce more computers, and consumption losses as the implicit tariff forces the home consumers to pay a higher price for cheaper imports of computers. By the surplus measure these two losses *together* constitute DWL as measured by the area *e'de*. Note that in calculating DWL it does not matter whether licenses are auctioned off or not. Because, in either case the scarcity rent accrues to economic agents within the home country, the government or the importers. But if foreign supply is monopolized by a single foreign firm, it can extract the entire scarcity rent from home importers by raising its supply price of computers from p^W to $\tilde{p}$. In such a case, the rectangular area in Figure 10.1 measuring the scarcity rent also constitutes DWL. Further, as we will see in a latter chapter, this scarcity rent that an import license promises to a potential license holder, leads to competition among potential license holders or the 'rent-seekers' for obtaining a license through wasteful lobbying. This constitutes an additional source of economic loss since the real resources are withdrawn from productive use elsewhere by the rent-seekers for lobbying.

What appears from the above discussion is that if we set aside the distribution of the scarcity rent and the consequent welfare implications of an import quota, the economic effects of an import quota and an import tariff are similar. Jagdish Bhagwati (1965) in his seminal work formalized this similarity in his *Price-Equivalence* theorem. The Price-Equivalence theorem states that under perfectly competitive conditions, if an import quota that allows $\overline{M}$ level of imports is replaced by an equal-import tariff (that is, an import tariff that generates the same $\overline{M}$ volume of imports), the domestic price will be larger than the world price by the same percentage points in both the cases. This is easy to understand. Refer back to Figure 10.1. If the import quota of $\overline{M}$ volume is replaced by an import tariff that generates the same volume of imports, neither less nor more, then the tariff rate must be set to the level so as to make the tariff-inclusive price exactly equal to $\tilde{p}$. Any other tariff rate will make the domestic tariff inclusive price larger or smaller than $\tilde{p}$ for any given world price. Correspondingly, the volume of imports will be either smaller or larger than $\overline{M}$. Therefore, an equal-import tariff should generate the same level of domestic price as the import quota. This further means that the equal-import tariff rate should be exactly equal to the implicit tariff rate defined in equation 10.1. Once the domestic prices are the same under an import quota and an equal-import tariff, all the economic effects are identical in magnitude.

A few comments are warranted in this context. First, the price-equivalence does not necessarily mean a welfare equivalence of an import quota and an equal-import tariff. As noted above, an import quota may inflict larger economic losses if a part of (or the entire) scarcity rent accrues to the foreign supplier of computers, and when rent-seekers engage in wasteful lobbying activities. Of course, under perfectly competitive conditions everywhere, the first source of additional economic loss will not be there. But the loss from the rent-seeking activity will still be there.

Second, the price-equivalence also extends to the TOT effect of an import quota and an equal-import tariff. Figure 10.2 illustrates this. Under an import quota imposed by the home country that restricts the import volume within the level $\overline{M}$, the home offer curve becomes $OQ\overline{M}$ and the global or international equilibrium shifts to E_Q from the free trade equilibrium E. The home country's exports decline as well because a lower volume of imports now needs a smaller volume of exports to finance the import bill. TOT improves for the home country, as shown by the steeper TOT line passing through E_Q.

When this import quota is replaced by an equal-import tariff, the tariff rate must be such that the tariff-ridden home curve crosses over the foreign offer curve at E_Q as well. This is shown by the broken offer curve OH'. Otherwise, for a larger tariff rate, the home offer curve shifts further to the left and the volume of imports under tariff falls below the level permissible under the import quota. Thus, the same TOT prevails under an equal-import tariff.

TOT improvement further implies that for a large importing country an import quota may raise its welfare. Similar to an import tariff, an import quota has a TOT and a VOT effect. For quota levels that do not restrict the volume of imports at a too small level, welfare increase on account of TOT improvement will be larger than the welfare loss on account of a decline in VOT. But for more stringent quota levels, a decline in VOT is large enough to lower the welfare of the country despite an improvement in TOT. Thus, similar to an optimum tariff, there exists an *optimum import quota* for which the large country's welfare is maximized.

Third, as Bhagwati (1965) himself demonstrated, market imperfection either in production or in trade may lead to a breakdown of price-equivalence. Subsequently, Hwang and Mai (1988) qualified this by showing that price-equivalence may still hold when international oligopolistic firms behave in a Cournot fashion. We will discuss these cases of equivalence and non-equivalence under market imperfection in the next chapter.

Box 10.3 Tariffication of QRs in India

An important policy shift was initiated in 1985 in India whereby QRs on import of capital and intermediate goods were replaced by tariff-based protectionism. But the tariff rates were not conditioned by the equal-import criterion since the intention was to allow the import of a larger amount of capital and intermediate goods at tariff-inclusive prices and thereby make Indian exports more efficient through technology upgradation. In many instances the tariff rates were actually higher than the equal-import rates so that the Indian market became more protective. Later in April 2001, as part of the structural adjustment programmes, QRs on most of the goods including consumer goods were replaced by *equivalent* tariffs. This policy shift is known as tariffication of QRs.

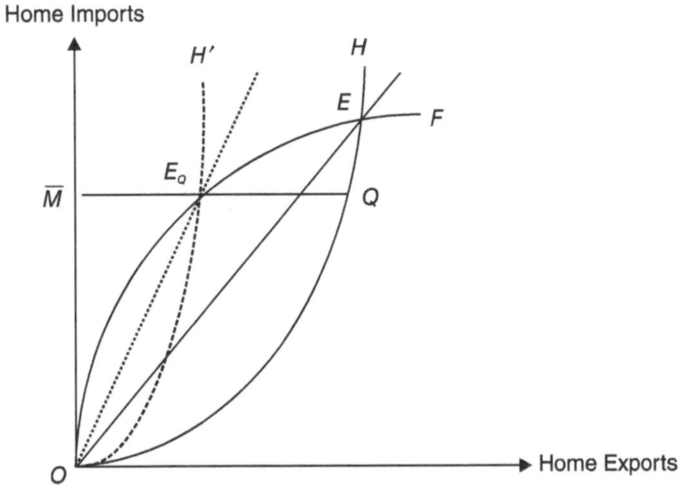

Figure 10.2 Tariff, Quota, and TOT

10.2 VOLUNTARY EXPORT RESTRAINTS

Voluntary export restraints (VER) are export quotas *negotiated* by an importing country with its trading partners. Under a successful negotiation, the trading partner or the exporting country *voluntarily* restricts its exports. There are many examples of VER being negotiated by countries. During the mid-1980s, the United States successfully negotiated a VER with Japan that restricted export of Japanese automobiles to the United States. Similar VER in textiles were negotiated by the United States with the East Asian exporting countries. The economic effects of a VER for a small exporting country are illustrated in Figure 10.3. Given the world relative price of computers, p^W, the foreign country was initially exporting X_f^* units of computers in panel *b* (or *bf* units in panel *a*). Domestic demand for computers and local production of computers in the foreign country were respectively p^Wb and p^Wf units. The consumers' surplus was the area ap^Wb and producers' surplus was the area Sp^Wf. Producers' surplus had two parts: surplus from domestic sales was the area p^WbjS, and from exports was

Box 10.4 QRs and Balance of Payments Objective

Countries often use QRs on imports under the balance of payments clause of the General Agreement on Trade and Tariff (GATT) in its Article XVIII (B). Since the early 1960s, India too had used GATT's balance of payments provision to justify her routine use of QRs. But since the 1990s, it became difficult for India to justify QRs on grounds of balance of payments as her current account and foreign exchange reserves improved significantly. Despite this, even in 1999–2000, 2,134 items (at the 8-digit sub-group levels) were subject to QRs, of which 1,589 items had QRs on imports, being maintained under the balance of payments provision. Soon India's unconstrained use of the balance of payments provision was challenged by the US, EU, and other developed countries in the Dispute Settlement Body of the World Trade Organization. India lost the case and had to remove QRs on almost all imports by 2001.

the area *bjf*. A VER of export volume $\overline{X}^*$ lowers the domestic price of computers in the foreign country to p_d^*. Note that this decline in the relative price is necessary to match the excess supply of *hi* units in panel *a* with the VER amount. A binding VER, $\overline{X}^* < X^*(p^W)$, induces foreign producers to sell $X^*(p^W) - \overline{X}^*$ in the domestic market. The consequent excess supply lowers the domestic price of the export good in the foreign country market. The lower domestic relative price raises consumers' surplus and lowers producers' surplus. A scarcity rent equal to the rectangular area *dcih* also arises because though for domestic sales the exporters get the lower price, for the export volume they get a higher world price. Like the import tariff, this scarcity rent under the binding VER can be appropriated by the exporters if export licenses are issued by the government without any charge; or can be appropriated by the government if the licenses are auctioned off. Foreign consumers' surplus increases by the area $p^W bgp_d^*$ plus the area *bgh*. The producers' surplus from domestic sales is now the area $p_d^* hkS$ and from exports the area *dcik* if the scarcity rent is appropriated by the exporters. Total loss in foreign producers' surplus is thus composed of the area $p^W bgp_d^*$, area *bdhg* and the area *cfi*. Of these losses, the area $p^W bgp_d^*$ and the area *bgh* are actually transfer of surplus to the foreign consumers as these two constitutes their increased surplus. Hence, areas *bdh* and *cfi* constitute DWL under a VER. Note that DWL would have remained the same if the scarcity rent would have been appropriated by the government, since it would then constitute just a transfer of surplus from foreign producers to their government.

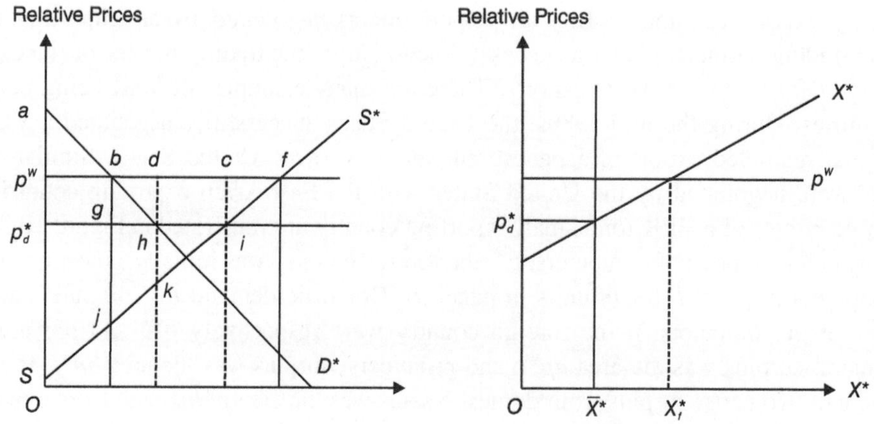

Figure 10.3 Economic Effects of VER in the Exporting Country

For a large exporting country, a VER will improve its TOT. Referring back to Figure 10.2, a VER imposed by the large foreign country that restricts its exports to $\overline{X}^*$ (= $\overline{M}$, say), makes its offer curve OE_QQ. Thus, the global equilibrium under VER shifts to point Q and TOT (the line segment joining the origin and point Q, which is not drawn though) moves in favour of the foreign country. The reason is simple. A VER imposed by the government of a foreign country on its exporters of computers lowers the supply of computers in the world market. At the initial TOT and hence given the import demand for computers by the home country, this lower supply creates an excess demand for computers and thus raises its world (relative) price. Since the foreign country exports computers, so this price rise is essentially a TOT improvement for it (and conversely a TOT deterioration for the home country). In Figure 10.3, TOT improvement means that the p^W-line shifts up. This raises the scarcity rent for foreign exporters. This additional scarcity rent or gain from a VER should now be weighed against the losses that are discussed above, which is in fact the VOT effect. On the whole, however, a VER will improve the welfare of the large exporting country if it is not too restrictive. This explains why VER may be *voluntary*.

We now turn to the effect of a VER in the *importing country* in comparison with an import quota. With only one source country for imports, a VER by that source country has similar effects that an import quota on such imports generates in the importing country. A similar equivalence result, as in case of import tariff and import quota, can be established between an import quota and an equal-import VER negotiated with the exporting country. The only difference is that a VER worsens the TOT for the importing country and thereby shifts the scarcity rent from the importing to the exporting country. To illustrate the equivalence result in a two country world economy, consider Figure 10.4 where the world market for the home import good, that is, computers, is shown with a downward sloping home import demand curve and an upward sloping foreign export supply curve. By construction, the foreign country is the only source of supply for home import of computers in this two country world. Under free trade, the world equilibrium relative price was Op with the volume of home imports or foreign exports being OF. When the home government imposes an import quota of OR, the effective home import demand in the world market becomes MQR. The world equilibrium shifts to V from E. The world relative price of computers thus falls to Ob, which is a TOT improvement for the importing home country, and the domestic relative price of computers in the home country rises to Oa.

The import quota creates a wedge between world and domestic prices in the importing country, and this is measured by the implicit tax or tariff rate $\frac{ab}{Ob}$. As explained earlier, home importers now enjoy the scarcity rent equal to the area $aQVb$. Note that, since the foreign country does not restrict its exports, the domestic price there, Ob, is aligned with the world price.

Now suppose the home country successfully negotiates an equal-import VER with the foreign country. Thus, instead of the home country restricting its import volume to OR, the foreign country restricts its export volume to OR. The effective foreign export supply curve is now X^*VQ. Given the home import demand curve MM', the world relative price of computers now rises to Oa as the global equilibrium under a VER shifts to Q from the global equilibrium under an import quota at V. This is a TOT improvement for the exporting foreign country but a TOT

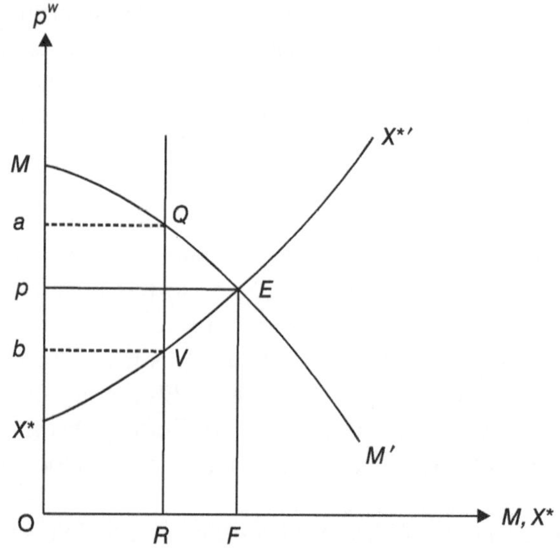

Figure 10.4 Equivalence between Quota and VER

deterioration for the importing home country. Since the home country no longer restricts its imports, so now the domestic relative price of computers there is aligned with the world price. Thus, again the domestic price rises to the same level *Oa* as under the import quota imposed by the home country, though now this is because the world relative price of computers rises. Hence, the effects of an equal-import VER on domestic production, consumption, and total surplus will be the same as those under quota discussed above and illustrated in Figure 10.1. In the exporting foreign country, however, the domestic relative price of computers declines to *Ob* and thus differs from the world price. The scarcity rent now accrues to foreign exporters. Thus, though a conversion of an import quota by an equal-import VER negotiated with the trading partner does not affect the domestic relative price and also the level of protection generated, it shifts the scarcity rent to the exporting country. Accordingly, *DWL under a VER is larger than the DWL under an equal-import quota.* Referring back to Figure 10.2, the conversion shifts the global equilibrium from E_Q to Q, and the home country unambiguously loses. This is because if we had drawn the home *TIC*s to indicate its welfare levels, the *TIC* passing through Q would lie strictly below the TIC passing through E_Q, thereby indicating a lower home welfare level.

There are quite a few caveats to this price-equivalence result though. The most important is that when there is more than one source of supply of a country's imports, then an import quota imposed by the country may be more restrictive and protective than a VER if the country is not able to negotiate VER with all its trading partners. Negotiating VER may be costly, and thus countries often negotiate VER with their major trading partners only, leaving smaller sources of supplies unrestrained. Thus, a VER is often source-specific and discriminatory. An import quota, on the other hand, restricts imports to a country regardless of the source of supply. It is much easier and less costly (in terms of both economic and political costs) to restrict importers than to negotiate VER with a large number of trading partners. Thus, an import quota is global and non-discriminatory though more restrictive. It is due to this restrictiveness of the import quota as compared to VER, that GATT (and now WTO) implicitly prefer VER negotiated with trading partners over import quotas used by countries to restrict their imports. A source-specific VER and a global import quota may also have different welfare effects. Extending the general equilibrium analysis of the two country model illustrated in Figure 10.2 to three countries, Dinopoulos and Kreinin (1989) showed the following welfare result. When a VER is negotiated by the importing country with one of its two trading partners, the welfare of the unrestricted exporter is higher but that of the VER-restricted exporting country is ambiguous.

Sometimes, the choice of trading partners with whom VER are negotiated may be strategic. For example, during the mid-1980s, the United States negotiated a VER for automobiles with Japan, leaving exports of automobiles by South Korea and Europe unrestrained. Part of this reason may be the relative cost efficiency (product superiority) of Japanese firms so that more intense competition was faced by the American firms from Japanese firms than from elsewhere. However, as we will see in a later chapter, strategic interactions among international oligopolists opens up another dimension to the equivalence aspect. As shown by Acharyya (1995), a source-specific and hence less restrictive VER may actually cause the domestic production to expand compared to a non-discriminatory and global import quota. That is, an import quota may be less protective despite restricting the volume of imports to a lower level than a VER does.

10.3 OTHER NON-TARIFF BARRIERS

Besides import quotas and VER (or export quotas), there are other non-tariff barriers (NTBs) to trade such as quality standards, environmental regulations, and technical barriers to trade (TBT). These regulations on trade are essentially related to the nature and standards of imported goods. For example, there are goods that degrade or pollute the environment while being produced or consumed. Such goods are called dirty goods or goods of poor environmental quality. Depending on the nature of the good, the per unit pollution emission varies, and accordingly we can categorize goods as dirtier to dirtiest. Examples of dirtiest goods include chemicals, iron and steel, paper and pulp, cement, wood products, glass products, leather products, and petroleum refineries. The developed countries often impose import quotas, pollution content tariffs, and minimum environmental standards on the import of such dirty goods from developing countries to protect their national environments. Imports of chemical products, for example, may not be allowed unless these meet a certain level of environmental standards or quality. The International Standard Organization's certifications for product standards are often set by the developed countries as the acceptable minimum standards for products produced and exported by developing countries. As we will elaborate in Chapter 18, while these import restrictions or green protectionism seem sensible, these restrictions cannot be actually justifiable in all cases of environmental degradation. Suppose, a good pollutes the environment only at the production stage, but not while it is consumed. Moreover, suppose that such pollution is confined within a small geographical area. Then, import of this good from a developing country will actually lower national pollution in the developed country by displacing the local production of the good there. Restrictions on imports then cannot be justified as protection of the national environment, but as protection for domestic producers just like the cases discussed above. That is, product standards in instances like this are essentially NTBs to trade in disguise to protect national industries.

SUMMARY POINTS

- Under an import quota, domestic consumers cannot buy foreign goods more than what is permitted by the quota regardless of how large the price that they pay is.
- Jagdish Bhagwati's Price-Equivalence theorem states that the economic effects of an import quota and an import tariff are the same. The only difference is that whereas an import tariff generates tariff revenue for the national exchequer, a binding import quota generates scarcity rent for import license holders. Part of this rent may, however, be extracted by the government.
- Price-equivalence also extends to the TOT effect of an import quota and an equal-import tariff.
- A VER worsens TOT for the importing country and thereby shifts the scarcity rent from the importing to the exporting country. Thus, a VER improves the welfare of the large exporting country if it is not too restrictive. This explains why VER may be *voluntary*.
- DWL under a VER is larger than the DWL under an equal-import quota for the importing country.
- When there is more than one source of supply of a country's imports, then an import quota imposed by the country may be more restrictive and protective than a VER if the country is not able to negotiate VER with all its trading partners. A VER is often source-specific and discriminatory.
- An import quota, on the other hand, restricts imports to a country regardless of the source of supply. Thus, an import quota is global and non-discriminatory though more restrictive.
- Besides import quotas and VER (or export quotas), there are other non-tariff barriers (NTBs) to trade such as quality standards, environmental regulations, and technical barriers to trade (TBT). These regulations on trade are essentially related to the nature and standards of imported goods.

KEYWORDS

- **Import quota** is a physical restriction on imports. It is the maximum permissible volume of a good that can be imported at the world price.
- **Voluntary export restraint (VER)** is the maximum permissible volume of exports negotiated between an importing and an exporting country.
- **Scarcity rent** (per unit) is the additional price (or revenue) over the world price that the importers get in the domestic market from selling the quota-restricted imported good.
- **Implicit tariff** rate is the rate at which the domestic relative price of the imported good under quota exceeds its world price.
- **Price-equivalence** between an import quota and an import tariff means that the domestic relative price of the imported good will be the same when the volume imported under a tariff is alternatively set as an import quota, or when a tariff generates the same level of imports as is allowed under an import quota. That is, when price- equivalence holds, the implicit tariff rate under the import quota is exactly equal to the tariff rate.
- **Dirty goods** are those that degrade the environment through pollution emission.

EXERCISES

1. Why does local production not increase by the same extent to which an import quota lowers the volume of imports below the free trade level?
2. Algebraically show that the domestic price under a *binding* import quota will be higher than the world price. Assume that the country imposing the import quota is small.
3. Consider the following import demand function of a small home country:

   $M = 100 - p_d$

   The world relative price of this import good is 50. If the home country government imposes an import quota of 40 units, is it binding? What will be the domestic relative price of imports for this quota level? Calculate the scarcity rent generated by this quota level.
4. What will be the equal-import ad-valorem tariff to replace an import quota of 30 units? Check the price-equivalence of these equal-import tariffs and quotas.
5. Algebraically prove that equal-import tariff and quota are (domestic) price equivalent.
6. Consider the following local market for soccer balls in Brazil:

   $D_B = a - 2p_B$, $S_B = c + p_B$

   If there is an import quota of (a – c)/5 units of soccer balls imported from Pakistan at the given world price of (a – c)/4, then:

   (a) How much does the local price of soccer balls rise in Brazil above this world price?
   (b) Calculate the implicit tax paid by buyers in Brazil.
   (c) Calculate the DWL.
7. In the above example, suppose import licenses are distributed directly to Pakistani exporters to sell soccer balls in Brazil, instead of to local importers. Will the import quota and an import-equivalent tariff then have the same welfare levels?
8. (a) Suppose to import a good, home country importers must obtain licenses from the customs officials which is distributed free of charge. Each license allows only one unit of import and each importer can get only one license. There is no ex ante restriction on the number of people who can obtain a license. If home import demand is $M = 100 - p^W$, and foreign supply is $X^* = 50 + p^W$, then how many importers will obtain licenses? At what price they will buy the good from the world market and at what price they will sell in the home country market?

   (b) Suppose on the day when issuing of license was to open, a fire broke out in the Customs Office which destroyed many documents including some licenses and only 50 licenses could be saved. Government decided not to print additional licenses till a fire extinguisher equipment is installed so that next day only those 50 licenses were distributed. At what prices the importers will now buy the good in the world market and sell in the domestic market? Does this natural calamity harm or benefit the importers? Intuitively explain your answer.
9. Even if an import quota leads to a large improvement in TOT or a large decline in the world relative price of imports, it always protects domestic industries. Why?
10. How will you relate an optimum import quota with an optimum import tariff?

(contd)

Exercises (*contd*)

11. If at the initial free trade equilibrium foreign import demand is inelastic, will an import quota and an equal-import tariff be price-equivalent?
12. Consider the following market for textiles in the home country:

$$p_T^d = 220 - 2Q_T, \; p_T^s = 100 + Q_T$$

Suppose the world price of textiles is Rs 180.

(a) If the foreign country negotiates a VER of 60 units of textiles with the home country, will it be binding?
(b) If a more stringent VER of 30 units is negotiated, what will be the domestic price of textiles in the home country?
(c) Calculate the scarcity rent accruing to home exporters.

SUGGESTED READING

Bhagwati, J.N., A. Panagariya, and T.N. Srinivasan. (1998). *Lectures on International Trade*. Cambridge, MA: MIT Press.

Vousden, N. (1990). *The Economics of Trade Protection*. Cambridge: Cambridge University Press.

ADVANCED READING

Acharyya, R. (1995). 'Protective Effects of Source-Specific VER and Global Quota under Oligopoly', *Keio Economic Studies*, 32(2): 65–70.

Bhagwati, J.N. (1965). 'On the Equivalence of Tariffs and Quotas', in R.E. Baldwain, G. Haberler, and F. Machlup (eds), *Trade Growth and Balance of Payments: Essays in Honour of G. Haberler.* Chicago, IL: Rand McNally, pp. 53–67.

Dinopoulos, E. and M.E. Kreinin (1989). 'Import Quotas and VERs: A Comparative Analysis in a Three-Country Framework', *Journal of International Economics*, 26: 169–78.

Hwang, H. and C.C. Mai. (1988). 'On the Equivalence of Tariff and Quota under Duopoly: A Conjectural Variation Approach', *Journal of International Economics*, 24: 373–80.

11 Market Imperfection and Trade Policy

Discussions of different modes of trade protection and promotion and their economic effects in Chapters 9 and 10 have been confined to perfectly competitive conditions in production. But domestic monopolies prevail for many reasons including protective trade policies themselves. That is, trade policies by themselves may determine the extent to which domestic monopolies may exert their market power. The nature of trade policy is also an important factor here. On the other hand, the monopolies discussed in Chapter 8 are large conglomerates and their market power is not confined to their respective domestic markets only. Such monopolies add an altogether different dimension to trade policies. In such cases trade policies can be used by national governments to influence international market share rivalry among these large monopolies to their national advantage. This chapter discusses these implications of trade policy issues for domestic and international monopolies and oligopolies. To keep things simple, for most of the discussions, we confine the discussion to the partial equilibrium analysis under the assumption of only one good being produced everywhere.

11.1 COMPETITIVE WORLD PRODUCTION AND DOMESTIC MONOPOLY

Consider the case of a small home country where the production of computers is monopolized by a domestic firm in the pre-trade situation. The pre-trade price p_a and units of computers produced X_a are standard monopoly levels as illustrated in Figure 11.1 for the marginal cost of producing computers which increases with the output level. But suppose this domestic monopolist is small enough and is a price taker in a perfectly competitive world market for computers. If the competitive world price of computers is below the lowest possible value of the marginal cost of this domestic monopolist (such as $p_O^W < Oa$), it cannot survive when trade opens up. Domestic demand for computers will then be entirely met through imports at this price. For a world price in the range $[c, p_a]$ the domestic monopolist survives after trade, but its monopoly power is restricted because it cannot charge a price higher than the world price of computers. Thus, *trade breaks up a domestic monopoly*. The domestic price will now be lower than the monopoly price and the total consumption of computers will be larger than the pre-trade (monopoly) level. Thus, by the total surplus measure, the home country will clearly gain due to this pro-competitive effect of trade.

International Economics. Rajat Acharyya, Oxford University Press. © Oxford University Press 2022.
DOI: 10.1093/oso/9780192865144.003.0011

There is, however, an important distinction to be made between world prices in the range $[c, b]$ and in the range $[b, p_a]$. For any world price in the range $[c, b]$, computers are imported. For example, consider the world price of computers being p_1^W. The domestic monopolist effectively becomes a price taker even in its own market. It now produces OX_d units of computers for which its marginal cost of production equals the world price p_1^W. The excess demand for computers at that price, X_dX_M units, is met through imports. The domestic monopolist's profit now falls to *acd* but the consumers' surplus increases from Dp_ah to *Dag*, which is larger than the profit loss. The economy thus gains from the pro-competitive effect of trade that breaks up the domestic monopoly.

Note that the price *Ob* represents the pre-trade domestic price of computers if computers were produced by perfectly competitive domestic firms. Thus, any world price lower than *Ob* is a reflection of the home country's (absolute) cost *dis*advantage in producing computers relative to the producers in the rest of the world. Hence, for any such world price, computers will be imported, and the country will gain from cheaper imports.

World price larger than *Ob*, on the other hand, is a reflection of the home country's (absolute) cost advantage in producing computers. The domestic monopolist, still being a virtual price taker, can now *export* computers. For example, for the world price p_2^W, the domestic firm produces *kf* units of computers for which its marginal cost of production equals the world (and domestic) price of computers. Of this total production, it sells *ke* units in the domestic market and exports *ef* units. Once again the economy gains as measured by the area *hefl*. The interesting point to observe here is that unlike the competitive case, export of computers *lowers* the price of computers in the home country. The reason is simple. Pre-trade, the domestic monopolist could charge the monopoly price p_a for the computers that it produced. But when the country opens up to international trade, competitive pressure from foreign producers forces it to lower the price to the level of the world price. This again reflects the pro-competitive effect of trade and constitutes a part of the gain for the economy. The other source of the welfare

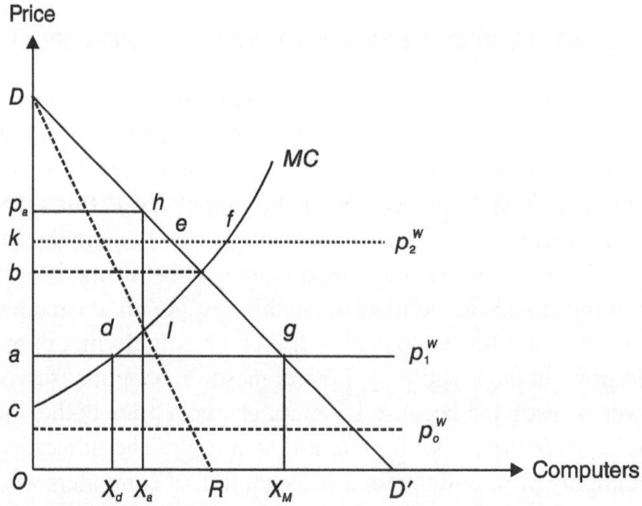

Figure 11.1 Trade, Domestic Monopoly, and Gains

gain is profit from exports for the domestic monopolist. Thus, all economic agents in the home country—consumers and the domestic monopolist—may gain if profit from exports is larger than the decline in profits from domestic sales.

To sum up, when computers are locally produced by a monopolist under autarchy, trade breaks up this domestic monopoly if the firm is small enough in the world market. The domestic monopolist must now charge the same price for the computers that it produces as producers abroad charge. The local price of computers thus falls, regardless of whether the country imports or exports computers, and the country gains from this pro-competitive effect of trade.

11.2 PROTECTION OF A DOMESTIC MONOPOLY

Sometimes even a domestic monopolist may need to be protected when its cost disadvantage is too large. Referring back to Figure 11.1, for a world price such as p_O^W, the domestic monopolist simply cannot survive foreign competition without protection. Even if we set aside the lobbying effort that a domestic monopolist may put in for its protection, there are employment concerns particularly when wages are downward rigid that prohibit workers displaced from this sector to be absorbed elsewhere. Under such a constraint, should the home country's government protect the inefficient domestic monopolist by imposing an import tariff or an import quota on import of computers? The answer depends on whether there are perfectly competitive foreign producers and suppliers (as discussed above) or a large monopolist foreign producer and supplier of computers. We discuss each of these cases in turn in the following sub-sections.

11.2.1 Competitive Foreign Supply: Non-equivalence of Tariff and Quota

When foreign supply is perfectly competitive, an import tariff should be a preferred mode of protection for the domestic monopolist rather than an import quota, both from employment and welfare objectives. The reason is simple. Though an import tariff protects the domestic monopolist and enables it to survive, it does not allow it to exercise its monopoly power. Since domestic consumers can still buy and consume any number of computers produced abroad at the tariff-inclusive price, the domestic monopolist cannot charge a price higher than what the tariff allows. But under an import quota, the volume of import of computers is restricted and domestic consumers cannot buy more computers than what the quota level permits. Thus, the domestic monopolist faces only restricted foreign competition, and can exercise its monopoly power in the residual market by charging a higher price than the tariff-inclusive price of computers produced abroad. Thus, an import tariff despite generating protection breaks up the monopoly and generates a higher welfare by its pro-competitive effect than an import quota. This in fact suggests the non-equivalence of an import tariff and an equal-import quota as demonstrated by Bhagwati (1965).

To illustrate, consider Figure 11.2. Under an ad-valorem tariff that raises the domestic import price of computers to $(1 + t)\,p_O^W$, the domestic monopolist produces OX_t number of computers and the country imports X_tX_M number of computers. When this import volume is alternatively set as an import quota, the available market for the domestic monopolist is indicated by the residual demand curve $D_RD'_R$. The residual demand at any price is the quantity demanded less the import quota level. Since the import quota level is a fixed amount, the residual demand curve is just a lateral (and parallel) displacement of the total demand curve by the level of the

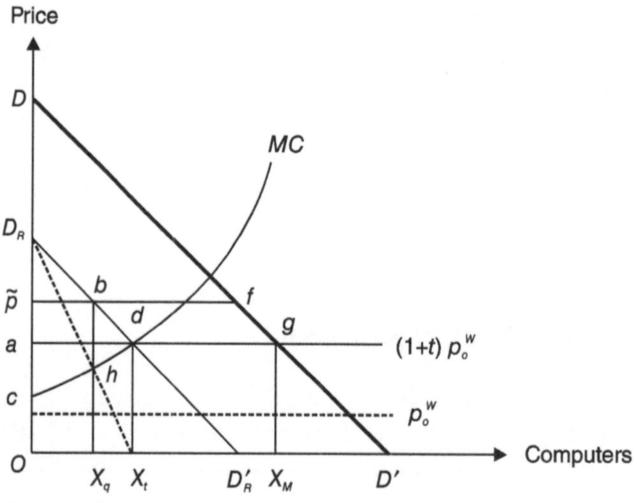

Figure 11.2 Protection of a Domestic Monopoly

import quota. For this residual demand, the domestic monopolist does not face any competition from suppliers even if it raises its price above the world price of computers. That is, under quota protection, the domestic monopolist can exercise its monopoly power in the residual market. It then produces less output than under tariff and raises the price to maximize its profit in this residual domestic market. By the standard monopoly profit maximization rule of MR = MC, it produces OX_q number of computers and charge the price $O\tilde{p}$. Thus, employment generated under an import quota is strictly less than that under an import tariff. Moreover, the total surplus or welfare under the quota, which equals the area *chbfD*, is also strictly less than the total surplus under a (equal-import) tariff, which equals the area *cdgD*. Hence, both in terms of employment generation and the cost of protection, a domestic monopolist should be protected, if at all, through an import tariff instead of an import quota.

From the above discussion it is also immediate that the price equivalence of an import tariff and an equal-import quota no longer holds. An equal-import quota leads to a higher domestic price, $\tilde{p} > (1 + t)\, p_O^W$, so that the implicit tariff under the quota is larger than the import tariff.

11.2.2 Monopoly Foreign Supplier and Strategic Competition

Consider now the case of a single and large foreign producer of computers. Suppose there is no importing agent in the home country and the foreign monopolist directly sells its output to home buyers. Thus, the supply of computers by the foreign monopolist is the volume of import of computers.

Under unrestricted imports of computers in the home country, this foreign producer competes with the domestic monopolist for the share of the home country market. To simplify the discussion, we assume that the marginal cost of this foreign supplier is the same as that of the domestic monopolist. Moreover, suppose the marginal cost is constant. If the firms behave in Cournot fashion (that is, each firm conjectures that when it changes its own output, the other firm does not change its output), the post-trade equilibrium market share will be the one shown in Figure 11.3. The downward sloping lines R and R^* are the Cournot output-reaction curves of the domestic and foreign monopolists respectively. The reaction curve R, for example, is the locus of profit maximizing (or best-response) output levels of the domestic monopolist for each output level (and exports) of the foreign monopolist. The reaction curves are drawn linear under the assumption of a linear demand function and a constant marginal cost function. The reason for the reaction curves being downward sloping, on the other hand, is as follows. For any given foreign output (and hence the level of imports), the domestic monopolist sets its output level by maximizing profit to be realized in the residual market, as illustrated in Figure 11.2. For a larger output of the foreign supplier and thus larger volume of imports, the residual demand for the domestic monopolist is smaller. Thus, the corresponding profit-maximizing output is smaller as well. That is, the best-response or profit-maximizing output level of the domestic monopolist varies inversely with the foreign monopolist's output level.

Note that when the foreign firm does not sell its computers in the home market (that is, the volume of imports is zero), the domestic monopolist produces the monopoly output level. Hence, the horizontal intercept of the reaction curve R equals the monopoly output, X_M. On the other hand, the maximum amount that the foreign monopolist can sell in the home country market is the one for which the market-clearing price equals the marginal cost (in which case it earns zero super-normal profit). This output level is the same as a competitive industry would have produced and supplied. The foreign supplier will not supply more than this because in such a case the market-clearing price will fall below the marginal cost and it will make losses. When the foreign monopolist supplies this maximum (competitive) output, the domestic monopolist's best-response is not to sell any amount at all. Otherwise, the market-clearing price will fall below the marginal cost and the domestic monopolist will make losses. Hence, the vertical intercept of the reaction curve for the domestic monopolist equals the competitive output level (of the foreign monopolist). The reaction curve for the foreign supplier can be explained similarly: it is negatively sloped with its vertical intercept being equal to the monopoly output of the foreign supplier, X^*_M (which is the same as X_M since costs are the

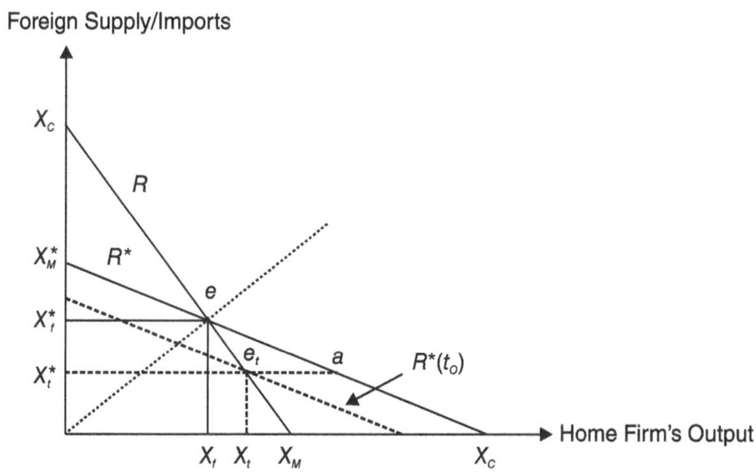

Figure 11.3 Foreign Monopoly Supplier and Protection

same) and the horizontal intercept being equal to the competitive output. It is now immediate that the domestic monopolist's reaction curve R would be steeper than the domestic monopolist's reaction curve R^* since the competitive output is larger than the monopoly output.

The equilibrium supplies by domestic and foreign monopolies in the home country market under unrestricted imports are then respectively X_f and X_f^* corresponding to the point e where these two reaction curves cross each other. Since the firms have identical marginal costs, the equilibrium point e lies on the 45° line through the origin meaning that $X_f = X_f^*$.

Given these initial market shares, consider now a per *unit* tariff at the rate t_0 imposed by the home country government on imports, that is, on the supply of the foreign monopolist to the home country market. Since the foreign monopolist directly sells its output to home consumers, so it has to pay this tariff to the home country government. An import tariff is thus like a sales tax (or a production tax) on the foreign monopolist. This unit tariff raises the foreign monopolist's marginal cost of production for such supplies, and consequently shifts *in* its best response supply of output for any given supply of output by the domestic monopolist. This is shown by the broken $R^*(t_0)$ curve. Note that the higher the rate of tariff, the lower will be the foreign reaction curve. At the new equilibrium e_t, the foreign supply or volume of imports declines to X_t^* and the domestic monopolist's supply rises to X_t. That is, a tariff raises the market share of the domestic monopolist. This is the *strategic effect* of an import tariff. Note that an import tariff also shifts part of the foreign profit to the domestic monopolist. Due to this redistribution of profits commensurate with the change in market shares, the strategic effect can also be interpreted as the *profit-shifting effect*. A part of the profit of the foreign monopolist is also transferred to the home country government in the form of tariff revenue. This is what Brander and Spencer (1985) termed the *rent-extracting effect* of a tariff. Both these profit-shifting and rent-extracting effects raise the home country's welfare over and above the free trade level. At the same time, there is a welfare loss for the home country. It is evident from Figure 11.3 that the local supply increases *less* than the decline in the foreign supply or imports. Thus, the tariff lowers the total supply of the good and consequently raises its price in the home country market. This is the cost of tariff to the economy. Consumers pay a higher price and consume less. Their surpluses fall and the economy loses. Thus, by the surplus measure, whether a tariff raises or lowers the welfare of the country depends on the magnitudes of the profit-shifting and the rent-extracting effects vis-à-vis the price (or consumption) effect.

An import quota triggers similar effects. In fact, the local supply will be the same when the import volume under tariff, X_t^*, is alternatively set as the import quota. Referring back to Figure 11.3, under the equal-import quota, the foreign reaction curve becomes the kinked $X_t^* aX_C$ because the foreign firm cannot supply more than the quota level. It is immediate then that the equilibrium market shares remain the same under equal-import quota as under tariff. This means the total supply and consequently the domestic price will remain the same as well. Hence, despite market imperfection, a tariff and an equal-import quota are price equivalent. This result, which extends Bhagwati's equivalence result, was demonstrated by Hwang and Mai (1988). However, this equivalence result holds *only when* the domestic and foreign monopolists have Cournot type conjecture that when one firm changes its output the other firm remains passive by not changing its output. The reason is simple. Under an import quota, the foreign firm cannot actually raise its supply above the quota level and, on the other hand, *will not like to lower its supply* as long as the domestic firm raises its output level within the range

$e_t a$. That is, the foreign monopolist's supply (or volume of imports) remains unchanged for any output level of the domestic monopolist in the range [0, *a*]. Thus, the Cournot conjecture of the domestic monopolist under the import tariff is actually being realized under an import quota. Hence, it does not change its supply of output under quota as long as the import volume under tariff is set as the quota level.

What this price equivalence under the Cournot conjecture implies is that the national government is indifferent between the mode of protection of the domestic monopolist on employment considerations. But, on the welfare consideration, the import tariff should be preferred because under the import quota there will be no rent-extracting effect. The part of the scarcity rent accruing to the foreign supplier cannot be transferred to the national exchequer.

11.3 INTERNATIONAL PRICE DISCRIMINATION AND DUMPING

International monopolies, or multinational corporations, often price discriminate across different country markets according to the country characteristics such as differences in per capita income. This is known as the pricing-to-market phenomenon and is reflective of the market powers of international monopolies. But often we find domestic monopolies that are protected in their own markets sell goods in the world market at a much cheaper price than the price at which they sell in their own domestic markets. This is known as the dumping of goods that benefit consumers but hurt competitive producers in importing countries.

To illustrate how a domestic monopolist practices price discrimination and dumping, consider Figure 11.4. Suppose the competitive world price p_O^W is high enough for the domestic monopolist to sell its output in the world market. If its own domestic market is protected through prohibitively high tariff on possible re-import of computers, it can fully exercise its monopoly power. The marginal revenue from domestic sales then varies inversely with the volume of sales (as indicated by the downward sloping curve *DR*), whereas the marginal revenue from exports is invariant at p_O^W. The latter indicates that the domestic monopolist is an insignificant seller and hence a price taker in the world market. For output levels up to X_D, the protected domestic market offers higher marginal revenue than exports. But beyond that output level exports fetch higher marginal revenue than domestic sales. The common (or total) marginal revenue is thus indicated by the kinked curve *Ddf.* By the standard rule of the profit maximizing output of a multi-market monopolist, the total output produced will be OX_E for which the marginal cost of producing computers is equal to the (common) marginal revenue. The division of this output in domestic sales and exports will then be such that the corresponding marginal revenues in the domestic and the world markets are equal. This is the output level X_D. Thus, OX_D number of computers is sold in the domestic market and X_DX_E number of computers is exported. Any other distribution lowers profits for the domestic monopolist.

Consider for example domestic sales less than OX_D. Clearly the marginal revenue from domestic sales is higher than that from exports for such a distribution of the total output. If an additional unit is now sold in the domestic market instead of being exported, the total revenue increases, and so does the profit. Similar reasoning shows that a smaller export volume than X_DX_E is profit reducing. Thus, the profit maximizing domestic sales to export ratio is $\frac{OX_D}{X_DX_E}$, for which the marginal revenues are equal to each other (and to the marginal cost). For such a

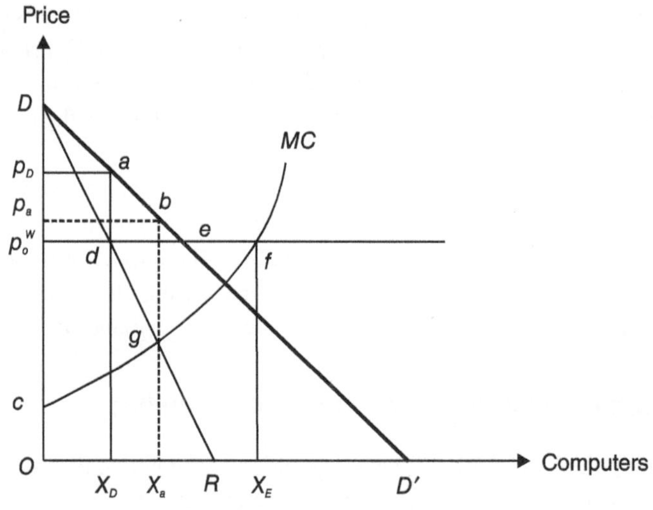

Figure 11.4 International Dumping

volume of domestic sales, the domestic monopolist charges the price p_D, even higher than the price p_a charged under autarchy. Thus, the domestic monopolist discriminates across markets. It charges a high price in its protected domestic market and dumps its output in the world market at the lower world price p_O^W.

Compared to the no-trade situation, the welfare of the home country is ambiguous. But for the importing country, dumping unambiguously raises the total surplus and thus should be good for it. In the context of reciprocal dumping by international monopolists discussed in Chapter 8, this is exactly what we have seen. Yet importing countries view dumping as unfair as it shuts down local firms producing similar or import-competing goods. These concerns have often led to anti-dumping tariffs and duties being imposed by importing countries against domestic monopolies of exporting countries.

On the other hand, these duties are often objected to and contested by importing countries in the World Trade Organization (WTO). The contentious issue here is that quite often simple practices of low-price sales resulting from lower costs or higher productivity are labeled *purposely* as dumping by importing countries and thus are subjected to anti-dumping duties in order to protect their own domestic import-competing industries. This has led to innumerable cases of complaints at the Dispute Settlement body of the WTO, both by importing countries against possible dumping and by the exporting countries against anti-dumping duties. We shall return to this issue in Chapter 19.

11.4 INTERNATIONAL MARKET SHARE RIVALRY AND STRATEGIC TRADE POLICY

It appears from the earlier discussion that trade policies can be used to the strategic advantage of domestic monopolies when it has significant market power. This opens up a new dimension of trade policies as national governments themselves can engage in strategic trade policy competition. This aspect of trade policy is all the more relevant when the large national monopolies can exert their market powers even in world markets. The typical example of export market share rivalry among large national monopolies is competition between Airbus and Boeing, the two giant manufacturers of passenger aircrafts from Europe and the United States. Similar competition for an export market share among national monopolies like Sony, Dell, Lenovo, Acer, and Toshiba can be observed in markets for laptops; among Samsung, LG, and Whirlpool in the home appliances segment; among Nokia, Samsung, Sony Ericsson, and Motorola in markets for mobile phones; and the like. Competition or rivalry among such monopolies for the share of export markets can be influenced for national advantages through trade policies like tariff and export subsidies. In the following, we discuss two such cases of the strategic use of trade policies to the advantage of national monopolies in export markets.

11.4.1 Export Subsidies and Market Share Rivalry

Consider two large national monopolies belonging to the home and foreign countries competing among themselves for market shares in a third country. Suppose these national monopolies produce identical goods and supply only to this third country export market. The firms have constant and identical marginal costs, and compete in terms of their respective levels of output or export supplies under the Cournot conjecture. There is neither any local producer of the good in the third country nor any producer elsewhere other than these two national monopolies. In such a context, Brander and Spencer (1985) demonstrated that each national government will provide export subsidies to its national monopolist to increase its export market share. Figure 11.5 illustrates this.

The equilibrium export market shares of these firms can be shown with the help of the reactions curves as specified earlier. The initial share of the export market for these monopolies under Cournot competition was at the point where the two bold reaction curves intersect each other. Thus, the home country's monopolist sells X_f units and the foreign country's monopolist sells X_f^* units in this export market. The firms, being identical, will have equal shares of the export market in the third country.

Box 11.1 Rules for Anti-dumping in Practice

It is often difficult to separate out dumping from the genuine cost advantage of suppliers. The EU law that adopts the GATT 1994 anti-dumping rules laid down in its Article VI considers a product being dumped if its export price to the European Union (EU) is less than the comparable price for a *like product* established in the ordinary course of trade within the exporting country. When the exporter in its country does not produce or sell a like product, comparison is made with the prices of other sellers or producers. The application of any anti-dumping duty, however, presupposes the presence of significant material injury to an EU industry. Such an injury may be caused to an industry established in the EU, or there may simply be the threat of injury to an industry. The determination of injury is based on the volume and the price of dumped imports, in particular to determine whether there has been significant price undercutting as compared with the price of a like product of the EU industry.

Box 11.2 Anti-dumping Duties

European Union imposed dumping duties (on top of normal duties) of 16.5 per cent and 10 per cent respectively, on European imports of certain leather footwear from China and Vietnam for a two-year period beginning 5 October 2006. There are similar anti-dumping duties being imposed by the United States. However, a study by Aggarwal (2002) reveals that the use of anti-dumping duty is no longer confined to a limited number of industrialized countries. The share of developing countries in the total cases of anti-dumping duties increased from 10 per cent at the beginning of the 1990s to almost 50 per cent by the turn of the year 2000. India has emerged as one of the most frequent users of anti-dumping measures among the developing countries. The first anti-dumping duty in India was levied in 1993. Between 1995 and 2000 India initiated 176 cases (individual country-wise) at the WTO, which is 12 per cent of the total number of cases initiated all over the world.

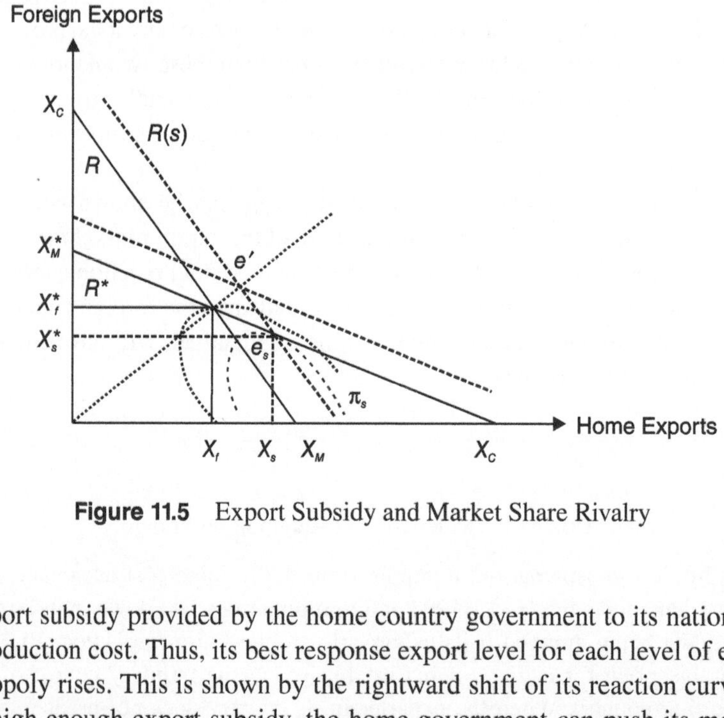

Figure 11.5 Export Subsidy and Market Share Rivalry

A unit export subsidy provided by the home country government to its national monopoly lowers its production cost. Thus, its best response export level for each level of exports by the foreign monopoly rises. This is shown by the rightward shift of its reaction curve. In fact, by providing a high enough export subsidy, the home government can push its monopolist to a position of Stackelberg leader. Note that the Stackelberg (leader-follower) equilibrium, when the home monopolist is the leader, is the one where the home monopolist's iso-profit curve (shown by the inverted U-shaped curves) is tangent to the foreign monopolist's (or follower's) reaction curve. Such an equilibrium is shown by point e_s with the corresponding profit level for the home monopolist being π_s. Thus, even though the firms behave as Cournot firms, the export subsidy enables the home monopolist to increase its export market share at the expense of the foreign monopoly and earn the same profit as a Stackelberg leader would have earned.

The profit gain for the home monopoly is, however, to be weighed against the amount of the subsidy provided since the subsidy is a loss to the national exchequer. For very small subsidy rates, this loss to the exchequer is small. Thus, the home country's welfare measured by the net benefit, $B = \pi(x, x^*, s) - sx$, rises, though less than proportionately with the increase in the home monopolist's profit and hence with the increase in the rate of subsidy. But as the rate of export subsidy is raised successively, the loss to the exchequer rises faster since the subsidy level, sx, rises due to an increase in both the rate of subsidy and the home monopolist's output (or export volume). Beyond a high subsidy rate, therefore, the net benefit of the home country declines. That is, the relationship between net benefit and the subsidy rate is non-monotonic, and the optimum rate of subsidy is strictly positive and finite.

The home country thus gains from the export subsidy, unless it is too high. This result is in sharp contrast to the welfare deteriorating effect of an export subsidy under perfectly competitive conditions discussed in Chapter 9. The difference can be explained as follows. An export subsidy lowers the price of the good in the export market because the home monopolist's output increases more than the foreign monopolist's output declines, so that the total supply (or export) in the third country market rises. Thus, we have a similar TOT deterioration as in a competitive world. Yet, the home country gains because of the price-cost margin for its firm that exists under Cournot or other non-competitive conditions but not under perfect competition. The expanded output of the domestic monopolist in the export market at a price above its marginal cost increases its profit that more than offsets the TOT loss from the export subsidy. In contrast, in a competitive world, free entry ensures that as an export subsidy lowers the effective marginal cost, the export price declines proportionately so that no price-cost margin exists.

However, the foreign country government will have a similar incentive for subsidizing the cost of export production of its own national monopoly. By providing an export subsidy in response to the home country's export subsidy, the foreign country government can restore the initial export market share for its national monopoly at point e'. In fact, the foreign government can push its monopolist to a Stackelberg leader position as well by providing an even higher subsidy that shifts its reaction curve further up (than the broken one shown in Figure 11.5) to a position where its iso-profit curve is tangent to $R(s)$.

What emerges from these unilateral incentives for providing export subsidies to national monopolies is an export subsidy competition (or retaliation) between the home and foreign country governments. Each government will choose a rate of subsidy that maximizes the country's welfare, $\pi(s, s^*) - sx(s, s^*)$ and $\pi^*(s, s^*) - s^*x^*(s, s^*)$ respectively for the home and the foreign country, given the subsidy provided by the other. James Brander and Barbara Spencer (1985) analysed such subsidy competition and derived the equilibrium optimum subsidies when, first, governments *simultaneously* choose subsidy levels, and then, given such subsidy levels, the home and foreign monopolists *simultaneously* choose their output (or export) levels. In such a context, subsidies are still optimal policy in the sense that given a positive subsidy by one country, it is desirable for the other to provide a positive subsidy as well. But the global subsidy equilibrium is Pareto inefficient compared to free trade, and this poses a Prisoners' Dilemma type problem. Though subsidies are unilaterally as well as bilaterally optimum, the total welfare of the countries is strictly lower than the welfare level when they do not subsidize their national monopolies.

11.4.2 Tariff as an Export Promotion Strategy

Another interesting trade policy dimension arises when production technologies exhibit increasing returns to scale (IRS) and the national monopolies compete both in their respective domestic markets and in export markets. In such a case, protecting national monopolies from foreign competition in their respective domestic markets through tariffs enable them to expand their export market shares. Thus, *tariff protection promotes exports*. This novel idea has been developed and formalized by Krugman (1984).

The reason is simple. When production technologies exhibit IRS, marginal costs decline with an expansion of total production. Note that when IRS or economies of scale are present, the domestic and export markets are not segmented as in the reciprocal dumping case discussed in Chapter 8. The markets are now connected from the production and the cost side and this forms the basis of this novel result. Tariff protection for the home country monopolist, for example, enables it to expand its production for the domestic market. For any level of production for export markets, its total production thus increases and this lowers its marginal cost of production. A tariff thus puts the home country monopolist in a cost advantage position vis-à-vis its rival firms in both its domestic and export markets. The tariff protected home monopolist's relative cost advantage is further reinforced by the fact that the tariff lowers the rival firms' market share in the home country. Their total production, for any level of production for the rest of export markets, thus declines. This raises their respective marginal costs. That is, *ceteris paribus* tariff protection for the home country monopolist generates a relative cost advantage for it in two ways. First, by expanding its own scale of production and thus lowering its own marginal cost, and second by reducing the scale of production of its competitors and thereby raising their marginal costs. Such a relative cost advantage will therefore cause the tariff-protected home monopolist's sales and market share in exports markets to rise. Referring back to Figure 11.5, the reaction curve of the home monopolist R shifts out whereas the reaction curve of the foreign monopolist R^* shifts in. Tariff protection thus appears as an export promotion strategy when production technologies exhibit IRS.

11.5 ADVANCED TOPIC: MONOPOLY, PARETO *SUB*-OPTIMALITY, AND GFT

The simplest way to extend some of the above discussed implications of imperfect competition is to consider an economy with a competitive sector, say textiles, and a monopolistic sector, say computers. Suppose the monopoly producer of computers is a domestic monopolist with no market power in the world market. Since under autarchy, the domestic monopolist charges a price above the marginal cost of production, it destroys the equality between the marginal rate of substitution in production and in consumption. The autarchic composition of output is thus Pareto sub-optimal. This is the cost of monopoly production of computers. Figure 11.6 illustrates this Pareto sub-optimal composition of output and the corresponding sub-optimal resource allocation. Note that since in the competitive textile sector, price equals marginal cost, for the autarchic equilibrium production (and consumption) bundle A_M, we have the following relationship between the marginal rates of substitution in production and in consumption:

$$MRT = \frac{MC_T}{MC_C} > \frac{P_{Ta}}{P_{Ca}} = MRS \tag{11.1}$$

Box 11.3 Evidence on Tariff Protection as Export Promotion

Studies of static economies of scale, learning-by-doing, and research competition (Bound et al. 1984; Hall 1988; Lieberman 1984) document increasing returns to scale in a wide range of industries. This suggests that the scope for strategic trade policy could be significant. But Dick (1994) finds little evidence of strategic export promotion for US import-competing industries that display the strongest increasing returns to scale in major industrialized trading partners. Instead, targeted non-tariff barriers and increased protected market size frequently have been export-deterring. The reason for this lack of evidence is that protection often fails to stimulate domestic output and promotes inefficient firm scale and entry. A study by Liang (1995), on the other hand, suggests that the import protection measure in South Korea is an integral element of its export-oriented trade policy.

Thus, in Figure 11.6, the autarchic price line p_a (the absolute slope of which reflects the relative price of textiles) cuts the PPF *from below*, but is tangent to CIC_m. Had the computer sector been perfectly competitive, marginal-cost pricing there as well would lead to the Pareto-optimal production bundle A, and push the economy on to a higher CIC_a. The point to note here is that the competitive textile sector is larger than it would have been if the computer sector was competitive. This is because the domestic monopolist produces less number of computers than a competitive industry would produce and pushes up the price of computers above the marginal cost of production. Thus, more resources are available for textile production and, through sectoral mobility of resources, this causes the textile sector to expand beyond the socially desirable (or Pareto optimal) size. The resource allocation is therefore Pareto sub-optimal as well.

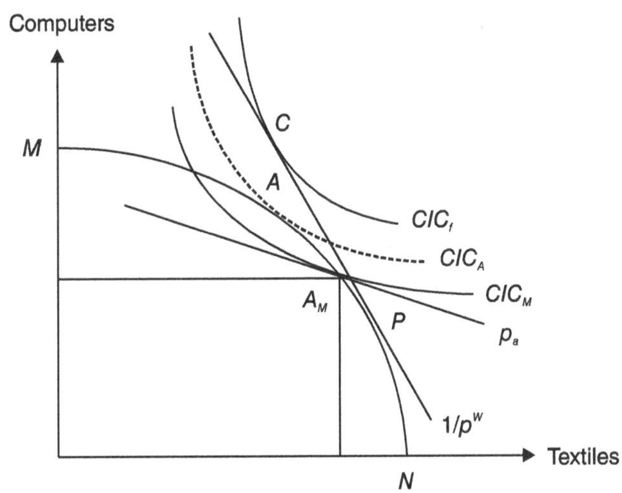

Figure 11.6 Domestic Monopoly and Pareto Sub-optimality

International trade benefits the country first by restoring the marginal condition for Pareto optimality as it breaks up the monopoly and forces the domestic monopolist to charge a price that equals marginal cost. On top of that we have the usual exchange and specialization gains. Suppose the home country has a comparative disadvantage in computers in the sense that the world relative price of computers is lower than the relative price that would have prevailed in the home country under autarchy if all its production sectors had been perfectly competitive.[1] If the country is small, opening up of trade will cause the domestic relative price of computers to fall (or conversely, the relative price of textiles to rise) to this world price level since the domestic monopolist can no longer exercise its market power. Now, depending on how low the world relative price is, the post-trade production bundle will be anywhere to the right of bundle *A*.

The point to note is that the home country may now produce less textiles than it was producing under autarchy. This happens when the price advantage in textiles is not too large such that the world price is tangent to PPF along the segment AA_M. For such small price differences, the domestic monopolist, now being a price taker, produces more computers, which leaves smaller resources for the textile sector than under autarchy. That is, after trade opens up, it is perfectly plausible that the home country expands the production of its comparative disadvantaged good (here, computers) and contracts the production of its comparative advantaged good (textiles). The monopoly-created price distortion led the home country to over-specialize in textiles under autarchy not only compared to what the competitive or marginal cost prices would have dictated (which is production bundle *A*), but even more than what is consistent with the comparative advantage of the country. Trade now removes this price distortion and the home country specializes to the correct extent that its comparative advantage leads to. The country thus gains despite the contraction of its export sector.

For a very large price difference as indicated by the absolute slope of the price line $1/p^W$ in Figure 11.6 (compared to the absolute slope of PPF at point *A*), on the other hand, free trade will lower the production of computers and raise that of textiles. Though the monopoly-created price distortion led the home country to over-specialize in textiles under autarchy than the competitive or marginal-cost prices would have dictated, a significantly large comparative advantage in textiles still leaves scope for further expansion.

There is an interesting caveat to the above GFT result when foreign firms are few and the domestic monopolist is sufficiently large to retain its market power even when imports are allowed. The example is the strategic Cournot competition between the domestic monopolist and a foreign monopolist in the home country market that we have analysed earlier. Import restrictions through tariffs, for example, are welfare improving over free trade in such a case. This sounds like the optimum tariff argument, but the difference is that the market power of the domestic monopolist itself is now another source of welfare improvement in addition to the TOT effect of a tariff for a large importing country. Thus, the optimum tariff rate when the local market is imperfectly competitive is larger than the optimum tariff rate under perfectly

[1] The reciprocal of the absolute slope of PPF at point *A* indicates such a relative price of computers.

competitive production conditions. This is immediate from the decomposition of the change in the real income of the home country as derived in Appendix A11:

$$dy = -Mdp^W + (p_d - p^W)dM + (p_d - \tilde{c})dX_C \tag{11.2}$$

where $\tilde{c}$ denotes the ratio of marginal cost of producing computers to that of textiles, or MRT, and p_d is the relative price of computers in the local market. When computers are produced under imperfectly competitive conditions even after trade, then their relative price exceeds the relative marginal cost: $p_d > \tilde{c}$. Thus, in addition to the usual TOT and VOT effects of an import tariff, as captured by the first two terms on the right hand side respectively, we have a third source of welfare change that arises when the local market is imperfectly competitive. Given the positive price-cost margin for the local producer, a tariff raises welfare further if it expands the imperfectly competitive domestic producer's output of computers.

Now recall from the discussion in Chapter 9 that the optimum tariff in a perfectly competitive economy is the one for which the TOT and the VOT wash out each other. But for that tariff, we still have the positive import-production effect. This means that the country's real income can still be raised through an even higher tariff. Algebraically, the change in real income evaluated at the optimum tariff for a competitive economy ($\bar{t}$) is positive:

$$dy|_{\bar{t}} = (p_d - \tilde{c})dX_C > 0 \tag{11.3}$$

Hence, the optimum tariff in a non-competitive economy is higher than the optimum tariff in a competitive economy.

APPENDIX A11

I. Decomposition of the Change in Real Income in a Non-competitive Economy

Recall the decomposition of the change in real income as specified in equation (A9.11) in Appendix A9 to Chapter 9, which is reproduced below:

$$dy = -Mdp^W + (p_d - p^W)dM + (dX_T + p_d dX_C) \tag{A11.1}$$

In a competitive economy, the third term equals zero since marginal cost pricing means $p_d = -MRT = -\frac{dX_T}{dX_C}$. But, when computers are produced under imperfect competition, $p_d > \tilde{c} = MRT = -\frac{dX_T}{dX_C}$. That is, the third term does not vanish. Adding and subtracting $\tilde{c}dX_c$ on the right hand side of equation (A11.1) now yields:

$$dy = -Mdp^W + (p_d - p^W)dM + (dX_T + p_d dX_C) + \tilde{c}dX_C - \tilde{c}dX_C$$

Since, $dX_T + \tilde{c}dX_C = 0$, so this boils down to the expression in equation (11.2) in the text:

$$dy = -Mdp^W + (p_d - p^W)dM + (p_d - \tilde{c})dX_C$$

SUMMARY POINTS

- If a domestic monopolist is small enough to have any market power whatsoever in a competitive world market, then international trade breaks up a domestic monopoly and the country gains due to this pro-competitive effect of trade. This is regardless of whether the country imports or exports the good that its domestic monopolist produces.
- When a domestic monopolist may need to be protected on employment considerations from competition from perfectly competitive foreign producers due to its cost disadvantage, a tariff should be a preferred mode of protection over an import quota. This is because the output of the domestic monopolist (and hence the employment generated by it) under an import quota is strictly less than that under an import tariff.
- This result implies the non-equivalence of an import tariff and an equal-import quota under imperfectly competitive conditions as demonstrated by Bhagwati (1965). The implicit tariff under quota is larger than the import tariff.
- In case of strategic competition in the home country market between the domestic monopolist and a single foreign supplier, the price equivalence result may still hold if the firms have Cournot conjectures. But, equal-import tariffs and quotas will not be welfare equivalent because the scarcity rent under quota is now shared by the domestic monopolist and the foreign supplier.
- Trade policies can be used by national governments to strategic advantage when large national monopolies can exert their market powers even in world markets. Export subsidies, for example, can be welfare improving in such cases by raising market shares of large national monopolies in export markets.
- When production technologies exhibit increasing returns to scale, protecting large national monopolies from foreign competition in their respective domestic markets through tariffs enable them to expand their export market shares. Thus, tariff protection promotes exports.
- The optimum tariff rate when the local market is imperfectly competitive is larger than the optimum tariff rate under perfectly competitive production conditions.

KEYWORDS

- **Domestic monopolist** is a single producer of a good in the local market but which has no market power whatsoever in the world market.
- **International monopolies** or oligopolies are multinational firms that are large enough to influence the world prices of the goods that they sell.
- **International dumping** is selling goods in the world market at a much cheaper price than the price at which firms sell in their own protected domestic markets. A product is considered to be dumped if its export price to the European Union (EU) is less than the

comparable price for a *like product* established in the ordinary course of trade within the exporting country.

- **Anti-dumping duty** is an import tariff imposed by the importing country government to protect its domestic import-competing good producers from dumping of goods by an exporter and the consequent 'unfair' trade.
- **Strategic or profit-shifting effect**, in the context of strategic competition amongst firms, arises when an import tariff transfers part of the foreign monopolist's profit to the domestic monopolist.

EXERCISES

1. A domestic monopolist, which is a price taker in the world market, produces computers at a marginal cost of $10Q_C$. If it faces a domestic demand function as:

   $Q_C = 588 - 2p_C$

   and a world price of Rs 150, should it export computers? If so, how many computers will be exported? How many computers will be sold in the domestic market and at what price? Calculate the firm's total profit.
2. In the above context, write down the export supply function of the domestic monopolist.
3. If for the above demand function and $p_c^W = 290$, the home market is fully protected from re-import, then calculate the following:
   (a) The total production of computers by the domestic monopolist.
   (b) Domestic sales and export volume of computers.
   (c) The domestic price of computers.
4. For the same domestic demand function and the marginal cost as in Question 1, what will be the local production of computers if the world price is Rs 200? Is the local production sufficient to meet all domestic demand at that price? What will be the total surplus for the home country at this price when trade is allowed?
5. Consider the following domestic demand function and the marginal cost function for a domestic monopolist:

   $Q_C^d = 200 - p_C$, $\text{MC} = 10 + 20Q_C$

   Suppose the world price of computers is Rs 90. If the home country government imposes a 20 per cent ad-valorem tariff on the import of computers, calculate the local supply and volume of imports. If the home country is small, does it gain from such a tariff? What is the source of its gains?
6. Suppose the volume of import under the tariff in the above problem is alternatively set as an import quota. Should the domestic firm produce the same number of computers? Calculate the implicit tariff paid by local consumers and compare it with the ad-valorem

(*contd*)

Exercises (*contd*)

tariff rate. What can you then infer about the price equivalence between the tariff and the equal-import quota in this context?

7. Suppose there is a single foreign supplier of computers, which has the same marginal cost of Rs 20 as the local producer. If the inverse demand function for computers in the local market is $p_C = 580 - 3Q_C$, determine the volume of imports and the price of computers in the local market when the firms have Cournot conjectures. How does your result change, if at all, when:
   (a) The foreign firm has a higher marginal cost of Rs 25?
   (b) The local government imposes a tariff of Rs 5 per unit of imports?
8. In the above context, with an identical marginal cost of Rs 20, find out the rate of tariff per unit of imports that will enable the domestic monopolist to earn the profit of a Stackelberg leader.
9. Does tariff quota equivalence hold when the domestic monopolist is a Stackelberg leader? Compare the implicit tariff under quota with the tariff rate.
10. Suppose the home and foreign monopolists producing identical goods compete in prices in the home country market. Compare the effects on market share and the domestic price of the good under a unit tariff and equivalent import quota. Explain your answer.

SUGGESTED READING

Caves, R.E., J. Frankel, and R.W. Jones (1995). *World Trade and Payments*. New York: HarperCollins College Publishers.

Helpman, E. and P. Krugman. (1989). *Trade Policy and Market Structure*. Cambridge, MA: MIT Press.

ADVANCED READING

Aggarwal, A. (2002). 'Anti Dumping Law and Practice: An Indian Perspective', ICRIER Working Paper No. 85.

Bhagwati, J.N. (1965). 'On the Equivalence of Tariffs and Quotas', in R.E. Baldwain, J. Bhagwati, R.E. Caves, and H.G. Johnson (eds), *Trade Growth and Balance of Payments: Essays in Honour of G. Haberler*. Chicago, IL: Rand McNally, pp. 53–67.

Bound, J., C. Cummins, Z. Griliches, B. Hall, and A. Jaffe (1984). 'Who Does R&D and Who Patents', in Z. Griliches (ed.), *R&D, Patents, and Productivity*. Chicago: University of Chicago Press, pp. 21–54.

Brander, J. and B. Spencer (1985). 'Export Subsidies and International Market Share Rivalry', *Journal of International Economics*, 18: 83–100.

Dick, A.R. (1994). 'Does Import Protection Act as Export Promotion? Evidence from the United States', *Oxford Economic Papers*, 46: 83–101.

Hall, R.E. (1988). 'Increasing Returns: Theory and Measurement with Industry Data', Discussion Paper, The Hoover Institute.

Hwang, H. and C.C. Mai (1988). 'On the Equivalence of Tariff and Quota under Duopoly: A Conjectural Variation Approach', *Journal of International Economics*, 24: 373–80.

Krugman, P. (1984). 'Import Protection as Export Promotion: International Competition in the Presence of Oligopoly and Economies of Scale', in H. Kierzkowski (ed.), *Monopolistic Competition and International Trade*. Oxford: Clarendon Press, pp. 75–86.

Liang, N. (1995). 'The Paradox of Export-Oriented Import Protection: Reassessing South Korea's Trade Policy', *The International Executive*, 37: 35–59.

Lieberman, M.B. (1984) 'The Learning Curve and Pricing in the Chemical Processing Industries', *Rand Journal of Economics*, 15: 213–28.

12 Political Economy of Trade Policy

Restrictive trade policies often trigger activities by economic agents that are directed at getting a share of the rents that such policies might generate. These rent-seeking lobbying activities use up scarce real resources that could otherwise be used for productive purposes. The economy thus produces less and thereby experiences a welfare loss when such activities are undertaken. As such, Bhagwati (1982) calls these activities directly unproductive profit-seeking, in short DUP, lobbying activities. Thus, the welfare cost of trade protection may be larger than is usually perceived and is discussed in earlier chapters when the DUP lobbying activities are taken into account.

Lobbying activities by economic agents can also be directed at influencing the trade policy choice of the government itself. For example, anti-liberalization interest groups can lobby for tariff protection for domestic import-competing industries. Such interest groups may include both owners of the import-competing firms and owners of the factors that are intensively used in the production of the import-competing goods. In fact, this leads us to a more general discussion of trade policies being chosen by national governments by explicitly taking into account political economy forces such as the political risk involved in committing to and pursuing a strong trade policy and the consequent loss of political support. Of course, such political economy considerations are more relevant in a democratic political regime and governance rather than in autocracies. The extent of ethno-linguistic fractionalization and income heterogeneity are also important elements in such political economy considerations for trade policy choices.

In this chapter we discuss these aspects of the political economy of trade policy and its choices. We begin with a discussion of DUP lobbying or rent-seeking activities and then move on to the political economy of trade policy choices.

12.1 DUP LOBBYING ACTIVITIES

We have learnt in an earlier chapter that an import quota imposes a dead-weight loss for a small open economy. It lowers the consumption of the imported commodity as domestic buyers have to pay a higher price and as it raises inefficient domestic production of the import-competing good. When the import-competing good is produced by a single domestic firm, the import quota imposes further costs on the economy by allowing it to exercise its monopoly power.

International Economics. Rajat Acharyya, Oxford University Press. © Oxford University Press 2022.
DOI: 10.1093/oso/9780192865144.003.0012

There may be costs in addition to these. As we have seen, an import quota generates a scarcity rent for import license holders. This may encourage people to compete among themselves to obtain an import license instead of working in production sectors. The gross output of the economy thus falls due to such rent-seeking behaviour of economic agents. Anne O. Krueger (1974) in her pioneering work pointed out this additional cost of an import quota. This has important implications for a large importing country as well. As we have seen earlier, an import quota improves the terms of trade (TOT) of the large importing country and thus may be welfare improving as long as the import quota is not too small (or stringent). But if we take into account the loss of output and real income from the rent-seeking activity triggered by the import quota, the welfare gain from an improved TOT *may* even get reversed. Thus, Anne Krueger's major contribution is to demonstrate that conventional dead-weight or volume-of-trade loss measures are underestimates of the actual loss of real income that arises from trade restrictions like import quotas.

To illustrate the rent-seeking DUP lobbying activity under an import quota in the simplest possible way, consider our home economy being completely specialized in the export of textiles.[1] Suppose labour is the only factor of production and α be the constant marginal (and average) product of labour in the production of textiles. Thus, if the home country possesses L number of workers, the total production of textiles is αL. Under competitive conditions, each worker is paid a real wage equal to its marginal product, α. Suppose the home country is small and the world relative price of computers is p^W. The line AB in Figure 12.1 with absolute slope equal to $1/p^W$ thus gives us the consumption possibilities for the small home economy when it exchanges its output of textiles ($OB = \alpha L$) with the rest of the world for computers. Under free trade, the home economy consumes at point C on AB with the volume of imports being OM_0 for exports of $OB - M_0C$ units of textiles. An import quota of M_Q pushes down the consumption point to C_Q along the consumption possibility line AB. The domestic price of computers rises to p which is indicated by the reciprocal of the absolute slope of the flatter line that is tangent to the CIC passing through C_Q. The consequent welfare loss from the import quota for the home country is shown by the lower social utility index U_Q.

The quota rent equals the amount $(p-p^W)M_Q$. Suppose import quota licenses are distributed by the government proportionate to the total applicants L_Q. Each applicant thus gets $\frac{(p-p^W)M_Q}{L_Q}$ as rent by obtaining a license that permits import of $\frac{M_Q}{L_Q}$ units of computers. However, applications for import quota licenses and finally getting the licenses take time, so that it is not possible for applicants (and rent-seekers) to work in the textile sector at the same time. The real wage foregone there thus constitutes the opportunity cost of being engaged in a rent-seeking activity. Free entry into the rent-seeking activity then implies that at equilibrium the number of rent-seekers L_Q must be such that the rent for each rent seeker is exactly equal to the real wage foregone:

$$\frac{(p-p^W)M_Q}{L_Q} = \alpha \tag{12.1}$$

[1] We here follow the simple exposition of Krueger's argument by Findlay and Wellisz (1982).

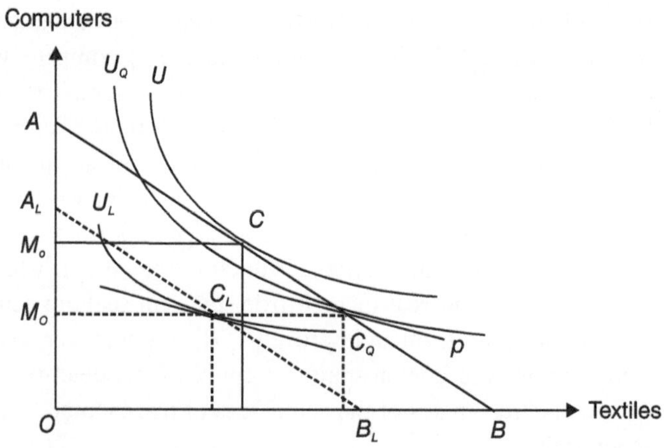

Figure 12.1 Welfare Loss from the Rent-Seeking Lobby

That is, for any given domestic relative price of computers, p, the above equality between the real wage and the (real) value of rent gives us the number of rent-seekers. Note that the number of rent-seekers varies positively with the domestic relative price of computers for any given import quota level. A higher domestic price of imports raises the return to each rent-seeker above the real wage. This attracts more people into the rent-seeking activity till the return to each rent-seeker declines again to the level of the real wage. This relationship is shown by the upward sloping curve L_QL_Q in Figure 12.2.

On the other hand, from the domestic market clearing condition for imports of computers we obtain the domestic relative price of computers that will prevail for any given number of rent-seekers:

$$M_d(p, y) = M_Q \tag{12.2}$$

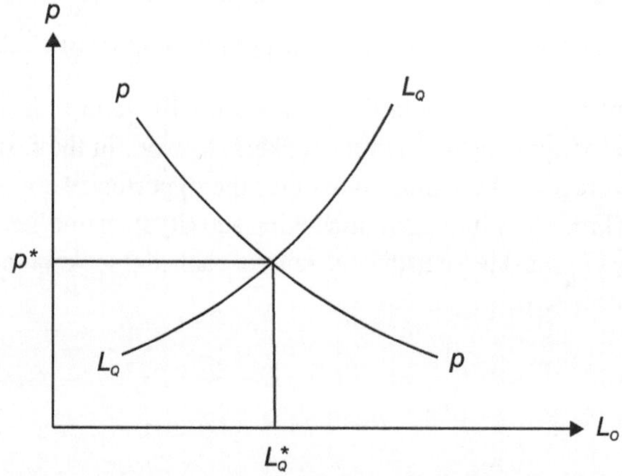

Figure 12.2 Rent-Seeking Equilibrium

where M_d (.) is the import demand function and y is the wage income from production of textiles, $\alpha(L - L_Q)$, plus the total rent, $(p - p^W)M_Q$:

$$y = \alpha(L - L_Q) + (p - p^W)M_Q \tag{12.3}$$

A larger number of rent-seekers lowers the wage income in the textile sector, and hence lowers the total income y for any given domestic relative price, p. This lowers the demand for computers, and accordingly given the import quota level, generates an excess supply of computers. This in turn lowers the domestic relative price of computers. That is, from the domestic market clearing condition in equation (12.2) we get an inverse relationship between the number of rent-seekers and the domestic relative price as indicated by the pp curve in Figure 12.2. The equilibrium number of rent-seekers and the domestic relative price of imports under the rent-seeking activity are thus determined as L_Q^* and p^* respectively.

The L_Q^* number of people now being engaged in the rent-seeking activity means a loss of output and real income by αL_Q^*. The home economy's consumption set thus shrinks and in Figure 12.1 this is shown by the line $A_L B_L$. Given the import quota level, the economy now consumes at point C_L and the utility loss from the rent-seeking activity is indicated by the lower utility index U_L. Thus, import quota inflicts further welfare losses due to the rent-seeking lobbying activity that it results in.

Extending Krueger's idea, Bhagwati and Srinivasan (1980), on the other hand, pointed out that a similar DUP-lobbying activity may arise under an import tariff, which they termed as revenue-seeking lobbying activity. The novelty of their analysis is the demonstration of a paradoxical result that such revenue-seeking lobbying activity may raise the welfare of a small economy over the welfare level under tariff without any lobbying activity. The logic is simple. As we have demonstrated, for a small economy with a standard two-commodity two-factor HOS type production structure, an import tariff is welfare reducing. The welfare loss arises from the tariff causing a shift of production composition towards the import-competing good that is not consistent with the country's comparative advantage. Now suppose the revenue-seeking activity requires both capital and labour resources. As the revenue-seeking activity withdraws capital and labour from the production of goods at the given world price ratio, the output levels of the two traded goods change. If lobbying requires more capital, say, and the import-competing good is relatively capital-intensive, then by the output magnification effect discussed earlier, the output of the import-competing good falls more than proportionately to the capital withdrawn from production relative to labour. But, at the same time, the output of the export good may rise. Thus, though the production point is dragged down inside PPF indicating a loss of real income due to the revenue-seeking lobbying activity, an increase in the output of the export good in which the country has a comparative advantage raises the country's welfare. If the export production rises sufficiently close to the level that would have been produced under free trade (and thus consistent with the country's comparative advantage), the welfare gain from the revenue-seeking activity will be larger than the welfare loss from resources being wasted in unproductive rent-seeking purposes. In such an event, the paradoxical result of the revenue-seeking lobbying activity under tariff raising the country's welfare is realized.

12.2 POLITICAL ECONOMY OF TRADE POLICY CHOICE

The main idea of the political economy of trade policy determination is the interconnectedness between economic and political markets in a country. Trade policies are essentially determined by political-economic forces that arise from such interconnectedness and interrelationships. In the political markets for trade policies, the demand for a particular type of trade policy comes from the preference pattern of the different socio-economic interest groups in an economy. The supply of a particular trade policy, on the other hand, comes from the preference patterns of decision-makers and the structure of governance. However, unlike competitive economic markets (goods market and factor markets in particular), the political market is usually imperfectly competitive since entry into the political market by agents (political parties, for example) is neither free nor easy. Given this perspective, there are five distinct approaches to the political economy of trade policy: political-support function approach, tariff-formation function approach, median voter approach, campaign contribution approach, and political contribution approach. But, as Rodrik (1995) points out, not all these take into account both the demand and supply side of political markets.

Whereas the political risk and the associated political-support function approach characterize the supply side, the tariff-formation function approach characterizes the demand side of the market. The third approach, the median voter approach pioneered by Mayer (1984), built a direct democracy model for trade policy determination where both the supply and the demand sides of the political market are taken into account. However, though in the history of evolution of the European Union (EU) voting has often played important roles (see Box 12.1), in general trade policies are rarely determined through voting. The other two approaches, campaign contribution and political contribution approaches, also take into account both sides of the political market. These approaches, like the tariff-formation function approach, emphasize on the lobbying expenditures undertaken by interest groups on the supply side. We elaborate below the political risk theory and the related political support function approach, and the lobbying or contribution approaches.

12.2.1 Democracy, Political Risk, and Political Support Approach

In democracies, economic policies are essentially determined by the interactions of pressure groups. Socio-economic fractionalization and political risks in democracies are the two key elements in such choices of economic policies in general, and of trade policies in particular. Greater socio-economic fractionalization of a country means serious conflict between competing fractions or groups each of them being concerned about its own group-interest at the expense of social welfare. In a democracy, fractionalization thus leads inherently to greater levels of political risk of being overthrown and losing any rents from being in power for a government if its policies exclude more groups than they include. Similar political risks may evolve from economic fractionalization or groups (such as income disparity) particularly when a policy increases the economic gap such as increased earnings inequality among different economic groups. In any case, political compulsions induce a democratic government to pursue policies to pacify all or most of the myopic pressure groups. This often limits the scope of long-term development policies and fundamental structural changes in economic policies.

Box 12.1 Voting and Policy Decision

The Maastricht Treaty in 1991 founded the EU and set the stage for the Economic and Monetary Union (EMU) of EU countries through the unification of their economies and adoption of a single currency by 1999. The new treaty raised a good deal of popular opposition and concern among the EU citizens. Danish voters turned down the ratification in a referendum, while French voters favoured the treaty by only a slim majority. In Germany a challenge to the treaty was lodged with the country's supreme court, saying that membership to the EU violated Germany's constitution. In an emergency meeting of the European Council, Denmark gained substantial concessions and exemptions, including the right to opt out of both EMU and any future common defence policy. Danish voters then approved the treaty in a subsequent referendum. In November 2011, USD 136 billion bailout loans for Greece sanctioned by the EU along with a 50 per cent debt write-off on the debt owed to its private creditors was put to referendum by the Greek Prime Minister George Papandreou.

Given such a perspective, it is easy to understand how the political risk theory can lead to a protectionist trade policy. Until the recent wave of globalization efforts, only a few countries in the developing world had been following free trade policies in the past few decades with India being no exception. Such a choice against free trade can be judged from the potential political risk involved in pursuing free trade as a development strategy. Free trade creates both winners and losers in a trading nation. GFT by itself cannot eliminate or minimize the political risk since in practice a compensation principle is difficult to apply to make sure that none lose from the free trade policy. Moreover, as we will explain in a latter chapter, trade may augment a country's output growth but at the initial stages of such trade-induced growth, income inequality is bound to rise. Thus, to the extent to which free trade promotes growth, it fuels inter-class conflict and thereby further increases the political risk for a democratic government.

Political pressure and lobbying from domestic industrialists and workers in the import-competing sectors under the threat of closing down of units and loss of jobs if a free trade policy is adopted also contributes to such a choice against free trade. Cassing and Hilman (1985)

Box 12.2 Ethno-linguistic Fractionalization and Government Spending

As argued by Anthony Annett (2001), a democratic government attempts to pacify the excluded groups by increasing the level of its expenditure (or subsidies), and thereby to reduce political risk. Thus, the policies with short-term benefits such as subsidy programmes or tax benefits are more often preferred to long-term policies targeting alleviation of poverty and lowering of income inequality in democracies. He finds strong empirical support for this basic premise using the indices of ethno-linguistic and religious fractionalization. That higher fractionalization within an economy, through greater political instability, leads to higher government consumption (or expenditure) has also been noted earlier by Velasco (1997). On the other hand, Blomberg (1996) finds the use of huge defence spending as a partial insurance against political instability.

provide an elegant formalization of how a democratic government that aims to maximize the political support that it can gather chooses the level as well as the mode of protection. In a small country, an import tariff raises the domestic relative price of imports above the free trade price level. If the domestic market is imperfectly competitive, profits of import-competing firms thus rise monotonically with the tariff rate, or with the price increase, $p - p^W$, as shown in Figure 12.3. Political support for the tariff policy from domestic import-competing firms thus increases with the price increase consequent upon successively higher tariff rates. But higher prices hurt domestic consumers and political support from them declines with the price increase. In other words, political support is an increasing function of the domestic industry's profit level and a decreasing function of the price level. This relationship can be captured graphically by a map of upward sloping (and convex downwards) iso-political-support loci with the property that a higher locus indicates larger political support. The level of protection for the domestic industry, $p_t - p^W$ (and the corresponding politically optimum tariff $t^* = \frac{p_t - p^W}{p^W}$) is then chosen by the government so as to maximize political support subject to the profit constraint $\pi\pi_m$. This is shown by the tangency point E_t in Figure 12.3 with corresponding maximum political support that the government gathers indicated by the index S_t^*.

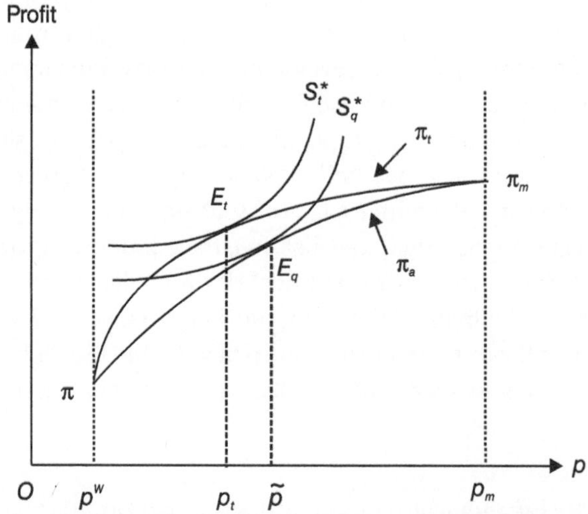

Figure 12.3 Political Support and Choice of Trade Protection

This political support maximizing approach enables us to choose between an import tariff and an import quota as the mode of protection. Like an import tariff, an import quota also raises domestic price. Consequently, the domestic industry's profit increases with the stringency of the import quota and so does its political support for such a policy from domestic firms. At the same time, a more stringent quota level leads to lower political support from domestic consumers. Thus, the same set of iso-political-support loci capture the political tensions generated by an import quota. But, an import quota that raises the domestic price above the free trade price to the same extent as does an import tariff, generates a *lower* profit for the domestic industry. This is illustrated in Appendix A12 with the example of a domestic monopolist. Thus, the profit locus is lower under an import quota than under an import tariff except for the extreme prices $p = p^*$ and $p = p_m$. This means that lower political support can be gathered when the domestic industry is protected through a politically optimum import quota corresponding to the tangency point E_q in Figure 12.3. However, note that the level of protection under quota, $\tilde{p} - p^W$, *may* still be larger than it is under tariff.

Whereas this political support approach is highly relevant, as we had pointed out earlier, it focuses only on the preference pattern of the government or the supplier of trade policy. The demand for protection, or trade policy in general, is not explicitly formalized. But conflicting interest groups hardly behave passively as is the case in this approach. Rather, they compete actively to influence the trade policy choice of the government through lobbying and other means. This is what the lobbying and contribution approaches emphasize upon, and we now turn to these approaches in the next section.

12.2.2 Lobbying and Contribution Approaches

That interest groups lobby for favourable government policies is a well-known fact. It is in fact rather naïve to think that interest groups do not lobby and government policymaking is not influenced by such lobbies. Even many monopolies in the world had been and are still the outcome of active lobbying. In such cases, the cost that the economy bears is not just in terms of the higher prices of goods and consequent redistribution of the total market surplus to domestic monopolies, but also in terms of real resources being spent in such lobbying activities just like the case of rent-seeking activities. In the trade policy context, the relevant example to illustrate such losses would be a monopoly seeking lobby by a domestic import-competing firm for prohibitive tariff protection as discussed by Bhagwati (1982). Suppose there is only one local producer of computers in the home country, but many and perfectly competitive producers of textiles. Under free trade, the domestic firm is a price taker for reasons spelled out in the earlier chapter. Given that the home country has a comparative advantage in textiles, the free trade equilibrium is shown by production point P and consumption point C in Figure 12.4. A lobby for protection shrinks in PPF to A_LB_L and entails real income losses indicated by a lower utility index U_L for the home economy. Note that this is purely the lobbying cost since the economy still trades with the rest of the world at the given world price indicated by the steeper line segments. Now if the lobby for a prohibitive tariff protected monopoly is successful, the domestic price of computers rises to the monopoly level and the equality between the price ratio and the marginal cost ratio breaks down. The price line cuts PPF *from below* and the output composition changes towards textiles since the domestic monopolist restricts the local production of computers to realize the price increase. The production now shifts from P_L to P_{Lm} and the welfare level falls further to U_{Lm}.

However, trade policies like this or any other type also hurt some economic groups. In the above case, domestic consumers are hurt by the prohibitive tariff because they are forced to pay the monopoly price for locally produced computers. So, one may expect that they will lobby for a liberal trade policy. What this suggests is that, in general, there can be conflict of interest among different economic groups regarding a particular trade policy and consequently there can be competition among these groups to influence the trade policy through lobbying. Different factor owners engaging in lobbying competition for pro- and anti-liberal

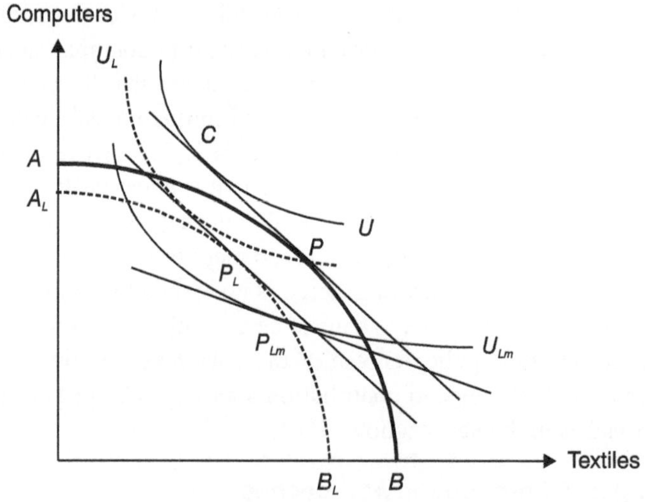

Figure 12.4 Monopoly Seeking Lobby

trade policies is perhaps the best suited example of contesting interest groups. The tariff-formation function approach of Findlay and Wellisz (1982) is based on this idea. To illustrate their argument, consider a small open economy with a specific factor production structure discussed in Chapter 7. The two goods, computers and textiles, are produced by sector-specific capital and homogeneous and mobile labour. As we had explained earlier, a tariff increase will unambiguously benefit the owners of capital in the import-competing computer sector and unambiguously hurt the owners of capital in the exportable textile sector. Suppose workers are not organized to lobby. Only the capitalists lobby for a higher or a lower tariff rate and such lobbying uses only labour. Given that the capitalists in each sector lobby *together*, which makes sense because otherwise lobbying effects may be diffused, suppose L_T units of labour is used in lobbying by the capitalists in the textile sector and L_C units by the capitalists in the computer sector. Findlay and Wellisz (1982) then make two assumptions. First, the level of tariff decided by the government depends on these lobbying efforts:

$$t = t(L_C, L_T), \frac{\partial t}{\partial L_C} > 0, \frac{\partial t}{\partial L_T} < 0, \tag{12.4}$$

This is the tariff-formation function and its properties specified in equation (12.4) follow from the identification of capitalists in the computer and the textile sectors as pro- and anti-protection lobbies respectively.

Second, the capitalists-lobbies compete in a Cournot fashion in terms of their lobbying efforts. This enables them to derive the lobbying-reaction functions. Starting with a particular tariff level, if capitalists in the textile sector raise their lobbying effort L_T, it only makes sense for the capitalists in the computer sector to raise their lobbying effort L_C as well. Otherwise, if L_C is not raised (and instead is kept unchanged or lowered), the government will lower the tariff rate in response to the higher lobbying effort from the textile sector. Thus, the best-response lobbying function for capitalists in the import-competing computer sector must be upward sloping as shown in Figure 12.5 by the $L_C\ L_C$ locus. Similarly, the best-response lobbying function for capitalists in the textile sector must be upward sloping as shown by the $L_T L_T$ locus. The Cournot-Nash equilibrium lobbying efforts are thus given by the pair (L_T^*, L_C^*), with the consequent level of equilibrium tariff being t (L_T^*, L_C^*).

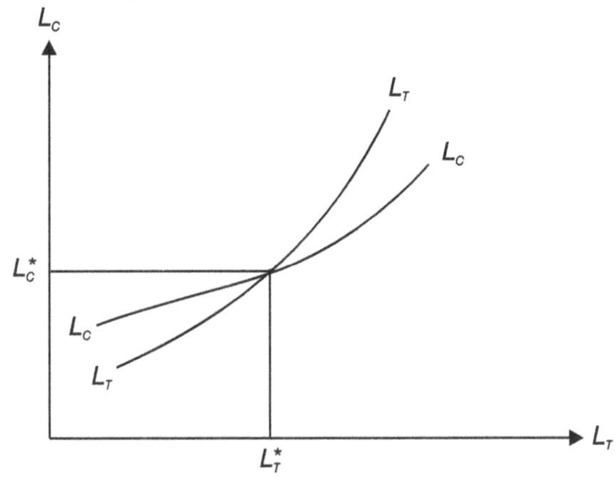

Figure 12.5 Lobbying Competition

However, while Findlay and Wellisz (1982) explicitly take into account lobbying competition among conflicting interest groups, they do not explicitly take into account the underlying preference pattern of the supplier of trade protection (which in their case is the government). Magee et al. (1989) in their campaign contribution approach join these two sides of the political market. They consider competition between two political parties to win an election, the probability of which depends on both the contributions that they receive and the trade policy they commit to for implementation after winning the election. The two lobbies, on the other hand, decide about the contribution they make to these two parties for their respective election campaigns. The parties move first and the lobbies move second. The equilibrium contributions, therefore, depend on tariff policies committed by the parties, which Rodrik (1995) terms as the inverse-tariff-formation-function.

Grossman and Helpman (1994), on the other hand, consider a multi-sector specific-factor production structure with an incumbent government deciding about the trade policy. The lobbies here are the group of owners of factors that are specific to each sector who may be hurt or may benefit from a change in the trade policy. The lobbies make political contributions to the incumbent government to influence the trade policy in their favour by maximizing the benefit that their respective members get from a particular trade policy net of the contributions. The government, on the other hand, decides about the trade policy by maximizing a weighted average of social welfare and the political contributions that it receives.

A nice summary of both these campaign contribution and political contribution approaches are provided in Rodrik (1995).

APPENDIX A12

I. Comparison of Profits Under Import Quota and Import Tariff

Consider a domestic monopolist producing the import-competing good with increasing marginal cost curve *MC* and facing the linear domestic demand curve as *DD'* as shown in Figure A12.1. As discussed in Chapter 11, for an import quota of the amount $D'_R D'$, it can exercise its monopoly power in the residual domestic market indicated by the residual demand curve $D_R D'_R$. It thus produces OX_q number of computers and charges the price $O\tilde{p}$. The realized profit equals the area $cea\,\tilde{p}$. Now consider an ad-valorem import tariff that raises the tariff-inclusive price $(1+t)p_o^W$ exactly to the level $O\tilde{p}$. The tariff now turns the domestic monopolist to a price taker for reasons spelled out earlier. The domestic monopolist, now being a price taker, raises its output level to OX_t and earns a higher profit equal to the area $cb\tilde{p}$.

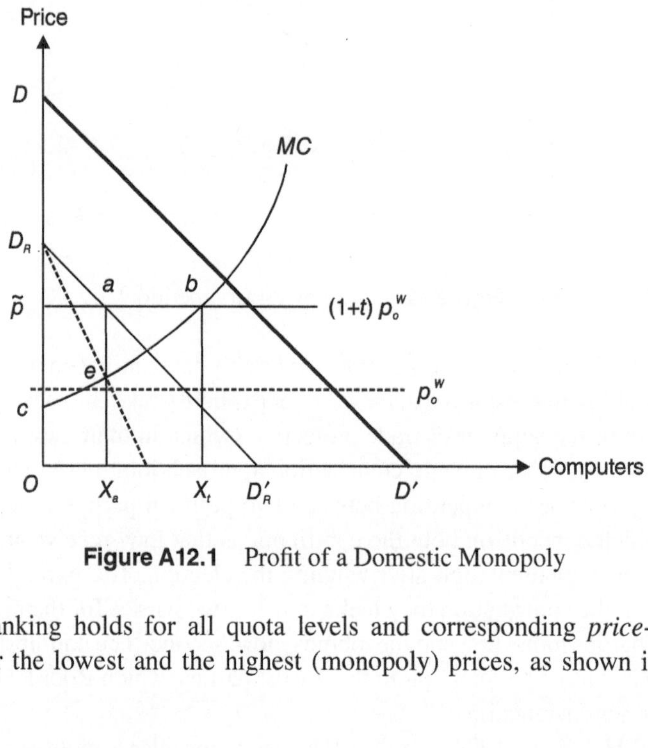

Figure A12.1 Profit of a Domestic Monopoly

This profit ranking holds for all quota levels and corresponding *price-equivalent* tariff levels except for the lowest and the highest (monopoly) prices, as shown in Figure 12.3 in the text.

SUMMARY POINTS

- Restrictive trade policies often trigger activities by economic agents that are directed at getting a share of the rents that such policies might generate. These rent-seeking lobbying activities use up scarce real resources that could have otherwise been used for productive purposes. The economy thus produces less and experiences a welfare loss when such activities are undertaken.
- An import quota generates rent-seeking activities, which unambiguously lower national welfare. On the other hand, revenue-seeking activities triggered by an import tariff may paradoxically improve national welfare.
- Lobbying activities by economic agents can also be directed at influencing the trade policy choice of the government itself.
- Trade policies are also chosen by democratic national governments by explicitly taking into account political economy forces such as the political risk involved in committing to and pursuing a strong trade policy and the consequent loss of political support. The extent of ethno-linguistic fractionalization and income heterogeneity are also important elements in such a political risk theory of trade policy choices.
- Lower political support is gathered when the domestic industry is protected through a politically optimum import quota than through a politically optimum import tariff. Thus, in the political support function approach an import tariff may be a preferred mode of protection for the domestic industry.
- In political markets for trade policies, the demand for a particular type of trade policy comes from the preference pattern of the different socio-economic interest groups in an economy. The supply of a particular trade policy, on the other hand, comes from the preference patterns of decision-makers and the structure of governance.
- The median voter approach, the campaign contribution approach, and the political contribution approach take into account both sides of the political market.

KEYWORDS

- **DUP lobbying activities** are directly unproductive profit-seeking lobbying activities using up scarce real resources that could have otherwise been used for productive purposes.
- **Revenue-seeking activity** is the lobbying activity undertaken by economic agents to get a share of the tariff revenue that otherwise accrues to the national exchequer.
- **Political risk theory** postulates that in a democracy socio-economic fractionalization leads inherently to greater levels of political risk of being overthrown and losing any rents from being in power for a government if its policies exclude more groups than they include.

EXERCISES

1. Consider the following lobbying reaction functions and tariff-formation function:

$$L_C - L_T = 700,\ L_C - 2L_T = 300,\ t = \frac{\sqrt{L_C} - \sqrt{L_T}}{100}$$

Find out the optimum lobbying expenses and the tariff rate.

2. Consider a political-support function as $S = S(\pi - \pi^W, p - p^W)$, where p^W is the world relative price of imports and π^W is the domestic monopolist's profit at that price. Write down the expression for an iso-political support function. Show that (a) it slopes upward in the (p, π) space, (b) a higher locus indicates higher political support.

3. Consider the following specific form of a political-support function: $S = (\pi - \pi^W) - (p - p^W)^2$. An import-competing good X is produced by a domestic monopolist in the economy under consideration at a marginal cost of X^2. The demand for the good in the local market is $p = 1000 - X$. In a perfectly competitive world market the same good is sold at a price of Rs 16 per unit. The local government has imposed an ad-valorem tariff at the rate t per unit of value which makes the domestic import price of the good in the local market $16(1 + t)$.
   (a) Calculate the domestic firm's profit π^W for $t = 0$.
   (b) What rate of tariff does the local government set to maximize its political support?
   (c) Find out the output produced by the local firm, the volume of import, the domestic price of the good, and the level of political support at that tariff rate.

4. Consider the following demand function for soccer balls in a local market:

   $P = 1600 - 20X$

   In the local market soccer balls are produced by a single firm at the total cost $100X + 5X^2$. The world market for soccer balls is perfectly competitive where each soccer ball is sold at a price of Rs 200.
   (a) If there is an import quota of 30 soccer balls, what price can the local firm charge in the local market?
   (b) Find out the rate of ad-valorem import tariff that results in the same price of soccer balls in the local market as the firm charges under the import quota.
   (c) Compare the profits earned by the local firm in each case.

5. Consider an economy producing and exporting mango and importing (but not producing) sugar. The production function for mango is $X = 5L_X$, where L_X is the labour used in production of mangoes (which is less than or equal to the total number of workers, L). The local import demand for sugar (S) is linear in its price and the country's income (I): $S = 1{,}000 - 10p + 0.01I$. In the world market, sugar is sold at Rs 50 per unit. There is an import quota of 100 units on sugar imports. If $L = 500$, how many of these workers will be engaged in rent-seeking activity?

6. A small open economy produces two goods, transport equipment and leather bags, using labour and capital. If both these factors of production are homogeneous and sectorally mobile, identify the pro- and anti-protectionist lobbies. How does your answer change when some workers have higher skills than others and production of transport equipment requires workers of higher skill? Justify your answer in each case.

SUGGESTED READING

Bhagwati, J.N., A. Panagariya, and T.N. Srinivasan (1998). *Lectures on International Trade*. Cambridge, MA: MIT Press.

Rodrik, D. (1995). 'Political Economy of Trade Policy', in G. Grossman and K. Rogoff (eds), *Handbook of International Economics*, Vol. III, chapter 20. Amsterdam: Elsevier Science.

ADVANCED READING

Annett, A. (2001). 'Social Fractionalization, Political Instability, and the Size of Government', *IMF Staff Papers*, 48(3): 561–92.

Bhagwati, J.N. (1982). 'Directly-Unproductive Profit-Seeking (DUP) Activities', *Journal of Political Economy*, 90: 988–1002.

Bhagwati, J.N. and T.N. Srinivasan (1980). 'Revenue Seeking: A Generalization of the Theory of Tariffs', *Journal of Political Economy*, 88: 1069–87.

Blomberg, S.B. (1996). 'Growth, Political Instability and the Defense Burden', *Economica*, 63: 649–72.

Cassing, J.H. and A.L. Hillman. (1985). 'Political Influence Motives and the Choice between Tariffs and Quotas', *Journal of International Economics* 19: 279–90.

Findlay, R. and Wellisz. (1982). 'Endogenous Tariffs, the Political Economy of Trade Restrictions, and Welfare', in J.N. Bhagwati and T.N. Srinivasan (eds), *Import Competition and Response*. Chicago: University of Chicago Press, pp. 223–34.

Grossman, G. and E. Helpman (1994). 'Protection for Sale', *American Economic Review*, 84: 833–50.

Krueger, A.O. (1974). 'The Political Economy of the Rent-Seeking Society', *American Economic Review*, 64: 291–303.

Magee, S.P., W.A. Brock, and L. Young (1989). *Black Hole Tariffs and Endogenous Policy Theory*. Cambridge, MA: Cambridge University Press.

Mayer, W. (1984). 'Endogenous Tariff Formation', *American Economic Review*, 74(5): 970–85.

Velasco, A. (1997).'A Model of Endogenous Fiscal Deficits and Delayed Fiscal Reforms', NBER Working Paper No. 6336.

13 Market Failure, Distortions, and Trade Policy

The efficiency and specialization gains from free international trade are realized when the pattern of trade is consistent with the comparative advantage of nations. But for that to happen the commodity prices must correctly reflect marginal benefits and marginal costs. Arbitrage and the consequent pattern of trade are guided by cross-country price differences. If prices do not correctly reflect marginal benefits and marginal costs, the pattern of trade may lead to a kind of specialization that is not exactly in line with the true comparative advantage of the country. This entails specialization losses rather than gains from such trade. In Chapter 2 we discussed such a case of *market failure* and a possibility of welfare losses from trade in the context of a negative production externality. There can be similar externalities in consumption as well, in which case the exchange gain may not be realized when trade opens up. The issue that arises then is: *should international trade be restricted in such cases*? Should an import tariff be imposed to correct the wrong specialization that free market leads to and to induce producers to specialize according to the true comparative advantage of the nation?

This issue of trade policy as a *corrective instrument* in cases of market failures of the above kind can be put in a much broader context. In general, market failures caused by production and consumption externalities are examples of distortions in an economy. Distortion is a situation of Pareto sub-optimal or socially sub-optimum production and consumption of commodities. Government intervention is therefore needed to improve social welfare through reallocation of resources and consequent changes in the otherwise sub-optimal production and consumption of commodities. Distortions can, however, arise in a free market for a variety of reasons and externalities driven market failures are only one set of reasons among those. Imperfectly competitive markets, both commodity and factor markets, are another important set of sources of distortions in an economy. For example, unionized money wages in some sectors may lead to an inefficient allocation of resources and composition of output. Given such a perspective, there is sizeable trade theory literature that examines the appropriateness of trade policies as instruments for correcting distortions in an economy. The general theoretical consensus reached by trade theorists in this regard is that except for the market power of a country in international trade, in all other cases of distortions trade restrictions or interventions

International Economics. Rajat Acharyya, Oxford University Press. © Oxford University Press 2022.
DOI: 10.1093/oso/9780192865144.003.0013

are *not* optimum policies. Trade restrictions *may* in fact lower social welfare further below the free trade level. Thus, free trade should be pursued but complemented by a set of domestic industrial policies that are appropriate for correcting the particular type of distortion. In this chapter, the focus is on these issues, which, as will be made clear, also provide an alternative justification of the optimum tariff argument for a large open economy.

However, for better understanding of these policy issues we need to first know the different types of distortions that may exist in an economy and their underlying causes. The latter is important for designing an optimal policy intervention and for judging whether such an optimal policy intervention should be a trade policy or a domestic industrial policy.

13.1 TAXONOMY OF DISTORTIONS

Distortions can be of various types and caused by various factors. The simplest way to understand the different types and causes is to look at the different ways the social optimum (or welfare maximizing) condition may be violated in an economy. Recall from our discussion in Chapter 2 that the socially optimum production and consumption bundles under autarchy in a home country are characterized by the following marginal (or tangency) condition:

$$MRS^h = p_a = MRT^h \tag{13.1}$$

That is, *at the optimum* the absolute slope of the community indifference curve (CIC), MRS^h, must be equal to the absolute slope of the production possibility frontier (PPF), MRT^h. Since under autarchy the home country must consume exactly what it produces, at the optimum CIC and PPF must be tangent to each other. This condition is in fact the *first order* condition for maximizing social welfare of the home country given the resource constraint of the

Box 13.1 The Market versus the State

In development policy debate, free market versus state regulation and intervention occupies a central position. Proponents of free markets argue that free and competitive markets promote efficiency and growth. The government should, therefore, keep its role to the bare minimum, related mostly to administrative activities. State intervention and regulation, on the other hand, are advocated for two reasons. First, efficiency does not necessarily mean *equity*. That is, a market allocation (or distribution) of two goods *X* and *Y* among a set of individuals $i = 1, 2, \ldots n$, $\{(x_1^*, y_1^*), (x_2^*, y_2^*), \ldots\ldots, (x_n^*, y_n^*)\}$, which is Pareto efficient, may be such that $x_i^* \neq x_j^*$ or $y_i^* \neq y_j^*$ or both $\forall\ i \neq j$. This allocation is then not an equitable allocation from an egalitarian perspective. If equity is valued more than efficiency in a society, then the state must intervene and redistribute goods among these individuals to achieve equitable allocation or distribution. Second, competitive markets often fail to promote efficiency. Externalities are plenty in the real world, and thus the resulting market failures and inefficient allocations need state intervention. Ronald Coase (1960), however, argued that market failures, particularly in cases of negative externalities, do not necessarily justify state intervention to achieve efficient allocations. His argument is explained in Box 13.2.

economy that is translated into PPF. Provided that the *second order* conditions for a maximum are satisfied, the marginal condition in equation (13.1), together with the requirement that consumption of each and every commodity is exactly equal to its domestic production and supply, ensures maximum social welfare under autarchy for our home country. The second order conditions require that the production set be strictly convex or PPF be strictly concave downwards and the CIC be strictly convex downwards. For example, recall our discussions on gains from trade in Chapter 2, where it was shown that there may not be gains from trade despite the tangency condition being satisfied, if the convexity condition in production is violated. In the rest of the discussion in this chapter we will assume that these second order conditions are satisfied and focus on the first order or marginal conditions like those in equation (13.1) as those will be the reference points for defining different types of distortions in an economy.

As explained earlier, international trade allows a country to consume beyond its production possibilities. Thus, our home country can exchange its domestically produced goods with a foreign country. The marginal condition in equation (13.1), with the post-trade world price p^W in place of the autarchic price p_a, need no longer be the point of tangency between the home country's CIC and PPF. That is, the production and consumption bundles now *differ*. But for each good, the total production in the two countries must be equal to the total demand made by the two countries. Thus, the resource constraint of the foreign country becomes relevant and accordingly the marginal (or first order) condition for optimum for a freely trading economy is specified as:

$$MRS^h = MRT^h = P^W = MRT^f \tag{13.2}$$

where $P^W = 1/p^w$ is the relative price of textiles.

Actually, for the home country, exchange possibilities are constrained by the offer made by the foreign country, and its offer curve reflects the rate at which the foreign country is willing to exchange one good for the other. That is, the MRT^f relevant for the home country is the (absolute) slope of the foreign offer curve. This interpretation of the MRT^f will be helpful in understanding trade distortions.

Underlying the above marginal condition in equation (13.2) there are several other marginal conditions that will be made explicit when we discuss sources or causes of each specific type of distortion.

13.1.1 Types of Distortions

There can broadly be three types of distortions according to the three ways in which the optimum marginal condition in equation (13.2) can be violated. Suppressing the world price for the time being, the different possible violations are:

$$MRS^h = MRT^h \neq MRT^f \tag{13.3}$$

$$MRS^h \neq MRT^h = MRT^f \tag{13.4}$$

$$MRT^h \neq MRS^h = MRT^f \tag{13.5}$$

The first type of distortion is called *foreign distortion* since the left hand side equality implies that there would have been no distortion in the economy if it did not participate in international trade. This is evident from comparing the optimum marginal condition in equation (13.1) under autarchy with the extreme left hand side equality in equation (13.3). The other two cases, on the other hand, indicate *domestic distortions* for similar reasons. Even if the home country had not participated in international trade with the foreign country, the marginal rate of substitution in consumption and the marginal rate of transformation in production in the home country would not have been the same. Thus, the distortions are in the sphere of domestic economic activities instead of arising while trading with the foreign country. The two types of domestic distortions are, however, distinctly different. In equation (13.4), the marginal condition is violated in the sphere of consumption but not in the sphere of production because the equality between MRT^h and MRT^f still holds but that between MRS^h and MRT^f does not. This type of domestic distortion is thus called *consumption distortion*. By similar logic the domestic distortion specified in equation (13.5) is the case of *production distortion*.

Note that in all these cases, free trade is sub-optimal since the violation of the optimum marginal condition in equation (13.2) means that the home country's welfare is not maximized. However, as demonstrated by Jagdish Bhagwati, Harry Johnson, T.N. Srinivasan, Gottfried Haberler, and others, this does not necessarily mean that trade should be prohibited or restricted. Only in case of foreign distortion, does a trade policy appear to be an optimal policy to correct the distortion. But in cases of domestic distortions, the optimal corrective policy should be domestic industrial policies. In general, however, for designing an optimal policy it is important to identify the exact underlying causes of these distortions. This is because of two reasons. First, different causes may be manifested in the same type of distortion and, second, any policy itself creates a distortion. Thus, the optimality of a policy largely depends on whether it can target the exact cause of the distortion.

13.1.2 Causes of Distortions

A distortion, regardless of its type, can either be policy created or be endogenous. A distortion is endogenous when it is caused by market powers of economic agents or the country as a whole, or is caused by technologies that exhibit externalities. In the latter case, the distortion arises because of the market failure.[1] On other hand, the same type of distortion may arise not due to market imperfection or market failure, but simply because of a trade or industrial policy such as import tariff, production subsidy, consumption tax, wage tax, or subsidy. Distortions are then policy created or exogenous. We elaborate below on these alternative causes or sources of distortion for each type specified above.

[1] Production of public goods (like roads, bridges, light-houses in a harbour) because of their indivisibility, non-rival consumption, and non-excludability also lead to market failure (though of a different kind) and production distortions thereof. The marginal condition in equation (13.1) itself is no longer the optimum condition in such cases. We, however, refrain from discussions on this particular cause of market failure and production distortions.

Foreign Distortion

Endogenous foreign distortion arises for a large trading nation. As spelled out in Chapter 3, a large home country, which has market power *in trade* in the sense that it is such a significant buyer and seller in the world market that it can influence its TOT by changing its trade volume, faces a concave downwards foreign offer curve. Along such an offer curve the absolute slope at any point (that is, MRT^f) is strictly less than the absolute slope of the line segment joining that point and the origin (or the autarchic point). By definition the latter gives us the average rate of transformation of one good into another in the foreign country. Hence, MRT^f is smaller than ART^f along the concave foreign offer curve that a large home country faces. At the free trade equilibrium for the large home country reproduced in Figure 13.1, its trade indifference curve (TIC) is tangent to the line segment *OE*, which represents both TOT and ART^f. Since, by construction the absolute slope of TIC represents the marginal condition in the home country $MRS^h = MRT^h$, so free trade violates the optimum condition in equation (13.2) and is sub-optimal:

$$MRS^h = MRT^h = P^W = ART^f > MRT^f \tag{13.6}$$

Any trade bundle in the region enclosed by the TIC and the foreign offer curve raises welfare of the home country above the free trade level. But if the home country had been a small or insignificant buyer and seller in the world market to influence its TOT, it would *perceive* the foreign offer curve as the line segment *OE*. Along such a perceived foreign offer curve, $ART^f = MRT^f$ so that the optimum marginal condition would have been satisfied for the free trade equilibrium bundle *E*. Hence, there would have been no endogenous foreign distortion for a small trading nation. Therefore, market power in the trade of a country is the cause of endogenous foreign distortion.

On the other hand, foreign distortion is policy imposed (or exogenous) when a small country pursues trade restriction policies like an import tariff or an import quota, or trade

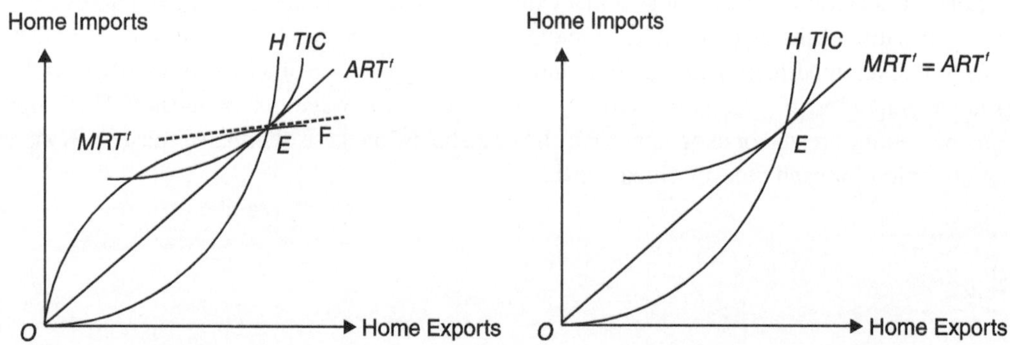

a: Large Home Country

b: Small Home Country

Figure 13.1 Foreign Distortion

promotion policies like export or import subsidies. For example, when a small home country imposes an ad-valorem import tariff it violates the marginal condition in equation (13.2) in the following way:

$$MRS^h = MRT^h = P^W/(1 + t) < p^W = ART^f = MRT^f \quad (13.7)$$

An import tariff lowers the volume of trade and at the same time creates a wedge between MRT^h and MRT^f. This explains why an import tariff is sub-optimal for a small country.

Production Distortion

There are two sources of endogenous production distortion. First is the production externality, both positive and negative, and second are imperfectly competitive product markets. Production distortion also arises from a factor market distortion such as sub-optimal or inefficient resource allocation. This, however, is discussed separately under factor market distortion. In order to delineate the cases of production distortion (and later consumption distortion) from a foreign distortion, we assume that the country is small so that there is no foreign distortion.

Recall from the discussions in Chapter 1 that negative (positive) production externalities arise when production of a particular good raises (or lowers) the cost of producing other goods. Examples of negative externality being caused by a production activity is the air pollution generated by an industrial production by emission of industrial ashes, which when deposited through rain on soil, adversely affects soil fertility and consequently agricultural productivity. The average and marginal cost of producing food grains thus rises. On the other hand, a positive production externality can arise in case of knowledge spillovers from an innovation that reduces production costs for an innovator as well as for other firms in the industry. In either case, the externalities are not internalized by the firm that is causing these externalities. But these costs are taken into account by a social planner and consequently the social cost of production and the private cost of production differ. To see how this divergence between social and marginal costs violates the optimum marginal condition in equation (13.2) and leads to a production distortion specified in equation (13.4), define the *social* cost of producing two goods X and Y as:

$$C_X = C_X(X, Y), \; C_Y = C_Y(X, Y) \quad (13.8)$$

The cost of producing good X depends on its own output level as well as on the output level of good Y (and vice-versa) because of the externalities generated by the production of these goods. The social planner calculates the social marginal cost of producing good X as the sum of change in the cost of producing good X and good Y as a consequence of an additional unit of good X being produced:

$$SMC_X = \frac{\partial C_X}{\partial X} + \frac{\partial C_Y}{\partial X} = MC_X + \frac{\partial C_Y}{\partial X} \quad (13.9)$$

Similarly, the social marginal cost of producing good Y is:

$$SMC_Y = \frac{\partial C_Y}{\partial Y} + \frac{\partial C_X}{\partial Y} = MC_Y + \frac{\partial C_X}{\partial Y} \tag{13.10}$$

where, MC_X and MC_Y are the own marginal costs estimated by the producers of good X and Y respectively. The second terms in equations (13.9) and (13.10) capture the external effects, which are positive if the relevant production generates a negative externality for the production of the other good and negative if otherwise. Now suppose the production of good X generates negative externality but the production of good Y does not generate any externality whatsoever. Hence, $\frac{\partial C_Y}{\partial X} > 0$ and $\frac{\partial C_X}{\partial Y} > 0$ so that:

$$\frac{SMC_X}{SMC_Y} = \frac{MC_X + \frac{\partial C_Y}{\partial X}}{MC_Y} > \frac{MC_X}{MC_Y} \tag{13.11}$$

Under perfectly competitive conditions, the world relative price of good X equals the ratio of private marginal costs. On the other hand, the absolute slope of the PPF being the opportunity cost of producing good X equals the ratio of the social marginal costs. Hence, in this example, under free trade the production externality causes a violation of the optimum marginal condition in equation (13.2) as:

$$MRT^h = \frac{SMC_X}{SMC_Y} > \frac{MC_X}{MC_Y} = P^W = MRS^h = MRT^f \tag{13.12}$$

Since the producers of good X underestimate the marginal cost of producing good X as long as they are not regulated or forced to internalize the costs they inflict upon others, they *over-produce* than what is socially desirable. This over-specialization in good X makes free trade sub-optimal. This is illustrated in Figure 13.2. Given the world relative price of good X as p^W, the economy would produce bundle P and consume bundle C had there been no production externality and thus no divergence between private and social marginal costs of producing good X. The welfare realized for the home country would have been the level indicated by CIC_S. But, when good X generates a negative externality, the competitive economy over-specializes in good X by producing bundle P'. The corresponding output level X_f is larger than the socially optimum level X_S. For such over-specialization, the opportunity cost of producing good X (or MRT^h) exceeds the rate p^W at which the market exchanges good X for good Y. The home country loses as a consequence of this underestimation of the (opportunity) cost and over-specialization.

A similar violation of the optimum condition and production distortion thereof may arise when good Y is produced by a domestic monopolist in the home country. Under autarchy, monopoly production of good Y means that the relative price of good Y will be higher than

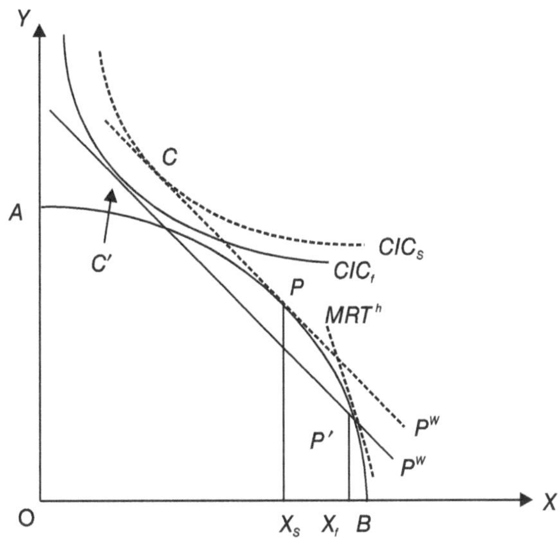

Figure 13.2 Production Distortion and Sub-optimality

the ratio of marginal costs due to the above-marginal-cost pricing of good *Y* by the domestic monopolist. Conversely, $P^W < \frac{MC_X}{MC_Y}$ so that the optimum condition in equation 13.1 under *autarchy* will be violated:

$$MRS^h = p_a < \frac{MC_X}{MC_Y} = \frac{SMC_X}{SMC_Y} MRT^h \tag{13.13}$$

But if the domestic monopolist has no market power in the world market, for reasons spelled out in Chapter 11, free international trade will break up the monopoly and the marginal-cost-pricing will restore the optimality. That is, the optimum condition in equation 13.2 under free trade will still hold. However, think of a situation where the domestic monopolist is large enough to have market power even after trade opens up. More specifically, consider that there are only two producers of good *Y* in the world—the domestic monopolist and a foreign monopolist—similar to the specification of Brander's (1981) reciprocal dumping model discussed in Chapter 8. Thus, post-trade, there will be Cournot pricing of good *Y* along with marginal-cost-pricing of good *X*. Hence:

$$MRT^h = \frac{SMC_X}{SMC_Y} = \frac{MC_X}{MC_Y} > P^W = MRS^h \tag{13.14}$$

However, in this case there will also be a foreign distortion because of the world market power of the domestic monopolist. Thus, whether production of the import-competing good by a single local firm creates distortion or not depends on the (world) market power of the firm under free trade.

Like foreign distortion, a production distortion may also be policy created. This may be the case, for example, when the local government imposes a production tax τ per unit of the value of good *X*. The price paid by domestic consumers is still the world relative price P^W, but the price retained by local producers after paying the tax to the government is $(1 - \tau)P^W$. Competitive local producers of good *X* thus produce a lower output for which $MC_X = (1 - \tau)P^W$. Hence, under free trade for this small open economy:

$$MRT^h = (1 - \tau)P^W < P^W = MRS^h = MRT^f \tag{13.15}$$

Similar cases of production distortion may arise from other domestic industrial policies.

Consumption Distortion

Similar to production externalities causing production distortions, consumption externalities are the primary sources of the endogenous consumption distortion specified in equation (13.4). Consumption externalities create a wedge between social and private marginal benefits from consuming goods. When consumption of a good by an individual raises the utility of others, the benefit from consuming the good is much higher than what is perceived by that individual. Thus, social marginal benefit or utility exceeds private marginal utility. But for generating such positive consumption externalities, the individual is not rewarded or paid by other individuals and hence she does not take into account these external benefits while deciding about the quantity of the good to be consumed. She is thus willing to pay the price that is at the most equal to her own marginal utility. Alternatively, given the price of the good, she will consume the quantity for which her own marginal utility is exactly equal to that price, which is *less* than the socially desirable or the optimum level. Thus, the ratio of private marginal utilities equals the world relative price (which in turn equals MRT^h in the absence of any production externality) under free trade. But MRS^h being the ratio of social marginal utilities, it now differs from MRT^h. Thus, again the optimum marginal condition in equation (13.2) under free trade is violated, but now in the sphere of consumption due to (positive) consumption externality. More precisely, if consumption of good *X* generates positive externality so that $SMU_X > MU_X$, but the consumption of good *Y* does not generate any externality whatsoever, under free trade we have:

$$MRS^h = \frac{SMU_X}{SMU_Y} > \frac{MU_X}{MU_Y} = P^W = MRT^h = MRT^f \tag{13.16}$$

The intuition for sub-optimality of free trade in this case is that consumers underestimate the marginal benefit of consuming good *X* and accordingly consume less than the socially optimum level. This is illustrated in Figure 13.3. Since there is no production externality, so the country's production specialization is optimum. But the country under-consumes good *X* at *C′* as compared to the optimum bundle *C*, resulting in a welfare loss.

On the other hand, by similar logic underlying why a production tax generates a policy-created or exogenous production distortion, it is easy to check that a tax on consumption of

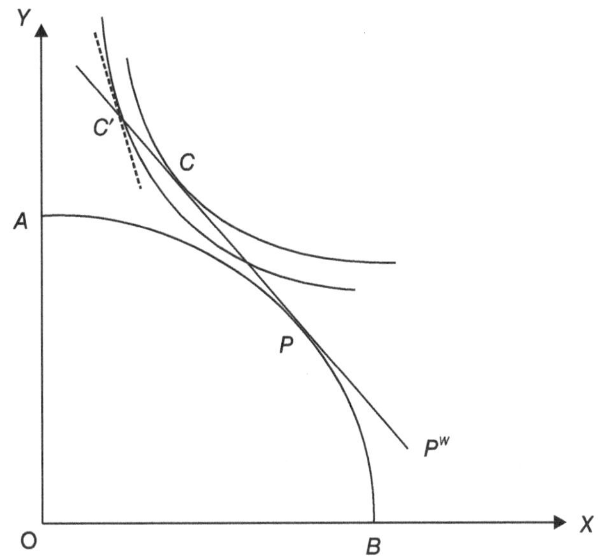

Figure 13.3 Consumption Distortion and Sub-optimality

good *X*, *ceteris paribus*, destroys the equality between MRS^h and MRT^h so that free trade is again sub-optimal. Now the consumption distortion is exogenous or policy-created. That is, if β is the rate of consumption tax per unit of expenditure on good *X*, then:

$$MRS^h = \frac{SMU_X}{SMU_Y} = \frac{MU_X}{MU_Y} = (1+\beta)P^W > P^W = MRT^h = MRT^f \tag{13.17}$$

Thus, here consumption distortion is generated by the tax policy. A consumption subsidy on good *Y* has a similar policy-created consumption distortion.

Factor Market Distortion

One important condition underlying the optimum marginal conditions in equations (13.1) and (13.2), or more specifically the efficient production condition, $p_a = MRT^h$ under autarchy or $P^W = MRT^h$ under free trade, is efficient resource allocation. A resource allocation is efficient if it raises the output of one good by lowering the output of the other good. The Edgeworth production box in Figure 13.4 illustrates the set of efficient resource allocations. The length of the two sides of the production box gives us the total labour force O_XL and total capital stock O_XK of the home country. X' and X'' are the two isoquants for good *X*, and Y' and Y'' are the two isoquants for good *Y*. Any point within this box represents a particular allocation of labour and capital in the two sectors. The concave downwards curve O_XO_Y is the *efficiency locus* or the *production contract curve*, which lies wholly above the diagonal indicating that good *X* is relatively capital-intensive as compared to good *Y* for all factor price ratios ρ.

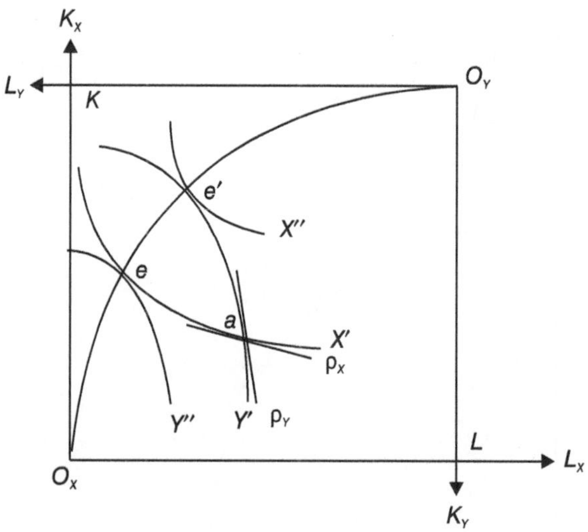

Figure 13.4 Efficient Resource Allocation

This is the locus of mutual tangencies of the isoquants, which is the efficiency locus because any resource allocation on this locus is efficient. To see why, consider the resource allocation at e for which the levels of output produced are X' and Y''. If more labour and capital are reallocated from sector Y to sector X resulting in an allocation like e', the output of good X rises to X'' but that of good Y falls to Y'. Thus, the resource allocation e is efficient by the above definition. By similar logic, all allocations along the contract locus are efficient. Now consider an allocation off the contract curve like allocation a. Many reallocations of resources of such an allocation are possible that can raise the output of one good without lowering the output of the other good. For example, any reallocation of labour and capital in the region enclosed by isoquants X' and Y' can raise the output levels of both the goods. Hence, by definition, allocation a is *not* an efficient allocation. What emerges is that an efficient (interior) resource allocation can be characterized by the following marginal condition that relates to the absolute slopes of the isoquants:

$$MRTS_{KL}^{X} = MRTS_{KL}^{Y} \tag{13.18}$$

where, $MRTS_{KL}^{X}$ and $MRTS_{KL}^{Y}$ are respectively the marginal rates of technical substitution between labour and capital in sector X and sector Y (or the absolute slopes of the isoquants).

Under perfectly competitive conditions, the least-cost choice of inputs requires that producers employ labour and capital for which the ratio of marginal products of labour and capital, which by definition is $MRTS_{KL}$ in that sector, equals the given factor price ratio. On the other hand, as long as labour and capital are homogeneous and can move freely from one sector to another, wages and rates of return to capital will be the same everywhere. This together with the least-cost choice of factors of productions implies that a competitive resource allocation will be such that:

$$MRTS_{KL}^{X} = \rho = MRTS_{KL}^{Y} \tag{13.19}$$

By equation (13.8) this means that a competitive resource allocation is efficient. But if sector *Y*, for example, is unionized where workers are paid a higher wage than the wage paid in sector *X*, the corresponding resource allocation will be inefficient:

$$MRTS_{KL}^{X} = \rho_X < \rho_Y = MRTS_{KL}^{Y} \tag{13.20}$$

An example of such an allocation that is consistent with the wage differential in the home country because some sectors are unionized while others are not, is allocation a in Figure 13.4. Thus, an imperfectly competitive labour market can be a source of inefficient resource allocation. There are two implications of this inefficient resource allocation. First, by definition the aggregate output is smaller at any interior inefficient allocation compared to the maximum feasible aggregate output corresponding to each interior efficient allocation. Thus, as shown in Figure 13.5, PPF for all feasible *inefficient* allocations will be below PPF for all feasible efficient allocations except for complete specialization cases. Note that along both PPF resources are fully employed, yet the aggregate value of production is smaller along *AP'B* because the resources are not efficiently utilized. The second implication of an inefficient resource allocation is that the tangency condition for an efficient output *composition* is violated, which in turn leads to a production distortion of the type specified in equation (13.5). More precisely, Appendix A13 shows that $P^W \neq MRT$ whenever $MRTS_{KL}^{X} \neq MRTS_{KL}^{Y}$. Hence, factor market distortions (or inefficient resource allocations) caused by wage differentials across sectors is another source of endogenous product distortions and sub-optimality of free trade. Thus, due to the unionized higher wage in sector *Y* and the consequent inefficient resource allocation, the home country produces the inefficient production bundle *P'* on the shrink-in PPF. Free trade is again sub-optimal.

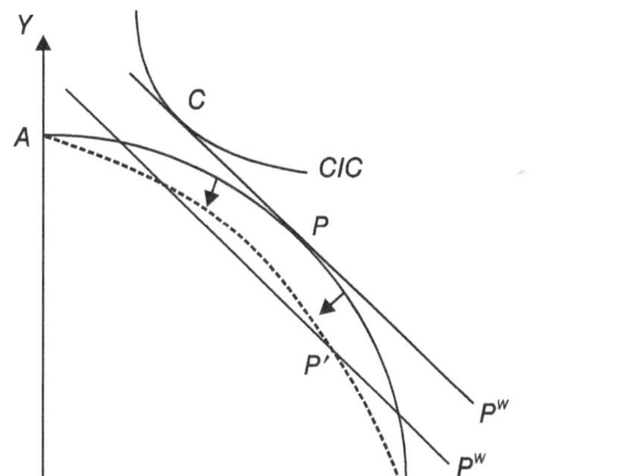

Figure 13.5 Wage Differential and Production Distortion

13.2 OPTIMAL INTERVENTION

The optimal intervention for correcting distortions and thus ensuring maximum welfare for the economy depends both on the type and the cause of distortion. As it should now be clear from the above discussion, any policy per se creates a distortion. Thus, in cases where the existing distortions are policy-created or exogenous, the optimal policy should be to dismantle or withdraw the policy itself. On the other hand, for endogenous distortions (arising from externalities and/or market imperfections of different kinds), a policy is needed to correct the existing distortions. The logic here is to create a policy-induced distortion deliberately to counter the existing distortion. A policy will thus be optimal only if it is targeted at the source of the distortion or in the sphere of economic activity where the distortion lies. The policy-created distortion must also be just enough to counter the existing distortion, no less and no more. This is what Harry G. Johnson (1965) calls the general rule for optimal intervention.

It immediately follows from this general rule for optimal intervention that a trade policy is an optimal intervention policy only in the case of a foreign distortion. But for domestic distortions of any kind, trade restriction is *not* an optimal policy even if free trade is sub-optimal. In fact, trade restrictions through an import tariff *may* lower the welfare further below the free trade level. This is because a tariff creates distortion in the sphere of international trade whereas the existing distortion is somewhere else. Thus, the policy-created distortion is not targeting the distortion at its source and therefore *may* accentuate the overall distortion instead of lowering or correcting it. Thus, for domestic distortions, free trade with relevant and appropriate domestic industrial policies is the optimal policy intervention to restore socially optimum production, consumption, and trade. In what follows, we identify the optimal policy intervention in each specific type of distortion and illustrate how trade restrictions may not even be a preferred policy over free trade.

13.2.1 Tariff or Quota as Optimal Policy Intervention for Foreign Distortion

Referring back to the sub-optimum condition in equation (13.6) and Figure 13.1, it is understandable that trade restrictions rather than trade promotion (through an export or import subsidy) should be an appropriate policy to correct the endogenous foreign distortion. An export subsidy that shifts the trade equilibrium to the right of E along the concave downwards foreign offer curve, lowers MRT^f further. On the other hand, the export subsidy expands the production of the export good in the home country and by the concavity of PPF, MRT^h rises further. Thus, given that at free trade, $MRS^h = MRT^h > MRT^f$, an export subsidy increases the divergence between MRT^h and MRT^f and cannot be an optimal policy. In fact, this offers another explanation for, in addition to the argument of TOT deterioration, why an export subsidy lowers welfare below the free trade level.

An import tariff, on the other hand, pushes the restricted-trade equilibrium to the left of E along the foreign offer curve and thereby raises MRT^f. Increase in the production of the import-competing good in the home country, on the other hand, lowers MRT^h. Thus, an import tariff lowers the wedge between MRT^h and MRT^f and consequently lowers foreign distortion. However, too large a tariff may again create a wedge between the two but now in the opposite direction. Thus, not all tariffs may be welfare improving. In fact, only the optimum tariff discussed earlier corrects the existing distortions fully without imposing additional distortions.

Box 13.2 State Intervention versus Market Solution

A.C. Pigou (1912) was the first to point out that government should tax those who inflict external costs and subsidize those whose acts generate positive externalities for society. This policy of tax or subsidy to correct externalities is known as the Pigouvian policy. But Ronald Coase (1960) argued that assigning property rights is an alternative market-based solution for the negative externality. Consider, for example, the case of industrial wastes being dumped into an adjacent water body, which is a source of drinking water for the local inhabitants. The water pollution causes health hazards for these people and raises their health expenditure or medical bills for curing the ailment. Since the industrial unit does not internalize these medical costs due to contamination of drinking water, this is a case of production externality. Now suppose the local inhabitants get the property right of the water body. Then, they can force the producers to compensate them for dumping industrial waste in the water body, provided of course that the legal system works efficiently. Producers being forced to provide compensation for health hazards, cut back production to the socially optimum level. If instead, the property right is assigned to the producers, the local inhabitants can bribe them for not dumping industrial waste in the water body. The amount of bribe will once again be the extent of utility loss from water pollution. Thus, there is now an opportunity cost of over-production since it will mean a corresponding bribe foregone, which makes their private cost calculations exactly the same as the social marginal cost.

This market-based solution, however, may fail to achieve socially optimum production levels if there are significantly high transaction costs involved in this kind of bargaining and if the parties involved are too many.

For such a tariff-restricted trade, the home country's TIC is tangent to the foreign offer curve. Thus, the optimum tariff restores the marginal condition enabling the country to attain the maximum welfare as illustrated in Figure 13.6. The only difference is that the optimum-tariff-inclusive domestic price is now the relevant price for home producers and consumers such that:

$$MRS^h = MRT^h = P^W/(1 + t_{opt}) = MRT^f \tag{13.21}$$

In Figure 13.6, the reciprocal of the slope of the line PP' gives us the optimum-tariff inclusive domestic price, $(1 + t_{opt})\ p^W$. But it is also the common tangent to the foreign offer curve at E_{opt} and TIC_{opt} passing through the same point. Thus, at the optimum-tariff-restricted trade equilibrium, the optimum marginal condition (13.21) is satisfied.

This provides an alternative explanation for why an optimum tariff maximizes the country's welfare. Also note that the foreign distortion could be corrected and the maximum welfare could be attained alternatively through an optimum import quota. But for a small country, a foreign distortion arises when it imposes a tariff or a quota, as we have explained above. Thus, for a small country, free trade is the optimal or first-best policy, provided of course there are no other distortions.

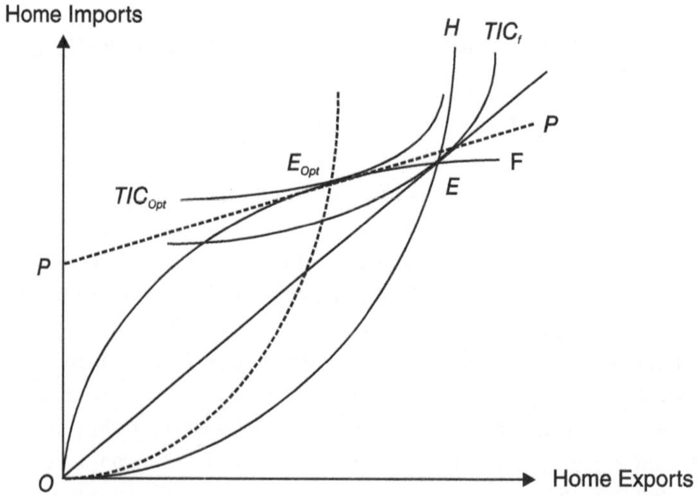

Figure 13.6 Foreign Distortion and Optimum Tariff

13.2.2 Optimal Policy Intervention for Production Distortion

Designing an optimal policy intervention in the case of a production distortion is not straightforward because it may be caused either by a production externality or factor market distortion. In the former case, a production tax-cum-subsidy with free trade is the first-best or optimal policy intervention. As explained earlier, in case of a negative externality generated by the production of good *X*, the unregulated competitive producers *over-produce* the good, which, in turn, means that the other good is under-produced compared to the socially optimum level. The consequent over-specialization in good *X* lowers the country's welfare. Thus, all that the government needs to do is to put a production tax on the producers of good *X* or provide production subsidies to the producers of good *Y* to correct this over-specialization. Note that given the full employment of resources, a subsidy on good *Y* achieves the same target level of specialization as does a tax on good *X*. Thus, *either* policy can be pursued. A production tax essentially forces the producers to internalize external costs that they inflict upon the rest of the economy. With the optimum tax rate being the difference between private and social marginal costs, the private marginal cost inclusive of the production tax equals the social marginal cost. Accordingly the producers of good *X* cut back their production levels to the level of social optimum.

But when the production distortion is caused by wage differentials and consequent inefficient resource allocations as we have explained in the earlier section, by the general rule of optimal intervention, a wage tax-cum-subsidy should be the optimal policy intervention. In our example of a unionized higher wage in sector *Y*, a wage subsidy given to the producers of good *Y* will lower the effective cost of hiring labour for them. This will induce them to choose more labour-intensive techniques of production. Additional workers are drawn from the non-unionized low-wage sector *X*. In the process, the ratio of effective wage—the wage paid net of the wage-subsidy—to the rate of return to capital in sector Y and the wage–rental ratio in sector X will be equalized. The corresponding resource allocations will thus be efficient.

Note that with fixed unionized money wage in sector Y, the money wage in sector X and the economy-wide uniform rate of return to capital is tied down by the given world prices of goods X and Y. The optimal wage subsidy then is the fixed amount ($\rho_Y - \rho_x$), such that $MRTS^X_{KL} = \rho_X = \rho_Y - (\rho_Y - \rho_x) = MRTS^Y_{KL}$. Referring back to Figure 13.5, the aggregate value of production should thus rise. On the other hand, the production distortion will be corrected as well. But, a production tax-cum-subsidy will only restore the tangency condition as shown in Figure 13.7. Since the factor prices are tied down by the given world commodity prices, it cannot alter the least-cost choice of techniques to increase the aggregate value of production. For a production tax imposed on good X or a production subsidy given to the unionized-wage sector Y, the economy thus still operates on the sub-optimal *shrink-in* PPF labeled A$P'B$ in Figure 13.7 and produces bundle P''. Thus, free trade with a production tax-cum-subsidy is *not* an optimal or first-best policy in this case, though it is a better policy option than free trade (without any domestic industrial policy).

The lesson from the above discussion is that *designing a production tax-cum-subsidy whenever a production distortion is manifested may be misleading*. Policymakers need to look at the underlying cause of it and accordingly design the optimal policy intervention.

How does an import tariff policy rank with a free trade underproduction externality? First of all note that for the small country an import tariff introduces a foreign distortion and thus lowers the country's welfare. On the other hand, it raises the production of the import-competing good. If this good generates negative externality, then the welfare falls further since the increase in production of the import-competing good imposes more external costs on the economy. The over-specialization is not corrected, rather it is magnified further. Thus, overall, the home country's welfare falls below the free trade level. That is, *an import tariff may not even be a second-best policy*. On the other hand, if it is the export good that generates negative

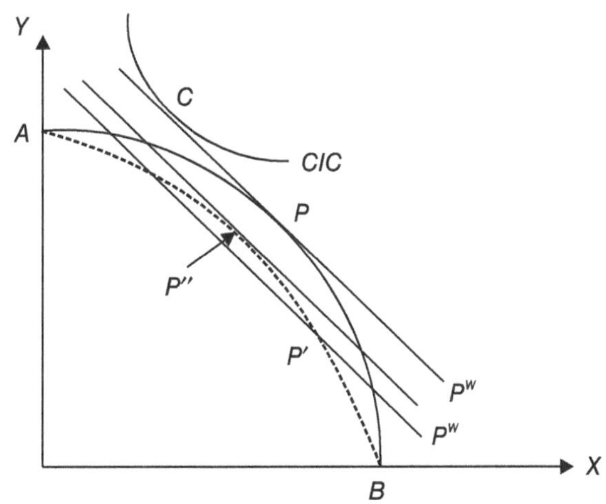

Figure 13.7 Wage Differential and Optimal Policy

externality, then an import tariff lowers the external costs as the production of the export good now contracts. The welfare on this account increases, though production distortion still exists because the tariff cannot restore the equality between the social and private marginal costs. It only reduces the divergence. This welfare gain then will have to be weighed against the welfare loss from (the policy-created) foreign distortion that is being introduced now. In general, an import tariff, or similar other trade restriction policies, reduces the welfare of the country below the free trade level under production externality.

13.2.3 Optimal Policy Intervention for Consumption Distortion

Again from the general rule for optimal policy intervention it follows that a consumption tax-cum-subsidy with free trade is the optimal policy intervention in case of a consumption distortion caused by consumption externality. Recall that in case of a *positive* consumption externality, the sub-optimality arises because of *under-consumption* of the good. A subsidy on the consumption of the good that benefits others then takes care of this problem by encouraging the consumers to consume more of the good up to the level that is socially desirable. Similarly, the good that creates negative externality in consumption, that is, lowers the utility of others, is over-consumed than is socially desirable and therefore such consumption should be taxed to attain the optimal level of consumption and the consequent maximum level of social welfare. Cigarette smoking and the negative externality generated through passive smoking is a typical example in this regard.

Once again, an import tariff may not even be a second-best policy for similar reasons as spelled out in case of production externality above.

APPENDIX A13

I. Product Distortion under Wage Differential

Consider an economy with a wage differential but no interest rate differentials. More precisely, suppose the money wage paid to workers employed in sector X is w_X and to those employed in sector Y is w_Y, with the following relationship between the two wages:

$$w_Y = \mu w_X,\ \mu \neq 1 \tag{A13.1}$$

If $\mu > 1$, higher wages are paid to workers employed in sector Y than those employed in sector X.

Given equation (A13.1) and $r_X = r_Y = r$, consider the total cost of producing the two traded goods:

$$C_X = w_X L_X + rK_X \tag{A13.2}$$

$$C_Y = w_X L_Y + rK_Y \tag{A13.3}$$

where, L_X and L_Y are labour allocated to (or employed in) sectors X and Y respectively. Similar is the interpretation of K_X and K_Y. These allocations must, however, be feasible. That is they satisfy the following resource constraint faced by the economy:

$$L_X + L_Y = L \tag{A13.4}$$

$$K_X + K_Y = K \tag{A13.5}$$

Total differentiation, holding factor prices constant, yields marginal costs as:

$$\frac{dC_X}{dX} = w_X \frac{dL_X}{dX} + r\frac{dK_X}{dX} \tag{A13.6}$$

$$\frac{dC_Y}{dY} = w_Y \frac{dL_Y}{dY} + r\frac{dK_Y}{dY} \tag{A13.7}$$

Note that changes in output levels (and consequent changes in the volume of trade) cannot change world commodity prices because the country is small. Thus, as long as the one-to-one correspondences hold, factor prices do not change as well.

But the changes in factor allocations or employment required for an expansion of good X must satisfy the resource constraints in equations (A13.4) and (A13.5). In other words, for an increase in labour (or capital) employment when the economy expands the output of good X, labour (or capital) available for production sector Y must fall. Consequently, as long as the marginal productivities are strictly positive, the output of good Y must fall as well. Total differentiation of the above resource constraints gives us such a trade off:

$$\frac{dL_X}{dX} + \frac{dL_Y}{dY}\frac{dY}{dX} = 0 \Rightarrow \frac{dL_X}{dX} = -\frac{dL_Y}{dY}\frac{dY}{dX} \tag{A13.8}$$

$$\frac{dK_X}{dX} = -\frac{dK_Y}{dY}\frac{dY}{dX} \tag{A13.9}$$

Substitution of equations (A13.8) and (A13.9) in (A13.6) yields:

$$\frac{dC_X}{dX} = -\frac{dY}{dX}\left[w_X \frac{dL_Y}{dY} + r\frac{dK_Y}{dY}\right] \tag{A13.6a}$$

Perfectly competitive producers of goods X and Y produce output levels for which the given world price of the goods equals the marginal cost to maximize their respective profits. Hence, using equations (A13.1), (A13.6a), and (A13.7), these profit maximizing conditions can be written as:

$$P^W = -\frac{dY}{dX}\frac{\left[w_X \frac{dL_Y}{dY} + r\frac{dK_Y}{dY}\right]}{\left[\mu w_X \frac{dL_Y}{dY} + r\frac{dK_Y}{dY}\right]}$$

By definition, $-\frac{dY}{dX} = \text{MRT}$ along PPF. Hence, denoting the second ratio term on the right hand side by β, the above profit maximizing condition boils down to:

$$P^W = \beta\,[MRT] \tag{A13.10}$$

Note that, $\mu \neq 1 \Rightarrow \beta \neq 1$. Thus, as long as wage differentials exist, $p^W \neq MRT$. That is, wage differentials, and consequent inefficient resource allocations, lead to a production distortion. More precisely, if $\mu > 1$ (i.e., $w_Y > w_X$), then $\beta < 1$, which in turn by equation (A13.10) implies that $P^W < MRT$. By similar reasoning, $P^W > MRT$ for $w_Y < w_X$.

SUMMARY POINTS

- Distortion is a situation of Pareto sub-optimal or socially sub-optimum production and consumption of commodities. In cases of distortion, government intervention is needed to improve upon social welfare through reallocation of resources and consequent changes in the otherwise sub-optimal production and consumption of commodities.
- Distortions are of various types. There may be foreign distortions or domestic distortions. The distinction is whether the distortion is in the sphere of international trade or in the sphere of domestic production or consumption.
- Each type of distortion may be policy created or may be endogenous. Endogenous distortions are those distortions that are caused by externalities in production and consumption or by market powers of firms, buyers, or of a country as a whole.
- In the case of a policy created distortion, the optimal rule is to dismantle the policy itself.
- In case of endogenous distortion, a distortion is created deliberately through a policy to take care of the existing distortion. The optimal rule here is that the policy-created distortion must be targeted at the source of the existing distortion and be just enough to counter it, no less and no more.
- By this general rule of optimal intervention, except for the case of foreign distortion, arising due to the market power of a country in international trade, in all other cases of endogenous domestic distortions trade restrictions or interventions are *not* optimum policies.
- A domestic distortion calls for free trade with a domestic industrial policy such as a production tax-cum-subsidy or consumption tax-cum-subsidy depending on whether it is caused by a production externality (or product market imperfection) or by a consumption externality.
- A factor market distortion may also imply a production distortion. But the optimal policy should be a wage tax-cum-subsidy.

KEYWORDS

- **Distortion** is a situation of Pareto sub-optimal or a socially sub-optimum production and consumption of commodities.
- **Distortion is endogenous** when it is caused by either market powers of economic agents or the market power of the country as a whole in trade, or by technologies that exhibit externalities.
- **Foreign distortion** arises when a country has *market power in trade* in the sense that it is such a significant buyer and seller in the world market that it can influence its TOT by changing its trade volume.
- **General rule for optimal policy intervention** in cases of distortions requires a policy to target the exact cause of an existing distortion and the policy created distortion must just be enough to counter the existing distortion, no less and no more. For domestic distortions of any kind, trade restriction is *not* an optimal policy even if free trade is sub-optimal in such cases.

EXERCISES

1. Consider a perfectly competitive firm producing an import-competing good at a domestic price of 25 per unit. There are 100 identical firms, each having a cost function $C = \frac{1}{2}x^2$. Production of this good generates negative externality for the rest of the economy such that for a social planner the cost of production for each firm is actually $SC = \frac{1}{2}x^2 + 5x$. Find out how much each firm produces at the unregulated equilibrium. Is this the socially optimum production level for each firm? If not, then how will you achieve the socially optimum level of production?
2. In the above example if this good is sold in the perfectly competitive world market at a price of 20 per unit, should unrestricted imports of the good induce domestic firms to produce the socially optimum level of output? If not, should you then recommend an import tariff?
3. Using the value of marginal product curves for labour, illustrate the optimal allocation of a fixed endowment of labour in two sectors producing traded goods.
    (a) Show that non-uniform wages mean a lower aggregate value of output.
    (b) If all sectors are unionized and demand the same money wage, can the maximum aggregate value of output be attained?
4. The ordinal utility functions of two consumers A and B in a small open economy are $U^A = U^A(x^A, y^A)$ and $U^B = U^B(x^B, y^B)$ respectively. If the consumption of good Y generates positive externality, write down the utility functions as evaluated by a social planner and the social marginal utility of consumption of an additional unit by individual A.

(contd)

Exercises (*contd*)

5. Consider a country, which is not engaged in international trade, producing two goods automobiles and wheat. If automobiles are produced only by Suzuki, but there are many perfectly competitive producers of bread, does the economy produce and consume the socially optimum product bundle? If not, what type of distortion arises at the unregulated market equilibrium?
6. In case of a production distortion generated by a monopoly under autarchy, should you recommend a production tax on the monopolist? Explain.
7. Suppose HMT is the sole producer of wrist watches in India. Its production cost increases at an increasing rate with the number of wrist watches produced: $\frac{1}{2}x^2$. If it faces a domestic demand for wrist watches as $p = a - x$ and import of wrist watches is not allowed, how many wrist watches does HMT produce? Would a social planner produce the same number of wrist watches? If not, how will the social planner induce HMT to produce the socially optimum number of wrist watches?
8. When distortions of any kind exist, if free trade in an unregulated market is welfare reducing compared to autarchy, should trade be prohibited or restricted?
9. Why is it that in case of domestic distortions, tariff-restricted trade is at the most a second-best policy?
10. A social planner observes that unregulated competitive producers produce relatively smaller quantities of rice and larger quantities of garments than the socially optimum levels. He imposes a production tax on garments and provides a subsidy to the farmers. Has he done the right thing to induce producers to produce socially optimum levels? Explain your answer.

SUGGESTED READING

Bhagwati, J.N., A. Panagariya, and T.N. Srinivasan (1998). *Lectures on International Trade*. Cambridge, MA: MIT Press.

ADVANCED READING

Brander, J.A. (1981). 'Intra-industry Trade in Identical Commodities', *Journal of International Economics*, 11: 1–14.

Coase, R.H. (1960). 'The Problem of Social Cost', *Journal of Law and Economics*, October: 1–44.

Johnson, H.G. (1965). 'Optimal Trade Intervention in Presence of Domestic Distortions', in R. Caves, H.G. Johnson, and P.B. Kenen (eds), *Trade, Growth and the Balance of Payments*. Rand McNally, pp. 3–34.

Pigou, A.C. (1912). *Wealth and Welfare*. London: Macmillan.

14 Multilateralism and Regionalism

Since the 1990s, there has been a spectacular upsurge in the number of regional trade agreements among group of nations in a particular region, usually neighbours, for freer trade and unified trade policies within that region. Bilateral trade negotiations between small and large countries are also growing rapidly. All these have been going hand-in-hand with the current wave of globalization and the World Trade Organization (WTO) rounds of multilateral negotiations for removal of trade and non-trade barriers with the ultimate objective of achieving global free trade. These two processes and approaches to trade liberalization are, however, conflicting with each other. This is because, as we will learn in this chapter, the regional approach is essentially a mix of trade cooperation among member countries and trade discrimination against non-members countries or the rest of the world. Globalization even in its narrowest interpretation, on the other hand, aims at integrating all economies with one another.

Since the early nineteenth century when Ricardo expounded the doctrine of comparative advantage, benefits of trade liberalization have influenced national trade policies. But globalization and trade liberalization have never been so universally and pervasively projected as a development policy as they were at the turn of the twenty-first century. One can observe a remarkable unanimity in the International Monetary Fund (IMF), the World Bank, and WTO in prescribing such policy rules as the only effective means of poverty reduction regardless of country-specific production and market structures. At the same time, the hue and cry regarding globalization as a policy rule and debates and controversies over the quantum of benefits of trade liberalization have never been so fierce and intense than ever before. There has been growing scepticism regarding the realization of true potentials of free trade under the existing set of rules and institutions in the world trading system.

Such scepticism along with political compulsions and narrow national interests of trading nations have been major causes of the recent upsurge in bilateral or regional trade agreements both within and across continents. But this regional approach has only slowed down the momentum in the multilateral approach to global free trade, and in many cases has undermined it. This has raised serious concerns over the direction of the world trading system in the future.

A study of the evolution of the world trading system around these conflicting trade negotiation approaches—regionalism and multilateralism—raises several questions. Why have countries been so sceptical to the multilateral approach to global free trade? Why have

International Economics. Rajat Acharyya, Oxford University Press. © Oxford University Press 2022.
DOI: 10.1093/oso/9780192865144.003.0014

bilateral or regional trading arrangements been the dominant approach to free trade in history as well as in contemporary times? Is the bilateral and regional approach to trade liberalization a stepping stone or a stumbling block to multilateralism and global free trade? In this chapter, we will find answers to these questions.

14.1 TYPOLOGY OF REGIONAL TRADING AGREEMENTS (RTAs) AND ECONOMIC COOPERATION

A regional trading bloc (RTB), or a regional trade arrangement (RTA), is a regional grouping among a few countries on the basis of reciprocated and coordinated trade policies vis-à-vis themselves and the rest of the world. A broader grouping or coalition among member countries goes beyond coordination of trade policies by unifying their fiscal and monetary policies. In general, regional economic cooperation has different forms depending on the different levels of cooperation and integration among the member countries. RTAs may also differ with respect to the scope and coverage of trade concessions and reciprocation. On the other hand, regional economic cooperation may have an open regionalism policy or a unanimous regionalism policy with respect to its accession policies for potential new members. Let us begin with the different stages of regional economic cooperation and thereafter we will discuss the differences in the scope and coverage of RTAs.

14.1.1 Different Stages of Regional Economic Cooperation

Jacob Viner (1950) conceived five different and successively higher stages of regional economic cooperation. The first is preferential trading arrangements (PTAs) among a group of countries, whereby member countries lower their respective tariff rates and other non-tariff barriers on their mutual trade, but keep the tariff and non-tariff barriers vis-à-vis the rest of the world the same. The PTA between ASEAN and China that has been in force from November 2004 and between Chile and India that has been in force from January 2009 are the most recent examples. Other examples include the PTA between Lao PDR and Thailand in force from 1991.

The next stage of cooperation is forming a free trade area (FTA), whereby all tariff and non-tariff barriers on mutual trade among the member countries are abolished. Major FTAs include the North American FTA (NAFTA) among Canada, Mexico, and the United States formed in 1994; and the Association of South East Asian Nations (ASEAN) among Brunei Darussalam, Cambodia, Indonesia, Laos, Malaysia, Myanmar, the Philippines, Singapore, Thailand, and Vietnam. ASEAN came into force in the late 1960s with Indonesia, Malaysia, the Philippines, Singapore, and Thailand as the five founder member countries and then expanded to include Brunei Darussalam in 1984, Vietnam in 1995, Laos and Myanmar in 1997, and Cambodia in 1999. FTAs in which India is involved include the ASEAN-India FTA signed in November 2009, and the proposed South Asia FTA (SAFTA) among Bangladesh, Bhutan, India, Maldives, Nepal, Pakistan, and Sri Lanka. There are, however, many more FTAs. According to the notifications in WTO, there are 182 FTAs that were *in force* till the end of 2010.

The third stage of economic cooperation (or a higher order RTA than the FTA) aims at forming a customs union (CU) whereby, in addition to fulfilling the requirements of an FTA, all members impose a common external tariff (and other NTBs) on imports by union members from the rest of the world. This is in contrast to both PTA and FTA in which trade policies of the member countries vis-à-vis the rest of the world remain unilateral and mostly unchanged, though relative and effective trade barriers increase for reasons spelled out later. Examples of major CUs include the Caribbean Community and Common Market (CARICOM), the Gulf Cooperation Council (GCC), MERCOSUR and the South African Customs Union (SACU). GCC, a political and economic union, was formed by Bahrain, Kuwait, Oman, Qatar, Saudi Arabia, and the United Arab Emirates in 1981. MERCOSUR was founded in 1991 by Argentina, Brazil, Paraguay, and Uruguay, which was later amended and updated by the 1994 Treaty of Ouro Preto. Bolivia, Chile, Colombia, Ecuador, and Peru currently have associate member status, and Venezuela signed a membership agreement on 17 June 2006. CARICOM, which came into effect on 1 August 1973, started with its first four signatories Barbados, Jamaica, Guyana, and Trinidad and Tobago. Currently CARICOM has 15 full members, five associate members, and seven observers. SACU, on the other hand, is the oldest and still existing CU in the world, which was established in 1910 as a Customs Union Agreement between the then Union of South Africa and the High Commission territories of Botswana, Lesotho, and Swaziland. After the independence for these territories, the agreement was updated and was re-launched as SACU that came into force on 1 March 1970. Namibia joined SACU as its fifth member in 1990 after its independence.

The fourth stage of economic cooperation is forming a common market, whereby unrestricted factor movements are allowed within the regional trading bloc. Thus, at this stage the member countries move from free commodity trade to free factor trade. Finally, the highest stage of cooperation, an economic and monetary union (EMU), is reached at when member countries unify their fiscal and monetary policies and switch over to a common currency system. The first ever economic union was formed by Belgium and Luxembourg as early as in 1921, and then in the post–World War II period by Belgium, and the Netherlands, and Luxembourg (BENELUX) after their 1958 BENELUX Treaty. The more recent example is that of the European Union (EU) when its 15 member countries unified their currencies in Euro in 1999. The United Kingdom is part of EU as well except for adopting the common currency Euro. EU offers an interesting case study of the political and economic forces that contributed to its evolution through the successive stages of economic cooperation and integration.

14.1.2 Evolution of the European Union through Successive Stages of Cooperation

EU, formally established on 1 November 1993, has a long history of cooperation and conflict among its member countries. The initiation of an integrated Europe can be traced back to the immediate post–World War II years. Two supra-national economic organizations marked such an early stage of economic integration. First, was the BENELUX customs union formed in 1948 between Belgium, the Netherlands, and Luxembourg. Political leaders of these countries have been the most ardent advocates of EU. Success of BENELUX as an economic union after the 1958 BENELUX Treaty has certainly been instrumental in the integrated Europe that we see today. Second, in 1950 the then French foreign minister Robert Schuman proposed the integration of French and German coal and steel industries and invited other nations to participate in it. The treaty establishing the European Coal and Steel Community (ECSC) was signed in 1951. It aimed at the elimination of tariffs and quotas on trade in iron ore, coal, coke, and steel within the community and a common external tariff on imports relating to the coal and steel industries from other nations. Thus, ECSC was intended to be a customs union though it was very narrow in its scope and coverage. In 1957 participants in ECSC signed the Rome Treaty on the European Economic Community (EEC). This was a big leap forward since the formation of EEC meant targeting the fourth stage of integration, the common market, straightway from a very narrowly defined CU in the form of ECSC. But the United Kingdom objected to the loss of control over its national policies implied in such an intense European integration and attempted to persuade European nations to create a free trade area instead. After the EEC Treaty was ratified, the United Kingdom, Norway, Sweden, Denmark, Switzerland, Austria, and Portugal created the European free trade area (EFTA) that, as we have already noted, was a much weaker union than the common market. UK's reluctance to give up its control over its national economic policies had in fact reversed the European integration process as it led to two separate unions within the West European contingent. In 1961, with the EEC's apparent economic success, the United Kingdom changed its mind and began negotiations for EEC's membership. But the then French president Charles de Gaulle vetoed British membership, primarily because of the United Kingdom's close ties to the United States. De Gaulle vetoed British admittance a second time in 1967. Finally, in 1973, during the tenure of the next French President, Georges Pompidou, UK, Ireland, and Denmark were admitted as members of EEC whereas Norway opted out (Figure 14.1).

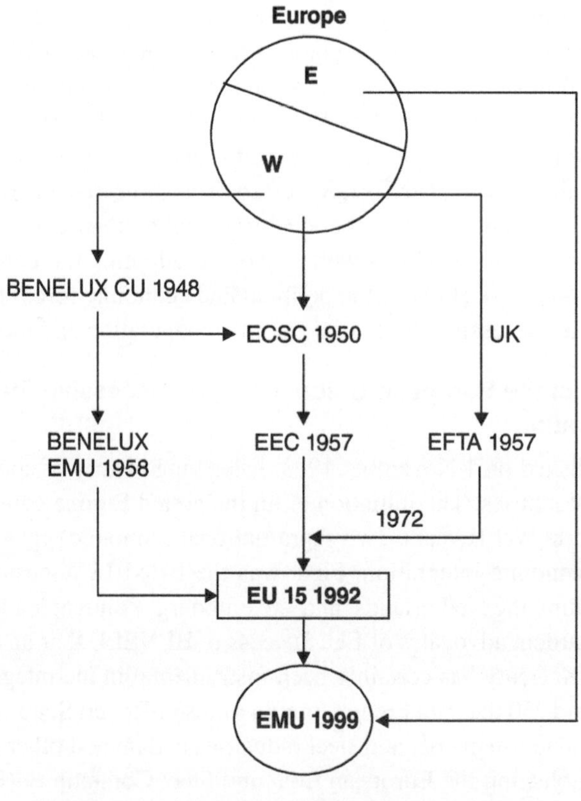

Figure 14.1 Evolution of European Integration

In 1986, the heads of EC member states signed the Single European Act (SEA), which was a package of amendments and additions to existing EC treaties. SEA required that EC adopt more than 300 measures to remove physical, technical, and fiscal barriers in order to establish a single market, where the economies of the member states would be completely integrated. In addition to this, member states agreed to adopt common policies and standards on matters ranging from taxes and employment to health and the environment. This started the countdown for creating the European Union.

The Treaty on European Union (often called the Maastricht Treaty) founded the EU and was intended to expand political, economic, and social integration among member states. After lengthy discussions, it was accepted by the European Council at Maastricht, the Netherlands in December 1991. It committed a transition of the EU to an Economic and Monetary Union (EMU). It was decided that under EMU the member nations will unify their economies and adopt a single currency by 1999. The Maastricht Treaty also set strict criteria that the member states had to meet before they could join EMU. In addition, the treaty created new structures designed to develop a more integrated foreign and security policy and to encourage greater governmental cooperation on judicial and police matters. The member states granted EU governing bodies more authority in several areas, including the environment, education, health, and consumer protection.

Popular reactions against some aspects and consequences of the Maastricht Treaty led to another inter-governmental conference among EU leaders that began in March 1996. It paved the way for the Amsterdam Treaty, which revised the Maastricht Treaty and other founding EU documents. These changes were intended to make the EU more attractive and relevant to ordinary people. The Amsterdam Treaty signed by the EU members on 2 October 1997, allowed the possibility of admitting Eastern European countries to EU.

The uneven progress of EU and EMU is in part due to the yet unresolved debate over whether to give priority to 'deepening' or 'widening'. That is, whether to concentrate on integrating the existing members further, or to welcome new members so that all can have an input into the kind of Europe they want.

14.1.3 Open and Unanimous Regionalism

An RTA can have a principle of either open regionalism or unanimous regionalism. In open regionalism, a potential member can join an existing RTA even without the consent of existing members. Under unanimous regionalism, on the other hand, member countries must unanimously agree on the accession of a new member. The rule of open regionalism is, however, hardly followed in principle as well as in practice by member countries. EU and the United States seemingly follow the open regionalism rule, provided some preconditions are satisfied by a potential member country. For example, EU membership is explicitly open to all European nations that meet the so-called Copenhagen membership criteria declared at the European Council meeting in Copenhagen, Denmark in June 1993. The criteria require that a country must have the institutions to preserve democratic governance and human rights, have a functioning market economy, and accept the obligations and intent of the EU. The US, on the other hand, now seems to offer FTAs to almost any nation provided the prospective partner country is willing to accept the US template FTA. This includes a great deal of market openings in sensitive areas like agricultural markets, intellectual property rights, and services. Thus, effectively the EU and the United States do not have an open regionalism rule.

14.1.4 Scope and Coverage of RTAs

Not all FTAs or CUs have the same scope and coverage with respect to policies regarding trade in goods and services. According to the WTO Secretariat, of the 102 agreements which were in force at the end of 1998, only 11 covered trade in services notified under the General Agreement on Trade in Services (GATS) in WTO. Moreover, of the agreements in force during 1990–98, only 43 had 100 per cent coverage in industrial products and more selective coverage in the agricultural sector (Crawford and Laird 2000).

Schaefer (2007), on the other hand, observes that many RTAs exclude agriculture from their coverage, at least to some extent. RTAs usually employ a positive list approach (not covered unless specifically included) for agricultural products. Interestingly, RTAs that exclude agricultural products allow member countries to obtain increased market access in industrial products in their respective markets. Another common feature of the new agreements, which have been in force after 1990, is that many of them now cover investment, intellectual property rights, and technical barriers to trade.

14.2 BILATERALISM AND REGIONALISM: OLD AND THE CONTEMPORARY

Today's EU, which started off with an economic union between Belgium, Luxembourg, and the Netherlands through the BENELUX Treaty in 1948, and the regional approach elsewhere in the form of NAFTA, ASEAN, or MERCOSOUR are not post–World War II phenomena. This regional approach to trade liberalization has its root in the late nineteenth century, when the bilateral approach and the unconditional MFN clause ushered in trade reforms and significant reductions in tariff rates throughout Europe. In fact, as articulated by Irwin (1993), since the mercantilist periods during the seventeenth century, bilateral and preferential trading arrangements have shaped trade policies in European countries.

14.2.1 Pre–World War I Bilateralism and Regionalism

The beginning of bilateralism in world trade can be traced back to the commercial treaty between England and Portugal in 1703. Portuguese wines had preferential access to the English market and English woolens to the Portuguese market. For England, such a treaty was motivated by the mercantilist idea of accumulation of specie through a trade surplus as Portugal at that time had a direct source of bullion through its new world colonies. Economists like Adam Smith, David Hume, and J.R. McCulloch, however, criticized this preferential trade arrangement as it meant loss of the French market for English woolen manufacturers and a diversion of wine import to Spain and Portugal where worse liquor at higher prices was bought.

The Anglo-French Accord of 1783 aimed at a modest reduction of duties on bilateral trade to eliminate smuggling and for raising tariff revenues. During the next 20 years, Britain attempted trade negotiations with Portugal, Spain, Poland, and Prussia, but failed to reach any agreement. The French Revolution and wars by Napoleon disrupted European trade thereafter. In 1823, through the Reciprocity of Duties Act, Britain attempted to negotiate bilateral and reciprocated tariff reductions. But this failed again. Thereafter, the Anglo-French Treaty in the 1860s was the most important of the treaties at that time which actually paved the way for multilateral free trade through bilateralism throughout Europe. According to the terms of the treaty, after 1865, France abolished all trade prohibitions and imposed specific ad-valorem duties not exceeding 30 per cent. Britain imposed duties on only 48 goods compared to 419 dutiable goods before the treaty. Most significantly, it reduced wine tariff. But, as Irwin (1993) observes, the critical element of the treaty was the unconditional most favoured nation (MFN) clause by which either country could extend to any other third country any favour regarding the importation of goods whether mentioned or not in the treaty. As France maintained a two-tiered tariff system, lower rates for Britain and higher rates for the rest, other European countries quickly sought agreements. France extended the unconditional MFN clause to Belgium in 1861, Italy in 1863, Switzerland in 1864, Sweden, Norway, Spain, and the Netherlands in 1865, and Austria in 1866. Thus the Anglo-French Treaty, which started purely as a bilateral arrangement, rapidly cascaded into a series of bilateral arrangements all linked by the inclusion of an unconditional MFN clause. This unconditional MFN set the stage for multilateral free trade in Europe. By 1908, Britain had MFN agreements with 46 countries, Germany with 30 countries, and France with more than 20 countries.

But with the outbreak of World War I in August 1914, trade restrictions and exchange controls were rapidly instituted throughout Europe to protect national interests. At the Allied Economic Conference in 1916, Britain, France, and Italy agreed to cooperate on their respective commercial policies after the war, but ruled out the extension of the MFN clause to Germany and other wartime opponents. After the war, however, UK did not return to its free trade policy. The United States also raised its import tariffs substantially.

14.2.2 Post–World War and Contemporary Regionalism

The post–World War period has two distinct phases of regionalism, which have been characterized by Ethier (2011) as *old* and *contemporary* regionalism. He marks RTAs signed and in force during the 1960s and 1970s as old regionalism and RTAs signed since 1990 as contemporary regionalism. The distinction between the two has been made in three ways. First, contemporary regionalism has grown at a time when multilateral liberalization of trade in manufactured goods among industrial countries is much more complete than it was in the 1970s. Second, during the late 1980s, many developing and less developed countries had begun their economic reforms, particularly trade policy reforms. Third, foreign direct investment is much more prominent now than in the days of old regionalism, and as explained later, this has been one of the main drivers of contemporary regionalism. There is now much more *fragmentation* of the production process, with different stages of the production of a final good being performed in different countries.

What Ethier further observes is that contemporary regionalism often involves one or more small countries linking up with a large country. It is usually the small partner that liberalizes the trade regime more whereas trade concessions on the part of the larger partner have been mostly modest. In general, contemporary regionalism involves deep integration. RTAs do not just aim at reduction or elimination of trade barriers, but also at harmonization of other broader economic policies. Finally, contemporary regional arrangements are mostly geographically regional. That is, the participants are neighbours. In sum, to quote Ethier (2011: 124), 'regional integration now usually involves reform-minded small countries "purchasing," with moderate trade concessions, links with a large, neighboring country that involve "deep" integration but that confer relatively minor trade advantages'.

14.3 REGIONAL TRADING AGREEMENTS: TRENDS, CAUSES, AND EFFECTS

RTAs have proliferated phenomenally during the last two decades. But the distribution of these RTAs has been highly uneven both across countries, within continents and across continents. On the other hand, RTAs are formed among a group of countries for a variety of reasons, both economic and political. Among economic reasons, national welfare considerations were perhaps the most important motive for regionalism in the pre–World War II era. But political reasons were the more dominant force for regionalism in the immediate post–World War II period, at least for the formation of the European Economic Community as discussed above. Contemporary regionalism, on the other hand, is driven more by economic reasons other than national welfare as argued by Wilfred Ethier (2011). To understand these different causes, however, we have to first learn about the perceived benefits of forming an RTA. We begin with a summary view of the trends and composition of RTAs across the globe and then discuss the perceived benefits from an RTA.

14.3.1 Growth, Composition, and Distribution of RTAs

According to notifications in WTO, the number of *active* RTAs had shot up to 230 by the end of 2003 from a mere 50 in 1992. The growth of RTAs slowed down thereafter, and yet by the end of the last decade the number of RTAs was more than five times what we had in 1992. Table 14.1 shows the composition of these active RTAs till the end of 2010 into FTAs, CUs, and economic integration agreements (EIAs). EIAs are regional trade arrangements that cover service trade in addition to goods trade.

Columns 2–5 in Table 14.1 indicate the WTO rule under which a particular RTA is formed by member countries. The Enabling Clause refers to the 1979 General Agreement on Tariffs and Trade (GATT) decision allowing preferential trade in goods among developing countries. It has continued to apply as part of GATT 1994 under the WTO. Article V of GATS governs the conclusion of RTAs in the area of trade in services, for both developed and developing countries. On the other hand, paragraphs 4 to 10 of Article XXIV of GATT provide for the formation and operation of customs unions and free-trade areas covering trade in goods.

Table 14.1 Composition of RTAs by Type

	Enabling Clause	GATS Article V	GATT Article XXIV	Grand Total
Customs Union (CU)	8		9	17
Economic Integration Agreement (EIA)		89		89
Free Trade Agreement (FTA)	12		170	182
Grand total	20	89	179	288

Source: Compiled from the WTO website (www.wto.org).

The number of FTAs negotiated by countries, however, differs significantly from one region to another. As noted by Faber and Acharyya (2010), till 2010 a majority of the countries had

FTAs negotiated with trading partners ranging from 12 to 15. Figure 14.2 illustrates the distribution of the number of FTAs concluded by countries. For example, nearly 30 countries had concluded 12 FTAs each and 25 countries had concluded 15 FTAs each.

Thus, FTAs have not been uniform across all countries. Neither has the number of RTAs signed by countries been uniform across different continents. Whereas signing FTAs had been rather rampant among the African countries in the 1970s, many of which have now become inactive, growth in the number of FTAs signed by Asian countries has been a more recent phenomenon of the 1990s. So not only has the number of FTAs being signed grown rapidly after 1990, the distribution of these RTAs has also been highly uneven across countries and continents.

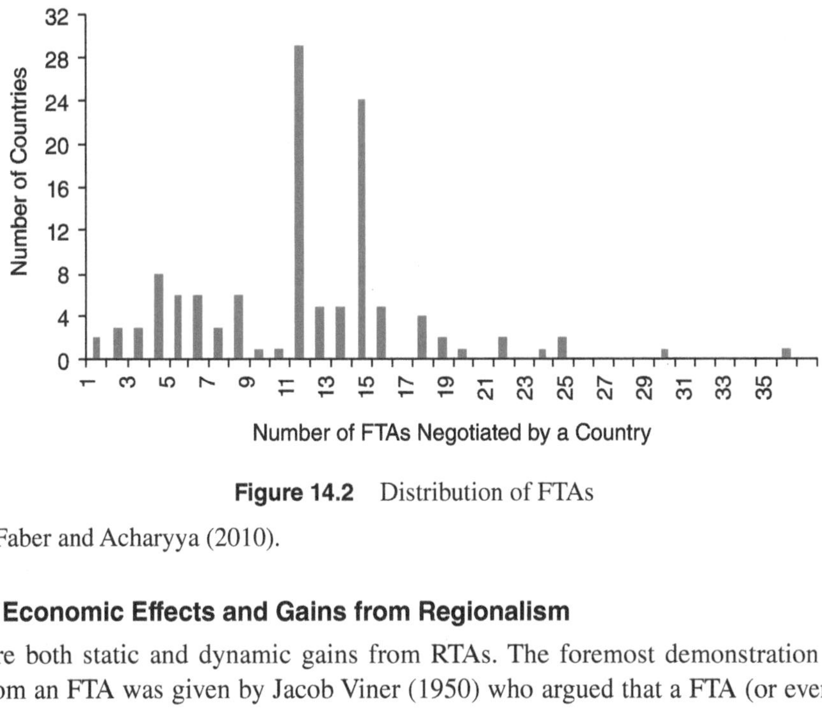

Figure 14.2 Distribution of FTAs

Source: Faber and Acharyya (2010).

14.3.2 Economic Effects and Gains from Regionalism

There are both static and dynamic gains from RTAs. The foremost demonstration of static gains from an FTA was given by Jacob Viner (1950) who argued that a FTA (or even a PTA) has two primary effects. It increases or *creates* trade among member countries as the tariffs on their mutual trade are abolished (or lowered in the case of a PTA). This is what Viner termed the *trade creation* effect of an FTA. At the same time, an FTA diverts trade from non-member countries to member countries. Lower tariffs on imports from member countries make them a relatively cheaper source of imports than non-member countries. Thus, goods previously imported from non-member countries may now be diverted to imports from member countries. This is Viner's *trade diversion* effect. Viner argued that whereas trade creation is good for member countries, trade diversion is necessarily bad. The beneficial effect of an FTA through trade creation among small countries is easily comprehensible. For small countries, tariffs are necessarily sub-optimal as we have learnt from our earlier discussion. Tariffs lower the volume of trade only, without any TOT effect for small countries. Thus, abolition of tariffs on mutual trade under the formation of an FTA (or tariff reductions on mutual trade under the formation of a PTA) raises the volume of trade among members and raises the welfare of *all* the member countries.

When member countries are large, abolition of tariffs and forming an FTA may not be welfare improving for *all* because of the TOT effect. Yet, free trade in the region raises the aggregate welfare of the region as a whole so that there is scope for compensating countries that lose through TOT deterioration after the formation of an FTA. This can be understood by recalling the tariff retaliation equilibrium discussed earlier in a two-country world economy reproduced below. The free trade regional equilibrium is at point E_{FTA}. The pair of TICs tangent to each other (and to the TOT line OE_{FTA}) indicates the welfare levels that can be attained by the two countries through FTA formation. The pre-FTA situation can be thought of as the non-cooperative tariff-equilibrium attained at the trade bundle at which the welfare reaction loci intersect each other. For such a pre-FTA equilibrium attained for trade bundle R, both countries unambiguously gain from the FTA.

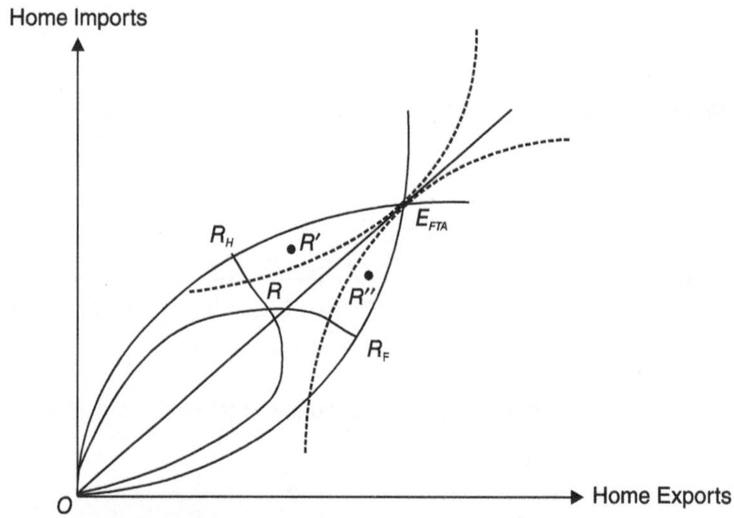

Figure 14.3 Gains from FTA for Large Partners

On the other hand, if one of the countries experienced welfare increase at the pre-FTA non-cooperative tariff-equilibrium (such as for trade bundle R' or R''), FTA formation will lower its welfare unambiguously. But the other country will gain from FTA formation substantially enough to make it possible to compensate the losing country through side payments.

The trade diversion effect of an FTA, on the other hand, can be illustrated with a simple example. Suppose there are three countries in a region: *A*, *B*, and *D*. Country *A* is completely specialized in textiles whereas countries *B* and *D* are completely specialized in computers. Country *D* is an efficient producer of computers in the sense that $P_Y^D < P_Y^B$. Suppose the government of country *A* had imposed tariff at the rate *t* regardless of whether computers are imported from *B* or *D*. Thus, initially computers were imported from country *D* by country *A* because $(1+t)P_Y^D < (1+t)P_Y^B$. Now in case of trade diversion, computers are imported from country *B* instead of from country *D* and this happens if after an FTA is formed between countries *A* and *B* the tariff-inclusive price of imports from country *D* is higher than the price of imports from the FTA partner country *B*: $(1+t)P_Y^D > P_Y^B$. To Viner this was bad because FTA between *A* and *B* replaces an efficient source of supply (country *D* in this example) by an inefficient source of supply. However, what he ignored is the gain for consumers from the lower price of computers imported. Thus, as if the FTA improves country *A*'s TOT. This led to a controversy between Richard Lipsey and Jagdish Bhagwati over why Viner overlooked the possibility of a TOT gain for importing country *A*. Lipsey interpreted Viner's numerical illustration of welfare decline through trade diversion as a case where textiles and computers are consumed in a fixed proportion. Bhagwati, on the other hand, was of the opinion that Viner meant fixed volume of import of computers. For more reflections on this debate, one may refer to Bhagwati et al. (1998).

The new trade theories, on the other hand, suggest that there are other sources of welfare gains from forming an FTA and consequently regional free trade. Recalling Krugman's love for the variety approach to international trade, FTA should increase product variety and real wages. This is due to the larger demand for varieties that integrated markets generate and economies of scale that it enables to achieve for the firms as explained earlier.

Besides these static gains from FTA, larger markets may also increase the rate of product innovations and growth of member countries. Adam Smith emphasized on larger markets through free trade as a source of productivity gain because larger markets enable large-scale production through division of labour, and division of labour raises the productivity of workers. Endogenous growth theories developed in the 1980s, on the other hand, argue that larger markets make innovations and development of new products more profitable. We will learn more about these growth effects in Chapter 15.

The primary gain from forming a customs union, on the other hand, arises from market power in international trade that the union confers upon its smaller member countries vis-à-vis non-member countries. For these small members, forming a customs union thus seems to be beneficial on this account. The usually higher external tariff also raises the aggregate welfare of union members as a whole by the optimum tariff argument. At the same time, there can be aggregate welfare losses from forming a customs union due to its trade diversion effect. If the countries had already formed a FTA, then further integration into a customs union will have no trade creation effect. But, there may still be trade diversion because of the common, and usually higher, external tariff imposed on imports from the rest of the world. However, as Krugman (1993) shows, welfare loss from the trade diversion effect of a customs union is relatively weak so that, overall, countries may gain.

The gain from forming a common market is conceived in the literature primarily in terms of free movement of factors within the region and consequent equalization of wages. However, as we have learnt earlier, if free commodity trade among member countries due to an FTA being formed at the earlier stage of cooperation equalized factor prices within the region, there will be no scope for such gains. There can still be other substantial gains through forming a common market arising from smaller transaction costs (in terms of visa and other travel documents) for movement of people within the region. This will facilitate service trade where the service provider himself must move from his native country to the service importing country to deliver the service such as doctors and surgeons in case of health services. We will return to this aspect in Chapter 18.

Box 14.1 Empirical Estimate of Gains from FTAs

Brown et al. (2002) estimated the gains from RTAs for Japan and the United States using a computable general equilibrium model. They considered three RTA expansions to estimate the welfare effects of a RTA: the Asia Pacific Economic (APEC) forum that involves both the United States and Japan, an ASEAN Plus 3 FTA that involves Japan, and an expansion of NAFTA to include Chile. In their simulation results they found almost no evidence of trade diversion for members due to the bilateral removal of APEC trade barriers and ASEAN Plus 3 trade barriers. But in case of the NAFTA-Chile FTA, there is some evidence of trade diversion. On the other hand, separate bilateral FTAs by Japan with Singapore, Mexico, Chile, and Korea and by the United States with Chile, Singapore, and Korea will have small but positive welfare effects on partner countries. There will also be significant trade diversion and detrimental welfare effects on some non-member countries for these bilateral FTAs. Kiyoto (2006), on the other hand, finds that the effects of regional FTAs are larger than those of bilateral FTAs. Moreover, among FTA member countries, the smaller member countries have larger benefits than the larger members. But the effects of multilateral free trade are significantly larger than those of bilateral and regional FTAs.

But when FPE does not hold even after free commodity trade equalizes commodity prices across countries for reasons spelled out earlier, formation of a common market that allows free movement of factors within the region will be unambiguously welfare improving. This is illustrated in Figure 14.4 where the loci representing the value of the marginal productivity curve for labour in the two countries are drawn. To illustrate in the simplest possible way, suppose labour is the only factor of production in both home and foreign countries which had earlier formed an FTA. Also suppose, despite abolition of all commodity trade barriers, wages were not equalized. This may be because, among other things, the countries have different production technologies. Given the total labour supply in the home country as OL_0 and that in the foreign country as O^*L_0 the equilibrium wages before forming the common market were w and w^* respectively. After the formation of a common market between these countries, migration within the region reallocates labour across the countries at L_C and equalizes the wages at w_C. Larger availability of labour in the home country raises the value of the output there as indicated by the area under the VMP_L curve: the area hcL_CL_0. But emigration of labour from the foreign country lowers the aggregate value of output there by the area cfL_CL_0. Since before the formation of a common market the value of marginal productivity of labour was higher in the home country, the output increase there will be larger than the output decline in the foreign country. Thus, through common market formation and labour migration the total value of output in the region increases by the triangular area *hcf*. This means, if the foreign country is compensated by the home country for its loss from emigration, then it is acceptable to both the countries.

Apart from this static welfare gain for the region *as a whole*, quite a few dynamic gains are also realized primarily through restructuring and agglomeration of industries. Removal of border restrictions on investment allows industries in different member countries to relocate

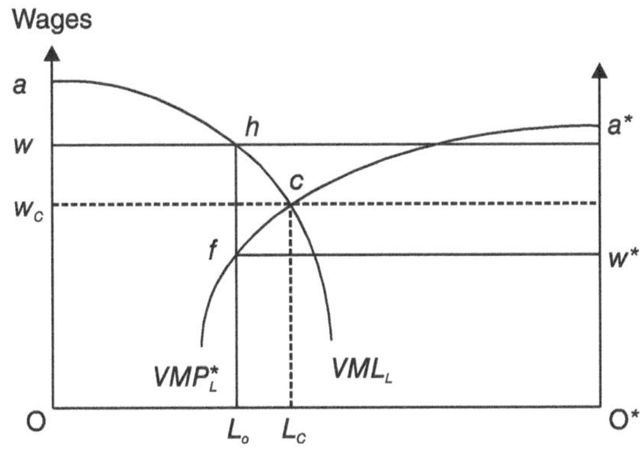

Figure 14.4 Gains from Labour Migration under Common Market

their plants in a particular region to exploit locational advantages. Consequent agglomerations also reduce transaction costs between the firms and entail external economies.

14.3.3 Why Are RTAs Formed?

Having learnt the effects and gains from forming an RTA, we can now answer the question why countries form RTAs in the first place. As mentioned earlier, there may be both economic and political reasons for this. Among the economic reasons one plausible motive is the gain in social welfare through the formation of a RTA. That is, a simple answer to the question *why* (and when) countries may prefer to form a RTA among them is that it confers upon them welfare gains. From the above discussions of economic gains, however, it appears that not always *all* countries are better off through the formation of a RTA. But if the aggregate welfare of the union as a whole increases then there is scope for compensating loser countries through side payments to make the RTA a Pareto superior trade arrangement.

There may also be purely *strategic reasons* for forming an RTA. First is the reciprocated market access argument. If a country unilaterally liberalizes its imports, it essentially provides market access to all exporting nations, but does not necessarily gain markets for its own exporters in those countries. Moreover, in not all those markets the unilaterally liberalizing country may have comparative advantage vis-à-vis other exporting countries and thus export potential. Instead, a bilateral or regional agreement can ensure reciprocated access to relevant export markets. At the same time liberalization of imports from within the region puts the domestic import-competing industries under less intense foreign competition than unilateral trade liberalization does.

The second strategic reason for forming an RTA is to link non-trade issues like environmental standards, labour standards, and TRIPS with trade gains that an RTA brings about. This is highly relevant when coordination and cooperation among the countries on these non-trade issues are required, but which are often difficult to achieve without attaching any potential economic loss in the event that a country defects from the coordinated and cooperative agreement. Examples of this strategic linking of non-trade issues with trade gains to be realized through RTAs are growing. As mentioned earlier, the United States has now linked these issues by requiring a potential FTA partner to commit to TRIPS and certain environmental standards.

The issue of trans-boundary pollution—pollution that is transported from the country of origin to another country through air (such as CO_2 emissions) and water—involving the United States and Mexico were linked to NAFTA agreements to free trade between these two countries. Similarly, MERCOSUR is also working on linking trade liberalization and environmental issues. On the other hand, patent protection, particularly in health drugs and medicines, have become a major hurdle in successful trade negotiations between the EU and India. Whereas India prefers to separate trade and the non-trade issues, the EU has so far taken a hard line in linking FTA gains with patent protection.

Apart from these welfare and strategic motives, many of the recent RTAs between the North–South (or developed–developing) countries have been aimed at *locking in* the Southern partner's economic reforms and stimulating inflows of foreign direct investment (FDI). Ethier (2011), for example, argues that *contemporary* regionalism among the small Asian countries and their larger trade partners has grown simply because of competition among these small countries to attract FDI from their larger developed-country trade partners. The developing countries foresee FDI as a key to success and growth (arguably though as we will elaborate in Chapter 16) as it brings with it better technology. Firms in developed countries, on the other hand, like to invest in the trade-reforming developing countries, because of the latter's comparative advantages. But they have many options about where to invest because there are many reformers in Asia, particularly in East Asia, with fairly similar economic characteristics. At the same time, because of the lumpiness of investment, firms like to invest only in one or two reforming countries. Thus, unilateral trade reforms by similar developing countries per se cannot attract FDI. Moreover, unilateral trade reforms are uncertain as it is likely that trade reforms may be reverted if such reforms are not successful. This reversal of trade reforms did happen in many Latin American countries in the late 1970s and 1980s. In such a context, a trade agreement between a developing country and a developed country creates a small and marginal but significant advantage for the developing country. Through bilateral or regional agreements it *commits* itself to trade and other economic reforms to the advantage of the developed-country partner. The preference and trade concessions granted by the developed-country partner, on the other hand, are often very marginal. But this small preference differentiates the developing-country partner from other similar developing countries in a significant way for firms in the developed-country partner that are looking out for

Box 14.2 Reciprocity Duties Act

The strategic motive was also evident in regionalism practised in late eighteenth and early nineteenth centuries. In early nineteenth century, for example, the UK attempted to negotiate reciprocal agreements with foreign governments for the most favoured nation (MFN) treatment for goods and shipping through its Reciprocity of Duties Act (1823). It kept external tariffs deliberately high on sugar, coffee, wines, and spirits simply to retain the bargaining power vis-à-vis European countries for negotiations with them. This helped initially but not in the long run. Soon the bargaining motive for setting differential tariffs was abandoned and external tariffs were applied without discrimination leaving other European countries free to determine their own tariff policies in 1846.

destinations for their foreign investments. Thus, a bilateral or regional agreement attracts all such investment from the developed-country partner. According to Ethier (2011) this explains why reforming countries enter into regional trade arrangements even though they typically receive only small trade concessions from their bigger partners. It is not to expand exports greatly to their partners and realize static welfare gains, but to compete with other *similar* countries for direct investment.

Besides these economic motives, internal political forces in a country also offer a significant explanation for preference for regional trade arrangements. In an earlier chapter we had discussed the political risk theory and lobbying groups in determining the trade policy choice of a democratic government. By similar logic, we can explain why RTAs are formed. Grossman and Helpman (1995) and Baldwin (2006), for example, argue that if RTAs provide large consumer benefits, governments can ignore the lobbies against RTAs. On the other hand, by the Domino theory, export sectors put pressure on governments to become members of an expanding RTA because reciprocated trade concessions through RTAs will enable them to sell more in the partner country at higher prices (Baldwin 2006). If the export lobby is stronger, its support and lobbying are expected to counter the resistance of import-competing groups in both trade creating and diverting sectors.

This argument can be explained in terms of Baldwin's (2006) *politically optimum* tariff. As we have learnt earlier, an import tariff raises the surplus for domestic producers of the import-competing good. The demand for protection thus rises with the level of import tariff. The cost of protection for the government, on the other hand, is the consequent efficiency or welfare loss. For a large country, welfare losses arise (and monotonically increase with the tariff rate) beyond the economically optimum, or welfare maximizing, tariff rate. Thus, the cost of tariff rises, which means the supply curve for protection is upward sloping as shown in Figure 14.5. The *unilaterally chosen* politically optimum tariff is thus given by the level of tariff t_{UL}, which is larger than the economically optimum tariff.

Now consider a preferential trading arrangement formed by two neighbouring countries whereby they reciprocate each other in lowering tariffs on their mutual trade. Suppose these countries practice open regionalism and announce reciprocated tariff reductions extended to any other potential member country. This will immediately increase the stake of the exporters in a non-member country in the region, because imports of member countries will now be diverted away from the exporters in the non-member country. This raises the cost of protection in the non-member country and the (regionally) politically optimum tariff falls to the level t_{RL}. Thus, the non-member country will now prefer to join the PTA because it is politically optimum to lower its tariff rate in reciprocation for similar tariff reductions and market access for its exporters by member countries.

This argument also builds the stage for expanding an existing PTA (or RTA in general) and offers a potential explanation for the argument that RTAs are actually stepping stones to multilateralism and global free trade. We will return to this aspect shortly.

RTAs may also be negotiated among neighbouring countries to mitigate potential political and military conflict among them. This had been one of the primary motives for initiating European integration in the immediate post–World War II years (see Box 14.3). A similar idea of achieving political stability and mitigating military conflict in the South Asian region through economic cooperation has largely motivated SAARC and the proposed SAFTA. In

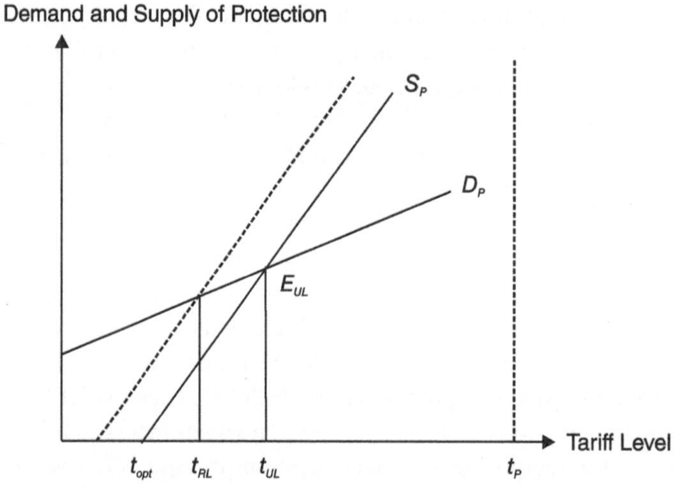

Figure 14.5 RTA and Politically Optimum Tariff

fact, if these efforts are successful, political stability will be the biggest gain for countries in this region, which is perhaps more important and significant than the trade and economic gains that such economic cooperation may lead to.

14.4 MULTILATERALISM IN THE POST-WTO ERA AND GLOBAL FREE TRADE

The essential idea of multilateral trade negotiations (MTNs) is to achieve global free trade among GATT members. MTN was initiated under GATT till the WTO replaced it in 1995. A round of multilateral trade negotiations was conducted during the Doha Development Agenda round. MTN was required primary for the following reason. In a distortion free world economy, multilateral free trade is globally efficient. But at the same time, there are incentives for countries, particularly large countries, to unilaterally restrict trade. Moreover, unilateral trade liberalization is not necessarily an optimal policy even for a small country as it may not induce reciprocation on the part of trading partners. As such, many countries adhered to inward-looking development strategies based on the infant industry argument and had their share of success during the 1970s and 1980s. These resulted in a restricted and Pareto inefficient world trading system.

But the slow progress in MTN and the failure of the Doha Development Round of negotiations to reach any consensus on trade and non-trade concessions led countries to negotiate trade agreements bilaterally and regionally. In fact, countries in Europe and America have not committed themselves unilaterally to negotiations in WTO rounds of talks on trade reforms and multilateral free trade. Even the World Bank in its report in 2001 recognized that higher than average tariff rates are imposed on major export products of developing countries like food and beverages, fruits, vegetables, textiles, clothing, and footwear. In most of the cases tariff peaks are in the range of 100–250 per cent. Tariff escalation, that is, tariff rates rising with the level of processing undergone along the vertical chain of production, are especially damaging for developing countries. They discourage diversification. Agricultural trade has been another area where historically subsidies to local farmers and preferential market access to developing countries provided by the Northern governments are in place. They stand tall even during the globalization era. In 2000, for example, rich countries subsidized their farmers five times the value of annual aid flows to developing countries.

This partly explains the upsurge in the number of RTAs and the growth in contemporary regionalism after 1990. However, the question still remains whether it is the quest for multilateral free trade that alone motivates countries to have regional agreements. Along with it has surfaced the related issue of whether regionalism is a stepping stone or a stumbling block to multilateralism.

14.4.1 From Regionalism to Multilateralism?

At the outset, economic motives behind regionalism do not necessarily suggest that it is a stepping stone to multilateral or global free trade. As we have elaborated above, RTAs are inherently discriminatory and protectionist trade practices, and thus are in contradiction with the principle of globalization and trade liberalization. Arguably the most important reason for forming an RTA is to gain a bargaining power vis-à-vis the countries outside the trading bloc through a unified external tariff.

Box 14.3 Political–Economic Factors in the Formation of the EU

After World War II, the economic motive for European economic integration rested on the argument that larger markets would promote competition and lead to higher productivity and standard of living. There were equally dominant political motives. First, it was believed that only a supra-national organization could eliminate the threat of war between the European countries. Second, was the view that if the European nations were to dominate world affairs, they must have at their command resources comparable to those of the United States. Soon, economic and political viewpoints merged as European countries realized that economic cooperation can mitigate conflicts between them and that economic strength is the basis of political and military power.

Robert Schuman's proposal to integrate of French and German coal and steel industries was essentially intended to monitor the German industry, which was reviving rapidly, since coal and steel are very important for many modern industries, especially the armaments industry. To allay fears of German militancy, West Germany immediately signed on and was soon joined by the Benelux nations and Italy. But the United Kingdom's non-participation marked the beginning of an internal conflict. The second major political-economic conflict was experienced during the accession of less developed agriculture-based Mediterranean countries—Greece in 1981, then Spain and Portugal in 1986. Inclusion of these countries meant that a large percentage of funds that the EU earmarked to support agriculture within the community would have to be redirected to the new members. This alarmed Ireland, who feared that its own share of these funds would be reduced.

Throughout the development of EU, there had been potential conflicts among the nations over the issue of supra-nationalism versus inter-governmentalism. Despite acceptance of the supra-national principle, national governments had been reluctant to cede all control in politically sensitive areas such as foreign policy and judicial affairs to EU institutions.

Box 14.4 The Doha Development Round

The Doha Development Round or Doha Development Agenda (DDA) is the current trade-negotiation round of WTO, which commenced at the WTO's Fourth Ministerial Conference in Doha, Qatar in November 2001. It was intended to be completed by 2004. But, as of now, talks have stalled over a host of contentious issues like agricultural subsidy, industrial tariffs and non-tariff barriers, services, and trade remedies. The most significant differences are between the developed nations, particularly EU, the US, and Japan, and major developing countries represented mainly by Brazil, China, India, South Korea, and South Africa. There is also a bone of contention between EU and the United States over their maintenance of agricultural subsidies. More specifically, three key issues have emerged: the United States to further reduce agricultural subsidies, EU to further reduce agricultural tariffs, and the industrial developing countries, particularly Brazil and India, to further lower tariffs and offer more liberalization in services trade. However, talks between the key Group of 6 countries—EU, the United States, Brazil, India, Australia, and Japan—failed to reach any consensus on these issues. As a result, the Doha Round was suspended at the end of July 2006.

Moreover, contemporary bilateralism and regionalism have not incorporated the unconditional MFN clause that spelled the success of achieving free trade throughout Europe via bilateralism in the pre-war period (Irwin 1993). This again takes us back to the view that it is the motive of achieving a liberal trade order *within* a small region and bargaining power vis-à-vis the rest of the world that drove countries to form RTAs in the post-war era. For example, more than two-third of EU's merchandise trade has been on an *in-house* preferential basis.

Recent developments in the theory of formation, size, and enlargement of RTAs also do not support the global free trade motive underlying the practice of regionalism. Levy (1995) and Krishna (1996) argue that under the *unanimous regionalism* rule, interests of the members confront the enlargement of a RTB. Similarly, Bloch (1996) demonstrated that a global trading bloc is not the optimal union structure. On the other hand, there are gains for members of an RTA only when their trading bloc merges with a larger or equal-sized RTB (Yi 1996). This means that there will be no incentive for a larger union to merge with a smaller union. All these analyses, therefore, do not argue strongly in favour of RTAs being stepping stones to global free trade under unanimous regionalism. While this optimism may be valid under *open regionalism* similar to the unconditional MFN clause of the late nineteenth century, such a rule is not followed in principle as well as in practice by member countries as we have mentioned earlier. Thus, bilateral or regional trade arrangements despite expediting free trade within a region have the risks of deteriorating into exclusionary, trade-diverting blocs that may possibly bring more harm than betterment to the world trading system.

Moreover, regional agreements have often overlapped leading to what Jagdish Bhagwati calls the spaghetti bowl effect, which is certainly not the best way of organizing world trade. However, Baldwin (2006) argues that political economy forces may actually transform spaghetti bowls into building blocks through Juggernaut and Domino effects. His argument can be summarized as follows. The starting point of the Juggernaut Effect is the unilaterally chosen politically optimum tariff illustrated in Figure 14.5. Given such a politically optimum tariff rate, consider an announcement of MTN based on the principle of reciprocity. Exporting firms in each country now become opponents of trade protection because a lower protection at home will imply greater market access in the foreign country under reciprocation. Thus, the announcement of a MTN raises the cost of protection in each country and shifts the supply curve to the left. MTN tariff at the new equilibrium is thus lower, That is, each nation finds it politically optimal to cut tariffs to some extent. This is the first part of the juggernaut logic.

The next element of the Juggernaut Effect arises from the size of domestic import-competing sectors. If there are fixed entry costs, a higher protection and hence a higher domestic price will allow a larger number of import-competing firms to survive at the zero-profit equilibrium. This positive relationship between the number of firms under free entry and the level of tariff is represented by the locus *FE* in Figure 14.6. On the other hand, a larger number of domestic import-competing firms mean that demand for protection will be larger as well resulting in a higher unilaterally chosen politically optimal tariff. This is represented by the PO_{UL} locus. Now as the MTN announcement lowers the politically optimum tariff at the initial size of the import-competing sectors, the PO_{UL} locus shifts down to PO_{MTN}. This alters the relative sizes of the import-competing sectors leading to a dynamics of adjustment in the political market and thus lowering the tariff rate. Thus, the tariff rate falls more than the initial decline (measured by the vertical distance between the PO_{UL} and PO_{MTN} loci) after MTN under reciprocation.

The Domino theory, on the other hand, starts with a political economy model of membership of a nation in an existing RTA. The key element here is the relative size of the export sectors. The decision of a nation to join a PTA is determined by a domestic political equilibrium that balances pro-membership forces (the export sectors) and anti-membership forces (import-competing sectors). Suppose at the initial political equilibrium, the outside nations decided against joining the RTA. Consider now a deepening of the existing RTA's integration. In non-member nations, exporters now have a greater stake in membership because they

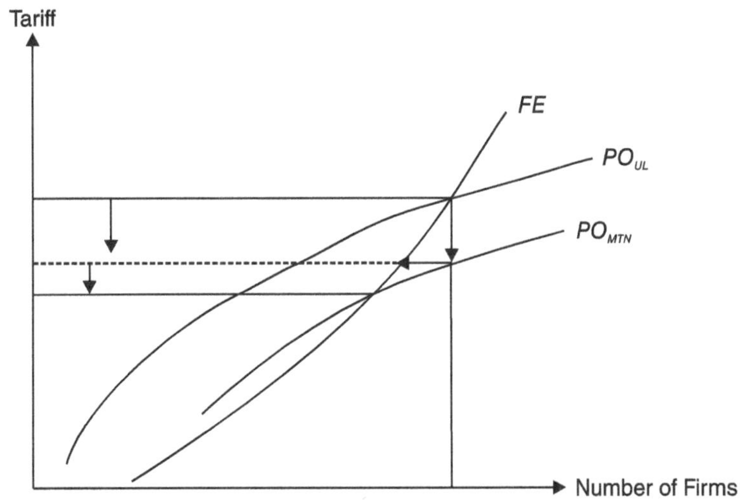

Figure 14.6 MTN and the Juggernaut Effect

will face larger discrimination if their nations stay out and larger gains if they join. Anti-membership forces (import-competing firms) also get strengthened because joining a more integrated RTA calls for larger market access in their own countries and thus more intensified import competition. But if the export sectors are larger than the import-competing sectors, and if political power is directly linked to the size of a sector, then we can expect pro-membership forces to grow faster than anti-membership forces. Thus, the nations who were almost politically indifferent to joining the PTA, will jump to the pro-joiner camp. This triggers a subsequent Domino Effect on the remaining outside nations. Their stakes now become even larger so that the within-nation pro-membership forces get even stronger. More nations will thus join and there will be successive enlargement of the RTA.

While this Domino theory is appealing and suggests that RTAs are stepping stones to global free trade, there is one important caveat to this argument. The Domino theory neglects the supply side of membership, that is, whether existing members will allow applicants to join the RTA. Essentially, the Domino theory seems to be based on the open regionalism rule, which is hardly practised as we have mentioned earlier.

SUMMARY POINTS

- Jacob Viner (1950) conceived five different and successively higher stages of regional economic cooperation: preferential trading arrangements (PTA), free trade areas (FTAs), customs union (CU), common market (CM), and economic and monetary union (EMU).
- EU offers an interesting case study of the political and economic forces that contributed to its evolution through successive stages of economic cooperation and integration.
- Two supra-national economic organizations marked such an early stage of economic integration in Europe: the 1958 BENELUX Treaty establishing the customs union between Belgium, the Netherlands, and Luxembourg as an economic union, and the European Coal and Steel Community (ECSC) signed in 1951.
- An RTA can have a principle of either open regionalism or unanimous regionalism. The rule of open regionalism is, however, hardly followed in principle as well as in practice by member countries. EU and the United States follow seemingly, but not effectively, open regionalism rules.
- RTAs differ in their scope and coverage with respect to policies regarding trade in goods and services. Many RTAs exclude agriculture as well as services from their coverage.
- Contemporary regionalism often involves one or more small countries linking up with a large country. It is usually the small partner that liberalizes the trade regime more whereas trade concessions on the part of the larger partner have been mostly modest.
- An FTA creates as well as diverts trade. According to Viner, the trade creation effect is welfare improving whereas the trade diversion effect is welfare reducing for member countries. Besides these static gains and losses from FTA, larger markets may also increase the rate of product innovations and growth of member countries.

- The primary gain from forming a CU arises from the market power in international trade that the union confers upon its smaller member countries vis-à-vis non-member countries.
- Apart from welfare motives, there may be purely *strategic reasons* for forming an RTA. First is the reciprocated market access argument. The second strategic reason is to link non-trade issues like environmental standards, labour standards, and TRIPS with trade gains that an RTA brings about.
- Contemporary regionalism (which we define below) among small Asian countries and their larger trade partners has grown simply because of the competition among these small countries to attract FDI from their larger developed-country trade partners.
- Contemporary bilateralism and regionalism have not incorporated the unconditional MFN clause that spelled the success of achieving multilateral free trade throughout Europe via bilateralism in the pre-war period. Recent developments in the theory of formation, size, and enlargement of RTAs also do not support the global free trade motive underlying the practice of regionalism.

KEYWORDS

- **Regional trade arrangement** (RTA) is a regional grouping among a few countries on the basis of reciprocated and coordinated trade policies vis-à-vis themselves and the rest of the world.
- **Free trade area** (FTA) is formed by two or more countries when they abolish all tariff and non-tariff barriers on their mutual trade.
- **Customs union** (CU) helps member countries, in addition to fulfilling the requirements of an FTA, impose a common external tariff on imports from the rest of the world.
- **BENELUX** is the economic union formed by Belgium, the Netherlands, and Luxembourg after their 1958 BENELUX Treaty.
- **Open regionalism** allows a potential member to join an existing RTA even without the consent of existing members.
- **Unanimous regionalism** is an arrangement where the member countries must unanimously agree upon the accession of a new member.
- **Economic Integration Agreements** (EIAs) are regional trade arrangements that cover service trade in addition to goods trade.
- **Enabling clause** refers to the 1979-GATT decision that allows preferential trade in goods among developing countries.
- **Trade diversion** Forming an FTA leads to trade diversion if the goods previously imported by a member country from non-member countries are now imported from other member countries.

(*contd*)

Keywords (*contd*)

- **Most favoured nation (MFN)** is a non-discriminatory trade policy commitment offered by one country to another on a reciprocal basis. Both countries apply the lowest import-duty and quota-restrictions on imports from each other that they apply on similar imports from any other country. Under Article I of GATT, all signatory states must extend this treatment to one another. But common markets, customs unions, and free trade areas are exempt from MFN provisions.
- **Rounds of multilateral trade negotiations** under GATT:
 1st Round: Geneva Tariff Conference, 1947
 2nd Round: Annecy Tariff Conference, 1949
 3rd Round: Torquay Tariff Conference, 1950–51
 4th Round: Geneva Tariff Conference, 1955–56
 5th Round: Dillon Round, 1960–61
 6th Round: Kennedy Round, 1963–67
 7th Round: Tokyo Round, 1973–79
 8th Round: Uruguay Round, 1986–94

EXERCISES

1. Distinguish between the trade creation and trade diversion effects of an FTA. Is trade diversion necessarily bad as claimed by Jacob Viner?
2. How is contemporary regionalism different in its nature and characteristics from the earlier regionalism?
3. Before an FTA agreement with Sri Lanka, India was importing garments from Bangladesh where the supply price of garments was 60 per unit, compared to the supply price of 70 per unit in Sri Lanka. India had imposed a uniform tariff of 40 per cent on imports of garments regardless of from where garments are imported.
   (a) Does the FTA agreement with Sri Lanka divert imports of garments by India?
   (b) If India's import demand for garments is p = 1000 – 5g, how much trade (or imports) is created and how much is diverted, if at all?
   (c) Calculate the gains or losses for India from the FTA agreement.
4. Consider two small countries A and B in a perfectly competitive world, producing only their respective export goods *X* and *Y* using labour as the only input. The production technologies for the two goods are $X = 40\sqrt{L_A}$ and $Y = 30\sqrt{L_B}$ respectively. The world prices of these goods are exogenously given. Good *X* is taken as the numeraire and the price of *Y* (expressed in terms of *X*) is 4 per unit:
   (a) If $L_A = 100$ and $L_B = 400$, find out the aggregate value of production and (real) wages in each country.

(b) If these countries form a common market whereby they allow labour migration within the common market, how many workers will migrate from one country to the other? What will be the real wage?

(c) Do both countries gain in terms of the aggregate value of output? Calculate the gains or losses.

5. Do you think that the politically optimum tariff will be smaller for a small country than for a large country? Justify your answer.
6. What are the distinguishing features of contemporary regionalism?
7. What do you think was the primary reason for bilateral agreements leading to multilateral free trade in Europe in the nineteenth century? Why are economists sceptical about attaining the same through bilateralism and regionalism in contemporary times?
8. What are the political economy forces that may potentially transform spaghetti bowls of regionalism into building blocks for multilateral free trade? On what crucial assumption does this logic depend?

SUGGESTED READING

Bhagwati, J.N., A. Panagariya, and T.N. Srinivasan (1998). *Lectures on International Trade*. Cambridge, MA: MIT Press.

ADVANCED READING

Baldwin, R. (2006). 'Multilateralizing Regionalism: Spaghetti Bowls as Building Blocs on the Path to Global Free Trade', *The World Economy*, 29(11): 1451–1518.

Bloch, F. (1996). 'Sequential Formation of Coalitions with Fixed Payoff Divisions', *Games and Economic Behaviour*, 14: 90–123.

Brown, D.K., A.V. Deardorff, and R.M. Stern (2002). 'Multilateral, Regional, and Bilateral Trade-Policy Options for the United States and Japan', Discussion Paper No. 490, School of Public Policy, Ann Arbour: The University of Michigan.

Crawford, J. and S. Laird (2000). 'Regional Trade Agreements and the WTO', Working Paper No. 00/03, Centre for Research in Economic Development and International Trade, University of Nottingham.

Ethier, W. (2011). 'Contemporary Regionalism', in M.N. Jovanović (ed.), *International Handbook on the Economics of Integration*, Volume I. UK: Edward Elgar, pp. 121–35.

Faber, G. and R. Acharyya. (2010). 'Political-Economic Explanations of Free Trade Agreements', mimeo, Utrecht School of Economics, The Netherlands.

Grossman, G. and E. Helpman. (1995). 'The Politics of Free-Trade Agreements', *The American Economic Review*, 85(4): 667–90.

Irwin, D.A. (1993). 'Multilateral and Bilateral Trade Policies in the World Trading System: An Historical Perspective', in Jaime De Melo and A. Panagariya (eds), *New Dimensions in Regional Integration*. UK: Cambridge University Press, pp. 90–118.

Kiyoto, K. (2006). 'An Analysis of the Potential Economic Effects of Bilateral, Regional, and Multilateral Free Trade', Working Paper, Repec.

Krishna, P. (1996). 'Regionalism and Multilateralism: A Political Economy Approach', Working Paper, Brown University.

Krugman P. (1993). 'Regionalism versus Multilateralism: Analytical Notes', in J. De Melo and A. Panagariya (eds), *New Dimension in Regional Integration*, UK: Cambridge University Press, pp. 58–78.

Levy, P. (1995). 'A Political Economic Analysis of Free Trade Agreements', Working Paper, Yale University.

Schaefer, M. (2007). 'Ensuring that Regional Trading Agreements Complement the WTO System: US Unilateralism a Supplement to WTO Initiatives?', *Journal of International Economic Law*, 10(3): 585–603.

Viner, Jacob. (1950). *The Customs Union Issue*. Carnegie Endowment for Intellectual Peace: NY.

Winters, A. (1996). 'Regionalism versus Multilateralism', Policy Research Working Paper Series 1687 (The World Bank).

The World Bank. (2001). *Global Economic Prospects 2001*. Washington DC: The World Bank.

Yi, S.S. (1996). 'Endogenous Formation of Customs Union under Imperfect Competition: Open Regionalism is Good', *Journal of International Economics*, 41: 153–77.

PART V

Input Trade, Services, and Growth

15 Trade, Growth, and Inclusion

International trade and growth of an economy are related in two ways. First, international trade effects the growth of the aggregate output of trading nations. This aspect of trade as an engine of output growth, or more precisely export-led growth, is largely based on dynamic gains from trade in terms of productivity improvement in contrast to static gains arising from an efficient resource allocation and exchange. However, as both theories and empirical evidence show, export-led growth depends much on *what* a country exports rather than on *how much* a country exports. Second, output growth caused by factors other than international trade such as technical progress, domestic capital accumulation, or population growth, affect the volume of trade. If the country is large in the world market in the sense discussed earlier, growth in output affects its terms of trade (TOT), which, however, may not always be favourable for the country. It is for this TOT effect that the welfare implication of the growth in output in an open economy contrasts with that in a closed economy.

Output growth may be of different types and not all types have the same implications for poor and unskilled workers. Certain types of growth may create very little opportunities for unskilled and low-skill workers and widen the gulf between them and skilled workers. Such types of growth has very little impact on poverty, since most of the poor either have no skill or have low levels of skill, and large adverse impacts on income inequality. Thus growth may be exclusive rather than inclusive. Faster output growth achieved by many countries in the present era of globalization and trade liberalization often has this inherent exclusiveness.

As growing evidence suggests, growth in exports of high-technology goods and services such as aerospace, chemicals, pharmaceuticals, scientific instruments, machineries and data processing, and office equipment seems to be one major source of export-led growth. This reflects a paradox of trade and development policies in the present era of globalization. To achieve faster output growth through exports, the export composition should be changed towards high-technology manufacturing goods. But this raises the demand for skilled labour more than that for unskilled workers since high-technology goods are usually skill-intensive as well. Such a growth pattern thus has less desirable implications for poverty and income inequality in a country, at least in the initial stages.

International Economics. Rajat Acharyya, Oxford University Press. © Oxford University Press 2022.
DOI: 10.1093/oso/9780192865144.003.0015

These intertwined issues of international trade and growth are discussed in this chapter. We begin with the different theories that talk about trade as an engine of growth, followed by the welfare implications of growth in a large open economy through its impact on TOT. Country experiences regarding export-led growth and the role of the nature and the composition of the export basket in this context are discussed thereafter. Finally, we examine whether export-led growth in the present era is inclusive or exclusive.

15.1 INTERNATIONAL TRADE AND GROWTH

Since the time of Adam Smith, economists have characterized positive effects of international trade or trade liberalization on output growth in several ways. These arguments and characterizations can be discussed under four broad categories.

15.1.1 Trade as an Engine of Growth

Though Sir Dennis Robertson (1940) was the first to characterize international trade as an engine of growth, a similar idea can be traced back to the writings of classical economists. For example, in his productivity theory Adam Smith viewed international trade as a dynamic force that widens the extent of the market and creates scope for further division of labour. This, in turn, raises the skills and dexterity of the workforce, encourages technical innovations, and enables producers to enjoy the gains from increasing returns. As Myint (1958) observes, in late nineteenth century Europe, this productivity theory was pushed into an export-led growth argument contending that a nation should *promote* exports instead of adopting a laissez-faire policy and allowing free trade.

Free input trade can also augment a country's growth by relaxing its resource constraint. For example, international trade provides an avenue for a capital scarce country to import intermediate and capital goods necessary for industrialization and growth. In general, import of foreign capital expands the productive capacity of a country and ushers in output growth. We will return to this aspect of input trade causing output growth in the next chapter.

David Ricardo and Thomas Malthus, on the other hand, perceived the contribution of international trade in the growth process of a nation in slightly different ways. For Malthus, *international trade offsets the diminishing returns in agriculture* and thereby steps up the rate of output growth. Without international trade, a growing population requires over-cultivation of agricultural land. Soon diminishing returns in agriculture set in and the per capita food availability declines. This in turn puts a constraint on overall faster growth. International trade in such a context allows food to be imported and thus frees up scarce resources from the agriculture sector to be used in manufacturing sectors. Consequently, diminishing returns in agriculture can be offset. A similar argument was provided by Ricardo. He viewed *international trade as a way to delay the stationary state* for the fast-growing industrialized nations. The increase in the rate of profit for exporters arising from their comparative advantages vis-à-vis foreign producers, raises the rate of capital accumulation and hence the rate of output growth. Imports lower profits in import-competing sectors, but efficient resource allocation according to the country's pattern of comparative advantage helps augment output growth.

15.1.2 Trade as Vent for Surplus

Adam Smith also argued that international trade provides vent for surplus productive capacities. He used the concept of unproductive or surplus labour to provide a supply side argument. Low productivity of labour in food production leads to low real wages in terms of food. This means the opportunity cost of leisure (which is the real wage foregone) is low, which induces workers to enjoy leisure more and work less. If food prices are higher abroad, international trade raises the opportunity cost of leisure. This is because one unit of food can now be exchanged for larger quantities of other (imported) goods, so that wages foregone for leisure now mean foregoing a larger consumption of other goods. This induces the workers to work for longer hours, which steps up the production of food and consequently the aggregate output.

A similar beneficial effect of international trade was perceived by Malthus. International trade expands the consumption set by making available foreign goods and therefore encourages people to increase their work effort (and enjoy less leisure time) at any given wage rate. That is, international trade increases the opportunity cost of leisure in terms of a wider set of consumption goods.

In contrast to these supply side arguments based on low productivity and work-leisure choice, John Maynard Keynes and later Michael Kalecki provided the effective demand argument for international trade as a vent for the surplus productive capacity of an economy. In their theories, the value of aggregate output, and hence aggregate employment, is determined by the effective demand for domestically produced goods. If the effective demand is small relative to the potential level of output that can be produced by fully utilizing the productive capacity of the economy, the value of output produced will be smaller and surplus labour (or involuntarily unemployed workers) will exist at the equilibrium. In a closed economy, private consumption demand, investment demand, and government demand together constitute effective demand for domestically produced goods. International trade provides an additional source of demand for domestic goods and thus raises the value of aggregate output and lowers unemployment of labour. But whereas exports (or foreigners' import demand for domestic goods) augment effective demand, imports (or demand for foreign goods) displace local production. Thus, as was first pointed out by Kalecki, international trade provides a vent for surplus productive capacity through an export *surplus*, rather than through exports per se.

The problem with this export (or trade) surplus argument is that all the trading nations cannot have export surpluses simultaneously. Thus, international trade cannot provide vent for surplus productive capacities for all trading nations. But when commodity prices are flexible, output and employment can expand even with an unchanged trade balance position through what is known as the Laursen–Metzler effect. We will return to this in the later part of this book.

15.1.3 Trade, Redistribution, and Growth

Neo-classical arguments for trade effecting the output growth of a nation evolve around the gains from trade and its income redistribution effect. As international trade raises the real income of trading nations, it allows a higher rate of savings, capital formation, and therefore output growth.

On the other hand, the income redistribution effect of trade alters the rate of output growth if people have different marginal propensities to save. Consider, for example, a HOS economy in which trade lowers the money wage and raises the rate of return to capital by the price magnification effect. Workers will thus save less whereas capital owners will save more. But since capitalists have a higher marginal propensity to save than wage earners, the aggregate savings of the economy will rise. There will consequently be a higher rate of capital accumulation and growth. Of course, if trade redistributes incomes in favour of workers, the rate of growth may be impeded. Thus, if trade patterns of countries are consistent with their respective endowment differences, then by this redistribution effect, international trade should increase the rate of growth in a capital-abundant country and lower the same in a labour-abundant country.

Finally, there is Corden's (1971) factor-weight effect. Under constant returns to scale technology, the rate of growth in output is a weighted average of the rate of capital accumulation and the growth in labour force. To check, suppose a country is completely specialized in its export good, y, and the CRS production function for this good is:

$$y = F(L, K) \tag{15.1}$$

Total differentiation yields:

$$dy = \frac{\partial F}{\partial L} dL + \frac{\partial F}{\partial K} dK \tag{15.2}$$

Denoting the real wage and the real rate of return to capital by w and r respectively, the marginal productivity conditions give us the following relationships:

$$w = \frac{\partial F}{\partial L}, \quad r = \frac{\partial F}{\partial K} \tag{15.3}$$

Substituting equation (15.3) in equation (15.2) and dividing throughout by y we obtain:

$$\hat{y} = \left(w\frac{L}{y} \right) \hat{L} + \left(r\frac{K}{y} \right) \hat{K} \tag{15.4}$$

where, $\hat{L}$ and $\hat{K}$ are the exogenous growth rates of labour force and capital stock respectively. Thus, when the economy opens up to international trade, it effects the rate of growth of output by altering their weights through the redistribution effect.

15.1.4 Trade, Variety, and Growth

Since the early 1980s, economists have found evidence on sustained productivity growth for a handful of countries including the newly industrialized countries of Asia (Romer 1990). Development of endogenous growth models were primarily motivated by this phenomenon which could not be explained by neo-classical growth models (such as the Solow growth model) as these theories predicted dampening productivity growth when diminishing returns set in.

Based on economies of scale and a monopolistically competitive environment, the New Growth Theories perceive growth as innovation of newer product varieties and better product quality. That is, growth is synonymous with the rate at which product qualities or product varieties are developed through research and development. In such a context, as international trade generates a scale effect, it lowers the average cost of producing existing and potential newer varieties. The economies of scale thus encourage innovation of newer varieties or products and consequently step up the rate of growth. An interesting result in this context has been demonstrated in Helpman (1993). When an innovating advanced country engages in commodity trade with a poor country, which imitates the products innovated and exported by the advanced country, the rate of product development and growth in the advanced country increases with the rate of imitation in the poor country. The intuition behind this result is simple. Once a product is successfully imitated by a local firm in the poor country, the producer of this good in the advanced country loses its monopoly rent. If the local firm in the poor country has a significant cost advantage arising due to its cheap labour, the firm in the advanced country is competed out through imitation. This induces the firm in the advanced country to innovate a newer variety. Thus, higher the rate of imitation, more firms in the advanced country lose their monopoly rent over their respective existing product varieties. This forces them to innovate at a faster rate than in a situation where there is no threat of imitation. Note that as long as the probability of a newer variety being imitated successfully is less than one, it pays the firms in the advanced country to invest in research and development to innovate newer varieties. This result has an interesting implication that a patent protection that prohibits imitation will lower the rate of innovation and hence product-growth rate in the advanced countries.

The other important implication of these new growth theories is that countries with a relatively diversified export basket and with better product qualities of such exports will experience a more rapid and sustained growth effect of openness than other countries. Thus, what matters is not exports per se, but what a country exports.

15.1.5 Import-led Growth (ILG)

For the developing countries, imports of oil, essential inputs, and technology are crucial to increase productive capacity and growth. Therefore, import may also be an engine of growth. This assertion is hypothesized as the import-led growth (ILG) strategy and cheaper and/or superior quality imported capital goods being the basis of such hypothesis. Growth of a country can also be led by the use of better and larger variety of intermediate products and capital equipments through imports. Endogenous growth models emphasize upon this Import-led Growth (ILG) hypothesis (Aghion and Howitt, 1992; Romer, 1987). In addition, since intermediate products and capital equipments embody foreign technical knowhow, so transmission of knowledge spillovers across countries through import of such goods also augment growth rates (Grossman and Helpman, 1991). Of course, there are standard learning effects (for example, reverse engineering) that encourages imitation or innovation of competing products.

15.1.6 Country Experiences

Empirical evidence of the impact of increased trade (or trade openness) on GDP growth of countries is mixed. Frankel and Romer (1999) find that the trade openness index (TOI), defined as the ratio of the value of exports plus imports to GDP, is strongly related to long-term growth though there is no reverse causation from growth to trade. Sachs and Warner (1995) consider an alternative openness variable based on import tariffs on machinery, import quota coverage, and distortions in the exchange rate. Their study finds that this measure of openness is positively correlated with more rapid growth.

Harrison (1996) and Rodriguez and Rodrik (1999), on the other hand, are sceptical about the positive impact of trade openness on growth. They show that the robustness of the correlation between the openness measure and output growth *declines* as other variables (such as property rights) are added to the analysis.

The most persuasive evidence in favour of the positive impact of trade openness was provided by Dollar and Kraay (2004). They have identified one-third of the developing countries in terms of an increase in their TOI over the last two decades of the twentieth century and labeled them as post-1980 globalizers. This group of countries had a particularly large increase in trade to the tune of 104 per cent compared to 71 per cent for the rich countries. These countries had also cut import tariffs by almost 34 points. These recent globalizers have experienced accelerated growth rates, much higher than what non-globalizers have achieved (see Figure 15.1). Thus, Dollar and Kraay conclude that in the 1990s, the globalizing developing countries were catching up with rich countries, whereas non-globalizers continued to lag further behind.

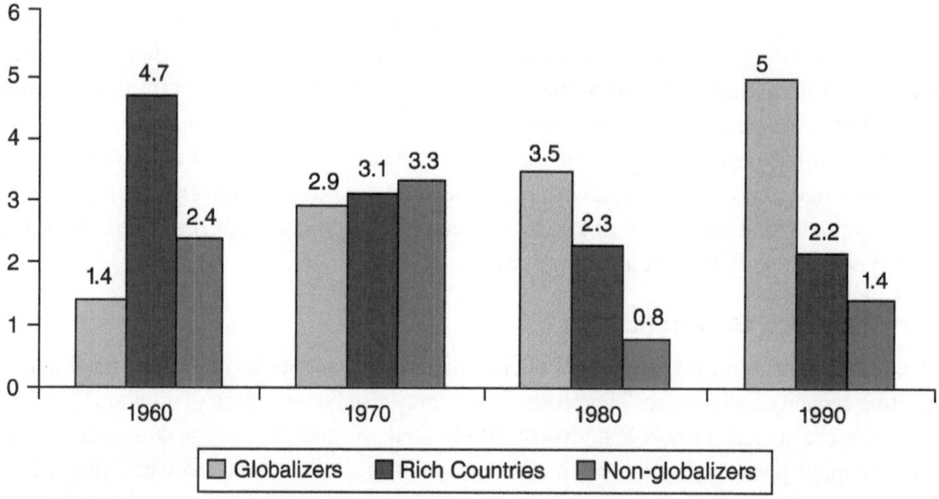

Figure 15.1 Per Capita GDP Growth Post-1980: Globalizers vs Non-globalizers

Source: Compiled from Dollar and Kraay (2004).
Note: Globalizers: 24 developing countries; non-globalizers: 49 developing countries.

However, the link between trade and growth depends much on the extent to which a country's export basket is diversified.[1] For example, Agosin (2007) found that export diversification was a significant explanatory factor for per capita GDP growth in Asia and Latin America over the period 1980–2003. But, at the same time, neither specialization nor diversification helps growth as long as the exports of a country comprise of low value added commodities. Thus, what may matter equally is *what* the countries export. Table 15.1 reports the correlation between GDP growth and exports of high-technology goods for some selected Latin American and Asian countries during the 1990s. For all these countries, the growth in GDP

[1] See Appendix A15 for a measure of diversification of export basket of a country.

was associated with a growth in high-technology exports. On the other hand, except for Brazil, Chile, Indonesia, and Mexico, the growth in GDP also correlates highly with the share of these exports in total manufacturing exports.

While analysing China's rapid growth during the 1990s and the early half of 2000, Rodrik (2006) observed that the export of a highly sophisticated product, which is usually not expected for a poor, labour-abundant country like China, has been the main driver of its rapid growth. Hausmann et al. (2007) provide more general evidence in this regard by using an indicator that measures the productivity level associated with a country's export basket (see Appendix A15). This measure was found to affect economic growth positively. Thus, countries that produce high-productivity goods experience faster growth than countries that produce low-productivity goods. More recently, in a cross-country regression analysis involving 65 countries for the period 1965–2005, Aditya and Acharyya (2011) show that both diversification and composition of exports are important determinants of economic growth. The relationship between GDP growth and the diversification of the export basket is a non-linear one with export specialization being important only beyond a threshold level. On the other hand, the higher the share of high-technology exports in manufacturing exports the larger is the aggregate value of the output of a country.

Table 15.1 Correlation between the Growth Rate and High-Technology Exports (HTX)

	Argentina	Brazil	Chile	China	Indonesia	Korea	Mexico	Singapore	Thailand
lnGDP & lnHTX	*0.75*	**0.82**	**0.86**	**0.99**	*0.67*	**0.87**	*0.69*	**0.99**	**0.90**
lnGDP & SHTX	*–0.72*	0.50	0.17	**0.97**	0.54	**0.82**	0.57	**0.97**	*0.65*

Source: Calculations based on the data reported in *WDI* (2007).
Note: Bold values are significant at the 1 per cent level; values in italics are significant at the 5 per cent level.

Chuang (1998) observed that for countries with greater shares of higher productivity products in the import basket, the trade induced learning and growth are likely to be higher. Similarly, what a country imports and from where it imports matters for its long-run growth. Veeramani (2014), on the other hand, constructs an index (termed as *IMKNOW*) to measure the level of knowledge embodied in a country's import basket of capital goods using the data for the period 1995–2005 and shows that a higher initial *IMKNOW* value of a country will lead to a faster subsequent economic growth. More recently, some very preliminary estimates arrived at by Marjit, Basu, and Veeramani (2019) covering 174 countries show that a 10 per cent improvement in openness index for intermediates trade raises per capita income growth rate by 23 per cent.

15.2 GROWTH, TOT, AND WELFARE

While growth may be desirable at the outset, not all types of growth may be actually beneficial for a country. Two situations deserve attention. First is Prebisch (1950) and Singer's (1950) hypothesis that TOT for countries that export primary goods deteriorate vis-à-vis countries that export manufacturing goods. Thus, whether export-led growth is good or bad depends on the nature of the export basket of a country. Second is Bhagwati's (1958) immiserizing growth hypothesis that export-biased growth, due to factor growth or technical progress, worsens the TOT of a large country. We elaborate upon each of these cases here.

15.2.1 Secular Deterioration in TOT for a Primary Good Exporter

The country experiences mentioned above suggest that exports of low-value addition goods such as primary goods and unskilled labour-intensive manufacturing goods, have very little impact on output growth. Growth in the exports of the primary good also has the perpetual problem of adverse terms of trade movement and price instability. As the *Oxfam Report 2002* observes, more than 50 developing countries were dependent on three or fewer primary

Box 15.1 Total Factor Productivity Growth in India

An alternative way of looking into the impact of trade on growth is through estimating total factor productivity (TFP) growth, which in some sense is based on Smith's productivity theory discussed above. There are quite a few such studies in the Indian context. Evidence, however, does not seem to be conclusively in favour of Smith's productivity theory. Whereas Krishna and Mitra (1998) find trade reforms augmenting productivity growth, Balakrishnan et al. (2000) and Das (2003) find the evidence on the other side. Das (2003) observes that TFP growth rates have been negative during 1991–2000 in most of the industries. Using panel data comprising firm-level information drawn from groups within the manufacturing industry that have experienced the most significant tariff reduction, Balakrishnan et al. (2000), on the other hand, find no evidence of a shift in productivity growth since the onset of reforms.

commodities for more than half of their export earnings during the 1990s. This narrow specialization in exports puts these countries in a vicious circle. With the demand for primary products less responsive to prices, a structural over-supply causes world prices to fall to abysmally low levels. In face of falling prices, developing countries attempt to export more to compensate for the consequent losses in their export earnings. This in turn depresses the prices further and completes the vicious circle. Dependence on exports of coffee beans and cocoa, sugar, and minerals by sub-Saharan African countries and some Latin American countries is a typical example.

The secular deterioration of TOT for primary good exporting countries was first documented by Prebisch (1950) and Singer (1950). Both of them observed that the net barter TOT for UK improved during 1876–1947. Since UK was the most industrialized country in that period and it imported raw materials and other primary commodities for its industrialization and manufacturing exportable production, the inverse of UK's barter TOT was taken as the proxy for the price of primary goods relative to the price of manufacturing goods. On this interpretation, the relative price of primary goods declined during 1876–1947. A major theoretical explanation for this deterioration of TOT put forward by Singer (1950) was that the demand for primary commodities is income inelastic. Trade among developed and developing countries according to their static comparative advantages in manufacturing and primary goods respectively led to gains from trade and income growth for all. Technical progress in manufacturing also generated output and income growth for developed countries. But since primary goods are income inelastic, their demand increased less than the demand for manufacturing goods as a consequence of such income gains. The relative price of primary goods thus declined.

Figure 15.2 illustrates this point in terms of the relative demand and relative supply analysis in Chapter 1. Consider a world consisting of only two countries Uganda and the United States

Box 15.2 Supply Management of Primary Exports

Over-supply of primary goods in the world market is another reason for the deterioration in their prices. There are several factors that drive the over-supply of primary goods. First, price instability and volatility make it difficult for producers to estimate future prices and plan production levels accordingly. Second, huge agricultural subsidies in rich industrialized countries in the production of sugar, cereals, and dairy and meat products results in over-production that is often dumped in the world market. The European Union's (EU) Common Agricultural Policy (CAP) is one glaring example. Third, development of new technologies in the West has lowered the demand for primary exports by developing countries. Demand for minerals, for example, has fallen due to the invention of fibre-optics for copper wires in the telephone industry and industrial plastics for aluminum.

Supply management through coordination among sub-Saharan and Latin American countries in cutting down production volumes is a plausible solution to this. However, coordination failure may be a major obstacle in its success. Emerging new suppliers outside the union or cartels also pose serious problems. For example, when African and Latin American governments targeted cutting the supply of coffee and cocoa by 10 per cent in 2000–01 to push up prices, the new low-cost producers in East Asia took advantage of such higher prices and increased their supplies.

exporting to each other coffee beans and textiles respectively. The curves d^W and s^W are the relative demand for coffee beans and relative supply of coffee beans by these countries taken together. Since there are no other countries in this example, these are essentially the world relative demand and supply of coffee beans. Now consider technical progress in the textile manufacturing sector in the United States that brings down the supply price of textiles by raising its production and supply. Alternatively speaking, the relative supply of coffee beans falls. *Ceteris paribus*, its relative price should rise as a consequence. But the income growth of countries consequent upon this technical progress raises the demand for both coffee beans and textiles, and since coffee beans are income inelastic in demand, their relative demand declines. If this decline in demand is larger than the decline in supply, the relative price of coffee beans falls. In Figure 15.2 this possibility is shown by a larger shift of the d^W curve to the left.

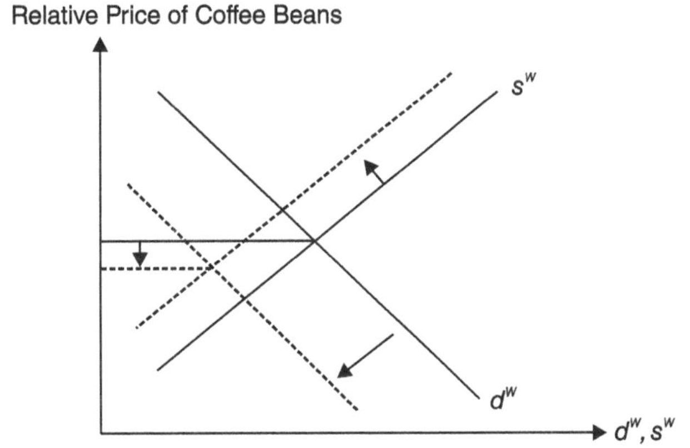

Figure 15.2 Deterioration of TOT of the Primary Good

Thus, inelastic demand for primary goods offers a plausible explanation for the secular deterioration of its relative price. Primary goods-exporting countries consequently experience welfare losses from their increased exports.

15.2.2 Immiserizing Growth

Jagdish Bhagwati demonstrated that even for a country that exports manufacturing good, TOT may worsen. The implication of this adverse TOT effect of growth is that if TOT deterioration is too large, the corresponding welfare loss outweighs the welfare gain from growth itself. Thus, growth may be immiserizing through adverse terms of trade effect.

To explain, suppose our home country was exporting relatively labour-intensive textiles and importing relatively capital-intensive computers. An exogenous growth in the workforce, *ceteris paribus*, enables the home country to produce more textiles for any given number of computers being locally produced. PPF in Figure 15.3 thus shifts outward though non-uniformly from *MN* to *M'N'*. At the initial TOT, the home country was producing at *P* and consuming at *C*. As the workforce grows exogenously and PPF shifts out, production shifts to

> **Box 15.3** Unionized Wages and Secular Deterioration in TOT
>
> Singer (1950) offered an alternative explanation of the secular deterioration of TOT. Strong labour unions in industrialized countries caused money wages in the manufacturing sector to increase during upswings in business cycles and corresponding price inflation. But during downswings, downward rigidity of money wages prevented wage cuts. On the other hand, relatively weaker labour unions in the primary good exporting developing countries failed to manage the same wage increase during upswings in business cycles. Wage cut also cannot be prevented during downswings and deflation. This means that the wage cost rises less during upswings and declines more during downswings in developing countries than in developed countries. Hence, there is a continuous decline in the relative cost of primary goods. Competition thus drives down prices through corresponding increased supply.

P' at this initial TOT. By the output magnification effect, the output of textiles increases and that of computers declines. Thus, growth here is *export biased.* On the other hand, increase in the real income consequent upon growth at this initial TOT, indicated by the higher parallel line tangent to *M'N'*, changes the local demand and consumption of textiles and computers.[2] If tastes are homothetic, the consumption point shifts to *C'* along the income consumption line through the initial consumption point *C*. Increased demand for computers together with the decline in their local production raises import demand for computers at the initial TOT. Consequently, the export offer rises too at the balanced trade. If the home country is large, the world price of computers thus should rise and that of textiles should fall. This worsening of TOT for the home country then lowers its welfare. Thus, export biased growth leads to a secondary welfare loss, and if this TOT deterioration is too large, overall welfare declines. This possibility is shown in Figure 15.3. TOT worsens to the broken flatter line. The production

[2] Recalling the algebra in the earlier chapter, the change in real income at the initial TOT and with no tariff equals $dy = p^W dX_C + dX_T$.

adjusts to P'' and consumption to C". The welfare of the home country now falls below the pre-growth level, as indicated by the utility index of CIC labeled U''.

Export-biased growth in a large country thus may be immiserizing. Bhagwati (1958) demonstrated that this paradoxical result is consistent with the stability conditions derived earlier. Note that export-biased growth shifts the home offer curve to the right along the foreign offer curve for the reasons spelled out above. As discussed earlier, a shift in the home offer curve produces a larger change in TOT along the backward-bending (or inelastic import demand) segment of the foreign offer curve than along the upward-sloping segment. Thus, if at the pre-growth equilibrium, foreign import demand is inelastic, it is likely that growth will be immiserizing. Yet, the stability condition may be satisfied because that requires the sum of the home and the foreign import demand elasticities be greater than one. Of course, growth may be immiserizing even when the foreign import demand is elastic.

A few comments are warranted at this point. First, growth is never immizerising if it is import biased. For example, had there been a *ceteris paribus* capital accumulation, at the initial TOT, the production of computers would have increased and that of textiles would have declined by the output magnification effect. Correspondingly, both export supply and import demand would have fallen leading to a TOT improvement for the growing home country. In such a case, the initial welfare improvement would have been augmented through an induced TOT improvement. Second, export-biased growth may be immiserizing for a large country even if tastes are non-homothetic. As long as the import-competing good is a normal good, growth-induced real income increase raises import demand and consequently worsens the country's TOT.

Third, even for a small open economy, growth may be immiserizing when trade is restricted by an import tariff. This was demonstrated by Harry G. Johnson (1967). In his case, it is not TOT deterioration which is the source of immiserization because for a small country (as

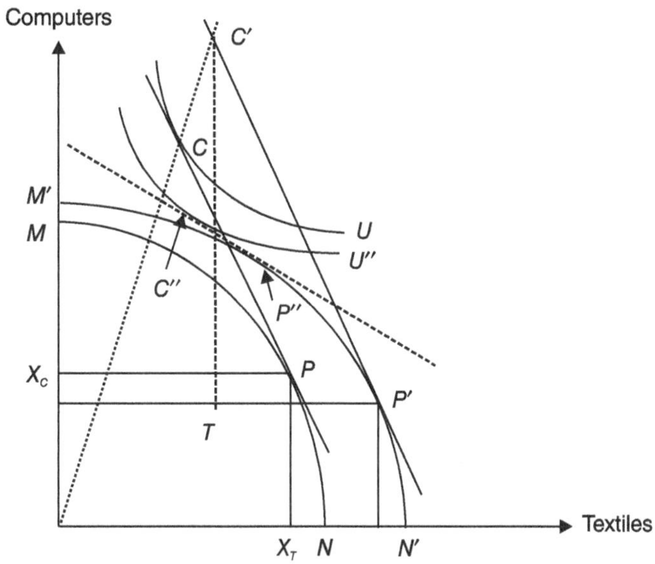

Figure 15.3 Immiserizing Growth in a Large Open Economy

long as it remains small even after growth) there is no change in its TOT. The possibility of immiserization arises because the tariff creates a pure distortion for the small country, which is accentuated through growth in factors of production and consequently in the aggregate value of output.

15.3 TRADE, GROWTH, AND INCLUSION

The important lessons that emerge from the above discussion is that output growth, whether induced by factor growth or through increased exports may not always be good for the country as a whole. However, even if it raises aggregate welfare, growth may still not be good for *all*. The question then is, does growth benefit the unskilled and the poor or does it bypass them by benefiting only a handful of the rich? In the latter case, we say that (trade-induced) *growth is not inclusive*. Inclusive growth essentially means pro-poor growth or broad-based growth that benefits particularly the unskilled and low-skill segment of the country's labour force. A related issue is how does trade-induced output growth redistribute incomes and thus change income inequality.

The key factor to both these questions is how growth effects the TOT of the country and the aggregate employment of the unskilled. For example, growth through primary exports for sub-Saharan African countries may not be inclusive since the deterioration of the TOT lowers the wages of unskilled workers by the price magnification effect. Since poor are either low skilled or unskilled, such export-led growth should lower the incomes of the poor. On the other hand, higher prices of manufacturing may make them impoverished. But if such growth generates larger employment for the unskilled, income losses may be compensated at the aggregate. Similarly, for reasons spelled out above, for the manufacturing goods exporting countries, growth may lower wage incomes of the unskilled and the poor if their exports are relatively unskilled-labour-intensive and (factor) growth is export-biased. Growth then raises income inequality and poverty, and is not inclusive.

Kuznets's observation on the impact of growth on intra-country income inequality provides an alternative argument of how trade may effect intra-country income inequality through its growth impact. The relationship between per capital income growth and inequality is described by the oft-quoted inverted-U hypothesis put forward by Kuznets (1955). Growth invariably shifts resources away from agricultural activities and towards industrialization and urbanization. As perceived by Kuznets, the dislocating effects of this reduction in agricultural activities and increased industrialization would be most unfavourable for the relative position of low-income groups. Thus, initially growth in per capita income is associated with rising inequality. But in the later stages as per capita income grows further, the pace of industrial growth slackens and the initial unfavourable forces become weaker. The benefits of such a growth spread out more widely to lower income inequality and the distribution of national income becomes more equal (Kuznets 1955).

Trade-induced growth processes in many nations over the last few decades have in fact increased the intra-country income inequality, particularly wage inequality between skilled and unskilled workers. As the empirical evidence mentioned above suggests, growth processes in the present era of globalization have been mostly driven by exports of high-technology products, which are relatively skilled-labour-intensive. Thus, whereas the demand for skilled

Box 15.4 Inequality and Growth

There is also a reverse causation running from inequality to economic growth. Alesina and Rodrik (1994), for example, have found a significant inverse relationship between initial inequality—particularly land inequality—and subsequent growth in per capita income. A similar result has been arrived at by Bruno et al. (1996) and Deininger and Squire (1996). However, it is important to note that different types of inequality have different, and sometimes opposing, effects on growth (Cornia and Court 2001). Inequality of earnings that rewards effort is likely to be pro-growth. But income or wealth accruing because of inheritance is likely to be anti-growth.

In India, regions with lower initial inequality tended to grow faster than regions with higher initial inequality, but the fast growing regions also experienced increasing inequality.

Box 15.5 Income Inequality and the Trickle Down Effect of Growth

Whether the benefits of growth, induced either by increased trade or factor growth, percolate or trickle down to have any sustained and persistent effect on poverty depends also on the pattern of income inequality. If the initial income distribution is highly unequal in favour of higher income groups, the poor will get only a very small share of the income growth induced by trade openness. Thus, initial high income inequality means that the income gain for the poorest will be far less than the income gain for the rich. If the income shares of different classes remain unchanged, this results in a lower rate of poverty reduction than would be achieved if such growth led to redistribution of income in favour of the poor.

labour has increased fast, such exports have increasingly marginalized unskilled workers and the poor. This has contributed towards a widening wage-gap in favour of skilled and semi-skilled workers. These developments reveal a paradox of export-led growth and poverty reduction. To generate strong linkages and dynamic effects with the rest of the economy, developing countries must enhance the product quality and specialize in high value addition activities. But this weakens the positive impact of export growth on poverty alleviation at the initial stages.

Bhagwati and Srinivasan (2003), however, have most persuasively argued that there has been a strong relationship between trade openness and growth and between growth and poverty alleviation. They cite examples of China and India as cases of growth reducing poverty quite significantly. At the early stages of the growth process, the poor may be marginalized, but at the later stages opportunities are also created for them and the benefits of growth trickle down. Their argument, like many others, is implicitly based on Kuznets' income mobility concept. High economic growth creates opportunities for more work and increased income. Demands for unskilled labour are also magnified with such growth. In a dynamic economy with rapid technological changes productive employment opportunities are generated as well as destroyed. In the process, some people move into the lower income groups relative to where they were at the beginning of the growth process. This is what Kuznets termed as *downward income mobility*. At the same time, there are people who move into higher income groups. They experience an *upward income mobility*. In the rapid growth process, as is usually argued, opportunities for upward mobility far outweigh downward mobility. Rapid economic growth, therefore, is pro-poor on the balance.

There is a caveat to this argument though. It is undeniable that growth is a necessary precondition for poverty alleviation and eradication. But it is not a sufficient condition in itself. If the poor cannot access the opportunities for upward mobility generated through the growth process, the potential favourable impact of economic growth on poverty is far from realized. Lack of education, training, and technical skills to cope up with the changes in technology and production structures that globalization and trade liberalization usher in is the most important constraint that delays access to opportunities for upward income mobility for the lower income groups. In fact, the increased income inequality that growth leads to in the initial stages itself reflects the persistent differences in the capacity of individuals to exploit market opportunities or to access productive employment and property rights. Thus, export-led growth policies need to be supplemented by domestic policies that ensure that the lower income groups and economically backward classes get access to education, and, more important, to opportunities for acquiring technical skills that help them exploit new market opportunities. Otherwise, benefits of growth will be concentrated in a few and will hardly trickle down. Growth will largely be exclusive then.

Box 15.6 Evidence on Trade and Poverty

Mohan Rao (1999) constructed a Trade Index from the residuals of regression equations which estimates the effects of population and income on the trade/GDP ratio, using a scale of 0 to 100. The idea is that population and income are the structural determinants of a country's capacity to trade. Thus, deviations of trade ratios from the structural relationship (between trade and these structural determinants) should indicate the influence of policies towards openness. Using this Trade Index measure of openness, Rao observed a statistically significant *positive* relationship between openness and poverty across countries during 1988–95: *poverty increases with increased openness of a country*. However, there had been more countries in which poverty actually declined with openness but such countries had on an average an openness trend of 0.1 per cent per annum. On the other hand, countries where poverty had increased had an average openness trend of 2.1 per cent per annum.

For India, there is some evidence on the statistically significant *negative* correlation between growth in GDP (and in per capita GDP) and *urban* poverty during the 1990s that coincided with its major economic reforms and trade liberalization policies. This was the period when India's average GDP growth had been as high as 6–7 per cent per annum.

APPENDIX A15

I. Diversification of the Export Basket

The standard measure of diversification of the export basket is Hirschman's (1945) coefficient of concentration, or the Commodity Concentration Index (CCI). For concentration of exports of a country, say of India, such an index is defined as:

$$CCI^h = [\Sigma_k (\alpha_{kj})^2]^{1/2} \times 100 \quad \text{(A15.1)}$$

where, α_{kj} = share of commodity k in total Indian exports to the world (or to a particular destination country j).

The value of CCI will be 100 if exports to the world (or to a particular destination) comprise of a single commodity. This is the case of highest commodity concentration. Smaller is its value, on the other hand, the more diversified the exports are in a particular market. However, this index is sensitive to the number of commodities included in the calculations and hence to the level of disaggregation of each commodity group.

II. Composition of the Export Basket: Manufacturing and High-Technology Exports

A first-hand indicator of the composition of a country's export basket is the share of manufacturing exports in its total merchandise exports. Similarly, the share of high-technology manufacturing exports in total manufacturing exports of a country can be used as an indicator of whether the country is specializing in low-technology (and unskilled-labour-intensive) manufacturing or in high-technology (and skilled-labour-intensive) manufacturing goods. This latter share is highly relevant in the trade-growth context because of its high value addition. Two definitions are used in current empirical literature to measure high-technology exports. First is the exports of machinery, transport equipment, and electronics goods; and the second is the measure defined by Sanjay Lall and used by the World Bank in its World Development Indicator that includes aerospace, computers, pharmaceuticals, scientific instruments, and electrical machinery.

Hausmann et al. (2007) offer an *EXPY* Index of the sophistication of a country's export basket, which is calculated from the weighted sum of measures of the productivity or sophistication level of each export sector, called *PRODY* values. The weights are the shares of each sector in the country's total exports. McCann (2007) calculates this index of the sophistication of a country's export basket to examine the trade and growth relationship for more than 100 countries. This index can be calculated through the following steps.

The first step is to calculate the index *PRODY* for the productivity or sophistication level of each export sector in a country. In calculating this index, Balassa's RCA Index (discussed in Chapter 1) is used as a weight. RCA is taken as a proxy measure of a product or a sector's total factor productivity. Given this, *PRODY* for a particular good or sector k is a weighted average of the per capita income of *countries* exporting that good, where the weights correspond to the RCA of each country in good k. Thus:

$$PRODY_k = \sum_j \left[\frac{X_{kj} / X_k^W}{X_j / X^W} \right] Y_j \quad \text{(A15.2)}$$

where, X_{kj} is the export of commodity k by country j, $X_j = \sum_k X_{kj}$ is country j's total exports of all commodities, X_k^W is the total world exports of commodity k, X^W is the total world exports of all commodities, and Y_j is the per capita GDP (or income) of country j. The ratio in the parenthesis is the RCA value for commodity k for country j.

The next step is to calculate EXPY for country j as the weighted sum of the PRODY values for each sector k where the weights are the shares of sector k in country j's export basket:

$$EXPY_j = \sum_k \left[\frac{X_{kj}}{X_j} \right] PROD_k \tag{A15.3}$$

The index will attain a lower bound if 100 per cent of a country's exports are in the sector with the lowest *PRODY* rating. Similarly, the higher bound will be attained if 100 per cent of a country's exports are in the sector with the highest *PRODY* rating. McCann (2007), for example, found the lower bound of USD 5,331 million for *EXPY* in 2003 for his sample of countries which will be attained if a country has 100 per cent of its exports in the agricultural raw materials sector. The upper bound of USD 16,579 million, on the other hand, will be attained if a country has 100 per cent of its exports in the insurance and financial services sector.

SUMMARY POINTS

- International trade and the growth of an economy are related in two ways. First, international trade effects the growth of aggregate output of trading nations. Second, output growth caused by factors other than international trade such as technical progress, domestic capital accumulation, or population growth, affect the volume of trade.
- Sir Dennis Robertson (1940) characterized international trade as an engine of growth. Much earlier, Adam Smith viewed international trade as a dynamic force that entails a productivity gain, which was later evolved into an export-led growth argument contending that a nation should *promote* exports instead of adopting a laissez-faire policy and allowing free trade.
- Malthus argued that *international trade offsets diminishing returns in agriculture* and thereby steps up the rate of output growth. Ricardo viewed *international trade as a way to delay the stationary state* for the fast growing industrialized nations.
- Adam Smith also argued that international trade provides vent for surplus productive capacities. International trade raises the opportunity cost of leisure and thereby induces workers to work for longer hours, which steps up the production of food and consequently aggregate output.

(contd)

Summary Points (*contd*)

- John Maynard Keynes and later Michael Kalecki provided the effective demand argument for international trade as a vent for surplus productive capacity of an economy. But what matters is not just exports but an export surplus.
- In neo-classical theory, international trade raises the real incomes of trading nations; it allows a higher rate of savings, capital formation and therefore output growth. The income redistribution effect of trade also alters the rate of output growth if people have different marginal propensities to save.
- The New Growth Theories perceive growth as innovation of newer product varieties and better product quality. In such a context, as international trade generates a scale effect, it lowers the average cost of producing existing and potential newer varieties and thereby encourages innovation of newer varieties or products.
- Empirical evidence of the impact of increased trade (or trade openness) on the GDP growth of countries is mixed. The link between trade and growth seems to depend much on the extent to which a country's export basket is diversified. Equally important is *what* the countries export.
- Not all types of growth may be actually beneficial for a country. Whether export-led growth is good or bad depends on the nature of a country's export basket. If the country exports primary goods, then it may not be beneficial because TOT for countries that export primary goods deteriorates vis-à-vis countries that export manufacturing goods. An export-biased growth, on the other hand, worsens the TOT of a large country, and consequently may be welfare reducing.
- Even if growth raises a country's aggregate welfare, it may still not be good for *all*, as it may bypass the unskilled and the poor and benefit only a handful of the rich. Thus, trade-induced growth may not be *inclusive*.
- Growth is a necessary precondition for poverty alleviation and eradication. But it is not a sufficient condition. If the poor cannot access the opportunities for upward mobility generated through the growth process, the potential favourable impact of economic growth on poverty is far from realized.

KEYWORDS

- **Export-led growth** argument postulates that a country should promote its exports instead of adopting a laissez-faire or free trade policy in order to augment its output growth. This is based on Adam Smith's premise that international trade leads to productivity gains.
- **Trade openness index** (TOI) is defined as the ratio of value of exports plus imports to GDP.
- **High-technology goods** are those which are technology as well as skill-intensive such as aerospace, chemicals, pharmaceuticals, scientific instruments, machineries and data processing, and office equipment.
- **Export-biased** growth takes place when exogenous factor growth or technical progress augments the production of export goods relatively more than of other goods.
- **Immiserizing** is experienced when the country's TOT worsens so much that the consequent welfare loss outweighs the beneficial effects of growth. This may happen when growth is export-biased.
- **Inclusive growth** essentially means pro-poor growth or broad-based growth that particularly benefits the unskilled and low-skill segment of the country's labour force.
- **Kuznets curve** is an inverted-U relationship between income inequality and per capita income growth. Initially, income inequality grows with an increase in per capita income, but after a threshold level of per capita income inequality starts declining.

EXERCISES

1. Distinguish between the supply side and demand side arguments for free trade as a vent for the surplus productive capacity of a country.
2. Do you think by the trade redistribution growth argument free trade will raise the rate of growth in a capital-rich and lower the same in a labour-rich country?
3. Consider Corden's factor-weight equation of growth of output specified in equation (15.4) in the text. If these rates of factor growth are the same and constant, at what rate does the economy's output grow? Suppose opening up of the economy to international trade raises the wage rate by 10 per cent but lowers the rate of return to capital by 5 per cent. How does the output growth rate change?
4. Based on empirical estimates of the export-led growth hypothesis, what aspects of the exports of a country seem to matter the most? Explain your answer.
5. What are the alternative theoretical explanations for the secular deterioration of TOT for primary good exporting countries?
6. Does factor growth have the same implication in an open economy as it has in a closed one? Explain.

(*contd*)

Exercises (*contd*)

7. Is it that export-biased growth is always immiserizing? If not, why not?
8. When is growth inclusive? Why is growth not always inclusive?
9. How did Kuznets argue that at the initial stages of growth in per capita income, income inequality in the growing country will worsen? What conditions must be satisfied for inequality to decline as per capita income growth crosses a threshold level?
10. Consider a two-country world. Countries have identical technology and identical and homothetic tastes. They produce and trade with each other two goods using internationally immobile capital and labour. If there is exogenous growth in the scarce factor in one of these countries, *ceteris paribus*, what can you infer about changes in the following?
    (a) Volume of trade between these two countries.
    (b) TOT and welfare of these two countries.
    (c) Income inequality in each country.

SUGGESTED READING

Bhagwati, J.N., A. Panagariya, and T.N. Srinivasan. (1998). *Lectures on International Trade*. Cambridge, MA: MIT Press.

ADVANCED READING

Aditya, A. and R. Acharyya (2011). 'Export Diversification, Composition and Economic Growth: Evidence from Cross-Country Analysis', *The Journal of International Trade and Economic Development*, November.

Aghion, Philippe and Peter Howitt. (1992). 'A Model of Growth Through Creative Destruction'. *Econometrica*, 60(2), 323–51.

Agosin, M.R. (2007). 'Export Diversification and Growth in Emerging Economies', Working Paper No. 233, Department of Economics, University of Chile.

Alesina, A. and D. Rodrik. (1994). 'Distributive Policies and Economic Growth', *Quarterly Journal of Economics*, 108: 465–90.

Balakrishnan, P., K. Pushpangadan, and M.S. Babu. (2000). 'Trade Liberalisation and Productivity Growth in Manufacturing: Evidence from Firm-Level Panel Data', *Economic and Political Weekly*, October, 35(41): 3679–82.

Bhagwati, J.N. (1958). 'Immiserizing Growth: A Geometric Note', *Review of Economic Studies*, 25: 201–5.

Bhagwati, J.N. and T.N. Srinivasan. (2003). 'Trade and Poverty in the Poor Countries', available at http://www.econ.yale.edu/~srinivas/trade_poverty.pdf.

Bruno, M., M. Ravallion, and L. Squire. (1996). 'Equity and Growth in Developing Countries: Old and New Perspectives on the Policy Issues', World Bank Policy Research Working Paper No. 1563.

Chuang, Yih-chyi. (1998). 'Learning by Doing, the Technology Gap and Growth'. *International Economic Review*, 39(3), 697–721.

Corden, M. (1971). *The Theory of Protection*. Oxford: Clarendon Press.

Cornia, A,G. and J. Court. (2001). 'Inequality, Growth and Poverty in the Era of Liberalization and Globalization' , Policy Brief No. 4, UNU/WIDER

Das, D.K. (2003). 'Manufacturing Productivity under Varying Trade Regimes: India in the 1980s and 1990s', ICRIER Working Paper No. 107.

Deininger, Klaus and Lyn Squire (1996). 'A New Dataset Measuring Income Inequality', *World Bank Economic Review*, 10(3): 565–91.

Dollar, D. and Art Kraay (2004). 'Trade, Growth, and Poverty', *Economic Journal, Royal Economic Society*, 114(493): F22–49, 02.

Frankel, J. and D. Romer (1999). 'Does Trade Cause Growth?', *American Economic Review*, 89(3): 379–99.

Grossman, Gene M and Elhanan Helpman. (1991)., *Innovation and Growth in the Global Economy*. The MIT Press, Cambridge MA.

Harrison, A. (1996). 'Openness and Growth: A Time Series, Cross-Country Analysis for Developing Countries', *Journal of Development Economics*, 48(2): 419–47.

Hausmann, R., Jason Hwang, and Dani Rodrik (2007). 'What You Export Matters', *Journal of Economic Growth*, 12(1): 1–25.

Helpman, E. (1993). 'Innovation, Imitation, and Intellectual Property Rights', *Econometrica*, 61: 1247–80.

Hirschman, A.O. (1945). *National Power and the Structure of Foreign Trade.* Berkeley: University of California Press.

Johnson, H.G. (1967). 'Economic Expansion and International Trade', *Manchester School of Economic and Social Studies*, 23: 95–112.

Krishna, P. and D. Mitra (1998). 'Trade Liberalisation, Market Discipline and Productivity Growth: New Evidence from India', *Journal of Development Economics*, 56: 447–62.

Kuznets, S. (1955). 'Economic Growth and Income Inequality', *American Economic Review*, 45: 1–28.

Marjit, S., Basu, A. and Veeramani, C. (2019). 'Growth Gains from Trade'. *CESifo Working Paper No. 7905, CESifo, Munich.*

McCann, F. (2007). 'Export Composition and Growth', mimeo, Dublin: School of Economics University College.

Myint, H. (1958). 'The Classical Theory of International Trade and the Underdeveloped Countries', *The Economic Journal*, 68(270): 317–37.

Oxfam International (2002). *Rigged Rules and Double Standards: Trade, Globalization and the Fight against Poverty*. Washington DC: Oxfam International Advocacy Office.

Prebisch, R. (1950). 'The Economic Development of Latin America and Its Principal Problems', reprinted in *Economic Bulletin for Latin America*, 7(1), 1962.

Rao, M. (1999). 'Openness, Poverty and Inequality', Background Paper, Human Development Report.

Robertson, D. (1940). *Essays in Monetary Theory*. London: P.S. King & Son.

Rodriguez , F. and D. Rodrik (1999). 'Trade Policy and Economic Growth: A Skeptic's Guide to Cross-National Evidence', NBER Working Paper No. W7081, April.

Rodrik, D. (2006). 'What's So Special about China's Exports?', NBER Working Paper No. 11947, Cambridge, MA: MIT Press.

Romer, P. (1987). 'Growth Based on Increasing Returns due to Specialization'. *The American Economic Review*, 77(2): 56–62.

Romer, P.M. (1990). 'Endogenous Technological Change', *Journal of Political Economy*, 98: S71–102.

Sachs, J. and A. Warner (1995). 'Economic Reforms and Process of Global Integration', Brookings Papers in Economic Activity.

Singer, H. (1950). 'U.S. Foreign Investment in Underdeveloped Areas: The Distribution of Gains between Investing and Borrowing Countries', *American Economic Review, Papers and Proceedings*, 40: 473–85.

Veeramani, C., (2014). 'World's Knowledge Spillovers: Beyond Openness and Growth'. *Journal of Economic Integration*, 29(2): 298–328.

16 Foreign Capital Inflow, Multinationals, and Migration

Inter-country immobility of capital and labour assumed in neo-classical trade models is not what we actually see around us. Rather large capital flows and labour migration could also be observed along with commodity movements much before the present waves of globalization. Despite this coexistence of commodity and factor trade, the assumption of inter-country immobility of factors of production serves two specific purposes in the models of comparative advantage. First, it enables us to locate the comparative advantage of nations, and thus the basis of commodity trade, in the endowments of *domestically owned* factors of production. Second, it delineates the effects of commodity trade on local production, distribution of income, national welfare, and output growth from the effects of factor flows. This delineation is important because the basis of commodity trade and factor flows (or factor trade), commodity price difference for the former and factor price differential for the latter, are interlinked as the Factor Price Equalization (FPE) theorem (and its complementary theorem known as the Goods Price Equalization (GPE) theorem that we will discuss here) shows. Now that we have learnt about the basis of commodity trade and its implications for national welfare, income distribution, and growth, we will discuss the causes and consequences of factor flows, separated from as well as in conjunction with commodity trade in this chapter.

Though factor flows, whether capital inflow or labour immigration, can be treated similarly in issues like their impact on commodity composition and the growth of output in the host country, there is one important asymmetry between the two. This is regarding their respective welfare implications for both the source and the host countries as we will discuss here. There are also completely asymmetric interests of the developed and developing countries over these two types of factor flows.

An important dimension of capital inflows is direct foreign investment by multinational corporations in host countries through fragmentation and outsourcing of production processes. This has some far-reaching policy implications as we will discuss in the later part of this chapter.

However, before discussing these issues, we begin with an interesting result derived by Robert Mundell (1957) known as the Goods Price Equalization (GPE) theorem, which is the reverse of the FPE theorem.

International Economics. Rajat Acharyya, Oxford University Press. © Oxford University Press 2022.
DOI: 10.1093/oso/9780192865144.003.0016

16.1 FACTOR FLOWS AND THE GOODS PRICE EQUALIZATION (GPE) THEOREM

As discussed in Chapter 6, under some fairly general conditions, free commodity trade leads to factor price equalization (FPE) across the trading nations. Thus, commodity trade acts as a substitute for factor flows or factor trade since inter-country factor flows would have achieved the same result. This remarkable result has far-reaching implications for factor flows. As long as factor flows are motivated or caused by factor price differentials, there will be no scope for such flows once commodity trade equalizes commodity prices and consequently factor prices across countries. The basis of this FPE, as we have seen earlier, is the one-to-one correspondence between commodity and factor prices.

A reverse result was established by Robert Mundell (1957). If countries allow only factor flows, but not any commodity trade, factor prices will be equalized across countries through arbitrage, provided of course labour and capital are homogeneous everywhere. If all countries share the same technology, such factor price equalization will also equalize commodity prices across the countries. Hence, there will be no scope for commodity trade even when countries allow such trade. This is known as the Goods Price Equalization (GPE) theorem. What is even more striking is that under the constant returns to scale technology, the movement of any *one* factor is sufficient to cause GPE. This can be proved in the following way.

Consider the standard two-commodity two-factor general equilibrium structure of a home country, as discussed in Chapter 3. Under the assumption of constant returns to scale technology, production functions of the two goods, computers and textiles, can be expressed simply as functions of relative capital-intensity choices, k_C and k_T:

$$X_C = L_C F(k_C),\ F'(k_C) > 0,\ F''(k_C) < 0 \tag{16.1}$$

$$X_T = L_T G(k_T),\ G'(k_T) > 0,\ G''(k_T) < 0 \tag{16.2}$$

where, L_C and L_T are the level of employment in the computer and textile sectors respectively ($L_C + L_T = L$). The positive signs of the first order partial derivatives, $F'(k_C)$ and $G'(k_T)$, indicate positive marginal productivity of the variable factor and the negative signs of the second order partial derivatives, $F''(k_C)$ and $G''(k_T)$, reflect diminishing marginal productivities. Taking textiles as the numeraire good, the marginal productivity conditions in the two sectors for labour and capital in the home country can be written as:

$$r = G'(k_T) = pF'(k_C) \tag{16.3}$$

$$w = [G(k_T) - k_T G'(k_T)] = p[F(k_C) - k_C F'(k_C)] \tag{16.4}$$

where, p is the relative price of computers in the home country. Note that since capital is mobile across the two sectors within the home country, it must earn the same (real) rate of return regardless of which sector it is employed in. Hence, at the equilibrium, the marginal productivities of capital measured in terms of textiles must be the same (and equal to the real rate of return to capital) in the two sectors even though the production functions are different for computer and textile production. Similarly, marginal productivities of labour must be the same in both the sectors and be equal to the real wage. This equalization of sectoral marginal productivities is indicated by the second equalities in the above conditions.

Denoting the foreign country variables with asterisks, similar marginal productivity conditions in the foreign country can be written as:

$$r^* = G'(k_T^*) = p^* F'(k_C^*) \tag{16.5}$$

$$w^* = G(k_T^*) - k_T^* G'(k_T^*) = p^*[F(k_C^*) - k_C^* F'(k_C^*)] \tag{16.6}$$

Note that since the technologies for computer and textile production are the same in the home and the foreign countries, so $F(.)$ and $G(.)$ functions are identical. But, the factor intensity choices may differ because of initial differences in factor prices. Suppose, prior to factor flows, the rate of return to capital is higher in the home country. The factor price frontier (or zero profit conditions) discussed in Chapter 6 then implies that the real wage must be lower in the home country. These inter-country differences in factor prices may reflect the relative capital scarcity (or labour abundance) in the home country.

If *unrestricted* factor flows are allowed, the assumed factor price differences will cause foreign capital to flow into the home country and home labour to migrate to the foreign country. Suppose, the home country allows inflow of foreign capital but does not allow its workers to emigrate. Unrestricted capital inflow will then equalize the rate of return to capital in the two countries, and consequently the factor intensities in the textile sectors in the two countries. This is immediate from the first inequalities in equations (16.3) and (16.5) rewritten as:

$$r = r^* \Rightarrow G'(k_T^*) = G'(k_T) \Rightarrow k_T^* = k_T$$

This in turn implies that the real wages must be the same in the two countries as well. This follows from the fact that the same capital intensities employed now in the production of textiles in the two countries should equalize the marginal productivity of labour in the two countries since the countries have identical technologies.

Thus, what we get is that foreign capital inflow equalizes both the rate of return to capital and the real wages in the two countries. There is thus equalization of relative wages as well: $\frac{w}{r} = \frac{w^*}{r^*}$. Consequently, home and foreign producers will choose the same factor intensities for producing computers, given their identical technologies: $k_C = k_C^* = \tilde{k}_C$. The value of the marginal productivity of labour in computer production will thus be equalized in the two countries. Referring back to the conditions in equations (16.4) and (16.6), it then follows that the commodity price ratios are equalized:

$$p[F(k_c) - k_C F'(k_C)] = p^*[F(k_C^*) - k_C^* F'(k_C^*)] \Rightarrow p = p^* \text{ since } k_c = k_c^*$$

Thus, a foreign capital inflow equalizes goods prices across the countries and leaves no scope for arbitrage and trade in commodities. The same GPE result can be obtained if we had allowed emigration of home labour. In other words, under identical and constant returns to scale technology, factor flows (or factor trade) act as a substitute for commodity trade.

The intuition behind this GPE result is simple. Suppose, home country has a comparative advantage in textiles: $p < p^*$. From the relationship between commodity prices and factor prices discussed in Chapter 6, it follows then that $\frac{w}{r} < \frac{w^*}{r^*}$ since textiles are relatively labour intensive. When factor flows are allowed instead of commodity trade, capital flows into the home country since its relative return is higher here than in the foreign country. Even if labour is not allowed to emigrate from the home country, inflow of capital raises the output of computers and lowers that of textiles in the home country by the output magnification effect. The relative price of textiles thus rises in the home country. By similar reasoning, the relative price of textiles falls in the foreign country. Thus, through capital inflow from the foreign country to the home country, (relative) commodity prices get equalized. By the HO theorem, commodity trade would have taken place because scarcity of capital in the home country would make computers scarce here as reflected in $p < p^*$. When capital imports (or inflow) are allowed, it erodes the scarcity of capital and consequently of the capital intensive computers. Relative price of computers thus falls and gets equalized with that abroad and thereby leaves no scope for arbitrage and commodity trade. Due to capital import by a capital scarce country, therefore, import of computers is no longer needed to meet its scarcity. That is, free capital imports substitute commodity trade.

16.2 FOREIGN CAPITAL INFLOW: CAUSES AND CONSEQUENCES

In a world with no uncertainty, capital movements are primarily induced by differences in the rates of return to capital across countries and regions. Of course, there are other compelling reasons for capital flows such as depreciation or appreciation of the value of the national currency of a country vis-à-vis the national currencies of other countries. Differences in environmental standards may also lead to capital flight from developed to developing countries. This is, however, linked to a much broader phenomenon of migration of dirty industries, and is discussed later.

In this chapter we confine our discussion to the differences in factor prices as the major driver of factor movements. The important point to note here is that capital inflows may take place even with commodity trade because commodity trade does not necessarily lead to factor price equalization. Recall our discussions in Chapters 6 and 7 that there are a host of reasons that prohibit FPE despite commodity price equalization through free commodity trade. These include significantly different factor endowments of countries that leaves them specialized in different sets of goods, the production of non-traded goods, different production technologies, and factor specificity. Thus, factor price differences may exist even after commodity trade. That commodity trade and factor trade do coexist is reflected in the fact that capital flows across nations occur even when they trade commodities among them. We will discuss the implications factor flows in this context where commodity trade leaves the scope for factor flows, rather than in the context of factor flows without any commodity trade among nations. In such a context, factor flows may, in fact, augment commodity trade as demonstrated by Markusen (1983).

Given such a perspective, four major effects of foreign capital inflow on the host country are discussed here—growth, distribution, employment, and welfare effects. Of course, these effects are often interrelated as we will see below. We, however, delineate the employment effect from the rest as it allows us to discuss growth and welfare implications of capital inflows in a standard HOS context.

16.2.1 Growth, Welfare, and Distributional Consequences of Foreign Capital Inflow

Consider a host country with the standard two-commodity, two-factor HOS production structure and full employment in both these domestic factors of production. For such a host country, two distinctions are to be made for discussing the implications of capital inflow for changes in output, growth, and welfare. First, how large the capital inflow is, and second, how large the host country is in the world commodity market. Whether trade is free or restricted also influences the welfare and distributional implications of foreign capital inflows. We begin with the case of a small host country under free trade.

Case of a Small Host Country under Free Trade

The GPE result discussed above rests on the premise that countries allow unrestricted capital inflows and outflows. Thus, as soon as capital flows are allowed, large capital flows occur at the instant point of time to equilibrate the rates of return to capital in the two countries. That is, arbitrage is instantaneous and full. While this may certainly be the case, this is not the case that we see always. Countries do restrict capital mobility. Not only countries, particularly smaller countries, take policies against capital flight, they also restrict foreign capital inflows even when they are capital scarce countries. Part of the reason for this is that income distributional and welfare consequences may not always be desirable as we will see below. Thus, even if we take a purely utilitarian approach, and set aside political factors, there may be compelling reasons for a cautious approach to allow foreign capital inflows. The interesting point that the existing theories make, however, is that the costs and benefits of foreign capital inflows depend on the amount of inflows allowed.

To illustrate, consider the case of a small host country producing two goods, computers and textiles, with the two domestic factors of production, labour and physical capital. The incomplete specialization by this country follows from the fact that its relative endowment ratio lies in the Chipman-McKenzie cone of diversification discussed earlier and reproduced in Figure 16.1. For the wage–rental ratio (corresponding to the world commodity price ratio) given by the absolute slope of the line AB, the cone of diversification k_COk_T is specified by the least-cost input choices in the computer and the textile sectors of the economy. Any foreign capital inflows that shift the relative capital availability ratio for this small host country within this cone of diversification will leave the wage–rental ratio unchanged and hence there will be no change in this small host country's welfare.

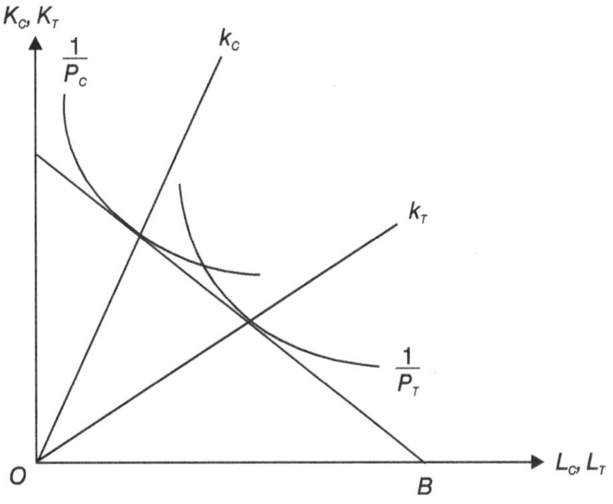

Figure 16.1 Capital Inflow and Factor Prices

The reason is as follows. A capital inflow leads to a growth effect, like the effect of accumulation of domestic capital. In both the cases, PPF shifts outward (though not uniformly for all levels of output) as a larger capital stock now enables the home country to produce more of both goods. But the difference is that the foreign capital is to be paid its value of marginal product under competitive conditions, which is repatriated back to the origin country. This payment to the foreign capital is thus a loss to the host country. That is, whereas the foreign capital-induced output growth is a source of welfare improvement for the host country, the competitive return to foreign capital is a source of welfare loss. If the rate of return to capital declines as foreign capital flows in, the foreign capital takes away less than its value of marginal product, and there will be a positive net growth effect on the welfare of the host country. But if factor prices do not change, the competitive return to foreign capital will leave the host country with no gain from output growth as the foreign capital takes all that it contributes. Since the capital inflow within the cone of diversification leaves the rate of return to capital unchanged, the growth effect on the host country's welfare is washed out by the payment to foreign capital.

Note, at the initial TOT, the foreign capital inflow changes the commodity composition towards the relatively capital-intensive good. This follows from the Rybczynski or output magnification result. Given the demand for goods, this produces an excess supply of the relatively capital-intensive good and an excess demand for the relatively labour-intensive good. The volumes of imports and exports thus change but since the host country is small, these changes will have no impact on its TOT. This is the reason why the factor prices in the host country remains unchanged.

But when the capital inflow is large enough to push the host country's relative capital availability ratio outside the cone of diversification, $k_C O k_T$, the host country no longer produces both the goods. It will be completely specialized in computers and textiles will now be entirely imported to meet local demand. Now it is easy to check that by the diminishing marginal productivity of the foreign capital, as more and more foreign capital flows in, the return to capital declines. Under perfectly competitive conditions, the value of the marginal product equals the rate of return paid to the foreign capital *at the margin*. But by diminishing returns to foreign capital, the value of the marginal product for *infra-marginal units* of foreign capital exceeds the competitive rate of return paid. That is, if $\tilde{K}_f$ is the amount of foreign capital flowing in, the contribution of this capital to total output of the host economy (which now produces only computers) is larger than the total amount paid to it. Thus, the host country now gains.

These welfare results are illustrated in Figure 16.2. The free trade welfare of the host country with no foreign capital inflow is *OF*. For foreign capital inflows that are smaller than K_f^*, the host country remains within the cone of diversification and the no-impact result illustrated in Figure 16.1 holds. The only effect of these small and moderately large capital inflows will be the change in commodity composition towards the relatively capital-intensive production of computers. Thus, the host country welfare remains unchanged at the free trade level. For capital inflows larger than this critical level, the home country is completely specialized in the production of computers, and diminishing returns to the variable factor (which is foreign capital here) then ensures that the rate of return to capital declines and foreign capital is thus paid less than what it contributes. The host country now gains as foreign capital flows in, and this gain monotonically increases with the amount of foreign capital that flows in.

The interesting point to note is that a foreign capital inflow can lower or increase the volume of trade depending on the initial trade pattern of the host country. If the host country was exporting the relatively capital-intensive computers prior to foreign capital inflow, such an inflow raises its volume of trade through the output magnification effect.[1] Thus, factor flows complement (or augment) commodity trade.

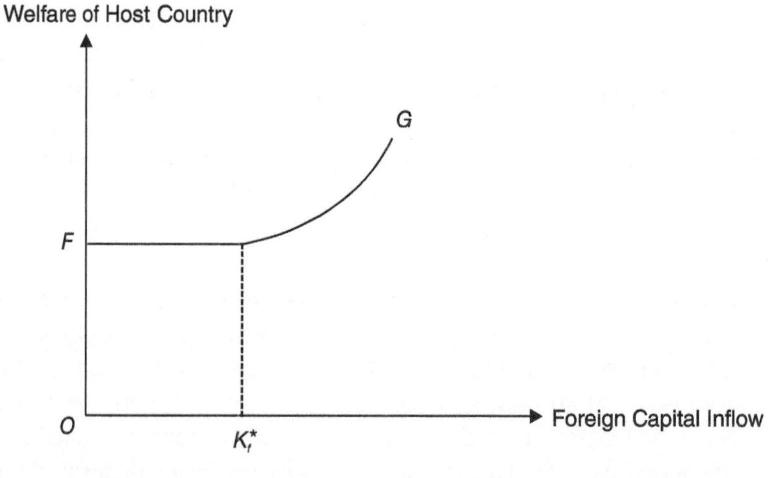

Figure 16.2 Foreign Capital Inflow and Welfare of Host Country

Case of a Small Host Country under Restricted Trade: Immiserizing Capital Inflow

The welfare effect of foreign capital inflow in a small country under restricted trade is, however, altogether different. Once again there will be no distributional consequences of small and moderately large capital inflows, but the country's welfare will unambiguously decline now.

Suppose, the host country was importing computers from the rest of the world and there was an ad-valorem tariff on such imports. Once again, the foreign capital inflow, as long as the host country produces both computers and textiles, cannot affect TOT and tariff-inclusive price. Thus, factor prices remain unchanged as under free trade discussed above. Yet, the welfare of the host country can change. To see how this happens, recall the algebra in Appendix A9 (Chapter 9) that defines the change in the real income of a country arising from three sources: TOT change, VOT change, and the growth of aggregate output. On top of that we will now have a welfare reducing effect in the change in the payments made to foreign capital. Thus, the change in the real income of the host country under tariff and foreign capital inflow can be expressed as:

$$dy = -Mdp^{W} + (p_d - p^{W})dM + (dX_T + p_d dX_C) - (rdK_f + K_f dr) \tag{16.7}$$

For the small host country, there is no TOT effect, so that the first term in equation (16.7) drops out. Now consider a very small foreign capital inflow that leaves the aggregate value of output unchanged and changes only the composition of output. Thus, the third term drops out as well. There will be no change in the payment to the foreign capital also because, first, the capital inflow is very small, and second, there is no change in factor prices. So all these leave us with the following expression for a change in the small host country's welfare under tariff for a very small foreign capital inflow:

$$dy = tp^{W} dM \tag{16.8}$$

Thus, the welfare change boils down to how a very small foreign capital inflow changes the volume of imports of the economy. Since the host country is assumed to import the relatively capital-intensive computers, by the Rybczynski (or output magnification) effect the foreign capital inflow lowers the volume of imports and consequently reduces the host country's welfare.

For moderately larger capital inflows, this VOT effect gets magnified. Though now we have a growth effect, as long as the capital inflow is not large enough to change the rate of return to capital (so that $K_f dr$ is still zero), this growth effect is washed out by competitive payments to foreign capital for the same reason as spelled out above. Thus, foreign capital inflow lowers welfare further:

$$dy = tp^{W} dM + (dX_T + p_d dX_C) - rdK_f < 0 \tag{16.9}$$

This remarkable result that a foreign capital inflow-led growth will be immiserizing was derived by Brecher and Diaz-Alejandro (1977). Thus, successive amounts of foreign capital inflows under tariff restricted trade lower the welfare of the small host country monotonically till all volume of imports vanish and the host country returns to its autarchic state.

After reaching the autarchic state, however, the domestic relative price of computers gets de-linked from its world relative price. The domestic price now jumps up to the pre-trade level above the world price. Moreover, this domestic relative price can now change if domestic supplies change even if the host country is small and faces a given set of world prices of computers and textiles.

Thus, further capital inflow (but still within the cone of diversification) lowers the domestic relative price of computers and with it the rate of return to capital by the price magnification effect because computers are relatively capital-intensive. This makes the net growth effect, captured by the last two terms in equation (16.7), positive. On the other hand, there will be no VOT effect as the capital inflow has already choked off all international trade. So now the welfare of the small host country rises with the capital inflow. The welfare increase continues till the domestic relative price falls to the level of the world relative price of computers. This is the free trade state and the welfare of the small host country is now constant at the free trade level of welfare for further inflows of foreign capital. Finally, when the capital inflow is large enough to push the economy's endowment outside the cone of diversification, its welfare rises again due to diminishing returns to foreign capital as spelled out above. These changes in the welfare of the small host country under tariff-restricted trade are illustrated in Figure 16.3. Note that since tariff restricted trade is sub-optimal for a small country, so before any foreign capital inflow took place, its welfare level was T, which was smaller than the free trade level of welfare F.

Case of a Large Host Country and TOT Change

For a large host country we have an additional TOT effect and with it a change in factor prices even for small or moderately large capital inflows that keep the country's endowment ratio within the cone of diversification. The TOT change now may be a source of welfare improvement or loss depending on the host country's pattern of specialization and trade. At the initial TOT, the foreign capital inflow changes the commodity composition towards the relatively capital-intensive good. As noted above, this follows from the output magnification effect. If the host country was initially exporting the relatively labour-intensive textiles, TOT improves in its favour since both its import demand and export supply will fall as foreign capital flows in. Thus, the welfare of the large host country improves on this account. The net growth effect is also positive in such a case since a TOT improvement, or a fall in the world relative price of capital-intensive imports, means a fall in the rate of return to capital by the price magnification effect. Thus, the foreign capital is paid less than it contributes to the total output. The only adverse effect of the foreign capital inflow is now through the fall in VOT.

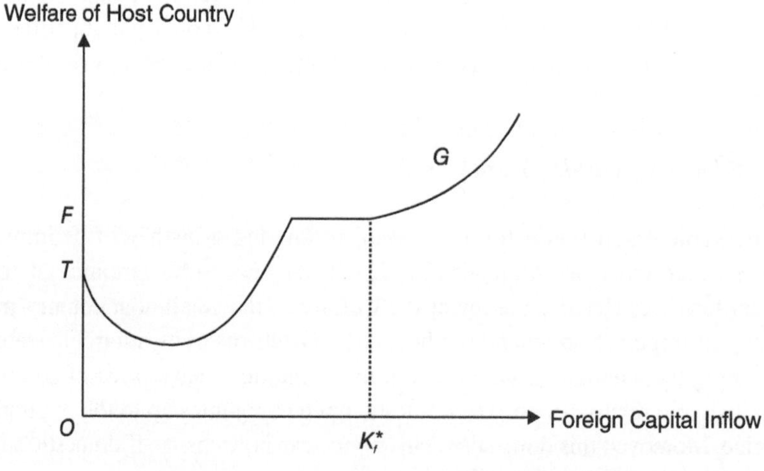

Figure 16.3 Foreign Capital Inflow under Tariff

It is immediate that when commodity trade is unrestricted, foreign capital inflow will unambiguously improve welfare if the large host country imports relatively capital-intensive computers. Under free trade the VOT effect does not exist. Every other effect remains the same. TOT improves if the host country imports the capital-intensive good, which in turn lowers the rate of return to capital and makes the net growth effect positive. But, if the large host country imports the relatively labour-intensive textiles, a foreign capital inflow will worsen its TOT, raise the competitive return to foreign capital and the host country will lose. Thus, in such a situation, foreign capital-led growth is immiserizing.

16.2.2 Foreign Capital Inflow and Aggregate Employment in the Host Country

Let us now turn to the effect of foreign capital inflow on aggregate employment in the host country. The employment effect largely depends on the production structure of the host economy as explained in Marjit and Acharyya (2003). We here discuss the case of a small dependent economy specified in Chapter 7. The host country produces a composite traded good (T) and a non-traded good (N). The money wage in the economy is rigid downward at a level higher than the one that ensures full employment of labour. The higher money wage causes a higher price of the non-traded good (which is relatively labour-intensive), which in turn lowers the demand for the non-traded good and consequently aggregate employment. The initial equilibrium with unemployment of labour under money wage rigidity in this dependent economy is shown in Figure 16.4. The level of aggregate employment L_e is indicated by the line through the point E, before foreign capital flew in.

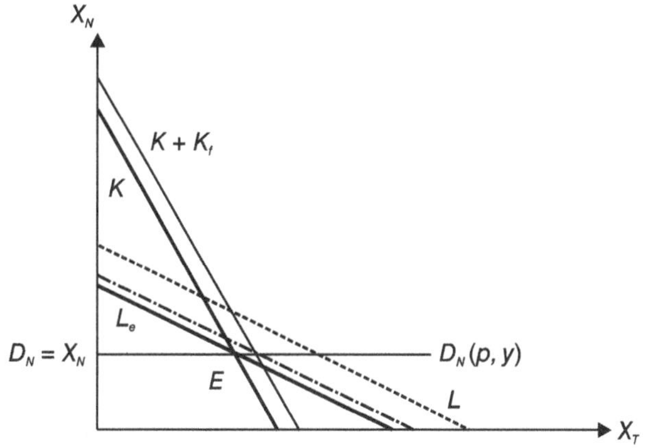

Figure 16.4 Foreign Capital Inflow and Employment

Note that under the rigid money wage, the rate of return to capital is determined by the world price of the composite traded good, and the price of the non-traded good is cost-determined. These are evident from the following zero profit conditions as specified earlier in Chapter 7:

$$P_T = a_{LT}\overline{W} + a_{KT}r \tag{16.10}$$

$$P_N = a_{LN}\overline{W} + a_{KN}r \tag{16.11}$$

Thus, restricted foreign capital inflows, regardless of size, neither affect the rate of return to capital nor the price of the non-traded good as long as the host country is small in the world commodity market. A very small capital inflow will have no growth effect either and hence the real income of the host country remains unchanged. This means, a very small capital inflow leaves the demand for the non-traded good and consequently its output unchanged. Only the output of the composite traded good expands due to greater availability of capital and aggregate employment unambiguously rises as a consequence. This is shown by the higher broken line to the immediate right of the bold line labeled K.

A large inflow, on the other hand, raises the aggregate value of output, but payments to the foreign capital at the competitive rate of return mean that there is no net growth effect. Once again, the real income remains unchanged. So, like the small capital inflow, aggregate employment increases through an increase in the production of the composite traded good.

16.3 FOREIGN DIRECT INVESTMENT AND MULTINATIONAL CORPORATION (MNC)

A large amount of world capital movement take place through foreign direct investment (FDI). During the 1970s and 1980s, FDI flows were predominantly within developed countries, with the United States heading the list of developed countries investing abroad. But, over the last two decades the direction of capital flows has changed significantly with an increasing share of FDI inflows in developing countries, particularly Asian countries. As Figure 16.5 shows, the share of FDI inflows in developed countries declined from 87 per cent in 1980 to 50 per cent in 2009. On the other hand, the share of FDI inflows in developing countries as a whole increased from a very low level of 12 per cent to 42 per cent over the same period. A large proportion of such FDI inflows have taken place in the Asian region, both from developed countries and, what is even more interesting, from developing countries in Asia itself.

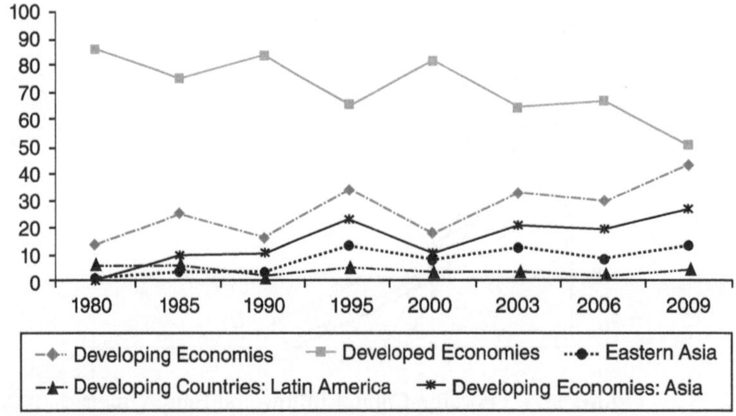

Figure 16.5 Share of FDI Inflow of Country Groups

Source: UNCTAD Trade Statistics.

According to the OECD definition, FDI is the net inflow of investments by a foreign MNC in an enterprise operating in another economy, the host country, with an aim to participate in the management of the enterprise through acquiring at least 10 per cent of the voting stock. FDI usually involves transfer of technology and expertise.

Box 16.1 Inward FDI in India

According to Reserve Bank of India's official figures of inward FDI from different source countries, majority of FDI comes from Mauritius, Singapore, The Netherlands, Japan, and the United States, contributing together on an average 75 per cent of total FDI received by India over the last 5–6 years. Share of UK in total inward FDI in India has declined significantly from 11 per cent in 2011–12 to little over 2 per cent in 2015–16. A sectoral decomposition of India's inward FDI, on the other hand, reveals some interesting facts (see Table 16.1 below). While manufacturing sector still attracts majority of FDI, its share has been declining. Services, including computer services, financial services, business services, and communication services, have attracted around 30 per cent of total FDI during 2011–16.

Table 16.1 Sector Composition of India's FDI

	2011–12	2012–13	2013–14	2014–15	2015–16
Manufacturing	39.78	35.70	39.75	38.84	23.40
Construction	11.22	7.21	7.95	6.63	11.48
Retail & Wholesale Trade	2.42	3.01	7.09	10.31	11.08
Electricity and other Energy Generation, Distribution & Transmission	5.94	9.04	8.00	5.19	3.78
Transportation	1.75	1.16	1.94	1.95	3.78
Sub Total	**61.10**	**56.13**	**64.73**	**62.91**	**53.52**
Services					
Computer Services	3.14	1.35	5.82	8.70	11.97
Financial Services	11.09	15.09	6.39	12.43	9.83
Business Services	6.77	3.52	3.25	2.75	8.40
Communication Services	6.21	0.50	7.82	4.34	7.31
Miscellaneous Services	3.41	3.02	5.86	2.37	2.83
Sub Total	**30.62**	**23.48**	**29.14**	**30.59**	**40.36**

Source: Author's compilation from RBI data.

FDI may take place in several forms, depending on the policy of the host country towards FDI. There may be a joint venture between a foreign MNC and a local firm in the host country. A typical example of FDI through a joint venture or collaboration in the insurance sector in India is Tata-AIG Insurance, which is a collaboration between the Indian enterprise—the Tata group—and the American enterprise—AIG. Takeovers, acquisitions, and mergers are other forms of FDI. An MNC may also invest through a subsidiary unit set up in the host country. Examples include foreign banks and financial intermediaries operating in India and other developing countries such as HSBC, Standard Chartered, and Citibank. In the automobile sector in India, Fiat, Ford, Hyundai, Nissan, Toyota, Volkswagen, and other foreign MNCs have set up subsidiaries to manufacture and sell their respective models of passenger cars.

There are many reasons that drive MNCs to operate through subsidiaries. FDI through a subsidiary operation can be viewed as a choice over producing the goods in the headquarter (located in the native country of the MNC) and then exporting the goods to the host country. From this perspective of FDI through a fully owned subsidiary as an *alternative* to exports by an MNC, the preference for FDI arises from low labour costs in the host country compared to the same in their own countries, high cost of transporting the final goods to the host country, and high tariffs and non-tariff barriers to imports by the host country. All these are compelling reasons as FDI through setting up of subsidiaries in the host country and producing goods there to serve the local market reduces the cost disadvantage that an MNC might face while competing with local producers by exporting its product.

Sometimes, a country may have a relative cost advantage in producing the basic stages or low value addition stages of a production activity. These stages are typically unskilled labour-intensive compared to higher order stages in a vertical chain of the production structure of a manufacturing good or a service product. Typically developing and low-income countries have relative cost advantages in these lower stages of production activities. This cost advantage often induces MNCs to fragment their production technologies and outsource low value addition production activities to these countries. The same can be done through the setting up of a subsidiary production unit in the host country and organizing the lower stages of production there using cheap local labour and raw materials. The intermediate goods produced through these subsidiaries (or by outsourced local firms in the host country) are then re-exported to the native country of the MNC as an input to the higher stages of production activities that produce the final good. This fragmentation of technology and production substantially reduces the overall cost of producing the final good for the MNC, provided transport costs of re-export are not significantly high, or service links between different production stages or blocks located in different countries are not too expensive. Thus, FDI through fragmentation of technology and outsourcing provides an MNC a competitive edge over its rivals in international export markets.

A typical reason for other modes of FDI, such as joint ventures, takeovers, acquisitions, and mergers, on the other hand, is to eliminate competition from local producers in the host country that the MNC would face had it exported its production to the host country. These forms of FDI also give rise to scale economies and synergy effects. In the case of a merger, for example, fixed costs are distributed over a large volume of production causing the unit cost of production to decline. Economies of scale may also arise from other indivisibilities such as production facilities, management functions, and management resources and systems. Synergy, on the other hand, refers to benefits other than those related to economies of scale such as enhanced managerial capabilities, innovativeness, R&D, and market coverage capacity due to the complementarity of resources and skills.

In the discussions below we briefly review the arguments of the tariff jumping theory of FDI and the outsourcing of production activities through fragmentation of production technology. We also discuss government policies for attracting FDI.

One such policy to attract FDI is lax environmental standards as the twin hypotheses of capital flight and pollution haven argue. We will review this dimension of government policy in Chapter 18. In this chapter we confine our discussion of government policy to Export Processing Zones.

16.3.1 Tariff Jumping Theory

Confronting a choice between setting up a production unit in the host country or exporting the good produced in its own country, an MNC may *ceteris paribus* take into consideration the

Box 16.2 Mergers and Acquisitions

Mergers can be of several types. A horizontal merger is a combination of two or more firms producing similar final or intermediate goods. A vertical merger is a combination of two or more firms involved in different stages of production or distribution of the same product. An example of a vertical merger is merger between a spinning company and a weaving company. A vertical merger may take the form of a forward or backward merger. When a manufacturing company combines with the supplier of the material, it is called backward merger and when it combines with the customer, it is known as a forward merger. A conglomerate merger, on the other hand, is a combination of firms engaged in unrelated lines of business activity. For example, a merger of different businesses like manufacturing of cement products, fertilizer products, electronic products, insurance investment, and advertising agencies is a conglomerate merger.

trade policy in the host country. When the host country government adopts a restrictive trade policy, but does not discriminate between local production and foreign production through subsidiary set ups, the MNC may well prefer FDI over exporting the good to the host country. The simplest way to capture this tariff jumping argument for FDI is to refer to the case of strategic Cournot competition between a domestic monopolist and a foreign monopolist discussed in Chapter 9. To focus on how a restrictive trade policy by itself can encourage FDI, suppose there is no cost advantage for the domestic monopolist that might arise from cheap local labour or other locational advantage. Thus, assume identical (and constant) marginal costs for domestic and the foreign monopolists. If the foreign monopolist produces the good in its own country and exports it to the home country, it pays a tariff to the home country government at the rate t per unit of exports to the home country. Reproducing Figure 11.3, the Cournot competition between the firms in the home country, given this tariff rate, yields $\frac{OX_t^*}{OX_t + OX_t^*}$ as the equilibrium market share for the exporter-MNC.

On the other hand, if the foreign MNC sets up a subsidiary production unit in the home country to produce the good there instead of exporting it, it can avoid the tariff payable to the home country government. If there is no tax imposed by the home country on FDI, there will be cost savings on the part of the foreign MNC and this will raise its market share and profit. This is shown by the equilibrium at point e. Note that R^* is the reaction curve of the foreign MNC when no tariff is imposed on its sales in the home country. However, local production through FDI is not costless. There are factory set-up costs and other operational costs, which do not vary with the level of output produced but are fixed or *sunk* in nature. Thus, the profit gain from local production through FDI instead of exporting goods, as indicated by a larger market share in Figure 16.6, is to be weighed against these operational costs.

These fixed or sunk costs do not effect the output choice of the foreign firm, but do effect the decision for FDI itself. Note that the domestic firm may be incurring similar operational costs, but that is not relevant here because as long as these costs do not vary with output levels, profit maximizing output choices remain unchanged. Denoting these fixed set-up costs by S, the net profit for the foreign MNC from local production through FDI is given by

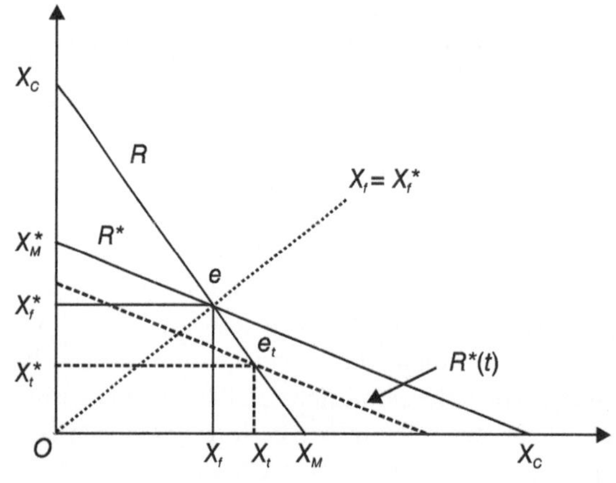

Figure 16.6 Market Shares under Exports and FDI Strategies

$\pi^*_{FDI} = \pi^*(x,x^*) - S$. Suppose the fixed cost is small enough to make the local production profitable, that is, $\pi^*_{FDI} > 0$. Now, the MNC will prefer FDI over exports if:

$$\pi^*_{FDI} = \pi^*(x,x^*) - S > \pi^*_{Exp} = \pi^*(x,x^*,t) \tag{16.12}$$

Since, the foreign MNC's profit decreases monotonically with an increase in the rate of tariff, the above condition is satisfied for high tariff rates given a particular level of fixed cost, *S*. This is the tariff jumping explanation of FDI. Figure 16.7 illustrates this. In the left-hand panel, the bold horizontal line gives us the net profit of the MNC from local production through FDI for a fixed set-up cost of S_0, and the downward sloping curve indicates its profit from exports. For all tariff rates higher than $t^*(S_0)$, the MNC will prefer local production of the good through FDI over exporting the good. Larger the set-up cost, higher is this critical tariff rate above which tariff jumping FDI takes place. This positive relationship is shown by the upward sloping curve *OA* in the right hand panel. That is, *OA* is the locus of pairs of set-up cost (*S*) and tariff (*t*) for which $\pi^*_{FDI} = \pi^*_{Exp}$ so that the MNC is indifferent between FDI and exports. For values of *s* and *t* in the right hand region, FDI is preferred over exports. That is, for all values of the set-up cost and tariff in this region, tariff jumping FDI takes place.

While tariff jumping FDI makes economic sense, with falling trade barriers all around in the present era of globalization, this explanation is no longer a relevant one. Rather, cheap local labour and economies of scale attained through fragmentation and outsourcing of production stages across different locations have become all the more relevant explanations for FDI.

The above analysis, however, can also be used to explain the transport cost argument for FDI. Interpret *t* as the rate of transport cost to be borne by the foreign MNC when it produces the good in its own country and exports the output to the home country. So even if trade is free, the foreign MNC's profit from exports to the home country will be the same as indicated by the downward sloping curve in the left hand panel in Figure 16.7: higher the transport cost per unit *ceteris paribus*, smaller is its profit from exports. The value t^* is now interpreted as the

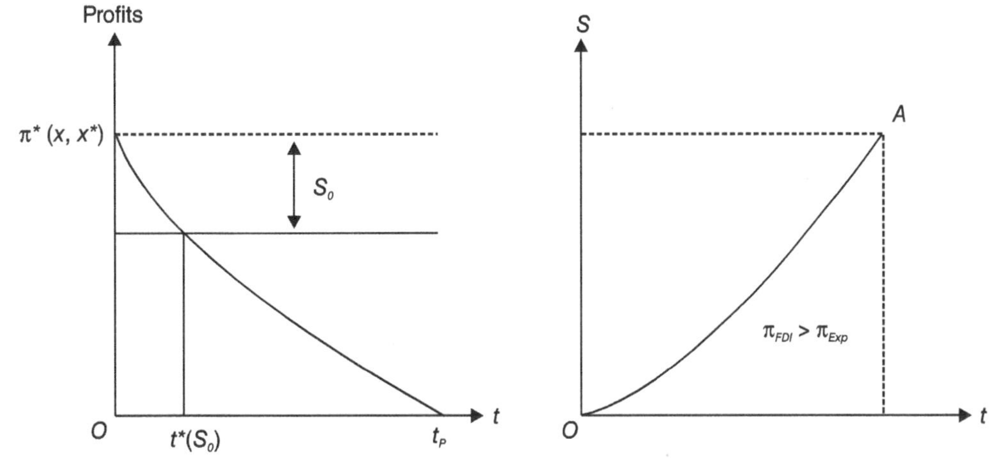

Figure 16.7 Tariff Jumping FDI

critical rate of transport cost above which local production through FDI will be preferred by the foreign MNC for a set-up cost of S_0.

16.3.2 Fragmentation, Global Value Chain and Economies of Scale

A large part of FDI is now driven by the economies of scale that can be achieved through fragmentation of production technology and outsourcing of the lower stages of production activities to the low-income developing countries. These stages are usually labour-intensive and thus a great deal of cost savings can be realized by outsourcing because of cheap labour in such countries. Outsourcing of low stages of IT & ITeS to Indian software companies by the US and European MNCs is a typical example. Other prominent examples include investments by US firms in assembly line production of automobiles in Mexico.

Fragmentation of the vertical chain of production processes and the outsourcing of different stages to different country locations, however, require service links to be established to connect these production stages or *blocks*. With the advent of IT technology, the cost of these service links has declined considerably over the past few decades. This has made fragmentation and outsourcing to even furthest locations cost-effective than ever before. Globalization and its scale effect, on the other hand, has made it possible to achieve economies of scale through larger fragmentation of production technologies. This idea has been elegantly captured by Jones and Kierzkowski (1990) in terms of a simple diagram reproduced below (Figure 16.8).

Lines *AB*, *CD*, *EF*, *GH*, and the like in Figure 16.8 represent total costs at different degrees of fragmentation and outsourcing of production activities. In each case, the marginal cost for the entire production activity may be constant (as reflected in the constant slopes of these lines). But, a higher degree of fragmentation should bring down the (constant) marginal cost because a better allocation of production activities across different locations can be made on the basis of comparative cost advantages (and productivity differences) of these locations. Thus, line *GH* in this example represents the highest degree of fragmentation and line *AB* the least. But, fragmentation requires service links in the form of communication and coordination among different production blocks. These costs are often invariant with respect to the scale of

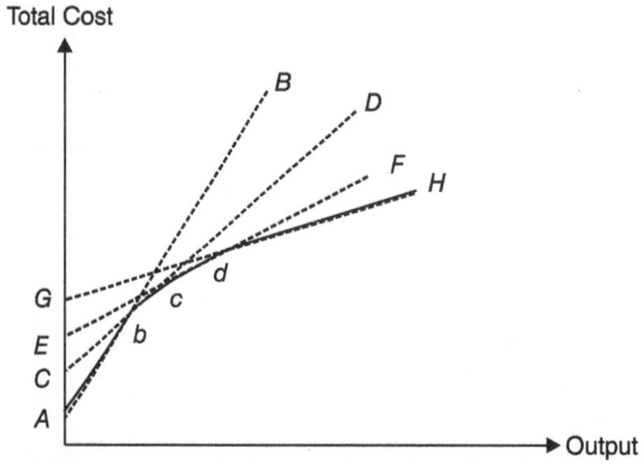

Figure 16.8 Fragmented Production Technology and IRS

operation. But the more fragmented a production technology is, larger are these fixed costs of service links. Thus, the most fragmented production technology indicated by line *GH* has the largest fixed cost. The lower envelope of these total cost curves, *AbcdH*, indicates that fragmentation of the production technology is an important source of economies of scale or increasing returns to production expansion.

Herein comes the role of globalization and growth. Globalization and trade liberalization expand the scope of the market and the scale of production. As the scale of production increases, more fragmented production technologies become cost minimizing. Of course, the total cost increases with the larger scale of operations and output, but at a decreasing rate (in a discrete manner though in Figure 16.8). Thus, increasing returns arise through the increasing order of fragmentation of production technologies made possible by globalization and the consequent increased market access for MNCs.

16.3.3 Fragmentation, Vertical Specialization, and Global Value Chain

One important dimension of fragmentation of vertical chain of production processes is global value chain (GVC). Many electronic goods, in particular, are now produced in fragments in different countries, starting from innovations and design in advanced industrial countries like USA and Japan, and then production of specialized inputs like semiconductors and processors by the NICs in East Asia like Republic of Korea and Chinese Taipei. Further value added, assembling and large scale production thereafter being organized in China for markets in the United States and in Europe. This chain of production processes is just one example of many similar but different combinations of countries performing different processes in vertical stages of production to manufacture the final consumable product. An obvious implication of GVC is many-fold increase in global trade in parts and components, or trade in manufacturing value added rather than global trade in finished products or gross value added (see, for example, Global Value Chain Development Report 2017). The nature of GVC participation by countries depends on their comparative advantages in different stages of the vertical chain of production. For example, the developed countries usually engage in high-end and intangible production activities, like research and development, design, and brand building, and in after-sales services and marketing stages. The developing countries, on the other hand, engage in low-end and tangible production activities, like manufacturing and assembly.

In this era of globalization, GVCs provide opportunities for the developing countries to increase their participation in global trade and, most importantly, to diversify their exports by specializing only in fragments of vertical stages of production according to their relative strengths and comparative advantages. Without the GVC, in order to diversify in their manufacturing exports the developing countries have to produce all the stages of a production process which may often be difficult given their resource constraints. In contrast, GVC allows them to divert their resources only to the production stages that they can do in best ways than other countries. Still the participation of developing countries in GVC has been rather limited. China is, of course, an exception. China tends to export more intermediate goods to other low-income downstream countries to support their final goods exports to the global market.

One of the reasons, as mentioned in the GVC Development Report (2017), is geographical proximity to the three main inter-connected hubs centred around the United States, around Germany in Europe, and around China, Japan, and South Korea in Asia. Only those developing countries trade in parts and components that are in closest proximity of any one of these hubs. Clearly, African countries are far from these hubs and rarely participate in such trade. The other important contributing factors for participation in GVCs include labour productivity in conjunction with wages and trade costs like tariffs and NTBs. Among the developing nations, those with relatively high labour productivities will also have relatively high wages, and yet may end up with having low unit labour costs if higher wages are not commensurate with higher productivities as may be the case when existing product and/or labour market conditions are imperfectly competitive. Conversely, low wages coupled with low labour productivity may cause a developing country a relatively high-cost producer of a fragment (or intermediate good) than a relatively high-wage developing country. That is, low wages may not be a driver of countries being able to participate in GVC. Non-tariff trade costs arising out of transport costs, insurance, country-specific regulations, licensing requirements, governance, and the like, also appear to be major impediments. Ad valorem tariff equivalents of these costs, though vary widely across sectors, are generally much higher than tariffs. Poor infrastructure and logistics for cross-border movements of parts and components add to these trade costs further.

The gains from GVC participation are, however, neither uniform nor always realized. Benefits of GVCs largely depend on whether a country operates at the high or at the low end of the value chain. Thus, given their respective comparative advantages in value chains, developed and developing countries may face asymmetric benefits and costs from joining GVCs (Baldwin, Ito, and Sato, 2014).

Measure of GVC uses multi-country input-output tables that helps identify the vertical structure of international production sharing. Hummels, Ishii, and Yi (2001) have made the GVC studies using input-output popular through the measurement of vertical specialization in terms of the amount of imported intermediate inputs used to produce an exported good. That is, the import content of exports has been taken by them as a measure of international production sharing. However, since the multi-country input-output tables essentially combines the national input-output tables of various countries at a given point of time, so transactions recorded are the domestic transactions. That is, production activities are territorial instead of national and accordingly it may be inappropriate to attribute value added in such activities as value added among countries.

An alternative to this measure of cross-border production-sharing activities is the value-added trade (Wang et. al. 2017). The value added method identifies two types of linkages in

GVC. One is the forward linkage, which is the domestic value-added embodied in intermediate exports that are further re-exported to third countries, expressed as a ratio of gross exports. It views a country's engagement in GVC activities from a producer perspective. The other is the backward linkage that views a country or sector's engagement in GVC activities from a user perspective, and is measured by the share of foreign value added in exports of a country.

However, a better index of international backward linkages is the foreign value-added in gross exports as a share of gross exports, which avoids double-counting possibility in case of the import-content measure. Since value added by an activity is the value of production less the value of intermediate goods used in that stage of production, so this foreign value-added measures the total value-added created in other countries together that enters the exports of the country under consideration.

Box 16.3 Import Intensity Measure of GVC Participation

Table 16.2 below reports the import intensity of exports of some selected developed and developing countries during 2006–16 as reported by OECD. Import content of exports reflects the extent to which a country is a user of foreign inputs, and is measured by the share of imported inputs in the overall exports of a country. This is often used an indicator of international backward linkages in GVC. The data on this measure indicates distinctly three different groups of countries. Countries having low international backward linkages like Australia, Brazil, Japan, and the United States; countries with medium international backward linkages like Canada, China, Germany, and India; and countries with high international backward linkages like the Newly Industrialized Countries (NICs) in Asia and America—South Korea, Singapore, Thailand, Viet Nam, and Mexico.

Table 16.2 Import Intensity of Exports and International Backward Linkage

	2006	2008	2010	2012	2014	2016
Low						
AUS	12.09	11.95	10.3	11.2	11.35	10.05
Brazil	10.94	11.01	9.6	10.63	11.53	10.22
Japan	12.24	15.18	12.16	13.95	15.81	11.38
USA	11.4	12.9	11.05	12.41	11.18	9.04
Moderate						
Canada	19.53	19.61	20.7	21.71	20.14	20.64
China	25.9	22.95	21.08	20.84	19.53	16.65
Germany	20.43	21.38	21.51	23.1	21.72	20.26
India	20.56	24.46	23.65	25.1	22.95	16.13
High						
Korea	34.18	41.19	38.19	42.0	37.34	30.37
Mexico	34.19	33.29	33.95	33.78	34.13	36.41
Singapore	44.58	45.2	41.27	43.76	43.03	39.45
Thailand	37.11	39.03	36.02	38.42	36.72	32.51
Viet Nam	38.07	41.51	40.51	40.85	42.42	43.6

Source: Author's compilation from OECD data.

16.3.4 Government Policies in Developing Countries: Export Processing Zones (EPZs)

Government policies in developing countries are often designed to attract FDI by facilitating assembly line production and re-export of finished products by foreign MNCs. A package of concessions is offered to foreign investors and MNCs to promote such activities by creating special economic zone (SEZs) or export processing zones (EPZs) in host countries. These concessions include free import of components, simplification of administrative procedures in setting up production units in the zone, tax holidays for foreign MNCs for a period ranging from 5 to 10 years, and different subsidy schemes that reduce fixed operation costs of the processing or assembly units. Infrastructure costs are also subsidized in most of the EPZs. Production units in these zones draw from the vast pool of cheap unskilled labour in the rest of the economy (or in the hinterland) of the host country.

In many developing countries, EPZs have played an important role in their growth and development processes. The prime example is *maquiladoras* in northern Mexico, where assembly line production is organized mostly by American MNCs for re-export to the United States. Initially *maquiladoras* were restricted to certain geographical locations or in the EPZs, but later these spread across different states of Mexico along the borders of the United States. These activities contribute 20–25 per cent of Mexico's GDP.

EPZs have played important roles in the development process in China as well. The package of concessions offered to investors in such EPZs has been combined with a control on labour inflow from the hinterland to the EPZs. Usually some specific (though simple) skills are required to work with foreign capital. In cases when such minimum skills are unavailable among local workers, migrating workers are trained to work with foreign capital. If the training cost increases with the number of workers migrating into these zones from the hinterland, then it makes sense for the local government to restrict the inflow of workers into these zones attracted by higher money wages there. This is the policy that the Chinese government adopted to keep the training costs borne by MNCs in check.

16.4 ASYMMETRY BETWEEN LABOUR MIGRATION AND CAPITAL FLOW

Though international labour migration in general has similar effects as capital flow, there is a basic asymmetry between the two when their welfare effects are considered. The asymmetry arises from whether the benefits of the migrants will be considered as part of the welfare of their country of origin or as a part of the host country. Like capital inflows in a host country, immigration of workers augments the value of aggregate output of the host country and thus benefits workers already residing and working there. For the country from where the workers emigrated, on the other hand, the value of aggregate output declines and this makes the workers left behind unambiguously worse-off. When the emigrants' incomes are counted in the national income of their native country, then the home country may actually gain. For the host country, on the other hand, the welfare change will be similar to what we have discussed above in case of a capital inflow.

The inclusion of emigrants' incomes in the national income of the country of origin makes sense for *temporary emigrants*. Temporary emigrants also remit back part of their earnings to their families back home. But for *permanent emigrants* from a home country to a host country, incomes earned by them should be a part of the national income of the host country. Yet the issue may not be that simple when the permanent immigrants to a host country retain their ties with their country of origin through frequent visits or even retaining the citizenship of their country of origin by birth. This has been the case with a large number of highly educated and skilled Indian immigrants in the United States.[2] There may thus be a convincing case for treating these permanent emigrants as part of the national population of their country of origin.

Box 16.4 EPZs as Engine of Growth in China

The International Labour Organization (ILO) defines EPZs as 'industrial zones with special incentives set up to attract foreign investors, in which imported materials undergo some degree of processing before being re-exported'. China's EPZs began as four SEZs in Shenzhen, Zhuhai, Shantou, and Xiamen in 1980 and later expanded to 14 open coastal cities. There are different types of EPZs in China and they are broadly called Development Zones. By the end of 2005, there were 210 national Development Zones (including 123 Enterprise Zones and 87 Industrial or Commercial Free Zones) and 1,346 provincial Development Zones. Production inputs entering EPZs are treated as exports and can take the duty drawback. The processing production and related work is free of value added tax and excise duties. All these concession policies have made the national Development Zones an efficient way of enhancing FDI inflow into China and thereby propelling its growth process.

Development Zones have become one of the main sources of China's industrial employment. Shares of all development zones in China's GDP and total trade were around 65 and 85 per cent respectively in 2005. The dark side of the EPZ-led growth in China is, however, a growing regional wage inequality among the coastal provinces (where most of the EPZs are being set up) and the hinterland.

SUMMARY POINTS

- A reverse of the FPE theorem, known as the Goods Price Equalization (GPE) theorem, was established by Robert Mundell (1957). If countries allow unrestricted factor flows, but not any commodity trade, and share the same technology, factor price equalization will also equalize commodity prices across the countries. Hence, there will be no scope for commodity trade even when countries allow such trade.
- Any small foreign capital inflow that shifts the relative capital availability ratio for a small host country within its cone of diversification will leave the wage–rental ratio unchanged and hence there will be no change in its national welfare.
- For larger capital inflows that push the host country's relative capital availability ratio outside the cone of diversification, the host country is completely specialized in its capital-intensive good. Then by the diminishing marginal productivity of foreign capital, as more and more foreign capital flows in, the return to capital declines, and the foreign capital is paid less than it contributes to the host country's output. The welfare of the host country thus rises with capital inflows.

(contd)

[2] Of late, the Government of India has decided to grant Overseas Citizenship of India (OCI) to persons of Indian origin who migrated from India and have taken up citizenship of a foreign country other than Bangladesh and Pakistan.

Summary Points (*contd*)

- If the host country exports the relatively capital-intensive good, foreign capital inflow raises its volume of trade through the output magnification effect. Thus, factor flows complement (or augment) commodity trade.
- Under tariff-restricted trade, the welfare of the small host country declines for small capital inflows if it imports the relatively capital-intensive good. This welfare loss comes from the VOT effect of the capital inflow. For moderately larger capital inflows, this VOT effect gets magnified. Though now we have a growth effect, it is washed out by competitive payments to foreign capital. Thus, foreign capital inflow lowers welfare further. That is, if a small host country imports the relatively capital-intensive good under tariff, a foreign capital inflow unambiguously lowers its welfare.
- When capital inflow chokes off all trade, further capital inflow lowers the domestic relative price of imports and with it the rate of return to foreign capital. In such a situation, the welfare of the small host country will rise.
- For a large host country we have an additional TOT effect and with it a change in factor prices even for small or moderately large capital inflows that keep the country's endowment ratio within its cone of diversification. The TOT change now may be a source of welfare improvement or loss depending on the host country's pattern of specialization and trade.
- A large amount of world capital movement takes place through foreign direct investment (FDI). FDI may take place in several forms, depending on the policy of the host country towards FDI. There may be a joint venture between a foreign MNC and a local firm in the host country. Other forms include mergers and acquisitions, setting up of wholly owned subsidiaries and fragmentation of production technologies, and outsourcing of lower stages of production activities.
- From the perspective of FDI through a fully owned subsidiary as an *alternative* to exports by an MNC, the preference for FDI arises from low labour costs in the host country compared to the same in their own countries, high cost of transporting the final good to the host country, and high tariffs and non-tariff barriers to imports by the host country.
- Government policies in developing countries are often designed to attract FDI by facilitating assembly line production and re-export of finished products by foreign MNCs. A package of concessions is offered to foreign investors and MNCs to promote such activities by creating SEZs or EPZs in host countries.
- Though international labour migration in general has similar effects as capital flow, there is a basic asymmetry between the two when their welfare effects are considered. The asymmetry arises from whether the benefits of the migrants will be considered as part of the welfare of their country of origin or as a part of the host country.

KEYWORDS

- **Goods price equalization theorem** asserts that if all countries share the same constant returns to scale technology, factor price equalization across countries through free movement of factors will equalize commodity prices across countries.
- **Foreign direct investment (FDI)** is the net inflow of investments by a foreign multinational company (MNC) in an enterprise operating in another economy, the host country, with an aim to participate in the management of the enterprise through acquiring at least 10 per cent of its voting stock.
- **Fragmentation** of technology means organizing different production stages of a vertical chain of production in different regions or countries to minimize the total cost of production and to attain economies of scale.
- **Merger** is an economic operation by two firms as one entity. A merger can be horizontal, vertical, or conglomerate, depending on the type of merged firms and economic operations.
- **Tariff jumping FDI** occurs when local production of goods in a host country through FDI by a foreign MNC is induced by high tariffs on imports of the same good.
- **Export processing zone (EPZ)** is an industrial zone with special incentives set up to attract foreign investors, in which imported material undergoes some degree of processing before being re-exported.

EXERCISES

1. In what sense does factor trade substitute commodity trade? Is there any situation where there will still be scope for commodity trade after factor trade?
2. Consider two countries freely trading two goods with each other. The goods are produced by labour and capital under constant returns to scale technologies and the countries have identical technologies for producing each good. Suppose, despite commodity price equalization through free trade, wages differ across these countries. If countries allow emigration and immigration, should the volume of trade be lowered or augmented by such labour migration?
3. Distinguish between the implications of a domestic capital accumulation-led growth and a foreign capital inflow-led growth in a country.
4. Algebraically derive the decomposition of a change in real income under restricted commodity trade and foreign capital inflow as specified in equation (16.7) in the text.

   [Hint: Under restricted foreign capital inflow, the value of GDP equals total domestic factor income and returns to foreign capital: $wL + rK + rK_f = X_T + pX_{C.}$]
5. Why is it that factor prices may change even for a small capital inflow that does not push a large country's endowment bundle outside its cone of diversification?
6. When can a capital inflow be immiserizing (or welfare reducing) for a large country under free trade? Is immiserizing more likely when capital flows in under tariff restricted commodity trade?

(contd)

Exercises (*contd*)

7. Consider a small open economy producing traded goods by homogeneous labour and sector-specific physical capital. The inputs are used in a fixed proportion in each sector.
   (a) Will all inputs be fully employed?
   (b) Suppose at the initial free commodity trade equilibrium, only labour was not fully employed. If the economy allows a small amount of foreign capital inflow, how does the aggregate employment change? Does your answer depend on which type of capital flows in?
8. In the above context, consider unrestricted inflow of foreign capital into the export sector.
   (a) Draw PPF for this economy and compare it with the PPF before the capital inflow (if there had been unemployment of labour).
   (b) Will the production of the import-competing good rise after the capital inflow?
   (c) How does the trade volume for this small economy change?
   (d) If there is a growth in the labour force in this economy, will the wage rate change? Compare your answer with a case where no capital inflow is allowed.
9. If an MNC produces a good in its own country and exports it to a foreign country, a fraction of output is lost in transit. The MNC can save on this loss of output and corresponding revenue if it produces the good in the foreign country through FDI, but has to incur a plant set up cost of Rs 100. The demand for the good in the foreign country is $p = 100 - X$, where X is the total supply. In either case, the MNC faces Cournot competition from a local supplier in the foreign country. The MNC has the same marginal cost of Rs 10 as the local firm regardless of where it produces the good. Should the MNC export the good or produce it in the foreign country through FDI?

SUGGESTED READING

Bhagwati, J.N. (1997). 'International Factor Movements and National Advantage', in V.N. Balasubramanyam (ed.), *Writings on International Economics*. New Delhi: Oxford University Press.

Caves, R.E., J. Frankel, and R.W. Jones. (1995). *World Trade and Payments*. New York: HarperCollins College Publishers.

Jones, R.W. (2000). *Globalization and the Theory of Input Trade*. Cambridge, MA: MIT Press.

ADVANCED READING

Baldwin, R., T. Ito, and H. Sato. 2014. *The Smile Curve: Evolving Sources of Value Added in Manufacturing*. Joint Research Program Series. Chiba City, Japan: Institute of Developing Economies—Japan External Trade Organization.

Brecher, R. and C.Diaz-Alejandro. (1977). 'Tariffs, Foreign Capital and Immiserizing Growth', *Journal of International Economics*, 7(4): 317–22.

Hummels, D., J. Ishii, and K-M. Yi. 2001. 'The Nature and Growth of Vertical Specialization in World Trade'. *Journal of International Economics* 54 (1): 75–96.

Jones, R.W. and H. Kierzkowski. (1990). 'The Role of Services in Production and International Trade: A Theoretical Framework', in R.W. Jones and A. Krueger (eds), *The Political Economy of International Trade*. Oxford: Basil Blackwell.

Marjit, S. and R. Acharyya. (2003). *International Trade, Wage Inequality and the Developing Economy*. Heidelberg: Physica/Springer Verlag.

Markusen, J. (1983). 'Factor Movements and Commodity Trade as Complements', *Journal of International Economics*, 14: 341–56.

Mundell, R. (1957). 'International Trade and Factor Mobility', *American Economic Review*, 47: 321–35.

Wang, Z., S.-J. Wei, X. Yu, and K. Zhu. 2017. 'Measures of Participation in Global Value Chains and Global Business Cycles'. Working Paper 23222, National Bureau of Economic Research, Cambridge, MA.

World Bank, 2017, Measuring and Analyzing the Impact of GVCs on Economic Development, Global Value Chain Development Report 2017.

17 Services Trade

Services account for more than 60 per cent of global production and employment. Compared to this, service exports account for much less, about 20–25 per cent of world exports of goods and services. But its importance is growing not only in developed countries but also in many developing countries. Part of the reason for this is that it is only after the recent advent of the telecommunications and transmission technology that many services, which had long been considered as purely domestic (or non-traded) activities, have become tradable. Thus, services are no longer just inputs to goods traded, but are themselves traded for final consumption. Being typically labour-intensive, services trade has the potential for generating substantial employment opportunities in the labour surplus developing countries. Unlike business and financial services, other categories of services like construction, transport and storage, and even telecommunications to a large extent, are unskilled- and semi-skilled-labour-intensive. Thus, growth in services trade can largely be beneficial for the labour-surplus developing nations.

Conceptually services trade is different from commodity trade in several ways. There are certain features of services that make their trade distinctly different from commodity trade. The determinants of comparative advantages of nations in services are also not exactly the same as those for commodities, though there are some broad similarities. Services trade has also been more restrictive than commodity trade and the multilateral negotiations on liberalizing services trade begun only recently after the formation of the World Trade Organization (WTO) in 1994. These differences, as we will discuss later, make it worthwhile to analyse services trade separately from commodity trade.

17.1 CONCEPTUAL ISSUES

The International Monetary Fund's (IMF's) 'Balance of Payment Manual' defines international trade in services as service transactions between the residents and non-residents of an economy. There are several plausible interpretations and definitions of service transactions. For example, the 'Manual on Statistics of International Trade in Services' of the European Statistical Agency defines the term 'services' as not separate entities over which ownership rights can be established. Services typically consist of changes in the condition of the consuming units realized by the activities of the producers at the demand of the customers. IMF's

International Economics. Rajat Acharyya, Oxford University Press. © Oxford University Press 2022.
DOI: 10.1093/oso/9780192865144.003.0017

definition of international trade in services also includes the value of services provided through foreign affiliates established abroad. Services are also supplied by individuals located abroad, either as service suppliers themselves or by being employed by service suppliers including those in the host country.

Services differ from goods in a number of ways. The most important difference is that many services cannot be separated from production activities. These are *joint products* as there is simultaneity in production, services, and consumption. Services also cannot be stored always and many services are non-transportable. This means that at least a significant part of services trade requires the physical proximity of the supplier and the customer in time as well as on location. These are trade in *personal* services. Thus, for international trade in such non-transportable personal services to take place, either the consumer must go the supplier or the supplier must go to the consumer. International trade agreements concerning services, in particular those embodied in the General Agreement on Trade in Services (GATS), make provisions for an agreement for suppliers moving to the country of the consumer. However, mainly because of the technical progress in telecommunications, certain types of services trade (such as banking, insurance, transcription of medical records, and call centres) can take place without physical contact between the service provider and the consumer. Improved telecommunications have also made it possible to establish cost-effective service links (such as distribution and communication) between different production blocks which is a crucial element for achieving economies of scale through fragmentation of production technologies and location of the different stages of production activities in different country locations according to their respective comparative advantages. These are *impersonal* services that do not require physical presence or face-to-face interactions between the service provider and the consumer (Mishra et al. 2011).

At the same time, there has been an increasing share of the services in the production of commodities whereby the services are traded in the form of trade in commodities. This is described as *embodied services trade*. A typical example is that the production and trade of automobiles requires service inputs like distribution and communication services. A study by Tucker and Sundberg (1988) reveals that in 1975 Australia and Thailand exported almost 50 and 32 per cent respectively of their services as embodied services in manufactured goods. But for Singapore, such embodied services export in 1973 was pretty low at around 18 per cent. Urata and Kiyota (2007) found that embodied services trade was significantly greater than disembodied services trade for both Japan and the United States in 1975 and 1985.

17.2 SERVICES TRADE: TYPES AND TRENDS

In development literature, conventional wisdom suggests that at a very early stage of the development of an economy, agricultural production constitutes the largest proportion of its GDP and national income. The next stage of development takes place through industrialization and growth in the production of manufacturing. Further development and growth shifts the composition of output more towards services. This pattern of development is evident from and reflected in a consistently larger share of service exports in the total exports and imports of goods and services for developed countries (see Figure 17.1). Their combined share increased from little over 20 per cent in 1990 to around 25 per cent in 2010. At the same time, the combined share of services was around 15 per cent of the total exports and imports of goods and services by developing countries. Some of the relatively advanced developing countries have share of services in GDPs far above this average for developing countries as a whole. For example, the service sector in India contributes more than 50 per cent to its GDP. India's service exports have also been quite high and comparable to those of UK and the US (see Box 17.1). This is somewhat contrary to the expected composition of aggregate output at India's stages of development. Similar service-led growth in East Asian countries like Thailand, Philippines, Singapore and South Korea, has also caused share of services in their total exports rising over the last two decades.

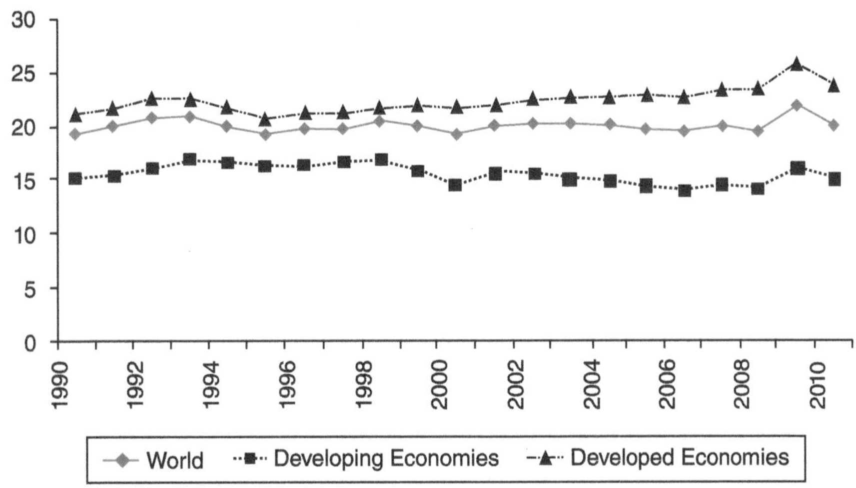

Figure 17.1 Percentage Share of Services Exports in Total Trade

Source: UNCTAD (2011).

Figure 17.2 reveals a similar picture but from a slightly different perspective. It shows the shares of high-income countries taken together, middle income countries taken together and lower-middle income countries taken together in world service exports. Not surprisingly, high income countries have the largest share—between 80–90 per cent—during the last three decades and a half. What is, however, interesting to observe is that the shares of these countries have declined steadily during these years. In contrast, the middle income countries have doubled their combined share of world service exports from 10 per cent in 1986 to 20 per cent in 2012.

Services are broadly classified into transportation, travel, and other services. Other services are further classified into construction, communication, insurance, financial, computer and information, other business services, personal, cultural and recreational services, and government services. Travel and transport services are typically low skill-intensive services, whereas insurance, financial, computer and information, and other business services are intensive in high skills. Thus, the changing composition of services exports of countries has some far-reaching implications for the pattern of job creation and employment generation. We will return to this in a later section of this chapter.

Box 17.1 India's Service Exports

It is often argued that India's development process has bypassed the phase of industrialization and shows the sign of a higher stage of development. Not only has the share of services in its GDP been more than 50 per cent during the last two decades, the share of services in the total exports of goods and services also increased significantly from 20 per cent in 1990 to 37 per cent in 2010. This is not only above the average share of all developing countries taken together but also much higher than the average share of all developed countries taken together. In fact, in terms of the importance of services in total exports, India is now comparable to the two major developed countries UK and the US with shares of service exports in their total trade in 2010 being 37 and 30 per cent respectively.

The largest components of India's service exports are computers and information services and other business services that account for 45 and 23 per cent of the services exports respectively. Both these categories of services are high and medium skill-intensive services. In contrast, traditional and low skill-intensive services like travel and transport account for 10 and 11 per cent of its total service exports respectively.

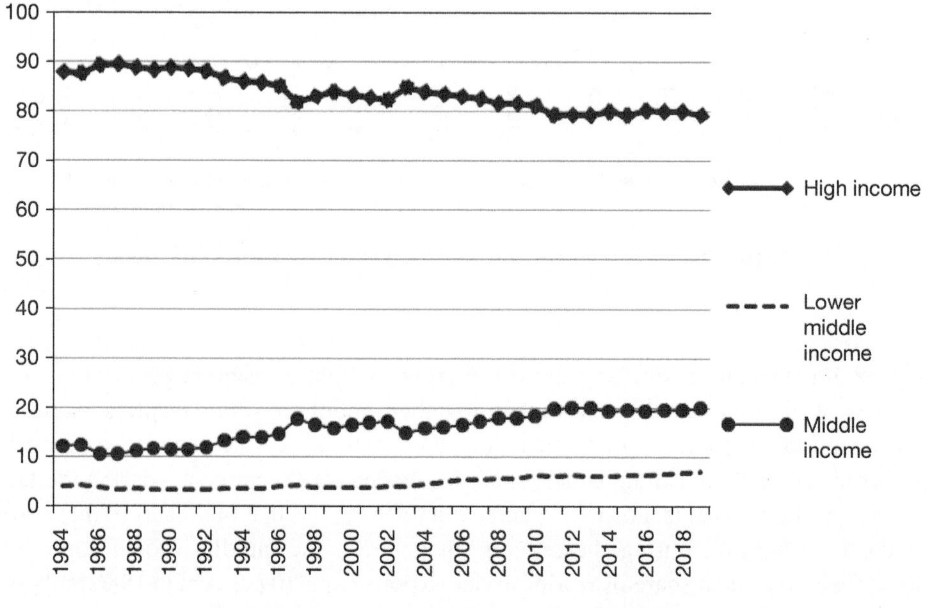

Figure 17.2 Share in World Service Exports

Source: Author's calculations from World Development Indicator 2020, World Bank.

By these broad classifications of services, a country may be a net exporter in some categories and a net importer in other categories of services depending on its pattern of comparative advantage and disadvantage within the service sector. For example, as is evident from Table 17.1, Japan was a net importer of transport services, communication services, insurance services and personal, cultural and recreational services during 2001–08. It also paid more to the rest of the world than it earned in royalties and license fees. However, overall, Japan was a *net exporter* of services.

Table 17.1 Net Exports of Services by Japan to the World (million USD)

	2001	2002	2003	2004	2005	2006	2007	2008
Total Services	736.51	1220.28	1817.22	510.38	517.76	885.81	1212.86	–477.66
Transportation	–1666.46	–1848.89	–2476.15	-3898.51	–4594.23	–4962.46	–5807.19	–6961.2
Travel	3361.88	3904.24	5137.78	4950.17	5593.10	6160.53	8145.28	8940.76
Other Services								
Communication	–340.84	–319.46	–173.81	–80.89	0	–4.41	–160.89	–199.40
Construction	53.27	67.91	62.90	77.95	94.69	97.89	68.61	68.78
Insurance	–90.51	–99.42	–121.27	–138.26	–146.62	–147.59	–169.02	–179.50
Financial	176.88	205.37	284.71	339.76	355.10	304.22	343.07	354.81
Computer and Information	10.86	98.33	76.52	155.17	83.23	126.75	45.52	108.55
Royalties and License Fees	–685.30	–862.23	–1057.78	–1223.75	–1451.73	–1560.06	–2096.77	–2296.19
Other Business Services	–22.24	120.07	184.18	609.67	846.14	1195.06	1274.86	237.71
Personal, Cultural, and Recreational	–133.44	–113.55	–156.94	–359.62	–334.48	–355.63	–430.52	–552.41
Government	72.40	67.91	57.07	78.69	72.54	30.87	0	0

Source: UNCTAD (2011).

On the other hand, GATS distinguishes between four modes of supplying services. These are cross-border trade (mode I supply), consumption abroad (mode II supply), commercial presence (mode III supply), and the presence of natural persons (mode IV supply). Cross-border supply is defined to cover service flows from the territory of one country into the territory of another country. Examples of cross-border or mode I supply of services are banking or architectural services transmitted via telecommunications or mail, tele-diagnosis of patients in India by medical teams in the United States, and call centres. Consumption abroad or mode II supply of services refers to situations where a service consumer moves into another country to obtain a service, such as tourists travelling in foreign countries, Indian and other Asian students receiving higher education in the United States or in UK, patients from Bangladesh travelling to Kolkata in India for their medical treatment, and foreign patients travelling to Costa Rica for dental procedures and to Singapore for cosmetic surgery.

Commercial presence or mode III supply refers to cases where a service supplier from one country establishes service units in another country to provide a service. This type of service includes domestic subsidiaries of foreign insurance companies, hotel chains, and establishing hospitals in a foreign country to provide medical services to foreign patients (such as India's Apollo Hospitals Group operating in Sri Lanka, Muscat, Dubai, Nepal, Tanzania, and Bangladesh). Finally, presence of natural persons or mode IV supply consists of persons from one country traveling to another country to provide a service. For example, professionals like accountants, doctors, and teachers rendering their services in a foreign country, and Indian engineers building roads in Afghanistan.

Developed country governments are keen to negotiate on commitments by the developing countries under the commercial presence, which is vital for their financial providers like banks and insurance companies, and for utility-service providers in water and electricity. On the other hand, developing countries will benefit the most in negotiating on the movement of people because they have a clear advantage in labour costs, both unskilled and skilled. But labour markets are still subject to the greatest restrictions resulting in a striking disparity between the development of global and highly mobile financial markets and immobile labour markets. This is certainly damaging for developing countries. The conflict of interest between developed and developing countries in liberalizing services trade is rooted in these distinct preferences for modes of service exports.

17.3 DETERMINANTS OF SERVICES TRADE

The comparative advantage of nations in services relative to goods or one type of service relative to the other type emanates from differences among countries in fundamentals. But since many services trade take place through factor movement and also a large part of services trade is actually embodied services trade, it may not be straightforward to say whether country differences and resulting comparative advantages will manifest in commodity flow, investment flow, or labour migration. In general, however, the basic motives and determinants of services trade are the same as that of goods trade. Thus, factor endowment, technology, taste, and economies of scale explanations discussed in earlier chapters should all be plausible explanations for services trade as well. For example, services are typically labour-intensive and so one can expect similar HOS explanations of goods trade. A country well endowed with labour should have comparative advantage in services. However, skill requirements vary widely across different types of services with financial and business services being highly skill- and technology-intensive. Thus, even within the service sector in general, we can expect countries specializing in different services according to the relative availability of workers with different skills. In fact, being relatively abundant in high skills, developed countries are

Box 17.2 The General Agreement of Trade in Services (GATS)

GATS was initiated in the Uruguay Round of negotiations under GATT and came into force in January 1995 after the formation of the WTO. This was intended to specify the rules for international trade in services and achieve trade liberalization across all GATT (and the WTO) member countries. GATS establishes a framework of rules to ensure that service regulations do not constitute unnecessary barriers to trade. It covers all the four modes of supply of services as defined earlier. But Article I(3) of GATS excludes services supplied 'in the exercise of government authority' such as social security schemes and other public services such as health and education that are provided 'at non-market conditions'. Article II of GATS, on the other hand, specifies the general obligations for all member countries of the WTO as an MFN treatment. By this MFN obligation the members must extend immediately and *unconditionally* 'treatment no less favourable than that accorded to like services and services suppliers of any other country' to services or service suppliers of all other members.

observed to specialize in financial and business services. On the other hand, with the notable exception of India, developing countries primarily specialize in traditional services like travel, transport and also in communication, which is not as skill-intensive as financial and business services. Asian developing countries like Korea, Singapore, Thailand, Malaysia, and Kuwait are major exporters of transport services, followed by some European economies like Turkey, Russia, Poland, Ukraine, and Latin American countries like Argentina, Brazil, and Mexico. Major developing country exporters of travel services are China, Mexico, Korea, Thailand, and Turkey.

But, India's exports of computing and data processing services and software services offer interesting case studies for a developing country having somewhat different specialization patterns in goods and services exports. High-technology and skill-intensive *goods* exports constitutes only about 5–6 per cent of the total exports of manufacturing goods for India, whereas low skill-intensive goods like leather manufacturing and cotton textiles still constitute the largest shares. In sharp contrast to this pattern of exports in manufacturing goods, India has been a significant player in the world market as far as the relatively skill-intensive service exports are concerned. For example, in 1998 India was the single largest supplier of computing and data processing services that the United States imported from developing countries (which constituted 30 per cent of the total imports by the United States). Indian software industry, its most dynamic export sector, is the most interesting success story of a developing country exporting skill-intensive services (see Boxes 17.1 and 17.3).

On the other hand, as observed by a UNCTAD study in 2004, countries like Egypt, Paraguay, and Turkey were successfully exporting certain kinds of services such as transport services, construction services, and royalties and license fees, though they were modest performers in exports of merchandise. Thus, for some of the developing countries, the pattern of export of services and of goods is not similar in terms of technology and skill intensities. Overall, however, major developing country exporters of services largely coincide with major developing country exporters of merchandise.

Comparative advantages in certain services are also linked to (or are derived from) the strength of a country in the industry relevant for those services. For example, the comparative advantage of many developing countries in maritime transport services (and commercial fleets) arises from the competitiveness of their national shipbuilding industries. Accordingly, major exporters of transport services are the newly industrialized and relatively advanced developing countries in Asia and Latin America.

Time zone differences of countries that are geographically far apart and belong to non-overlapping time zones are observed to engage in a lot of services trade, though virtually. The typical example is virtual trade in intermediate services, mainly in business processing services, between India and the United States. Marjit et al. (2020) call this time zone differences constituting the basis of services trade as the fourth dimension, since even if the fundamentals discussed in Chapter 1 are the same, time zone itself establishes comparative advantage for these countries in different stages of the production process. Non-overlapping time zones enable a production process to be completed virtually in 24 hours (or one-day time) and thus make it cost efficient through trade in production processes between India and the United States. Thus, geographical distance, which usually constrains international trade in goods by increasing the cost of transporting goods from one country to the other, may actually promote virtual trade in intermediate services by placing countries in different and non-overlapping time zones. There are, however, two pre-requisites for such a virtual trade in services to take place. First, a service production activity can be performed in fragments or in different vertically segmented stages; and second, the technology should be such that the service output at each fragmented stage can be transported quickly with little costs to another country. While for many service activities fragmentation is feasible, such as software development, revolution in the IT sector has reduced the delivery costs to almost zero. Of course, a well-developed information communication network connecting the two countries is needed for this, a condition that is satisfied for both India and the United States. In fact, as Marjit et al. (2020) specify, these countries essentially engage in *periodic intra-industry trade* in services. The idea is that the night-time demand in one time zone is fulfilled by using daytime supply in another time zone. The day-time service in the home country can be purchased from day-time service providers there and night-time service providers in the foreign country. As the night shift wage is higher in both countries, so the day-time service providers have a cost advantage. That is, the home country will be a net exporter of services during its day time and the foreign country will be a net exporter of services during home's night time. Thus a periodic intra industry trade occurs between the two countries mainly due to the time zone differences, and such trade could be gainful.

Another important determinant of services trade is the trust between the service exporter and importer. Services being more relationship specific, the trust factor is often a crucial element of a country's service export growth. Empirical estimates of the determinants of comparative advantages in services by van der Marel (2012), for example, suggests that exporters who enjoy a higher level of trust by importers tend to trade more services. Sharing a similar language and culture with the importing country is also important for certain types of service exports. India's comparative advantage in IT-enabled services exports and front-office category of business process outsourcing (BPO) like customer interaction services largely arises from English

Box 17.3 India's Comparative Advantage in Services

As Chanda (2002) observes, India's significant comparative advantage lies in the mode IV supply of services and also in mode I supply (cross-border services exports such as BPO). India is the largest supplier of IT professionals to the United States and a major supplier to Canada, Germany, Austria, Japan, and Singapore. Despite recent trends of software services being imported from India through offshore and outsourcing activities, the movement of software engineers has remained the major mode of India's software service exports to the United States. India's comparative advantage over other developing countries (as well as over many relatively developed countries) in exports of mode IV-based professional and business services like health, engineering, accountancy, and management, is also evident from the larger number of H1B visas being granted by the United States to Indian professionals. Moreover, among all countries, Indian doctors working abroad are the largest in number.

In mode I supply, primarily offshoring and outsourcing, India is a leading destination for many developed countries. India has the largest exports of outsourced services in the United States, primarily due to complementary time zones that India and the United States belong to. It also exports large outsourced services to Europe and Japan.

as a language being taught in Indian schools and being the medium of instruction in higher education in many disciplines, a legacy of British colonial rule in India, that have resulted in a sizeable English-speaking educated urban population.

Recent estimates of revealed comparative advantage (RCA) of European countries by Lundstrom and Mishra (2011) reveal that EU-15 has RCA in services and the gap between goods and services is increasing.

17.4 SERVICES TRADE, WELFARE GAINS, AND GROWTH

17.4.1 Welfare Gains and Income Distribution

Mutual gains from services trade and the within-country distribution of such gains may, however, depend on the pattern of specialization and services trade. When services trade takes place between two countries as cross-border supplies (such as India providing call centre services to British Airways and e-banking service provided by British banks to Indian customers), both countries will gain just like in goods trade. Service consumers everywhere will benefit from the lower price due to increased competition, and service providers will gain from the larger markets and the increased price of their services. On the other hand, the observed pattern of services trade between developed and developing countries, in general, is expected to cause income gains being distributed in favour of skilled workers in the former and against them in the latter group of countries. Developing countries like India may, however, have a similar distributional experience as developed countries because of their similar pattern of services trade.

In general, countries importing services will gain unambiguously regardless of the mode of supply and the pattern of service specialization, provided of course that such a pattern of trade is consistent with their comparative advantages. That service importing countries unambiguously gain but service exporting countries may not always gain can be illustrated in the context of services trade through mode IV supply, which in essence is the same as the gains from labour migration. Consider as an illustration the world comprising of India and the United States. The countries have different endowments of the only two factors of production, IT professionals and physical capital that they work with to produce goods like software as well as to provide IT-enabled-services. In Figure 17.3, the total number of IT professionals equal OO^*, with O^*L_0 professionals in India and OL_0 in the United States. Given the prices of the good that is being produced and the stock of physical capital in these countries, the two concave curves labeled VMP_L^{Ind} and VMP_L^{USA} represent the *value* of marginal product of the Indian and the American IT professionals respectively. Further, suppose that these professionals are equally skilled and the difference in their (physical) marginal productivities, if any, arises solely from the different endowment of physical capital in the two countries. That is, Indian and American professionals are perfect substitutes. Given the larger number of IT professionals in India at a particular point of time under consideration, before any migration and services trade between these countries, the wage for IT professionals in India is lower than that in the United States. If now labour migration is allowed, Indian professionals will migrate to the United States till wages in the two countries are equalized at OW^* (= O^*f). Thus, L_0L_1 professionals will immigrate to the United States. India thus exports the service of IT professionals.

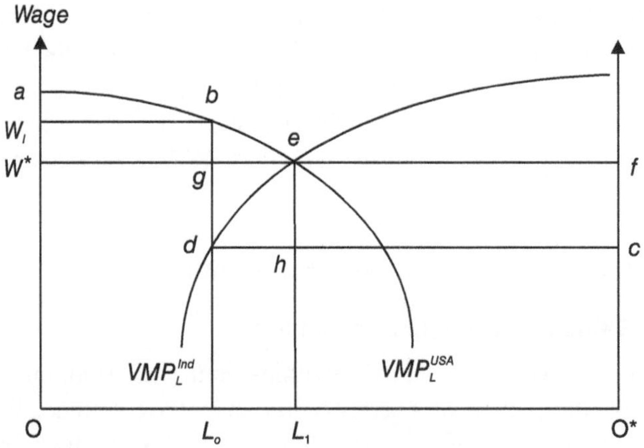

Figure 17.3 Gains from Mode IV Services Trade

As a consequence of this service export by India through migration of IT professionals, the global output of IT professionals increases by the area *bed*. This global output (and welfare) gain arises through efficient allocation of IT professionals and their services. The United States unambiguously gains from this import of services through immigration of IT professionals from India. By the surplus measure—value of output less wage bill—his gain equals the area *beg*. The service exporting country India may gain or lose depending on permanent or temporary migration of IT professionals. If this emigration is temporary, or in case of permanent migration if the entire income of the IT professionals emigrating to the US is repatriated to India, India's welfare increases by the area *dge*. Otherwise, India (and those IT professionals who stay back) lose by the area *edh*.

17.4.2 Services Export-Led Growth

Service exports just like merchandise or goods exports can be an important source of growth for countries. China and India's growth experiences for the last couple of decades, in fact, offer two interesting but different routes to achieve and sustain high growth rates. Whereas China has followed the high-technology manufacturing-led growth strategy, India's impressive growth has been mainly driven by its service sector. Thus, growth in service exports itself can be an alternative source of rapid output growth in developing countries. Though there is not much of theory that explicitly formalizes the causal link between service exports and output growth, similar mechanisms in general should underlie such a link as those that link the exports of goods and output growth. At the same time, there is an important distinction between goods and service exports that warrants a separate theoretical analysis for service exports and output growth relationship. As we have mentioned earlier, many services cannot be stored and thus cannot be accumulated over time. Thus, the factor accumulation theories may not be directly applicable to study the causal link between services exports and output growth.

There are not too many empirical studies as well. Two studies deserve mention here. First is the UNCTAD (2004) study that analysed the services-exports-growth relationship for 114 countries over the period 1980–2000. The study found that the link between services export and the output growth varied across developed and developing countries. Moreover, the export elasticity of GDP was much higher in the case of goods exports than in the case of service exports. For developing countries, transport and travel services were potentially the most important drivers of output growth. However, for travel services, there was a significant leakage effect as a large part of export receipts from travel services accrued to foreign agents. Thus, often the link between travel service exports and output growth was weak. The relatively stronger link between the services export and output growth for developed countries, on the other hand, was partly attributable to the nature of service exports of these countries, namely, financial and the business services that are both technology- and skill-intensive and are most dynamic service sectors.

What appears from UNCTAD's study is very similar to what has been pointed out in Chapter 15 for goods exports. For a stronger causal link between service exports and output growth, the nature of service exports may be more important. A more recent study by Mishra et al. (2011) finds precise empirical support for this dimension of service exports. By constructing an index of service exports sophistication in a similar way as the *EXPY* index of the sophistication of a country's merchandise export basket constructed by Hausmann et al. (2007), they find not only that export sophistication promoted growth in per capita income for 103 countries over the period 1990–2007, but that it also predicted *subsequent* growth.

However, this once again poses the development challenge. A developing country like India that chooses the services-led growth strategy needs to promote skill-intensive service exports to achieve faster growth. But that means marginalization of the unskilled and the poor, both in terms of employment and income opportunities at least in the initial stages of the growth. Like the high-technology-intensive manufacturing exports driven growth, this type of service export-led growth is also exclusive.

Virtual trade in services driven by non-overlapping time zones also has the potential to increase growth for both the trading partners. Marjit et al. (2020) discuss several channels through which growth may be promoted. First, virtual trade in production processes will increase output per unit of time and hence cause growth. Second, a time saving technological advance in one of the countries will increase marginal productivity of capital in both countries

Box 17.4 Jobless Growth in India

Growth in the service sector and services exports has not been accompanied by any significant employment growth in India. IT, ITeS, and financial services have grown more rapidly than other services. Consequently, India's composition of service exports has shifted from traditional services like transportation and travel towards business and financial services that are relatively high skill-intensive services. This has created employment opportunities for skilled workers rather than for unskilled ones. The only sub-sector that has grown to generate some employment for unskilled workers is construction services. In 2008 the IT and BPO sectors which accounted for almost 25 per cent of India's services exports directly employed less than 0.5 per cent of its labour force. *Indirect job creation* has been estimated to be only 1.8 per cent.

at the same rate. The interesting implication of this is a terms of trade improvement for the other country where no technological improvement has taken place because of an increase in demand for its intermediate services. This terms of trade improvement promotes economic growth there. Third, growth potentials vary positively with the geographical distance. Since more distant the two trading countries are from each other, less overlapping are the time zones of the countries concerned, so when distance between two countries is the largest, virtual trade is most beneficial. This increases both production and profits, which can in turn be reinvested to stimulate growth.

However, virtual trade in services is almost certain to worsen within-country inequality by increasing relative demand for skilled labour.

SUMMARY POINTS

- After the recent advent of the telecommunications and transmission technology many services, which had long been considered as purely domestic (or non-traded) activities, have become tradable. Thus, services are no longer just inputs to goods traded, but are themselves traded for final consumption.
- Many services cannot be separated from production activities. These are joint products as there is simultaneity in production, services, and consumption. Services also cannot always be stored and many services are non-transportable. This means that at least a significant part of the services trade requires the physical proximity of the supplier and the customer in time as well as on location. These are trade in *personal* services.
- Certain types of services trade (such as banking, insurance, transcription of medical records, and call centres) can take place without physical contact between the service provider and the consumer. These are trade in *impersonal* services.
- Some services are traded in the form of trade in commodities. These are *embodied services trade*. A typical example is that the production and trade of automobiles require service inputs like distribution and communication services.
- GATS distinguishes between four modes of supplying services. These are cross-border trade (mode I supply), consumption abroad (mode II supply), commercial presence (mode III supply), and the presence of natural persons (mode IV supply).
- Developed country governments are keen to negotiate on commitments under commercial presence, whereas developing countries will benefit the most in negotiating on the movement of people because they have a clear advantage in labour costs, both unskilled and skilled.
- Skill requirements vary widely across different types of services with financial and business services being highly skill- and technology-intensive. Thus, even within the service sector in general, we can expect countries specializing in different services according to their relative availability of workers with different skills.

- Comparative advantages in certain services are also linked to (or are derived from) the strength of a country in the industry relevant for those services.
- Services being more relationship specific, another important determinant of services trade is the trust between the service exporter and importer.
- Sharing a similar language and culture with the importing country is also important for certain types of service exports.
- When services trade takes place between two countries as cross-border supplies, both countries will gain just like in goods trade.
- In general, countries importing services will gain unambiguously regardless of the mode of supply and the pattern of service specialization provided of course such pattern of trade is consistent with their comparative advantages.
- The observed pattern of services trade between developed and developing countries, in general, is expected to cause income gains being distributed in favour of skilled workers in the former and against them in the latter group of countries.
- Like merchandise or goods exports, service exports can be an important source of growth for countries. India's impressive growth has been mainly driven by its service sector.
- Many services cannot be stored and thus cannot be accumulated over time. This means factor accumulation theories may not be directly applicable to study the causal link between service exports and output growth.

KEYWORDS

- **Trade in services,** as defined in the International Monetary Fund's 'Balance of Payment Manual', is service transactions between residents and non-residents of an economy.
- **Embodied services trade** refers to services being traded as inputs to or as an integral part of traded commodities.
- **General Agreement on Trade in Services** (GATS), which came into force in January 1995, was intended to specify rules for international trade in services and achieve trade liberalization across all GATT (and the WTO) member countries. GATS establishes a framework of rules to ensure that service regulations do not constitute unnecessary barriers to trade.
- **Cross-border supply** is defined to cover service flows from the territory of one country into the territory of another country.
- **Consumption abroad** or mode II supply of services refers to situations where a service consumer moves into another country to obtain a service.

(*contd*)

Keywords (*contd*)

- **Commercial presence** or mode III supply refers to cases where a service supplier from one country establishes service units in another country to provide a service.
- **Presence of natural persons** or mode IV supply consists of persons from one country traveling to another country to provide a service.
- **IT-enabled services** (ITeS) are a broad category of services covering different kinds of data processing and voice interactions that use some IT infrastructure as inputs, but do not necessarily involve the production of IT outputs.
- **Business process outsourcing** (**BPO**) is a sub-set of outsourcing that involves the contracting of operations and responsibilities of specific business processes replacing in-house services with labour from an outside firm. It is typically categorized into *back office outsourcing*, which is outsourcing of internal business functions such as human resources or finance and accounting, and *front office outsourcing*, which is a customer-related service such as call centre services.

EXERCISES

1. Distinguish between personal and impersonal services. Give examples to clarify your answer.
2. Distinguish between the different types of supply of services as laid down in GATS.
3. Categorize the supply of services in the following instances:
   (a) Anne and Mary, two British nationals, visiting the Sphinx and Pyramids.
   (b) The chief chef of Le Meurice, Paris, teaching a course in French cuisine to apprentices in Delhi through tele-conferencing.
   (c) McDonald's outlets in New Delhi and Bangalore.
   (d) Pandit Ravi Shankar, the Indian sitar maestro, performing in the city of New York during his music tour of the United States.
   (e) Diego Maradona coaching the Indian national soccer team.
   (f) Indian cricketer Yuvraj Singh travelling to the United States for treatment for his lung cancer.
   (g) The State Bank of India opening its overseas branch in the city of Berlin.
   (h) Flight information service provided to British Airways passengers by a call centre in Bangalore.
4. How can language and culture be a determinant of service exports? Give an example of service exports where these are relevant.
5. Should service exports be beneficial for unskilled workers in an economy?
6. How can service exports promote the growth of a country? What are the country experiences in this regard?
7. How different are Chinese and Indian growth processes?

SUGGESTED READING

Chanda, R. (2002). *Globalization of Services: India's Opportunities and Constraints*. New Delhi: Oxford University Press.

Mattoo, A., R.M. Stern, and G. Zanini (eds). (2008). *A Handbook of International Trade in Services*. Calrendon: World Bank/Oxford University Press.

Raychaudhuri, A. and P. De. (2012). *International Trade in Services in India: Implications for Growth and Inequality in a Globalized World*. New Delhi: Oxford University Press.

ADVANCED READING

Hausmann, R., Jason Hwang, and Dani Rodrik. (2007). 'What You Export Matters', *Journal of Economic Growth*, 12(1): 1–25.

Lundstrom, S. and S. Mishra. (2011). 'Service Export Sophistication and Europe's New Growth Model', Policy Research Working Paper No. 5793, World Bank Europe and Central Asia Region.

Marjit, S., B. Mandal, N. Nakanishi. (2020). *Virtual Trade and Comparative Advantage—The Fourth Dimension*. Kobe University Monograph Series in Social Science Research (Series Editors: Takashi Yanagawa). Springer Singapore and Kobe University.

Marel, E. Van der (2012). 'Determinants of Comparative Advantage in Services', Working Paper No. 087, FIW Working Paper Series, Austrian Institute of Economic Research, March, Vienna.

Mishra, S., S. Lundstrom, and R. Anand. (2011). 'Service Export Sophistication and Economic Growth', Policy Research Working Paper No. 5606, World Bank South Asia Region Economic Policy and Poverty.

Tucker, K. and M. Sundberg. (1988). *International Trade in Services*. London: Routledge.

UNCTAD (2004). 'Exports of Services and Economic Growth in Developing Countries', available at http://www.unctad.org/en/docs/ditctncdmisc20036_en.pdf

——— (2011). *UNCTAD Trade Statistics*, available at www.unctad.org.

Urata, S. and K. Kiyota. (2007). 'Services Trade in East Asia', in T. Ito and A.E. Krueger (eds), *Trade in Services in the Asia-Pacific Region*. University of Chicago Press, pp. 378–419.

PART VI

Standards, Regulations, and Multilateral Trade Agreements

18 Product Standards, Regulations, and Trade

The goods traded among countries are more often subjected to different sets of international standards and regulations. For example, the richer countries often impose a minimum quality restriction on the goods imported from poor countries. Such minimum quality standards may require the International Standard Organization's ISO 9000 series certifications or country-specific norms and standards. Richer and advanced industrialized countries also require that the imported goods are more eco-friendly and emit pollution per unit of production and consumption at least to the level comparable with the import-competing goods produced in their own countries. Goods produced in developing countries must be compliant with the universally accepted core labour standards set by the International Labour Organization (ILO) is another important product standard that advanced industrialized countries often set as a precondition for imports.

Regulating trade through these labour, quality, and environmental standards is intended to create a level playing field by removing an undue comparative advantage of the poorer countries that arises from differential product standards. Poorer countries, on the other hand, perceive these standards and regulations as essentially non-tariff barriers in disguise. This trade restrictive nature of product standards has often led countries to negotiate at GATT and later at the WTO on the level and nature of the standards without hindering the volume of trade. For example, the Agreement on Technical Barriers to Trade (TBT), also known as the Standards Code, was negotiated at the Tokyo Round of trade negotiations (1973–79). The agreement emphasized on transparency and non-discrimination in the preparation, adoption, and application of technical regulations and standards. During the Uruguay Round (1986–94), some modifications were made to the TBT Agreement. An Agreement on Sanitary and Phytosanitary Measures (SPS), which is an agreement on food safety and animal and plant health standards, was also negotiated. Food safety measures relate to bacterial contaminants, pesticides, inspection, and labelling. This agreement allowed countries to set their own standards, but country-specific standards triggered quite a few conflicts even among the richer countries. For example, EU guidelines that prohibited the import and sale of meat and meat products treated with certain growth hormones was challenged by the United States and

International Economics. Rajat Acharyya, Oxford University Press. © Oxford University Press 2022.
DOI: 10.1093/oso/9780192865144.003.0018

Canada in the WTO's Dispute Settlement Body in 1996. We shall return to this issue in the next chapter.

The dimensions and implications of environmental and health standards of products are, however, different from those of quality and labour standards. In the following discussion, we distinguish between these different types of product standards and regulations in terms of their implications for trade and investment flows across nations.

18.1 QUALITY STANDARDS, TRADE, AND EMPLOYMENT

Quality standards imposed by importing countries may be related not only to the intrinsic quality of the products but also to the finishing and packaging of the products. An example of trade sanctions against India's leather exports is the ban imposed by Germany (which is a major importer of Indian leather) and EU countries on all items containing Pentachlorophenol (the cheapest anti-fungal preservative used by Indian leather manufacturers) of more than 5 mg/kg.

Recall from our discussions in Chapter 8 that there are many reasons for low quality phenomena in developing countries. One explanation is that better quality products are usually intensive in physical and human capital that are relatively scarcer factors in developing countries and have relatively higher market rates of return. These countries thus specialize in low quality products. In such a context, a minimum quality standard set by richer countries for their imports may have an adverse effect on the employment of unskilled workers in developing countries. There are two ways in which such an adverse effect can realize. First, in the very short run, with exports of low quality products being prohibited, the composition of output will shift towards import-competing production, which is relatively capital-intensive in capital-scarce developing countries. Unskilled workers are displaced as a consequence from the contracting export sector and only a handful of them can be absorbed in the expanding import-competing production. Overall, the aggregate unemployment of unskilled workers should rise.

Second, since higher quality varieties make less use of unskilled labour than lower-quality varieties, quality enhancement by itself displaces unskilled labour. One should, therefore, weigh this adverse *technique* effect against the favourable foreign-demand induced *scale* effect in tracing the net change in the aggregate employment of unskilled workers that quality standards and regulations may result in.

Minimum quality standards may also lower welfare and may accentuate wage inequality. Recall the quality choice in an extended HOS model discussed in Chapter 8. If the minimum quality restriction is binding in the sense that the equilibrium quality in an economy is lower than the minimum quality required for the good to be exported to another country, then it violates the marginal condition for quality choice. A higher minimum quality $\bar{Q}$ requires larger capital and thus raises its rate of return, which is greater than the rate at which this quality would have been the optimal choice for exporters. That is, for $\bar{Q}$, marginal cost exceeds marginal revenue from quality:

$$a'_{KZ}(\bar{Q})r' > P_Z^{W'}(\bar{Q})$$

The minimum quality restriction is, therefore, distortionary for the exporting country leading to a loss of real income and welfare for it. Figure 18.1 illustrates this.

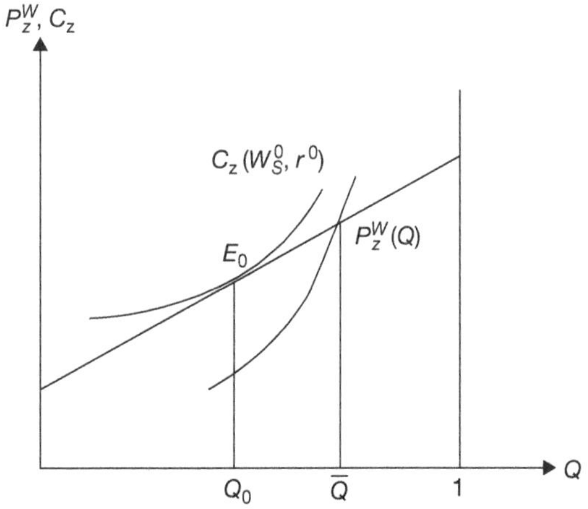

Figure 18.1 Binding Minimum Quality Restriction and Distortion

On the other hand, it can be easily checked that both the skilled and the unskilled wages will fall in the exporting country as a consequence of minimum quality restrictions on its exports. Thus, unskilled workers lose in absolute terms. They may lose in relative terms if their wages decline more than the skilled wage.

Minimum quality standards that require product labeling such as the ISO 9000 series certification, however, may be beneficial for developing countries when the quality of their export products can be judged by foreign buyers only after buying and consuming the products. Foreign buyers' marginal willingness-to-pay for such *experience* goods is usually based on the country-of-origin of such products and their perceptions about the average industry quality in the country concerned. The general perception is that developing countries produce and export goods of lower quality and this often induces foreign buyers to pay less at the margin for goods produced by these countries. This, in turn, lowers the incentive for a potentially high-quality producer to raise the quality of its product above the industry average and produce the socially optimum quality. Thus, there is a negative information externality leading to a *lemons* problem: bad quality products drive out good quality products from the market. Herein comes the role of the ISO 9000 series certification for exporting firms in developing countries. It acts as a signal to foreign buyers as a better quality product than their perceived average industry quality. To the extent to which the foreign buyers are willing to pay more for products having

Box 18.1 Search and Experience Goods

Nelson (1974) classified goods into search goods and experience goods. Search goods are those the true qualities of which can be judged by buyers *before* they actually buy and consume these goods. There is thus no asymmetry in information across the producers and consumers regarding the true quality of the product. Items of daily consumption such as fruits and vegetables fall in this category of search goods. On the other hand, there are goods such as automobiles, home appliances, computers, and scientific instruments, for which buyers can judge true product qualities only *after* buying and experiencing these products. These goods are called *experience goods.*

the ISO 9000 certificate, it raises the incentive for the exporting firm to raise its product quality above the average industry quality.

18.2 LABOUR STANDARDS AND TRADE SANCTIONS

In international and multilateral forums for trade negotiations, the United States has time and again pressed for the use of trade sanctions against countries that are not implementing core labour standards (see Box 18.3) ever since its first attempt in 1953 to include labour standards in GATT's Articles of Agreement. It continued with its efforts for inclusion of such an article in the Tokyo and Uruguay Rounds of negotiations under GATT and later in the WTO Ministerial Conferences in Singapore in 1996, Geneva in 1998, and Doha in 2001, without much success. Though in recent times the United States has got some support on this issue of inclusion of labour standards in the agenda for trade negotiations from Canada, EU, and Japan, the strongest opposition has come from developing countries.

The primary argument for trade measures by the United States and other industrialized countries against countries with lower labour standards is to achieve a level-playing field. It is often contended that the comparative cost advantage of developing countries in labour-intensive products is rooted in suppressed wages due to unfair labour practices, and in many cases in the use and exploitation of child labour, rather than due to fundamentally low wages. Trade sanctions and measures used to enforce labour standards and a ban on imports of commodities using child labour from developing countries are thus seen as effective policy instruments to prohibit such unfair trade.

But there is not much empirical support for this argument that lower labour standards lead to trade competitiveness. The OECD (1996) study of Trade, Employment and Labour Standards concludes that there is no evidence that countries with low standards have better global export performance than countries with high standards. On the other hand, a study of imports by the United States from 10 major developing countries in 1994 by Aggarwal (1995) revealed that core labour standards are often lower in less export-oriented or non-traded sectors such as agriculture and services. Similarly, within an export-oriented sector, labour conditions in firms

Box 18.2 Quality Uncertainty and Akerlof's Lemons Problem

George Akerlof (1970) formalized this problem of quality uncertainty using the market for used cars as an example. In the United States, good used cars are known as cherries and the defective ones as lemons. Since many important mechanical parts and other elements of a car are not easily accessible for inspection, and information regarding past history of accidents is not available to a potential buyer, she does not know beforehand whether a used car is a cherry or a lemon. So her best guess for a used car is that it is of average quality and she is willing to pay for it accordingly. This means that the owner of a well maintained, cautiously driven used car will not get a high enough price to make selling of that car worthwhile. Consequently, the owners of good cars will not place their cars in the used car market. Thus, due to asymmetric information and consequent quality uncertainty, lemons or defective used cars drive out good used cars or cherries from the market for used cars.

that are more involved in exporting are at least similar to those in firms that are less involved in exporting.

However, the caveat here is that these dual standards for domestic production and for export may be the outcome of a more stringent requirement of the importing countries that the goods imported must have been produced in conformity with core labour standards.

On the other hand, the diversity in labour standards does not call for trade sanctions or restrictions either. Srinivasan (1995), for example, strongly opines that the diversity of labour standards between nations reflects differences in their factor endowments and levels of income. Moreover, to the extent to which poor labour standards reflect labour market failures, by the discussion of the general rule for optimal intervention in cases of market failures in Chapter 13, it requires government intervention in the form of income transfers and domestic wage tax or subsidies. Similarly, Brown et al. (1996) also do not justify harmonization of labour standards. Their argument rests on the logic that labour market failures are likely to differ across countries, which require different rates of labour market interventions resulting in different levels of labour standards that are nationally optimal. That is, diversity of labour standards is merely a reflection of different national conditions and is *not unfair* as long as they are consistent with efficient resource allocations across sectors within each nation.

However, it is interesting to observe that in a number of cases developing countries have in fact much higher levels of legal protection for their workers than in developed countries such as collective wage bargaining and minimum wages. The problem lies in the implementation and enforcement of such laws. In many cases, excessively complex labour standards force firms and workers to operate in the *informal* economy. With production in the formal sector generating only a handful of employment opportunities under very rigid labour standards and laws, workers in labour surplus economies have little choice but to accept informal sector jobs that have no labour codes and standards. Trade sanctions can do little in such circumstances, and in fact, may add to the misery of the workers by not allowing the export of goods produced in the informal sector and thus violating the core labour standards.

Similarly, whether trade sanctions can actually lower the incidence of child labour is a debatable issue, simply because trade sanctions do not address the problem of child labour appro-

Box 18.3 Core Labour Standards

Labour standards vary from one country to the other depending on the stage of development, and political, social, and cultural conditions of the country. Despite these differences, in ILO's conventions a consensus on a group of core labour standards has been achieved that should ideally apply universally. These core labour standards include: (a) prohibition of forced labour, (b) freedom of association, (c) the right to organize and bargain collectively, (d) elimination of child labour exploitation, and (e) non-discrimination in employment. There are other less universally accepted labour standards related to acceptable conditions of work such as a minimum wage, limitations on hours of work, and occupational safety and health in the workplace.

priately.[1] These sanctions, like legislative, policy and social actions, target the demand side of the problem when it is necessary to address supply side factors or the causes for the incidence of child labour. It is now general consensus among economists that abject poverty is a major cause of child labour. It is hard to find middle and high income parents in developing countries sending their children to work. But parents with low incomes often send their children to work in order to achieve a subsistence level of consumption, and evidence towards such a cause of child labour is growing (Grootaert and Patrinos 1999; Edmonds 2004). Once we understand this, it is easy to comprehend that trade sanctions may actually aggravate the incidence of child labour. Evidence is growing that in many developing countries, trade sanctions on exports that used child labour have forced children to move into many non-traded activities in the informal segments of the economy and even pushed them to do abusive work.

This may happen for two reasons. First, trade sanctions lower adult and household incomes and as a consequence induce more children to be sent to work by their parents (Basu 2004). Second, a poor parent has no or limited access to formal credit markets and is thus dependent

Box 18.4 Magnitude of Child Labour

The incidence of child labour is pervasive and growing in many countries in Latin America, East Asia, and in the Indian subcontinent. According to the Census report, 14.5 per cent of the children below 14 years of age were in some form of employment in India in 1961. Despite the Child Labour (Prohibition and Regulation) Act, 1986, by which the Government of India can fine a person or a firm employing children in contravention of the provisions of the Act, at the beginning of the present century, the percentage of working children had increased to more than 20 per cent. In Bangladesh, India, and Pakistan most of the children work under compulsion from their parents. A sizeable proportion of them, at least 15 million among the 70–80 million working children in India across all age groups by the most conservative estimates of Human Rights Watch Asia (1996), work as *bonded* child labour in order to pay off their parents' debts. In all the cases, the creditor-employer offers loans to destitute parents to secure the labour of a child which is even cheaper under bondage. Consequently, the highest concentration of child labour can be found in agriculture. According to a recent report by the International Labour Organization, about 80 per cent of the child labourers in India are employed in the agriculture sector. The next three sectors that account for most of the child labour in India are glass factories, the match box industry, and the carpet industry. In China, reports reveal that most of the children are employed in toy manufacturing, textiles, construction, and food production.

Among India's major export goods, carpet, diamond cutting and finishing, garments, and footwear have high concentrations of child labour. Similarly, high child labour can be observed in the export of soccer balls by Pakistan, export of wood furniture and garments by Indonesia, and export of garments and footwear by Bangladesh.

on informal credit markets for borrowing to smooth out consumption during the period of a child's education. Trade sanctions raise this cost of borrowing in informal credit markets and thus the opportunity cost of sending children to school (Jafarey and Lahiri 2002). Whatever be the most plausible reasons empirically, the fact remains that trade sanctions are not the best way of addressing the problem of child labour in many poor nations. These sanctions may do more harm than good to the children.

Using cross-country data, Cigno et al. (2002) observe that the trade-share in GDP, the standard measure of openness, raises the labour participation ratio in the age group of 10–14

Box 18.5 Incidence of Child Labour: Supply Side and Demand Side Explanations

Like market for any commodity, the incidence of child labour too has two dimensions: supply of child labour, which essentially is a parental decision; and, the demand for child labour, which is the firm's/employer's decision. In majority of the empirical studies it has been observed that abject poverty is the major cause of child labour. Despite being altruist, parents send their children to work instead of to schools merely because they cannot afford to forego the child's income in order to achieve a subsistence level of consumption. If sending children out to work is an act of desperation on the part of the parents, then one can expect that parents would not send their children to work if their own wages were higher or employment prospects better. This is what Basu and Van (1998) calls Luxury Axiom. Poverty in combination with credit constraints is another major supply-side explanation for prevalence of child labour. In developing countries, informal credit markets work mainly for short-term loans to meet unforeseen contingencies. But, poor households need long-term credit to be able to substitute for the foregone earnings of their children when they are sent to school. Poverty essentially makes opportunity cost of sending children to school (which is the child wage foregone) very high. Opportunity costs also include the implicit costs of the time that children devote to schooling, including the time they spend in the classroom, in travelling to school and in doing schoolwork at home. On the demand side, non-pecuniary and non-economic factors are often very important reasons why employers hire children in the carpet, gems, and diamond industries, in particular: child workers are more docile and less troublesome; children show greater willingness to do repetitive monotonous jobs; children have greater innocence, do less absenteeism; children do not join trade unions or agitate for their rights.

Children not only work at private firms (the child labour market), but a substantial proportion of child workers work at the household and in own family farming, handicraft, and other businesses, and in informal markets (such as domestic help, or in road side garages or tea stalls). In such cases, the supply and demand for child labour emanate within the family or household. Accordingly, even in economies with a low rate of child labour supplied to private firms, the existence of child labour in the household may lead to a high incidence of child labour.

years, but has no significant effect on the primary school non-attendance rate. Edmonds and Pavcnik (2005), on the other hand, find that an increase in the world price of rice exports by Vietnam has lowered the incidence of child labour there. This suggests that trade sanctions against exports produced by child labour (which should lower export earnings) may induce more parents to send their children to work.

To avoid trade sanctions, countries that are known to have high incidence of child labour have started adopting product labeling to distinguish products produced by child labour from those that are 'child labour free' to influence buyers' choice. RUGMARK and KALEEN label carpets produced in India for export to Germany and the US and CARE and FARE and DIP are the other labeling organizations for goods produced in India, Kenya, and Nepal. Certificates for fair labour standards and child-labour free produce are provided by STEP in Switzerland for manufacturing goods imported from India, Nepal, and Pakistan. Soccer balls produced in Pakistan are also labeled for exports to the US. These product labels enable buyers to get product-specific information instead of relying solely upon their country-of-origin perception when they buy such goods.

18.3 ENVIRONMENTAL STANDARDS, TRADE, AND FDI

Environmental standards are different in dimension than quality and labour standards because these are essentially policy responses to negative externalities generated by an economic activity and to possible ecological dumping. As we had mentioned in Chapter 1, many production activities such as leather manufacturing, cement industry, chemicals, iron and steel, and non-ferrous metals, are highly polluting activities. Air or water pollution emitted during the production of these goods degrades the environment and causes harm to the rest of the economy. But such environmental costs are not internalized by producers and as such the profit maximizing production level is sub-optimal in the sense defined in Chapter 13. Such a (production) distortion requires a pollution-emission tax or standard on production, which forces the producers to internalize the negative externality so that the socially optimum production level is attained. But, optimal pollution-emission taxes or environmental standards vary across countries according to their fundamentals and this variation has far-reaching implications on how the nations trade with each other.

The interrelationship between international trade and environmental standards is, however, complex as they have a two-way causal relationship with each other. First, lax environmental standards may establish a comparative advantage for a nation in dirty goods that use the environment as a free input. This is supply side causation. Second, increased trade and gains therefrom may generate a demand for higher environmental quality and therefore a higher environmental standard or regulation. This is demand side causation running in the *opposite direction*.

Environmental standards may also have far-reaching implications on capital inflow and FDI. The twin hypotheses of capital flight and pollution havens formalize this implication as we will discuss later.

18.3.1 Standards, Comparative Advantage, and Unfair Trade

The logic of low environmental standards causing international trade is similar to the case of low labour standards (or suppressed wages) making relatively labour-intensive goods cheaper. At the same time, the dimension of the problem is different because in the case of low environmental standards, comparative advantage is rooted in the negative externality that production or consumption of dirty goods generates. Exogenous differences in the property rights regime can also be a source of comparative advantage in dirty goods (Chichilnisky 1994). Usually, the poor countries do not assign any property rights to environmental resources, while rich countries do so. As a result, poor countries gain a comparative advantage in dirty goods that takes environmental resources as free inputs.

To illustrate how lower environmental standards or pollution taxes can establish a comparative advantage recall the argument in Chapter 1. Leather manufacture generates water pollution and imposes a cost on society in terms of low catch of fish and polluted drinking water, in addition to the usual production costs incurred by producers. These costs are, however, not internalized by unregulated private producers, and accordingly the estimated private cost of leather manufacture is smaller than the social cost of production. Under competitive conditions, leather manufacture is thus priced at a lower private marginal cost in an economy that does not implement environmental standards strictly to force private producers to internalize external costs. This establishes a comparative advantage for this economy compared to an economy where, *ceteris paribus*, environmental standards are strictly enforced so that the same good is priced at a higher social marginal cost. This comparative advantage is perverse and the export of the dirty good essentially reflects ecological dumping as the export good is priced *below* the social marginal cost.

This ecological dumping and unfair trade have been the bone of contention between developed and developing countries. Trade sanctions or restrictions are often imposed by developed countries as countervailing measures against this unfair trade or ecological dumping. Developing countries, on the other hand, perceive these measures as non-tariff barriers in disguise to protect the interests of import-competing firms in developed countries than to protect their environment. This concern and apprehension of the developing countries is not unreasonable at least in some specific cases. If environmental degradation is caused by production pollution, exports of dirty goods by developing countries actually benefit the developed countries by displacing the local production of dirty goods there and thereby shifting the pollution load from these countries to the exporting developing countries. Thus, as long as *production* of dirty goods generates pollution that is localized in nature and does not transmit to the importing countries through air or water (such as local air pollutants like SO_2, CO, and NO_X), it is difficult to rationalize the imposition of trade sanctions to protect the environment of importing countries. Trade sanctions in such cases surface merely as non-tariff barriers. The trade sanctions may, however, be justified in two cases. First, the dirty goods generate *consumption pollution* so that unfair trade and ecological dumping shift the pollution load to the importing developed countries from the developing countries. Second, the production of dirty goods generates pollution that is *trans-boundary* or global in nature, such as emission of carbon dioxide (CO_2), and thus affect the developed countries.

At the same time, there are two caveats to the argument of unfair trade and ecological dumping. First, the comparative advantage of developing countries in dirty goods per se does not mean that such an advantage is rooted in lax environmental standards and thus in pricing below the social marginal cost. Such comparative advantage may actually be based on fundamentals like tastes, technology, and factor endowment. That is, *ex post*, looking at the cross-country price differences it may be premature to talk about either unfair trade or ecological dumping. Second, by similar logic, countries with stricter environmental standards may export the dirty goods if they have significant cost advantages emanating from technology or a factor endowment bias (Copeland and Taylor 2003). The richer countries have both larger endowments of physical (as well as human) capital and stricter environmental regulations relative to the poorer nations. Thus, if a dirty good is relatively capital-intensive such as iron and steel, the capital abundance of the richer nations creates a supply bias for them in such goods in the HO sense discussed earlier. Stricter regulations in the rich countries, on the other hand, make the cost of producing dirty goods relatively higher in these countries. Alternatively speaking, lax environmental standards in the poorer nations create a supply bias of the same good for them. If the rich nations are too rich in capital, we can expect a supply bias for the richer nations to be stronger. The end result is that the price of dirty goods will be lower in the richer nations and they will specialize in and export dirty goods to the poorer nations. Therefore, trade shifts the production of dirty goods from the poor countries with weak pollution regulations to rich countries where regulations are more stringent.

Empirical evidence, on the other hand, does not conclusively suggest that weak environmental standards establish a comparative advantage in dirty goods and increase the export of such goods.[2] In one of the earliest works on pollution havens, Tobey (1990) found no statistical significance of his environmental regulation measures on the net exports of five pollution-intensive industries for 23 countries. A similar conclusion was reached by Grossman and Krueger (1993) who examined the environmental impacts of NAFTA. In a more recent study Xu (2000) examines whether more stringent domestic environmental policies reduce the international competitiveness of environmentally sensitive goods (ESGs) for 34 countries (including the OECD countries and major East Asian developing economies) from 1965 to 1995. The time series evidence does not indicate that there were any systematic changes in trade patterns of ESGs since the 1970s despite the introduction of more stringent environmental regulations in most of the developed countries since then.

18.3.2 Trade, Income Gains, and Demand for Higher Standards

Unlike the supply side argument that lax standards lead to increased trade, the demand side argument emphasizes on the reverse causation. Stringency of environmental regulations accompanies higher per capita incomes. The logic for stricter environmental standards is based on the premise that if people increase their demand for a clean environment as their incomes rise, then they will tolerate higher levels of pollution only if the effluent charge is higher. Moreover, income growth beyond a high enough level shifts preferences toward cleaner goods. That is, clean goods are *relatively* income elastic. At low levels of income, increased consumption is valued highly relative to the environmental quality. But when a country achieves a sufficiently high per capita income level and standard of living, people value the environment more and as a consequence regulatory institutions become more effective since implementation of stricter environmental regulations becomes politically easier. Income gains from international trade also increase the ability of governments to afford costly investments in environmental protection. The

Box 18.6 Trans-boundary Pollution

The most common example of trans-boundary pollution is CO_2 emission, which is actually a global pollutant. Long-distance transportation of airborne particles has also been documented around the world. For example, dust from the Gobi Desert in Mongolia travels far out into the Pacific Ocean. A Japanese research group in 1971 concluded that a single surge of dust from the Gobi had drifted across the Pacific for well over 10,000 kilometres. An example of trans-boundary water pollution is the Ganges (that flows through India and Bangladesh) carrying water pollution caused by chemical plants, leather manufacturing units, and other industrial units in India through to Bangladesh. The Nile and its tributaries that flow through Uganda, Sudan, Egypt, Ethiopia, Zaire, Kenya, Tanzanian, Rwanda, and Burundi before flowing into lake Victoria Nyanes, is another example of transmitting water pollution from an upstream country to downstream countries.

[2] For a survey of the empirical estimates see Acharyya (2013).

empirically observed inverted-U relationship between per capita income and the pollution level, known as the Environmental Kuznets Curve (EKC), provides support to this demand side relationship (Copeland and Taylor 2003; Roca 2003; Selden and Song 1994).

18.3.3 Capital Flight, Pollution Havens, and Migration of Dirty Industries

Over the last few decades two phenomena have occurred almost simultaneously that have prompted many to make a cause-and-effect link between the two. First, developing countries have emerged as net exporters of dirty goods and developed countries their net importers. This phenomenon has been termed as migration of dirty industries. Second, since 1990, there has been a remarkable and sustained increase in capital inflow into developing countries. It is often argued that a major explanation of both the capital inflow and the displacement of dirty industries is the difference in environmental standards across developed and developing countries. The demand for a better environment in developed countries has raised the cost of operation of dirty industries there. Preference for faster growth, on the other hand, often causes the environmental standards being loosely implemented in the poor and developing countries. Accordingly, capital finds better returns in dirty industries in developing countries than in developed countries. That is, low environmental standards attract foreign capital into the dirty industries in developing countries. This is known as the *capital flight hypothesis*.

The *pollution haven hypothesis* extends this argument further by postulating that developing countries deliberately keep their environmental standards low in order to attract foreign capital. That is, developing countries *choose* to remain pollution havens for dirty industries. Moreover, as the argument goes, developing countries engage in active competition in lowering their environmental standards to attract foreign capital, which leads to a race-to-the-bottom situation.

Theoretically all this makes sense if it is weaker regulation that alone attracts foreign capital. But, empirical evidence regarding the causes and nature of capital inflow and FDI does not seem to validate these arguments. It is true that East Asian countries, in particular, compete for attracting FDI through successive liberalization of their trade and investment regimes as features of contemporary regionalism suggest. But there is not much evidence that such competition for FDI is motivated by the development and export of dirty goods or that in such competition lax environmental standards have been a major policy instrument. Moreover, a large part of FDI inflows in East Asian countries in fact has been intra-region in character rather than being from advanced industrialized countries of North America and Western Europe. Among the Asian developing countries, relatively high income countries attract most of the FDI inflows. As the empirically observed EKC suggests, the demand for a cleaner environment, and consequently the demand for stricter environmental regulations, increases with the per capita income level of a country. This means that large inflows of capital in the high income Asian developing countries cannot be characterized as being caused by lower environmental standards, at least as much as the capital flight hypothesis postulates.

SUMMARY POINTS

- The goods traded among countries are more often subjected to different sets of international labour, quality, and environmental standards. Advanced industrialized countries impose these standards and regulations on imports from developing countries to create a level-playing field by removing an undue comparative advantage of the poorer countries that arise from differential product standards.
- The poorer countries perceive these standards and regulations as essentially non-tariff barriers in disguise.
- A minimum quality standard set by richer countries for their imports may have an adverse effect on the employment of unskilled workers in developing countries.
- Minimum quality standards requiring product labeling such as the ISO 9000 series certification may be beneficial for developing countries when the quality of their export products can be judged by foreign buyers only after buying and consuming the products.
- The diversity in labour standards, which reflects differences in factor endowments and levels of incomes of the countries, does not call for trade sanctions or restrictions. To the extent to which poor labour standards reflect labour market failures, it requires government intervention in the form of income transfers and domestic wage tax or subsidies.
- Trade sanctions may actually aggravate the incidence of child labour. In many developing countries, trade sanctions on exports that use child labour have forced children to move into many non-traded activities in the informal segments of the economy and even pushed them to abusive works.
- The interrelationship between international trade and environmental standards is complex as they have a two-way causal relationship with each other.
- As long as the *production* of dirty goods generates pollution that is localized in nature and does not transmit to the importing countries through air or water, it is difficult to rationalize the imposition of trade sanctions to protect the environment of the importing countries. Trade sanctions in such cases surface merely as non-tariff barriers.
- The comparative advantage of developing countries in dirty goods per se does not mean that such an advantage is rooted in lax environmental standards and thus in pricing below the social marginal cost.
- Countries with stricter environmental standards may export dirty goods if they have significant cost advantages emanating from technology or a factor endowment bias.
- Stringency of environmental regulations accompanies higher per capita incomes. The logic for stricter environmental standards is based on the premise that if people increase their demand for a clean environment as their incomes rise, then they will tolerate higher levels of pollution only if the effluent charge is higher.
- Developing countries have emerged as net exporters of dirty goods and developed countries their net importers. This phenomenon has been termed as migration of dirty industries.

KEYWORDS

- **ISO 9000 series standards** is a well-known Quality Management System developed by the International Standards Organization in Geneva in 1987 with the first revision in 1994 and the second in 2000. The eight quality management principles upon which the ISO 9001 series certification (applicable in contractual situations) is based are customer focused organization, leadership, involvement of people, process approach, system approach to management, continual improvement, factual approach to decision making, and mutually beneficial supplier relationship. The ISO 9004 series certificates are applicable in non-contractual situations.
- **Core labour standards** include prohibition of forced labour, freedom of association, the right to organize and bargain collectively, elimination of child labour exploitation, and non-discrimination in employment. There are other less universally accepted labour standards related to acceptable conditions of work such as a minimum wage, limitations on hours of work, and occupational safety and health in the workplace.
- **Child labour**, according to the ILO, is defined as work that deprives children of their childhood, of the opportunity to attend school, or obliging them to leave school prematurely, and that is harmful to their physical and mental development. In India, the various laws relating to labour prohibit a person under the age of 14 years to work.
- **Ecological dumping** occurs when an environmentally polluting good is exported at a price below its social marginal cost.
- **Green protectionism** refers to protectionist trade policies in the disguise of environmental regulations and preservation of the environment.
- **Trans-boundary pollution** is pollution that originates in one country and then transmits to other countries through pathways of water or air, and thereby causes damages to the environment in other countries.
- **Migration of dirty industries** refers to a phenomenon whereby the share of dirty industries in industrial production in the developing countries increase and the same in the developed countries decline.
- **Pollution haven hypothesis** postulates that the poor and developing nations deliberately keep their environmental taxes and standards low and thus choose to remain as pollution havens in order to attract FDI in their dirty industries.

EXERCISES

1. How can you reason the general apprehension that minimum quality standards imposed on exports by developing countries may lower aggregate employment there?
2. How do product quality certifications like ISO 9000 series certificates benefit exporters in developing countries?
3. Why is trade policy not a Pareto optimum (or first-best) policy for violations of labour standards?

4. Why do you think the incidence of child labour is persisting in many poor developing nations despite innumerable legislations, fines imposed on employing firms, social boycotts, and trade sanctions?
5. Using relative demand and relative supply (or marginal cost) curves illustrate that in case of consumption pollution the cross-country differences in the consumption-pollution tax create a comparative advantage for countries even when they have identical tastes, technology, and factor endowment.
6. How will you show that a nation may export dirty goods despite having a higher pollution tax or stricter environmental regulation?
7. How does international trade lead to stringency of environmental regulation in a country?
8. Why is it that developing countries may choose to remain pollution havens?

SUGGESTED READING

Acharyya, R. (2013). *Trade and Environment*. New Delhi: Oxford University Press.

Copeland, B.R. and M.S. Taylor. (2003). 'Trade, Growth and the Environment', NBER Working Paper No. 9823. National Bureau of Economic Research, Cambridge, MA.

ADVANCED READING

Aggarwal, Mita. (1995). 'International Trade, Labor Standards, and Labor Market Conditions: An Evaluation of the Linkages', USITC, Office of Economics Working Paper No. 95-06-C (June).

Akerlof, G.A. (1970). 'The Market for Lemons: Qualitative Uncertainty and the Market Mechanism', *Quarterly Journal of Economics*, 84: 488–500.

Basu, Kaushik and Pham Hoang Van. (1998). 'The Economics of Child Labor'. *American Economic Review*, 88.3, June, pp. 412–27.

Basu, K. (2004). 'Child Labour and the Law: Notes on Possible Pathologies', Discussion Paper No. 2052. Harvard Institute of Economic Research, Harvard University, Cambridge, MA.

Bhagwati, J.N. and T.N. Srinivasan. (1996). 'Trade and the Environment: Does Environmental Diversity Detract from the Case for Free Trade?', in J. Bhagwati and R.E. Hudec (eds), *Fair Trade and Harmonization: Economic Analysis,* Volume 1. MIT Press.

Brown, Drusilla K., Alan V. Deardorff, and Robert M. Stern. (1996). 'International Labor Standards and Trade: A Theoretical Analysis', in Jagdish N. Bhagwati and Robert E. Hudec (eds), *Harmonization and Fair Trade: Prerequisites for Free Trade?* Cambridge: MIT Press: 227–80.

Chichilnisky, G. (1994). 'Global Environment and North-South Trade', *American Economic Review*, 84: 851–74.

Cigno, A., F.C. Rosati, and L. Guarcello. (2002). 'Does Globalization Increase Child Labour?', *World Development*, 30: 1579–89.

Edmonds, E.V. (2004). 'Does Child Labour Decline with Improving Economic Status?', *Journal of Human Resources*, 40(1).

Edmonds, E.V. and N. Pavcnik. (2005). 'The Effect of Trade Liberalization on Child Labour', *Journal of International Economics*, 65: 401–19.

Grootaert, C. and H. Patrinos. (1999). *The Policy Analysis of Child Labour*. New York: St. Martin's Press.

Grossman, Gene M. and Alan B. Krueger (1993). 'Environmental Impacts of a North American Free Trade Agreement', in P. Garber (ed.), *The U.S.-Mexico Free Trade Agreement*. Cambridge, MA: MIT Press, pp. 13–56.

Human Rights Watch Asia (1996). 'The Small Hands of Slavery: Bonded Child Labour in India.

Jafarey, S. and S. Lahiri (2002). 'Will Trade Sanctions Reduce Child Labour? The Role of Credit Markets', *Journal of Development Economics*, 68: 137–56.

Nelson, P. (1974). 'Advertising as Information', *Journal of Political Economy*, July/August, pp. 729–54.

OECD (1996). *Trade, Employment and Labour Standards: A Study of Core Workers' Rights and International Trade*, OECD Publishing.

Roca, J. (2003). 'Do Individual Preferences Explain Environmental Kuznets Curve?', *Ecological Economics*, 45(1): 3–10.

Selden, T.M. and D. Song (1994). 'Environmental Quality and Development: Is There a Kuznets Curve for Air Pollution Emissions?', *Journal of Environmental Economics and Management* 27:147–62.

Srinivasan, T.N. (1995). 'International Trade and Labour Standards', in Pitou van Dijck and Gerrit Faber (eds), *Challenges to the New World Trade Organization*. Amsterdam: Martinus Nijhoff/ Kluwer, pp. 239–43.

Tobey, J. (1990). 'The Effects of Domestic Environmental Policies on Patterns of World Trade', *Kyklos*, 43(2): 191–209.

Xu, X. (2000). 'International Trade and Environmental Regulation: Time Series Evidence and Cross Section Test', *Environmental and Resource Economics*, 17: 233–57.

19 World Trade Organization and Trade Agreements

With accelerated growth in world trade volumes and an increasing number of countries integrating their national economies with the world economy from the 1980s, the importance of establishing and monitoring rules for international trade in goods and services became paramount. For this purpose, the World Trade Organization (WTO) was established through the Marrakech Agreement, which came into force on 1 January 1995. This replaced GATT, which concluded its last round of multilateral negotiations, known as the Uruguay Round, in 1994. WTO introduced new rules of trade policy that extend beyond the coverage of GATT and multilateral and the plurilateral agreements. These new rules and agreements now govern the world trading system.

Till 2011, the WTO had 157 member countries and 26 observer governments like Algeria, Belarus, Bhutan, Lao PDR, Libya, Sudan, and Uzbekistan. These observer countries are actually the ones who applied for accession to the WTO and are currently negotiating their accession. The latest members of the WTO are Russia, Samoa, Vanuatu, and Montenegro. The process of becoming a WTO member is unique to each applicant country and the terms of accession depend on the country's stage of economic development and the current trade regime. The accession process is done through establishing a working party of WTO members and a process of negotiations.

In this chapter we discuss the functions, aims, and structure of the WTO and the trade policy rules and agreements that it implements and administers.

19.1 STRUCTURE AND FUNCTIONS OF THE WTO

19.1.1 Structure of the WTO

WTO is composed of several bodies like the Ministerial Conference, the Secretariat and Director General, the General Council, the Trade Policy Review Body, the Dispute Settlement Body, and the Councils on Trade in Goods and Trade in Services. The Ministerial Conference, which is composed of international trade (or commerce) ministers from all the member

International Economics. Rajat Acharyya, Oxford University Press. © Oxford University Press 2022.
DOI: 10.1093/oso/9780192865144.003.0019

countries, is WTO's governing body. It sets the strategic direction of the organization and makes all final decisions on agreements under its coverage. The Ministerial Conference meets at least once every two years. The Secretariat and Director General of the WTO is located in its headquarter in Geneva, and it undertakes the administrative functions of running all aspects of the organization. The Secretariat has no legal decision-making powers though, but provides important inputs to decision-making by relevant bodies. The Director General, who is elected by the members, heads the Secretariat.

The General Council looks after WTO's day-to-day business and management. This is WTO's key decision-making body for most issues. The different bodies that address specific issues report directly to this General Council. It is composed of senior representatives of all member countries and is based at the WTO headquarters in Geneva.

The Trade Policy Review Body is essentially a monitoring body of the WTO on the mechanism and implementation of the trade policy rules by members. It periodically reviews trade policies and practices of all member states and how they are adhering to WTO obligations. This body is composed of all the WTO members.

The Dispute Settlement Body looks into the effectiveness of the dispute resolution process for all WTO agreements, and implementation of the decisions on WTO disputes. The permanent Appellate Body established in 1994, along with dispute resolution panels chosen individually for each case that is filed by a member, hears the dispute and gives a verdict on it. The final decision of the Appellate Body can only be reversed by a full consensus of the Dispute Settlement Body.

The Councils on Trade in Goods and Trade in Services operate under the mandate of the General Council and provide a mechanism to oversee the details of the general and specific agreements on trade in goods and trade in services. There is also a Council for the Agreement on Trade-Related Aspects of Intellectual Property Rights (TRIPS). Other bodies that deal with specific issues are the Committee on Trade and Development and the Committee on Trade and Environment.

19.1.2 Functions of the WTO

There are three main functions of the WTO. First, is to set, implement, and administer the WTO agreements regarding rules of international trade policy and patent protection. Second, is to provide a forum for negotiations among member countries. Third, it acts to resolve international trade disputes among members and provides a forum for the dispute settlement mechanism. The primary goal of these functions is to promote international trade and to ensure that national policies of member countries do not distort or hinder international trade in goods and services. At the same time, it aims to ensure that growth in trade, output, and employment are achieved through protection and preservation of the global environment. The preamble to the 1994 Marrakech Agreement sets out more specific goals for the WTO and its functions, such as raising the standard of living and ensuring full employment through securing a growing share of the world trade for the least developed countries. Promotion of international trade among member countries is aimed to be achieved through negotiations among the members regarding lowering of tariff and non-tariff barriers and thereby ensuring reciprocated market access for each other.

Box 19.1 Dispute Settlement Mechanism at the WTO

The WTO's dispute settlement mechanism provides a level-playing field for the disputing countries. A WTO dispute proceeds through three main stages: consultation, formal litigation, and implementation. All disputes start with a request for consultations, and the complainant and the defendant are then required to consult for 60 days with the goal of negotiating a mutually satisfactory solution to the dispute. About 40 per cent of all disputes brought to the WTO end at this stage, of which nearly 75 per cent yield at least partial concessions from the defendant. If consultations fail, the complainant can request a panel proceeding. Panels are comprised of three to five persons who are experts in trade law and are agreed to by the parties on a case-by-case basis. There are typically two rounds of testimony, including from other countries (*third parties*) that notify WTO of a substantial interest in the case. For example, in a dispute over anti-dumping duties imposed by the US (the defendant) on imports of shrimps from Vietnam (the complainant) in 2010, China, EU, India, Japan, South Korea, Mexico, and Thailand joined as third parties.

19.2 DECISION MAKING

Decisions in the WTO are generally taken by consensus. WTO describes itself as 'a rules-based, member-driven organization…all decisions are made by the member governments, and the rules are the outcome of negotiations among members'. Consensus dominates the decision making process. Consensus for policy rules is usually negotiated in informal meetings (the so-called Green Room process), which are well represented and influenced by the Quad countries—Canada, EU, Japan, and the United States. As many researchers and observers argue, although WTO's consensus governance model provides law-based initial bargaining, the trading rounds actually conclude through power-based bargaining that favours the Quad countries.

But, reaching a consensus can at times be difficult, particularly in a body composed of 157 very different members. Where consensus cannot be reached, the WTO Agreement allows for votes. The WTO is based on the system of 'one country, one vote', in contrast to the 'one dollar, one vote' governance of the International Monetary Fund (IMF) and the World Bank. But again the influence of Quad countries is most substantial.[1] As such, rules and agreements may not lead to Pareto improvement.

The failure of the Seattle Ministerial Conference (see Box 19.3) suggests that decision making needs to be more inclusive, representative, and efficient than the Green Room process. Its dispute settlement procedures, on the other hand, need to improve as well; the compliance provisions particularly need to be fixed to ensure that countries comply with WTO rulings and

[1] The WTO budget is financed by membership fees determined according to each member's share of total world trade in the previous three years, including trade in goods, services, and intellectual property rights, with a minimum contribution of 0.015 per cent. But contributions from Quad countries finance over half of its total budget. So the influence of Quad countries is understandable.

Box 19.2 Dispute Settlement: Complaint by India against the Customs Bond Directive of the United States

In view of the enhanced bond requirements imposed by the United States on imports of frozen warm-water shrimp from India, consultations with the United States on this matter were requested by India on 6 June 2006. India considered that the amended bond directive in general and the enhanced bond requirement (EBR) in particular, were inconsistent with the Articles of the Anti-Dumping Agreement and of the Subsidies and Countervailing Measures (SCM) Agreement of the WTO. Soon, Brazil, China, and Thailand requested to join the consultations as third parties. In its report submitted in February 2008, the dispute resolution panel set up for investigating into this complaint upheld India's claims that EBR on shrimp import from India was inconsistent with Articles 1 and 18.1 of the Anti-Dumping Agreement and that 'the United States violated Article 18.5 of the Anti-Dumping Agreement and Article 32.6 of the SCM Agreement because it failed to notify the Amended CBD to the Anti-Dumping and SCM Committees'. On 17 April 2008, India notified its decision to request the Appellate Body to review certain issues of the law covered in the panel report and certain legal interpretations developed by the panel. In its report on 16 July 2008, the Appellate Body, however, upheld the panel's conclusion and recommended that the Dispute Settlement Body request the United States to bring its measure into conformity with its obligations under Anti-Dumping Agreements.

bring their trade policies more quickly into conformity with its rules. This need was evidenced in the dispute between EU and the United States over banana and beef. In 1996, EU directives that prohibited the import and sale of meat and meat products treated with certain growth hormones was challenged by the United States and Canada in the WTO Dispute Settlement Body (DSB). These countries alleged that these directives violated several provisions of the Agreement on Sanitary and Phytosanitary Measures. EU, on the other hand, contended that the presence of banned hormones in food may present a risk to consumers' health. Despite the Appellate Body ruling in 2000, EU refused to lift its ban on hormone-treated beef imports from the United States. This led the United States to impose 100 per cent import tariffs on EU goods worth USD 115 million. In addition, it imposed 100 per cent duties on EU products worth USD 190 million in retaliation against EU's failure to implement the WTO decision on importation, distribution, and sale of bananas.

19.3 WTO RULES AND PRINCIPLES OF TRADE POLICY

The WTO establishes a framework for trade policies based on five principles, some of which are actually a continuation of GATT's principles. These five principles are non-discrimination, reciprocity, binding and enforceable commitments, transparency, and safety valves.

Non-discrimination, which is embedded in the main WTO rules on goods, services, and intellectual property, has two major components: the most favoured nation (MFN) rule, and the national treatment policy. As defined in Chapter 14, the MFN rule requires that a WTO member country must apply the same conditions on all trade with other WTO members.

That is, if a special favour regarding importation of goods and services and regarding trade related intellectual property rights is granted by a member country to any other WTO member country, it must be granted to *all* WTO member countries. Exceptions to the MFN principle, however, allow for preferential treatment of the least developed countries, regional free trade areas, and customs unions. There are several implications of the MFN rule. First, it provides smaller countries an insurance against larger countries exploiting their market power by raising tariffs against their products in periods of bad times. Second, the MFN rule raises the cost of defecting from a trade commitment for a country and thus indirectly enforces the multilateral rule. Note that working backwards, if a country deviates from its trade policy commitment by raising its tariff and non-tariff barriers then it must apply such changes to all the members. And this raises the political cost of defection.

National treatment means that imported goods should be treated no less favourably than similar domestically produced goods. This policy rule was introduced to limit the use of non-tariff barriers to trade such as technical standards and security standards to discriminate against imported goods.

The reciprocity principles are intended to ensure increased access for WTO members in each other's markets and for providing incentives to members in complying with the WTO obligation of trade liberalization by ensuring larger gains than if they had unilaterally liberalized their trade regimes. This is particularly important for countries where internal political forces and lobbies influence trade policy decisions. As explained in Chapter 12, greater trade concessions obtained from trading partners in reciprocation of allowing market access for their exporting firms means that national governments can secure greater political support from their own exporters to counter anti-liberalization domestic forces such as the import-competing firms.

Binding and enforceable commitments refer to tariff commitments made by WTO members in a multilateral trade negotiation and on accession which are enumerated in a schedule of concessions. These schedules are ceiling bindings, which a country can change only after

Box 19.3 Seattle Ministerial Conference

The third Ministerial Conference was held in Seattle, USA, during 30 November to 3 December 1999. The focus of the conference was on launching 'New Rounds', which would be the next round of negotiations to follow the Uruguay Round of GATT negotiations, and a corresponding decision on the scope and modalities of the new round. But it ended in a failure. The four-day meeting did not reach a conclusion and discussions were suspended. There were many issues of differences and contentions. The United States and EU differed with each other on the issue of eliminating export subsidies and on the extent of reduction of domestic supports. The strengthening of the disciplines in the Anti-dumping Agreement demanded by many developing countries was opposed by the United States. On the other hand, many developing nations refused labour and environmental standards to be linked to trade rights and obligations. Resentment among developing countries also grew about the efficiency and transparency of the WTO decision making process, as they were unable to participate in Green Room sessions that attempted to build momentum for the meeting.

negotiating with its trading partners. In reciprocation, the country must compensate trade partners for their loss of trade. In the event of dissatisfaction, the trade partners can invoke the WTO dispute settlement procedures.

The principle of transparency requires that WTO members must publish their trade regulations to allow for the review of administrative decisions affecting trade, to respond to requests for information by other members, and to notify changes in trade policies to the WTO. These transparency requirements are supplemented and facilitated by periodic country-specific reports through the Trade Policy Review Mechanism (TPRM).

Safety valves allow national governments to restrict trade under specific circumstances as laid down in three types of provisions. First, there are articles that allow the use of trade measures to attain non-economic objectives such as public health and national security. Second, articles aimed at ensuring fair competition. The countries are allowed to impose countervailing duties on imports that are subsidized in the exporting country and to impose anti-dumping duties. Third, there are provisions that permit intervention in trade for economic reasons such as a balance of payments crisis and protecting an infant industry.

19.4 WTO AGREEMENTS

Besides the existing GATT agreements, the 1994 Marrakech Agreement incorporated several new substantive agreements in WTO's legal text. First of all, the WTO introduced new rules on agriculture and textiles, known as the Agreement on Agriculture (AoA), and a more specific Agreement on Textiles and Clothing. WTO agreements and rules of trade policy also extend beyond the coverage of GATT as trade in services (through GATS) and intellectual property rights and patent protection (through TRIPS) were brought into the multilateral trading system. Plurilateral agreements like Agreements on Government Procurement (GPA) have also been made part of multilateral negotiations, though these are not put under general obligations for member countries. WTO agreements can be divided into four broad categories: Multilateral Agreements on Trade in Goods, General Agreement on Trade in Services (GATS), Agreement on Trade-Related Aspects of Intellectual Property Rights (TRIPS), and Plurilateral Trade Agreements. In Chapter 17 we discussed GATS and its implications. In the following subsections, we discuss some of the other major agreements under the Multilateral Agreements on Trade in Goods, along with TRIPS and GPA.

19.4.1 Multilateral Agreements on Trade in Goods

Multilateral Agreements on Trade in Goods include the GATT 1994 agreements and new major agreements like AoA, Agreement on Textiles and Clothing, Agreement on the Application of Sanitary and Phytosanitary Measures (SPM), Agreement on Technical Barriers to Trade (TBT), Agreement on Trade-Related Investment Measures, Agreement on Rules of Origin (ROO), Agreement on Subsidies and Countervailing Measures, and Agreement on Safeguards.

Agreements on Agriculture (AoA)

AoA was signed by members in 1994 in the Uruguay Round multilateral trade negotiations and came into force on 1 January 1995 as part of the WTO Multilateral Agreements on Trade in Goods. This agreement was intended to correct the distortions in agricultural trade caused by huge farm subsidies provided by industrialized countries. Such subsidies lead to over-production, which in turn necessitates export subsidies to dump the excess agricultural produce in the international markets (see Box 9.4 in Chapter 9). The most glaring example of this is EU's Common Agricultural Policy (CAP) that was intended to stabilize agricultural markets across the region through a common levy on all agricultural imports from abroad and setting an artificially high guaranteeing price, which created massive over-production. The surplus production bought by the EU is often sold at very low prices in international markets. Such protectionism, distortion of prices, and dumping of surplus produce in world markets attracted the criticism of the United States, which itself provides huge farm subsidies, and also other major food producers. Farm subsidies or domestic support stand tall even during the so-called globalization process. In 2000, for example, the rich countries subsidized their farmers five times the value of annual aid flows to developing countries. Throughout the decade of the 1990s, subsidies provided by EU and the US government in fact increased. Thus, fair trade in agriculture required reduction of domestic subsidies (or domestic support) and export subsidies by industrialized countries, and increased market access for agricultural products. AoA incorporates these three elements of the agricultural trade policy.

Regarding market access, the agreement has two basic elements: tariffication of all non-tariff barriers and a minimum level for imports of agricultural products by member countries as a share of domestic consumption. Tariffication requires conversion of all non-tariff barriers (NTBs) such as quantitative restrictions and export and import licensing into equal-import tariffs. These tariffs and other existing tariffs on agricultural imports are to be reduced subsequently by a simple average of 36 per cent over 6 years in the case of developed countries and 24 per cent over 10 years in the case of developing countries. Under the requirement of a minimum level for imports of agricultural products, member countries are to maintain levels of access for each individual product that were in place in 1995, with the minimum access being not less than 3 per cent of domestic consumption. This minimum access level was to rise to 5 per cent by 2000 for developed countries and by 2004 for developing countries.

WTO provisions on reduction of domestic support, on the other hand, require, as a first step, to quantify the aggregate value of domestic support or subsidy given to each category of agricultural product, known as Aggregate Measurement of Support (AMS), and then to make commitments to reduce such support. AMS consists of a calculation of both product-specific subsidies (such as guaranteeing price under CAP in EU and procurement price of food grains in India) and the total level of support for the agricultural sector as a whole such as subsidies on fertilizers, electricity, irrigation, seeds, and agricultural credit. These are called Amber Box measures. Commitment on the part of countries to lower their domestic support, on the other hand, requires a 20 per cent reduction in the total AMS for developed countries over 6 years and a 13 per cent reduction for developing countries. The least developed countries are exempted from making any commitments. The base period external reference price on which the reductions were calculated was 1986–88.

Finally, under the provisions for export subsidies, member countries are required to reduce the value of direct export subsidies to a level of 36 per cent below the 1986–90 base period level over a 6 year implementation period commencing in 1995. The quantity of subsidized exports, on the other hand, is to be reduced by 21 per cent over the same period. In the case of developing countries, the reductions are two-thirds those for the developed countries over a 10 year period and there are no reductions required for least developed countries.

There is, however, an inherent unfairness in AoA, particularly with regard to domestic support. Many developed countries provide domestic subsidies which are as high as 100 per cent. The requirement of 20 per cent reduction in the total AMS allows these countries to continue with their domestic subsidies or support up to 80 per cent after the 6 year period commencing in 1995. In contrast, most developing countries are now prohibited from having subsidies beyond the *de minimis* level of 10 per cent of the total agriculture value, except in some specific cases. The exemption of Blue Box measures also allows developed countries to continue with most of their domestic support. On the other hand, as the Oxfam (2005) report noted, EU could increase its expenditure on export subsidies for wheat by more than ten times, and still be within the allowed limits. The implications for this bias in favour of developed countries are far-reaching. WTO figures themselves indicate that farm subsidies by developed countries are almost exclusively responsible for trade distortions. Agricultural support in developing countries, on the other hand, is marginal. By WTO's own notifications, the total aggregated support in developing countries is 14 times *lower* than that of the United States and EU combined. Given that 90 per cent of the world farmers live in the developing and the least developed countries, these figures mean that the largest part of world subsidies target only a small percentage of the world population living on agriculture.

Box 19.4 Special Safeguards for Developing Countries

AoA allows quite a few exemptions for developing countries known as Special Safeguards Provisions. First of all, there is the balance of payments (BOP) cover for developing countries under the principle of the Safety Valve. For example, under such BOP considerations, India did not undertake any commitments with regard to market access and this had been clearly stated in its schedule filed under GATT. The only commitment that India had undertaken was to bind its tariffs on primary agricultural products at 100 per cent, on processed foods at 150 per cent, and on edible oil at 300 per cent.

Second, Special Safeguards Provisions allow for the application of additional duties when shipments are made at prices below certain reference levels or when there is a sudden import surge. The market access provision also does not apply when the commodity in question is a traditional staple of a developing country.

Third, there are three categories of exemption for domestic support measures. First, Green Box measures which include government assistance on (i) research, pest and disease control, training, extension, and advisory services; (ii) public stock holding for food security purposes; (iii) domestic food aid; and (iv) direct payment to producers like governmental financial participation in income insurance and safety nets, relief from natural disasters, and payments under environmental assistance programmes. Second, Special and Differential Treatment box measures which include (i) investment subsidies which are generally available to agriculture in developing countries; and (ii) agricultural input services generally available to low income and resource poor producers in developing countries. Third, Blue Box measures such as direct payments to farmers to compensate them for programmes to limit their production, which are relevant from the developed countries' point of view only.

Agreement on Rules of Origin (ROO)

The WTO Agreement on ROO defines the rules of origin as laws and regulations to determine the country of origin of goods. With growing input trade across the globe, fragmentation of production technologies and outsourcing of manufacturing production to different country locations, determining where a product comes from is no longer an easy task. In such cases, Rules of Origin are the criteria needed to determine the national source of a product. Their importance is derived from the fact that duties and restrictions in several cases depend on the source of imports. Thus, Rules of Origin are important in implementing trade policy instruments like anti-dumping and countervailing duties, origin marking, and safeguard measures.

There is a wide variation in the practice of governments with regard to the Rules of Origin. While the requirement of substantial transformation of a product is universally recognized to determine its country of origin, some governments apply the criterion of change of tariff classification, and others the criterion of manufacturing or processing operations. In a globalizing world, harmonization in these practices by member countries has become all the more important. A Technical Committee on Rules of Origin, created under the World Customs Organization, meets at least once a year to carry out harmonization work and to deal with any matter concerning technical problems related to the Rules of Origin. The membership to this committee is open to all WTO members. By the Agreement on ROO, a country is to be determined as the origin of a particular good where the good has been *wholly* obtained. The primary task of the technical committee is to provide a harmonized definition of goods that are to be considered as wholly obtained in one country. When more than one country is involved in the production of a good (as in the case of fragmentation of production technology and outsourcing of different stages of production to different country locations) the country where the final substantial transformation has been carried out will be considered as the origin country.

Till the harmonization work on the Rules of Origin is complete, the Agreement on ROO requires WTO members to permit a potential exporter (of another country) to request an

Box 19.5 Price Support Estimate as an Alternative Measure of Domestic Support

OECD's measure of support, known as the Price Support Estimate (PSE), is based on the annual monetary transfers to farmers from policy measures that maintain a difference between domestic prices and the prices at the country's border. The difference of PSE with WTO's Aggregate Measure of Support (AMS) is two-fold. First, PSE covers *all* transfers to the farmers from agricultural policies in contrast to AMS, which is based only on Amber Box measures. Second, the market price support in PSE is measured at the farm-gate level using actual producer prices and border prices for commodities in a given year. This is in contrast to AMS market price support which is calculated by the difference between the domestic *administered* support price and a world reference price fixed in terms of a historical base period. There are, however, some methodological problems with PSE such as the risk of over-stating border support. The difference in the estimates of domestic support by these alternative measures is huge. Whereas PSE shows that between 1986 and 2001, EU and US subsidies increased, by the AMS model the subsidies *decreased* for the same years.

assessment of the origin of its product from that country's customs service. The importing country must issue its origin assessment within 150 days from such a request. Assessments are valid for three years and changes in origin rules cannot be applied retroactively.

19.4.2 Agreement on Trade Related Intellectual Property Rights (TRIPS)

The Agreement on TRIPS (and GATS), which came into effect from 1 January 1995, is the new rule that governs the world trading system. This sets out the minimum standards of protection to be provided by each member country and allows them to provide more extensive protection of intellectual property. The areas of intellectual property that it covers are copyright, trademarks including service marks, patents including the protection of new varieties of plants, the layout-designs of integrated circuits, and undisclosed information including trade secrets and test data. The agreement sets the standards by requiring that the Paris Convention for the Protection of Industrial Property and the Berne Convention for the Protection of Literary and Artistic Works in their most recent versions must be complied with. Members are allowed to determine the appropriate method of implementing the provisions of the agreement within their own legal system and practice.

Regarding patent protection, the TRIPS Agreement requires member countries to make patents available for any inventions, whether products or processes, in all fields of technology. Such patents shall be granted without discrimination whether the products are imported or

Box 19.6 Agreements on TBT and SPS

During the Tokyo Round of trade negotiations (1973–79), participating countries raised concerns on how the environmental measures in the form of technical regulations and standards were hindering trade. The Tokyo Round Agreement on Technical Barriers to Trade (TBT) was then negotiated. This required non-discrimination in the preparation, adoption, and application of technical regulations and standards. Transparency in such technical regulations and standards was also sought. During the Uruguay Round (1986–94), modifications were made to the TBT Agreement. Later the WTO mandate on transparency required that member countries 'shall notify their draft technical regulations and conformity assessment procedures and allow a reasonable time to make comments on them'. It also provides that the members shall publish their TBT measures. In a meeting of the TBT Committee in November 2011, members discussed trade concerns regarding standards and certification to labeling of tobacco products (Australia's measures), alcoholic drinks (Thailand, Brazil, EU, Colombia, South Africa, and Kenya), drinks with added caffeine (Mexico), food additives (China), and genetically modified organisms in food (Peru, EU).

The Agreement on Sanitary and Phytosanitary Measures is an agreement on food safety and animal and plant health standards. Food safety measures relate to bacterial contaminants, pesticides, inspection, and labeling. It allows countries to set their own standards, but these regulations must be applied only to the extent 'necessary to protect human, animal or plant life or health', and should not 'arbitrarily or unjustifiably discriminate between countries where identical or similar conditions prevail'. But as we have mentioned above, country-specific standards created acrimonious disputes amongst countries in many instances.

locally produced, subject to the normal tests of novelty, inventiveness, and industrial applicability. The exclusive rights that must be conferred by a product patent should cover making, using, and selling, with some exceptions though. Notably, the provisions of the agreement require that a process patent protection must give rights not only over the use of the process but also *over the products obtained directly by the process*. Moreover, patent owners shall have the right to assign, transfer by succession, and license the patent to any other firm.

There are certain exceptions that are allowed to countries under the TRIPS Agreement. The most notable is that countries may implement their own rules of exhaustion of patent rights once an on-patent product is *marketed*. Article 6 of TRIPS states that once the patent holder markets an on-patent product, its exclusive rights to *sell* exhausts, and what remains is its exclusive right to produce (and license). Thus, countries can allow parallel imports of an on-patent product from low-priced low-income regions or countries without the permission of the patent holder MNC. Understandably, however, wide variations in national rules for exhaustion among the rich countries are observed. For example, in the market for healthcare and patented pharmaceutical products, Japan allows international exhaustion and EU allows only regional exhaustion of patented goods.[2] Thus, Japanese importers can parallel import a patented product from any other country, whereas importers in UK, say, can do so only from any other EU member country. But, the United States allows only national exhaustion of patents and copyrights. These variations in the use of Article 6 of the TRIPS Agreement are understandable. Parallel imports lead to arbitrage and consequently limit the scope for cross-country price discrimination by a patent holder MNC. Prices in different countries converge and differ only by the extent of transport costs. Since prices are usually set high in rich countries and low in poorer countries under price discrimination, so consumers in rich countries benefit from such price convergence and those in the poorer countries lose. This benefit is particularly important for markets in healthcare and for poor patients in rich countries. But, the patent holder pharmaceutical MNC loses as its profit declines with price convergence as a consequence of parallel trade allowed by countries. The United States being one of the major exporter countries for medicines and drugs, it is obvious then that it will not allow parallel imports to protect the interests of its pharmaceutical MNCs. In fact, the United States goes beyond this by implementing the so called TRIPS-Plus provisions as part of its bilateral FTA negotiations with developing countries. Among these clauses there is a commitment required on the part of the developing country trade partner not to allow parallel imports. Some of the major pharmaceuticals MNCs being located in some European countries, EU also now include this provision in its bilateral FTA negotiations with other countries.

Article 7 of TRIPS states that the protection and enforcement of TRIPS should be 'conducive to social and economic welfare'. This has given member countries certain flexibilities and exceptions and country-specific variations in the implementation of a stronger IPR regime within the scope of TRIPS. On the other hand, the exception that is particularly relevant for developing countries is *compulsory licensing* by which a non-patentee can obtain a license

[2] Allowing for parallel trade as the rule of the internal market in EU emerged out of the Treaty of Rome, and has found endorsement in the European Court of Justice which held that a patent holder's rights are exhausted EU-wide once the on-patent product is placed anywhere in the EU market.

Box 19.7 Copyright Protection

The provisions of the Berne Convention that are incorporated into the TRIPS Agreement deal with questions such as subject matter to be protected, the minimum term of protection, and the rights to be conferred and the permissible limitations to those rights. It is stated that copyright protection shall be applicable only to 'expressions and not to ideas, procedures, methods of operation or mathematical concepts as such'. In the TRIPS Agreement, copyright protection is extended to computer programmes. These programmes are treated as literary works and thus are protected by copyright under those provisions of the Berne Convention (1971) that apply to literary works. The term of protection for any copyright protected work shall be the life of the author and 50 years after his death.

and compete with the patent holder by paying a nominal (or often non-existent) royalty to the patent holder through the national government. A large number of countries had allowed compulsory licensing in the pre-TRIPS era and a strong case has often been made in favour of its continuation under the new patent protection regime. Canada has successfully implemented compulsory licensing since the 1920s. In the 1923 Patent Act of Canada, compulsory licensing allowed the licensee the right to manufacture, use, or sell a patented innovation before the patent expired without the consent of the patent holder and in exchange the licensee was required to pay a royalty. This royalty was then paid to the patent holder.

The strongest case for patent protection under TRIPs is that it is a precondition for innovation that is essential for growth and prosperity. But what this argument overlooks is that for a potential innovator this is not a sufficient condition. The potential benefit of patent protection is often misunderstood, sometimes purposely blown up, because the major impediments to innovation levels in developing countries are not lack of patent protection but financial, infrastructural, and skill-based. Moreover, since industrialized countries account for more than 90 per cent of the global R&D, the principal beneficiaries of the TRIPs Agreement will be the industrialized countries.[3]

There is also the danger of sleeping patents on related products by multinational corporations aimed at eliminating any indirect competition from local producers.

The worst effect of patent protection seems to be in the area of public health. The high cost of basic medicines that TRIPs will result in, may in fact drive a vast majority of the poor out of the healthcare system. Of course, prices will rise not because of innovation or patent costs, but because of elimination of competition and concentration of market power that the TRIPs agreements will lead to. For example, countries with strong generic industries that provide copies of brand names or patented drugs such as India and Brazil are a major source of medicines for countries lacking a manufacturing base. Competition between these

[3] Evidence does not seem to suggest that TRIPS will have any significant positive impact on healthcare innovation in the developing world (Primo Braga 1990). This is because not only investments in basic R&D and costs of full development of a commercial drug are very high, but also most of the developing countries, with notable exceptions like India, lack technological capabilities and skills to undertake basic R&D (Lall 2003).

Box 19.8 Indian Patent Act (1999), Mailbox Facility, and Compulsory Licensing

India was granted a 10 year transition period, beginning on 1 January 1999, to comply with all provisions of TRIPS by the year 2005. There were a series of Amendments of the Indian Patent Act of 1970, first in 1999, and then in 2002 and 2005. In the 1999 amendment of Act, a mailbox facility was created in accordance with the *mailbox* provisions in Article 70.8 of TRIPS by which all applications claiming pharmaceutical inventions during this 10 year transition period would be accepted and put away in a mailbox to be examined in 2005. By this *mailbox facility*, applications would be judged for novelty on the basis of the filing date and not with reference to 2005. The act provides that in regard to the *mailbox applications* that result in the grant of patents, an automatic compulsory licensing would be issued to those generic companies that made significant investment and were producing and marketing a drug covered by the mailbox application prior to 2005.

generic drug companies and patented drug companies has significantly lowered the prices of medicines for HIV/AIDS and blood diarrhoea. India, having a strong and well-developed pharmaceutical sector based on its expertise and skills in chemicals, took full advantage of the flexibility granted in the TRIPS Agreement to wage its own war against malaria, tuberculosis, AIDS, and other diseases. India's generic drug production and export benefits millions of poor patients worldwide so much so that it is termed as the pharmacy of the developing world.

To consider a specific example, an Indian pharmaceutical firm, introduced the AIDS drugs Zidovudine, Stavudine, and Lamivudine between 1993 and 1998 and offered these drugs at significantly lower prices than other companies. The original product of the British firm sold for more than double the price in India, Pakistan, and Indonesia and cost five to six times more in the United States and Great Britain. Given that more than 95 per cent of all HIV-infected people live in developing countries, patent protection for medicines and drugs simply implies denying many of these poor patients access to available drugs and consequently their right to live. In India alone, 8 million people are estimated to be HIV-positive of which 500,000 people have already developed AIDS.

The situation is further worsened for them by high and upper-middle income countries like Australia, EU, Japan, Hong Kong, New Zealand, and Singapore which allow parallel imports of patented drugs from low income developing countries. Drug prices across countries tend to converge but at a level higher than what would have prevailed in the low income developing countries without parallel imports. Thus, poor patients in high income countries gain at the expense of even poorer patients in low income countries. Worse still, to prevent price arbitrage through parallel imports, pharmaceutical MNCs may price patented drugs high enough to exclude low income countries from accessing the drugs altogether and thus preventing these countries from becoming potential sources of parallel imports. Malueg and Schwartz (1994) have theoretically established such a possibility for low income countries with large income and demand disparities.

What is needed, therefore, is an international agreement on the protection of intellectual property rights in general with special rules for innovations and market access for poor patients in areas of life and death. While access to cheap and effective medicines for poor patients should have priority, research in therapies for tropical diseases has to be stimulated as well.

19.4.3 Plurilateral Trade Agreements: Agreement on Government Procurement (GPA)

Government procurement was originally omitted from the scope of the main multilateral trade rules for opening up market access. But government procurement of goods and services typically accounts for 10–15 per cent of the GDP for developed countries, and up to as much as 20 per cent of the GDP for developing countries. These volumes are significant enough to indicate a considerable gap in the multilateral trading system that the omission of this dimension of trade from the scope of the multilateral trade rules has created. Many countries place restrictions on government procurement of both goods and services to encourage domestic industries.

These concerns resulted in a plurilateral Agreement on Government Procurement (GPA) at the Uruguay Round in 1994 which was signed by WTO members. This is only binding to WTO members *who choose to sign*. The agreement is based on the 1979 Tokyo Round government procurement agreement. Currently, there are 26 signatories, including Canada, the EU, the United Kingdom, and the United States. The rest of the signatories are predominantly developed countries. Developed countries see this agreement as an opportunity to increase market shares for their own firms, allowing them to bid for foreign government purchases on a 'level-playing field'. Thus, many of them want the GPA to become a *multilateral* agreement. The most vocal proponents of a multilateral GPA are EU and the United States. There are, however, some concerns raised by several developing countries, particularly India, Pakistan, and Egypt, and relief organizations such as Oxfam. These parties see the opening of government procurement not as a way to gain a level-playing field, but rather as a situation in which the developing and the least developed countries are likely to lose ground to expanding industrial countries. The apprehension is that growing industries in developing nations will be at a disadvantage if large

Box 19.9 Goods in Transit versus Patent Infringement: India versus the EU

On 11 May 2010, India launched a WTO dispute against EU and the Netherlands on the seizure of a shipment of generic drugs in transit from India to Brazil by Dutch customs officials on patent infringement grounds of generic drugs originating in India. The medicine in question is the generic version of the hypertension drug *Losartan potassium* that is patent protected in EU but not in India or in Brazil. DuPont is the patent owner, while Merck & Co. has the manufacturing and marketing rights. India alleges that the measures at issue are, in several respects, inconsistent as such and as applied with the obligations of the European Union and the Netherlands under Articles V and X of GATT 1994 and under various provisions of the TRIPs Agreement together with the provisions of the August 2003 decision on TRIPs and Public Health.

On 28 May 2010, Brazil, Canada, and Ecuador requested to join the consultations. On 31 May 2010, China, Japan, and Turkey requested to join the consultations. Subsequently, the European Union informed DSB that it had accepted the requests of Canada, China, Ecuador, India, Japan, and Turkey to join the consultations.

and established foreign companies are allowed to bid for government contracts alongside their own domestic firms.

GPA establishes an agreed framework of rights and obligations among its parties with respect to their national laws, regulations, procedures, and practices in the area of government procurement. An important element of this is the principle of non-discrimination. Government decisions regarding the purchase of goods and services must not depend on where the good is produced or the service rendered, or upon the supplier's foreign affiliations. The agreement also places considerable emphasis on procedures for providing transparency in laws, regulations, procedures, and practices regarding government procurement.

In February 2010 India became an observer in the WTO Agreement on Government Procurement (GPA). Increasingly, in the context of FTA negotiations, demands are being made on India for accepting bilateral obligations on government procurement. The scope of obligations requested by some of India's trading partners includes transparency requirements and market access commitments.

It has been pointed out that there could be both gains and losses for developing countries like India on account of accession to GPA or accepting bilateral commitments on government procurement. Due to an increase in the number of sellers, participation in bilateral government procurement agreements and multilateral GPA will result in pro-competitive gains manifested in lower prices and higher consumer welfare. Benefits may also accrue from increased market access, particularly in services, in significant foreign markets. This, however, may not be fully realized on account of supply side constraints in India and the fact that import penetration in government procurement markets in large industrialized economies is rather modest.

On the other hand, accepting international rules on government procurement has associated costs. First, there could be costs linked to switching over from the existing procurement regime to new systems mandated under international rules. Second, there will be a 'leakage' in the government's attempts to boost the economy through increased spending during a downturn. Accession to bilateral government procurement agreements and GPA will also restrict the development policy space available to India. The ability to assist local companies, and particular socio-economic groups or ethnic communities, or under-developed regions, through government procurement and spending will also be curtailed.

APPENDIX A19

I. Tariff Reductions and Market Access for Non-agricultural Products (NAMA)

Regarding increasing market access for non-agricultural products (NAMA), countries have agreed to reduce or eliminate tariff peaks, high tariffs, and tariff escalation, as well as non-tariff barriers on products of export interest to developing countries. The modalities of such reductions, however, could not be universally agreed upon. In the Tokyo Round of GATT negotiations, the participating countries agreed to cut tariffs across the board, whereas in the Uruguay Round, they negotiated product-by-product tariff cuts. There has also been a discussion on a Swiss formula for tariff reduction. But again a general consensus is yet to be achieved. Reduction methods that have come up for negotiated tariff reductions are:

Flat-rate percentage reductions: This is the same percentage reduction for all products, no matter whether the starting tariff is high or low.

Uruguay Round approach: Tariff reductions for industrial goods can take place along the lines of AoA. In the 1986–94 Uruguay Round negotiations on agriculture an agreement was reached for developed countries to cut tariffs on agricultural products by an average of 36 per cent over six years with a minimum of 15 per cent on each product for the period. Thus, tariff rates are to be reduced at the rate 6 per cent per annum.

Harmonized reductions: These are designed principally to make steeper cuts on higher tariffs, bringing down the final tariffs closer together. One example is the *Swiss formula*. Interestingly, though the formula was proposed by Switzerland in the 1973–79 Tokyo Round negotiations, it itself opposed using this formula in negotiations on agriculture. Instead it preferred the Uruguay Round approach.

The key element in the Swiss formula is a number A, called the Swiss coefficient, which determines the maximum final tariff rate after reductions:

$$t_T = \frac{At_{T-1}}{A + t_{T-1}},\ T = 0, 1, 2, 3, \ldots \tag{A19.1}$$

where, t_T is the resulting lower tariff rate after the end of period T, t_{T-1} is the previous period tariff rate and A is the coefficient and the maximum tariff rate *after* reduction. This coefficient is to be negotiated and applies to all countries. Tariff reductions by this formula lead to a narrow range of final tariff rates from a wide set of initial tariffs across countries.

Note that if t_{T-1} is infinitely high, $t_T = A$. However, many countries argue that the formula is too simple for use in tariff negotiations and that it does not lead to proportionate reduction in tariffs across all countries. The Asia-Pacific Economic Cooperation (APEC) countries adopted the Swiss formula for tariff reductions for industrial goods in the 2005 meeting of APEC Ministers Responsible for Trade at Jeju Island, Korea.

An example of reduced tariff rates over a 6-year period for a coefficient value of 20 and different initial tariff rates is shown in Table A19.1.

Table A19.1 Reduced Tariff Rates under the Swiss Formula for a Coefficient of 20

Coefficient	20	20	20	20	20
Starting Year (T = 0)	100	75	50	25	10
Year 1 (T = 1)	20.00	18.75	16.67	12.50	7.14
Year 2 (T = 2)	11.11	10.71	10.00	8.33	5.56
Year 3 (T = 3)	7.69	7.50	7.14	6.25	4.55
Year 4 (T = 4)	5.88	5.77	5.56	5.00	3.85
Year 5 (T = 5)	4.76	4.69	4.55	4.17	3.33
Year 6 (T = 6)	4.00	3.95	3.85	3.57	2.94

Note that, higher the value of A, lower are the reduction commitments and vice-versa. Thus, the selection of the coefficient is crucial in order to determine the effect of the formula on the final tariff profile of any WTO member.

SUMMARY POINTS

- The WTO was established for the purpose of monitoring rules for international trade in goods and services through the Marrakech Agreement, and came into force on 1 January 1995. This replaced GATT.
- Till 2011, there were 157 member countries in WTO and 26 observer governments.
- The functions of the WTO include implementing and administering WTO agreements regarding the rules of international trade policy and patent protection, providing a forum for negotiations among member countries, and resolving international trade disputes among members.
- Decisions in WTO are generally taken by consensus, which is usually negotiated in informal meetings (the so-called Green Room process), and are well represented and influenced by Canada, EU, Japan, and the United States.
- Where consensus cannot be reached, the WTO Agreement allows for votes. WTO is based on the system of 'one country, one vote'.
- WTO establishes a framework for trade policies based on five principles, some of which are actually a continuation of GATT's principles. These five principles are non-discrimination, reciprocity, binding and enforceable commitments, transparency, and safety valves.
- The WTO agreements and rules of trade policy extend beyond the coverage of GATT as trade in services (through GATS) and intellectual property rights and patent protection (through TRIPS) were brought into the multilateral trading system.
- WTO agreements can be divided into four broad categories: Multilateral Agreements on Trade in Goods, General Agreement on Trade in Services (GATS), Agreement on Trade-Related Aspects of Intellectual Property Rights (TRIPS), and Plurilateral Trade Agreements.
- The TRIPS Agreement requires member countries to make patents available for any inventions, whether products or processes, in all fields of technology. Such patents shall be granted without discrimination whether the products are imported or locally produced. The exclusive rights that must be conferred by a product patent should cover making, using, and selling.
- There are certain exceptions that are allowed to countries under the TRIPS Agreement. Article 6 of TRIPS states that once the patent holder markets an on-patent product, its exclusive rights to *sell* exhausts, and what remains is its exclusive right to produce (and license). Thus, countries can allow parallel imports of an on-patent product from low-priced low-income regions or countries without the permission of the patent holder MNC.
- The plurilateral Agreement on Government Procurement (GPA) at the Uruguay Round in 1994 signed by WTO members is binding only to WTO members *who choose to sign*. The agreement is based on the 1979 Tokyo Round government procurement agreement. Currently, there are 26 signatories, including Canada, the EU, the United Kingdom, and the United States. In February 2010 India became an observer.

KEYWORDS

- **Ministerial conferences,** composed of international trade (or commerce) ministers from all member countries, form the WTO's governing body. Ministerial conference meets at least once every two years. So far eight meetings have been held:

  First Ministerial Conference in Singapore, 9–13 December 1996.
  Second Ministerial Conference in Geneva, Switzerland, 18–20 May 1998.
  Third Ministerial Conference in Seattle, USA, 30 November–3 December 1999.
  Fourth Ministerial Conference in Doha, Qatar, 9–13 November 2001.
  Fifth Ministerial Conference in Cancun, Mexico, 10–14 September 2003.
  Sixth Ministerial Conference in Hong Kong, 13–18 December 2005.
  Seventh Ministerial Conference in Geneva, Switzerland, 30 November–2 December 2009.
  Eighth Ministerial Conference in Geneva, Switzerland,15–17 December 2011.
- **Dispute Settlement Body** of the WTO resolves international trade disputes among member countries and provides a forum for the dispute settlement mechanism.
- **Green Room process** refers to consensus for policy rules negotiated in informal meetings among a small group of member countries.
- **Aggregate Measurement of Support** (AMS) is a measure to quantify the aggregate value of domestic support or subsidy given to each category of agricultural product. This is based on product-specific subsidies (such as the procurement price of food grains) and the total level of support for the agricultural sector as a whole (such as subsidies on inputs).
- **Amber Box measures** are domestic support to farmers that are trade distorting and have effects on production such as input subsidies and price support. Subsidies under the Amber Box are calculated under AMS and are subject to reduction.
- **Green Box measures** are domestic supports that are assumed to have no effect on production such as support for research, pest control, marketing assistance, and the like.
- **Blue Box measures** are domestic supports that involve direct payments to farmers to compensate them for programmes to limit their production.
- **Price Support Estimate** (PSE) of OECD is an alternative measure of domestic support or subsidy which quantifies annual monetary transfers to farmers from policy measures that maintain a difference between domestic prices and prices at the country's border. PSE covers *all* transfers to farmers from agricultural policies in contrast to AMS which is based on only product-specific subsidies and input subsidies (the Amber Box ones).
- **Rules of origin** are the criteria needed to determine the national source of a product or the country of origin of goods. These are important in implementing trade policy instruments like anti-dumping and countervailing duties, origin marking, and safeguard measures.
- **Parallel imports** refer to imports of an on-patent product from low-priced countries without the permission of the patent holder MNC. *This is not smuggling* but is allowed

under the provisions of Article 6 of the TRIPS Agreement. It states that once the patent holder markets an on-patent product, its exclusive rights to sell exhausts, and what remains is its exclusive right to produce (and license).

- **Compulsory licensing** is the system whereby a non-patentee firm can obtain a license by paying a nominal royalty to the patent holder through its national government to compete with the patent holder.

EXERCISES

1. How are the decisions taken in the WTO? Is the decision making inclusive and participatory?
2. On what principles are WTO rules for trade policies based?
3. What is the MFN rule? What are its implications?
4. Why is the reciprocity principle perceived to be important for the success of multilateral trade negotiations?
5. How do farm subsidies given by industrialized countries distort international trade?
6. Discuss the main elements of AoA. Why is it often alleged that AoA is discriminatory?
7. What are the Amber Box, Green Box, and Blue Box domestic support measures? Do all these supports come under the reduction in WTO's provisions on AoA?
8. Suppose the Microsoft corporation outsources initial and low value addition stages of a software development to India and its own research office in the United States carries out the final stages of the development of the software. The new software is then exported to European countries. Which country should be regarded as the country of origin for the new software under WTO's ROO agreement? Explain.
9. What is parallel import? Is it illegal under the provisions on TRIPS? What are its implications for the pricing policy of a patent holder MNC? Why is it that not all rich nations allow parallel imports?
10. Consider the markets for a copyrighted commercial software in China and the UK as defined by the following linear demand functions:

    $S_C = 100 - 5P_C$, $S_U = 200 - 5P_U$

    where, S_C and S_U are respectively the number of the commercial software demanded in China and the UK, and P_C and P_U are respectively the country specific prices charged by the MNC.

    (a) If both countries strictly implement patent protection to rule out any piracy of this software, determine the country-specific prices charged by the MNC.

    (b) Which of the two countries will have the incentive to allow parallel imports? Why?

    (c) If countries allow parallel imports, what will be its effect on the price of the software and consumer welfare? Assume that there is no transport cost.

    (d) Should both countries have an incentive to allow parallel imports based on gains for their respective consumers?

(contd)

Exercise (*contd*)

(e) If the software MNC is located in the UK, how does your answer in (d) change, if at all?

11. [Advanced] Consider a product of quality q to be innovated by an MNC by investing a sum C that varies quadratically with the target level of innovation: $C = \frac{1}{2}q^2$. The MNC obtains a patent for its innovation and sells this patented product in the United States (U) and Australia (A), which comprise the world. There are n_j number of identical buyers in each country (j = U, A), and each buyer buys only one unit of the product if at all. If a representative buyer in a country buys the good, it derives a net utility which is additively separable in the quality and the price of the product in the following way: $u_j = \alpha_j q - p_j$, $\alpha_u > \alpha_A$. A consumer buys the good only if $u_j \geq 0$.
   (a) If there is no production cost except for the product innovation cost, write down the profit function of the monopolist if it caters to both the markets under strict implementation of TRIPS.
   (b) Find out the profit maximizing price and innovation (or quality) levels.
   [Hints: Given the zero reservation utility, the MNC extracts all surpluses from a representative consumer by charging its reservation price: $p_j = \alpha_j q$. Thus, its profit equals: $\pi = [n_U \alpha_U + n_A \alpha_A]q - \frac{1}{2}q^2$.]

12. In the above context, suppose the countries allow parallel trade of this innovated product that compels the MNC to charge the same price in both markets.
   (a) Find out the price and the innovation level when the monopolist continues to cater to both the markets. Is the innovation level higher or lower than that under market discrimination?
   (b) Will it be profitable for the MNC to cater to both the markets?

   [Hints: (a) Under parallel imports, the MNC must charge $p = \alpha_A q$ to all if it caters to both the markets. This results in a profit of $\bar{\pi} = [n_U + n_A]\alpha_A q - \frac{1}{2}q^2$.

   (b) Alternatively, the MNC can cater only to buyers in the United States by charging their reservation price to all $p = \alpha_U q$. Buyers in Australia are then priced out of the market and there will be no scope for parallel imports. This pricing policy (and single-market coverage) yields a profit of $\tilde{\pi} = n_U \alpha_U q - \frac{1}{2}q^2$. Find out the profit-maximizing innovation level $\tilde{q}$ and then compare $\tilde{\pi}$ with $\bar{\pi}$.]

13. In adopting the Swiss formula for reduction of tariffs on non-agricultural imports, each country will try to negotiate as high a value of coefficient A as possible. Do you agree? If so why?

SUGGESTED READING

Hoekman, B. (2002). 'The WTO: Functions and Basic Principles', in B. Hoekman, B.A. Mattoo, and P. English (eds), *Development. Trade and the WTO: A Handbook*, Part I. The World Bank, chapter 6. Available at http://www.wto.org.

ADVANCED READING

Acharyya, R. and M.D.C. Garcia-Alonso. (2011). 'Parallel Imports, Drug Innovation and International Patent Protection: A Policy Game', *Journal of International Trade and Economic Development*, October 2011.

Lall, S. (2003). 'Indicators of Relative Importance of IPRs in Developing Countries', *Research Policy*, 32: 1657–80.

Malueg, D.A. and M. Schwartz. (1994). 'Parallel Imports, Demand Dispersion and International Price Discrimination', *Journal of International Economics*, 37: 167–96.

Oxfam. (2005). 'A Round for Free: How Rich Countries Are Getting a Free Ride on Agricultural Subsidies at the WTO', Oxfam Briefing Paper No. 76.

Primo Braga, C. (1990). 'The Developing Country Case for and against Intellectual Property Protection', in Wolfgang E. Siebeck (ed.), *Strengthening Protection of Intellectual Property in Developing Countries: A Survey of the Literature.* Washington, DC: The World Bank.

Valletti, T.M. (2006). 'Differential Pricing, Parallel Imports and the Incentive to Invest', *Journal of International Economics*, 70: 314–24.

PART VII

Theory of Balance of Payments and Open Economy Macroeconomics

20 Balance of Payments and National Income Accounting

Balance of payments (BOP) is a record of values of all economic transactions of a country with the rest of the world in a particular year. The values are usually expressed in the domestic currency of the country under consideration and also in terms of an internationally accepted currency like the US dollar. India's BOP as recorded and published by the Reserve Bank of India, for example, is expressed in both Indian rupees and US dollars. The transactions recorded in BOP include those undertaken by private economic agents like exporters, importers, asset traders, and by the government. BOP also defines different sub-accounts and balances thereof such as the trade account, the current account, and the capital account. Transactions that earn foreign currencies, such as export of goods and services, inward remittances, foreign direct investments, and receipts of loans, are recorded as credit or positive items in BOP. On the other hand, transactions that spend foreign currencies such as import of goods and services, outward remittances, investment in foreign countries, loan repayments, and debt servicing are recorded as debit or negative items. This chapter discusses these different components of BOP accounts and the concepts of balance and equilibrium in the external payments of a country.

The chapter also discusses how basic national income identities can be extended to include external trade and transfers of a country. An important distinction that is made in this context is between Gross National Product (GNP) and Gross Domestic Product (GDP).

20.1 CLASSIFICATION OF TRANSACTIONS AND SUB-ACCOUNTS

The BOP account is usually classified by the nature of transactions into a current account and a capital account. Figure 20.1 illustrates such classifications of the transactions. The first distinction is between current account transactions and capital account transactions. Current account transactions are essentially those that do not give rise to any future claims. There are two broad types of current account transactions. First, transactions that relate to cross-border sale and purchase of goods and extension of services, or exports and imports of goods and services. Service exports and imports are termed as invisibles in contrast to goods trade as visible.

International Economics. Rajat Acharyya, Oxford University Press. © Oxford University Press 2022.
DOI: 10.1093/oso/9780192865144.003.0020

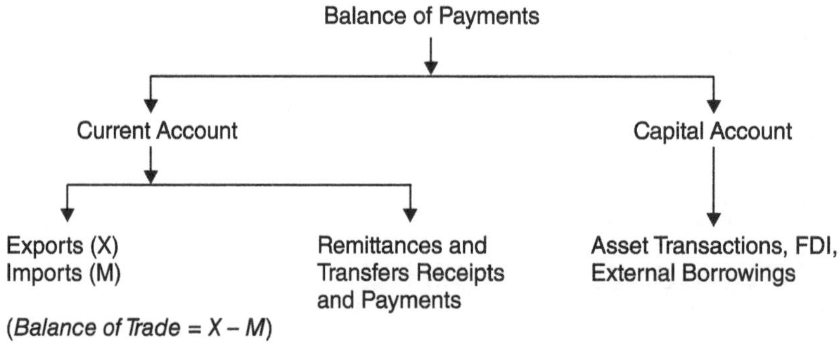

Figure 20.1 Classification of International Transactions in BOP

The net receipts from these exports and imports constitute the balance of trade (BOT). If in a particular year, the value of export of goods and services to the rest of the world by a country exceeds the value of its import of goods and services, the country experiences a surplus in its trade account, or a trade surplus in short. Similarly, a trade deficit for a country arises in a particular year if the value of its exports is smaller than the value of its imports. The second type of transactions in the current account is those payments (or receipts) for which there are no corresponding receipts (or payments). These are called unrequited payments and receipts. For example, incomes from assets held abroad by domestic citizens, remittances sent by domestic citizens working abroad, and war compensations received by the country. Similarly, there may be payments made by the country such as interest paid on external loans or on domestic assets held by foreign citizens and remittances sent by foreign citizens working in the domestic country under considerations. Note that unlike exports (or imports) of goods and services, these transactions do not involve any exchange even at present. Exports of goods involve an exchange in the sense that foreign exchange is earned in exchange for goods and services being exported by the country. In contrast, these transactions as exemplified earlier are unilateral transfers. The net receipts from these transactions together with the transactions in the trade account constitute the *balance of current account*. Once again, positive net receipts imply a current account surplus and negative net receipts—payments exceeding receipts—imply a current account deficit.

Capital account transactions, on the other hand, give rise to *future claims* such as acquiring foreign assets or shares in companies located abroad. These transactions yield interest incomes for domestic citizens and shareholders (and constitute a part of current account transactions) from the next period onwards. Advancing loans to foreign countries, which is another capital account transaction, also yields interest incomes in the next period. Though these capital account transactions are export of capital by the country under consideration, these are actually debit items since foreign exchange flows *out* rather than flowing in. Import of capital such as direct investment by foreign companies through setting up of subsidiary production units, portfolio investment by foreign citizens, and external borrowings by the domestic country are credit items since the country now earns foreign exchange through these capital account transactions. Note that these *imports of capital constitute claims of the rest of the world* on the domestic country under consideration. Thus, interest payments on loans taken—that is, debt servicing—and on interest bearing assets acquired by foreigners will be debit items in the current account in the next year.

A capital account surplus arises when the import of capital is larger than the export of capital. But there is a fundamental difference between a current account surplus and a capital account surplus. The current account reflects the net income of a country. On the other hand, *the capital account indicates a net change in national ownership of assets*. A surplus in the capital account means there is a net inflow of foreign currency, but that constitutes a net claim of foreigners on the domestic economy. This is because net inflows are effectively outcomes of larger borrowing than lending and a larger sale of domestic assets than purchase of foreign assets. Therefore, in terms of asset creation, a capital account surplus, *unlike* a surplus in the current account, indicates a country's weakness rather than its strength. A deficit in the capital account, on the other hand, means a net claim on foreign assets and thus reflects a country's strength.

The final category of transactions listed in the capital account is changes in the stock of gold and foreign currency *reserves* held by the central bank of the country. An increase in such reserves is considered as import of capital and is thus listed as a credit item in BOP accounts. On the other hand, a decrease in reserves is considered as export of capital and is thus listed as a debit item. Note that these transactions will either appear on the credit side or on the debit side of a country's BOP account since the stock of gold and foreign currency reserves can *either* increase *or* decrease. These transactions are actually official settlement transactions that act as a balancing factor in the sense explained later. These are listed on either the debit or the credit side as may be required to balance the value of all other transactions on the credit side with those on the debit side.

Box 20.1 IMF Classifications

The International Monetary Fund (IMF) uses a slightly different set of definitions for BOP accounts. It uses the term *current account* to describe the same set of transactions as mentioned earlier. But it decomposes the current account slightly differently into three sub-accounts: the *goods and services account*, which is the overall trade balance; the *primary income account*, which relates to interest incomes such as from loans and investments; and the *secondary income account*, which considers transfer payments or remittances.

Similarly, IMF defines some of the capital account transactions mentioned earlier as transactions in *financial account* and the rest as transactions in capital account. That is, IMF uses the term *capital account* to designate only a sub-set of transactions that other classifications would consider under capital account. Debt forgiveness for a country, which in a sense is the transfer of ownership of an asset, is the largest component of IMF's capital account transactions. All other transactions that would feature as capital account transactions in the standard classification such as foreign direct investment, portfolio investment, and the like are classified by IMF under financial account. These classifications are also used by the Organisation for Economic Cooperation and Development (OECD) and the United Nations System of National Accounts (SNA). Thus, by the IMF definition, the BOP account is composed of current account, financial account, and capital account.

Finally, BOP of a country is the sum of current account and capital account transactions *including* the official settlement term.

20.2 BOP ACCOUNTING: AN EXAMPLE

Table 20.1 reports India's provisional BOP account for the financial year 2019–20. The main items of transactions are shown with some simplifications to exemplify the classifications of transactions discussed in the earlier section. The total receipts in the trade account that comprise earnings from export of goods and services, were USD 5,33,622 million, whereas payments for import of goods and services were USD 6,06,206 million. Thus, as per the provisional estimates, India had a trade deficit to the tune of USD 72,584 million during 2019–20. An asymmetry in the trade account is to be noted in this context. Whereas merchandise exports were much less than merchandise imports, service exports by India were much larger than service imports. This reflects India's emergence as a net service exporting country over the last two decades. A decomposition of services reveals several interesting features of this. Major

Table 20.1 India's Balance of Payments: 2019–20 P (USD million)

Receipts/Credit		Payments/Debit	
A. Current Account			
Exports of Goods	320,431	Import of Goods	477,937
Exports of Services	213,191	Imports of Services	128,269
Of which		*Of which*	
Travel	29,998	*Travel*	22,011
Transportation	20,988	*Transportation*	24,285
Software services	93,102	*Software services*	8,459
Business services	45,716	*Business services*	46,881
Financial services	4,734	*Financial services*	2,919
Communication services	2,723	*Communication services*	1,296
Total Trade Account	**533,622**	**Total Trade Account**	**606,206**
Transfers	83,356	Transfers	8,147
Investment Income received	19,542	Investment Income paid	49,752
Total Current Account	**636,520**	**Total Current Account**	**664,105**
B. Capital Account			
Foreign Direct Investment	77,794	Investment Abroad	34,780
Portfolio investment	290,741	Portfolio investment	289,337
Commercial Borrowing & short term loans	46,149	Commercial lending	39,785
Assistance/Aid Received	9,330	Aids given	5,579
Other capital imports	62,549	Other capital imports	44,087
Total Capital Account	**486,563**	**Total Capital Account**	**413,568**
C. Errors & Omissions	**1,856**	**C. Errors & Omissions**	**882**
Overall Receipts (A+B+C)	**1,124,939**	**Overall Receipts (A+B+C)**	**1,078,555**
		Official settlements	
		(Decrease in foreign exchange reserves)	46,384

Source: Compiled from the BOP statement of the Reserve Bank of India.

Note: Some items of transactions are omitted for simplification so that actual balances in current and capital accounts may differ from those reported here.

components of service trade are travel, transport, software services, and business services. Larger incomes were earned from foreigners visiting India for vacation and business than foreign currency spent by Indians who travelled abroad. But, the most significant contributor in earnings from service exports is software services. Whereas we have provided software services to the world totalling US $ 93,102 million in value, we have taken software services from the world totalling only US $ 8,459 million in value. The other two types of services in which we had a surplus and emerged as net exporter were financial services and communication services. But their net contributions were rather small.

By adding transfer receipts and incomes from investment abroad to the transactions in the trade account, we arrive at current account receipts. Similarly, transfer payments and incomes from investment paid to foreigners are added to payments in the trade account to arrive at current account payments. On the current account also India had a deficit though to a lesser extent than the trade deficit. Once again there was an asymmetry regarding the two types of transactions, and this can be related to the asymmetric movements in labour and capital. Much larger transfer receipts than payments may partly mean larger emigration of Indian workers abroad than immigration of foreign workers to India. Thus, inward remittances (which are part of transfer receipts) were significantly higher. On the other hand, the growth in FDI inflows and/or portfolio investments in India may have contributed to more investment incomes being paid to foreigners than earned through investing abroad.

In the capital account, the two main types of transactions on the credit (or receipt) side are foreign investments and borrowings from abroad. As mentioned earlier, these are import of capital, but unlike import of goods and services, these are listed on the credit side because import of capital means foreign exchange earned. The corresponding items on the debit (or payments) side of the capital account of BOP are investments abroad and lending. An interesting dimension of total foreign investment deserves attention. The portfolio investment in India by foreigners is almost four times the foreign direct investment. Our portfolio investment abroad is larger than our long-term investment abroad to an even larger extent. But, contribution of foreign direct investment in the net import of capital was much larger than that of portfolio investment. Taking into account other capital imports and exports, we arrive at the total capital account receipts and payments. Note that *in this example*, India had a capital account surplus during 2019–20. Sometimes errors and omissions arise in compilation of statements. Some of these may be related to over-statement or under-statement of the recorded components. In BOP, the standard practice is to show separately an item for net errors and omissions. In the above example, errors and omissions on the credit side were USD 1,856 million and on the debit side were USD 882 million. The current account balance, the capital account balance, and net errors and omissions together define the overall balance, which is in surplus in the above example by the amount USD 46,384 million. But, BOP is a double-entry bookkeeping which requires that the debit and the credit sides must match each other. This is done through the official settlement of USD 46,384 million listed on the debit side. Thus, the official settlement term is a balancing factor necessitated by the double-entry bookkeeping principle of BOP accounting. The logic is as follows. An overall surplus means that India has a claim on the rest of the world. The listing of official settlement on the debit side then means that India buys its claim on the rest of the world in exchange for its foreign currency reserves (that is, through export of capital). The overall surplus is thus settled. Thus, in this example, India's foreign exchange reserves declined by the value of USD 46,384 million.

On the other hand, had there been an overall deficit—that is, if the total receipts had been smaller than the total payments—the official settlement by the exact amount of the deficit would have been recorded on the credit side. A deficit means that the rest of the world has a claim on India and this is an asset for the rest of the world. That is, as if India has *sold* equivalent claims to the rest of the world against which there will be foreign exchange inflow or import of capital. The deficit is thus officially settled by a corresponding entry on the credit side as import of capital or increase in foreign currency reserves.

20.3 AUTONOMOUS AND ACCOMMODATING TRANSACTIONS AND BOP EQUILIBRIUM

As mentioned earlier, a country's BOP account follows the double-entry book keeping method, which balances both the credit and the debit sides. By this accounting method, therefore, a country's BOP is always in balance. In the example of India's BOP position for the financial year 2019–20 reported in Table 20.1, the total receipts equal USD 1,124,939 million and match with total payments *including* the official settlement of USD 46,384 million. Thus, *ex post*, there is no imbalance in India's BOP position for that year. Yet, we can say that India had a BOP surplus in 2019–20, and this surplus was to the tune of USD 46,384 million. This is because the total receipts were larger than the total payments *excluding* the official settlement exactly by this amount. The official settlement does not reflect transactions that were undertaken by relevant economic agents purely on the basis of maximization of their economic objectives. Instead, these were undertaken to balance the debit side with the credit side in order to meet the accounting principle of a balance sheet by the double-entry book keeping method. That is, the official settlement by the amount of USD 46,384 million was just a *balancing factor*. Accordingly, in the *ex post* sense after taking into account the official settlement or the balancing factor, the BOP statement becomes an identity. But, *ex ante*, taking into account all transactions up to the final entry of the official settlement (or the change in the reserve position of the country's central bank) but not including it, we can indeed talk about a BOP imbalance, either a BOP deficit or a BOP surplus. It is in this *ex ante* sense that economists use these deficit or surplus concepts. Thus, *the official settlement or the balancing factor itself indicates the BOP position of a country*. If this entry appears on the debit side (as in the above example), it indicates that the country is having a BOP surplus, and otherwise a BOP deficit.

An alternative classification of transactions listed in a country's BOP is useful in identifying whether the country is running a BOP surplus or deficit or has it truly achieved a balance (or equilibrium). This classification distinguishes between autonomous and accommodating transactions. Autonomous transactions are outcomes of optimizing decisions of individual economic agents (and of the government). These transactions are thus *planned ex ante* regardless of the BOP position of the country. Of course, these transactions may be constrained and influenced by the policies taken by the government for BOP considerations, but are not caused *directly* by BOP considerations or are not intended to meet the principles of a double-entry balance sheet. All current account transactions and some capital account transactions are autonomous transactions.

On the other hand, accommodating transactions are *directly caused* by BOP considerations. These are not *ex ante* planned but are *ex post* in nature since these are undertaken with an intention to match the credit and the debit sides of BOP or the total receipts and payments of a country. These transactions are undertaken only by the central bank of a country after taking into account all autonomous transactions and observing whether the receipts from and the payments for such transactions match or not. These accommodating transactions (or official settlements) take the form of accommodating capital movements like changes in gold or foreign currency reserves held by the central bank and official borrowing from abroad or extending loans to other countries. That is, *accommodating transactions are purely capital account transactions* and are undertaken only at the official level.

What follows from the above definitions is that whereas current account transactions are all autonomous, capital movements or capital account transactions can be both autonomous and accommodating transactions. The mismatch between total autonomous receipts and autonomous payments indicates the nature and extent of the imbalance (or disequilibrium) in BOP and of corresponding accommodating capital movement. In our earlier example, the total autonomous capital account receipts was USD 4,88,419 million (including errors & omissions), total autonomous capital account receipts (including errors and omissions) was USD 4,14,450 million, and the accommodating capital account *payments* was USD 46,384 million. This accommodating capital account *payment* indicates a BOP *surplus*.

To summarize, accommodating capital movements (or official settlements) indicates the BOP position of a country. If it is an inflow (or accommodating capital imports) and is thus listed on the credit side, it indicates a BOP deficit because it means that the total autonomous receipts are less than the total autonomous payments. On the other hand, if it is an outflow (or accommodating capital exports), it indicates a BOP surplus because now the total autonomous receipts are larger than total autonomous payments. But, *ex post*, BOP of a country always balances in the book keeping sense and is thus an *identity*.

20.4 BASIC IDENTITIES IN BOP AND NATIONAL INCOME ACCOUNTING

Having understood the different types of transactions and BOP accounting principles, we now relate the national income accounting with BOP accounting. Since accounting deals with ex-post values, so every relationship that we consider below is an identity. At the outset, however, it is important to distinguish between the basic national income identity in a closed economy and in an open economy. In a closed economy, gross national product (GNP) and gross domestic product (GDP) are the same. GDP is the aggregate value of all domestically produced goods in a particular year and GNP is the total income received by all domestically owned factors of production in a particular year. Since in a closed economy only nationally owned factors of production are used to produce the goods by a country and nationally owned factors of production engage themselves only in domestic production activities, so the aggregate value of all goods domestically produced must exactly match the total income received by all factors of production. Thus, if we denote India's GDP by Y and GNP by $\tilde{Y}$ then if India does not trade commodities and factors with the rest of the world, by the expenditure method, we have the following basic GDP identity:

$$Y \equiv \tilde{Y} \equiv C + I + G \tag{20.1}$$

where, C is the total expenditure on consumption goods by all residing in India, I is the total expenditure in India on investment goods, and G is the Government of India's total expenditure on goods and services.

But when India trades with the rest of the world, this basic GDP (or GNP) identity needs to be modified in two directions. First of all, factor trade (or migration of labour and capital movements across countries) means that some foreign nationals may be producing goods and services in India and some Indian workers may be working abroad. Thus, the value contributed by foreign workers (and income earned by them) working in India is a part of India's GDP but not a part of India's GNP. On the other hand, the value contributed by Indian workers (and income earned by them) working abroad is not a part of India's GDP but a part of India's GNP.[1] Similarly, interest income earned on investments abroad by Indian investors is a part of India's GNP but not a part of its GDP, and interest paid to foreign capital invested in India is not a component of India's GNP. That is, factor trade causes the GDP and GNP of a country to differ. If we denote income earned by Indian workers working in the United States, Europe, and in Middle East Asia, and interest income earned by Indian capital invested in Bangladesh, by R_d, and similarly income earned by foreign workers working in India and foreign capital invested in India by R_f, then India's GDP and GNP differ in the following way:

$$\tilde{Y} \equiv Y + (R_d - R_f) \equiv Y + R \tag{20.2}$$

where, R is India's *net* factor income from abroad. Thus, GNP > GDP if $R > 0$.

The second modification in the basic GDP identity in equation (20.1) is needed due to commodity trade. When goods trade takes place, the total consumption expenditure by consumers residing in India is no longer just on goods produced in India, but also on goods produced elsewhere and imported to India. Similarly, the total expenditure on investment goods may comprise of machines and other intermediate goods produced in India as well as imported from the rest of the world. Thus, if we denote the expenditure on domestically produced final consumption goods and intermediate goods by those residing in India together by D and that on imported final consumption goods and intermediate goods together by M, then:

$$C + I \equiv D + M \tag{20.3}$$

Thus, by the expenditure method, since India's GDP is the aggregate value of expenditure on domestically produced consumption and investment goods, so no longer the entire value of $C + I$, but only a part of it, which is, $D \equiv C + I - M$, will be a component of India's GDP. The Government of India may also spend on imported goods, but we abstract from that. So the entire part of G is still a component of GDP. Finally, India also exports consumption and investment goods that it produces. This is the foreigners' expenditure on goods produced in India and thus should now be a new component of India's GDP. Let this be denoted by X. Therefore, when India trades commodities with the rest of the world, its basic *GDP identity* becomes:

$$Y \equiv D + G + X \tag{20.4}$$

which upon substitution of values from equation (20.3) boils down to:

$$Y \equiv C + I + G + (X - M) \tag{20.5}$$

Note that $C + I + G$ in equation (20.5) now denotes the aggregate expenditure by private individuals residing in India and the government on *all* goods—domestically produced as well as imported. But the expenditure on imported goods is a leakage from the circular flow of India's *domestically produced* national income (or GDP). Hence, the value of imports must be subtracted from the aggregate expenditure $E \equiv C + I + G$ to calculate India's GDP. Similarly, the value of exports must be added because this reflects foreigners' expenditure on Indian goods and is an addition to the circular flow of national income.

Now recall that trade balance (denoted by TB) for India is the net value of exports $X - M$. Thus, from equation (20.5) we arrive at the first basic identity between GDP or *domestically produced* national income of a country and its BOP:

$$TB \equiv Y - E \tag{20.6}$$

If there is no factor trade, GDP is also the national income or GNP. In that case, $Y - E$ is the aggregate savings of the economy so that the identity in equation (20.6) means that the trade balance of a country equals its aggregate savings. When a country earns more than it spends, that is, it saves a positive amount, it experiences a trade surplus. Similarly, if the country dis-saves, it experiences a trade deficit. These are, however, not cause-and-effect statements since the values considered here are actual or *ex post*. In the next chapter, when we will discuss how national income is *determined* by considering *ex ante* or planned expenditures, we will make some cause-and-effect statements.

When factor trade exists, as we have explained above, GNP or national income of India is not just Y but $Y + R$ as defined in equation (20.2). On the other hand, with factor incomes, the relevant BOP component now is the current account balance (denoted by CA). To extend the analysis further, suppose TR denotes *net* transfers—transfer receipts (such as inward remittances) less transfer payments (such as remittances from India to the rest of world). Thus:

$$CA \equiv (X - M) + R + TR \tag{20.7}$$

Hence, adding $(R + TR)$ on both sides of equation (20.5) we arrive at the relationship between national income or GNP with the current account balance:

$$\begin{aligned} \tilde{Y} &\equiv Y + R + TR \equiv C + I + G + [(X - M) + R + TR] \\ &\equiv C + I + G + CA \end{aligned} \tag{20.8}$$

Further, if there are lumpsum income taxes, denoted by T, collected by the Government of India on both factor income in India and from abroad, $\tilde{Y}_d \equiv Y + R + TR - T$ constitutes India's disposable national income. Accordingly, the above identity changes to:

$$\tilde{Y}_d \equiv C + I + (G - T) + CA \tag{20.9}$$

A little manipulation of the above identity relates the current account surplus with aggregate savings of the economy as:

$$\begin{aligned} CA &\equiv \tilde{Y}_d - (C + I) + (T - G) \\ &\equiv (S - I) + (T - G) \end{aligned} \tag{20.10}$$

The first term on the right hand side in equation (20.10) is net private savings, whereas the second term is net government savings. If private savings equal private investment, then the above identity implies that a current account deficit ($CA < 0$) is exactly equal to the budget deficit ($G - T > 0$). Once again, this is an *ex post* statement and is premature at this point to say that government budget deficit *causes* current account deficit.

Further, if there is no autonomous capital account transaction, the current account deficit in this instance must be balanced by an official settlement or official capital import through sale of foreign assets held by the central bank. Let $\Delta NFACB$ denotes change in net acquisition of foreign assets or accommodating capital transactions. Then, the current account balance is equal in magnitude with the net acquisition of foreign assets:

$$CA \equiv \Delta NFACB \tag{20.11}$$

Thus, a current account deficit (which could be linked to budget deficit) means a corresponding sale of foreign assets held by the central bank ($\Delta NFACB < 0$). The official import of capital (or foreign currency earned) in exchange is listed on the credit side in BOP accounts and BOP balances. Substitution of equation (20.11) then relates the net acquisition of foreign assets by the central bank with the country's aggregate savings:

$$\Delta NFACB \equiv (S - I) + (T - G) \tag{20.12}$$

When autonomous capital transactions exists, the above identity changes as follows. First of all, a country's capital account balance (KA) equals the net acquisition of foreign assets by *private citizens*:

$$KA \equiv -\Delta NFAPR \tag{20.13}$$

Note that a capital account surplus means that the import of capital is larger than the export of capital. That is, there is a *negative* net acquisition of foreign assets by private citizens. This explains the negative sign in equation (20.13).

Second, the book keeping identity of a BOP account requires that the sum of capital account balance and current account balance should equal the accommodating capital movement ($\Delta NFACB$):

$$CA + KA \equiv CA - \Delta NFAPR \equiv \Delta NFACB \tag{20.14}$$

A country's current account balance therefore equals the aggregate (net) acquisition of foreign assets by the country:

$$CA \equiv \Delta NFAPR + \Delta NFACB \equiv \Delta NFA \tag{20.15}$$

Accordingly, the aggregate savings of the economy now relate to the aggregate (net) acquisition of foreign assets by the country:

$$(S - I) + (T - G) \equiv (\Delta NFAPR + \Delta NFACB) \equiv \Delta NFA \tag{20.16}$$

Finally, if we denote the overall balance of payments (excluding the official settlement) by B, then:

$$B \equiv CA + KA \equiv \Delta NFACB \tag{20.17}$$

An overall BOP surplus ($B > 0$) means $\Delta NFACB > 0$, that is, *as if* the country buys foreign assets. In the example given in Table 20.1, $B \equiv \Delta NFACB =$ 46,384.

SUMMARY POINTS

- The BOP account is broadly classified into the current account and the capital account. Current account transactions are essentially those that do not give rise to any future claims. Capital account transactions give rise to future claims.
- There is a fundamental difference between a current account surplus and a capital account surplus. The current account reflects the net income of a country. On the other hand, *the capital account indicates a net change in national ownership of assets.* A capital account surplus, *unlike* a surplus in the current account, indicates a country's weakness rather than strength.
- The BOP account follows the double-entry book keeping method, which balances both the credit and the debit sides. By this accounting method, BOP of a country is always in balance. Such a balance is achieved through an official settlement.
- The mismatch between total autonomous receipts and autonomous payments indicates the nature and extent of the imbalance in BOP and of corresponding accommodating capital movement.
- Alternatively, accommodating capital movements or official settlement indicates the BOP position of a country. An accommodating capital inflow indicates a BOP deficit and an outflow indicates a BOP surplus.
- In a closed economy, gross national product (GNP) and gross domestic product (GDP) are the same. But in an open economy, *net* earnings from abroad for domestically owned factors of production must be added to GDP to arrive at GNP.
- Expenditure on imported goods is a leakage from the circular flow of a country's *domestically produced* national income (or GDP). Hence, the value of imports must be subtracted from the aggregate expenditure.
- The value of exports must be added because this reflects foreigners' expenditure on Indian goods and is an addition to the circular flow of national income.
- A country's current account balance equals the aggregate (net) acquisition of foreign assets by the country.
- A country's capital account balance (KA) equals the net acquisition of foreign assets by *private citizens.*

KEYWORDS

- **Balance of payment** (BOP) is a record of values of all economic transactions of a country with the rest of the world for a particular year. It is the sum of current account and capital account transactions including the official settlement term.
- **BOP account** follows the double-entry book keeping method, which balances both the credit and debit sides. By this accounting method, BOP of a country is always in balance.
- **Current account transactions** are essentially those that do not give rise to any future claims. Examples include export and import of goods and services, remittances, factor incomes from abroad, and return on investments abroad.
- **Unrequited payments** (or receipts) are those for which there are no corresponding receipts (or payments). For example, incomes from assets held abroad by domestic citizens, remittances sent by domestic citizens working abroad, and war compensations received by the country.
- **Capital account transactions** give rise to future claims such as acquiring foreign assets or shares in companies located abroad, which yield interest incomes for domestic citizens and shareholders (and constitute a part of current account transactions) in the next period onwards.
- **Balance of trade** (BOT) is the receipts from exports less payments for imports of a country.
- **Current account balance** is the country's net receipts from trade in goods and services together with the difference between unrequited receipts and payments.
- **Capital account balance** is the difference between the import and export of capital. In terms of asset creation, a capital account *surplus*, unlike a surplus in the current account, actually indicates a country's weakness rather than its strength.
- **Autonomous transactions** are outcomes of optimizing decisions of individual economic agents (and of the government). These transactions are *planned* regardless of the BOP position of the country. All current account transactions and some capital account transactions are autonomous transactions.
- **Accommodating transactions** are directly caused by BOP considerations. These are *ex post* in nature since these are undertaken with an intention to match the credit and debit sides or total receipts and payments in BOP. These transactions (also called ***official settlement***) are undertaken only by the central bank in the nature of capital movements or changes in reserves of foreign currency. Thus, accommodating transactions are often treated as a part of capital account transactions.
- **Gross domestic product** (GDP) is the aggregate value of all domestically produced goods in a particular year.
- **Gross national product** (GNP) is the total income received by all domestically owned factors of production. Factor trade (or migration of labour and capital movements across countries) means that GNP differs from GDP.

EXERCISES

1. Distinguish between current account and capital account transactions.
2. What does a capital account surplus indicate about a country's economic position? Explain.
3. In what sense does a BOP always balance? Discuss the role of official settlement in this context.
4. If the BOP always balances, how can we explain BOP deficit or surplus of a country?
5. How is the distinction between autonomous and accommodating transactions relevant for understanding the BOP position of a country?
6. Identify which of the following transactions are current account transactions and which are capital account transactions:
   (a) Soccer balls made in Pakistan and supplied for the London 2012 Olympics.
   (b) Royalty paid to an Indian author by a Europe-based publisher for books sold in the US and EU.
   (c) Capital raised by a Chinese firm by selling its shares in the global capital market.
   (d) Shares of a British firm sold by foreigners to realize capital gains.
   (e) Interest paid by an Indian firm on bonds and shares held by an American citizen residing in the United States.
   (f) Debts of a country being forgiven by IMF.
   (g) Interest paid by the Government of India on loans taken from the World Bank.
   (h) Repayment of external debts by Bangladesh.
   (i) Apollo Gleneagles taking lease of land in Bangladesh to set up a hospital.
   (j) UN Global Fund distributing malaria and AIDS drugs in Ethiopia.
7. With reasons classify the following transactions into autonomous and accommodating transactions:
   (a) Loans taken by the Government of India in the early 1990s to manage the BOP crisis and avoid defaulting on international debt repayments.
   (b) Annual license fee paid to a US-based pharmaceutical firm for producing and selling a patented drug by an Indian firm.
   (c) Imports of music albums by Beatles.
   (d) Payments made to Amazon.com for buying used books.
   (e) Foreign assets sold by RBI in exchange for foreign currency.
   (f) The Korean automobile manufacturer, Hyundai, making new investments in its subsidiary in India.
8. Consider the following international transaction by India (value in million USD):

Merchandise Exports	8,500
Merchandise Imports	10,290
BPO services provided to British Airways	430
Medical transcriptions services	360
Net remittances received	250
Interest paid on external loans	975
FDI inflow	10,100
External lending	650

(contd)

Exercise (*contd*)

(a) Calculate the balance of trade and balance of current account.
(b) Is the capital account in surplus or deficit?
(c) Find out the change in reserves held by the Reserve Bank of India.

9. Following are the values in million USD of international transactions undertaken by India in a particular financial year:

Exports of manufacturing goods	9,625
Exports of fruits and vegetables	350
Imports of machinery and other equipments	875
Imports of consumer goods	9,055
Amount remitted by Indians working in the Gulf	660
Earnings on investment abroad	230
Purchase of shares in Microsoft corporation by Indian software companies	105
Loans taken from the World Bank for development projects	900

Calculate the net autonomous receipts for India and change in reserves held by the Reserve Bank of India.

10. How does goods trade modify the basic GDP identity of a country?
11. Define the GDP and GNP of a country. How do these concepts differ from each other in the presence of international factor movements?
12. Calculate India's GDP and GNP in the following contexts (all values are in million USD):

Total consumption spending by people residing in India	5,000
Purchase of machines and intermediate goods by Indian manufacturers	2,500
Import of intermediate goods	2,000
Import of household appliances and other consumer goods	2,900
Exports of manufactured goods	4,100
Medicines and food aid to UN Global Fund	1,700
Royalty received by Indian authors from publishers in Europe	130

13. If in addition to transactions listed in the table above, the budget deficit of the Government of India is USD 7,000 million, calculate India's disposable national income and current account balance.

SUGGESTED READING

Dornbusch, R. (1980). *Open Economy Macroeconomics*. New York: Basic Books.

Gondolfo, G. (2002). *International Finance and Open-Economy Macroeconomics*. Heidelberg: Springer Verlag.

21 National Income and Current Account Balance

The Income Approach

In Chapter 20 we discussed the *ex post* relations between the different components of national income and balance of payments (BOP). They were accounting identities since the relations were specified in terms of realized or actual values, rather than planned or *ex ante* values. Accordingly, the accounting identities cannot be used as cause-and-effect relations. A study of cause-and-effect relations and *determinations* of national income in an open economy require actual or *ex post* values being replaced by plans of relevant economic agents. This chapter does this by specifying the relationship between national income and trade or current account balances in terms of plans or behavioural functions.

Three main issues are discussed. First, how an equilibrium in an open economy evolves where the plans of all economic agents are simultaneously realized. The level of national income and trade (or current) account position of a country at equilibrium are the two elements that are of particular interest in this context. Second, is how the equilibrium national income and trade balance change when the spending pattern of private economic agents as well as the government changes. These *effects* are discussed both in the absence and presence of international transmission mechanisms by which a change in the national income of a country affects the national incomes of its trading partners and vice versa. Third, we discuss an interesting debate over plausible effects of a unilateral transfer of income from one country to the other. The context of this debate that started between John Maynard Keynes and Bertil Ohlin in 1929 was war reparations or compensations to be paid by Germany to Allied countries in Europe (see Box 21.1). Subsequent analyses by economists, however, show that the debate over a secondary loss or gain for Germany can essentially be resolved by a stability analysis. These three issues are addressed and explained in a simple Keynesian macroeconomic or effective demand framework. This is also known as the income approach for determining national income and BOP.

International Economics. Rajat Acharyya, Oxford University Press. © Oxford University Press 2022.
DOI: 10.1093/oso/9780192865144.003.0021

21.1 EFFECTIVE DEMAND, NATIONAL INCOME, AND TRADE BALANCE: INCOME APPROACH

The income approach based on the simple Keynesian effective demand analysis has some simplifying assumptions. First, rates of exchange between national and foreign currencies are assumed to be fixed and normalized to one. Thus, for example, one unit of Indian rupees exchanges for one unit of US dollars or one unit of euros. Second, commodity prices are assumed to be constant because of under-employed resources everywhere. Again, the constant prices are normalized to one. Thus, the real and money magnitudes of different variables and components of effective demand are the same. These two assumptions together mean that the price of a good produced in the domestic economy under consideration relative to the price of a good produced in its trading partner is constant. That is, if we consider trade between India and the United States, and P_i, P_u and e denote respectively the rupee-price of goods produced in India, the dollar-price of goods produced in the United States, and the rupee-dollar exchange rate, then $p \equiv \frac{eP_u}{P_i} = 1$. Thus, the effective demand for goods produced in India, and its components, depends only on the national income of India, Y_i, and under international transmission possibility, on the national income of the United States. Hence, it is an *income approach*. The third assumption is that only transactions in the trade account—trade in goods and services—are considered. This means India's GDP and GNP are the same, and that BOP is essentially the trade balance. Transfers and hence current account balance are discussed in the later part of this chapter, whereas asset transactions are discussed in Chapter 24.

In this income approach based on the simple Keynesian effective demand analysis, India's aggregate output or national income is determined by effective demand. Recalling the GDP identity discussed in Chapter 20, the effective demand has four components: consumption demand (or expenditure), investment demand, government demand, and *net* exports. Both investments and the Government of India's expenditure are assumed to be exogenously given in this simple Keynesian framework and these levels are denoted by $\bar{I}_i$ and $\bar{G}_i$. The total consumption expenditure by residents in India, C_i, the total expenditure on goods *produced in India* by residents in India, D_i, and import of goods produced in the United States, M_i, all vary positively with India's national income (Y_i):

$$C_i = C_i(Y_i),\ 0 < c_i \equiv \frac{\partial C_i}{\partial Y_i} < 1 \tag{21.1}$$

$$D_i = D_i(Y_i),\ 0 < d_i \equiv \frac{\partial D_i}{\partial Y_i} < 1 \tag{21.2}$$

$$M_i = M_i(Y_i),\ 0 < m_i \equiv \frac{\partial M_i}{\partial Y_i} < 1 \tag{21.3}$$

where, c_i, d_i, and m_i are the marginal propensity to consume all goods (*MPC*), the marginal propensity to consume domestically produced goods, and the marginal propensity to consume imports (*MPI*) respectively. Note that by definition, $c_i = d_i + m_i$ and since income is either spent or saved so denoting the marginal propensity to save by residents in India (MPS) by s_i, we must have $1 = d_i + s_i + m_i$. Finally, India's exports being the import demand by US consumers, so:

$$X_i = M_u = M_u(Y_u),\ 0 < m_u < 1 \tag{21.4}$$

where, m_u is the marginal propensity to consume imports by US consumers.

To begin with, let us assume that the national income of the United States is constant and thus, India's exports or M_u are also exogenously given at the level $\bar{M}_u$. This allows us to abstract from the international transmission mechanism. We will later relax this assumption and draw implications of the international transmission mechanism. The equilibrium aggregate value of India's output (or national income) must equal effective demand. Recalling the definition of India's GDP, the equilibrium condition can be specified as:

$$Y_i = D_i(Y_i) + \bar{G}_i + \bar{M}_u \tag{21.5}$$

Since by definition $D_i = C_i + \bar{I}_i - M_i$, the above equilibrium condition can be restated as:

$$Y_i = C_i(Y_i) + \bar{I}_i + \bar{G}_i + [\bar{M}_u - M_i(Y_i)] \tag{21.6}$$

Further, since aggregate expenditure E_i (or what is known as *absorption*) equals consumption, investment and government expenditures, so:

$$Y_i - \bar{E} - E_i(Y_i) = [\bar{M}_u - M_i(Y_i)] \tag{21.7}$$

where, $\bar{E} = \bar{I}_i + \bar{G}_i$ is the autonomous (or exogenously given) aggregate expenditure. Note that, $e_i \equiv \frac{\partial E_i}{\partial Y_i} \equiv \frac{\partial C_i}{\partial Y_i} \equiv c_i$.

From all the above alternative specifications of the equilibrium national income emerges an important implication of international trade. Trade *surplus* or positive net exports, $\bar{M}_u - M_i(Y_i) > 0$, is all that matters for augmenting aggregate output and national income through trade. An export-led growth argument is thus built into this income approach. The intuition is simple. Import demand for Indian goods by US citizens augments India's output and national income. Thus, India's exports of goods and services have favourable effects on its effective-demand-determined output. But India's imports or consumption of US goods and services substitutes the consumption of domestically produced goods. Thus, imports mean a decline in the demand for Indian goods. Therefore, if exports exceed imports, international trade augments the *net* demand for goods and services produced in India and consequently raises its aggregate output and national income. Trade surplus, however, is not independently determined. For any exogenously given US import demand (or India's exports), India's import demand, and consequently a trade surplus or deficit, depends on India's national income level. Alternatively, from equation (21.7) we can say that if all economic agents together spend less than they earn, $Y_i - \bar{E} - E_i(Y_i) > 0$, India will have a trade surplus. This is the essence of what is known as *the absorption approach* to BOP. A trade (or BOP) surplus and deficit essentially depend on a country's total absorption or aggregate expenditure (E) relative to its produced income (Y).

What emerges from the above discussion is that national income and trade balance position are interdependent and have to be determined simultaneously. This is illustrated in Figure 21.1 by plotting the two sides of the equilibrium condition in equation (21.7). To keep things simple, both the $[Y_i - \bar{E} - E_i(Y_i)]$ and the TB curves are drawn as straight lines. The $[Y_i - \bar{E} - E_i(Y_i)]$ line has a negative vertical intercept of $\bar{E} = \bar{I}_i + \bar{G}_i$ and a positive absolute slope equal to $(1 - e_i) = s_i > 0$. The TB curve, representing the right hand side of equation (21.7), has a positive vertical intercept $\bar{M}_u$ and a negative slope equal to $(-m_i)$. As long as the marginal propensity to save and the marginal propensity to import are constant values, these curves will be straight lines as depicted in Figure 21.1. India's equilibrium national income, $\bar{Y}_i$, and its equilibrium trade balance position, $TB = \bar{M}_u - M_i(\bar{Y}_i)$, are simultaneously determined at point A where these two curves cross each other and thereby satisfy the equilibrium condition (21.7).

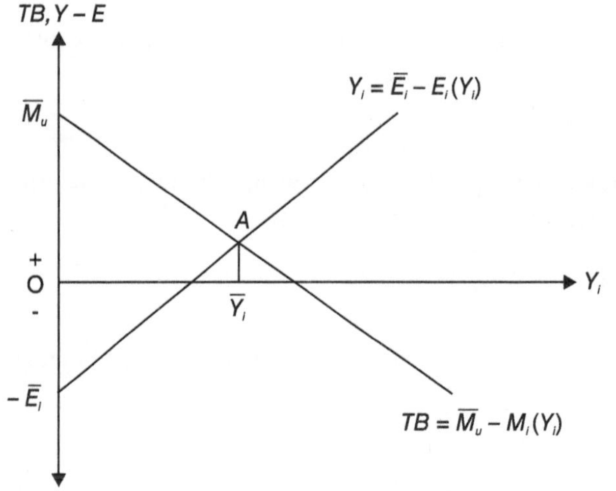

Figure 21.1 Simultaneous Determination of National Income and Trade Balance

The way the two curves are drawn, India runs a trade surplus by the magnitude of $A\bar{Y}_i$. However, depending on the levels of exogenous aggregate spending $\bar{E}$ and US import demand $\bar{M}_u$, and the relative slopes of these curves, there are two other possibilities: the curves cross each other *on* the income-axis, which means trade is balanced at the equilibrium; or the curves cross each other at some point *below* the income-axis, which means a trade deficit at the equilibrium.

21.2 EXPENDITURE AND FOREIGN TRADE MULTIPLIERS WITHOUT THE INTERNATIONAL TRANSMISSION EFFECT

Having determined the national income and trade balance of a country simultaneously, we now examine how increased trade affects the national income and trade balance of a country. The discussion will bring out the importance of an increase in net exports (or a trade surplus), rather than exports per se, in augmenting the national income of a country. As we will see, like investment or government expenditure multipliers in an effective demand framework, an exogenous increase in net exports will have a multiplier effect as well. That is, a 1 per cent increase in net exports will result in more than a 1 per cent increase in national income.

Apart from these *foreign trade multipliers*, we will also discuss two expenditure multiplier effects. First is an exogenous increase in aggregate spending (E), which can be driven by either an exogenous rise in investments or in the Government of India's expenditure or both. Second is a change in the spending patterns of consumers without any exogenous increase in aggregate spending. A discussion of these expenditure multipliers brings out the dampening effect of international trade in the sense that multiplier expansions are now smaller in magnitude than if there had been no trade.

21.2.1 Foreign Trade Multipliers

There are several ways in which we can consider an exogenous increase in *net* exports for a country. We will, however, confine our discussion to two specific cases in the above context—a *ceteris paribus* exogenous increase in US import demand and an exogenous decline in India's import demand. But as we will see the latter may have an altogether different implication.

An Exogenous Increase in India's Export or US Import Demand

Consider a *ceteris paribus* exogenous increase in US import demand by the magnitude $\Delta\bar{M}_u > 0$. As evident from equation (21.5), at the initial income and the corresponding demand by Indian consumers for Indian goods D_i, this will proportionately raise the effective demand for Indian goods. India's national income will thus rise proportionately. But this rise in national income will now have subsequent demand augmenting effects since larger incomes will enable Indian consumers to spend more on domestically produced goods. If we denote the initial rise in national income by ΔY_{io}, which equals $\Delta\bar{M}_u$, then it induces an additional spending on domestic goods by the amount $d_i(\Delta Y_{io})$, where d_i is the marginal propensity to consume Indian goods by Indian consumers. Consequently, effective demand and national income rise proportionately by $d_i(\Delta Y_{io})$. This in turn again induces consumers to raise their spending on Indian goods by $d_i\{d_i(\Delta Y_{io})\} \equiv d_i^2(\Delta Y_{io})$. There will be further subsequent proportional rise in the national income induced by this additional consumption spending and such expansion in the national income will in turn lead to another round of increase in domestic demand for domestic goods by the amount $d_i^3(\Delta Y_{io})$. Thus, the initial income increase induced by an exogenous increase in the US import demand leads to a chain of subsequent increases in domestic demand for domestic good (D_i) and corresponding proportional increases in national income. However, the marginal propensity to consume domestic goods (d_i) being strictly less than one, the national income expansion in each round will be smaller than that in the previous round. Thus, the induced effects will converge to zero for an infinitely large sequence of events. Algebraically, the final change in national income will be the sum of the initial expansion ΔY_{io} and the induced expansions:

$$\Delta Y_i = \Delta Y_{io} + d_i(\Delta Y_{io}) + d_i^2(\Delta Y_{io}) + d_i^3(\Delta Y_{io}) + d_i^4(\Delta Y_{io}) + \ldots\ldots$$

$$= (1 + d_i + d_i^2 + d_i^3 + d_i^4 + \ldots\ldots.)\ \Delta Y_{io} = \frac{1}{1-d_i}\Delta\bar{M}_u$$

Recalling that $1 = d_i + s_i + m_i$, this boils down to:

$$\Delta Y_i = \frac{1}{s_i + m_i}\Delta \bar{M}_u \tag{21.8}$$

It is immediate from the above discussion that the final change in the national income is more than the exogenous increase in US import demand due to the subsequent induced consumption demand and corresponding increase in national income. This is also evident from the fact that since $(s_i + m_i) < 1$, so $\Delta Y_i > \Delta Y_{io} = \Delta \bar{M}_u$. That is, there will be a multiplier expansion of national income. Note that both savings and import spending are leakages in the circular flow national income. The magnitude of the multiplier expansion is thus inversely related to the total leakage as measured by the marginal propensity to save and the marginal propensity to import.

What implication does this multiplier expansion of national income have on the trade balance position? Note that a *ceteris paribus* exogenous increase in US import demand (or India's exports) will initially improve India's trade balance proportionately: $\Delta TB_i = \Delta \bar{M}_u$. But income expansions will augment India's imports and hence subsequently the trade balance should worsen. Is the chain of induced spending on imports from the United States larger than the initial improvement so that India's trade balance worsens at the end? To find an answer, note that each round of national income expansion raises import demand by the marginal propensity to import m_i. That is, the trade balance worsens in each round by m_i times the national income expansion in the previous round. Algebraically:

$$\Delta TB_i = \Delta \bar{M}_u - [m_i(\Delta Y_{io}) + m_i d_i(\Delta Y_{io}) + m_i d_i^2(\Delta Y_{io}) + m_i d_i^3(\Delta Y_{io}) + \ldots\ldots]$$

$$= \Delta \bar{M}_u - m_i(1 + d_i + d_i^2 + d_i^3 + d_i^4 + \ldots\ldots\ldots)\ \Delta Y_{io} = \Delta \bar{M}_u - \frac{m_i}{1 - d_i}\Delta \bar{M}_u$$

$$= \frac{s_i}{s_i + m_i}\Delta \bar{M}_u \tag{21.9}$$

Thus, the trade balance does improve despite induced multiplier expansion of imports by the magnitude $\frac{m_i}{s_i + m_i}\Delta \bar{M}_u$. The initial trade balance improvement is only dampened through subsequent increases in India's imports. This is because the multiplier expansion of India's imports is strictly *less* than proportional to its initial increase in exports:

$$\frac{m_i}{s_i + m_i}\Delta \bar{M}_u < \Delta \bar{M}_u$$

The above logical derivation of multiplier expansion in India's national income and a corresponding change in its trade balance position can also be verified from the equilibrium condition (21.7) by the method of calculus, as shown in Appendix A21. Graphically, we illustrate the expansion in national income and a less than proportionate improvement in the trade balance in Figure 21.2. We begin with India's initial equilibrium national income $\bar{Y}_i$ such that its trade is balanced. An exogenous increase in US import demand shifts the *TB* curve upward to the one shown by the broken line. The new equilibrium is shown by point *B* with increased national income being Y_i' and a trade surplus of BY_i'. But this is less than the initial trade surplus $A'\bar{Y}_i = \Delta \bar{M}_u$.

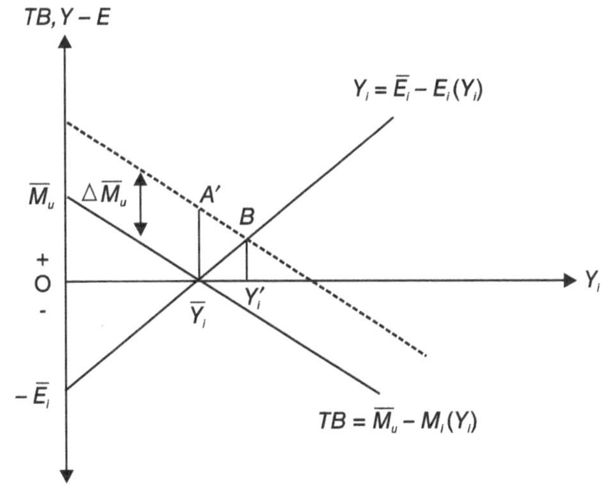

Figure 21.2 Increase in Exports, National Income, and Trade Balance

An Exogenous Increase in India's Import Demand

An exogenous increase in India's import demand has an altogether different implication. Since import expenditure is part of the aggregate expenditure or absorption, E_i, so the relevant issue is whether an exogenous increase in India's import demand changes the aggregate expenditure or not. This, in turn, depends on how this increased import demand and expenditure is financed at the initial level of national income. There are two alternative ways that the additional import expenditure can be financed by the domestic consumers: either by lowering savings, or by lowering domestic expenditure on domestic goods (D_i). In the former case, the aggregate expenditure E_i increases as the Indian residents spend more on US goods at their respective initial income levels *without substituting and reducing their spending on goods produced in India*. Thus, the increased expenditure being on US goods, there will be no change in the effective demand for goods produced in India, and consequently, *India's aggregate value of output and national income will remain the same.* This can be verified by rewriting the effective demand condition (21.7) as:

$$Y_i = D_i(Y_i) + G_i + \bar{M}_u \tag{21.10}$$

In Figure 21.3, a *ceteris paribus* exogenous increase in the import expenditure will shift both the $[Y_i - \bar{E} - E_i(Y_i)]$ and *TB* curves down by the same magnitude without changing the equilibrium value of Y_i.

The only impact of this exogenous increase in India's import demand will, therefore, be a worsening of India's trade balance by an equal magnitude:

$$\Delta TB_i = -\Delta \bar{M}_i \tag{21.11}$$

But if the exogenous increase in the import expenditure is financed by a corresponding *decline in the expenditure on goods produced in India*, $\Delta \bar{M}_i = -\Delta D_i$, then this will mean a decline in India's aggregate output and national income. Note that in this case, the aggregate expenditure or absorption remains the same, but its composition changes away from domestically produced goods. Graphically, in Figure 21.3, there will be no shift of the $Y_i - \bar{E}_i - E_i(Y_i)$ curve. Only the TB_i curve will shift down, thereby changing the equilibrium to the left of point A and lowering the national income. There will, however, be a *multiplier contraction* of India's national income as a consequence of this fall in expenditure on domestically produced goods to finance the additional import expenditure. That is, Y will fall more than proportionately. Algebraically, the national income will fall initially by the exact magnitude of the decline in the expenditure on domestically produced good:

$$\Delta Y_{i0} = \Delta\bar{D}_i = -\Delta\bar{M}_i < 0$$

Subsequently, following the similar logic as in case of the export multiplier, this fall in national income will trigger a chain of lower spending on domestically produced goods and consequent lowering of the national income. The final change in India's national income in this particular case will, therefore, be the sum of the initial contraction and the induced contractions:

$$\begin{aligned}\Delta Y_i &= \Delta Y_{i0} + d_i(\Delta Y_{i0}) + d_i^2(\Delta Y_{i0}) + d_i^3(\Delta Y_{i0}) + d_i^4(\Delta Y_{i0}) + \ldots \\ &= (1 + d_i + d_i^2 + d_i^3 + d_i^4 + \ldots)\Delta Y_{i0} = -\frac{1}{1-d_i}\Delta\bar{M}_i = -\frac{1}{s_i + m_i}\Delta\bar{M}_i\end{aligned}$$

The decline in national income will subsequently improve the trade balance as import demand will fall. But again it is easy to check that an improvement in the induced trade balance will be less than the initial worsening of trade balance as specified in equation (21.11).

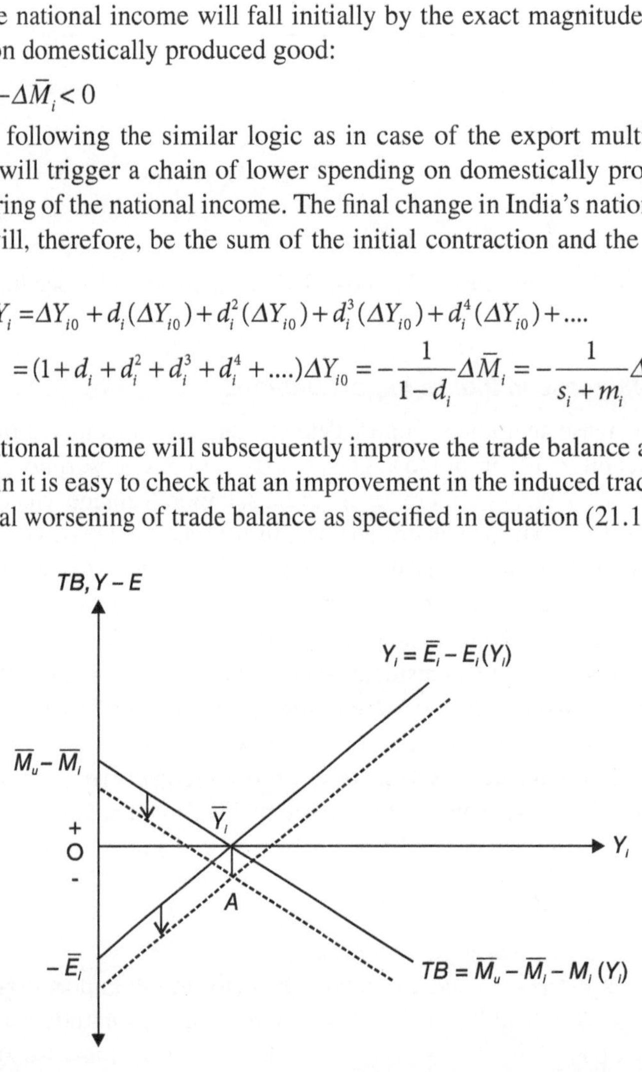

Figure 21.3 Increase in Imports, National Income, and Trade Balance

21.2.2 Expenditure Multipliers

Like the exogenous increase in import expenditure, two cases are relevant in the context of expenditure multipliers. First is an exogenous change in aggregate expenditure E_i brought about by an exogenous increase in consumption expenditure, or in investment expenditure or in government expenditure on domestically produced goods. Second is a shift in the spending *pattern* or an exogenous change *only in the composition of aggregate spending* over domestic and foreign goods. In the former case, an exogenous increase in aggregate spending or absorption lowers national savings and shifts the $[Y_i - \bar{E} - E_i(Y_i)]$ curve down (or to the right) as shown by the broken line in Figure 21.4. The national income rises but now a trade deficit for India develops by the amount CY_i'. The reason is that with no change in US import demand, the expansion in national income raises only the import demand by India and thus worsens its trade balance.

Algebraically, these changes in national income and trade balance position are given as:

$$dY_i = \frac{1}{s_i + m_i} d\bar{E}_i > 0 \tag{21.12}$$

$$dTB_i = -m_i dY_i = -\frac{m_i}{s_i + m_i} d\bar{E}_i < 0 \tag{21.13}$$

The multiplier income expansion specified in equation (21.12) brings out the dampening effect of international trade. Had there been no trade, income would have expanded by a larger magnitude $dY_i = \frac{1}{s_i} d\bar{E}_i$. The reason is simple. The increase in income raises import demand, which is a leakage from the circular flow of income.

A change in spending patterns or the composition of aggregate spending, on the other hand, has an altogether different implication. If the composition of spending shifts in favour of domestic goods and away from imports or US goods, then given that the aggregate expenditure remains the same, it must mean $\Delta\bar{D}_i = -\Delta\bar{M}_i$. This change in the composition of aggregate expenditure without a change in its level leaves the $[Y_i - \bar{E} - E_i(Y_i)]$ curve unchanged but shifts the TB_i curve upward. India's national income rises again but now the trade balance improves by the amount BY_i' in Figure 21.4. That is, a shift in the spending pattern has a similar effect as foreign trade or the net exports multiplier. If the shift is away from imports, it is essentially an exogenous increase in net exports, which, for reasons spelled out earlier, expands India's national income and improves its trade balance. But if the shift in spending pattern is away from domestic goods, it means a decline in net exports. There will thus be a multiplier *contraction* of national income and a deterioration of trade balance.

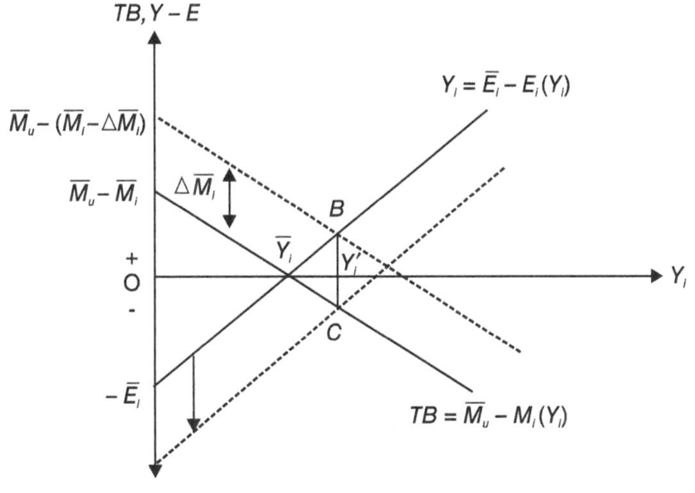

Figure 21.4 Increase in Aggregate Spending, National Income, and Trade Balance

21.3 INTERNATIONAL TRANSMISSION MECHANISM

So far we have assumed that the national income of the United States remains the same regardless of the external shock that effects India's national income and import demand. But that is not a realistic assumption because any change in India's import demand will mean a corresponding change in the demand for goods produced in the United States. This should change the national income of the United States by the same logic as any (exogenous) change in US import demand changes India's national income. What is more, a change in US national income and consequently in its import demand will induce *further* changes in India's national income. Thus, the national incomes of countries are interdependent through *international transmission of effects* of the shocks that originate in one country. Such international transmission leads to further multiplier expansion of national incomes.

To illustrate, consider the following two effective demand conditions for India and the United States and the trade balance condition for India:

$$Y_i = C_i(Y_i) + \bar{I}_i + \bar{G}_i + [M_u(Y_u) - M_i(Y_i)] \tag{21.14}$$

$$Y_u = C_u(Y_u) + \bar{I}_u + \bar{G}_u + [M_i(Y_i) - M_u(Y_u)] \tag{21.15}$$

$$TB_i = M_u(Y_u) - M_i(Y_i) \tag{21.16}$$

Note that by definition, $TB_i = -TB_u$. From equations (21.14) and (21.15), the aggregate output levels and the national incomes of the two countries are *simultaneously* determined. Figure 21.5 illustrates the equilibrium national incomes. The curve labeled Y_iY_i represents the different combinations of national incomes, (Y_i, Y_u), that satisfy the effective demand condition (21.14) for India. Similarly, the curve labeled Y_uY_u represents the different combinations of national incomes, (Y_i, Y_u) that satisfy the effective demand condition (21.15) for the United States. Both these curves are positively sloped. An increase in Y_u raises US import demand and thus raises India's net exports at the initial level of its national income. This increase in net exports leads to a multiplier expansion of India's national income. By similar logic, an increase in India's national income results in a multiplier expansion of the US national income. Algebraically, the slopes of these two curves are given as:

$$\left.\frac{dY_u}{dY_i}\right|_{Y_iY_i} = \frac{s+m}{m^*} \tag{21.17}$$

$$\left.\frac{dY_u}{dY_i}\right|_{Y_uY_u} = \frac{m}{s^* + m^*} \tag{21.18}$$

Note that the Y_iY_i curve is steeper than the Y_uY_u curve. For existence of an equilibrium we must assume that the values of the exogenous variables in equations (21.14) and (21.15) be such that the Y_uY_u curve has a larger vertical intercept than the Y_iY_i curve. The equilibrium national incomes Y_i^e and Y_u^e are the ones that correspond to the intersection of these two curves. India's trade balance position (and correspondingly that of the United States) is shown by the broken line drawn through the intersection point. This line represents an iso-trade-balance curve, which is the locus of different combinations of (Y_i, Y_u) for which India's trade balance, negative, positive or zero, *remains the same* in value. This locus again reflects a positive relationship between the national incomes of the two countries. An increase in Y_u, raises US import demand and thus India's net exports at its initial national income level. To maintain India's trade balance at the same level, its national income and correspondingly imports must rise. Algebraically, the slope of such an iso-trade-balance curve can be obtained by totally differentiating equation (21.16) holding the value of TB_i at a particular level:

$$\left.\frac{dY_u}{dY_i}\right|_{TB_i} = \frac{m}{m^*} \tag{21.19}$$

Thus, the locus is flatter than the Y_iY_i curve but is steeper than the Y_uY_u curve as drawn in Figure 21.5. Note that since a larger national income of the United States, for any given national income of India, worsens its trade balance, so successively higher iso-trade-balance curves than the one drawn in Figure 21.5 will reflect successively lower values of trade balance for the United States (or higher values of trade balance for India).

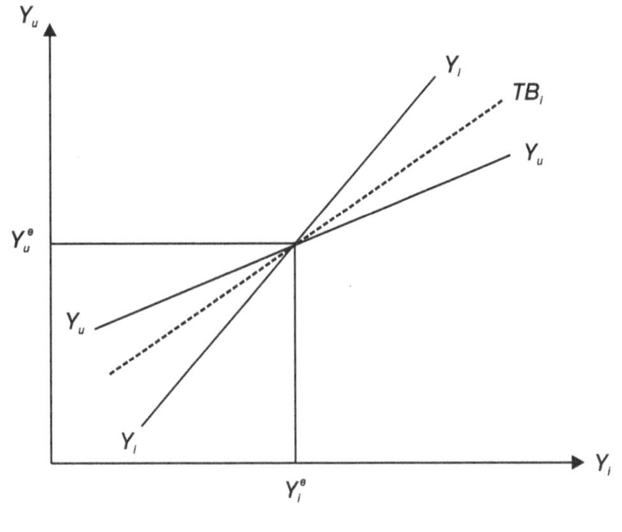

Figure 21.5 Simultaneous Determination of National Incomes

Suppose, the parametric configurations be such that at the equilibrium shown in Figure 21.4, trade is balanced, that is, $TB_i = -TB_u = 0$. Thus, any combinations of national incomes in the region above the iso-trade-balance curve drawn in Figure 21.4, India's trade is in surplus and below it India's trade is in deficit.

Given this assumption, consider now a *ceteris paribus* exogenous increase in expenditure by Indian residents on goods produced in India, $\Delta D_i > 0$. As explained earlier, this leads to a multiplier expansion of India's national income by the magnitude of $\frac{1}{s_i + m_i}\Delta D_i$, *at the initial level of the national income of the United States*. This is shown by the rightward shift of the Y_iY_i curve in Figure 21.6, and increase in India's national income to the level Y_i' at $Y_u = Y_u^e$.

But this increase in India's national income will increase its imports and correspondingly raise the national income of the United States. This in turn will trigger a chain of increase in national incomes of the two countries through increase in import demand of each country in each round of income expansion. That is, increase in the national income of each country transmits to the other country through trade. But again the import demands decline successively since only a fraction of the income expansion is spent on imports in each round. That is, the transmission of national incomes fades out after infinitely large sequences of induced changes. At the end, we have further multiplier expansion in India's national income as shown by the increase to the level Y_i''. In other words, in the presence of an international transmission (or repercussion) effect, the multiplier expansion of national incomes will be larger. Algebraically, it is easy to check from Appendix A21 that:

$$\frac{dY_i}{dD_i} = \frac{s_u + m_u}{s_i s_u + s_i m_u + s_u m_i} > \frac{1}{s_i + m_i} \tag{21.20}$$

Starting from balanced trade, the multiplier expansion of India's national income leads to a trade deficit. The reason is simple. The Y_uY_u curve being flatter than the $TB_i = 0$ curve means that an expansion in India's national income raises the equilibrium national income of the United States to a smaller extent than is required to maintain balanced trade. Accordingly, India's import demand rises more than the US import demand resulting in a trade deficit measured by

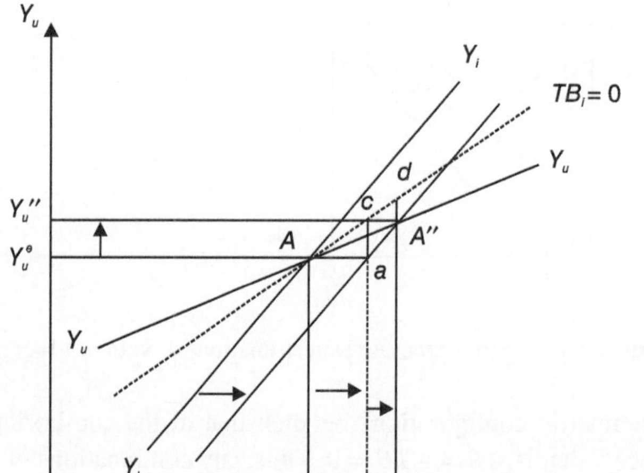

Figure 21.6 International Transmission and Foreign Trade Multiplier

dA'' in Figure 21.6. At the initial equilibrium US national income, the increase in spending on domestic goods worsens India's trade deficit by raising its national income and imports. This is measured by *ca*. Subsequent expansion of the US national income raises its import demand and thus India's exports, which reduces India's trade deficit to some extent, though it cannot reverse it since India's national income rises as a consequence as well.

21.4 TRANSFERS AND TRADE BALANCE: THE TRANSFER PROBLEM

As we have explained in Chapter 20, transfers are payments or receipts by a country without any corresponding exchange of goods, services, or assets. These are unrequited receipts and payments raising the purchasing power of the recipient and lowering the same for the donor. Thus, transfers have two effects on the current account position of countries. First, a transfer payment of USD 1,000, for example, by the United States to India improves India's current account balance but lowers that of the United States by equivalent amounts. But this transfer payment raises India's purchasing power and lowers that of the United States. Consequently, India will import more goods and services and the United States will import less. There is thus a *secondary effect* on the current account of both the countries. The trade balance (and hence, current account) worsens for India and improves for the United States as volumes of imports and exports change following the transfer. From the donor's perspective, the United States in this example, if the trade surplus is smaller than the amount of transfer itself (by which its current account initially worsened), then overall its current account is in deficit and the transfer is said to be *under-effected.* Otherwise, if the subsequent trade surplus is larger than the amount of transfer itself, overall the current account of the donor is in surplus and the transfer is said to be *over-effected.* For example, if transfer of USD 1,000 and corresponding fall in the purchasing power in the United States lowers its value of import (at initial prices) from India by USD 550 whereas India's increased purchasing power raises its imports (or US exports) by USD 310, the current account balance of the United States worsens by USD 140. Its transfer to India is thus under-effected. But if the value of its imports would have fallen by USD 650 and its exports risen by USD 500, say, then its transfer of USD 1,000 to India would have been over-effected since its current account would have improved by USD 50.

In either case, however, the current account (and the balance of payments) is in disequilibrium, which in turn will affect world prices and the terms of trade (TOT). If world commodity prices change in a way that worsens the TOT for the donor, the United States in the above example, there will be a *secondary burden* of the transfer for the donor. The TOT change will bring in further changes in the trade balance and in the current account. In terms of welfare or real income change, on the other hand, the primary burden is the loss of real income or purchasing power by the transfer amount itself. In addition, if subsequent changes in trade volumes worsen the TOT for the donor, then there will be further loss of real income and welfare.

Since the time of John Stuart Mill, economists have been divided in opinion regarding these two effects of a transfer—effects on the current account balance and TOT for the donor. The first part of the age-old controversy, known as the *transfer problem*, has been regarding whether a transfer is under-effected or over-effected. James Meade (1951) derived his famous sum-of-MPC-minus-one condition for an under-effected or over-effected transfer under the assumption

Box 21.1 War Reparations

After World War II, Germany was obliged to pay war reparations to Allied governments to the tune of USD 23 billion, mainly in machinery and manufacturing plants. In addition, large numbers of civilian factories were dismantled for transport to France and the UK. German reparations were also partly to be in the form of forced labour. German prisoners of war and civilians were used as reparation labour or enforced labour in the Soviet Union, France, the UK, Belgium, and in Germany in the US run Military Labour Service Units. By the Paris Peace Treaties in 1947, Italy agreed to pay reparations of about USD 125 million to the then Yugoslavia, USD 105 million to Greece, USD 100 million to the Soviet Union, USD 25 million to Ethiopia, and USD 5 million to Albania.

A more recent example of war reparations is that paid by Iraq after the Gulf War and damage caused by its invasion of Kuwait. Iraq accepted the United Nations Security Council resolution in this regard and USD 350 billion in claims were filed by governments, corporations, and individuals.

that national income levels of the donor and the recipient change by the exact amount of the transfer. In a world with under-employed resources and effective demand determined output levels, such an assumption will always mean that a transfer is under-effected. Allowing the aggregate output to change, Lloyd Metzler (1942) and Machlup (1943) arrived at the same result that a transfer will always be under-effected for the donor.[1] But, in a competitive full-employment world with flexible prices, a transfer may well be over-effected.

The second part of the transfer problem has been regarding whether the transfer improves or worsens the TOT for the donor. The orthodox position of A.C. Pigou, F.W. Taussig, Denis Robertson, and John Maynard Keynes was that the TOT will worsen for the donor. There will thus be a secondary burden of the transfer. Bertil Ohlin, on the other hand, was of the opinion that the TOT will improve in favour of the donor. These arguments led to another controversy between John Maynard Keynes and Bertil Ohlin in 1929 over German reparations (or war compensations) after World War I. Keynes was of the opinion that the secondary burden of a TOT deterioration will be so large as to make the transfer or war compensation *economically unviable* for Germany. But if TOT improves in favour of Germany instead, can it be so large as to make it better off even after taking into account the initial transfer of real purchasing power or income? That is, *is it better to give than to receive*?

However, subsequent research has settled the second part of the transfer problem once and for all. Whether a transfer improves or worsens the TOT for the donor is essentially a stability issue.[2] Stability requires that in a situation of trade (and current account) deficit, the TOT should deteriorate. Thus, if a transfer is under-effected and the current account is in deficit, the TOT must deteriorate for the donor in a stable world market. To check this, suppose instead that TOT improves for the donor when the transfer is under-effected. This means that the

[1] A.C. Pigou was the foremost economist to provide a rigorous formal analysis of the transfer problem in a pure exchange model and arrived at the orthodox conclusion of an under-effected transfer.

[2] See, for example, Samuelson (1954) and his correspondence principle.

donor will buy more Indian goods as these are relatively cheaper now. On the other hand, its exports will fall since India will now buy less US goods which have become relatively dearer. Thus, the trade and current account deficit widens further and we move further away from the pre-transfer balanced trade equilibrium, meaning that the world market is unstable. That is, if the world market is stable, an under-effected transfer should lead to a subsequent worsening of TOT for the donor (and corresponding trade surplus to restore the equilibrium). By similar reasoning, an over-effected transfer should lead to a subsequent improvement in TOT for the donor (and corresponding trade deficit to restore the equilibrium).

What appears from the above argument is that given the stability condition the *orthodox position follows if a transfer is under-effected.* The second part of the transfer problem—controversy regarding whether TOT worsens or improves for the donor after the transfer—thus boils down to the first part of the problem—whether the transfer is under-effected or over-effected. In other words, by the stability condition, the transfer problem is essentially a one part problem. In the next sub-section we examine whether a transfer is under-effected or over-effected.

21.4.1 The Classical Case

James Meade provided his well-known condition for a change in the current account balance of the country making the transfer under the assumption that the aggregate output and the produced income of the countries remain constant *after* the transfer. Suppose the United States makes a transfer of T amount to India, which is financed by a lump-sum income tax collection. Thus, the aggregate disposable income in the United States falls by the amount of this transfer. On the other hand, suppose the T amount received by India is distributed to its residents in a lump-sum way. Thus, the aggregate disposable income in India rises by the exact magnitude of the transfer. Given these changes in the aggregate disposable incomes by the exact amount of the transfer under the assumption that the aggregate output and the produced income remain constant, there are *three* effects on the current account balance of the United States. First, the transfer worsens its current account by the amount T. Second, the fall in its disposable income lowers its import expenditure by $m_u T$. This improves its current account. Finally, the rise in India's disposable income raises its import expenditure and thus exports of the United States by $m_i T$. This further improves its current account. So given that there had been no transfer initially ($dT = T$), the net change in the current account balance of the United States equals:

$$dCA = -T + m_u T + m_i T = -(1 - m_i - m_u)T \tag{21.21}$$

Thus, current account improves or transfer is over-effected if $m_i + m_u > 1$. Otherwise, transfer is under-effected. This is Meade's criterion.

As explained above, this condition should also determine whether the TOT of the donor worsens or improves. In particular, in a stable world market, TOT should worsen if $m_i + m_u < 1$. Algebraically, this can be verified from the following relationship in a two-country two-commodity world with instantaneous market clearing (see Appendix A21):

$$\frac{dp^W}{dT} = \frac{1-(m_i + m_u)}{M_i\left[1-(\varepsilon_i + \varepsilon_u)\right]} \tag{21.22}$$

where, p^W is the world relative price of imports by India and M_i is its volume of imports.

Recall from Chapter 4 that $\varepsilon_i + \varepsilon_u > 1$ is the Marshall-Lerner stability condition. Hence, a transfer worsens the TOT for the United States, $\frac{dp^W}{dT} < 0$, if $m_i + m_u < 1$, which is the condition for the transfer being under-effected. On the other hand, if $m_i + m_u > 1$, which means that the transfer is over-effected, TOT improves for the donor, $\frac{dp^W}{dT} > 0$.

There is, however, a relationship between the stability condition and Meade's condition stated above. The Walrasian stability in the world market, say, for goods imported by India (the recipient) requires, as noted earlier, that the excess demand must fall as the relative price of that good rises. A rise in the relative price of India's import good produces four effects. First is a substitution effect in demand by which Indian buyers buy less of the relatively dearer US good. Similar substitution effect causes US buyers to buy less of their own good. So by both these substitution effects, world demand for the US good declines. There are, in addition, two income effects. If the US good imported by India is a normal good, increase in its price and consequent decline in the real income of Indian buyers will induce them to buy even less of the US good. So by the income effect of Indian buyers, the world demand for the US good falls further. But, the income effect for US buyers induced by the price rise will move in the opposite direction. Since the United States is a seller of its good in the world market, so increase in the relative price of its good means a rise in its real income. Thus, US buyers will buy *more* of their good. World demand thus rises by the income effect of US buyers. If this income effect is large enough, overall the world demand will rise following a rise in the relative price of the good imported by India (or exported by the United States). Since a pure income transfer does not change the production levels in either country, so in such a case excess demand in the world market rises. But this means that the world market is unstable. Hence, the seller's income effect is a source of instability. In particular, a necessary condition (though not sufficient) for instability in the world market is that the seller's income effect be larger than the buyer's income effect. Since the former is captured by the marginal propensity to consume exports by the United States, $1 - m_u$, and the latter is captured by the marginal propensity to consume imports by India, m_i, so a necessary condition for *in*stability is:

$$1 - m_u > m_i \Rightarrow m_i + m_u < 1$$

But this is the condition for a transfer being under-effected. By similar logic, a *sufficient condition* (though not necessary) for stability is that the buyer's income effect be larger than the seller's income effect. This means:

$$1 - m_u < m_i \Rightarrow m_i + m_u > 1$$

But this is the condition for transfer being over-effected.

In sum, both an under-effected transfer and an over-effected transfer are compatible with the stability condition. However, even if a transfer is over-effected causing the TOT to improve for the donor, it is easy to verify from the change in the real income of the United States (as derived in Appendix A21) that such an improvement in TOT *cannot* be so large as to make it better off:

$$dy_u = \frac{(\varepsilon_i + \varepsilon_u) - (m_i + m_u)}{1 - (\varepsilon_i + \varepsilon_u)} dT \tag{21.23}$$

Recall now the decomposition of import demand elasticity into pure substitution elasticity (η), the marginal propensity to consume imports (m), and the elasticity of supply of import-competing production (e). Since a transfer does not change the production levels in either country as long as it is a pure transfer of income rather than a transfer of resources, so $\varepsilon_i = \eta_i + m_i$ and $\varepsilon_u = \eta_u + m_u$. Substitution of these values in equation (21.23) reveals that $dy < 0$ since η_i and η_u are positive:

$$dy_u = \frac{\eta_i + \eta_u}{1 - (\varepsilon_i + \varepsilon_u)} dT < 0 \tag{21.23a}$$

Thus, it is *not* better to give than to receive.

21.4.2 Under-Effected Transfer in a Keynesian World

We have seen above that in a market clearing flexible price scenario, a transfer may be under-effected or over-effected. Both possibilities are compatible with the world market being stable. But in a world with under-employed resources and effective demand determined outputs (or GDP) with constant prices, a transfer is always under-effected. To see this, recall from the discussion earlier that aggregate output and national income in such a world are determined by the demand for domestic goods by domestic citizens and by foreigners:

$$Y_u = D_u(Y_{du}) + M_i(Y_{di}) \tag{21.24}$$

$$Y_i = D_u(Y_{di}) + M_u(Y_{du}) \tag{21.25}$$

where, $Y_{du} = Y_u - T$ and $Y_{di} = Y_u - T$ are disposable national incomes of the United States and India respectively. Totally differentiating the above effective demand conditions, holding GDPs constant under the Meade assumption of constant output levels even after the transfer, we obtain the following relationship between the marginal propensities:

$$0 = \frac{\partial D_u}{\partial Y_{du}} \frac{\partial Y_{du}}{\partial T} + \frac{\partial M_i}{\partial Y_{di}} \frac{\partial Y_{di}}{\partial T} \Rightarrow d_u = m_i \tag{21.26}$$

$$0 = \frac{\partial D_i}{\partial Y_{di}} \frac{\partial Y_{di}}{\partial T} + \frac{\partial M_u}{\partial Y_{du}} \frac{\partial Y_{du}}{\partial T} \Rightarrow d_i = m_u \tag{21.27}$$

Now substitution of equation (21.27) in equation (21.21) yields:

$$dCA = -(1 - m_i - d_i)T = -s_i < 0 \tag{21.28}$$

Hence, *transfer is unambiguously under-effected.* The reason for this result is that taxes in the United States to finance the transfer are actually paid by consumers there not by lowering their consumption expenditure but by lowering their savings. Thus, imports do not fall by the amount of the tax (or the transfer). Similarly, the increased income in India is partly absorbed in larger savings so that its import expenditure and hence exports of the United States do not increase by the full amount of the transfer received.

Moreover, as explained above, this means that by the stability condition, TOT must worsen for the United States to improve its trade balance and arrive at the equilibrium position. Thus, the orthodox position, that there is a secondary burden of the transfer, follows from the classical assumption of constant output levels in a Keynesian effective demand or income approach.

The above results hold even when we allow aggregate output levels to change after the transfer as shown by Metzler (1942) and Machlup (1943). As can be verified from Appendix A21:

$$\frac{dY_u}{dT} = \frac{s_u m_i - s_i d_u}{(s_u + m_u)(s_i + m_i) - m_u m_i} \tag{21.29}$$

$$\frac{dY_i}{dT} = \frac{s_u d_i - s_i m_u}{(s_u + m_u)(s_i + m_i) - m_u m_i} \tag{21.30}$$

$$\frac{dCA}{dT} = -\frac{s_u s_i}{(s_u + m_u)(s_i + m_i) - m_u m_i} \tag{21.31}$$

Since $(s_u + m_u)(s_i + m_i) - m_u m > 0$, so the current account again worsens for the United States after it transfers income to India. On the other hand, changes in aggregate output levels of the donor and the recipient are ambiguous. But disposable income falls for the donor and rises for the recipient though less than proportionately:

$$\frac{dY_{du}}{dT} = -\frac{s_i}{(s_u + m_u)(s_i + m_i) - m_u m_i} \tag{21.32}$$

$$\frac{dY_{di}}{dT} = \frac{s_u}{(s_u + m_u)(s_i + m_i) - m_u m_i} \tag{21.33}$$

Thus, regardless of whether the output levels change or not, a transfer of income is unambiguously under-effected in a world of effective demand determined output.[3] The orthodox position thus holds.

[3] Harry G. Johnson (1956) established that if the marginal propensities change with changes in disposable incomes instead of being constant as in the above derivation, a transfer may well be *over-effected*.

APPENDIX A21

I. Foreign Trade and Expenditure Multipliers without Transmission Mechanism

Recall the equilibrium condition from equation (21.7) reproduced below:

$$Y_i - \bar{E}_i - E_i(Y_i) = [\bar{M}_u - M_i(Y_i)] \tag{A21.1}$$

Total differentiation of this effective demand condition yields:

$$dY_i - d\bar{E}_i - c_i dY_i = d\bar{M}_u - m_i dY_i$$

Changing sides and using $c_i + s_i = 1$, we obtain:

$$dY_i = \frac{d\bar{M}_u + d\bar{E}_i}{s_i + m_i} \tag{A21.2}$$

By setting $d\bar{E}_i = 0$, we obtain the export multiplier as specified in equation (21.8) in the text. Similarly, by setting $d\bar{M}_u = 0$ we obtain the expenditure multiplier as specified in equation 21.12.

On the other hand, total differentiation of the trade balance for India $TB = \bar{M}_u - M_i(Y_i)$ yields:

$$dTB = d\bar{M}_u - m_i dY_i$$

Substitution of value of dY_i from equation (A21.2) for $d\bar{E}_i = 0$ yields the magnitude of improvement in India's trade balance following a *ceteris paribus* increase in its exports:

$$dTB = d\bar{M}_u - \frac{m_i}{s_i + m_i} d\bar{M}_u = \frac{s_i}{s_i + m_i} d\bar{M}_u$$

II. Expenditure Multiplier with Transmission Mechanism

Rewrite the system of effective demand and trade balance conditions in equations (21.14)–(21.16) in the text as:

$$Y_i = \bar{D}_i + D_i(Y_i) + \bar{M}_u + M_u(Y_u) \tag{A21.3}$$

$$Y_u = \bar{D}_u + D_u(Y_u) + \bar{M}_i + M_i(Y_i) \tag{A21.4}$$

$$TB_i = \bar{M} + M_u(Y_u) - M_i(Y_i) \tag{A21.5}$$

Total differentiation of these conditions for no change in exogenous exports yield the following system of equations of change:

$$(1 - d_i)dY_i - m_u dY_u = d\bar{D}_i$$

$$-m_i dY_i + (1 - d_i)dY_i = d\bar{D}_u$$

Hence, using $1 = d_i + s_i + m_i$ and writing these equations in matrix notation we obtain:

$$\begin{bmatrix} s_i + m_i & -m_u \\ -m_i & s_u + m_u \end{bmatrix} \begin{bmatrix} dY_i \\ dY_u \end{bmatrix} = \begin{bmatrix} d\bar{D}_i \\ d\bar{D}_u \end{bmatrix} \tag{A21.6}$$

Check that the Jacobian determinant is non-vanishing:

$$|J| = \begin{vmatrix} s_i + m_i & -m_u \\ -m_i & s_u + m_u \end{vmatrix} = (s_u + m_u)(s_i + m_i) - m_u m_i = s_u s_i + s_u m_i + s_i m_u > 0$$

Hence, by Cramer's rule we can solve for changes in aggregate output and incomes as:

$$dY_i = \frac{\begin{vmatrix} d\bar{D}_i & -m_u \\ d\bar{D}_u & s_u + m_u \end{vmatrix}}{|J|} = \frac{(s_u + m_u)d\bar{D}_i + m_u d\bar{D}_u}{s_u s_i + s_u m_i + s_i m_u} \tag{A21.7}$$

$$dY_u = \frac{\begin{vmatrix} s_i + m_i & d\bar{D}_i \\ -m_i & d\bar{D}_u \end{vmatrix}}{|J|} = \frac{(s_i + m_i)d\bar{D}_u + m_i d\bar{D}_i}{s_u s_i + s_u m_i + s_i m_u} \tag{A21.8}$$

Now consider that $d\bar{D}_i > 0 = d\bar{D}_u$. Hence, equation (A21.7) boils down to equation (21.20) in the text. Note that equation (A21.7) can be rewritten as:

$$\frac{dY_i}{d\bar{D}_i} = \frac{(s_u + m_u)}{(s_u + m_u)s_i + s_u m_i} = \frac{1}{s_i + \left(\dfrac{s_u}{s_u + m_u}\right)m_i} > \frac{1}{s_i + m_i} \text{ since } \frac{s_u}{s_u + m_u} < 1$$

Finally, totally differentiating equation (A21.5) holding exogenous exports constant and using equations (A21.7) and (A21.8) for $d\bar{D}_i > 0 = d\bar{D}_u$ we obtain the change in India's trade balance as:

$$\frac{dTB_i}{d\bar{D}_i} = m_u \frac{dY_u}{d\bar{D}_i} - m_i \frac{dY_i}{d\bar{D}_i}$$

$$= \frac{m_u m_i - m_i(s_i + m_i)}{s_u s_i + s_u m_i + s_i m_u} = \frac{-s_i m_i}{s_u s_i + s_u m_i + s_i m_u} < 0 \tag{A21.9}$$

III. Transfer, TOT, and Real Income of the Donor

Consider the trade balance condition for the recipient (India):

$$p^W M_i(Y_{di}, p^W) = M_u(Y_{du}, p^W) + T \tag{A21.10}$$

Due to the income transfer received, India can import more than its value of exports. Note that unlike the income approach, we should allow world relative prices to vary to trace out the TOT effect of a transfer of income. We take the export good of the US (say good 2 in a two-commodity world) as the numeraire good.

Total differentiation of equation (A21.10) yields:

$$M_i dp^W + p^W\left(\frac{\partial M_i}{\partial Y_{di}}dY_{di} + \frac{\partial M_i}{\partial p^W}dp^W\right) = \frac{\partial M_u}{\partial Y_{du}}dY_{du} + \frac{\partial M_u}{\partial p^W}dp^W - dT$$

Using $Y_{du} = Y_u - T$ and $Y_{di} = Y_u + T$, and the assumption that pure income transfer does not change aggregate output levels, that is, $dY_i = dY_u = 0$, this boils down to:

$$M_i\left[1 + \frac{p^W}{M_i}\frac{\partial M_i}{\partial p^W} - \frac{1}{M_i}\frac{\partial M_u}{\partial p^W}\right]dp^W = [-m_u - m_i + 1]dT$$

Note that $p^W\dfrac{\partial M_i}{\partial Y_{di}} = m_i$ because Y_{di} is measured in different units than the imported good. Finally, assuming that initially there was no transfer so that $p^W M_i = M_u$, and using the definitions of import demand elasticity, we arrive at the change in the world relative price of the good imported by the recipient country (or exported by the transferring country, the US) as specified in equation (21.22) in the text:

$$\hat{p}^W = \frac{1-(m_i + m_u)}{p^W M_i[1-(\varepsilon_i + \varepsilon_u)]}dT \qquad \text{(A21.11)}$$

On the other hand, from the national budget constraint of the donor expressed in terms of its own export good (good 2), $p^W D_{1u} + D_{2u} = p^W X_{1u} + X_{2u} - T$, proceeding as in Appendix A9 (Chapter 9) under the assumption that output levels do not change since the transfer is a pure income transfer, we can arrive at the change in donor's welfare (or real income, measured in its own export good) as sum of TOT effect and the direct effect of the transfer:

$$dy_u = M_i dp^W - dT \qquad \text{(A21.12)}$$

Substitution of equation (A21.11) in (A21.12) yields the expression in equation (21.23).

IV. Under-Effected Transfer in an Effective-Demand Model

Consider the following effective demand equations and current account balance condition for the donor and the recipient:

$$Y_u = E_u(Y_{du}) + M_i(Y_{di}) - M_u(Y_{du}) \qquad \text{(A21.13)}$$

$$Y_i = E_i(Y_{di}) + M_u(Y_{du}) - M_i(Y_{di}) \qquad \text{(A21.14)}$$

$$CA = M_i(Y_{di}) - M_u(Y_{du}) - T \qquad \text{(A21.15)}$$

Given $Y_{du} = Y_u - T$ and $Y_{di} = Y_u + T$, total differentiation of equation (A21.13), using $\equiv \frac{\partial E_i}{\partial Y_i} \equiv \frac{\partial C_i}{\partial Y_i} \equiv c_i$, $c_i = d_i + m_i$ and $1 = d_i + s_i + m_i$, yield:

$$dY_u = \frac{\partial E_u}{\partial Y_{du}}[dY_u - dT] + \frac{\partial M_i}{\partial Y_{di}}[dY_i + dT] - \frac{\partial M_u}{\partial Y_{du}}[dY_u - dT]$$

$$\Rightarrow (1 - c_u + m_u)dY_u - m_i dY_i = (m_u - c_u)dT + m_i dT$$

$$\Rightarrow (s_u + m_u)dY_u - m_i dY_i = (m_i - d_u)dT$$

Similarly, from equation (A21.14) we obtain:

$$-m_u dY_u + (s_i + m_i)dY_i = (d_i - m_u)dT$$

Finally, from equation (A21.15) we obtain:

$$\begin{aligned} dCA &= \frac{\partial M_i}{\partial Y_{di}}[dY_i + dT] - \frac{\partial M_u}{\partial Y_{du}}[dY_u - dT] - dT \\ &= m_i dY_i - m_u dY_u + (m_i + m_u - 1)dT \end{aligned}$$

These equations of changes can be rewritten in matrix form as:

$$\begin{bmatrix} s_u + m_u & -m_i & 0 \\ -m_u & s_i + m_i & 0 \\ m_u & m_i & 1 \end{bmatrix} \begin{bmatrix} dY_u \\ dY_i \\ dCA \end{bmatrix} = \begin{bmatrix} m_i - d_u \\ d_i - m_u \\ m_u + m_i - 1 \end{bmatrix} dT \qquad \text{(A21.16)}$$

Check that the Jacobian determinant is non-vanishing:

$$|J| = \begin{vmatrix} s_u + m_u & -m_i & 0 \\ -m_u & s_i + m_i & 0 \\ m_u & m_i & 1 \end{vmatrix} = (s_u + m_u)(s_i + m_i) - m_u m_i = s_u s_i + s_u m_i + s_i m_u > 0$$

Hence, applying Cramer's rule, we can solve for changes in output levels as specified in equations (21.30) and (21.31) in the text. Changes in disposable incomes can then be derived $dY_{du} = dY_u - dT$ and $dY_{di} = dY_u - dT$. On the other hand, since:

$$dCA = m_i\, dY_{di} - m_u\, dY_{du} - dT$$

so substitution of values for changes in disposable incomes (see equations [21.32] and [21.33] in the text) yield:

$$dCA = \left[\frac{m_i s_u}{(s_u + m_u)(s_i + m_i) - m_u m_i}\right] dT + \left[\frac{m_u s_i}{(s_u + m_u)(s_i + m_i) - m_u m_i}\right] dT - dT$$

$$= \left[\frac{m_i s_u + m_u s_i - s_u s_i - s_u m_i - s_i m_u}{(s_u + m_u)(s_i + m_i) - m_u m_i}\right] dT = -\left[\frac{s_u s_i}{(s_u + m_u)(s_i + m_i) - m_u m_i}\right] dT < 0$$

SUMMARY POINTS

- Trade *surplus* or positive net exports is all that matters for augmenting aggregate output and national income through trade. Exports augment local production whereas imports substitute local production. Thus, only if exports exceed imports, international trade augments the *net* demand for goods and raises aggregate output and national income.
- A trade (or BOP) surplus and deficit essentially depends on a country's total absorption or aggregate expenditure relative to its produced income.
- An exogenous increase in net exports will have a multiplier expansion of aggregate output and income. The magnitude of the multiplier expansion is inversely related to the total leakage as measured by the marginal propensity to save and the marginal propensity to import.
- If Indian residents spend more on US goods without substituting their spending on domestically produced goods, India's aggregate value of output and national income will remain the same.
- A shift in the spending pattern of consumers away from imports, like an exogenous increase in net exports, expands the national income and improves the trade balance. But if the shift in spending pattern is away from domestic goods, it means a decline in net exports, and accordingly there will be a multiplier *contraction* of national income and a deterioration of trade balance.
- In the presence of international transmission (or repercussion) effect, the multiplier expansion of national incomes will be larger.
- The first part of the transfer problem has been regarding as whether a transfer is under-effected or over-effected. The second part of the transfer problem is regarding as whether the transfer improves or worsens the TOT for the donor, and if TOT improves whether it can be so large as to make it better off even after taking into account the initial transfer of real purchasing power or income.
- But by the stability condition, the transfer problem is essentially a one part problem. Whether TOT worsens or improves for the donor after the transfer is essentially related to whether the transfer is under-effected or over-effected.
- In a world with under-employed resources and effective demand determined output levels, a transfer is always under-effected under the assumption that the national income levels of the donor and the recipient change by the exact amount of the transfer.
- Allowing the aggregate output to change, Lloyd Metzler (1942) and Machlup (1943) arrived at the same result that a transfer will always be under-effected for the donor.

KEYWORDS

- **International transmission** of income means that a change in the national income of one country brought about by parametric changes there causes change in the national income of its trading partner. This happens because of the interdependence of the national incomes of trading partners through international trade between them. Thus, international trade between countries provides us such a transmission mechanism.
- **Under-effected (over-effect) transfer**: A transfer of income from one country to the other is said to be ***under-effected*** (***over-effected***) if the transfer worsens (improves) the current account of the donor.
- **Transfer problem** refers to the debate over whether a transfer of income is under-effected and over-effected, and whether it worsens or improves the donor's TOT.

EXERCISES

1. Determine the national income and aggregate savings of Bangladesh using the following information set (all values in million USD):

   Autonomous aggregate expenditure = 2,000
   Consumption expenditure is proportional to national income
   with the marginal propensity to consume = 0.7
   Value of autonomous exports = 400
   Marginal propensity to consume imported goods = 0.3

   Does Bangladesh have a trade surplus?
2. Given the above set of information, if the autonomous export value increases by USD 120, how much should Bangladesh's national income increase? Should its trade balance improve? Explain your answer.
3. Consider two economies of which one does not trade with the external world. Both countries have identical savings propensity equal to 0.2. The country that is engaged in international trade has a marginal propensity to import equal to 0.4. If the national governments of both the countries increase their respective expenditures by USD 200, which country will experience a larger increase in its national income and why?
4. Chinese consumers spend respectively 60 and 10 per cent of their incomes on goods produced locally and abroad. In 2010, the Chinese government spent 1,000 million yuan on purchase of Chinese goods and foreign goods in the ratio 65:35. Purchase of locally produced capital goods for investment was 500 million yuan. If foreigners spent 1,500 million yuan on Chinese goods in the same year, calculate China's national income in 2010. In 2011, the Chinese government increased its expenditure on locally produced goods by 20 per cent over that in the previous year with a corresponding equi-proportionate decline in expenditure on goods produced abroad. What will be the impact of this on China's national income and trade balance in 2011?
5. In the above example, how much would the trade balance change if there had been: (a) a *ceteris paribus* 20 per cent increase in Chinese government's expenditure on locally

produced goods, (b) a *ceteris paribus* 20 per cent increase in the Chinese government's expenditure on imported goods?

6. (a) Suppose the marginal propensity to consume Indian goods by Indian citizens is 0.5, the marginal propensity to consume by Indian citizens is 0.7, GoI spends Rs. 500 only on Indian goods, the marginal propensity to import Indian goods by the rest of the world (RoW) is 0.3 and the aggregate income of the RoW is Rs. 1000. There is no investment expenditure. Calculate—(i) India's GDP and NI; (ii) India's trade balance.

   (b) Suppose GoI now buys goods from the RoW worth Rs. 200. How do India's NI and trade balance change?

7. Suppose national incomes of India and Sri Lanka are interdependent through trade between them. The two countries completely specialize respectively in cloth and rice. Consumers in both the countries have identical tastes. They spend 50 per cent of their incomes on rice and 30 per cent on cloth. The Government of India buys cloth worth USD 200 million and rice worth USD 300 million to distribute among unemployed Indians. The Sri Lankan government, on the other hand, purchases rice worth USD 200 million. Determine India and Sri Lanka's national incomes. What is the trade balance for India?

8. In the above example of India–Sri Lanka trade, suppose the Government of India redistributes more rice by purchasing an additional USD 100 million worth of rice. How does it affect the national incomes of the two countries? Compare your result with the case when the national income of Sri Lanka is USD 3,000 million.

9. Why is it that while an exogenous increase in exports raises the national income of a country, an exogenous increase in its imports, *ceteris paribus*, does not change the national income for a given national income of its trading partner?

10. Why does an exogenous increase in India's exports increase its national income more than proportionately? How is the magnitude of such an income expansion related to marginal propensities?

11. Why is it that net exports, rather than exports per se, matter for an income expansion?

12. Suppose India makes a transfer of income worth USD 2,000 million to Bangladesh. This is a pure income transfer and has no impact on the produced income of the two countries. Consumers everywhere spend 30 per cent of their incomes on locally produced goods. Consumers in Bangladesh and in India save 20 per cent and 15 per cent of their incomes respectively. Using this information, can you say whether the transfer is under-effected or over-effected?

13. In what sense is the transfer problem a two-part problem? Can the first part of the problem help resolve the second part?

14. Why does an under-effected transfer mean that TOT worsens for the donor country?

15. Consider the following effective demand conditions for India and China:

$$Y_i = 990 + C_i + M_c - M_i$$
$$Y_c = 620 + C_c + M_i - M_c$$
$$C_i = 0.6\,Y_{di},\ C_c = 0.7\,Y_{dc},\ M_i = 0.3\,Y_{di},\ M_c = 0.4\,Y_{dc}$$

If there is a transfer of income worth USD 300 million by India to China, will it be under-effected or over-effected when income levels can change?

SUGGESTED READING

Bhagwati, J.N., A. Panagariya, and T.N. Srinivasan. (1998). *Lectures on International Trade*. Cambridge, MA: MIT Press.

Caves, R.E., J. Frankel, and R.W. Jones. (1995). *World Trade and Payments*. New York: HarperCollins College Publishers.

Dornbusch, R. (1980). *Open Economy Macroeconomics*. New York: Basic Books.

ADVANCED READING

Johnson, H.G. (1956). 'Transfer Problem and Exchange Stability', *Journal of Political Economy*, 64(3): 212–25.

Keynes, J.M. (1929). 'The German Transfer Problem', *Economic Journal*, *39*: 1–7. Reprinted in H.S. Ellis and L.A. Metzler (eds). (1949). *Readings in the Theory of International Trade*. Philadelphia: Blakiston.

Machlup, F. (1943). *International Trade and the National Income Multiplier.* Philadelphia: Blakiston.

Meade, J. (1951). *The Balance of Payments*. London: Oxford University Press.

Metzler, L.A. (1942). 'The Transfer Problem Reconsidered', *Journal of Political Economy*, 59: 397–414. Reprinted in H.S. Ellis and L.A. Metzler (eds). (1949). *Readings in the Theory of International Trade.* Philadelphia: Blakiston.

Samuelson, P.A. (1954). 'The Transfer Problem and Transport Costs: Analysis of Effects of Trade Impediments', *Economic Journal*, 64: 264–89. Reprinted in R.E. Caves and H.G. Johnson (eds). (1968). *Readings in International Economics*. Irwin: Homewood IL.

22 International Currency Systems and Exchange Rate Regimes

Early trade in history used precious metals such as gold and silver (called bullion) for buying and selling goods. Later, the use of coins in place of bullion approximately since the fourth century BC and the spread of trade between different regions or empires using different coins led to the emergence of an economic class of money-changers to facilitate such cross-region trade. In the present day, the international currency system that defines the parameters of the foreign exchange market—a market where national currencies are exchanged and traded—acts as the money-changers of yesteryears.

Prices of goods produced in different countries are now expressed and quoted in different national currency units. Apple iPad 3 is priced in US dollar (USD), Sony digital camera is priced in yen, German cars priced in euro, and Darjeeling tea priced in Indian rupees provide a few examples. To facilitate international exchange of these goods and corresponding payments and receipts, a system of convertibility of one currency into another is needed. The international currency system is such a facilitator that provides a set of internationally agreed rules and means of payment acceptable between buyers and sellers of different nationalities.

The international currency system has been marked by three different phases. The first was the *gold standard system* during 1875–1944 in which values of national currencies were determined by a fixed amount of gold, which was the *reserve asset* with the national monetary authorities. The use of this gold standard marked the first use of formalized *exchange rates* in history. The second phase was the Bretton Woods system (1944–71) during which the gold standard system was replaced by the *gold-USD exchange standard*. Values of all the national currencies were pegged to the US dollar and the value of the US dollar was convertible to gold at a fixed rate. Thus, the US dollar (henceforth, USD) became reserve (currency) assets for nations instead of gold. This system also created two international monetary institutions, the International Monetary Fund and the World Bank. The current phase begins with the abandonment of the Bretton Woods system during the 1970s and adoption of a flexible exchange rate system by many countries with the USD and the euro being the major reserve currencies for nations across the globe.

International Economics. Rajat Acharyya, Oxford University Press. © Oxford University Press 2022.
DOI: 10.1093/oso/9780192865144.003.0022

This chapter discusses these different phases of the international currency system, the flexible exchange rate regime, and departures from it due to interventions of different kinds in foreign exchange markets by countries to protect their national interests. India's exchange rate policies in the 1990s to mitigate its balance of payment (BOP) crisis are discussed as a case study.

22.1 THE INTERNATIONAL MONETARY SYSTEM

22.1.1 Gold Standard

Gold standard is a monetary system in which gold is the reserve asset against the coins and currencies in circulation. A country's government allows its currency unit to be freely converted into fixed amounts of gold and vice-versa. The exchange rate between two different national currencies under the gold standard monetary system is determined by the difference in the value of these currencies for an ounce of gold as fixed by the national governments. Thus, though coins and paper currencies were used in trade in place of bullion, these were backed by reserves of gold. This is in contrast to present-day *fiat money*, which a national government declares to be a legal tender but which has no intrinsic value and is not backed by reserves of gold, silver, or other precious metals. It is based on faith and if people lose faith in a nation's paper currency, the money will no longer hold any value.

The gold standard system characterized the international currency system for almost half a century during 1875–1914 and during the interwar years. But it collapsed entirely during the Great Depression of the 1930s. Part of the reason for this was the inherent flaw in the system. The system required countries to hold large amounts of gold in reserve to cope with volatile demand and supply of currencies, which had prevented monetary authorities from expanding their money supplies rapidly enough to revive economic activities during times of economic depression.

22.1.2 Bretton Woods and Thereafter

After World War II, the representatives of 43 nations met at Bretton Woods, New Hampshire, in 1944 to create a new international monetary system. The United States at that time accounted for over half of the world's manufacturing capacity and held most of the world's gold. So the participating nations agreed upon pegging their currencies to the USD, which, in turn, was made convertible into gold at USD 35 per ounce. Compared to the fixed exchange rate regime under the gold standard, this system allowed some flexibility. The exchange rates between currencies were still fixed but now could be adjusted through fixing a new value of a national currency in terms of the USD. So in effect the Bretton Woods system was a gold-USD exchange standard. The countries accumulated USDs as their *reserves*, and consequently the US Federal Reserve Bank largely determined the world money supply. Thus, under the Bretton Woods exchange rate or currency system, USD assumed the central role. The new exchange rate system allowed countries facing economic hardship after World War II to devalue their currencies by up to 10 per cent against the dollar, and more if approved by the International Monetary Fund (IMF), an institution created specifically for the purpose of bringing the international monetary system in order. A system of capital controls was introduced to protect countries from the damaging effects of capital flight and to allow them to pursue independent macroeconomic policies while still allowing the capital inflows intended for productive investments.

There was an in-built asymmetry in this currency system. The United States was not allowed to devalue the USD vis-à-vis other currencies. But under conditions of fundamental disequilibrium, other nations could devalue their currencies vis-à-vis the USD. In contrast, the pegged exchange rate regime based on the gold standard had no such asymmetry. As we will discuss later, a country losing its gold reserves through a BOP deficit experienced a corresponding contraction in its domestic money supply. But it also meant a corresponding gain in the gold reserves by trading partners and consequent expansion of money supply in these countries.

Bretton Woods also created two important Institutions—the World Bank and the IMF. John Maynard Keynes, US Treasury Secretary Henry Morganthau, and his chief economic advisor Harry Dexter White were the chief architects of these institutions. The purpose was to establish a post-War economic order with consensus-based decision making and cooperation in international trade, and developing a multilateral framework that was needed to overcome the destabilizing effects of the pre-War Great Depression and tariff wars. IMF was perceived to harmonize monetary policies of member countries and maintain exchange rate stability. It would also provide temporary financial assistance to countries experiencing balance of payments crises. The World Bank, on the other hand, was assigned the task of lending money to the war-ravaged and impoverished countries for reconstruction and development projects and thereby improving their capacity to trade.

The central role of the USD as both the currency of reserve as well as intervention became a problem as huge international demand eventually forced the United States to run a persistent trade deficit. This undermined people's confidence in the USD. A parallel market for gold also emerged where its price rose above the official US mandated price. This, in turn, led speculators to run down the US gold reserves. The United States urged Germany and Japan, both of which had favourable payment balances, to appreciate their currencies vis-à-vis USD, but they were reluctant to do so since that would increase prices of their goods and hurt their exports. Eventually President Nixon decided to end the regime of convertibility of the USD into gold on 15 August 1971, abandoned the fixed value of the USD, and allowed it to float vis-à-vis other currencies. The value of USD declined quite significantly. This marked the effective end of the Bretton Woods system. The United States also abandoned capital controls in 1974, followed by Great Britain in 1979, and by most other major economies subsequently. By the end of the 1970s, many major countries of the world had switched to floating or flexible exchange rate regimes, but were still trying to manage and stabilize exchange rate volatility, a system known as managed float as will be explained later.

By the turn of the present millennium, many economists and policymakers had started thinking about reviving the Bretton Woods system of international currency management. A consensus is now growing that the present system of unrestrained foreign exchange markets and flexible exchange rates in the developed world has failed. Voices in favour of Keynes's idea of a centrally managed global reserve currency, called bancor, are also rising across the globe. Keynes's idea was that national currencies are unsuitable for use as global reserve currencies since it is difficult to simultaneously achieve domestic monetary policy goals and meet other countries' demand for a reserve currency. In March 2009, Zhou Xiaochuan, the governor of the

People's Bank of China, proposed a gradual move towards an increased use of IMF's Special Drawing Rights (SDRs) as a centrally managed global reserve currency similar to Keynes's reserve currency bancor. His proposal attracted much international attention and has emerged as one of the plausible basis for a new international currency system. A consensus, however, is yet to be achieved.

22.1.3 Different Currency and Exchange Rate Regimes in the Post-Bretton Woods Era

The ratio at which the currency of a country is exchanged for the currency of another country is called the exchange rate. If, for example, the currencies under consideration are the Indian rupee (INR) and the US dollar (USD), then the rupee-dollar exchange rate is defined as the number of units of INR that are exchanged for one unit of USD. It is a unit free measure. An exchange rate of 50 means one USD exchanges for 50 INR. Essentially, the exchange rate is the price of one currency in terms of another currency. In this example, it is the price of USD in terms of INR.

It is obvious then that like any other price, the exchange rate will also be determined in a market, called the foreign exchange market, by the interactions of the demand for and supply of USD in exchange for INR. However, monetary authorities of countries often intervene in the foreign exchange market to influence and manipulate the exchange rate for various reasons

Box 22.1 Special Drawing Rights (SDR)

SDR is an international reserve asset which was created by IMF in 1969 to support the Bretton Woods fixed exchange rate system. It serves as a unit of account of the IMF. The value of SDR was initially defined as equivalent to one USD or 0.888671 grams of fine gold. At present, it is defined as a weighted average or a basket of four major currencies—euro, Japanese yen, pound-sterling, and USD. A country participating in the Bretton Woods system needed official reserves—central banks holdings of gold and USD —that could be used to buy the domestic currency in foreign exchange markets in order to maintain the pegged exchange rate for its currency. But expansion of world trade and financial development could not be supported by the international supply of these two reserve assets. The international community thus decided to create a new international reserve asset in the form of SDR under the auspices of IMF. Holders of SDR can obtain any other currency in exchange for their SDR either through voluntary exchanges between member countries or by the IMF designating the member countries with strong external positions to purchase SDR from members with weak external positions.

The USD-equivalent of SDR is posted daily on the IMF's website. It is calculated as the sum of the four basket currencies valued in USD, on the basis of exchange rates quoted each day in the London market. The basket composition is reviewed every five years by IMF to ensure that it reflects the relative importance of currencies in the world's trading and financial systems. The weights of the currencies in the SDR basket are revised on the basis of the value of the exports of goods and services and the amount of reserves denominated in the respective currencies that were held by other IMF members. The latest review was done in November 2010.

as we will learn in this chapter. The nature of interventions varies widely across the countries. Such variations have resulted in a wide range of currency regimes that we observe across the globe. Figure 22.1 illustrates such variations in currency or exchange rate regimes.

The three broad classifications of currency systems and exchange rate regimes are defined in respect of whether the exchange rate is market determined or exogenously determined by the monetary authority of a country. In the former case we have a flexible or floating exchange rate regime, which many countries, particularly developed countries, have adopted now. In case of an exchange rate exogenously fixed by the monetary authority of a country at a particular value, usually at a level lower than the foreign exchange market clearing value, we have a system of a fixed or pegged exchange rate regime. The third broad type of exchange rate regime is a mix of floating and pegged regimes, known as the Target Zone. Within each of the first two broad classifications there exist different types of other exchange rate regimes and currency systems.

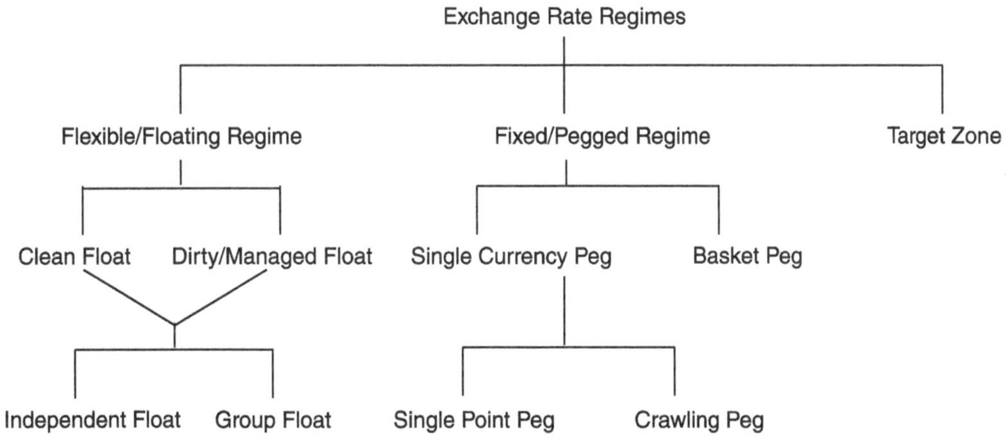

Figure 22.1 Different Currency Systems and Exchange Rate Regimes

Among the floating exchange rate regimes, a *clean float* is a regime where the monetary authority of a country does not intervene in the foreign exchange market in any way whatsoever and allows the price of a particular foreign currency in terms of its own currency (or conversely, allows the price of its own currency in terms of a particular foreign currency) to adjust to market conditions. Very few countries in the world, however, adopt such a clean float regime. New Zealand adopted a clean float regime in 1985 abandoning its pegged currency regime. However, most of the countries adopting a floating regime often moderate the adjustment in the price of their respective currencies vis-à-vis a foreign currency (usually the USD or the euro) to changing foreign exchange market conditions through buying and selling foreign currencies. This results in what is called a *dirty or managed float*. Even the United States, through its Federal Reserve Bank, has made massive interventions in the past to moderate the fluctuations of the USD price vis-à-vis foreign currencies like euro or pound-sterling. The present Indian currency system since the 1990s is also a managed or dirty float.

A currency is usually floated vis-à-vis another currency independent of any other currency. Alternatively, a group of currencies with their values being pegged to each other can be floated vis-à-vis another currency. This is called a system of group float, clean or managed. The example of such a group float is the European Monetary System (EMS) introduced on 19 March 1979. The German mark, French franc, Italian lira, Belgium-Luxembourg franc, Danish kroner, Dutch guilder, and Irish pound were pegged to each other but were together floated against the USD. This group float or EMS (along with the currencies of Austria, Finland, Greece, Spain, and Portugal) was later replaced by the common currency euro in 2002 (see Box 22.2).

The most commonly observed regime, however, is the pegged regime. Till 1990 most of the developing countries had adopted this currency system. When the value of the domestic currency is pegged to a single major currency, the regime is called a *single currency peg*. When a domestic currency is pegged to a major single currency at a particular value by the monetary authority over a long period of time, till a major intervention is made, the system is called *single point peg*. On the other hand, if the pegged rate is periodically adjusted and revised, we have a *crawling peg* regime. The Indian currency system in the late 1980s was a crawling peg system. A currency may also be pegged to some major currencies collectively. In such a case we have the *basket peg* currency regime. An example is a currency pegged to IMF's Special Drawing Rights (SDRs). A country usually follows a basket peg in order to avoid over-exposure of its currency to fluctuations of a single currency. For example, except during the period from 5 January 2003 until 20 May 2007, Kuwait has preferred a regime of basket peg. During these four years, the Kuwait dinar was pegged to only the USD. But in 2007 dinar was re-pegged to a weighted currency basket (comprising of euro, pound-sterling, Swiss franc, and USD) because the USD was weak at the time and its fluctuations resulted in high inflation in Kuwait. Kuwaiti dinar is the world's highest-valued currency unit worth about more than USD3.

Finally, a Target Zone sets a band for the exchange rate movement. The exchange rate is allowed to adjust freely to market conditions within this band, but not beyond the upper and lower limits. That is, whenever the exchange rate has a tendency to depreciate in value over and above the upper limit set by the monetary authority, the depreciation is arrested through

Box 22.2 The Euro

Euro is the common currency and the unit of account of EU member countries except UK. On 1 January 1999, the euro came into force for accounting purposes and electronic fund transfers in 11 participating EU member countries—Austria, Belgium, Finland, France, Germany, Italy, Ireland, Luxembourg, the Netherlands, Spain, and Portugal. Greece did not officially adopt the euro till 1 January 2001. Between 1999 and 2002, the euro coexisted with the currencies of the participating countries. On 1 January 2002, euro-denominated coins and bills went into circulation in 12 EU countries replacing the currencies of these nations. The adoption of the euro was the final step in the EU's plan for an Economic and Monetary Union (EMU). EMU was designed to establish a single currency and a single monetary authority for EU member states, and was an integral part of the 1991 Maastricht Treaty that founded EU. In order to make the euro a stable currency, EU set stringent economic criteria such as levels of inflation, amount of budget deficit and government debt, and stability of the existing national currency that member countries had to meet before they could adopt the euro.

appropriate interventions in the foreign exchange market. Similarly, whenever the exchange rate tends to appreciate in value below the lower limit set by the monetary authority, the appreciation is checked through appropriate interventions. EMS was an example of a kind of Target Zone regime, with a moving or crawling band of exchange rates, since it allowed group float of seven European currencies vis-à-vis USD within a spread of 2.25 per cent between USD rates of the strongest and weakest participating currencies. The Italian lira was, however, allowed a 6 per cent spread (or band) for its fluctuations.

Choice of an appropriate exchange rate regime for an open economy has always been a major concern for policymakers. This task has been made more difficult by an inconclusive theoretical literature which has not been able to pick a single regime as an unconditionally superior one over other regimes. In practice as well, different regimes have worked for different countries. Thus, the study of exchange rate regimes still remains an interesting subject matter of international economics. In the remainder of this chapter, each of these currency systems and exchange rate regimes and their implications for trade balance and foreign exchange reserves are discussed in more detail.

22.2 EXCHANGE RATE UNDER A CLEAN FLOAT

Under a clean float, competition among agents in the foreign exchange market—buyers and sellers of foreign currency for domestic currency—determines the value of the exchange rate. Recall that an exchange rate is defined as the price of a foreign currency in terms of the domestic currency.

To fix ideas, consider a foreign exchange market in a world comprised of only India and the United States, where INR and USD are traded for each other. Though neither of these countries has adopted a clean float, and there are many restrictions in India on the purchase and sale of foreign currencies by Indian citizens even today as we will discuss later, to concretize the idea of a clean float, these countries are taken as specific examples. In such a context, the demand for USD comes from four groups of agents. First, Indian importers who plan to import goods from the United States and must pay for such imports in USD, buy USD in exchange for INR. Second, American professionals who are working in India as, for example, a visiting professors at Delhi School of Economics or the Indian Institute of Management, and are paid salaries in INR, will buy USD in exchange for INR to repatriate savings out of their salaries to their families in the United States. The third category of demand for USD is related to travel or health services, or in general, related to *import* of services. Indian students travelling to the United States for higher studies and Indian patients traveling there for cancer treatment will demand USD in exchange for INR. Demand for USD by Indian tourists planning a vacation in the United States is another example. Indian currencies will not be accepted for a bus ride from New York city to Niagara County for a visit to the great Niagara Falls. Finally, wealth holders will demand USD to buy shares in American companies or other assets in the United States. Asset traders and speculators will also demand USD if they anticipate that its price vis-à-vis INR is going to rise in the future so that there will be capital losses on holding of rupee denominated assets. In sum, the demand for USD in the foreign exchange market comes from India's import of goods and services, American professionals working in India, Indians travelling to the United States, and wealth holders and asset traders or speculators.

The supply of USD in the foreign exchange market, on the other hand, comes from the counterparts of the above mentioned agents. Indian exporters are paid in USD for the goods they export to the United States. They sell their dollar earnings for INR because USD is not accepted in local markets for buying vegetables, or for payments of electricity bills in India. The supply of USD (and correspondingly the demand for INR) also comes from Indian professionals like doctors, software engineers, or accountants on assignments in the United States and repatriating part of their savings back home. American tourists coming to India to visit the Taj Mahal will sell USD to obtain INR for spending on local goods and services during their visit. Finally, wealth holders and asset traders will sell USD in exchange for INR if they plan to buy assets in India or anticipate the price of the dollar to fall and a consequent capital loss on their holding of dollar denominated assets.

Now to study how the rupee-dollar exchange rate is determined under a clean float, let us simplify things by considering only the demand for currency coming from exporters and importers. We shall draw implications of wealth holders' demand for dollar and speculative activities later. Under this simplification, the demand for USD equals the value of imports of US goods (or the value of India's imports) and the supply of USD is the export revenue for Indian exporters. Let P_i, P_u, and e denote the rupee-denominated price (index) of goods produced in India, dollar-denominated price (index) of goods produced in the United States, and the rupee-dollar exchange rate or the units of INR per unit of USD respectively. Given these notations, assuming that the real incomes of the two countries are fixed, the import demand in each country depends on the relative price or TOT, $p \equiv \frac{eP_u}{P_i}$:

$$M_i^d = M_i^d(p),\ M_i^{d'}(p) < 0 \tag{22.1}$$

$$M_u^d = M_u^d(p),\ M_u^{d'}(p) > 0 \tag{22.2}$$

Thus, the demand for USD being the dollar value of imports and the supply of USD being the dollar value of exports, the equilibrium condition in the foreign exchange market is essentially the trade balance condition expressed in USD:

$$P_u M_i^d(p) = \frac{P_i}{e} M_u^d(p) \tag{22.3}$$

Note that at equilibrium, India's export volume equals the import volume of the United States. For any given set of prices, the trade balance condition in equation (22.3) determines the equilibrium exchange rate. This is illustrated in Figure 22.2. The dollar demand curve D is downward sloping because by equation (22.1), a *ceteris paribus* increase in the value of the exchange rate worsens the TOT for India and thus lowers its demand for goods imported from the United States. An increase in the value of the exchange rate means larger units of INR now exchange for one unit of USD. That is, US goods are now dearer when converted into INR relative to the goods produced in India. This induces Indian consumers to substitute consumption of goods imported from the United States with that of domestic goods.

But, the dollar supply curve may be positively or negatively sloped. A *ceteris paribus* increase in the value of the exchange rate improves TOT for United States and thus raises its demand for goods imported from India and correspondingly India's volume of exports. At the same time, Indian exporters now earns less dollars per unit of exports because of the fall in the dollar price of India's exports, $\frac{P_i}{e}$. Thus, whereas a *ceteris paribus* increase in the value of the exchange rate raises India's *volume* of exports (or import volume of the United States), it lowers the dollar price of exports. The *value* of exports thus rises making the dollar supply curve positively sloped *only if* the US import demand is elastic ($\varepsilon_u > 1$). Otherwise, the dollar supply curve is downward sloping. Note that the demand for and supply of dollar curves are not the usual demand and supply curves, but *value* curves, and that is why the elasticity conditions are important in determining their slopes.

In Figure 22.2, the supply curve *S* is drawn positively sloped under the assumption of elastic US import demand for Indian goods. This also ensures stability of the equilibrium exchange rate, though it is not a necessary condition. As shown in Appendix A22, the same Marshall-Lerner condition as discussed in Chapter 3 ensures that the equilibrium exchange rate is stable. Given these dollar demand and supply curves, the equilibrium exchange rate under clean float is e_o with Om_o being the equilibrium (dollar) value of India's imports as well as (dollar) value of India's exports (or dollar value of imports by the United States). Alternatively, Om_o units of USD are exchanged for e_o times Om_o units of INR.

By definition, trade is necessarily balanced at the equilibrium exchange rate e_o. Note that since we have considered the demand for and the supply of USD only on the trade account (or from importers and exporters of goods and services), so the relevant balance is the trade balance. If we had incorporated in the above partial equilibrium framework the demand for and the supply of USD on account of remittances, the equilibrium in the foreign exchange market would mean the current account balance. Similarly, inclusion of asset transactions would make the balance of payments (BOP) of the countries in equilibrium (in the sense defined in Chapter 20) at the foreign exchange market equilibrium. Keeping these distinctions in mind, henceforth, as a simplification of course, we shall use the terms trade balance and BOP interchangeably.

The advantage of a clean float regime is that there is no BOP problem for the country adopting this regime. In the above context, the rupee-dollar exchange rate instantaneously and fully adjusts to clear the foreign exchange market and therefore to equate the demand for and the supply of USD. Hence, by the above mentioned definitions, BOP for India or its trade or current account, as may be relevant, will always be balanced. An external shock is absorbed through changes in the value of the exchange rate without any corresponding change in dollar reserves (or foreign currency in general) held by the Reserve Bank of India (RBI). For example, a BOP deficit caused by some external shocks means the demand for dollars exceeds the supply of dollars. This raises the price of USD in terms of INR. Thus, the value of the exchange rate rises or INR depreciates in value vis-à-vis the USD. This makes imports costlier for India but cheaper for the United States. The decrease in India's import *volume* and increase in its export *volume* (or the US import volume) wipes out the excess demand for the dollar and consequently the BOP deficit. Note that the assumption of elastic US import demand causes India's export value to rise as well. Similarly, if an external shock generates a BOP surplus for India, the value of the exchange rate declines or INR appreciates and at the new equilibrium the initial excess supply of USD is wiped out. Thus, under a clean float, the country under

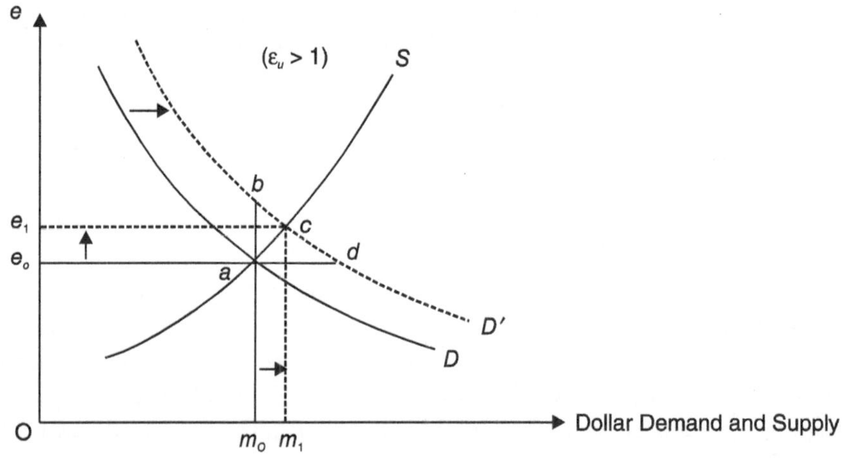

Figure 22.2 Equilibrium Spot Exchange Rate under Clean Float

consideration need not worry about BOP deficit or surplus. Consequently, dollar reserves (or foreign currencies in general) with the central bank of the country remain unchanged. At the same time, however, the exchange rate becomes volatile with far-reaching implications for the monetary and real sectors of the economy, as we will see later.

To see how different external shocks change the equilibrium exchange rate without changing the dollar reserves held by RBI, consider the following two cases. First, suppose the dollar-price of a good imported by India from the United States rises *ceteris paribus*. If the good has an inelastic demand, its lower import demand consequent upon the increase in its price will be less than proportionate so that the import bill, *ceteris paribus*, increases. The dollar demand curve in Figure 22.2 thus shifts to the right to D' following this price shock. The excess demand for dollars at the initial equilibrium exchange rate, *ad* in magnitude in the diagram, causes a depreciation of INR by the magnitude *ab*. This depreciation triggers two effects. First, it raises US import demand since Indian goods are now cheaper when converted into dollar prices. Again, the elastic US import demand ensures that its import bill and consequently India's export *value* rises. Dollar supply (or dollars sold by Indian exporters) in the foreign exchange market thus rises along the supply curve *S* (from *a* to *c*). Second, it lowers India's imports of *all* goods as rupee prices of imports now increase. The demand for USD thus falls, but now *along* the demand curve D' (from *d* to *c*). Dollar demand and supply are matched at the exchange rate e_1 with a larger amount of dollar Om_1 being exchanged in the foreign exchange market for e_1 times Om_1 units of INR. Note that the depreciation induced increase in dollar supply and decline in dollar demand moderate the initial rise in the value of the exchange rate. Thus, the dollar-price shock and consequent excess demand for USD induces a larger supply of USD in the foreign exchange market through depreciation of INR and consequent increased export earnings for Indian exporters, without requiring the RBI to sell USD from its reserves. BOP is again in equilibrium. Hence, under a clean float, a dollar-price shock depreciates the domestic currency of the importing country without affecting the dollar reserves held by RBI.

Note that if US import demand had been inelastic, export earnings and hence dollar supply by Indian exporters would have declined. This would have led to the further depreciation of

Box 22.3 Spot and Forward Exchange Rates

The exchange rate that we are talking about here is called the *spot* exchange rate. Under clean float, when economic agents are uncertain about the exchange rate movement and thus about the spot exchange rate at a future date, they might want to insure their returns from an asset denominated in a particular currency if they expect the value of the currency to depreciate in the future. They would then negotiate a forward contract for buying and selling of this currency for another currency at a future date at an exchange rate quoted today. This exchange rate is called the *forward* exchange rate. The spot and forward exchange rates are related with each other through a condition known as the *covered interest parity* condition or no-arbitrage condition as we will learn in Chapter 24. On the other hand, the efficient market hypothesis states that the forward rate is the optimal predictor of the future spot rate under risk neutrality. Essentially the forward exchange rate and the covered interest parity conditions eliminate the exchange rate risk involved in asset trading that arises from unanticipated changes in the exchange rate in the future.

INR than moderating it. But as long as the market is stable (requiring that the dollar demand curve be flatter than the dollar supply curve as in Figure 22.3), depreciation induced decline in dollar demand would have been larger than the decline in dollar supply in the foreign exchange market. Thus, again through depreciation of INR the demand for and supply of dollars would have matched. But in contrast to the case of US import demand being elastic, now INR would depreciate *more* resulting in a smaller amount of dollar transactions relative to the pre-shock level. However, dollar reserves with RBI would still remain unchanged and BOP would return to equilibrium.

The second example of an external shock that one may consider is short-term capital inflow and portfolio investment. One of the determinants of such a capital inflow and portfolio

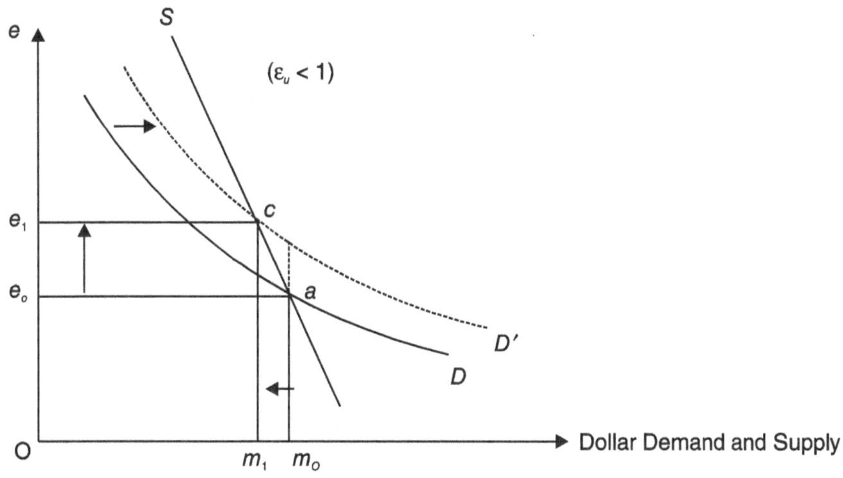

Figure 22.3 Equilibrium Exchange Rate for Inelastic Import

investment is the cross-country interest rate differential. Of course, we also need to take into account capital gains or losses arising from exchange rate movements. At this point we abstract from such considerations. Suppose an expansionary monetary policy by the Federal Reserve Bank in the United States depresses down the interest rate there on dollar-deposits and dollar-denominated assets below the rate of interest offered in India on deposits and rupee-denominated assets. For any given exchange rate this will attract portfolio investment in rupee-denominated assets. With asset-holders attempting to convert their wealth into these assets, USD is sold for INR in the foreign exchange market. The increase in the supply of USD thus lowers the value of the exchange rate. The Indian currency now appreciates in value vis-à-vis USD. Indian exports become costlier since the dollar-price of Indian goods rises. This lowers the import demand by the United States and hence the dollar earnings of Indian exporters. On the other hand, appreciation of INR makes US goods relatively cheaper, which in turn raises India's import demand and correspondingly the demand for USD. The initial excess supply thus is wiped out through appreciation of INR. The foreign exchange market attains a new equilibrium with a larger amount of USD exchanged for INR. BOP is once again in equilibrium and there is no change in the dollar reserves held by RBI either.

To summarize, under a clean float regime, whereby the monetary authority of a country does not intervene in the foreign exchange market, BOP is always in equilibrium. Any shock that leads to either an excess demand for dollars or an excess supply of dollars, causes the exchange rate to adjust *instantaneously and fully* to bring back the foreign exchange market in equilibrium through induced changes in the demand for and the supply of dollars, without requiring the dollar reserves held by the monetary authority to deplete down or pile up.

22.3 INTERVENTIONS IN THE FOREIGN EXCHANGE MARKET

As mentioned earlier, countries rarely allow their domestic currencies to float freely vis-à-vis other currencies. More often than not they intervene in the foreign exchange market. Such interventions vary from managed float and Target Zone that aim at moderating the exchange rate movement though allowing some degree of flexibility, to a pegged regime that allows no flexibility by pegging the value of their currencies vis-à-vis a particular currency or a basket of currencies. In this section we elaborate upon these market interventions by monetary authorities and their implications for BOP (or trade balance) and foreign currency reserves.

22.3.1 A Dirty or Managed Float

Under this regime, the monetary authority or a central bank of a country attempts to moderate exchange rate fluctuations *as and when it thinks* that the domestic currency is appreciating (or depreciating) too much following a shock such as the ones exemplified above. This is achieved through buying or selling foreign currencies in the foreign exchange market. In contrast to a clean float, therefore, foreign currency reserves with the central bank *change* under a managed float. Foreign currency reserves deplete when a currency depreciation is moderated through selling a foreign currency and increase when a currency appreciation is moderated through buying a foreign currency. But, under this regime, *there is no pre-commitment* by the central bank to defend a particular level of the exchange rate or the value of the domestic currency vis-à-vis a the foreign currency under consideration. The central bank intervenes *as and when it finds it necessary or desirable to do so*. Most of the major currencies in the world after the breakdown of Bretton Woods are under managed float. The Indian currency regime is also a managed float since 1994. We will elaborate on the Indian currency system in a later section.

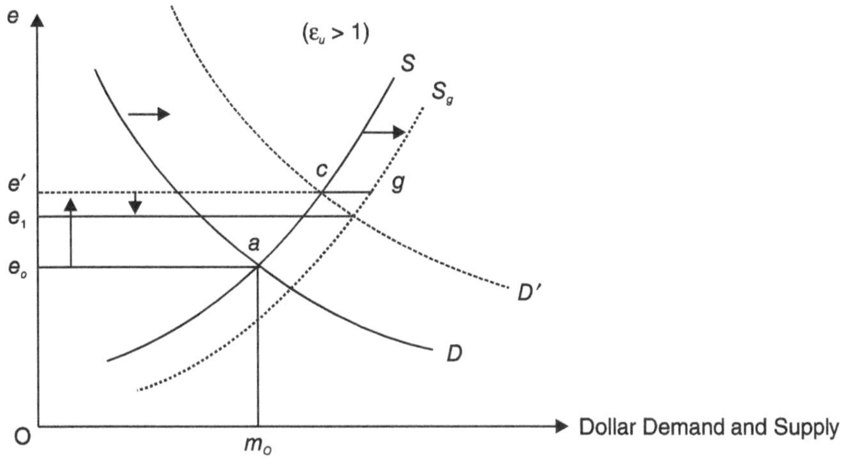

Figure 22.4 Intervention under Managed Float

To explain how a managed float works, consider again the example of an increase in the dollar-price of a good imported by India, which is inelastic in demand. The increased import bill and consequent increase in the demand for dollars increases the exchange rate to e' for reasons spelled out above (see Figure 22.4). But if RBI considers this magnitude of depreciation of the Indian currency too large then it sells, say, *cg* units of dollars, from its reserves. This shifts the dollar supply curve to S_g and lowers the exchange rate to e_1. Thus, under this managed float, the world price shock is absorbed partly in depreciation of the Indian currency (from e_0 to e_1) and partly through depletion of dollar reserves held with RBI.

There may be many valid reasons for such moderation of currency depreciation through depletion of foreign exchange reserves. One reason is that developing countries like India import large volumes of intermediate and capital goods. Currency depreciation raises the rupee price of these imports, which in turn raises the cost of producing the final goods. Imports of petroleum, oil, and lubricants also become dearer with a cost-cascading inflationary impact on the real sector of the economy. Moreover, many exported goods are import-intensive. For example, as estimated by Bhat et al. (2007), the average import-intensity of India's manufacturing exports was more than 16 per cent in 1998–99, of which non-ferrous basic metals was the most import-intensive (24 per cent), followed by electrical and electronic machine tools (20 per cent), plastic and rubber products (17 pėr cent), drugs and pharmaceuticals (15 per cent), and leather and leather products (12 per cent). A large depreciation of the Indian currency makes these exports less competitive in the world market by raising their imported-input costs.

Appreciation of the domestic currency also makes final exports (that do not use any imported inputs) less competitive in the world market as foreign buyers now have to pay more in their own currencies for the same units of goods imported. This induces them to demand less of the imported goods. As has been explained in Chapter 21, lower exports mean lower aggregate employment. In labour-abundant underemployed developing countries this is a significant cost inflicted by currency appreciation. Too much of currency appreciation and consequent loss of employment may also be politically difficult to negotiate by democratic governments in developing countries which are constrained by resources to provide compensation for such job losses.

Box 22.4 Depreciation of Indian Rupee, Currency Speculation and RBI Intervention

A recent example of a central bank or monetary authority of a country intervening in the foreign exchange market to moderate depreciation of its domestic currency is the intervention by the Reserve Bank of India (RBI) during April–May 2021. Rise in the international prices of metals and crude oil caused India's import bills to soar up in the first quarter of 2021. This raised the demand for US Dollar and depreciated the Indian Rupee (INR). Depreciation of INR was further fuelled by the speculators who were buying US Dollars anticipating further rise in the price of it and consequent capital gains in the future from holding of it. Potentially, this triggered the fear of inflation not only because of surge in INR liquidity as the buying of US Dollars by importers and speculators in the spot market led to injection of more INR into the system, but also through increased cost of essentials inputs for domestic production. To counter these potential threats, and as part of its inflation management strategy, the RBI intervened in the forward swap market by selling US Dollar to a bank with an undertaking to buy it back at a premium. This increased the supply of US Dollar and appreciated INR by 154 basis points between 12 April and 7 May 2021.

22.3.2 Over-Valued Pegged Exchange Rate Regime

Under the pegged exchange rate regime, the central bank of a country pegs a fixed value of its currency vis-à-vis a particular foreign currency (the single currency, single point peg), or to a basket of currencies (the basket peg), and *commits* itself to defend this value by its intervention in the foreign exchange market as may be necessitated by shocks. Usually, the value of the exchange rate is fixed at a level lower than what would have been the market-clearing level under a (clean) floating regime. This is the *over-valued* pegged regime because a lower than equilibrium value of the exchange rate means that lesser units of the domestic currency are now required in exchange for one unit of the foreign currency under consideration, than the free market forces would require. That is, the domestic currency is *artificially over-valued* vis-à-vis the foreign currency. This has some far-reaching implications that are discussed and explained with the help of Figure 22.5.

Suppose RBI pegs the value of INR vis-à-vis USD at the level $\bar{e}$. This over-valued exchange rate creates an excess demand for USD. The demand for goods imported from the United States rises since buyers now need to pay less in INR for the same dollar-priced US goods. That is, US goods become cheaper in Indian rupees. By the same logic, India's exports fall because Indian goods are now dearer when rupee-denominated prices are converted into dollars. Consequently, dollars earned and sold by Indian exporters decline. Thus, over-valuation of the rupee creates an excess demand for dollars by the amount *ab* in Figure 22.5, which in turn puts an upward pressure on the exchange rate. If the monetary authority does not intervene in

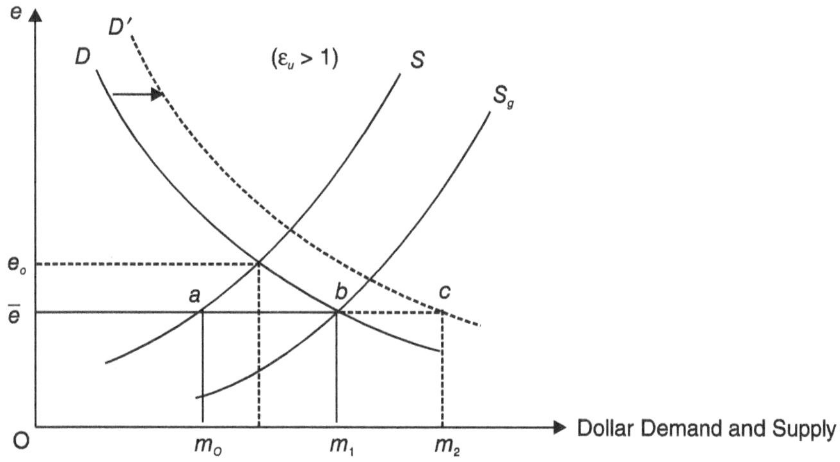

Figure 22.5 Over-Valued Pegged Exchange Rate Regime

the market to manage this excess demand, the pegged rate cannot be sustained. Note that the excess demand for dollars at the over-valued exchange rate arises regardless of whether the US import demand is elastic or inelastic for reasons spelled out.

There are two ways that RBI can ensure that the exchange rate does not move away from the pegged rate $\bar{e}$. First is to sell dollars from its reserves to meet the excess demand *ab*. Thus, the total dollar supply is now indicated by the curve labeled S_g, so that at the pegged rate $\bar{e}$ the demand for and the supply of dollars match with each other. The foreign exchange market clears again and BOP equilibrium is restored.

The other alternative to defend the pegged rate is through import tariffs (that lower excess demand for dollars at the over-valued rate as the curve *D* in Figure 22.5 shifts to the left) and through an exchange control that puts a cap on foreign currency buying (such as m_0 in Figure 22.5). This exchange control had been a major component of India's exchange rate regime prior to its BOP crisis that culminated in 1991, and though it had been relaxed in the mid-1990s, is not completely done away with. We will return to this in the next sub-section.

Under this over-valued pegged exchange rate regime any external shock changes only the reserves of the foreign currency held by the central bank of a country. For example, the import price shock that raises the demand for the foreign currency necessitates further sale of this currency by the central bank from its reserves in exchange for domestic currency. In Figure 22.5, in the context of the rupee-dollar exchange rate, the dollar amount *bc* needs to be sold by RBI to defend or maintain the pegged exchange rate $\bar{e}$ when an increase in the dollar-price of goods imported by India raises its dollar demand as indicated by the curve labeled *D'*. On the other hand, a supply shock that raises the supply of dollars such as a surge in the short-term capital flow from the United States to India, requires RBI to buy the consequent excess supply of dollars to prohibit the exchange rate to fall below $\bar{e}$ and the domestic currency to appreciate.

Thus, in contrast to a managed float, the central bank of a country must commit itself to buying and selling the foreign currency in terms of which it has pegged the value of its domestic currency. This commitment results in changes in the reserves of the foreign currency in the

Box 22.5 Pegged Renminbi, BoP surpluses and Supply Management in China

Since 1995, China has been experiencing current account surplus with a steep rise in it after 2002 (see Figure 22.6) primarily due to steady growth in exports. The extent of surplus, however, sharply declined during 2009–11, but increased again thereafter till 2015. On the other hand, speculative capital inflows during the last two decades have resulted in capital accounts surpluses as well. In face of such surpluses China has to keep purchasing excess supply of foreign currencies in order to defend the crawling peg exchange rate system that it adopted in 2005, and prevent its domestic currency Renminbi from abrupt appreciations. As a result, the country has been accumulating foreign reserves at a rapid pace.

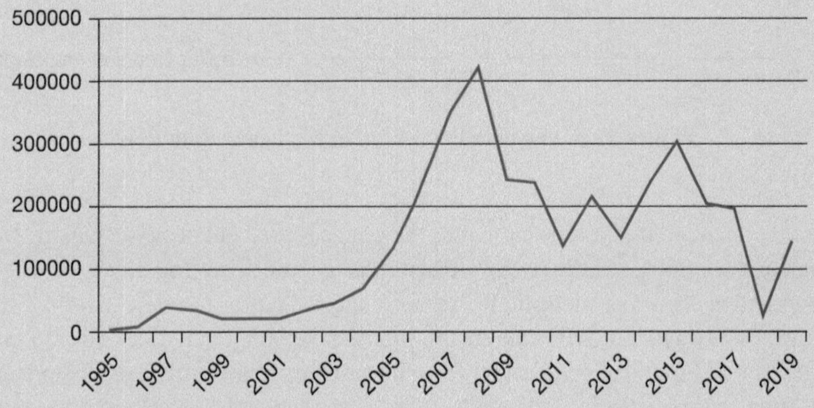

Figure 22.6 Current Account Balance of China (Million USD)

face of shocks that push the foreign exchange market into disequilibrium and thus put pressure on the pegged exchange rate. Thus, in terms of adjustment in the foreign exchange market, the pegged exchange rate regime is the polar opposite of a clean float regime. In the case of a clean float, any external shock changes *only* the exchange rate leaving the foreign exchange reserves unchanged. Under a pegged regime, on the other hand, any external shock changes *only* the foreign exchange reserves leaving the exchange rate unchanged.

22.3.3 Exchange Control and Black Market for Foreign Exchange

A central bank can defend its over-valued and pegged domestic currency through an exchange control that does not allow its importers and others to buy more than a fixed amount of a foreign currency. Refer to Figure 22.7. An exchange control that allows purchase of only Om_0 amount of dollars makes the demand curve Ddm_0. Given the dollar supply curve S, the foreign exchange market thus clears at the pegged exchange rate $\bar{e}$. This is a *demand management* (or demand rationing) policy in contrast to the supply management policy discussed earlier to defend an over-valued pegged exchange rate. The excess demand by the amount *ab* at the pegged rate is managed through the rationing of demand for dollars, instead of selling dollars from the reserve.

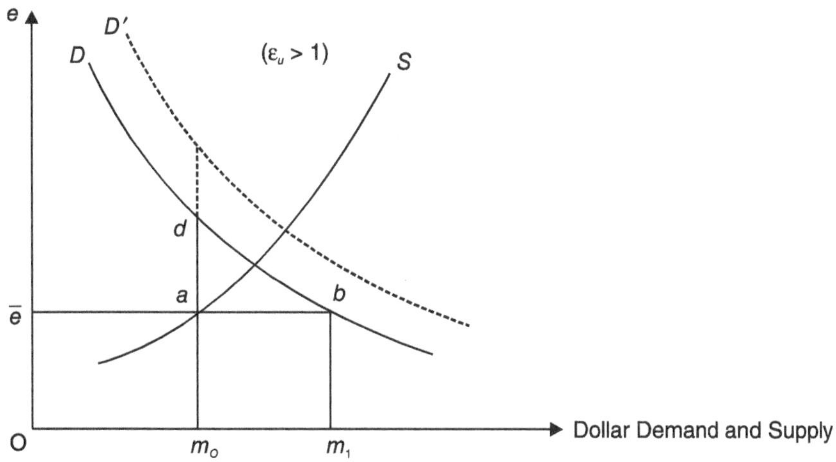

Figure 22.7 Exchange Control

Usually an exchange control is administered in many ways in tandem with restrictive trade policies. First, domestic citizens are required to buy foreign currencies only from authorized dealers of foreign exchange such as nationalized banks in India. Similarly, exporters and other earners of foreign currency are required to sell all their foreign currency earnings to these authorized sellers. Second, merchandise import demand is rationed through import quotas and import licenses issued to the importers. That is, trade restrictions are used to curb and ration the demand for foreign currency and thus to defend an over-valued pegged exchange rate regime. The glaring example is trade protection in India during the 1970s and 1980s, both in the form of high tariff and non-tariff barriers, that were designed partly to achieve the target of defending the over-valued pegged rupee-dollar exchange rate. Thus *trade protection was supplementary to the pegged exchange rate regime in India.* Third, the demand for foreign currency can be rationed through restrictions on outward remittances, buying of foreign currencies for business and academic tours and travel abroad and, above all, restricting foreign-asset trading and capital account transactions. India's exchange rate policies and exchange control offer a point in case for all these different types of restrictions.

However, an exchange control leads to a larger problem than selling of USD does. An over-valued officially pegged exchange rate and binding exchange control together generate a scarcity of dollars. In Figure 22.7, the exchange control that prohibits buying of dollars more than the stipulated amount Om_0, which is binding, leaves importers and other buyers with an unsatisfied demand for dollars. This induces them to look for unofficial or illegal sources wherefrom they can meet their excess demand for dollars even at a premium. Their willingness to pay a premium over the pegged official rate to obtain additional dollars over and above the amount permitted by the exchange control, on the other hand, induces exporters to *under-invoice* their value of exports and sell part of their dollar earnings in an unofficial or black market for foreign exchange. Thus, a *black market for foreign exchange emerges as a direct consequence of an exchange control* that is intended to sustain the over-valued pegged rate. Accordingly, the supply curve S in Figure 22.7 no longer reflects the amount of dollars

Box 22.6 FERA and FEMA in India

The Foreign Exchange Regulation Act (FERA) was implemented in India in 1974, primarily to put restrictions on the purchase and sale of foreign currencies in order to manage India's foreign exchange reserves under a pegged exchange rate regime. After the amendment of FERA in 1993, the Foreign Exchange Management Act (FEMA) came into force, which was intended to relax the controls on foreign exchange. Transactions in the current account for external trade no longer required RBI's permission. But exporters were needed to furnish their export details to RBI. The Act empowered RBI to restrict payments made to any person outside India or receipts from them. Restrictions were also imposed on people living in India who carry out transactions in foreign exchange, foreign security, or who own or hold immovable property abroad. RBI is empowered by this Act to impose restrictions on capital account transactions.

actually earned by exporters and sold in the (official) foreign exchange market. At the officially pegged rate, the amount Om_0 may still represent the dollars (or foreign currency, in general) earned by exporting goods, but the dollars *reported* and sold to RBI (or to authorized dealers) is strictly lower than this amount. Larger the premium over the pegged exchange rate offered by buyers, smaller is the proportion of actual dollar earnings being reported and sold in the legal market. This leakage of scarce foreign currency earnings into the illegal black market for foreign exchange, in fact, requires further interventions in the official foreign exchange market to defend the officially pegged exchange rate.

Two facts emerge from the discussion above. First, even a demand management policy to defend an over-valued pegged exchange rate through a binding exchange control such as Om_0 in Figure 22.7 means a leakage from dollar reserves or other foreign currencies held by RBI or a central bank of a country. Official dollar reserves are now smaller not because dollars are being sold by the central bank (directly or through its authorized dealers such as nationalized banks in India) to meet the excess demand at the pegged rate, but because foreign currency earners conceal part of their earnings and sell it in a black market at a premium over the officially pegged rate. That is, less dollars are sold to the central bank or to its authorized dealers. Official foreign currency reserves are thus less than what they could have been had there been no black market for foreign currency.

Second, the black market premium on foreign currency depends on how stringent or binding the exchange control is and consequently on the extent to which there is potential excess demand for dollars in the official foreign exchange market. Black market premium on foreign currency in turn determines the extent to which foreign currency earners conceal their earnings and thus the official reserves fall below the level Om_0. That is, official dollar reserves or any other foreign currency, the exchange control to defend the pegged rate, and the black market premium on the dollar are all *interdependent*.

Following Acharyya (1998), a simple illustration of the determination of black market premium on dollar can be presented as follows. Let e_b denote the black market exchange rate. Define the black market premium (BMP) on dollar as the proportion by which the black market exchange rate exceeds the officially pegged rate, $\frac{e_b - \bar{e}}{\bar{e}}$. Let α be the proportion of actual

Box 22.7 Under-invoiced Trade in Bangladesh, China, India, and Sri Lanka

The quantum of mis-invoicing and smuggling by Indian exporters in 1990–91 according to Kumar (1999) was worth at least USD 15 billion that amounted to 80 per cent of official exports. Raychaudhuri et al. (2003) estimated the extent of under-invoicing of exports of Bangladesh, India, and Sri Lanka to major advanced industrialized countries for the period 1980–96. They used a mean-difference analysis of the free-on-board (FOB) export value and a transport-cost adjusted cost-of-insurance-and-freight (CIF) export value as an indirect measure of under-invoicing. CIF exports by a country are imports from that country as reported by partner countries. If for any product category, the mean difference between FOB and transport-cost adjusted CIF exports is statistically significant, then such differences indicate the incidence of mis-invoicing of exports. In case of under-invoicing of exports, mean differences should be positive. Raychaudhuri et al. (2003) found that in all their estimates, mean differences were positive and for exports to a large number of countries such mean differences were statistically significant as well. A study by Beja (2008), on the other hand, reveals large trade mis-invoicing between China and its trade partners to the tune of USD 287.6 billion between 2000 and 2005. The full magnitude of unrecorded trade was estimated to be USD 1.4 trillion during that period.

dollar earnings by exporters that is reported and sold to the central bank. Thus, the export value is under-invoiced and unreported exports are smuggled out of the country. Under-invoicing and smuggling involve costs that may include bribes paid to dishonest customs officials. Alternatively, the cost may be viewed as the probability of being caught while concealing a part of the actual dollar earnings and thus payment of fine and confiscation of goods being smuggled. Whatever is the form, as long as the marginal cost of smuggling and under-invoicing is increasing with the volume of under-invoicing, legal and illegal sales of dollars will coexist.[1] Exporters decide what proportion of actual dollar earnings is to be reported and how much is to be concealed and sold in the black market depending on BMP and the cost of smuggling or under-invoicing. For any given cost of smuggling, we can expect that a larger BMP premium will induce a larger proportion of actual dollar earnings being concealed and sold in the black market. This allocation decision is shown in Appendix A22 for a specific form of the cost of smuggling. Hence, the black market dollar supply increases with BMP. Denoting $\phi \equiv \frac{e_o}{e_b}$ and hence BMP by $\frac{1}{\phi} - 1$, the curve labeled S_b in Figure 22.8 represents such a supply curve.

On the other hand, how many dollars will be demanded in the black market depends on consumers' optimal allocation of a given expenditure on home and foreign goods, as illustrated in Appendix A22. In particular, the aggregate demand for dollars in the black market (M_b) depends on the officially pegged exchange rate, the black market rate, (real) national income (y), and the stringency of the exchange control. Suppose the exchange control is such that the

[1] A similar case can be found in Pitt (1984) where legal and illegal trade in goods coexist unlike that in Bhagwati and Hansen (1973).

central bank sells up to β fraction of its (net) dollar receipts (from exporters selling dollars) to importers. That is, if αM_u is the value of exports reported and thus dollars sold by Indian exporters to RBI, Indian importers are allowed to buy *together* only up to $\beta\alpha M_u$ amount of dollars. The smaller is this proportion β, the more stringent is the exchange control since a smaller amount of dollars is sold by RBI to importers. Thus, the black market dollar demand function can be written as:

$$M_b = M - \bar{M} = M_b(e_o, e_b, y, \beta), \frac{\partial M_b}{\partial e_o} < 0, \frac{\partial M_b}{\partial e_b} < 0, \frac{\partial M_b}{\partial y} > 0, \frac{\partial M_b}{\partial \beta} < 0 \qquad (22.4)$$

where, M is the demand for dollars, or under the above simplifying assumption, the value of import demand, and $\bar{M} = \beta\alpha M_u$ is the exchange control or the maximum amount of dollars that can be bought by importers in exchange for INR from authorized dealers.

It is obvious that a more stringent exchange control and a higher national income would both mean a higher black market demand for dollars. That the black market dollar demand falls as the official pegged rate is devalued (that is, the value of the pegged rate is raised above $\bar{e}$) is also comprehensible. A currency devaluation raises the value of exports, if foreign import demand is elastic. It also thus raises the proportion of dollar earnings reported and sold to authorized dealers. Both these increase the sale of dollars to authorized dealers and consequently RBI's dollar reserves. This enables the central bank to allow purchase of a larger amount of dollars to defend the devalued pegged rate. That is, a devaluation of the domestic currency relaxes the exchange control and hence lowers the black market dollar demand.

But the black market dollar demand may fall or rise as the black market exchange rate depreciates. A rise in the black market exchange rate (or a depreciation of the Indian rupee vis-à-vis the dollar in the black market) means a rise in the *average* rupee denominated price of US goods for Indian buyers. Note that buyers now pay the price $\bar{e}P_u$ for legally imported US goods and e_bP_u for smuggled US goods. Thus, *ceteris paribus*, an increase in e_b raises the

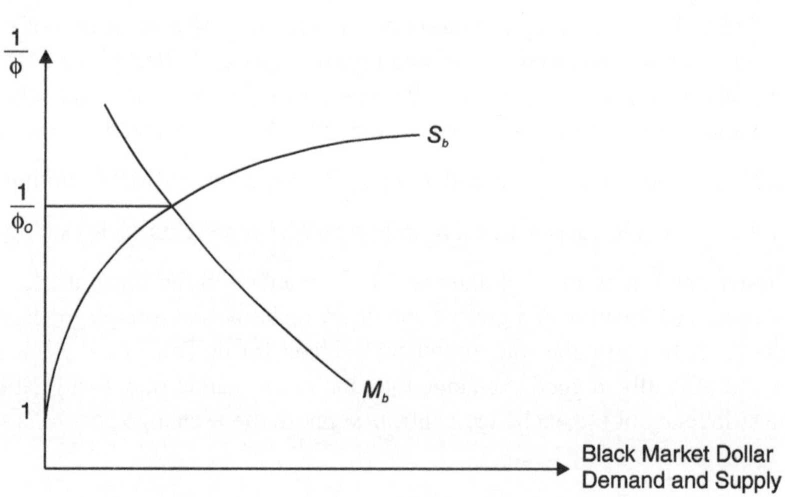

Figure 22.8 Black Market Premium on Dollar

average rupee denominated price that they pay for goods imported from the United States. The demand for foreign goods, and hence dollar demand, both legal and black market, thus falls by this *price effect*. On the other hand, a larger proportion of actual dollar earnings are now concealed since BMP rises for any given official exchange rate. This makes the exchange control more stringent. Thus, the black market dollar demand rises on this account. In equation (22.4) we assume that the price effect is larger so that overall the black market dollar demand falls as the black market exchange rate depreciates. This also ensures stability in the black market for foreign exchange since for any given official exchange rate $e_o, \frac{\partial M_b}{\partial e_b} < 0$ means that M_b is decreasing in $\frac{1}{\phi}$ as shown in Figure 22.8. However, this is only a sufficient but not a necessary condition for stability in the black market for foreign exchange.

Given these dollar demand and supply curves, the equilibrium black market exchange rate and BMP $\frac{1}{\phi_o}$ then correspond to the intersection of these curves such that the black market clears at that rate.

22.3.4 BOP Crisis under Over-Valued Pegged Exchange Rate Regime

From the above discussions it is understandable that neither the supply management nor the demand management policy to defend the over-valued pegged rate is sustainable in the long run. If the country adopting such a currency system cannot raise its exports at least as rapidly as its imports, the trade deficit, and hence the excess demand for dollars, will persist and may even grow over time. Under the supply management policy, the central bank of the country will have to sell dollars at each time period to maintain the pegged rate. A persistent and growing trade deficit will thus mean a steady depletion of dollar (or, in general, foreign currency) reserves held by it, which potentially leads to a situation of foreign exchange reserves drying up at some point of time in the not-so-distant future, and thereby generating a BOP crisis.

The demand management policy is no better either. As explained before, an exchange control to defend the over-valued pegged exchange rate leads to a black market for foreign exchange and under-invoicing of exports. Such under-invoicing puts the official reserves of foreign currencies far below the potential. Persistent and growing trade deficit now requires stricter and stricter exchange controls, which raise the black market premium offered by importers and consequently induces exporters to conceal an even larger proportion of their dollar earnings. This accentuates the leakage of dollars into the black market and lowers the actual reserves with the central bank further.

Thus, a country adopting an over-valued pegged exchange rate regime and running a persistent trade or BOP deficit, will soon find its foreign currency reserves depleting down to zero. Of course, the time length of emergence of such a BOP crisis will depend on the level of official reserves at the time of adopting an over-valued pegged regime and the rate at which the dollar is to be sold to defend this pegged rate. The crisis can also be delayed through a nominal devaluation of the domestic currency or through a crawling peg. A nominal devaluation, for example, lowers trade deficit or excess demand for dollars so that a less amount of dollars need to be sold from its reserves by the central bank under its supply management policy to defend the pegged exchange rate. On the other hand, when the central bank pursues a demand management policy through an exchange control to defend the pegged exchange rate, a nominal devaluation *may* lower BMP and thus induce exporters to under-invoice less. This raises the official dollar reserves. However, there is a caveat to this argument as mentioned in Box 22.8. But even if a nominal devaluation and similarly a crawling peg are able to slow down the depletion (or leakage) of official reserves, these are only *temporary measures* and can only postpone the complete run-down of reserves and the resulting BOP crisis.

Sooner or later, the central bank has to abandon the pegged exchange rate regime and allow the exchange rate to depreciate and settle at the higher market clearing level. As explained earlier, such a switch to a floating or flexible exchange rate regime will allow the central bank of the country not to bother about maintaining and losing foreign currency reserves since the BOP will always be in equilibrium through adjustments in the exchange rate. However, the transition from a pegged to a floating regime poses another problem that actually deepens the BOP crisis before resolving it. If wealth holders anticipate an imminent BOP crisis and expect the central bank to devalue the domestic currency or abandon the pegged exchange rate itself, they will sell the domestic currency for the foreign currency to avoid capital losses from holding the domestic currency well before the BOP crisis is actually realized. This puts more pressure on the pegged exchange rate and forces the central bank to sell larger amounts of foreign currency than otherwise. This is called the *speculative attack* on the domestic currency. The foreign currency reserves deplete even faster and the BOP crisis is realized much earlier than it would have without the speculative attack.

Box 22.8 Devaluation and Black Market Premium (BMP)

The standard theoretical argument is that a nominal devaluation of the domestic currency lowers the black market premium on the foreign currency and thus raises the official reserves of foreign currency by inducing exporters to report a larger proportion of their actual foreign currency earnings (Kamin 1993). But empirical evidence regarding the effect of a currency devaluation on BMP is mixed. A study by Dean et al. (1994) reveals that BMP increased for Brazil, China, Colombia, India, Indonesia, and Sri Lanka whereas it declined only marginally for Bangladesh and Chile after their respective trade and exchange rate reforms during 1986–91. Kiguel and O'Connell (1995), on the other hand, observed that in the case of Sudan the impact of devaluation was only transitory. BMP significantly declined immediately after each of the four maxi-devaluations in the 1980s, but rose again till the next dose of devaluation was administered.

Theoretically also it is quite possible that a nominal devaluation raises BMP instead of lowering it contrary to the standard result. See Acharyya (1998, 2012) for such a possibility that may arise because a nominal devaluation may raise the aggregate output and income of a country, which in turn raises import demand and black market demand for the dollar. The standard result and the premise that a nominal devaluation *always* lowers BMP, on the other hand, are based on the presumption that the aggregate output (and income) is fixed at the full employment level through flexibility of wages and prices. But this does not seem to be a very realistic assumption particularly for developing countries where mis-invoicing of trade is much more significant.

22.3.5 Target Zone

A Target Zone is a regime where the central bank allows the exchange rate to move within a pre-determined band and commits itself to buying or selling of a foreign currency whenever the exchange rate has a tendency to move beyond this band. In Figure 22.9, the exchange rates $\bar{e}$ and $\bar{\bar{e}}$ define such a band or *Target Zone*. The exchange rate is allowed to float within these two limits. That is, for any change in dollar demand or supply that changes the equilibrium exchange rate within this target zone, the central bank does not intervene in the foreign exchange market in any way. But if an increase in the demand for dollars (at the initial equilibrium exchange rate e_0) is too large such as the one indicated by the curve D', the central bank sells *ab* amount of dollars to prohibit the exchange rate to depreciate beyond $\bar{\bar{e}}$. Similarly, the central bank buys dollars to prohibit the exchange rate to appreciate below $\bar{e}$ for a large inflow of foreign capital, for example, and a consequent increase in dollar supply.

In essence, a Target Zone is a combination of floating and pegged exchange rate regimes. So, under this system both the exchange rate and the reserves of foreign currency may change similar to a managed float. The difference is that in a managed float the central bank does not define any band for exchange rate movement for its intervention. That is, there is no pre-commitment on its part to defend any particular exchange rate. As and when it feels that the exchange rate depreciation or appreciation is too excessive and thus needs to be moderated, it intervenes either through its supply management or demand management policies. But under Target Zone, the central bank pre-commits itself to intervene in the foreign exchange market whenever the exchange rate depreciates or appreciates beyond the target zone.

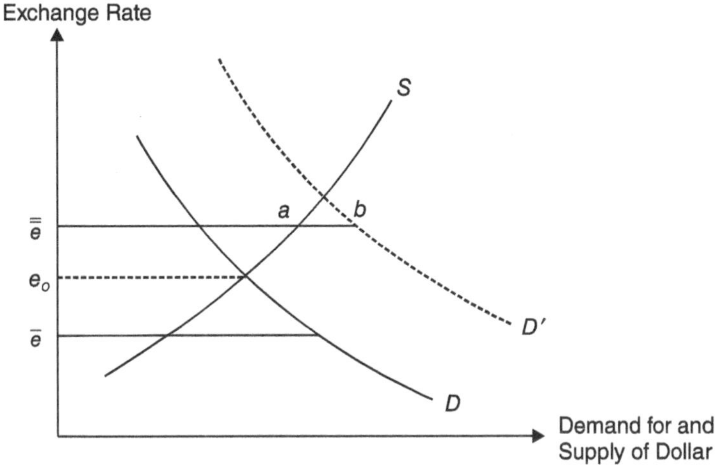

Figure 22.9 Target Zone

Note that a BOP crisis may also arise under a Target Zone if demand shocks, after the market reaches the upper bound, $\bar{\bar{e}}$, persist. Each such shock requires depletion of dollar reserves to prohibit the domestic currency to depreciate beyond this level. There may also be a speculative attack if at any point of time wealth holders anticipate that the dollar reserves with the central bank are too paltry to defend the exchange rate $\bar{\bar{e}}$ in the event of a further demand shock in the future.

At the same time, speculative attack under Target Zone may actually help the monetary authority of a country to stabilize the exchange rate within the announced (or targeted) bands. As the exchange rate changes in value and approaches the band following the changes in the fundamentals, speculators expect an imminent intervention by the central bank or the monetary authority so that its value does not cross over the band.[2] For example, as soon as changes in the fundamentals cause the value of the domestic currency to approach the upper limit $\overline{e}$, the speculators anticipate that the central bank will sell US Dollar to stop the domestic currency from depreciating further above this limit. Of course, *the speculators must believe that the central bank genuinely commits to the target zone management*, that is, *will* intervene in the market to prohibit the exchange rate to depreciate above $\overline{e}$ or appreciate below $\overline{e}$. Given such *credible commitment* on part of the central bank of the country, the speculators expect that the domestic currency will gain in value against US Dollar than losing, that is, will appreciate rather than depreciate further vis-à-vis US Dollar, since the central bank will sell US Dollar. Conversely, they expect US Dollar to depreciate in value vis-à-vis the domestic currency due to such target zone management. Accordingly, they start selling their holdings of US Dollar as they anticipate a capital loss from such holdings in near future. This moderates the depreciation of the domestic currency *before* actually reaching the upper limit. That is, speculation narrows down the range of exchange rate fluctuations even before the central bank actually intervenes in the market. Consequently, the central bank can intervene to prohibit the exchange rate to breach the upper limit for even larger changes in fundamentals in presence of speculative attack on currencies than without such attack. Similar argument holds when changes in the fundamentals cause the domestic currency to appreciate and approach the lower limit $\overline{e}$. Given the credible commitment by the central bank of the domestic country, speculators will now expect the domestic currency to depreciate in near future rather than appreciating further. They thus start buying US Dollar anticipating capital gains, which in turn actually moderates appreciation of the domestic currency.

The credibility of target zone management is, however, crucial for speculative attacks to moderate exchange rate variations near the bands. This, in turn, depends on the amount of the foreign exchange reserves of the central bank. If it has only a paltry stock of US Dollar, selling of US Dollar to prohibit the domestic currency to depreciate further above the upper limit will not be feasible and credible then.

22.4 INDIA'S BOP CRISIS AND ITS EXCHANGE RATE POLICIES

During the first quarter of 1991, India's foreign currency reserves came down at USD 1.1 billion that were barely enough to meet two weeks of the import bill. India also came closer to defaulting on its international debt commitments. As is generally argued, the crisis was an outcome of a combination of forces: trade, exchange rate, and fiscal policies that were adopted during the 1970s and 1980s, external events like the Gulf War and the loss of a huge export market in the erstwhile USSR during the 1980s (Acharyya 2012; Rakshit 2004). Since its Independence in 1947, India has adopted a pegged exchange rate regime along with exchange control. Restrictions on commodity trade, particularly quantitative restrictions on import of

2 Krugman (1991) had developed this idea very elegantly in terms of the S-type movement in the exchange rate against the fundamentals like money supply.

capital, intermediate, and consumer goods, and on capital account transactions were intended to supplement the pegged exchange rate regime. But these policies were unsustainable for reasons spelled out above. During the 1970s and 1980s, India's exports did not increase as rapidly as its imports. Consequently, the trade deficit, and the excess demand for dollars, persisted and even grew over these decades. Under the supply management policy, selling dollars to maintain the pegged rate thus meant a steady depletion of foreign currency reserves held by RBI leading potentially to a situation of foreign exchange reserves drying up, and thereby generating a BOP crisis. Under the demand management policy, on the other hand, exchange control that was implemented through the issue of import licenses permitting only a stipulated amount of import of goods resulted in a black market (known as the *hawala* market) where dollars and other foreign currencies were sold at a huge premium. This meant the supply of foreign currencies to RBI through nationalized banks (who were the authorized dealers) and an addition to the reserve of foreign currencies was much less than the potential. Financing the ever growing budget and fiscal deficits of the Central Government through issuing new money also contributed to the depletion of foreign currency reserves. We will learn more about the adverse impact of such deficits on foreign currency reserves in a latter chapter.

The problem of shrinking official reserves of foreign currency was further compounded by the breakdown of the erstwhile USSR and the outbreak of the Gulf War in the late 1980s. A large proportion of India's import requirements of capital goods was met by countries of East Europe and bilateral agreements often allowed India to make payments in Indian rupees and receive the same in exchange for goods exported to this region. The breakdown of USSR and the political turmoil in the East Europe meant loss of this rupee payment account trade with this region, and a corresponding increase in imports of essential intermediate and capital goods from the general currency area markets, where payments must be made in relevant foreign currencies. This raised the demand for dollars in India significantly. The Gulf War, on the other hand, had two impacts. First was the increase in oil prices, and second was a decline of inflow of remittances coming from the Middle East. Both these worsened the inflow of reserves and India's merchandise and invisible trade balances further. By the early 1990s when all these adverse situations culminated in a potential crisis, in anticipation of a capital loss on their loans (and rupee holdings), foreign depositors and investors withdrew large sums of foreign currency leading to a self-fulfilling speculative attack.

India's BOP crisis that culminated in early 1991, triggered major shifts in its trade and exchange rate policies, followed by a host of other domestic policy changes. The first major exchange rate policy was about 18 per cent devaluation of the Indian rupee vis-à-vis the US dollar during July–August 1991. Then there was a switch to a market-driven exchange rate regime, abandoning the over-valued pegged regime through the Liberalized Exchange Rate Management System (LERMS). Exchange controls on current account transactions were also relaxed to a large extent, though not completely dispensed off. But restrictions on capital account transactions were strictly maintained.

The present currency system, however, is at best a managed (or dirty) float, whereby RBI does not prohibit the rupee to appreciate or depreciate but moderates too much fluctuation in its value vis-à-vis the USD by buying or selling of USD, as the case may be. At the same time, this regime should not be confused with the convertibility of Indian rupee on the trade or current account. This is because exchange controls that are still in place prohibit unrestricted purchase of foreign currency which is an essential condition for a domestic currency to be fully convertible (Article VIII, IMF).

Box 22.9 Liberalized Exchange Rate Management System (LERMS)

The transition from a pegged to a managed float was achieved through a policy of Liberalized Exchange Rate Management System (LERMS). Beginning the fiscal year in March 1992, a 40:60 conversion formula was put in place whereby all Indian exporters were allowed to sell 60 per cent of their dollar earnings at the market-determined exchange rate—the one quoted by authorized dealers given the market conditions and the reference rate issued by RBI—and the rest at the officially pegged rate to authorized dealers. Thus, a dual exchange rate regime was introduced. As noted by Basu (1993), this rate was collusively set at a mark up by oligopolistic authorized dealers over the reference rates. On 1 April 1993, this conversion formula was changed to 0:100, thereby completing the transition from an over-valued pegged regime to a managed float.

It provided an implicit subsidy to exporters intended to reduce under-invoicing of exports. Under LERMS, every dollar earned would fetch more rupees for Indian exporters since the effective exchange rate was a weighted average of the higher market-rate and the officially pegged rate. Alternatively, given that a nominal devaluation of the rupee is, in effect, equivalent to a combination of the across-the-board (ad-valorem) export subsidy and import tariff, LERMS can be interpreted as a one-way devaluation. On both interpretations, it is easy to understand that LERMS was intended to improve India's trade balance during the transition from an over-valued pegged regime to a (managed) float.

APPENDIX A22

I. Existence, Uniqueness, and Stability in the Foreign Exchange Market under Clean Float

Though in Figure 22.2 an equilibrium exchange rate is shown to exist, for reasons similar to that explained in Chapter 4, an equilibrium exchange rate may not always exist. The condition of existence can be conveniently expressed in terms of an excess demand (for dollars) function $E(e)$:

$$E(e) = P_u M_i(p) - \frac{P_i}{e} M_u(p) \tag{A22.1}$$

where, $p = \dfrac{eP_u}{P_i}$.

By definition, an equilibrium exchange rate e_o is such that, $E(e_o) = 0$. Then, if the excess (dollar) demand function is continuous in e, the following conditions ensure that $e_o > 0$ (that is, an equilibrium exchange rate exists):

(a) there exists an exchange rate $e' > 0$ such that $E(e') > 0$
(b) there exists an exchange rate $e'' > 0$ such that $E(e'') < 0$

The explanation for this existence condition is similar to that for the existence of an equilibrium world price as detailed out in Appendix A4 (Chapter 4).

On the other hand, though the assumed elastic foreign import demand ensures uniqueness of equilibrium, it need not be the case. A linear US import demand function will mean varying import demand elasticity along the US import demand curve resulting in a non-monotonic import-*value* or dollar supply curve. This may imply multiple equilibrium in the foreign exchange market. For the dollar demand function, there is no such problem of non-monotonicity because an increase in the value of the exchange rate means a decline in the volume of import demand and thus, given the dollar price of imported goods, a decline in the value of imports by India regardless of whether its import demand is elastic or inelastic.

Finally, turning to the stability of equilibrium in the foreign exchange market, a Walrasian stability requires that the excess demand for dollars be decreasing in the exchange rate: $E'(e) < 0$. To check what this condition boils down to, differentiate equation (A22.1) holding export and import prices constant and letting $P_i = P_u = 1$:

$$\frac{\partial E}{\partial e} = \frac{\partial M_i}{\partial e} - \frac{1}{e}\frac{\partial M_u}{\partial e} + \frac{1}{e^2}M_u$$

$$= \frac{M_u}{e^2}\left[\frac{e^2}{M_u}\frac{\partial M_i}{\partial e} - \frac{e}{M_u}\frac{\partial M_u}{\partial e} + 1\right]$$

$$= \frac{M_u}{e^2}\left[1 + \frac{eM_i}{M_u}\left(\frac{e}{M_i}\frac{\partial M_i}{\partial e}\right) - \frac{e}{M_u}\frac{\partial M_u}{\partial e}\right]$$

Since, $\varepsilon_i = -\frac{e}{M_i}\frac{\partial M_i}{\partial e}$ and $\varepsilon_u = \frac{e}{M_u}\frac{\partial M_u}{\partial e}$ are respectively import demand elasticities for India and the United States, so the above expression boils down to:

$$\frac{\partial E}{\partial e} = \frac{M_u}{e^2}\left[1 - \frac{eM_i}{M_u}\varepsilon_i - \varepsilon_u\right] \tag{A22.2}$$

Thus, the equilibrium exchange rate is stable if:

$$\frac{eM_i}{M_u}\varepsilon_i + \varepsilon_u > 1 \tag{A22.3}$$

Since at equilibrium, trade is balanced, so $eM_i = M_u$, and accordingly equation (A22.3) boils down to the Marshall-Lerner condition that the sum of import demand elasticities be equal to one.

II. The Optimal Under-Invoicing of Exports

Let α proportion of actual dollar earnings M_u (that equals value of foreign import demand for prices normalized to unity) is reported and exchanged for INR with authorized dealers at the officially pegged rate $\bar{e}$. Thus, $(1 - \alpha)M_u$ is unreported and sold in the black market. Let there be n identical and perfectly competitive Indian exporters. Suppose for a representative exporter, the marginal cost (MC) of under-reporting actual dollar earnings and selling them in the black market is an increasing function of the unreported amount x_b:

$$\text{MC} = ce_b x_b \tag{A22.4}$$

Given such costs of illegal trading, the representative exporter's allocation of foreign exchange earnings, $m_u = M_u/n$, is determined by the equality of marginal returns from selling dollars in the official and black markets:

$$\bar{e} = e_b(1 - cx_b) \tag{A22.5}$$

The right hand side is the (net) marginal return from illegal trading of dollars. Substitution of $x_b = (1 - \alpha)\, m_u$ in equation (A22.5) yields the proportion of dollars sold in the black market:

$$(1-\alpha) = \frac{e_b - \bar{e}}{ce_b m_u} \tag{A22.6}$$

The aggregate black market dollar supply thus equals:

$$X_b = n(1-\phi)/c \tag{A22.7}$$

where, $\phi \equiv \dfrac{\bar{e}}{e_b}$.

Given that $BMP = \dfrac{1}{\phi} - 1$, the black market dollar supply varies positively with BMP as illustrated in Figure 22.7 in the text.

III. Allocation of Expenditure and Black Market Dollar Demand

For any given real income (y), Indian consumers allocate their consumption expenditure $C(y)$, measured in INR, on a domestically produced good and an imported good. Let d_i and m be respectively the quantities of domestically produced good and imported good purchased by a representative consumer. Normalizing the given prices, the consumer chooses these quantities to maximize his utility such that:

$$C(y) = d_i + \bar{e}m \tag{A22.8}$$

The optimal allocation, without any exchange control and hence black market for the dollar, is shown by the consumption bundle c in Figure A22.1. The budget line AB represents the relation in equation (A22.8) and its absolute slope equals $\dfrac{1}{\bar{e}}$. For a binding exchange control that allows each consumer to buy a quantity of imported goods not more than $\bar{m}$, the relevant budget constraint is given by $A'DB$. For imports up to $\bar{m}$, the consumer pays $\bar{e}$ per unit of legal imports. But for additional units of consumption of the imported good, which is to be obtained illegally, it must pay the price e_b since these units of (smuggled) imports are to be financed through dollars obtained in the black market. This changes the optimal allocation of the given consumption expenditure as shown by the consumption bundle c^*.

The total demand for the imported good is thus m^*, which given the official import restriction of $\bar{m}$ means that m_b units are to be obtained illegally. Given the normalized dollar price of imports, this is also the *value* of illegally obtained imports or the demand for dollars in the black market. What follows from this optimization exercise is that the black market dollar demand depends on the officially pegged exchange rate, $\bar{e}$, the black market exchange rate, e_b, the import restriction (or the stringency of the exchange control), $\bar{m}$, and real income, y. As spelled out in the text, how many dollars will be allowed to be purchased for imports (and hence how many dollars will be sold by RBI from its reserves) depends on the policy parameter β.

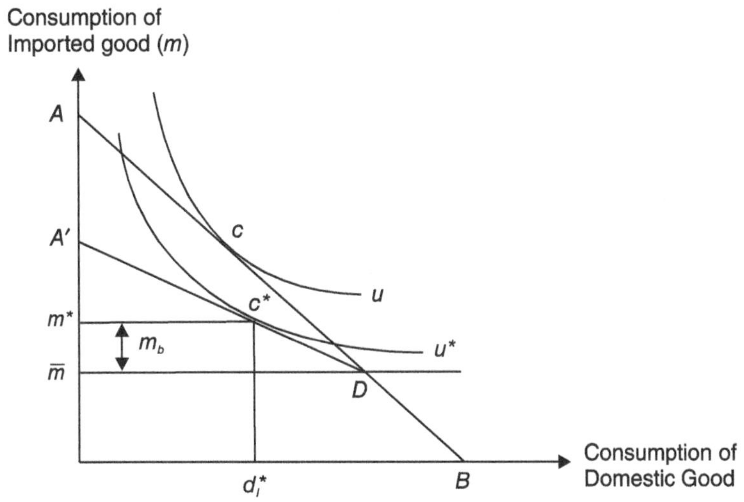

Figure A22.1 Black Market Dollar Demand

Hence, aggregating individual black market dollar demand m_b over all consumers we can write the total black market demand for dollars as:

$$M_b = M_b(e_o, e_b, y, \beta)$$

which is as specified in equation (22.4) in the text.

SUMMARY POINTS

- The international currency system has been marked by three different phases. The first was the gold standard system during 1875–1944. The second phase was the Bretton Woods system or the gold-USD exchange standard (1944–71). The current phase begins with the abandonment of the Bretton Woods system during the 1970s and adoption of a flexible exchange rate system by many countries with the USD and the euro being major reserve currencies for nations across the globe.
- Currency systems and exchange rate regimes are defined and distinguished broadly with respect to whether the exchange rate is market determined or exogenously determined by the monetary authority of a country.
- The advantage of a clean float regime is that the BOP of the country adopting this regime is always in equilibrium. Following any external shock, the exchange rate instantaneously and fully adjusts to clear the foreign exchange market and therefore to equate the demand for and the supply of foreign currency. The reserve of foreign currencies with the central bank of the country remains unchanged.
- Countries rarely adopt a clean float. Instead they adopt a dirty or managed float regime in which the central bank of a country attempts to moderate exchange rate fluctuations as and when it thinks that the domestic currency is appreciating (or depreciating) too much following a shock. But there is no pre-commitment by the central bank to defend a particular level of the exchange rate.
- Under a pegged exchange rate regime, the central bank of a country pegs a fixed value of its currency vis-à-vis a particular foreign currency, and commits itself to defend this value by its intervention in the foreign exchange market as may be necessitated by shocks.
- An over-valued pegged exchange rate regime creates an excess demand for foreign currencies, which is managed by the central bank of the country either by selling foreign currencies from its reserves or by rationing the demand for foreign currencies through an exchange control.
- An over-valued officially pegged exchange rate together with binding exchange control gives rise to a black market for foreign currencies.
- Neither the supply management nor the demand management policy to defend an over-valued pegged rate is sustainable in the long run. Under the supply management policy, a persistent and growing trade deficit will mean a steady depletion of foreign currency reserves held by the central bank. The demand management policy is no better either, as it leads to leakage of foreign currencies into the black market, and lowers the actual reserves with the central bank.
- A country adopting an over-valued pegged exchange rate regime and running a persistent trade or BOP deficit will sooner or later find its foreign currency reserves depleting down to zero and a BOP crisis emerging. The situation may be worsened further by a speculative attack on the domestic currency.
- India's BOP crisis that culminated in 1991 was an outcome of a combination of forces: trade, exchange rate, and fiscal policies that were adopted during the 1970s and 1980s,

external events like the Gulf War and the loss of a huge export market in the erstwhile USSR during the 1980s.

- The BOP crisis triggered major shifts in India's trade and exchange rate policies, followed by a host of other domestic policy changes. Among the exchange rate policies were nominal devaluation of the rupee in 1991, relaxing exchange controls on current account transactions, and a transition to a market-driven exchange rate regime through the Liberalized Exchange Rate Management System (LERMS) during 1993–94.

KEYWORDS

- **International currency system** defines the parameters of the foreign exchange market where national currencies are exchanged and traded.
- **Gold standard** was an international monetary system in which gold was the reserve asset against coins and currencies in circulation in different countries.
- **Fiat money** is money that a national government declares to be legal tender but which has no intrinsic value. This is not backed by reserves of gold, silver, or other precious metals, but is based solely on faith.
- **The Bretton Woods system** was a gold-USD exchange standard that defined the international currency system during 1944–71. Currencies of different countries were pegged to the USD, which, in turn, was convertible into gold at USD 35 per ounce.
- **Bancor** was a centrally managed global reserve currency proposed by John Maynard Keynes.
- **Special Drawing Rights** (SDR) is an international reserve asset created by IMF in 1969 to support the Bretton Woods fixed exchange rate system. At present it is defined as weighted average of four major currencies—euro, Japanese yen, pound-sterling, and USD.
- **Fixed or pegged exchange rate regime** is a regime where the exchange rate between a national and a foreign currency is exogenously fixed by the monetary authority of the country at a particular value, usually at a level lower than the foreign exchange market clearing value.
- **Clean float** is a regime where the monetary authority of a country does not intervene in the foreign exchange market in any way whatsoever and allows the price of its own currency in terms of a particular foreign currency to adjust to market conditions.
- **Spot exchange rate** is the market price of one currency in terms of another currency that prevails today.
- **Forward exchange rate** is the rate agreed upon today at which economic agents are willing to exchange one currency for another at some specified future date.
- **Exchange control** is a cap imposed by the monetary authority of a country on foreign currency buying by its domestic importers and other buyers.

(*contd*)

Keywords (*contd*)

- **Target Zone** is a regime where the central bank allows the exchange rate to move within a pre-determined band and commits itself to buying or selling a foreign currency whenever the exchange rate has a tendency to go beyond this band. In essence, a target zone is a combination of floating and pegged exchange rate regimes.
- **Black market for foreign exchange** is a market where foreign currencies are exchanged for the national currency of a country at a premium over the rate at which the value of the national currency is pegged by its monetary authority. A black market for foreign exchange is an outcome of an over-valued pegged exchange rate regime together with binding exchange control.
- **Black market premium** on dollars is the proportion by which the black market exchange rate exceeds the officially pegged rate.
- **BOP crisis** is a situation where foreign currency reserves held by the central bank of a country dry up and the country defaults on payment for its imports and debt repayment. A BOP crisis emerged for India in early 1991 when it had foreign currency reserves that could barely finance a week's imports.
- **Speculative attack** on the domestic currency occurs when anticipating a BOP crisis wealth holders sell the domestic currency for the foreign currency to avoid capital losses from holding domestic currency assets. This puts more pressure on the domestic currency and pre-pones the crisis.

EXERCISES

1. What was the gold standard system? Was this system analogous to the floating or fixed exchange rate regime that we observe today? Why was this system abandoned?
2. Why did the US dollar assume a central role under the Bretton Woods currency system? How does this system compare to the gold standard?
3. Why is it that under a clean float, a country need not worry about its BOP problem?
4. How can a pegged exchange rate regime potentially lead to a BOP crisis? Does this depend on how the central bank defends the pegged exchange rate?
5. Consider the following import demand functions for India and the United States (for $P_i = P_u = 1$):

   $M_i = 100 - 10e, M_u = 80 + 5e^2$

   where, e = units of rupee per unit of US dollar. Suppose there are no other international transactions than import and export of goods.

   (a) Write the demand function for dollar and the supply function of dollar, and discuss their properties.

   (b) Find out the equilibrium value of the exchange rate under clean float. Is it unique?

   (c) Check the Walrasian stability of the equilibrium.

6. Suppose, in the above context, the Reserve Bank of India pegs the exchange rate at value 4. How many dollars should it sell from its reserves to defend this pegged rate?
7. Suppose the prices of both the imported and exported good double, that is, $P_i = P_u = 2$. How does it affect the reserve position of the Reserve Bank of India? Why?
8. For any given set of commodity prices, how does a reduction in tariff by India on imports from the United States affect the rupee–dollar exchange rate under clean float?
9. In the above context, how would a tariff reduction by India have affected the foreign currency reserves held by RBI under an over-valued pegged supplemented by supply management policy?
10. Consider the import demand functions specified in Question 5. If the Reserve Bank of India imposes an exchange control to defend the pegged exchange rate $e = 4$, what should be the maximum amount of dollars to be allowed to be purchased by importers from authorized dealers? If this exchange control is administered through an import quota, rewrite the import demand function.
11. Suppose US import demand function is $M_u = 40 - \frac{30}{e}$. If $P_u = 1$, the officially pegged exchange rate is 2, the black market exchange rate is 10, and the marginal cost of under-reporting export earnings is $e_b X_b/5$, where $X_b = (1 - \alpha)M_u$, find the value of α or the extent of under-invoicing.
12. Do you think that BMP on a foreign currency arises due to the over-valued pegged exchange rate regime?
13. [Advanced] Let there be 100 identical consumers in India. Utility derived by a representative consumer from consuming Indian and imported US goods is $U = d_i^{0.5} d_u^{0.5}$. A representative consumer maximizes her utility subject to the budget constraint $100 = d_i + \bar{e} d_u$. Suppose, $P_i = P_u = 1$ and the official pegged exchange rate is 4.
    (a) Find out the import volume and dollar demand.
    (b) Suppose RBI rations demand for dollars by not allowing each consumer to buy imported goods worth more than USD 10. Is this exchange control binding?
    (c) Rewrite the budget constraint of a representative consumer under this exchange control.
    (d) If the black market exchange rate is 10, how many dollars will be demanded in the black market?
14. In what sense does a Target Zone combine elements of floating and pegged exchange rate regimes?
15. What is a speculative attack on a currency? How does it deepen the BOP crisis under a pegged regime? Can this be avoided if a country adopts a Target Zone regime?
16. What was the nature of India's BOP crisis in the early 1990s? How could this crisis be attributed to the exchange rate regime that RBI adopted in the 1970s and 1980s? What are the other factors that could possibly have contributed to deepen the BOP crisis?
17. What was the policy of LERMS that was introduced in India during 1992–93? What specific purposes did it serve? What effect could LERMS possibly have on BMP on USD?

SUGGESTED READING

Acharyya, R. (2012). 'India's Trade and Exchange Rate Policies: Understanding the BOP Crisis and the Reforms Thereafter', in C. Ghate (ed.), *Oxford Handbook on Indian Economy.* UK: Oxford University Press.

Krugman, P.R. (1995). *Currencies and Crises*. MIT Press.

ADVANCED READING

Acharyya, R. (1998). 'Exchange Control, Black Market for Foreign Exchange and Employment in a Model with a Non-traded Good', *Review of Development Economics*, 2(3): 305–17.

Basu, K. (1993). 'Structural Reforms in India,1991–93: Experiences and Agenda', *Economic and Political Weekly*, 27 November, 28(48): 2599–605.

Beja, E.L. (2008). 'Estimating Trade Mis-invoicing from China: 2000–2005', *China and the World Economy*, 16: 82–92.

Bhagwati, J.N. and B. Hansen. (1973). 'A Theoretical Analysis of Smuggling', *Quarterly Journal of Economics*, 87: 172–87.

Bhat, T.P., A. Guha, M. Paul, and P.P. Sahu. (2007). 'Estimates of Import Intensity in India's Manufacturing Sector: Recent Trends and Dimensions', Working Paper No. 2007/08, Institute for Studies in Industrial Development.

Dean, J., S. Desai, and J. Riedel. (1994). 'Trade Policy Reform in Developing Countries since 1985', World Bank Discussion Paper No. 267.

Kamin, S.B. (1993). 'Devaluation, Exchange Controls, and Black Market for Foreign Exchange in Developing Countries', *Journal of Development Economics*, 40: 151–69.

Kiguel, M. and S.A. O'Connell. (1995). 'Parallel Exchange Rates in Developing Countries', *The World Bank Research Observer*, 10: 21–52.

Krugman, P.R. (1991). 'Target Zones and Exchange Rate Dynamics'. *Quarterly Journal of Economics*, 56(3): 669–82.

Kumar, A. (1999). 'The Black Economy: Missing Dimensions of Macro Policy-Making in India', *The Economic and Political Weekly*, 20 March, 34(12): 681–94.

Pitt, M.M. (1984). 'Smuggling and the Black Market for Foreign Exchange', *Journal of International Economics*, 16: 243–57.

Rakshit, M.K. (2004). 'Some Macroeconomics of India's Reforms Experience', in K. Basu (ed.), *India's Emerging Economy: Performance and Prospects in the 1990s and Beyond*. Cambridge, MA: MIT Press, pp. 83–113.

Raychaudhuri, A., R. Acharyya, S. Marjit, and M. Rahman (2003). 'Trade Potentials of the South Asian Economies under the New Global Trade Regime—The Role of Some Non-price Factors: A Case Study of India, Bangladesh and Sri Lanka', Project Report submitted to SANEI.

23 BOP Adjustment Policies in a Pegged Exchange Rate Regime

In the income approach in Chapter 21 it was shown that at the effective demand equilibrium, with or without international transmission of effects, balance of payments (BOP) may be in deficit or in surplus. The underlying assumptions of the income approach were constant commodity prices and a fixed exchange rate. These assumptions prohibit automatic adjustments towards a BOP equilibrium. This was elaborated upon in Chapter 22 where it was shown that under a clean float, the foreign exchange market always adjusts to equilibrate the demand for and the supply of foreign currency and consequently the value of imports and exports. Thus, countries face no BOP problem. But when the exchange rate is pegged with an over-valuation of the domestic currency vis-à-vis the foreign currency, the country's BOP is in deficit. Under such circumstances of BOP deficit under pegged exchange rate regimes, national governments or monetary authorities may undertake policies that aim at lowering the BOP deficit. In this chapter we will discuss such policies that aim at correcting the BOP imbalances under a pegged exchange rate regime. These policies can be categorized broadly into expenditure reducing and expenditure switching policies. Of course, similar to the arguments in Chapter 22, these policies are only temporary in nature and can hardly be a solution to the BOP crisis in the long run.

Expenditure reducing and switching policies are associated with the income (or absorption) approach of Chapter 21 and the elasticity approach of Chapter 22 respectively. But both these approaches are restrictive and incomplete. Whereas the income or absorption approach assumes constant prices (and hence terms of trade or TOT), the elasticity approach assumes constant national incomes and makes a partial equilibrium analysis. An effective demand framework with variable TOT (but with constant commodity prices) provides us a complete and more comprehensive approach wherein these two types of adjustment policies can be analysed. This is also what we discuss in this chapter. The advantage of this *synthesis approach* is that it enables us to examine a policy conflict in attaining internal balance (or full employment) and external balance (or BOP equilibrium) for a country simultaneously.

International Economics. Rajat Acharyya, Oxford University Press. © Oxford University Press 2022.
DOI: 10.1093/oso/9780192865144.003.0023

23.1 TWO TYPES OF ADJUSTMENT POLICIES

BOP adjustment policies primarily target lowering import demand and import expenditure to reduce a country's BOP deficit. Given the country's exports (which are determined by the import expenditure of its trading partner), its import expenditure can be lowered and thus the BOP deficit (or the trade deficit) can be improved in two ways. First, domestic consumers can be induced to spend less in general through, for example, taxing their incomes. This is the expenditure *reducing* the adjustment policy as it targets reducing aggregate expenditure, and consequently import expenditure. Second, an adjustment policy may aim at inducing domestic consumers to change the composition of their total expenditure away from foreign goods. This can be achieved by making foreign goods relatively dearer than domestically produced goods such as through tariffs and a devaluation of the domestic currency. These are expenditure *switching* policies.

However, both expenditure reducing and switching policies that primarily target the lowering of a country's import expenditure can also affect its exports or its trade partner's import demand. This is evident from the following trade balance condition for India in the context of India–US trade:

$$TB_i = M_u(Y_u, p) - pM_i(Y_i, p) \tag{23.1}$$

An expenditure reducing policy adopted by India lowers its import demand and import value for any given TOT (or value of p) by lowering its national income. The trade balance thus improves. But, recalling the international transmission mechanism in an effective demand framework as discussed in Chapter 21, fall in Y_i lowers Y_u and hence the import demand by the United States. India's export value thus falls and the trade balance worsens on this account. Similarly, an expenditure switching policy like devaluation, for example, affects both the value of import and exports for India, for any given set of national incomes.

23.1.1 Expenditure Reducing Policies: Absorption Approach

In an income or absorption approach discussed in Chapter 21, the trade balance position of a country depends on its level of absorption (or aggregate expenditure) relative to its produced income: $TB = Y - E$. Thus, by this approach a BOP adjustment policy under a fixed exchange rate requires reduction of the aggregate expenditure or absorption, E. As the aggregate expenditure is reduced through either an income tax or a reduction in government expenditure, the national income falls, which in turn lowers import expenditure. Consequently, BOP (or the trade balance) improves. In macroeconomic policy discussions, these two policies, taxes and lower government expenditure, fall in the category of contractionary fiscal policies. Contractionary monetary policy can also serve the purpose of lowering aggregate expenditure or absorption.

To illustrate how expenditure reducing policies work, reconsider the diagrammatic determination of India's national income and trade balance position in Figure 23.1. Without any international transmission, suppose initially India had a trade deficit of the amount *ab*. Recall that aggregate expenditure or absorption is the sum of consumption expenditure (C), investment expenditure (I), and government expenditure (G). A reduction in government expenditure then means an exogenous reduction in aggregate expenditure or absorption. The $Y_i - \overline{E}_i - E_i(Y_i)$ curve in Figure 23.1 thus shifts *up*. Lower expenditure reduces India's national income and correspondingly its import demand. Given the US import demand for Indian goods, this results in a fall in the trade deficit to *cd*. Thus, a lower government expenditure (or budget deficit, for any given tax revenue) as an expenditure reducing policy improves India's trade balance.

A lump-sum income tax, or an increase in the rate of such tax, on the other hand, improves the trade balance in two ways. First, as it lowers disposable income at the initial income of the consumers, they demand less of US goods. The import expenditure thus falls *at the initial national income level*. Second, the lump-sum tax also induces consumers to buy less of Indian goods. This lowers India's national income and thus lowers its import expenditure further.

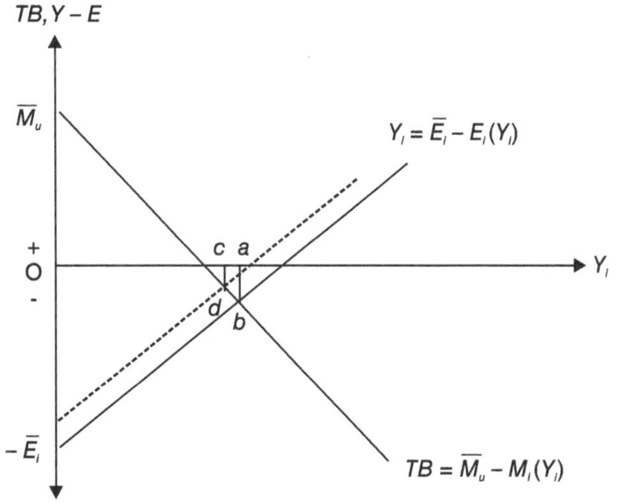

Figure 23.1 Expenditure Reducing Policy

A contractionary monetary policy as an expenditure reducing policy is better explained in the next chapter where we introduce money demand and money supply in the effective demand approach. However, a simple example will help us understand how it improves the trade balance. A reduction in the supply of domestic money by the Reserve Bank of India (RBI) will cause the desired holding of cash by people to exceed their actual holding of cash. For any given interest rate, people will thus sell some of their domestic assets (like bonds) to meet their desired cash holdings for carrying out day-to-day transactions and also for speculative buying and selling of assets in the future. Sale of bonds lowers their prices and consequently raises the interest rate. But this means that the cost of borrowing rises. Private investment expenditure thus falls, and with it falls the aggregate expenditure or the absorption of the country. The $Y_i - \overline{E}_i - E_i(Y_i)$ curve in Figure 23.1 again shifts up from its initial position. India's national income falls, and this in turn, lowers its import expenditure and trade deficit.

In sum, expenditure reducing policies improve the trade balance of a country by lowering its national income and correspondingly its import expenditure.

23.1.2 Expenditure Switching Policy: Elasticity Approach

In contrast to expenditure reducing policies, expenditure switching policies such as a nominal devaluation of the domestic currency aim at improving the trade balance through changes in the composition of consumption (or aggregate) expenditure away from imported goods, for any given national income level and aggregate expenditure or absorption. However, as discussed in Chapter 22, whether a nominal devaluation improves the trade balance or not depends on the values of the import demand elasticity. This is thus known as the elasticity approach.

To explain, reconsider India's trade balance condition in equation (23.1) expressed in Indian currency, with constant national incomes and constant prices of Indian and US goods, all normalized to one:

$$TB_i = M_u(e) - eM_i(e) \tag{23.2}$$

where, e is the rupee-dollar exchange rate.

A devaluation of the Indian rupee makes Indian goods cheaper when their prices are converted into USD but US goods dearer when their prices are converted into Indian rupee. That is, Indian consumers now need to pay more in Indian rupee per unit of imports from the United States, whereas US consumers need to pay less in USD per unit of imports from India. Consequently, US import volume and import value rise. But though India's import *volume* falls, its import bill, $eM_i(e)$, does not necessarily decline following a nominal devaluation. If India's import demand is elastic, the fall in the import volume is more than proportionate to the rise in the rupee price of imports per unit. India's import bill falls in such a case. This along with the rise in its export value causes its trade balance to improve. But when its import demand is inelastic, devaluation raises its import bill. Trade balance can still improve provided India's import demand is not too inelastic. In particular, as shown in Appendix A23, a nominal devaluation of the rupee vis-à-vis USD improves India's trade balance if the following elasticity condition holds:

$$\frac{\partial TB_i}{\partial e} = M_i\left[\frac{1}{\alpha}\varepsilon_u + \varepsilon_i - 1\right] > 0 \text{ if } \frac{1}{\alpha}\varepsilon_u + \varepsilon_i > 1 \tag{23.3}$$

where, α is the proportion by which the value of imports and the value of exports differ from each other such that $eM_i = \alpha M_u$. The initial trade deficit for India means a greater than one value of α. Thus, this elasticity condition is more stringent than the Marshall-Lerner condition for stability of the foreign exchange market, which requires $\varepsilon_u + \varepsilon_i > 1$.[1]

There are, however, a few caveats. First, this elasticity approach is based on the premise that the import demand in India and the United States will respond quickly to the rise in the rupee-price of US goods and decline in the dollar-price of Indian goods as a result of the devaluation

[1] If we had an initial balanced trade, condition (23.3) would have boiled down to the Marshall-Lerner condition. But that is not an appropriate presumption in the present context of a policy to reduce the *initial trade deficit*.

of the rupee.[2] But this may not be the case. In fact, there is much evidence that demand and supply adjust to price changes with a time lag. The sluggishness in export and import volumes immediately following the devaluation of the domestic currency may be due to several reasons. For example, production of many goods takes time to increase. Thus, unless there are stocks of goods, India's exports respond to a larger import demand from the United States only with a time lag. On the other hand, delay or lag in search time for a cheaper substitute to dearer US goods, or simply non-availability of such a substitute, may cause India's import demand to decline only marginally even after the price rise. That is, in periods immediately after the devaluation, we can expect India's exports and imports to change very slowly. Elasticity values thus remain far below the values required to satisfy the condition in equation (23.3), resulting in a worsening of the trade balance. Over time, finding a cheaper substitute and increasing production cause the import demand and export supply to change in larger magnitudes. The elasticity values grow larger and the trade balance thus improves. In sum, a country's trade balance changes in a J-curve like fashion after a devaluation—it immediately worsens since the elasticity values remain small, but improves over time as demand and supply adjust fully to price changes resulting in larger elasticity values.

Second, when intermediate goods are imported, a nominal devaluation raises production costs and affects the resource allocation in a way that may worsen the trade balance instead of improving it. Third, when the money wage is rigid and some of the goods produced are non-traded, whether a nominal devaluation of the domestic currency improves trade balance or not depends on how it changes the real exchange rate. This, in turn, depends on the relative capital-intensity of the traded good vis-à-vis non-traded goods.

Branson (1983) also doubts the effectiveness of devaluation in improving trade balances of many developing countries that display trade patterns with very low trade elasticities. For example, many of the African countries export only one or two commodities with inelastic export supply. Their import of capital goods and intermediate inputs also has inelastic demand. Trade elasticities in these countries are thus substantially low. This calls into question the effectiveness of devaluation as a policy for restoring trade balance.

An import tariff is another expenditure switching policy. By raising the tariff-inclusive domestic currency price of the imported US goods, an import tariff induces Indian consumers to substitute such imported goods by goods produced in India. Since the trade balance is evaluated at world prices of US goods being imported, so despite the increase in domestic tariff-inclusive price of imported goods, India's import bill payable to the United States (or the value of India's imports) declines unambiguously. Hence, a tariff unambiguously improves India's trade balance.

As we will see later, the change in tariff and consequent change in the tariff inclusive price of imports will change the effective demand for goods produced in India (the direction of change being dependent on an elasticity condition) unless the tariff revenue collected by the Indian government is spent entirely on these goods. This change in national income brings in further changes in India's trade balance.

[2] Another important presumption is that the domestic currency prices of foreign goods rise proportionately with the rate of depreciation of the domestic currency. This is known as (complete) exchange rate pass-through. But as country experiences reveal, the exchange rate pass-through is seldom complete and sometimes may even be perverse. We will return to this issue in Chapter 24.

Box 23.1 The J-Curve Phenomenon

The J-curve phenomenon indicates that supply and demand adjust slowly so that immediately following a nominal devaluation the trade deficit of the country worsens. This is exactly what happened to India's trade and current account balance in the immediate periods after the major devaluation of its currency in July 1991. Trade deficit as a percentage of GDP worsened from 0.97 in 1991 to 1.88 in 1992. Trade deficits grew larger till 1997 and declined marginally thereafter. A similar effect was observed for UK when it devalued its currency, pound, by almost 15 per cent after it came out of the European Exchange Rate Mechanism in 1992. Import volumes did not decline much, whereas its exports responded to larger demand from abroad with a time lag.

23.2 SYNTHESIS APPROACH

From the discussions of the absorption and elasticity approaches to BOP adjustment policies under fixed exchange rate it appears that both the approaches rest on some restrictive assumptions. The absorption approach ignores price effects by assuming a fixed TOT. The elasticity approach to BOP adjustment, on the other hand, is essentially a partial equilibrium analysis whereby it neglects the income effect of expenditure switching policies like nominal devaluation and import tariff. The effective demand framework with a variable TOT (but still with constant goods prices) provides us a synthesis of these two approaches and allows us to examine both types of BOP adjustment policies in terms of the same analytical framework. This is what we discuss here. However, since our focus is on BOP adjustment policies, we abstract from the international transmission of effects of such policies by assuming constant national income of the United States. But still its import demand (and India's value of exports) can change through changes in TOT.

With variable TOT, we rewrite the effective demand condition discussed in Chapter 21 as:

$$Y_i = \overline{E} + E_i(Y_i) + TB_i \tag{23.4}$$

where, TB_i is India's trade balance, which varies with TOT, $p \equiv \frac{eP_u}{P_i}$, and its national income:

$$TB_i = M_u(p) - pM_i(Y_i, p) \tag{23.5}$$

Note that though the aggregate expenditure or absorption E_i is assumed to be dependent only on national income, as in the income approach in Chapter 21, any policy induced change in TOT changes the absorption by changing the national income as we will see now. Later we will examine the implications of aggregate expenditure or absorption being *directly* affected by a change in TOT.

At equilibrium, if it is achieved, trade must be balanced, so that for $TB_i = 0$, the above two conditions simultaneously determine India's national income and TOT. The equilibrium is illustrated in Figure 23.2. The Y_iY_i curve is the locus of different combinations of India's national income level and TOT that maintains the effective demand equilibrium in equation (23.4). On the other hand, the $TB_i = 0$ curve is the locus of different combinations of

India's national income level and TOT that maintains balanced trade. It is straightforward to check from Appendix A23 that both these curves slope upward in the (p, Y_i) space as long as the world market for traded goods is stable, with the Y_iY_i curve being flatter than the $TB_i = 0$ curve:

$$\left.\frac{dY_i}{dp}\right|_{Y_iY_i} = \frac{M_i\left[\frac{1}{\alpha}\varepsilon_u + \varepsilon_i - 1\right]}{s_i + m_i} \tag{23.6}$$

$$\left.\frac{dY_i}{dp}\right|_{TB_i=0} = \frac{M_i\left[\varepsilon_u + \varepsilon_i - 1\right]}{m_i} \tag{23.7}$$

Recall that $\varepsilon_u + \varepsilon_i > 1$ is the Marshall-Lerner stability condition. Hence, given positive marginal propensity to import, the $TB_i = 0$ curve slopes upward. Starting from an initial balanced trade situation ($\alpha = 1$), an increase in p or a deterioration of TOT for India improves its trade balance if the elasticity values satisfy the Marshall-Lerner stability condition for external equilibrium. To maintain trade balance then, India's value of imports must rise, which in turn necessitates its national income to rise. Hence, both p and Y_i must increase along the $TB_i = 0$ curve. Along the Y_iY_i curve, on the other hand, trade is not necessarily balanced. For reasons spelled out in the context of the elasticity approach, a TOT deterioration (or increase in the value of p) raises the net export value (or improves the trade balance) and consequently the effective demand for goods produced in India if $\frac{1}{\alpha}\varepsilon_u + \varepsilon_i > 1$. This increase in the effective demand raises the aggregate value of output and national income. Hence, both p and Y_i must also increase along the Y_iY_i curve if $\frac{1}{\alpha}\varepsilon_u + \varepsilon_i > 1$. Note that since $\alpha = 1$ when trade is balanced, so the stability condition $\varepsilon_u + \varepsilon_i > 1$ implies that the Y_iY_i curve is positively sloped in the neighbourhood of equilibrium. On the other hand, since the region below the $TB_i = 0$ curve is the trade surplus region (and thus $\alpha < 1$), so the Marshall-Lerner condition again ensures a positive monotonic relationship between India's national income and its TOT along that part of the Y_iY_i curve. This is because, for $\alpha < 1$, $\varepsilon_u + \varepsilon_i > 1$ implies $\frac{1}{\alpha}\varepsilon_u + \varepsilon_i > 1$. But we require a more stringent elasticity condition $\frac{1}{\alpha}\varepsilon_u + \varepsilon_i > 1$ to ensure the positive slope of the segment of the Y_iY_i curve that lies above the $TB_i = 0$ curve which is the trade deficit region for which $\alpha > 1$.

In Figure 23.2, the equilibrium national income of India and its TOT are given by the values Y_i^e and p^e respectively that correspond to the intersection point of the two curves representing balanced trade and an effective demand equilibrium. Note that with constant goods prices, this equilibrium with balanced trade would have been automatically achieved if the rupee-dollar exchange rate had been flexible. But under a fixed exchange rate, an automatic adjustment towards this equilibrium is not possible. Suppose the RBI pegs its exchange rate at an overvalued level in the sense defined in Chapter 22. In the present context this means pegging a value of the exchange rate that results in a lower relative price of US goods than p^e such as p'. India will then have a trade deficit for reasons spelled out earlier. Without some policy changes introduced by the Government of India, this trade deficit will persist.

Further, what is evident from Figure 23.2 is that India's aggregate output and national income will also be lower than what could have been attained with balanced trade. This is not surprising because the trade deficit caused by an over-valued pegged exchange rate essentially means that domestic consumers prefer to spend more on the relatively cheaper foreign goods than on domestic goods so that the effective demand for domestic output is now lower.

Starting from such an initial trade deficit position of the Indian economy with an over-valued rupee-dollar exchange rate as at point *A* in Figure 23.2, we now examine the effects of expenditure reducing and switching policies on India's national income and trade balance.

23.2.1 Expenditure Reducing Policy

Consider an exogenous reduction in spending by the Government of India that lowers absorption. Given the pegged exchange rate and corresponding TOT, p', at the initial effective demand equilibrium, the effect of this expenditure reducing policy will be exactly the same as in the income approach discussed in Chapter 21 and also earlier in this chapter. That is, the exogenous reduction in government spending will lower the effective demand for goods produced in India and hence lower the aggregate value of output and national income. The Y_iY_i curve in Figure 23.3 thus shifts down and the economy moves to a position like *B*, with a smaller trade deficit.

With a pegged exchange rate and constant goods prices, there will be no further effect on trade deficit and national income. The exact magnitude of the downward shift (or decline in India's national income) is given by the expenditure multiplier times the reduction in government spending, $\frac{1}{s_i + m_i} d\bar{G}$, and the magnitude of reduction in the trade deficit will equal $\frac{m_i}{s_i + m_i} d\bar{G}$. Taxes and other types of expenditure reducing policies can be similarly analysed as in the income approach.

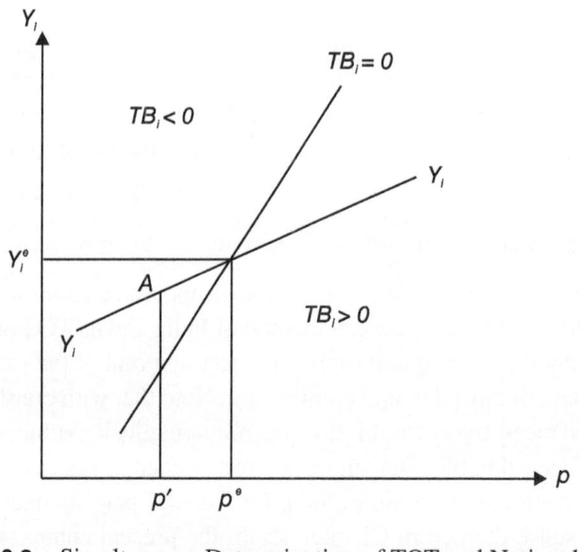

Figure 23.2 Simultaneous Determination of TOT and National Income

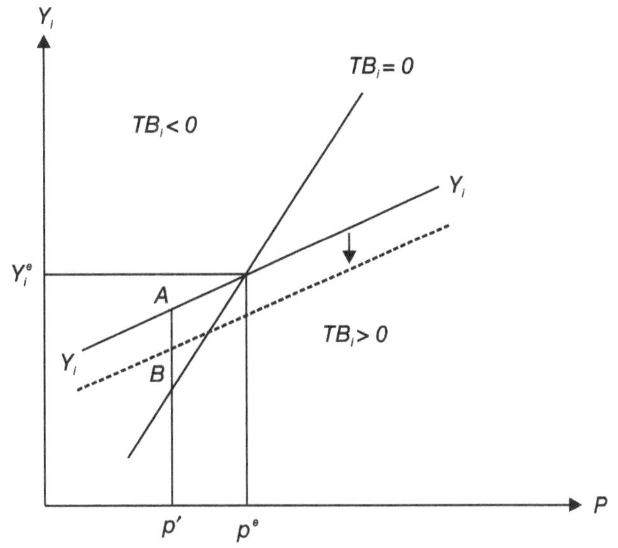

Figure 23.3 Expenditure Reducing Policy in Synthesis Approach

23.2.2 Expenditure Switching Policies

There are broadly two types of expenditure switching policies. First is the exchange rate policy like nominal devaluation of the Indian currency, and second are trade policies like import tariff, export subsidy, or quantitative trade restrictions.

Nominal Devaluation of the Indian Currency

Given constant goods prices, a devaluation of the Indian currency or an increase in the value of the rupee-dollar exchange rate raises the relative price of US goods (or worsens India's TOT) proportionately: $\hat{p} = \hat{e} > 0$. Under the assumption that $\frac{1}{\alpha}\varepsilon_u + \varepsilon_i > 1$, this lowers India's trade deficit and consequently raises the effective demand for Indian goods. This triggers a multiplier expansion of the national income and a consequent increase in imports. However, since only a fraction of this income expansion is spent on imports, the initial decline in India's trade deficit is not reversed by a subsequent rise in its import expenditure. This is evident from Figure 23.4. A devaluation that raises the relative price from p' to p'', moves the economy from A to C along the Y_iY_i curve. National income expands and trade deficit as measured by the vertical distance between the Y_iY_i curve and the $TB_i = 0$ curve, declines from the pre-devaluation level AA' to Cd. But the decline in trade deficit is smaller than if devaluation would not have raised India's national income. Increase in the value of India's imports consequent upon increase in its national income is measured by Cc. Thus, without the income expansionary effect of a devaluation, the trade deficit would have declined more. This multiplier expansion of national income and the corresponding *smaller* decline in trade deficit brings out the essence of the effective demand approach in contrast to the partial equilibrium nature of the elasticity approach.

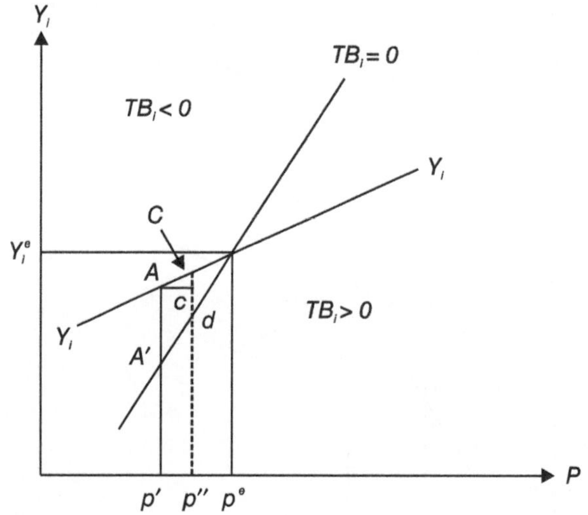

Figure 23.4 Devaluation, Income Expansion, and Trade Balance

Algebraically, given that $\hat{p} = \hat{e} > 0$, national income expansion will simply be as specified in equation (23.6). On the other hand, as shown in Appendix A23, a decline in trade deficit equals:

$$dTB_i = \frac{s_i}{s_i + m_i} M_i \left[\frac{1}{\alpha} \varepsilon_u + \varepsilon_i - 1 \right] de \tag{23.8}$$

Comparison with improvement in trade balance under the elasticity approach specified in equation (23.3) reconfirms that devaluation is less effective in improving the trade balance when it raises national income.

Import Tariff

An ad-valorem import tariff (t) imposed by the Indian government creates a wedge between the relative prices of US goods in the world market (p) and in India (p_d). Indian consumers now pay the tariff-inclusive higher price p_d for US goods though these goods are imported at the world price. Thus, India's import bill to the rest of the world (or to the United States in this two-country world) and its trade balance are still evaluated at the world relative price, p. But its import demand now varies inversely with the tariff inclusive price. Hence, India's trade balance should now be rewritten as:

$$TB_i = M_u(p) - pM_i(Y_i, p_d) \tag{23.9}$$

where, $p_d = (1 + t)p$.

On the other hand, for effective demand for domestic goods, import *expenditure* by Indian consumers evaluated at the tariff-inclusive price of US goods will now be relevant. This is because the excess over the world price that they pay goes to the exchequer as tariff proceeds. As long as the tariff proceeds are not redistributed to consumers and the government spends them by itself entirely on goods produced in the United States, tariff proceeds should be subtracted from the aggregate expenditure to arrive at the effective demand for Indian goods. Hence, condition (23.4) should now be rewritten as:

$$Y_i = \overline{E} + E_i(Y_i) + [M_u(p) - pM_i(Y_i, p_d)] - tpM_i(Y_i, p_d) \tag{23.10}$$

That is, tariff constitutes an additional leakage from the circular flow of income. Using $p_d - p = tp$, the effective demand condition in equation (23.10) reduces to:

$$Y_i = \overline{E} + E_i(Y_i) + M_u(p) - p_d M_i(Y_i, p_d) \tag{23.11}$$

Given these changes in the trade balance and effective demand conditions, let us now examine how an ad-valorem tariff on imports of goods from the United States affects India's trade balance and national income. Suppose initially no tariffs were in place and due to an over-valued exchange rate India's trade was in deficit. If now an import tariff is imposed, the trade deficit should decline *at the initial level of India's national income*. This is because a higher tariff-inclusive price of US goods induces Indian consumers to buy less of US goods. With constant goods prices and a pegged exchange rate, India's import bill payable to the United States should decline. Note that US import demand (and consequently India's exports) does not change since tariff does not affect TOT.

But as the tariff changes the national income, there will correspondingly be a further induced effect on import demand, import bill, and India's trade deficit. From equation (23.11) it is immediate that the effective demand for goods produced in India and hence the aggregate value of output and national income will rise only if the net exports *evaluated at the tariff-inclusive relative price* improve. But this depends on the import demand elasticity because whereas consumers pay more per unit of imports, they demand less than before. If their import demand is elastic, their import expenditure, $p_d M_i(Y_i, p_d)$, declines. With US import demand remaining the same, India's net exports *evaluated at the tariff-inclusive relative price* improve. Hence, an import tariff raises India's national income only if its import demand is elastic. This can be algebraically verified from the following (see Appendix A23):

$$\frac{dY_i}{dt} = \frac{(\varepsilon_i - 1)\alpha M_u}{s_i + m_i} \tag{23.12}$$

Hence, $\frac{dY_i}{dt} > 0$ if $\varepsilon_i > 1$. Note that there is again a multiplier expansion in India's national income.

This multiplier expansion in India's national income induces an increase in its import demand and worsens its trade deficit on that account. But again, the increase in imports being just a fraction of the income expansion, overall the trade deficit should decline:[3]

$$\frac{dTB_i}{dt} = \frac{(\varepsilon_i s_i + m_i)\alpha M_u}{s_i + m_i} > 0 \tag{23.13}$$

[3] When $TB_i < 0, \frac{\partial TB_i}{\partial t} > 0$ indicates that the magnitude of the trade *deficit* declines.

An interesting point to note here is that if India's import demand had been inelastic, the decline in its national income would have lowered its trade deficit by a larger magnitude. This is because the (multiplier) contraction in its national income would mean a consequent fall in import demand. Thus, regardless of whether India's import demand is elastic or inelastic, an import tariff unambiguously lowers its trade deficit. This is in fact reflected in equation (23.13). However, the magnitude of the reduction in trade deficit varies positively with the value of India's import demand elasticity. Larger the value of India's import demand elasticity, *ceteris paribus*, smaller is the decline in its trade deficit.

Diagrammatically, an unambiguous improvement in trade balance can be illustrated by plotting the trade balance condition in equation (23.9) and the effective demand condition in equation (23.11) in the (p_d, Y_i) space as in Figure 23.5. The balanced trade locus is positively sloped regardless of the stability or elasticity condition. Given constant goods prices and a pegged exchange rate, TOT remains unchanged whereas the *domestic* relative price of imports varies proportionately with the tariff rate. By the law of demand, successively higher tariffs and a consequently higher domestic relative price of imports lowers import demand and improves the trade balance unambiguously. To maintain balanced trade, the national income must then rise. Thus, regardless of any condition, tariff (or p_d) and Y_i must both increase along the $TB_i = 0$ curve. On the other hand, by equation (23.12), the Y_iY_i curve is positively sloped (as in panel *a*) if India's import demand is elastic. Otherwise it is downward sloping (as in panel *b*).

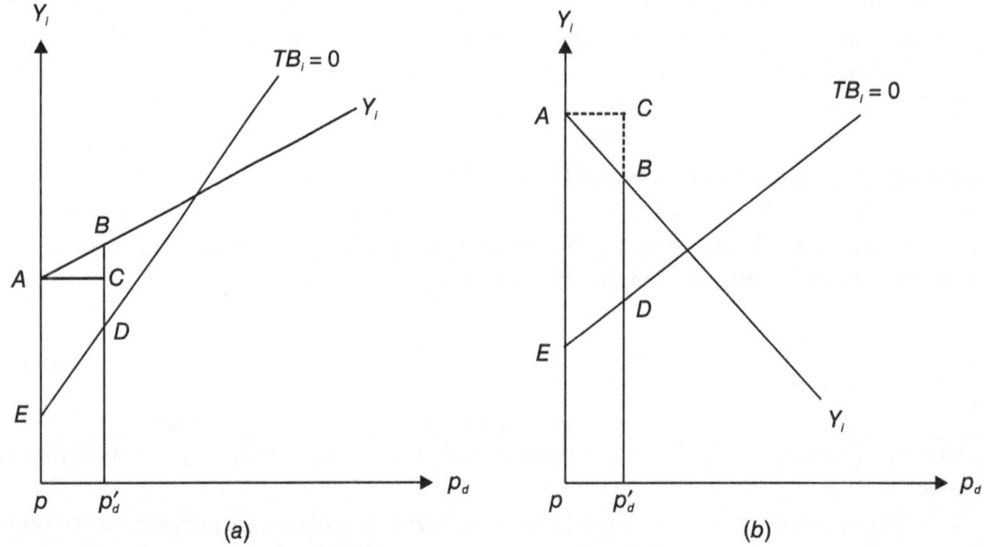

Figure 23.5 Tariffs and Trade Balance

With $t = 0$ and hence $p_d = p$, initially the economy was at point *A*, with the magnitude of trade deficit indicated by *AE*. An imposition of tariff raises p_d above p to p_d' and pushes the economy to point *B*. Trade deficit unambiguously falls in both cases. But the magnitude of decline in trade deficit is smaller in panel (a) than in panel (b). At the initial level of national income, tariff pushes the economy to point C with the trade deficit declining to the level CD.

But, in panel (a), given elastic import demand, tariff raises national income, which in turn raises import demand and thus worsens the trade deficit to some extent. Hence, the final decline in trade deficit is smaller than that at the initial national income level. In panel (b), on the other hand, tariff lowers national income, which lowers import demand and consequently the trade deficit further. Note that BD is the final magnitude of trade deficit after tariff in both panels.

23.3 INTERNAL AND EXTERNAL BALANCE AND THE POLICY CONFLICT

Macroeconomic policy targets for an open economy have an additional dimension compared to that in a closed economy. Apart from maintaining internal balance or full employment, policies should also target at maintaining external balance. In general, the policy target should be to attain internal and external balances *simultaneously*. But as we have learnt, these two balances are not independent of each other. Internal balance means aggregate effective demand, of which trade surplus (or deficit) is an integral part, must equal the full employment output (or potential output in Keynes' terms):

$$\bar{Y}_i = \bar{E} + E_i(Y_i) + M_u(p) - pM_i(Y_i, p) \tag{23.14}$$

On the other hand, the trade balance of a country depends largely on its level of national income. Hence, the two balances are interdependent. At the same time, an internal balance does not necessarily mean that external trade is balanced and vice-versa. It is possible that external trade is balanced and yet effective demand is smaller than full employment or potential output so that a part of the workforce remains unemployed. Similarly, the workforce may be fully employed but external trade may be in deficit.

Moreover, under a pegged exchange rate and constant goods prices, there is no mechanism of automatic adjustment towards the desired situation where the country attains both these balances simultaneously. Thus, it is perfectly plausible that at any point of time and for any set of government policies (like a pegged value of the exchange rate and the level of government expenditure), a country attains only one of these balances. Policy changes are then needed to attain the desired situation. But given the interdependence of the two balances, policy changes that target correcting the internal imbalance may affect the external balance that may already have been achieved. Similarly, in cases of external imbalances, policies that target corrections of such imbalances may actually cause internal imbalance. Thus, there is a *policy conflict*. T.E. Swan (1955) and W.E. Salter (1959) were the foremost to talk about such a policy conflict in cases of economic unhappiness, which is a situation where neither of these two balances is attained. Their argument was further developed by Max Corden (1960). From this policy conflict it follows that policymakers need *two distinct policies to maintain the two balances simultaneously*. James Meade (1951) made an explicit argument that expenditure reducing and expenditure switching policies provide us such a pair of policies to simultaneously attain internal and the external balances.[4]

[4] The general principle that attaining two different policy targets requires two independent policy tools originated with Jan Tinbergen (1952). Robert Mundell (1968), as we will discuss in the next chapter, applied this principle in terms of fiscal and monetary policies under capital mobility.

To illustrate, consider government expenditure as an expenditure reducing policy and nominal devaluation as an expenditure switching policy. We plot the internal balance in equation (23.14) and external balance $TB_i = 0$ in the policy space in Figure 23.6, which is known as the Swan diagram. As explained before, an increase in the Government of India's expenditure on goods produced in India raises the effective demand for such goods. But output being at full employment level, $\overline{Y}_i$, this increase in government spending creates an excess demand for goods. To maintain the internal balance, an appreciation of the Indian currency is needed. An appreciation of the value of the Indian currency vis-à-vis USD (which means a fall in the value of the exchange rate *e* since less units of Indian rupees now exchange for one unit of USD), lowers US import demand for Indian goods (now dearer in USD). On the other hand, it raises India's import demand for US goods (now cheaper in the Indian currency) though India's import expenditure may rise or fall. Overall, for any given national income of India, by the elasticity condition $\frac{1}{\alpha}\varepsilon_u + \varepsilon_i > 1$ the currency appreciation worsens its trade balance. This in turn leads to a multiplier contraction in the effective demand and brings it back to the full employment output level. That is, given $\frac{1}{\alpha}\varepsilon_u + \varepsilon_i > 1$, an increase in government spending must be matched by a fall in the value of the rupee-dollar exchange rate to maintain the internal balance condition in equation (23.14). This is shown by the downward sloping Y_iY_i curve in Figure 23.6.

On the other hand, an increase in the value of exchange rate *e* (or devaluation) improves India's trade balance (or creates a trade surplus), given the Marshall-Lerner condition $\varepsilon_u + \varepsilon_i > 1$. Note that for external balance $TB_i = 0$, the value of α is one. Thus, the Marshall-Lerner elasticity condition is relevant in the context of external balance when RBI changes the value of its exchange rate. To maintain the external balance, import demand must be raised, which necessitates an increase in the government expenditure and a corresponding increase in effective demand and real income. Thus, the $TB_i = 0$ curve in Figure 23.6 is positively sloped as a devaluation must be combined with an increase in government expenditure to maintain the external balance as long as the Marshall-Lerner condition holds.

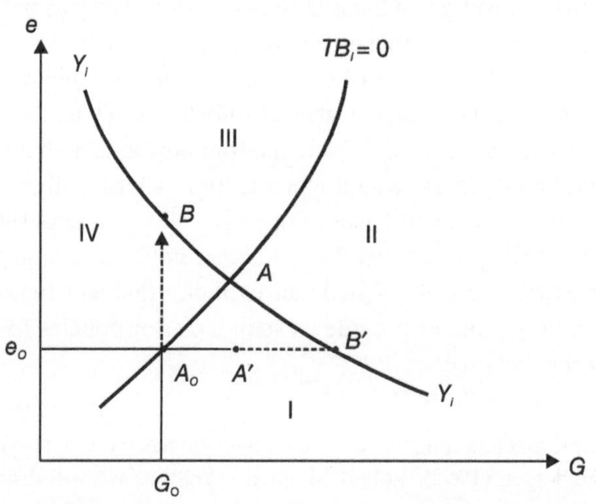

Figure 23.6 Policy Conflict in Swan Diagram

These two loci divide the entire policy space into four zones of economic unhappiness. For all policy combinations in Zone I, India's trade is in deficit along with effective demand falling short of the full employment output. Some workers will therefore remain unemployed. The reason is simple. Consider any policy combination (G, e) in Zone I such as the combination A'. Given the value of the exchange rate pegged at e_0, the level of government expenditure is *larger than* G_0 *required to maintain the external balance*. This means that India's national income and its import demand will be larger at A' than at A_0. At the same time, this level of government expenditure is *smaller than that required to maintain the internal balance* for the exchange rate pegged at e_0 so that the effective demand for India's produced goods will be less than the amount that would have ensured full employment of all workers. Thus, for policy combination A', there will be trade deficit along with unemployment. By similar reasoning, in Zone II India again experiences trade deficit but now with an excess demand for domestic output. In Zones III and IV, on the other hand, India's trade is in surplus along with excess demand for goods and unemployment respectively. These are the four zones of economic unhappiness because for policy combinations in either of these zones, neither of the balances can be attained. If policy combinations are not correct, the economy will be in any one of these zones of economic unhappiness. It is also plausible that the economy may attain only one balance such as for policy combination (G_0, e_0). In this instance, India's trade is balanced but its workforce is not fully employed.

A policy conflict in cases of economic unhappiness is apparent in Figure 23.6. For example, suppose initially the policy combination was (G_0, e_0). Thus, whereas external balance had been achieved, not all workers were employed. The Government of India can raise its expenditure to attain internal balance at point B' or can devalue its currency to attain internal balance at point B. In either case, internal balance is attained at the cost of external balance: a trade deficit in the former and a trade surplus in the latter. Thus, *both policies must be changed* to attain internal and external balance *simultaneously* at point A, even if the economy had initially attained one of these balances. But designing and implementing appropriate policy changes are not easy. This is because the same policy change may not be appropriate starting from any point in Zone I. An initial position very close to A_0 requires an increase in government spending on domestic goods along with a devaluation of the Indian currency to attain both balances at point A. But if the initial position of the Indian economy had been close to point B', a devaluation of the Indian currency must be combined with a *smaller* government spending on domestic goods.

That is, a particular zone of economic unhappiness (and corresponding nature of imbalances) does not by itself reveal enough information to design an appropriate combination of expenditure reducing and switching policies. Figure 23.7 illustrates this by dividing the policy space into four *policy sectors—a, b, c,* and *d*—rather than into the four zones of economic unhappiness. These policy sectors are obtained once the optimal combination of policies (G_i^*, e^*) is identified. Thus, for an initial position of the economy anywhere in the policy sector a, both the value of the exchange rate and the level of government spending on domestic goods are less than optimal levels. Accordingly, the government must raise its spending on domestic goods and at the same time devalue its currency. For the economy's initial position in the policy sector b, the appropriate policy combination should be a reduction in government spending with a devaluation of the domestic currency. Similarly, for initial positions in policy sectors c and d, appropriate policies should be a reduction in government spending with a revaluation (or appreciation) of the domestic currency and an increase in government spending with a revaluation of the domestic currency respectively.

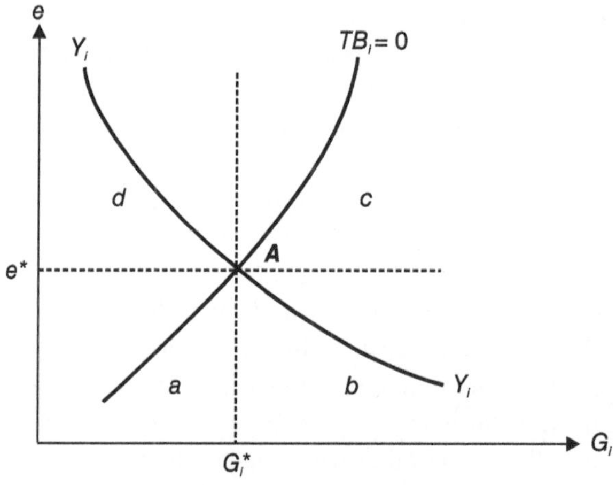

Figure 23.7 Policy Sectors

Note that the policy sectors overlap with the different zones of economic unhappiness. For example, policy sector *a* overlaps with Zones I and IV in Figure 23.6. That is, the same set of policy changes may be appropriate for different combinations of imbalances or economic unhappiness. On the other hand, Zone I in Figure 23.6 overlaps with policy sectors *a* and *b* in Figure 23.7. This illustrates that different types of policy combinations may be required for similar kinds of imbalances or economic unhappiness. This takes us to a related issue known as the *assignment problem* as discussed in Box 23.2.

23.4 ADVANCED TOPICS ON DEVALUATION

23.4.1 The Laursen–Metzler Effect

An important underlying assumption in evaluating the effect of a nominal devaluation and the consequent change in a country's TOT as discussed earlier is that the allocation of income over consumption expenditure and savings do not change. A TOT change only affects consumers' allocation of expenditure on domestic and the foreign goods. To explain, note that a devaluation of domestic currency worsens India's TOT (or raises the relative price, p). This reduces its real expenditure proportionately at the initial level of its national income. Thus, there is no immediate adjustment in aggregate savings by Indian consumers. Aggregate savings change only subsequently when the national income changes resulting in an adjustment in aggregate expenditure. But this need not be the case. An increase in the relative price of foreign goods vis-à-vis domestic goods may have a direct bearing on savings. Part of the real income shock due to the increased price may be borne by reducing savings instead of being absorbed entirely through a proportionate decline in the real aggregate expenditure. That is, aggregate expenditure may *rise* with the rise in the relative price of foreign goods *even at the initial income level.* This had been pointed out by Laursen and Metzler. In such situations, the effective demand equation (23.4) should be rewritten as:

$$Y_i = \overline{E} + E_i(Y_i, p) + TB_i, \frac{\partial E_i}{\partial p} > 0 \quad (23.15)$$

Box 23.2 Assignment Problem and the Principle of Effective Market Classification

In a decentralized economy the central bank determines (or manages) the exchange rate and the government or the fiscal authority determines the fiscal policy or tax and expenditure through its budgetary provisions. Often these two authorities do not act in a coordinated way. In such a case it is often difficult to decide which authority should be assigned to correct the internal balance and which one to correct the external balance. This is known as the *assignment problem* and was first coined by Mundell in the context of fiscal and monetary policies under a pegged exchange rate. His solution was the *principle of effective market classification*, which means that each authority should be assigned to maintain the balance on which its policy instrument has the largest impact. This choice, however, depends on the parametric configurations of the economy. Suppose the central bank is to manage the external balance and the government the internal balance. The central bank devalues (or revalues) whenever a trade deficit (or surplus) arises, whereas the government raises (or lowers) its expenditure whenever the effective demand falls short of (or exceeds) the full employment output level. Starting from a position of trade deficit but internal balance, it is easy to check that this assignment rule can work to attain both the balances through successive adjustments in the policy instruments only if the Y_iY_i curve in Figure 23.6 is steeper than the $TB_i = 0$ curve. Otherwise, this assignment rule will result in a divergent adjustment process. In such a case, the central bank (and its exchange rate policy) should be assigned the task of maintaining the internal balance and the government and its expenditure policy should take care of any trade deficit or surplus.

where, TB_i is as defined in equation (23.5). It is then easy to verify that a nominal devaluation expands the national income by a larger magnitude when this Laursen–Metzler effect, $\frac{\partial E_i}{\partial p} > 0$, is taken into account:

$$dY_i = \frac{M_i\left[\frac{1}{\alpha}\varepsilon_u + \varepsilon_i - 1\right] + \frac{\partial E_i}{\partial p}}{s_i + m_i}de \tag{23.16}$$

Improvement in trade balance, on the other hand, will be smaller in magnitude as the larger income effect raises the demand for imports subsequent to income expansion by a larger magnitude than in the absence of such an effect.

23.4.2 Non-traded Good, Real Exchange Rate, and Devaluation

For reasons explained in Chapter 7, if some goods that are produced in an economy are non-traded, the effect of a nominal devaluation of the domestic currency on the country's trade balance essentially depends on how the relative price of the traded to the non-traded goods changes and consequently how the resources are reallocated across these sectors. We explain this dimension of the effect of a nominal devaluation following the analysis of Ronald Jones and Max Corden (1976), based on the two-good analytical framework of a small open economy as outlined in Chapter 7. Suppose India produces a composite traded good *T*—which is a composite of all goods that it trades with the rest of the world—and a non-traded good (N). These goods are produced by the same set of factors, labour and capital. Suppose, the money wage is predetermined at a level $\overline{W}$. Assume that this level of wage is just sufficient to ensure full employment of labour. However, the money wage rigidity prevents automatic adjustment of excess demand and excess supply of labour that any policy change may result in. Given the target of maintaining full employment, a nominal devaluation thus has to be followed by an appropriate fiscal policy.

To fix the idea, consider the following set of conditions to specify this composite traded good non-traded good framework as discussed in Chapter 7:

$$P_T = a_{LT}\overline{W} + a_{KT}r \tag{23.17}$$

$$P_N = a_{LN}\overline{W} + a_{KN}r \tag{23.18}$$

$$a_{ij} = a_{ij}(\overline{W}/r),\ i = L, K;\ j = T, N \tag{23.19}$$

Note that the money wage rigidity now makes the price of the non-traded good cost determined. Given the fixed exchange rate, the rupee price and the dollar price of the composite traded good, P_T and P_T^* respectively, are related as:

$$P_T = eP_T^* \tag{23.20}$$

A devaluation raises the rupee-price of the composite traded good proportionately and consequently raises the rate of return to capital in India. This in turn raises the capital cost of producing the non-traded good and consequently its competitive price. Thus, a nominal devaluation of the rupee raises both the prices. If the composite traded good is relatively capital-intensive, then the relative price of the composite traded good, $\frac{eP_T^*}{P_N}$, or the real exchange rate (R), rises. Algebraically, as shown in Appendix A23:

$$\hat{R} \equiv \hat{P}_T - \hat{P}_N = \frac{(\theta_{KT} - \theta_{KN})}{\theta_{KT}}\hat{e} \tag{23.21}$$

Note that the dollar price of the composite traded good does not change under the assumption that India is a price taker in the world market. Thus, a devaluation raises the value of the real exchange rate (or depreciates it) if $\theta_{KT} > \theta_{KN}$. Resources in such a case shift to the traded sector as its production expands, but the demand switches in favour of the non-traded good as its price falls. This creates a situation of excess demand for labour. To maintain internal balance, the government must reduce the demand for the non-traded good through a contractionary fiscal policy or expenditure reducing policy. The aggregate expenditure (E_i) thus falls below the produced income (Y_i) and, consequently, a trade surplus develops:

$$Y_i - E_i = TB_i > 0 \tag{23.22}$$

Note that under small country assumption the aggregate value of output and income remain the same.

Alternatively, had the non-traded good been relatively capital-intensive, $\theta_{KT} - \theta_{KN}$, the real exchange rate would have appreciated leading to a situation of excess supply of labour at the given money wage. To maintain internal balance, the government would have to pursue an expansionary fiscal policy and thereby raise the demand for the non-traded good. In such a case, the economy would spend more than its produced income, $Y_i < E_i$, causing a trade deficit.

In sum, given a rigid money wage and the production of non-traded good(s), whether a nominal devaluation of the domestic currency improves the trade balance or not depends on how it changes the real exchange rate, which, in turn, depends on the relative capital intensity of the (composite) traded good vis-à-vis the non-traded good(s). A nominal devaluation improves the trade balance only when the composite traded good is relatively capital-intensive. This is known as the Jones–Corden condition.

APPENDIX A23

I. Elasticity Approach

With constant prices normalized to unity and aggregate national income held constant at the full employment level, India's trade balance depends only on the rupee-dollar exchange rate:

$$TB_i = M_u(e) - eM_i(e) \tag{A23.1}$$

Differentiating with respect to the exchange rate we get:

$$\frac{\partial TB_i}{\partial e} = \frac{\partial M_u}{\partial e} - e\frac{\partial M_i}{\partial e} - M_i$$

$$= M_i\left[\frac{1}{M_i}\frac{\partial M_u}{\partial e} - \frac{e}{M_i}\frac{\partial M_i}{\partial e} - 1\right] \tag{A23.2}$$

If initially trade is not balanced, then $eM_i \neq M_u$. Let $eM_i = \alpha M_u$. Initial trade deficit (surplus) for India then would mean a greater (less) than one value of α. Substitution of this in equation (A23.2) yields:

$$\frac{\partial TB_i}{\partial e} = M_i\left[\frac{e}{\alpha M_u}\frac{\partial M_u}{\partial e} - \frac{e}{M_i}\frac{\partial M_i}{\partial e} - 1\right]$$

$$\Rightarrow \frac{\partial TB_i}{\partial e} = M_i\left[\frac{1}{\alpha}\varepsilon_u + \varepsilon - 1\right] \tag{A23.3}$$

Hence, a nominal devaluation improves the trade balance if $\frac{1}{\alpha}\varepsilon_u + \varepsilon > 1$.

II. *Synthesis Approach*: Slopes of Y_iY_i and $TB_i = 0$ Curves

Consider the effective demand and balanced trade conditions in equations (23.4) and (23.5) reproduced here:

$$Y_i = \overline{E} + E_i(Y_i) + M_u(p) - pM_i(Y_i, p) \qquad \text{(A23.4)}$$

$$TB_i = M_u(p) - pM_i(Y_i, p) = 0 \qquad \text{(A23.5)}$$

Total differentiation of equation (A23.4) yields:

$$dY_i = d\overline{E}_i + \frac{\partial E_i}{\partial Y_i}dY_i + \frac{\partial M_u}{\partial p}dp - M_i dp - p\left[\frac{\partial M_i}{\partial Y_i}dY_i + \frac{\partial M_i}{\partial p}dp\right]$$

For $d\overline{E}_i = 0$, and noting that $\frac{\partial E_i}{\partial Y_i} \equiv c_i$, we get the slope of the internal balance as:

$$(1 - c_i + m_i)dY_i = \frac{\partial M_u}{\partial p}dp - M_i dp - p\frac{\partial M_i}{\partial p}$$

$$\Rightarrow (s_i + m_i)dY_i = M_i\left[\frac{1}{M_i}\frac{\partial M_u}{\partial p} - 1 - \frac{p}{M_i}\frac{\partial M_i}{\partial p}\right]dp$$

Using $eM_i = \alpha M_i$, this boils down to the slope of the internal balance as:

$$\left.\frac{dY_i}{dp}\right|_{Y_iY_i} = \frac{M_i\left[\frac{1}{\alpha}\varepsilon_u + \varepsilon_i - 1\right]}{s_i + m_i}$$

On the other hand, totally differentiating equation (A23.5) we obtain:

$$0 = \frac{\partial M_u}{\partial p}dp - M_i dp - p\left[\frac{\partial M_i}{\partial Y_i}dY_i + \frac{\partial M_i}{\partial p}dp\right]$$

$$\Rightarrow p\frac{\partial M_i}{\partial Y_i}dY_i = \frac{\partial M_u}{\partial p}dp - M_i dp - p\frac{\partial M_i}{\partial p}dp$$

$$\Rightarrow m_i dY_i = M_i\left[\frac{1}{M_i}\frac{\partial M_u}{\partial p} - 1 - \frac{p}{M_i}\frac{\partial M_i}{\partial p}\right]dp \qquad \text{(A23.6)}$$

But now, $eM_i = M_u$ along the external balance curve so that the above boils down to:

$$\left.\frac{dY_i}{dp}\right|_{TB_i=0} = \frac{M_i\left[\varepsilon_u + \varepsilon_i - 1\right]}{m_i}$$

III. Devaluation and Trade Balance

With constant prices, the relative price changes proportionately with the change in the value of the exchange rate: $\hat{p} = \hat{e}$. Using this, total differentiation of the trade balance condition $TB_i = M_u(p) - pM_i(Y_i, p)$ yields:

$$dTB_i = \frac{\partial M_u}{\partial p}dp - M_i dp - p\left[\frac{\partial M_i}{\partial Y_i}dY_i + \frac{\partial M_i}{\partial p}dp\right]$$

$$= M_i\left[\frac{1}{M_i}\frac{\partial M_u}{\partial p} - \frac{p}{M_i}\frac{\partial M_i}{\partial p} - 1\right]dp - p\frac{\partial M_i}{\partial Y_i}dY_i \qquad \text{(A23.7)}$$

Given the initial trade deficit, $eM_i = \alpha M_u$ with $\alpha < 1$ and by equation (23.6), this boils down to:

$$dTB_i = M_i\left[\frac{1}{\alpha}\varepsilon_u + \varepsilon_i - 1\right]de - m_i dY_i$$

$$= M_i\left[\frac{1}{\alpha}\varepsilon_u + \varepsilon_i - 1\right]de - \frac{m_i}{s_i + m_i}M_i\left[\frac{1}{\alpha}\varepsilon_u + \varepsilon_i - 1\right]de$$

$$= \frac{s_i}{s_i + m_i}M_i\left[\frac{1}{\alpha}\varepsilon_u + \varepsilon_i - 1\right]de$$

IV. Tariff, National Income, and Trade Balance

Under tariff, import expenditure incurred by Indian consumers is evaluated at the tariff-inclusive domestic relative price $p_d = (1 + t)p$. Recall the effective demand condition from equation (23.11) in the text:

$$Y_i = \overline{E} + E_i(Y_i) + M_u(p) - p_d M_i(Y_i, p_d)$$

Total differentiation with constant commodity prices and a pegged exchange rate yields:

$$dY_i = d\overline{E}_i + \frac{\partial E_i}{\partial Y_i}dY_i + \frac{\partial M_u}{\partial p}dp - M_i dp_d - p_d\left[\frac{\partial M_i}{\partial Y_i}dY_i + \frac{\partial M_i}{\partial p_d}dp_d\right]$$

Assuming that initially there was no tariff, and substituting $d\bar{E}_i = 0$, $dp = 0, dp_d = pdt$ and the initial condition $p_d = p$, this boils down to:

$$dY_i = \frac{\partial E_i}{\partial Y_i} dY_i - pM_i dt - p\left[\frac{\partial M_i}{\partial Y_i} dY_i + p\frac{\partial M_i}{\partial p_d} dt\right]$$

$$\Rightarrow (s_i + m_i) dY_i = -pM_i dt - p^2 \frac{\partial M_i}{\partial p_d} dt = pM_i \left[-\frac{p}{M_i}\frac{\partial M_i}{\partial p_d} - 1\right] dt$$

$$\Rightarrow \frac{dY_i}{dt} = \frac{(\varepsilon_i - 1)\alpha M_u}{s_i + m_i} \tag{A23.8}$$

which is equation (23.12) in the text.

But the trade balance should be evaluated at the world relative price as in equation (23.9) in the text and reproduced here, since India as a whole pays this price to the rest of the world for its imports:

$$TB_i = M_u(p) - pM_i(Y_i, p_d) \tag{A23.9}$$

Again total differentiation yields:

$$dTB_i = \frac{\partial M_u}{\partial p} dp - M_i dp - p\left[\frac{\partial M_i}{\partial Y_i} dY_i + \frac{\partial M_i}{\partial p_d} dp_d\right]$$

By the initial conditions and relations as above this reduces to:

$$dTB_i = -p\left[\frac{\partial M_i}{\partial Y_i} dY_i + \frac{\partial M_i}{\partial p} dp\right] = -m_i dY_i - pM_i \frac{p}{M_i}\frac{\partial M_i}{\partial p_d} dt$$

$$= \left[-\frac{m_i(\varepsilon_i - 1)\alpha M_u}{s_i + m_i} + \alpha M_u \varepsilon_i\right] dt$$

$$\Rightarrow \frac{dTB_i}{dt} = \frac{(\varepsilon_i s_i + m_i)\alpha M_u}{s_i + m_i} \tag{A23.10}$$

which is equation (23.13) in the text.

V. Devaluation and the Real Exchange Rate

Total differentiation of the zero profit conditions in equations (23.17) and (23.18) yields:

$$\hat{P}_T = \theta_{KT}\hat{r},\ \hat{P}_N = \theta_{KN}\hat{r} \tag{A23.11}$$

Under the small country assumption, $\hat{P}_T = \hat{e}$. Hence, from equation (A23.11) follows that the change in the rate of return to capital is more than proportionate to the rate of devaluation:

$$\hat{r} = \frac{1}{\theta_{KT}}\hat{e} \tag{A23.12}$$

Hence:

$$\hat{R} \equiv \hat{P}_T - \hat{P}_N = (\theta_{KT} - \theta_{KN})\hat{r}$$

$$= \frac{(\theta_{KT} - \theta_{KN})}{\theta_{KT}}\hat{e}$$

SUMMARY POINTS

- BOP adjustment policies primarily target lowering import demand and import expenditure to reduce a country's BOP deficit. The expenditure *reducing* adjustment policy targets reducing aggregate expenditure and consequently import expenditure.
- Expenditure *switching* policies are targeted at inducing domestic consumers to change the composition of their total expenditure away from foreign goods. Exchange rate and tariff policies are examples of expenditure *switching* policies.
- Absorption and elasticity approaches to BOP adjustment policies under a fixed exchange rate rest on some restrictive assumptions. The absorption approach ignores price effects by assuming a fixed TOT. The elasticity approach, on the other hand, is essentially a partial equilibrium analysis whereby it neglects the income effect of expenditure switching policies.
- In the synthesis approach, as long as the tariff proceeds are spent by the government itself and on goods produced abroad, it constitutes an additional leakage from the circular flow of income. In such a case, an import tariff raises the country's national income only if its import demand is elastic.
- But regardless of whether India's import demand is elastic or inelastic, an import tariff unambiguously lowers its trade deficit.
- Macroeconomic policy targets in an open economy have an additional dimension compared to that in a closed economy. Apart from maintaining internal balance or full employment, policies should also target maintaining external balance.
- Given the interdependence of the two balances, there is a *policy conflict* in the sense that a policy change that targets correction for internal imbalance may affect the external balance that may already have been achieved and vice versa. Thus, policymakers need two distinct policies to maintain the two balances simultaneously.
- In some cases, the same set of policy changes may be appropriate for different combinations of imbalances or economic unhappiness. In other cases, different types of policy combinations may be required for similar kinds of imbalances or economic unhappiness.

KEYWORDS

- **Expenditure reducing policy** for BOP adjustment is one that reduces import expenditure and consequently improves the trade balance by reducing aggregate expenditure and absorption of the economy. Examples are income tax, reduction in government expenditure, and a contractionary monetary policy.
- **Expenditure switching policy** for BOP adjustment is one that improves the trade balance by inducing domestic consumers to change the composition of their total expenditure away from foreign goods. Nominal devaluation, import tariffs, and export subsidies are examples of expenditure switching policies.
- **J-curve phenomenon** means that a country's trade balance changes in a J-curve like fashion after a devaluation of its currency. Supply and demand adjust slowly so that immediately following a nominal devaluation the trade deficit of the country worsens, but this improves over time as demand and supply adjust fully to price changes resulting in larger elasticity values.
- **Laursen–Metzler effect** postulates that part of a real income shock due to increased price is borne by reduction of savings resulting in aggregate expenditure (or absorption) rising with the rise in the relative price of foreign goods even at the initial income level.
- **Jones–Corden condition** states that a nominal devaluation of currency improves the country's trade balance by raising the real exchange rate only if the traded goods are capital-intensive relative to non-traded goods.

EXERCISES

1. Consider the following import demand functions for India and France:

   $$M_i = \frac{100}{e},\ M_f = 50 + 3e$$

   (a) Write down the trade balance condition for India expressed in its domestic currency.
   (b) Find out the value of the rupee–euro exchange rate for which trade is balanced.
   (c) If initially the exchange rate is one, what is the value of trade deficit or surplus for India, whichever the case may be?
   (d) If the rupee is devalued vis-à-vis the euro, does India's trade balance improve?
2. Suppose in the above example India's imports from France depend in addition on its national income such that $M_i = \frac{100 + Y_i}{e}$. If initially there was a tariff on imports from France, does India's national income rise when this rate is raised? What would be the impact of this increase in tariff rate on India's balance of trade with France?
3. When and why should tariff revenue be subtracted from the total expenditure to arrive at the effective demand for domestically produced goods?

4. Show that a tariff improves the trade balance by the exact amount of the tariff revenue when import demand is unitary elastic, by more than the tariff revenue when import demand is elastic, and less than the tariff revenue when import demand is inelastic.

   [Hints: Use initial free trade condition $t = 0$ so that $dt = t$ and $pM_i = M_u$ to rewrite condition (23.13).]

5. Write down the effective demand condition when the tariff proceeds are spent by the government entirely on domestic goods. What will be the effect of an increase in the tariff rate on the national income and trade balance of a country?

6. Work out the effect of a tariff on the trade balance if tariff proceeds are redistributed in a lump-sum manner to domestic citizens.

7. [Advanced] Suppose India subsidizes its exporters at the ad-valorem rate s such that the (relative) price that US buyers pay for goods imported from India is $p_u = \frac{eP_u}{(1-s)P_i} = \frac{p}{1-s}$.

   Find out the effect of such an export subsidy on India's national income and trade balance assuming an initial free trade situation.

   [Hints: The effective demand condition remains the same as under free trade except for the fact that US import demand now depends on p_u. On the other hand, India's trade balance is now evaluated at p_u since India receives the price p_u per unit of its goods sold abroad. Now, India's national income will increase unambiguously, but its trade balance improvement depends on the value of US import demand elasticity. Thus the effects are just opposite to those of an import tariff.]

8. In a particular year Japan experiences a deficit in trade with China though it is able to maintain its internal balance. If the Japanese yen was pegged vis-à-vis Chinese yuan at an over-valued rate, should you recommend a devaluation of the yen to attain the external balance? Does this expenditure-switching policy help Japan to maintain both the balances? Explain.

9. Explain why by pursuing only an expenditure-reducing policy or an expenditure-switching policy a country cannot attain both internal and external balances simultaneously.

10. In a particular year India experienced both trade deficit and unemployment. RBI then devalued the rupee and the Government of India raised its expenditure. Yet, both these imbalances could not be corrected. Why?

11. [Advanced] Suppose India produces a composite traded good with labour, capital, and an imported input. It also produces a non-traded good with labour and capital. The money wage is rigid and the Government of India maintains full employment (or internal balance) through a fiscal policy. In such a context, when does a nominal devaluation of the rupee improve its trade balance? Compare your condition with the Jones–Corden condition. How does your result change when the non-traded good also uses the same imported input in its production?

12. In the above context, what would have been the impact of LERMS that was implemented in India during 1992–93 as discussed in Chapter 22 on India's trade balance?

SUGGESTED READING

Caves, R.E., J. Frankel, and R.W. Jones. (1995). *World Trade and Payments*. New York: HarperCollins College Publishers.

Dornbusch, R. (1980). *Open Economy Macroeconomics.* New York: Basic Books.

Advanced Reading

Branson, W. (1983). 'Economic Structure and Policy for External Balance', in A. W. Hooke, ed., Exchange Rate Regimes and Policy Interdependence (International Monetary Fund, 1983), pp. 39–74.

Corden, W.M. (1960). 'The Geometric Representation of Policies to Attain Internal and External Balance', *Review of Economic Studies*, 28: 1–22.

Jones, R.W. and W.M. Corden (1976). 'Devaluation, Non-flexible Prices and the Trade Balance for a Small Economy', *Canadian Journal of Economics*, 9: 150–61.

Meade, J. (1951). *The Theory of International Economic Policy: I. The Balance of Payments.* London and New York: Oxford University Press.

Mundell, R.A. (1968). *International Economics* (chapter 8). New York: The Macmillan Company.

Salter, W.E. (1959). 'Internal and External Balance: The Role of Price and Expenditure Effects', *Economic Record*, 35: 226–38.

Swan, T. (1955). 'Longer-Run Problems of the Balance of Payments', Paper delivered at the Congress of the Australian and New Zealand Association for the Advancement of Science. Published in H.W. Arndt and W.M. Corden (eds). (1963). *The Australian Economy: A Volume of Readings*. Melbourne: Cheshire Press, pp. 384–95.

Tinbergen, J. (1952). *On the Theory of Economic Policy*. Amsterdam: North Holland.

24 Money, Price, and Exchange Rate

This chapter discusses three important elements of the analyses of BOP adjustment and exchange rate determination that have been set aside so far in the earlier chapters: flexible commodity prices, monetary policy of a country's central bank, and capital account transactions such as capital mobility or asset trading. Without these elements being explicitly taken into account, we have an incomplete analysis of BOP adjustment and a theory of exchange rate determination. The elasticity and absorption (or income) approaches and their synthesis discussed in Chapter 23 merely remain as theories of adjustment in balance of trade rather than adjustment in BOP without consideration of capital account transactions.

We consider two variants of these relationships. First is the monetarist approach to BOP that, in contrast to the elasticity and the absorption approaches, postulates that a BOP imbalance is essentially a monetary phenomenon and is *transient in nature*. By this monetarists in the tradition of David Hume mean that BOP imbalances simply reflect monetary disequilibrium and adjustments of actual and desired holding of money and other stock of assets rather than being permanent flows determined by the national income and the corresponding absorption. Price change constitutes an important element of monetary adjustment in this so-called monetarist model, which is based on the quantity theory of money and wage-price flexibility in the tradition of classical macroeconomics.

Second is the Mundell–Flemming tradition of monetary approach under the Keynesian assumption of sticky wages and prices with capital mobility. Income change is the key element in monetary adjustments in this approach. This approach is essentially the open economy extension of the Keynesian IS–LM framework, known popularly as the Mundell–Flemming model. The main point of discussion here is the relative efficacy of fiscal and monetary policies in changing output levels, with BOP adjusting under a fixed exchange rate through *endogenous* capital mobility.

Another dimension of discussions in this chapter is the monetarist approach to exchange rate determination. The exchange rate of a country and its price level are closely linked with domestic money supply. Under clean float, changes in money supply change the interest earnings on domestic assets relative to earnings from foreign asset holdings. The portfolio of assets held by wealth holders thus changes, which affects the demand for foreign currency and consequently the exchange rate. This is the essence of the monetarist or asset approach to

International Economics. Rajat Acharyya, Oxford University Press. © Oxford University Press 2022.
DOI: 10.1093/oso/9780192865144.003.0024

exchange rate determination that we discuss in the later part of this chapter. These discussions also suggest that it is not possible for a country to target the exchange rate, run an independent monetary policy, and allow full capital mobility simultaneously. This is known as the *impossible trinity* paradigm of an open economy.

We further discuss the theoretical validity and empirical support for purchasing power parity (PPP), which is one of the building blocks of the monetarist approach to BOP and exchange rate determination. Purchasing power parity is also known as the Law of One Price: due to international arbitrage, bananas must be sold everywhere at the same price. One implication of this purchasing power parity and the Law of One Price is complete exchange rate pass-through by which exchange rate variations must be fully reflected in price changes. But neither purchasing power parity nor the exchange rate pass-through seem to be self-enforcing propositions. There are many plausible explanations for this purchasing power parity puzzle, some of which we elaborate upon in this chapter.

24.1 THE MONETARIST APPROACH TO BOP

In contrast to the absorption and elasticity approaches, the essence of the monetarist approach is that any BOP imbalance is only a *temporary* phenomenon that reflects an adjustment of the actual to desired holding of money and other stocks of assets by wealth holders. That is, neither is a trade deficit (or surplus) permanent nor can it be managed through changing national income and corresponding absorption. It is purely a *monetary phenomenon*. Flexible commodity prices, however, play an important role, as we will see below, in such automatic monetary adjustments that restore BOP equilibrium. This basic idea originated with the price-specie flow mechanism of David Hume, who was an eighteenth century philosopher and economist. Later in the twentieth century, Robert Mundell revived his idea and translated it into an income-specie flow mechanism under the assumption of constant commodity prices in the Keynesian tradition. His was an attempt to reconcile the monetarist approach with the Keynesian income approach. We first describe Hume's price-specie flow mechanism of automatic adjustments in BOP and then discuss the basic tenets and postulates of latter formulations of the monetarist approach. Mundell's synthesis is discussed in the next section.

24.1.1 Hume's Price-Specie Flow Mechanism

In seventeenth and eighteenth century England there emerged a school of thought known as mercantilism, which floated the idea of maintaining a trade surplus as a means of acquiring precious metals like gold and silver, or the specie, and increasing a country's wealth. Thus, according to mercantilists, exports should be promoted and imports should be discouraged. David Hume criticized this idea by arguing that this policy could not work in the long run because a country's stock of gold will automatically adjust to its demand through changes in commodity prices. Suppose a country pursues export promotion and import restriction policies to create a BOP surplus. The country thus experiences an inflow of gold and other specie. This inflow of gold causes the actual holdings to exceed the desired holdings of gold by domestic citizens and induces them to spend more on both domestic and foreign goods. Imports rise whereas increased spending that raises prices of domestic goods in the short-run lowers exports because foreigners now demand less. BOP of the country worsens and specie flows out of the country. People reduce their spending as a consequence and prices fall. The outflow of specie will continue till prices return to their original levels and BOP returns to its equilibrium. In the long run, the country's stock of gold or specie will return to its initial level. This is Hume's price-specie flow mechanism by which it is not possible for a country to acquire specie or wealth through a BOP surplus. This price-specie flow mechanism, which is the cornerstone of the monetarist model, depends on several crucial assumptions to which we now turn.

24.1.2 Building Blocks of the Monetarist Model

There are three basic assumptions or building blocks of the monetarist model. First is the perfect wage-price flexibility, typical of a classical macroeconomic system. This guarantees that the entire workforce will always be fully employed and the aggregate output and income will remain invariant at the full employment level. So in our two-country example:

$$Y_i = \bar{Y}_i,\ Y_u = \bar{Y}_u \tag{24.1}$$

The second crucial monetarist assumption is that of purchasing power parity, which means that:

$$P_i = eP_u \tag{24.2}$$

where, P_i and P_u are the price levels in India and the United State, expressed in their respective domestic currencies. This assumption, however, requires full flexibility of prices in the two countries. It states that for any given rupee-dollar exchange rate, a change in the price level in the United States is matched by a proportionate change in the price level in India, and vice-versa. However, this need not always be the case. But if P_i and P_u are considered to be the rupee and dollar price of the same good, say bananas, produced in the two countries, then it may seem logical that the rupee price of bananas produced in the United States, eP_u, should be the same as the price of bananas produced in India. PPP then can be interpreted as the

> **Box 24.1** Mercantilism and International Trade Policy
>
> Mercantilism was the first systematic body of thought on international trade issues that emerged during seventeenth and eighteenth centuries England in particular. The mercantile system served the interests of merchants and producers such as the British East India Company. In exchange for paying taxes to support the armies of the nation-states, the mercantile classes induced governments to enact policies that would protect their business interests against foreign competition. Two key ideas are associated with mercantilism. First, a nation should promote favourable balance of trade through export promotion and import restriction. Second, a nation should encourage a particular commodity composition of trade in which exports of manufacturing commodities should be promoted and imports of raw materials should be allowed. But imports of manufacturing should be prohibited. Better employment opportunities in manufacturing than in mining and the need to develop domestic industries to strengthen the nation-state were the primary justifications for such a particular commodity composition of trade.

Law of One Price and should follow from international arbitrage, provided that there are no transport costs and other barriers to trade. The other implication of the PPP condition is that if the rupee depreciates vis-à-vis the dollar (that is, the value of e rises), but the price of bananas in the United States does not change, then the rupee price of US bananas (and Indian bananas) sold in India should rise proportionately. This is known as the complete exchange rate pass-through. However, both large deviations from PPP or the Law of One Price and incomplete (and sometimes perverse) exchange rate pass-through have been empirically observed. We shall return to these empirical observations and the plausible explanations in the later part of this chapter.

The third crucial assumption of the monetarist approach is non-sterilization of the flow of foreign currencies. Sterilization is a process by which the central bank of a country adjusts domestic lending and borrowing to match the foreign exchange reserves in a way that keeps the stock of high-powered money or the monetary base unchanged. This can be explained in terms of the following balance sheet of a central bank:

$$NFACB + DC \equiv H \tag{24.3}$$

where, $NFACB$ is net foreign assets (or foreign exchange reserves) held by the central bank as defined earlier in Chapter 20; DC is the domestic credit extended by the central bank through commercial banks; and H is high-powered money or the monetary base of a country. High-powered money is the total currency issued by the central bank.[1] This is a liability of the central bank. On the other hand, $NFACB$ and DC are the total assets of the central bank.

Now recall from the discussion in Chapter 20 that a change in net foreign assets (or foreign exchange reserves) held by the central bank, $\Delta NFACB$, is the official settlement term or the *accommodating* capital flow that indicates a country's BOP position. Thus, from the balance sheet identity of a central bank emerges a relationship between a country's BOP deficit or surplus, a change in domestic credit, and a change in the stock of high-powered money:

$$\Delta NFACB + \Delta DC \equiv \Delta H \tag{24.4}$$

A BOP surplus means $\Delta NFACB > 0$. That is, the country buys foreign assets or accumulates foreign exchange reserves. If domestic credit is held constant by the central bank, $\Delta DC = 0$, then the stock of high-powered money rises. On the other hand, if the country experiences a BOP deficit, net foreign assets or foreign exchange reserves decline, which in turn lower the stock of high-powered money. That is, by keeping the domestic credit unchanged, the central bank allows its monetary base to change with the change in foreign exchange reserves. This is called non-sterilization of reserve flows. Algebraically, under non-sterilization:

$$\Delta NFACB \equiv \Delta H \tag{24.5}$$

[1] The total money supply in a country is much larger than this monetary base or high-powered money, because one unit of currency changes hands more than once through a commercial bank's lending. By the M1 definition, the total money supply is currency held by the public plus demand deposits. Given the money multiplier, larger the monetary base, larger is the money supply in a country.

The exact mechanism by which the stock of high-powered money or the monetary base changes with the BOP position and accommodating capital flows can be explained as follows. Recall from the discussion of exchange rate regimes in Chapter 22 that a BOP imbalance is not automatically corrected under a pegged exchange rate. A BOP deficit means an excess demand for foreign currency, which puts an upward pressure on the exchange rate. To defend the pegged rate, the central bank must then sell foreign currency from its reserves in exchange for domestic currency. Thus, domestic currency is withdrawn from circulation leading to a fall in the monetary base and correspondingly in money supply. On the other hand, a BOP surplus means an excess supply of foreign currency. The central bank must now buy foreign currency to defend the pegged exchange rate in exchange for the domestic currency. Thus, more domestic currencies are put in circulation now, which means a rise in the monetary base and consequently the money supply. That is, under non-sterilization of reserve flows, money supply contracts in a BOP deficit country and expands in a BOP surplus economy. On this non-sterilization process rests Hume's price-specie flow mechanism and the basic tenet of the monetarist approach that a BOP surplus or deficit is essentially a monetary phenomenon.

If, however, the central bank wishes to sterilize the reserves flow, that is, does not wish the monetary base to change with the BOP position, it adjusts its domestic credit accordingly. For example, in case of a BOP deficit, the sale of foreign currency to defend the pegged exchange rate is matched by an increase in domestic credit by the central bank through its open market operations like buying of bonds previously issued by it to the public. Through such extension of domestic credit, the domestic currency is again put back into circulation. Thus, under sterilization:

$$\Delta NFACB \equiv -\Delta DC \tag{24.6}$$

There are, however, practical limits to and fiscal costs of sterilization. Sometimes, sterilization may be self-defeating as well. We will return to these issues later.

24.1.3 Monetary Adjustment under Fixed Exchange Rate

Given the above set of assumptions, the starting point of the monetarist approach is the quantity theory of money, which in our example of Indo-US trade is described by the following set of conditions:

$$H_i = k_i P_i Y_i,\ H_u = k_u P_u Y_u \tag{24.7}$$

where, k_i and k_u are constant fractions of total expenditures that people in aggregate in India and the United States respectively, desire to hold in their respective domestic currencies (that is, in cash) to carry out necessary transactions during the time gap between receipts and payments. Thus, the right hand side in quantity equations for India and the United States represent transactions demand for money. These are the stocks of domestic currencies that people desire to hold. On the other hand, on the left hand side we have the actual stocks of currencies or high-powered money issued by the central banks in the two countries. Since currencies issued by the central bank that are in circulation must be held by some people or the other, equation

(24.7) describes money market equilibria in India and the United States: the actual and desired holding of stock of money must be equal at equilibrium.[2]

This quantity theory of money can also be interpreted as the product market equilibrium in a closed economy that requires that the full employment output must be equal to real expenditure or demand for output. Substituting equation (24.1) in equation (24.7) under the assumption of perfect wage-price flexibility, and defining $v_i \equiv \frac{1}{k_i}$ and $v_u \equiv \frac{1}{k_u}$ as the expenditure (or income) velocity of money, or the number of times a unit of currency changes hands through transactions (or purchase and sale of goods) during a given time period, in India and the United States respectively, the quantity equations can be rewritten as:

$$\bar{Y}_i = \frac{v_i H_i}{P_i},\ \bar{Y}_u = \frac{v_u H_u}{P_u} \tag{24.8}$$

The right hand side in both the equations in (24.8) now represent *real* expenditure on domestically produced goods in India and the United States. Note that aggregate expenditure cannot exceed total money supply, which is the monetary base or the stock of money in circulation times the (average) number of times a unit of currency changes hands. Thus, equation (24.8) represents product market equilibrium in the two countries as well: full employment output levels equal real expenditures or aggregate demand.

Two comments are warranted at this point. First, the quantity equation of money indicates a proportional relationship between the stock of high-powered money (or money supply) and the price level of a country. As is evident from equation (24.7), an increase in H_i (and a corresponding increase in the total money supply), raises the price level in India proportionately since by definition k_i is constant and the output remains invariant at the full employment level by the assumption of wage-price flexibility. On the other hand, to keep the demand for labour at the full employment level, money wage rises proportionately as well. That is, an increase in the stock of money raises (proportionately) only the money variables. This is the *neutrality of money* postulate of classical macroeconomics or the monetarist approach. This proportionality rule also means that the aggregate demand or real expenditure always equals the full employment output level. Thus, product market equilibrium can always be maintained.

Second, the stock of high-powered money changes with the excess demand for money, which by equations (24.7) and (24.8) means:

$$\dot{H}_i = P_i Y_i - v_i H_i,\ \dot{H}_u = P_u Y_u - v_u H_u \tag{24.9}$$

That is, excess demands for money in aggregate in India and the United States, $P_i Y_i - v_i H_i > 0$ and $P_u Y_u - v_u H_u > 0$, are matched by more currencies being put in circulation by the Reserve Bank of India (RBI) and the Federal Reserve Bank of the United States respectively. Thus, the money market (as well as the product market) equilibrium conditions in the two countries under autarchy can be stated as $\dot{H}_i = 0$ and $\dot{H}_u = 0$.

[2] We here assume away demand deposits held by people in commercial banks. Thus, high-powered money is also the total money supply by the M1 definition.

But when trade takes place, the above domestic market clearing conditions need not hold because total national income is now spent on both domestic and foreign goods. That is, the aggregate expenditure in India, vH_i, now includes import expenditure by Indian consumers. Similarly, domestic output is also sold abroad, that is, exported. Thus:

$$P_iY_i - P_iM_u = v_iH_i - eP_uM_i\,,\; P_uY_u - P_uM_i = v_uH_u - P_iM_u \tag{24.10}$$

Rearranging, and using equation (24.9), this boils down to:

$$\dot{H}_i = TB_i\,,\; \dot{H}_u = TB_u \tag{24.11}$$

Thus, now an excess demand for money can be met through selling a larger value of goods abroad than the expenditure on foreign goods, that is, running a trade surplus. However, since in this two-country world one country's trade surplus is the other country's trade deficit and in equilibrium such surplus and deficit must match each other so the world equilibrium condition is stated as the world value of output must equal the world expenditure (or money supply):

$$P_iY_i + eP_uY_u = v_iH_i + ev_uH_u \tag{24.12}$$

The left hand side is the world value of output, whereas the right hand side is the world stock of money, both measured in Indian currency. Alternatively, the above world equilibrium condition can be stated as:

$$\dot{H}_i = -\,e\dot{H}_u \tag{24.13}$$

These alternative statements of the world equilibrium condition essentially follow from Walras' Law described in Chapter 2. An excess demand for money (or trade surplus) in one country must be exactly matched by a corresponding excess supply (or trade deficit) in the other.

International trade equalizes prices of traded goods. Using the PPP condition in equation (24.2), the common post-trade price level measured in Indian currency (hereafter, rupee price level) is determined by the world money supply and world output level:

$$P_i = \frac{v_iH_i + ev_uH_u}{Y_i + Y_u} \tag{24.14}$$

The short-run equilibrium with a trade surplus for India and a corresponding trade deficit for the United States is shown in Figure 24.1. The excess demand functions $\dot{H}_i$ and $(-\,e\dot{H}_u)$ are plotted against the rupee price level. Note that both $\dot{H}_i$ and $e\dot{H}_u$, given the PPP condition, vary positively with the rupee price level. Domestic price levels in the two countries (measured in Indian currency) at the no-trade equilibria are E_i and E_u, for which $\dot{H}_i = 0$ and $e\dot{H}_u = 0$. When trade opens up, world equilibrium is attained at the point of intersection of $\dot{H}_i$ and $(-\,e\dot{H}_u)$ curves, E_S, where the equilibrium condition in equation (24.13) is satisfied. Note that

India having a trade surplus in Figure 24.1 is just one of the three possibilities, the other being the United States having a trade surplus, or trade being balanced at the short-run equilibrium. The equilibrium rupee price level at the depicted short-run world equilibrium is P_i^*.

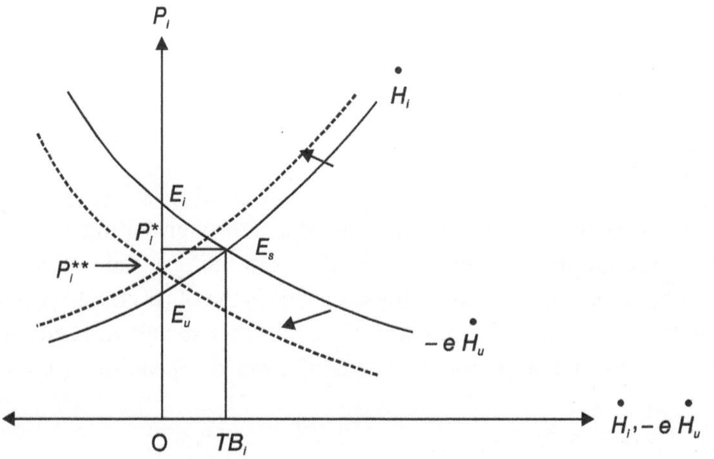

Figure 24.1 Short-Run Equilibrium

But this trade surplus for India and the corresponding trade deficit in the United States are purely temporary as automatic adjustments in the money supply will result in a trade balance in both these countries. The process of adjustment is as follows. A trade surplus for India means a flow of USD from the United States to India, which puts a downward pressure on the rupee-dollar exchange rate. RBI thus starts buying dollars in exchange for rupees. That is, now more Indian currency is put in circulation, which under the assumption of non-sterilization, raises the stock of the Indian currency (and corresponding money supply in India). This shifts the $\dot{H}_i$ curve up and to the left. On the other hand, an outflow of dollars due to trade deficit for the United States lowers the stock of currency in circulation or high-powered money there. This shifts the $(-e\dot{H}_u)$ curve down and to the left. The process continues till the two curves intersect each other on the vertical axis as shown by the two broken curves. Thus, trade is balanced in the long run through these automatic adjustments in money stock in the two countries. This indicates that BOP is essentially a monetary phenomenon, which is the essence of the monetarist approach.

But whether the rupee price level falls (as shown in Figure 24.1) or rises depends on the expenditure velocity in the two countries. Dollar outflow and inflow simply redistribute the total world stock of currency in the two countries. Yet the total money supply may change if $v_i \neq v_u$. Suppose, $v_i > v_u$. Then a redistribution of high-powered money from the United States to India raises expenditure in India more than it lowers expenditure in the United States. Thus, at the initial rupee price level (and corresponding dollar price level by the PPP condition) arises an excess demand for goods in the world market. This raises the rupee price level. By similar reasoning if $v_i < v_u$, a redistribution of high-powered money from the United States to India creates an excess supply of goods in the world market, which lowers the rupee price level. All these can be algebraically verified from equation (24.14), given that $dH_i = -edH_u$:

$$dP_i = \frac{(v_i - v_u)}{\bar{Y}_i + \bar{Y}_u} dH_i \quad (24.15)$$

Diagrammatically, the expenditure velocities determine the relative shifts of the $\dot{H}_i$ and the $(-e\dot{H}_u)$ curves. The latter shifts more if $v_i < v_u$. Figure 24.1 is thus drawn on this assumption such that during the monetary adjustment, the $(-e\dot{H}_u)$ curve shifts more than the $\dot{H}_i$ curve resulting in a price fall, $P_i^{**} < P_i^*$.

These automatic adjustment mechanisms under the assumptions of wage-price flexibility, PPP, and non-sterilization of reserve flows, also suggest that the mercantilist idea of export promotion to maintain a trade surplus and acquiring specie will be self-defeating in the long run. Consider, for example, a nominal devaluation of the Indian rupee vis-à-vis the US dollar. Starting from a global trade balance equilibrium with the rupee-dollar exchange rate e_0 and price levels being $P_i^{**} = e_o P_u^{**}$, a devaluation that raises the value of the exchange rate to e_1 shifts the $(-e\dot{H}_u)$ curve to the right in Figure 24.2. A trade surplus for India thus emerges at the short run equilibrium at E_S. Note that the devaluation causes the aggregate world expenditure in Indian currency to rise at the initial equilibrium stocks of high-powered money in the two countries as is immediate from equation (24.14). Alternatively, the world stock of money (expressed in the Indian currency) rises. This raises the rupee price level from its initial equilibrium value from P_i^{**} to P_i^*, which in turn generates an excess demand for money in India by equation (24.9). This excess demand is then met through a trade surplus. But as the US dollars flow in, to keep the exchange rate at the devalued level e_1, RBI must buy dollars in exchange for Indian rupees. The stock of high-powered money thus rises in India. Accordingly, the $\dot{H}_i$ curve shifts up and to the left. In the United States, on the other hand, reserves outflow due to trade deficit caused by the devaluation of the Indian currency and this lowers the stock of high-powered money. This shifts down the $(-e\dot{H}_u)$ curve. Again at the long run equilibrium both countries achieve trade balance. The essence of the monetarist argument here is that a trade surplus cannot be maintained in the long run. Thus, the wealth acquired by India in the short run through a trade surplus will flow out in the long run. The only effect of a nominal devaluation will be changes in price levels.

How does the price level change at the new global equilibrium with balanced trade? Initially, the nominal devaluation of the Indian currency raises the rupee price level proportionately. But monetary adjustments in the two countries cause the price level to change further. Algebraically, it is straightforward to check from equation (24.14) that:

$$dP_i = \frac{1}{Y_W}\left[(v_i - v_u)dH_i + v_u H_u de\right] \quad (24.16)$$

where $Y_W = Y_i + Y_u$.

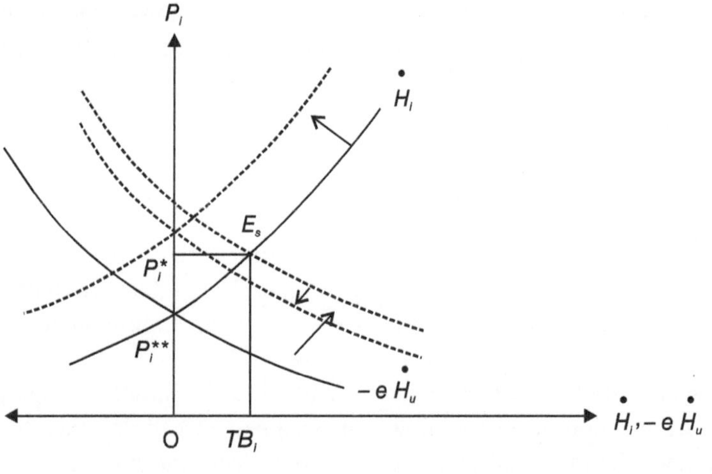

Figure 24.2 Devaluation in the Monetarist Model

For reasons spelled out, if $v_i > v_u$, the initial increase in the rupee price level is magnified by the monetary adjustment, as shown in Figure 24.2. But if $v_i < v_u$, monetary adjustments in the two countries lower the rupee price level from its short run equilibrium level P_i^*. At the end, the rupee price level still rises since this subsequent price fall only moderates the initial price rise but cannot reverse it. On the other hand, given $\frac{1}{e}dH_i = -dH_u$, the change in the dollar price level can be evaluated as:

$$dP_u = \frac{1}{Y_W}\left[(v_u - v_i)dH_i - \frac{v_i H_i}{e^2}de\right] \tag{24.16a}$$

Again, a devaluation initially lowers the dollar price level. A subsequent change in the dollar price induced by monetary adjustments is proportional to the change in the rupee price by the PPP condition at the devalued pegged exchange rate e_1. Thus, whereas the dollar price rises subsequently if $v_i > v_u$, it declines if $v_i < v_u$.

That the rupee price must rise and the dollar price must fall at the new global equilibrium is also evident from the fact that a devaluation raises the world stock of money measured in rupees, $(v_i H_i + e v_u H_u)$, but lowers the world stock of money measured in dollars, $\left(\frac{v_i H_i}{e} + v_u H_u\right)$. Thus, the world aggregate rupee expenditure rises but the dollar expenditure declines.

Like devaluation, any other trade policy will only temporarily create a trade surplus. Effects of any monetary policy on a country's trade balance will also be only temporary. To exemplify, suppose the US Federal Reserve Bank issues new currencies, which raises its stock of high-powered money. At the initial price level, this means the actual holding of money balances exceeds the desired holding. That is, such issue of currencies creates an excess supply of money and the undesired holding of money is spent on goods (since there are no other assets).

With increased spending on both domestic and foreign goods, a trade deficit thus emerges for the United States. This is also evident from equations (24.9) and (24.11). There will thus again be an outflow of dollars, which will lower the excess supply of money. The inflow of dollars in India, for reasons similar to that explained here, raises the stock of high-powered money there. This causes the actual holding of money balances to exceed the desired holding in India. Indian wealth holders spend their undesired holdings, which, in turn causes India's trade to be in deficit. Thus, the trade surplus that emerged for India initially due to spending of the undesired holding of money balances by US consumers now dwindles away by increased spending. Thus, again trade is balanced in the two countries. The only effect of an expansionary monetary policy of the Federal Reserve Bank will be to raise both the price levels, given the exchange rate. This is evident from equation (24.14). Initially issue of new currencies by the US Federal Reserve Bank raises the world stock of currency (measured in rupees). Accordingly, the rupee price level rises, which in turn, by the PPP condition, causes the dollar price level to rise. Subsequently, monetary adjustments will cause both prices to rise further if $v_i > v_u$. Diagrammatically, shifts in the $\dot{H}_i$ and the $(-e\dot{H}_u)$ curves will be similar to that illustrated in Figure 24.2.

In sum, under a fixed exchange rate the stock of money in each country changes with trade imbalance. The stock of high-powered money and consequently money supply falls in the deficit country as reserves flow out and rises in the surplus country under the non-sterilization assumption. *During the process of monetary adjustment*, rupee price rises (falls) if expenditure velocity is larger (smaller) in value in India than in the United States. Prices remain constant during the monetary adjustment, on the other hand, if values of expenditure velocity are the same in the two countries. In any case, however, the reserve outflows and inflows move the global equilibrium towards balanced trade. Thus, BOP is a monetary phenomenon and any imbalance is essentially temporary in nature. In the long run, a trade deficit or a trade surplus cannot persist.

An important policy dimension that arises from this discussion is that when the central bank of a country pegs the exchange rate, the nominal money supply becomes an endogenous rather than a policy variable. That is, the central bank loses its autonomy over the money supply. In general, the central bank of a country cannot simultaneously peg the exchange rate and control the money supply. Of course, if the central bank sterilizes the reserve flow, the monetary base (and thus the total money supply in the economy) can be controlled through open market operations. But, as we will discuss later, there are some practical limits to the sterilization policy.

24.1.4 Monetary Adjustment under Flexible Exchange Rate

Recall from the discussion in Chapter 22 that under a flexible exchange rate (or clean float), reserves held by central banks do not change and any BOP imbalance and consequent excess demand or supply of currencies are corrected through appreciation or depreciation of the exchange rate. The central banks need not buy or sell foreign currencies to defend the exchange rate (except under a managed float) and thus can maintain a fixed stock of high-powered money or fixed units of currencies put in circulation. Thus, instead of a monetary adjustment, now the long run global equilibrium with balanced trade is achieved through changes in the exchange rate.

To illustrate, consider again an initial short run equilibrium with trade surplus for India as shown in Figure 24.3. By equation (24.9), there is an excess demand for money in India. The exchange rate being the price of the Indian currency per unit of the US currency, the excess demand for money pushes up the price of the Indian currency. That is, the rupee-dollar exchange rate appreciates, or the value of the exchange rate falls. Alternatively, as we had explained in Chapter 22, a trade surplus means India earns more US dollars through exports than it spends through imports. This excess supply of dollars in the foreign exchange rate market lowers the price of dollars vis-à-vis rupees. The appreciation of the Indian currency (or depreciation of the US dollar) does not shift the $\dot{H}_i$ curve but shifts down the $(-e\dot{H}_u)$ curve till the global balanced trade equilibrium is reached with no excess demand or supply of either currency.

Note that now the rupee price level P_i *unambiguously declines*. This is also evident from equation (24.14). Given constant stocks of high-powered money, an appreciation of the exchange rate (or fall in the value of e) means a fall in the aggregate world expenditure measured in the Indian currency. Thus, the goods market clears at a lower rupee price. By similar reasoning, since an appreciation of the rupee-dollar exchange rate means a depreciation of the value of the US dollar vis-à-vis the Indian rupee, the aggregate world expenditure measured in US dollars rises. Hence, the dollar price rises. However, as shown in Appendix A24, both these price changes are less than proportionate to the rate of appreciation of the rupee-dollar exchange rate:

$$\hat{P}_i = (1-\lambda)\hat{e} < 0, \; \hat{P}_u = -\lambda\hat{e} > 0 \tag{24.17}$$

where, $\lambda = \dfrac{v_i H_i}{P_i Y_w}$ is the share of India's in aggregate world expenditure measured in rupee.

Two comments are warranted at this point. First, the relative price $p \equiv \dfrac{eP_u}{P_i}$ remains constant:

$$\hat{p} = \hat{e} + \hat{P}_u - \hat{P}_i = \hat{e} - \lambda\hat{e} - (1-\lambda)\hat{e} = 0 \tag{24.18}$$

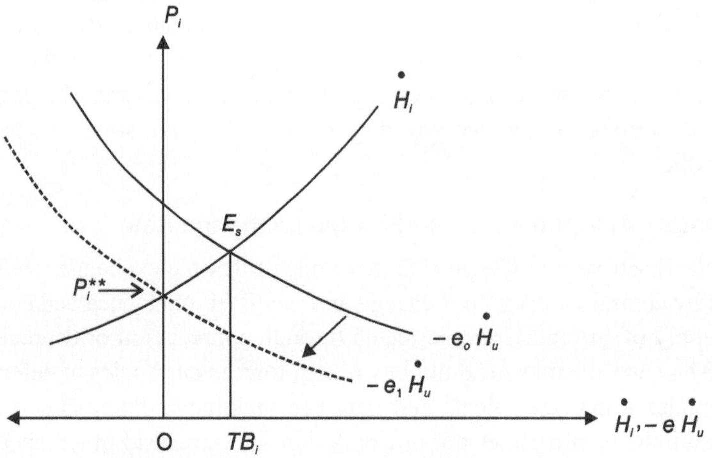

Figure 24.3 BOP Adjustment under Clean Float

This is obvious from the PPP condition as it means that $p = 1$. Second, under a flexible exchange rate (or clean float) BOP adjustment in the long run takes place through changes in money demand rather than through changes in money supply as under a fixed exchange rate. An initial trade surplus for India or an excess demand for money, $\dot{H}_i = P_iY_i - v_iH_i > 0$ is now adjusted through a fall in the rupee price level and the corresponding fall in money demand. Under a fixed exchange rate, on the other hand, excess money demand was adjusted through an increase in the stock of high-powered money, H_i. This is the distinguishing feature of the BOP adjustment process under a clean float. However, the essence of the monetarist argument remains: BOP imbalance is a monetary phenomenon and is transitory in nature.

24.2 MONETARY ADJUSTMENT UNDER KEYNESIAN ASSUMPTION

The monetary approach of Robert Mundell (1961, 1963) and J.M. Flemming (1962), in contrast to the monetarist model discussed earlier has been in the tradition of Keynesian income adjustment rather than classical price adjustment. The basic monetarist proposition still holds though in their extension of the IS–LM analytical framework: BOP imbalance is a temporary phenomenon and adjusts automatically through changes in the money stock over time. However, the major difference is in the *other variable* that adjusts with the money stock. In the monetarist model, prices adjust with endogenous changes in the money stock, whereas in Mundell's analysis it is the national income that adjusts under the assumption of sticky wages and prices. Thus, in contrast to Hume's price-specie flow mechanism, a BOP imbalance adjusts over time through an *income-specie flow* mechanism.

The other important proposition of the Mundell–Flemming IS–LM analysis is the relative efficacy of fiscal and monetary policies as stabilizers of income changes in the presence of capital mobility. Mundell and Flemming differed in their assumptions regarding the degree of capital mobility and accordingly arrived at different policy conclusions. For example, assuming perfect capital mobility in the sense defined later, Mundell showed that under a pegged exchange rate regime, capital flows offset an increase in money stock so that an expansionary monetary policy is ineffective in changing aggregate output and national income.

24.2.1 Mundell's Income-Specie Flow Mechanism

Consider an extension of the simple Keynesian effective demand approach with constant prices discussed in Chapter 21 by including a money market and linking the product and money markets in two ways. First, investment demand (or expenditure) is an inverse function of the domestic rate of interest. Thus, the effective demand condition for product market equilibrium in India is now rewritten as:

$$Y_i = C(Y_i) + I(r_i) + \bar{G}_i + \left[M_u(e) - eM_i(e, Y_i)\right] \tag{24.19}$$

Note that we have assumed that the US income remains constant so there is no international transmission of policy effects.

Second, people demand cash or money for speculative purposes, in addition to carrying out day-to-day transactions related to purchase and sale of goods. This is a major departure from the monetarist model in the tradition of the quantity theory of money. In contrast to the quantity equation of money market equilibrium condition in equation (24.7), we now have the following equilibrium condition:

$$H_i = L_i(Y_i, r_i),\ H_u = L_u(Y_u, r_u) \tag{24.20}$$

where, $L_i(Y_i, r_i)$ and $L_u(Y_u, r_u)$ are the Keynesian aggregate money demand or liquidity preference functions in India and the United states respectively. By constant prices, normalized to one, real and money balances are the same.[3] Money demand increases with income but falls with the increase in interest rate. Interest rate is the opportunity cost of holding money instead of putting it into interest-bearing assets like bonds. An increase in the interest rate means the opportunity cost of holding money rises and this lowers the aggregate demand for cash for speculative purposes.

For any given money stock of a country and an exchange rate, these two equilibrium conditions in equations (24.19) and (24.20) simultaneously determine the national income and the national interest rate. Graphically, these conditions are represented as the familiar *IS* and *LM* curves in Figure 24.4. Note that the IS curve shifts up and down with change in the exchange rate, whereas the LM curve shifts up and down with change in the money stock.

To explain the income-specie flow mechanism, suppose at the initial equilibrium E_s, India had a deficit in trade with the United States due to an over-valued pegged exchange rate. The consequent excess demand for dollars forces RBI to sell dollars from its reserves in exchange for domestic money. Under non-sterilization, with less currency being in circulation (or a fall in the money supply), the LM curve shifts to the left, which causes the interest rate to rise. The intuition is simple. A fall in money supply means the actual holding of currency falls below the desired holding of currency *at the initial rate of interest and national income*. People then sell part of their bond holdings to meet their excess demand for cash. This lowers the bond price and raises the interest rate. The rise in interest rate causes a multiplier contraction of the national income of India through a decline in domestic investment. Consequently, import demand falls and with it falls the trade deficit. These adjustments through changes in the stock of money continue till India's trade with the United States is balanced at the new equilibrium *E*. This is Robert Mundell's income-specie flow mechanism.

Thus, similar to the monetarist model, a BOP imbalance is only a temporary phenomenon and adjusts over time through adjustment in the stock of money and corresponding changes in the national income. The only difference is that the national incomes instead of prices now adjust under the Keynesian assumption of sticky wages and prices and a corresponding less than full employment equilibrium. In the monetarist model, on the other hand, the wage-price flexibility maintained aggregate output at the full employment level and thus only prices adjusted with changes in the money stock.

Note that even if we had allowed the national income of the United States to change, the trade balance would have been achieved. Since the initial trade deficit for India (or trade

[3] Recall that we also assume that the money multiplier is constant and is normalized to one. Accordingly H_i and H_u are also the total money supply in the two countries. These assumptions mean that the money supply can be affected only through changes in high-powered money by open market operations. All these, however, are simplifying assumptions and have no bearing on the policy effects that we discuss here.

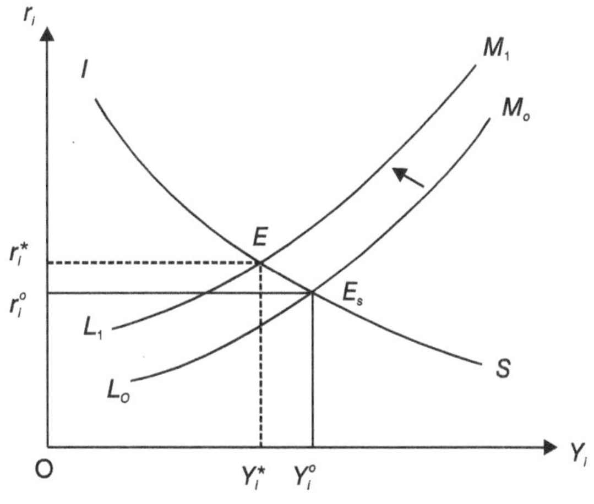

Figure 24.4 Income-Specie Flow Mechanism

surplus for the United States) causes money supply to increase in the United States so her national income would have increased. This would have raised US import demand and improved India's trade balance.

24.2.2 Capital Mobility and Stabilization Policies under Pegged Exchange Rate

Now consider the possibility of autonomous capital mobility in the above context. The actual mechanism through which foreign capital flows in or flows out of a country can be explained in terms of a portfolio holding of domestic and foreign assets, which are perfect substitutes of each other, by domestic wealth holders. The portfolio choice or allocation of wealth over domestic and foreign assets depends, among others, on the interest differential. We elaborate on this portfolio choice in the next section. At this point, without elaborating too much on *how* capital flows in or out, we simply assume that a higher domestic interest rate than abroad attracts foreign capital into India and a lower rate leads to capital flight or outflow from India. Moreover, suppose that India is a small country in both the world product and asset (or capital) markets. Thus, like incomes abroad, interest rates on foreign bonds are also exogenously given such that India's domestic policies can change neither incomes abroad nor interest rates on foreign bonds. We assume that a common interest rate r_w prevails in the global capital or asset market. Capital mobility, however, may be perfect or imperfect. If capital mobility is perfect, then any domestic policy induced increase in r_i over r_w instantaneously attracts an infinitely large capital inflow to restore back the parity between domestic and world interest rates. Thus, the only possible asset market and BOP equilibrium will be $r_i = r_w$. But the *actual* capital inflow, as determined by the extent of trade imbalance, may be *finite* as we will see now. Under imperfect (or sluggish) capital mobility, on the other hand, the interest differential though will be lower but will still persist.[4]

[4] Perfect and imperfect capital mobility can be related to perfect and imperfect substitutability of domestic and foreign assets as we will see later.

With capital mobility, BOP cannot simply be defined in terms of trade or current account balance. The capital account balance will now have to be explicitly taken into account. Since a capital inflow creates a capital account surplus, and by the above assumption, capital flows in whenever $r_i > r_w$, so the BOP equilibrium condition can be written as:

$$B = [M_w(e) - eM_i(e, Y_i)] + k_i(r_i - r_w) = 0,\ 0 \leq k_i' \leq \infty \qquad (24.21)$$

The first term in the parenthesis on the right hand side is the trade balance position for India, whereas the second term is its capital account balance position. Under the assumption that India is a small country in the goods market, its trade balance depends only on its own national income and the exchange rate. The capital account, on the other hand, depends on the interest rate differential. For reasons spelled out above, for a domestic interest rate higher than the rate in the rest of the world, $r_i > r_w$, capital flows in and consequently the capital account improves. But for a lower domestic interest rate, capital flows out and the capital account worsens. Thus, for any given trade balance, BOP varies positively with the interest differential, $r_i - r_w$. The magnitude of change in the capital account, however, depends on the degree of capital mobility, which is captured by the value of k_i'. Graphically, the degree of capital mobility influences the relative slope of the BOP equilibrium locus $B = 0$ as shown in Figure 24.5. If capital mobility is perfect, then starting from a point like A, for an increase in Y_i that worsens the trade balance and hence BOP, an infinitesimally small rise in domestic interest rate r_i is sufficient to induce instantaneous large capital inflows to improve the capital account and restore the BOP equilibrium. Thus, the $B = 0$ locus is perfectly elastic at $r_i = r_w$. But if capital mobility is imperfect, a *finite* rise in r_i is required to induce capital flows and improve the capital account to restore the BOP equilibrium following an increase in Y_i. Hence, the $B = 0$ locus is positively sloped. Moreover, smaller the degree of capital mobility, the larger is

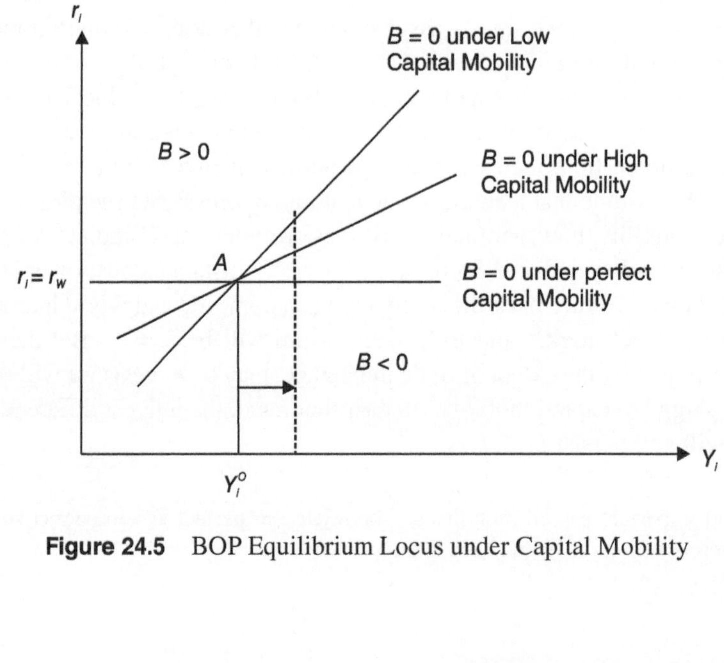

Figure 24.5 BOP Equilibrium Locus under Capital Mobility

the required rise in r_i and consequently steeper is the $B = 0$ locus. Algebraically, the slope of the $B = 0$ locus being,

$$\left.\frac{dr_i}{dY_i}\right|_{B=0} = \frac{m_i}{k_i'} \tag{24.22}$$

a perfect capital mobility which means $k_i' = \infty$, the $B = 0$ locus is horizontal in the (Y_i, r_i) space. At the other extreme, when there is no capital mobility, $k_i' = 0$, and the $B = 0$ locus is vertical. In fact, with no capital mobility, BOP varies inversely with national income for any given value of the exchange rate.

Note that regardless of the degree of capital mobility, for any pair of (Y_i, r_i) in the region below $B = 0$ locus, India's BOP is in deficit. To check, consider $B = 0$ locus under perfect capital mobility. Given the national income Y_i^o, a higher r_i than r_w (that pushes the economy in the region above $B = 0$ locus) attracts foreign capital and thus improves India's capital account and BOP. By similar reasoning, for any other pair of (Y_i, r_i) in the region above $B = 0$ locus, India's BOP is in surplus.

Incorporating this $B = 0$ locus in the IS–LM diagram, we can now analyse the effects of fiscal and monetary policies on India's national income in the presence of capital mobility. We start with the perfect mobility case. Suppose initially the economy was at point E in Figure 24.6 with BOP being in equilibrium. Consider now an increase in money supply by RBI as a result of which the LM curve shifts to the right. The domestic interest rate declines for reasons similar to that explained earlier. Increase in the money supply raises the actual cash holdings of people above their desired cash holdings at the initial interest rate r_i^o. They spend this undesired holding of money on bonds. Since everyone wishes to buy bonds, price rises and the interest rate on domestic bonds declines. The monetary expansion thus pushes the economy to a BOP deficit situation at the short run equilibrium E_S. Note that the decline in the domestic

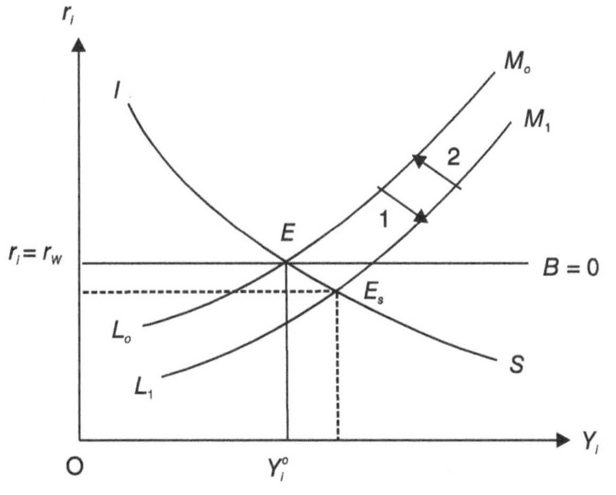

Figure 24.6 Monetary Policy under Perfect Capital Mobility

interest rate adversely affects India's BOP in two ways. First, larger investment leads to a multiplier expansion in national income that worsens India's trade balance. Second, capital now flows out, which worsens the capital account.

The lower domestic interest rate at the short run BOP deficit equilibrium induces wealth holders to substitute their domestic bond holdings by foreign bonds and thus demand more foreign currency. To prohibit the rupee-dollar exchange rate to depreciate from its pegged level due to this excess demand for foreign currency, RBI then must sell dollars in exchange for rupees. The foreign currency reserves thus flow out and, under non-sterilization, the stock of domestic money in circulation declines. The LM curve shifts back to its initial position and BOP returns to its equilibrium. The important point to note here is that the initial income expansion cannot be sustained either. That is, a monetary policy is totally ineffective in changing the aggregate output under perfect capital mobility and a fixed exchange rate. This was one major result established by Mundell (1963). In fact, this result again shows that when the central bank of a country pegs the exchange rate for its currency vis-à-vis a foreign currency, it loses its autonomy over the supply of its currency.

But a fiscal policy will be fully effective. This is illustrated in Figure 24.7. An increase in its expenditure by the Government of India raises both the national income and domestic interest rate by shifting the IS curve to the right along the LM curve. The increase in the domestic interest rate lowers domestic investment. That is, increased government expenditure *crowds out* a part of the domestic private investment. Consequently, income expansion realized at the short run equilibrium E_S will be far less than what could have been achieved had there been no change in the interest rate. In the long run, higher domestic interest brings in foreign capital into the Indian economy as wealth holders sell off their foreign bond holdings to buy domestic bonds. To defend the pegged exchange rate from appreciating in face of such an inflow of USD, RBI should now buy USDs for rupees. More domestic currency is thus put into circulation, which shifts the LM curve till the long run BOP equilibrium is attained at point E_1. The domestic interest rate returns to its initial value and gets equalized with the world interest rate. Private investment rises and consequently, national income and aggregate output

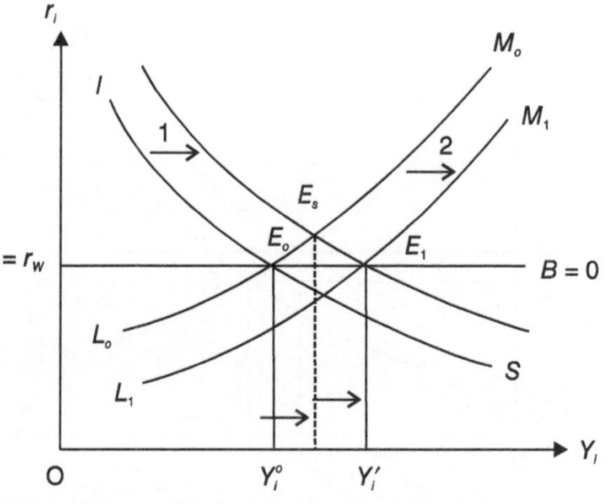

Figure 24.7 Fiscal Policy under Perfect Capital Mobility

expand further. Thus, perfect capital mobility under a fixed exchange rate regime prevents the crowding out effect of an expansionary fiscal policy by bringing down the domestic interest rate to its initial level and thereby making the fiscal expansion fully effective.

The short-run BOP surplus generated through an expansionary fiscal policy again vanishes in the long run. The nature of BOP adjustment now, however, is altogether different from that in case of a monetary expansion. At the short run equilibrium, the increase in national income worsened the trade balance but the increase in domestic interest rate improved the capital account balance through inflow of capital. Overall, BOP improved as explained before (see Figure 24.5). But, in the long run, as capital inflow raises the national income further through increase in money supply, the trade deficit magnifies and this worsens BOP. At the long run equilibrium, deficit on the trade account exactly matches with the surplus in the capital account, and BOP is in equilibrium again.

Flemming (1962), on the other hand, had obtained a different set of results under the assumption of imperfect capital mobility. Under imperfect capital mobility a rise in domestic interest rate caused by a fiscal expansion is only *moderated* by a capital flow instead of being brought down to its initial level (which is also equal to the world interest rate). Thus, capital mobility cannot fully mitigate the crowding out of private investment by fiscal expansion. Accordingly, output changes less than it does under perfect capital mobility, the extent of which depends on the degree of capital mobility. Two cases are relevant here. First is a high enough capital mobility so that the required rate of increase in the domestic interest rate to attract foreign capital and maintain BOP equilibrium when the national income rises following any policy change is *smaller* than that to maintain the money market equilibrium. In this case, the $B = 0$ locus is flatter than the LM curve as in Figure 24.8a. Second is the case of a sufficiently low capital mobility for which the required rate of increase in the domestic interest rate to maintain BOP equilibrium when the national income rises following any policy change is *larger* than that to maintain the money market equilibrium. In this case, the $B = 0$ locus is steeper than the LM curve as in Figure 24.8b.

For high capital mobility, a fiscal expansion pushes the economy to a short run equilibrium at E_S along the L_0M_0 curve with a BOP surplus. For reasons spelled out, the fiscal expansion raises both the national income and interest rate. The increase in national income worsens the trade balance whereas the rise in interest rate improves the capital account as it attracts foreign capital. Overall, BOP improves at the short run equilibrium E_S because capital mobility is very high. This BOP surplus causes foreign reserves to flow *in* which forces RBI to buy the excess supply of the foreign currency to prevent the exchange rate from appreciating. This raises the stock of the Indian currency in circulation, and the LM curve shifts to the right till the long run equilibrium at E_1 is attained. Thus, again the subsequent rise in the money stock raises output and income further. But the income expansion is now less than that under perfect capital mobility since the interest rate rises at the long run equilibrium, thereby crowding out part of the private investment. In contrast, for a very low capital mobility in the sense defined earlier and illustrated in panel (b), the fiscal expansion causes a BOP deficit at the short run equilibrium E_S. Now, capital mobility being low, the capital account surplus is smaller in magnitude than the trade deficit. The overall BOP deficit causes foreign currency to flow *out*, forcing RBI to sell the foreign currency to defend the pegged exchange rate. This lowers the stock of the Indian currency in circulation and shifts the LM curve to the left. This monetary

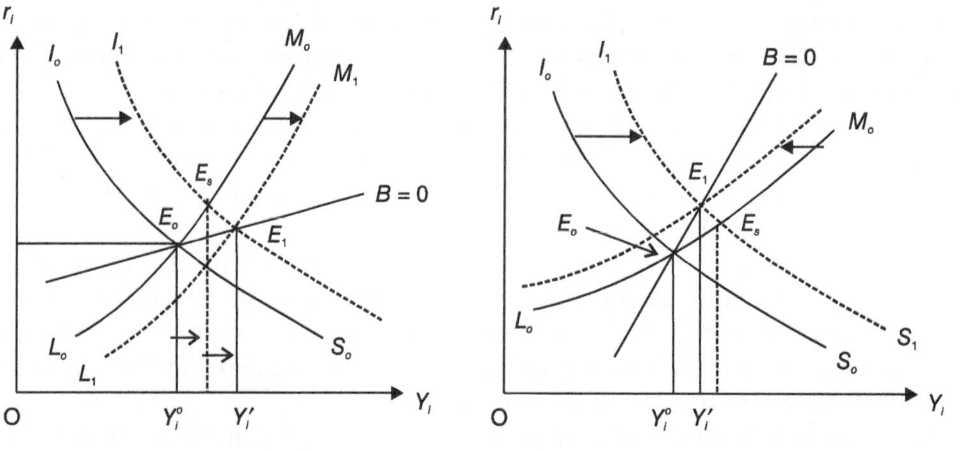

(a) High Capital Mobility (b) Low Capital Mobility

Figure 24.8 Fiscal Policy under Imperfect Capital Mobility

contraction causes the national income to contract. Hence, at the long run equilibrium, the initial income expansion gets moderated.

In sum, under imperfect capital mobility, the effects of a fiscal expansion get moderated by the degree of capital mobility. On the other hand, it is easy to check that the Mundell result—that capital mobility offsets effects of a monetary expansion—still holds regardless of the degree of capital mobility.

24.2.3 Capital Mobility and Stabilization Policies under Clean Float

Under clean float, like the monetarist model, the BOP imbalance is adjusted not through a change in the money stock but through exchange rate appreciation or depreciation, as the case may be. RBI does not need to sell or buy foreign currencies and in the process change the stock of money to defend the exchange rate. That is, unlike the case of a pegged exchange rate, RBI will now have autonomy over controlling its money supply. Thus, with the exchange rate allowed to change, a monetary expansion will be fully effective in raising the aggregate output, whereas a fiscal expansion will be totally ineffective. These are the dual of Mundell's results under pegged exchange rate regime discussed here.

To illustrate, consider Figure 24.9. A monetary expansion at the initial BOP equilibrium E_0 shifts the LM curve and pushes the economy to a short run equilibrium at E_S with a BOP deficit. The decline in the domestic interest rate below the world interest rate leads to a capital outflow and thereby worsens the capital account. A trade deficit arises as well due to the corresponding income expansion. The BOP deficit creates an excess demand for foreign currencies, which in turn depreciates the rupee-dollar exchange rate. As explained in an earlier chapter, by the Marshall-Lerner stability condition, exchange rate depreciation lowers trade deficit and raises effective demand and hence aggregate output. The IS curve now shifts to the right till the long run equilibrium is attained at E_1. Note that with the domestic interest rate in India remaining the same at the long run equilibrium, capital mobility and consequent exchange rate depreciation mitigates the crowding out effect to make the monetary policy fully effective.

A fiscal expansion, on the other hand, cannot change the aggregate output. At the initial BOP equilibrium, a fiscal expansion raises the domestic interest rate as well as income and output. Now foreign capital flows in and since capital mobility is perfect so the consequent capital account surplus over-compensates for the increase in trade deficit due to income expansion. BOP is thus in surplus at the short run equilibrium. The consequent excess supply of foreign currency (as the country earns more than it spends) appreciates the exchange rate. This magnifies the trade deficit further till the BOP equilibrium is restored with the domestic interest rate being equalized with the world interest rate again. The trade deficit now lowers effective demand and output and fully cancels out the initial increase due to fiscal expansion. Graphically, since RBI does not intervene in the foreign exchange market by buying or selling dollars, so the money stock does not change and the LM curve does not shift. In Figure 24.10, the IS curve initially shifts to the right due to fiscal expansion, and subsequently gets back to its initial position through exchange rate appreciation. Aggregate output and income thus remain at the same initial level. Exchange rate appreciation and consequent decline in the effective demand completely washes out the favourable effect of a fiscal expansion.

In sum, under perfect capital mobility, relative effectiveness of fiscal and monetary expansions under clean float is just opposite to that under a pegged exchange rate regime. These results are thus dual of Mundell's results.

The case of imperfect capital mobility is now slightly different than under a pegged exchange rate. Exchange rate appreciation or depreciation now shifts the $B = 0$ locus as well along with the IS curve. This is evident from (24.21). However, the important point to note is that the shift of the IS curve will be *smaller* than the $B = 0$ locus. This can be algebraically verified from the following (see Appendix A24):

$$dY_i\big|_{IS} = \frac{M_i\left[\varepsilon_u + \varepsilon_i - 1\right]}{s_i + m_i} de < dY_i\big|_{B=0} = \frac{M_i\left[\varepsilon_u + \varepsilon_i - 1\right]}{m_i} de \tag{24.23}$$

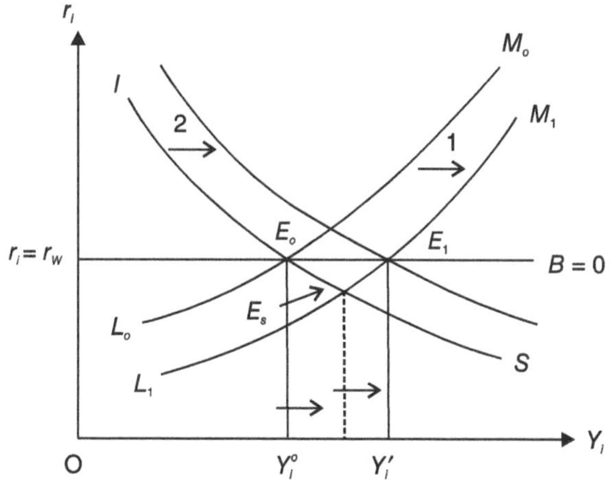

Figure 24.9 Monetary Policy under Clean Float

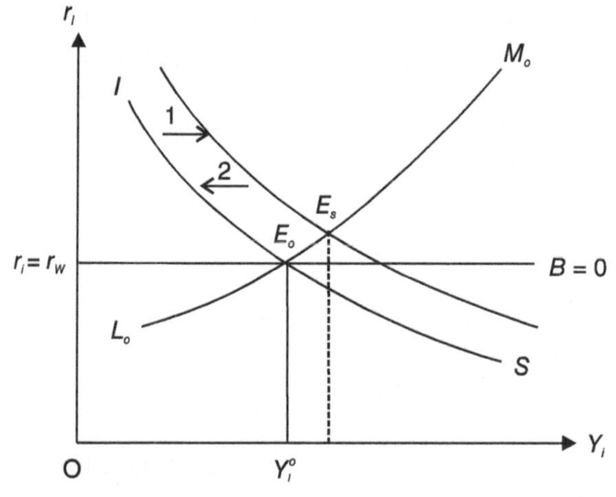

Figure 24.10 Fiscal Policy under Clean Float

As we illustrate below, because of this a fiscal expansion will be able to change output under imperfect capital mobility. Once again two cases are relevant as above. We, however, illustrate in Figure 24.11 only the case of a relatively high degree of capital mobility in the sense defined earlier. Panel (a) depicts monetary expansion and panel (b) depicts fiscal expansion. In case of a monetary expansion at the initial equilibrium exchange rate, the domestic interest rate falls below the world rate along the I_0S_0 curve, which worsens India's capital account through an outflow of capital. Income expansion worsens BOP further through larger imports and consequent trade deficit. Consequent excess demand for foreign currency depreciates the exchange rate, which in turn lowers the trade deficit and raises the effective demand for goods produced in India. Thus, both the IS curve and $B = 0$ locus shift to the right. The long run equilibrium is obtained at E_1 with the BOP again in equilibrium. The initial income expansion thus gets reinforced through currency depreciation.

For a fiscal expansion, on the other hand, the initial expansion gets dampened because now a BOP surplus emerges at the short run equilibrium E_S, which appreciates the exchange rate. Thus, subsequent trade deficit lowers the effective demand and hence the aggregate output. Graphically, with the $B = 0$ locus shifting faster to the left than the IS curve, the long run equilibrium is obtained to the right of E_0, which means an expansion of income relative to the initial equilibrium level. Thus, unlike the case of perfect capital mobility, a fiscal expansion raises output and income. Output and income changes following monetary and fiscal expansions under low degree of capital mobility can similarly be analysed.

In sum, whereas under perfect capital mobility, a fiscal expansion is totally ineffective and a monetary expansion is fully effective, under imperfect capital mobility, both fiscal and monetary expansions are effective in raising output.

24.3 ASSET MARKET, PORTFOLIO CHOICE, AND THE EXCHANGE RATE

Much of the argument earlier has implicitly, and sometimes explicitly, used the portfolio choice of assets and its implication on the stock of money under a pegged exchange rate regime. On

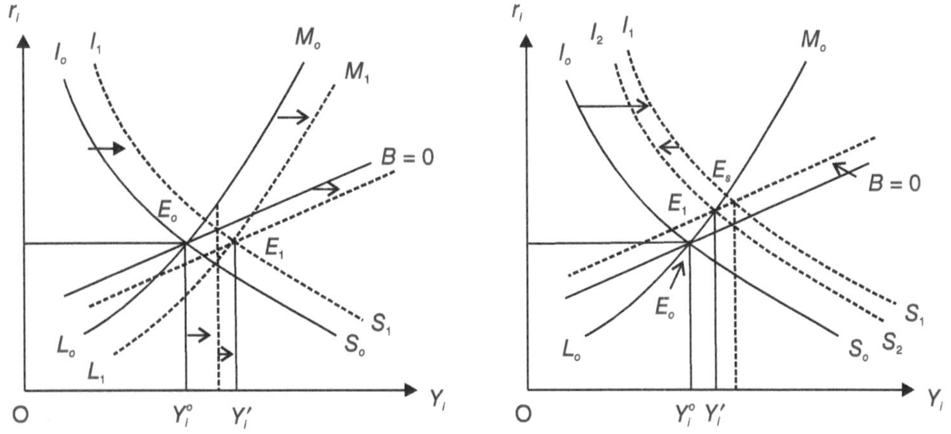

(a) Monetary Expansion (b) Fiscal Expansion

Figure 24.11 Monetary and Fiscal Policy under Clean Float and High Capital Mobility

the other hand, the analysis of a monetary expansion under clean float indicates that a change in the money supply changes the exchange rate. Thus, it appears that money supply and the exchange rate are closely related through market interest rates on bonds and the portfolio choice of domestic and foreign assets. This section brings out these relationships explicitly, by considering the asset approach or portfolio choice theory of exchange rate determination. The essence of this approach is that the exchange rate is the price of foreign assets vis-à-vis domestic assets. Alternatively, demand for foreign currency arises from wealth holders' demand for foreign assets. Accordingly, allocation of their wealth over domestic and foreign assets (or portfolio of assets) determines the exchange rate.

The starting point of the asset approach is, therefore, the optimal allocation of wealth over different assets. Suppose all wealth holders are identical. A representative Indian wealth holder compares returns on rupee-assets and dollar-assets, these being the only two assets that she may buy or sell. Let r_i and r_u denote the interest rates or rates of returns on these assets. If prices are constant and the wealth holder does not expect the exchange rate to change, as in case of a pegged exchange rate regime implemented by RBI, she will be indifferent between holding dollar-assets and rupee-assets when these two interest rates are equal. But under clean float, her choice of assets will in addition be governed by her expectation regarding an appreciation or depreciation of the domestic currency. If she expects that the rupee will depreciate vis-à-vis the dollar in the next period at the rate $\phi \equiv \dfrac{\tilde{e} - e}{e}$, then she expects to get $r_u + \phi$ on each rupee invested in dollar-assets or put in dollar deposits. The reason for this is simple. Suppose, one rupee exchanges for one unit of dollars. Then on each rupee put in dollar deposits, she expects to get in the next period the sum $(1 + \phi)$ as principal and r_u as interest earned. That is, by putting one rupee in a dollar deposit, she expects to get a return of $r_u + \phi$. Accordingly, she will be indifferent between investing a rupee in domestic assets and in dollar-assets if:

$$r_i = r_u + \phi \tag{24.24}$$

This is known as the (uncovered) interest parity condition for asset market equilibrium: at equilibrium, the *expected* rates of returns on assets must be equal. Of course, the assets must be perfect substitutes. Otherwise, even for the same rate of return, a wealth holder may prefer one asset over the other (see Box 24.3). Note that ϕ is positive or negative accordingly as she expects the rupee to depreciate or appreciate vis-à-vis the dollar in the next period.

This interest parity condition is also the condition for equilibrium in the foreign exchange market, for any given expected rate of change in the exchange rate, ϕ. To see why, suppose for a particular value of the current exchange rate, $r_i > r_u + \phi$. This means that rupee-assets or deposits offer higher rates of return than does dollar-assets or deposits. Thus, wealth holders convert their dollar-assets into rupee-assets, which means an excess supply of dollars or excess demand for rupees. By similar reasoning, if $r_i < r_u + \phi$, there will be an excess demand for dollars or excess supply of rupees. But when the interest parity condition holds, wealth holders are indifferent between holding rupee-assets and dollar-assets. There will thus neither be an excess demand for nor an excess supply of dollars. The foreign exchange market thus attains its equilibrium.

Once it is understood that the interest parity condition in equation (24.24) determines the exchange rate under clean float, it is easy to relate a country's money stock with the exchange rate. Recall that the interest rates in the two countries are determined by the money market equilibrium conditions in equation (24.20). Thus, for any given pair of income levels in the two countries, the stock of money in circulation determines domestic interest rates, which in turn determine the exchange rate. This is illustrated in Figure 24.12 where equilibrium in the money and asset markets are shown in panels (a) and (b) respectively. Note that the price level is normalized to one under the Keynesian assumption of sticky prices so that money and real balances are the same. The downward sloping curve in panel (b) represents the inverse relationship between the expected rate of return on dollar deposits ($\tilde{r}_u$) and the current exchange rate, for any given expected exchange rate in the future ($\tilde{e}$) and the stock of money issued by

Box 24.2 Uncovered and Covered Interest Parity

The equalization of the expected rates of return based on the expected spot exchange rate in the future in equation (24.24) is known as the *uncovered* interest parity condition. This is so called because it does not cover the wealth holder against *unexpected* depreciation of the rupee vis-à-vis the dollar. But when a wealth holder wants to cover herself from such an unexpected depreciation of the domestic currency in the future, she may buy dollar-assets or deposits with rupees and at the same time sell the principal and the interest on dollar deposits at a *forward exchange rate* for the rupee. That is, by agreeing upon selling her dollar deposits at a forward exchange rate, quoted today, she covers herself from unexpected depreciation of the rupee in the future. In such a case, she will be indifferent between holding rupee-deposits and dollar deposits only if $r_i = r_u + \dfrac{e^f - e}{e}$. This is the *covered* interest parity condition. Uncovered and covered interest parity conditions may hold simultaneously only when the expected future spot exchange rate and the forward exchange rate, quoted at present, are equal: $\tilde{e} = e^f$. In fact, the efficient market hypothesis states that the forward rate is the optimal predictor of the future spot rate under risk neutrality.

the US Federal Reserve Bank (H_u). On the other hand, an increase in the stock of money issued by the US Federal Reserve Bank lowers the actual interest rate on dollar-assets or deposits and thus lowers the expected rate of return, given the expected exchange rate in the future. Thus, $\tilde{r}_u$ varies inversely with the exchange rate depreciation and the stock of currency issued by the Federal Reserve Bank.

In Figure 24.12, the initial equilibrium exchange rate is e^* for which the interest parity condition in equation (24.24) and the money market equilibrium conditions in equation (24.20) are satisfied together, given the stock of money supplied by RBI. Note that given the money market equilibrium interest rates, for any exchange rate larger in value than e^*, the rupee-assets offer a higher return than dollar-assets. Wealth holders will thus demand rupee-assets in exchange for their holding of dollar-assets. The consequent excess supply of dollars, as they sell off their dollar-assets, will lower the price of the dollar vis-à-vis the rupee or appreciate the exchange rate. The asset market will thus adjust towards the equilibrium value e^*. On the other hand, for any $e < e^*$, the wealth holders will demand dollars as they would like to convert their rupee-assets into dollar-assets which now offer a relatively higher expected rate of return. The exchange rate now depreciates and the market again adjusts towards the equilibrium value e^*.

Now consider a decrease in money supply by RBI. This will have two effects. First, the actual holding of the cash balance is now smaller than the desired holding of the cash balance at the initial equilibrium interest rate r_i^*. Wealth holders will then sell their assets to meet their excess demand for cash. This raises the interest rate on rupee-assets. This is shown in Figure 24.12 by the movement up along the $L(Y_i, r_i)$ locus in panel (a) and the vertical shift of the domestic interest rate locus in panel (b). Second, the rise in the rate of interest on rupee-assets now makes it more profitable for wealth holders than dollar-assets. This causes the exchange rate to appreciate as the portfolio of assets shift in favour of rupee-assets. Thus, a contractionary monetary policy by RBI appreciates the rupee-dollar exchange rate. By similar reasoning, a monetary expansion by RBI will depreciate the exchange rate. On the other hand,

Box 24.3 Uncovered Interest Parity and Perfect Assets Substitutability

Assets are said to be perfect substitutes when wealth holders are indifferent between the portfolio of their assets that yield the same expected returns. Thus, when we say that for the uncovered interest parity condition in equation (24.24), the wealth holders are indifferent between holding rupee-assets and dollar-assets and thus this condition constitutes the equilibrium condition in the foreign exchange market, we assume that these assets are perfect substitutes. In contrast, when assets are imperfect substitutes such as differentiated by the element of *risk* and its degree, the expected returns may differ. Or, to put it the other way, wealth holders are *not* indifferent between assets with different degrees of risk, and thus being imperfect substitutes for each other, even when they yield the same expected rates of return. Wealth holders may prefer to hold a very risky asset only if it yields a very high expected return relative to a less risky asset. Therefore, in a world of perfect asset substitutability only the expected rates of return and the interest parity condition matter, whereas in a world of imperfect asset substitutability both the expected rates of return and the risk associated with assets matter.

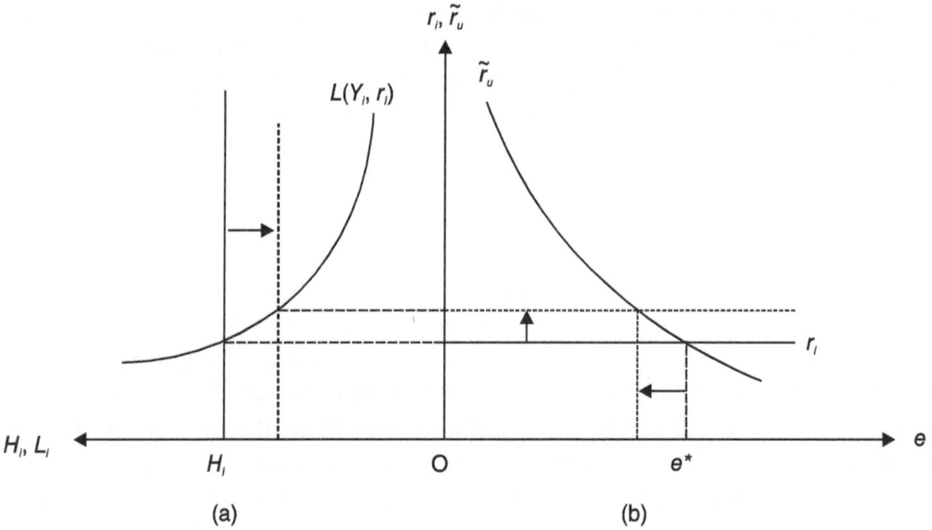

Figure 24.12 Money, Assets, and Exchange Rate

a monetary expansion by the US Federal Reserve Bank lowers the interest rate on dollar-assets or deposits. Given the expected rate of depreciation, this lowers the expected returns from such assets and consequently the portfolio of assets shifts in favour of rupee deposits. The exchange rate now appreciates. That is, monetary expansions by RBI and by the US Federal Reserve Bank have the opposite effect on the rupee-dollar exchange rate.

These effects of monetary expansion and contraction on the exchange rate are, however, incomplete if by the wage-price stickiness in the two countries output (and income) levels are below full employment levels and thus change with such expansion or contraction. This is because, in such cases, monetary expansions raise the output level and result in further changes in interest rates and consequently in the exchange rate. At the same time, exchange rate changes also affect the effective demand and income of the countries. This is evident from the effective demand condition in equation (24.19) for India and a similar condition for the United States. Thus, the output (or income) level and the exchange rate should be simultaneously determined. To illustrate, first of all note that by the Marshall–Lerner condition, the effective demand condition in equation (24.19) gives us a positive relationship between the aggregate output (and income) in India and the exchange rate. A currency depreciation raises the trade balance in Indian currency and consequently raises the effective demand and output level. This is shown by the positively-sloped Y_iY_i curve in Figure 24.13. On the other hand, from the asset and money markets depicted in Figure 24.12 emerges an inverse relationship between India's national income and the rupee-dollar exchange rate. For any given stock of money, an increase in the national income raises the (transactions) demand for money, and to meet this additional demand for cash Indian wealth holders sell part of their bond holdings, and thereby lower bond prices and raise the interest rate on bonds. This rise in the rate of interest on rupee-assets (or bonds) appreciates the exchange rate for reasons spelled above. This inverse relationship is shown by the *ee* curve in Figure 24.13.

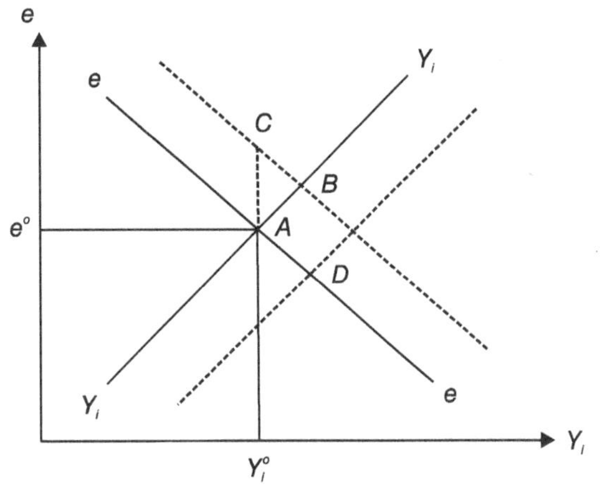

Figure 24.13 Output Changes and Exchange Rate

The initial equilibrium pair of exchange rate and India's national income is (e^o, Y_i^o) corresponding to the point of intersection *A* between the (bold) Y_iY_i and *ee* curves. Now, an increase in money supply by RBI depreciates the exchange rate for any given output and income. Thus, the *ee* curve shifts up and pushes the equilibrium from *A* to *B*. But the currency depreciation raises income, and this moderates the initial exchange rate depreciation (as indicated by the increase in the value of the exchange rate from *A* to *C*). Thus, when income changes of a monetary expansion are taken into account, the exchange rate depreciation is moderated. Figure 24.13 also brings out the effect of fiscal expansions like an increase in expenditure by the government (or a decrease in income taxes) on the exchange rate. Such a fiscal expansion raises effective demand, output, and income at the initial equilibrium exchange rate. The Y_iY_i curve now shifts to the right and the exchange rate appreciates at the new equilibrium point *D*. The logic is as follows. An increase in income due to a fiscal expansion raises the transactions demand for money. With RBI not increasing the stock of money, wealth holders meet their additional demand for cash by selling domestic bonds. This raises the domestic rate of interest and shifts the portfolio of assets in favour of rupee-assets. The demand for dollars declines and as a consequence the exchange rate appreciates. Thus, the asset or portfolio choice approach to exchange rate determination links exchange rate movements with both monetary and fiscal variables.

This approach also brings out the loss of autonomy for a central bank over its money supply under a pegged exchange rate regime. To illustrate, suppose, RBI pegs the exchange rate or the value of the rupee vis-à-vis the dollar at e^*. Under a pegged exchange rate regime, the wealth holders do not expect the home currency to depreciate or appreciate as long as they believe that RBI is committed to defending the pegged rate. Thus, the expected rate of return on dollar-assets $\tilde{r}_u$ is simply the US interest rate r_u, and the $\tilde{r}_u$-curve in Figure 24.12 is no longer relevant. Suppose, for a given stock of dollars in circulation, H_u^*, and liquidity preference of US wealth holders, r_u^* is the US money market equilibrium rate of interest on dollar-assets. This is shown in the lower right hand side panel in Figure 24.14. Then given the money demand function in India, RBI must supply the stock of money H_i^* that results in a domestic interest rate r_i^*

exactly equal to this US interest rate on dollar-assets *at any level* of the pegged exchange rate. If RBI puts a smaller stock of money in circulation, such as H_i', the domestic interest rate rises above r_u^*. This will induce wealth holders to sell dollar-assets and buy rupee-assets. To prohibit the exchange rate from appreciating, RBI must buy dollars and thereby put back in circulation the domestic currency withdrawn earlier. The money stock thus returns to its initial level H_i^*. Note that in the process the rate of interest on rupee-assets falls back to its initial equilibrium level $r_i^* = r_u^*$. On the other hand, given H_u^* and the corresponding US interest rate r_u^*, if RBI puts a larger stock of domestic currency in circulation than H_i^*, the rate of interest on rupee-assets will fall below the US interest rate. Wealth holders' attempts to convert their rupee-assets into dollar-assets will create an excess demand for dollars. To prohibit the exchange rate from depreciating, RBI must sell dollars and thereby withdraw currencies that were put in circulation. The stock of money again returns to its initial level. Thus, RBI cannot control the money supply and peg the exchange rate simultaneously.

From the previous discussion it appears that the insulation property of a pegged exchange rate regime no longer holds. To see this, suppose there is a money contraction by the US Federal Reserve Bank from the stock of US currencies in circulation H_u^* to H_u'. This raises the US interest rate on dollar deposits and puts an upward pressure on the rupee-dollar exchange rate for reasons spelled above. To prohibit the exchange rate from depreciating, RBI now must raise the rate of interest on rupee deposits to match the higher US interest rate through a corresponding contraction of the money supply from H_i^* to H_i'. That is, a contractionary monetary policy pursued by the US Federal Reserve Bank must be matched by a corresponding monetary contraction by RBI. Similarly, a monetary expansion in the United States must be matched by a corresponding monetary expansion by RBI to defend its pegged exchange rate.

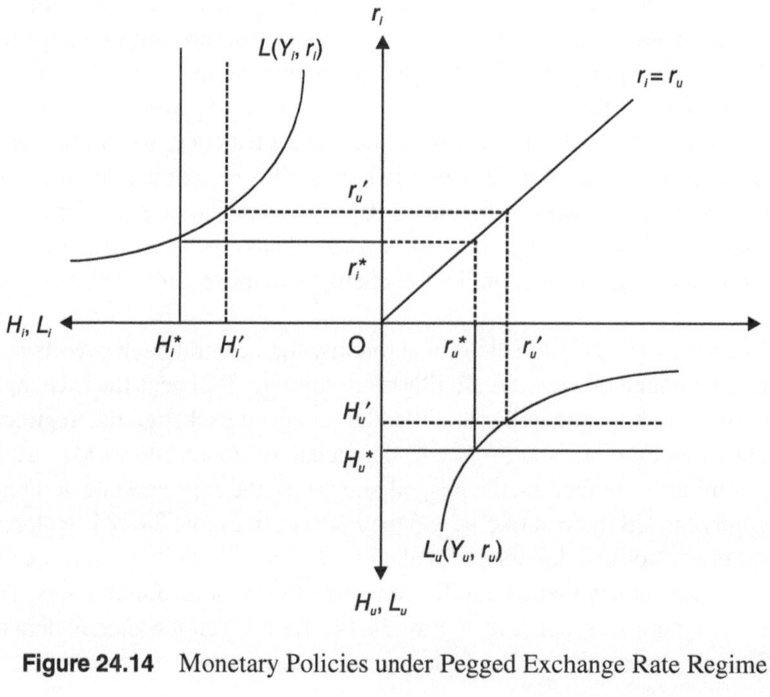

Figure 24.14 Monetary Policies under Pegged Exchange Rate Regime

A monetary contraction is deflationary and when prices are flexible, a monetary expansion is inflationary. Thus, under a pegged exchange rate regime, India imports inflation or deflation from the United States. The real sector of the economy is no longer insulated from the external shock as well since expansionary and contractionary monetary policies affect aggregate output and income under the assumption of sticky real wages.

24.4 PURCHASING POWER PARITY AND THE EXCHANGE RATE

As we have seen in our discussion in the earlier sections of this chapter, the PPP condition is an important building bloc of both the monetarist model and Mundell and Flemming's monetary approach. Under wage-price flexibility, this PPP condition provides us a theory of a long run exchange rate in the monetarist tradition. In the sub-section below this monetarist theory is elaborated upon. However, how far PPP holds in the short run as well as in the long run is itself empirically questionable. Evidence does not seem to favour the PPP condition even for countries that produce a single good so that PPP would essentially mean the Law of One Price. Bananas are not sold everywhere at the same price when converted into the same currency unit. A related issue is of an incomplete exchange rate pass-through. Economists offer several theoretical explanations for this PPP puzzle and incomplete exchange rate pass-through, which we discuss in subsequent sub-sections.

24.4.1 Wage-Price Flexibility and the Long-Run Exchange Rate

In the asset or portfolio choice approach, we have seen that changes in money supply affect the exchange rate under clean float. An extreme position in this regard is that of the monetarists who claim that the exchange rate is solely determined by relative money supplies. In the tradition of the quantity theory of money, under the assumption of wage-price flexibility, a monetary expansion proportionately changes prices and the exchange rate. Thus, an exchange

Box 24.4 Sterilization and the Autonomy of Monetary Policy

The central bank of a country can sterilize its reserve flow through open market operations to keep the monetary base constant. Thus, its control over money supply (or its autonomy over monetary policy) can be retained under a pegged regime by resorting to sterilization. But, such a sterilization policy will fail when domestic and foreign assets are perfect substitutes. In the above example, a contraction in the money supply in the United States causes RBI to lower its money supply. Suppose now that RBI sterilizes this by buying domestic assets, injecting more money and thus keeping the monetary base constant. But as soon as it does so the bond prices rise and the interest rate on domestic assets declines. Everyone would then try to convert rupee-assets into dollar-assets and thus raise their dollar demand. RBI then must sell dollars in order to prevent the exchange rate from depreciating. This means that RBI has to withdraw domestic money *again* from the economy. Thus, a policy of sterilization to retain control over domestic money supply is *self-defeating* when assets are perfect substitutes. Such a policy may work only when assets are imperfect substitutes (or capital mobility is imperfect) since interest differentials can persist in such a case even at the equilibrium.

rate is purely a monetary phenomenon. To illustrate the monetarist position, note that from the PPP condition in equation (24.2) the exchange rate can be expressed as the ratio of price levels of India and the United States:

$$e = \frac{P_i}{P_u} \tag{24.25}$$

Now by the monetary theory, the price levels vary with money supply (or money stock):

$$P_i = \frac{H_i}{L_i(Y_i, r_i)},\ P_u = \frac{H_u}{L_u(Y_u, r_u)} \tag{24.26}$$

Substitution of these equilibrium conditions in equation (24.25) yields the exchange rate as functions of money stocks:

$$e = \frac{H_i}{H_u} \frac{L_u(Y_u, r_u)}{L_i(Y_i, r_i)} \tag{24.27}$$

Since the wage-price flexibility ensures that output is fixed at the full employment level, so changes in money stock do not have any effect on output levels. The interest rate is also unaffected. That is, money is neutral in the classical macroeconomic tradition. This means that changes in the exchange rate are governed only by changes in money stocks:

$$\hat{e} = \hat{H}_i - \hat{H}_u \tag{24.28}$$

This is the basis of the monetarist claim that the long run exchange rate is a monetary phenomenon. Two comments are warranted here. First, if both RBI and the US Federal Reserve Bank raise their stocks of money in circulation by the same proportion, the exchange rate in the long run will remain unchanged. Second, a *ceteris paribus* change in the money stock in India depreciates the exchange rate and raises the rupee price level proportionately:

$$\hat{e} = \hat{P}_i = \hat{H}_i \tag{24.29}$$

This proportionality rule follows from equations (24.26) and (24.28).

24.4.2 The Purchasing Power Parity Puzzle

The PPP condition in equation (24.2) explained earlier is the absolute version of PPP, whereas the relative version of PPP states that the real exchange rate *R*, or TOT, is equal to one:

$$R \equiv \frac{eP_u}{P_i} = 1 \tag{24.30}$$

The monetarist claim that the exchange rate changes proportionately with price levels or with the stock of money also follows directly from this relative PPP. Furthermore, this version of PPP postulates that the rate of appreciation or depreciation of the rupee vis-à-vis the dollar is equal to the difference in inflation rates between India and the United States.

Empirical evidence, however, does not seem to support either version of the PPP condition. Two consensuses have emerged from empirical observations. First, real exchange rates tend to their PPP values in the very long run. Second, short run deviations from PPP are large and volatile. This is the PPP puzzle, because the PPP condition when interpreted as the Law of One Price may seem logical as we had explained earlier. Economists have offered quite a few explanations for these observations and the PPP puzzle.

One obvious explanation is trade costs such as tariffs, non-tariff barriers, and transport costs, which create a wedge between prices of the same good in two countries when expressed in the same currency unit. Imported goods having a non-traded or localized input is another major explanation. The price of imported bananas in supermarkets also includes transportation from sea ports to the supermarkets, labour costs, taxes, and insurances. That is, what we pay is the price of *value added bananas*. Like the non-traded input component, the existence of non-traded final goods and productivity differences across traded and non-traded sectors of trading nations can also explain the PPP puzzle. To illustrate, consider the composite traded good and non-traded good framework discussed earlier, with capital being internationally mobile across India and the United States. Thus, in both countries, the same rate of return to capital prevails, which is denoted by r^*. Moreover, suppose labour is equally productive in the non-traded sector in both the countries, but it is more productive in the production of the traded good in the United States than in India. Given these simplifying assumptions, a perfectly competitive product and factor markets in the two countries imply the following zero-profit conditions:

$$P_T^c = a_{LT}^c W^c + a_{KT} r^*, \; c = i, u \tag{24.31}$$

$$P_N^c = a_{LN} W^c + a_{KN} r^* \tag{24.32}$$

If consumers spend the same ρ fraction of their incomes on the traded good and $(1-\rho)$ fraction of their incomes on the non-traded good everywhere, the price level (or index) can be defined as $P^c = (P_T^c)^{\rho}(P_N^c)^{1-\rho}$, $c = i, u$. Suppose the exchange rate is fixed and normalized to unity. By arbitrage and the consequent Law of One Price, international trade equalizes the prices of the composite traded good: $P_T^i = P_T^u$. Hence by the assumption made above that $a_{LT}^u < a_{LT}^i$, the money wage must be lower in India: $W^i < W^u$. This in turn means that the price of the non-traded good must be lower in India than in the United States. Therefore, $P^i < P^u$, and thus PPP does not hold.

Paul Krugman (1987), on the other hand, argues that deviations from PPP essentially reflect producers' ability to price discriminate across countries. This is what he calls the pricing-to-market phenomenon. In many instances monopolistic firms segment international markets and limit the scope of arbitrage between these markets by limiting warranty of durables within specific geographical locations or political boundaries. For example, warranty on Macintosh laptops manufactured and bought in the United States is not negotiable in case of trouble-shooting while using it in China. Such a limited geographical warranty of products, limits the scope of arbitrage, and enables MNCs to charge different prices of the same product in different countries. This pricing-to-market phenomenon (or international price discrimination) is a major explanation of deviations from the PPP condition in an imperfectly competitive world.

24.4.3 Exchange Rate Pass-Through

Under the Law of One Price, we can expect that a depreciation of the rupee should lower the dollar price of Indian goods in the US market proportionately given the same rupee price. Similarly, an appreciation of the rupee should raise prices of Indian goods sold in the US markets proportionately. That is, $\hat{P}_u = -\hat{e}$. This is known as the exchange rate pass-through. The effect of a change in the exchange rate is fully reflected in prices. In fact, this *complete* exchange rate pass-through is the basic premise underlying the argument that a nominal devaluation of the domestic currency will boost the volume of exports and lower the volume of imports. But often the exchange rate pass-through is incomplete in the sense that price changes are less than proportional.

In some cases, the price change is even perverse. For example, during 1980–84, the USD appreciated vis-à-vis the German currency, mark. Given the mark-price, German cars should have been sold in the United States at a lower dollar-price. But, instead, German cars were sold at a higher dollar price during that period. Thus, German exporters were unable to pass-through the exchange rate variation in their price of exports to the United States.

These instances of incomplete and sometimes perverse exchange rate pass-through can also be explained in similar terms as mentioned earlier because an incomplete (or perverse) exchange rate pass-through essentially means a deviation from the PPP condition. The most important explanation is, however, again the pricing-to-market phenomenon. Rudiger Dornbusch (1987) has shown such possibilities in Brander's strategic trade model, Krugman's monopolistic competition model, and in a circular city model of characteristics approach with transport costs. Consider, for example, the strategic trade model of Brander (1981) discussed in Chapter 8. An identical good is produced by two monopolies in India and the United States with identical constant marginal costs. To be more specific, suppose only labour is used to produce this good and one unit of labour produces one unit of the good. Suppose w_i and w_u are the money wages in India and the United States respectively in their respective currencies. Thus, by assumption these are unit and marginal costs in the two countries. Recall that by reciprocal dumping, both firms supply (or export) to each other's markets. However, by the market segmentation property, the equilibrium supplies in the two markets are independent of each other. To start with, consider only the market in India where the US firm exports its output produced in a factory in the United States. Consider the following linear demand for the good in India:

$$p_i = a - (q_i + q_u) \tag{24.33}$$

where, p_i is the rupee-price of the good and q_i and q_u are quantities sold by the Indian firm and the US firm in India respectively. The profits of the two firms from selling the good in the Indian market, expressed in their respective national currencies, are:

$$\pi_i = (p_i - w_i)q_i,\ \pi_u = \left(\frac{p_i}{e} - w_u\right)q_u \tag{24.34}$$

Profit maximization yields the following equilibrium output levels and the rupee-price of the good in India's domestic market:

$$q_i^* = \frac{1}{3}[a - 2w_i + ew_u],\ q_u^* = \frac{1}{3}[a - 2ew_u + w_i] \tag{24.35}$$

$$p_i^* = \frac{1}{3}[a + w_i + ew_u] \tag{24.36}$$

It is now straightforward to check that:

$$\hat{p}_i^* = \frac{1}{3}\frac{ew_u}{p_i^*}\hat{e} \tag{24.37}$$

Since under market imperfection $ew_u < P_i^*$, so depreciation of the domestic currency raises the rupee-price of imports from the United States less than proportionately. That is, the exchange rate pass-through is incomplete. The reason is simple. Currency depreciation raises the rupee-cost of producing the good for the US firm. Under perfect competition this would have meant a proportionate rise in the rupee price of India's imports from the United States. But when the US firm has market power, as in the above example, it absorbs part of the cost increase (measured in Indian rupee) in reduced profit by raising its price less than proportionately to make up for the loss in its market share due to the increased rupee-cost and price.

If the demand for the good in the US market is the same as defined in equation (24.33), except that the price p_u is measured in dollar units, then by the market symmetry property the export price of the Indian firm in the US market is given by:

$$p_u^* = \frac{1}{3}\left[a + \frac{w_i}{e} + w_u\right] \Rightarrow \hat{p}_u^* = -\frac{1}{3}\frac{w_u}{ep_u^*}\hat{e} \tag{24.38}$$

Box 24.5 Incomplete Pass-Through in the US Import Price

Using data on currency and prices for US imports, Gopinath et al. (2008) find that there is a large difference in the pass-through into the US import prices of the average good priced in dollars versus the average good priced in non-dollar currencies. One month after a change in the exchange rate, the pass-through is nearly zero for goods priced in dollars and nearly complete for goods priced in non-dollar currencies. Thus, in the short run when prices are rigid, the pass-through into import prices of goods priced in the producer's currency is 100 per cent and it is 0 per cent for goods priced in the local currency. But, 24 months after the shock, pass-through is only 0.17 for dollar priced goods and 0.98 for non-dollar priced goods. That is, when in the longer run prices adjust the difference in pass-through declines.

That is, depreciation of the Indian currency lowers the price of the good imported by the United States from India, but by less than proportionately. Thus, again, the exchange rate pass-through is incomplete.

This benchmark case of international duopoly can be extended to any number of domestic and foreign oligopolists. For example, if there were n_i and n_u number of Indian and US firms respectively, a currency depreciation again would have raised India's import price less than proportionately:

$$\hat{p}_i^* = \left[\frac{n_u}{n_i + n_u + 1}\right]\frac{ew_u}{p_i^*}\hat{e} \tag{24.39}$$

Note that the larger had been the ratio of Indian to US firms, the smaller would have been the price rise. That is, the extent to which pass-through is incomplete now depends on the relative number of US firms.

APPENDIX A24

I. Price Changes in Monetarist Model under Flexible Exchange Rate

From equation (24.14) in the text reproduced as equation (A24.1):

$$P_i = \frac{v_i H_i + ev_u H_u}{Y_i + Y_u} \tag{A24.1}$$

differentiation with respect to the exchange rate yields:

$$dP_i = \frac{v_u H_u}{Y_W} de \Rightarrow \hat{P}_i = \frac{ev_u H_u}{P_i Y_W}\hat{e} = (1-\lambda)\hat{e}$$

where, $(1-\lambda) = \frac{ev_u H_u}{P_i Y_W}$ is the share of expenditure by the United States in aggregate world expenditure on goods measured in rupee.

On the other hand, by the PPP condition, $P_u = \frac{P_i}{e}$:

$$dP_u = -\frac{v_i H_i}{Y_W e^2} de \Rightarrow \hat{P}_u = -\frac{v_i H_i}{eP_u Y_W}\hat{e} = -\frac{v_i H_i}{P_i Y_W}\hat{e} = -\lambda\hat{e}$$

where, $\lambda = \frac{v_i H_i}{P_i Y_W}$ is the share of India's expenditure in aggregate world expenditure on goods measured in rupees.

II. Mundell–Fleming Model under Flexible Exchange Rate: Shift of the IS Curve and the B = 0 Locus

Recall the equation of the IS curve and the $B = 0$ locus from equations (24.19) and (24.21) reproduced as (A24.2) and (A24.3):

$$Y_i = C(Y_i) + I(r_i) + \bar{G}_i + [M_u(e) - eM_i(e, Y_i)] \tag{A24.2}$$

$$B = [M_u(e) - eM_i(e, Y_i)] + k_i(r_i - r_w) = 0 \tag{A24.3}$$

Shifts of these curves, when measured horizontally, are essentially changes in the income levels for any given domestic interest rate. Thus, differentiating equation (A24.2) holding r_i constant we obtain:

$$dY_i = cdY_i + \left[\frac{\partial M_u}{\partial e} - e\frac{\partial M_i}{\partial e} - M_i\right]de - e\frac{\partial M_i}{\partial Y_i}dY_i \Rightarrow dY_i\big|_{IS} = \frac{M_i[\varepsilon_u + \varepsilon_i - 1]}{s_i + m_i}de$$

Similarly, from equation (A24.3) we obtain:

$$0 = \left[\frac{\partial M_u}{\partial e} - e\frac{\partial M_i}{\partial e} - M_i\right]de - e\frac{\partial M_i}{\partial Y_i}dY_i \Rightarrow dY_i\big|_{B=0} = \frac{M_i[\varepsilon_u + \varepsilon_i - 1]}{m_i}de$$

SUMMARY POINTS

- The essence of the monetarist approach is that any BOP imbalance is only a *temporary* phenomenon that reflects an adjustment of actual to desired holding of money and other stocks of assets by wealth holders. It is purely a *monetary phenomenon.*
- David Hume's price-specie flow mechanism, which demonstrated that the mercantilist idea of export promotion to maintain a trade surplus and acquiring specie will be self-defeating in the long run, is the cornerstone of the monetarist model.
- Wage-price flexibility, purchasing power parity, and non-sterilization of the flow of foreign currencies are the three basic assumptions or building blocs of the monetarist model.
- Under a fixed exchange rate, BOP adjustment in the long run takes place through changes in the supply of money or the stock of high-powered money, whereas under

(*contd*)

Summary Points (*contd*)

a flexible exchange rate (or clean float) BOP adjusts through changes in the money demand.

- The important implication of the monetarist model is that a country's central bank loses its autonomy over the monetary policy under a pegged exchange rate regime. That is, it cannot control both money supply and exchange rate.
- In Robert Mundell and J.M. Flemming's monetary approach, the basic monetarist proposition still holds but now a BOP imbalance adjusts over time through changes in income rather than in prices. Mundell's income-specie flow now constitutes the basic adjustment mechanism.
- The other important proposition of the Mundell-Flemming IS–LM analysis is the relative efficacy of fiscal and monetary policies as stabilizers of income changes in the presence of capital mobility.
- A monetary policy is totally ineffective in changing aggregate output under perfect capital mobility and fixed exchange rate regardless of the degree of capital mobility.
- A fiscal expansion is effective in raising aggregate output and income though its effects get moderated by the degree of capital mobility under a fixed exchange rate regime.
- Under clean float, a monetary expansion will be fully effective in raising aggregate output, whereas a fiscal expansion will be totally ineffective. These are the dual of Mundell's results.
- The asset or portfolio choice approach to exchange rate determination demonstrates that the exchange rate itself is a monetary phenomenon. It also links exchange rate movements with both monetary and fiscal variables.
- The PPP puzzle is the empirical observation that real exchange rates tend to their PPP values in the very long run whereas deviations from PPP in the short run are large and volatile.
- Trade costs such as tariffs, non-tariff barriers, transport costs, value addition by non-traded or localized inputs, productivity differences across traded and non-traded final goods sectors, and pricing-to-market are some of the major explanations of the PPP puzzle.
- Explanations for incomplete exchange rate pass-through are similar by which changes in the exchange rate cause less than proportionate changes in prices.

KEYWORDS

- **David Hume's price-specie flow mechanism** postulates that it is not possible for a country to acquire specie or wealth through a BOP surplus since in the long run the country's stock of gold or specie will return to its initial level through a rise in the prices of goods.
- **Purchasing power parity** states that price levels of trading partners expressed in their respective currencies must be the same when expressed in a common currency. Often termed as the Law of One Price, this means bananas must be sold at the same price everywhere when converted into a common currency.
- **Sterilization** is a process by which the central bank of a country adjusts its domestic lending and borrowing to match changes in its foreign exchange reserves in a way that keeps the stock of high-powered money or the monetary base unchanged.
- **High-powered money** or **the monetary base** of a country is the total currencies issued by its central bank. This is a liability of the central bank.
- **Neutrality of money** is an important postulate of the classical macroeconomic system. It states that changes in the stock of money change money variables—prices and money wages—proportionately without changing real variables like output, savings, and investment.
- **Capital mobility is perfect** when any domestic policy induced increase in the domestic interest rate over the world interest rate instantaneously attracts an infinitely large capital inflow to restore back the parity between domestic and world interest rates.
- **Uncovered interest parity** is the equalization of the expected rates of return on domestic and foreign assets based on an expected spot exchange rate in the future. This is so called because it does not cover the wealth holder against *unexpected* depreciation of the domestic currency vis-à-vis the foreign currency.
- **Covered interest parity** condition is the equalization of the expected rates of return based on a forward exchange rate for the domestic currency that fully covers the investor from capital losses from any unexpected depreciation of the domestic currency.
- Assets are said to be **perfect substitutes** when wealth holders are indifferent between portfolios of their assets that yield the same expected returns.
- Assets are said to be **imperfect substitutes** when these are differentiated by the element of risk and its degree, and thus wealth holders are *not* indifferent between assets when they yield the same expected rates of return.
- **Exchange rate pass-through** means that the effect of a change in the exchange rate is fully reflected in the price levels of the trading nations. This follows from the PPP condition. But often exchange rate pass-through is incomplete in the sense that price changes are less than proportional.

EXERCISES

1. How did David Hume criticize the mercantilist view that a country should promote exports and discourage imports to acquire species?
2. Consider the following production functions in Canada and the United States:

   $$Y_C = \frac{1}{50} L_C^2, \quad Y_u = 1000 L_u^{0.5}$$

   Number of workers in Canada and the United States are 500 and 400 respectively. Canadians hold 20 per cent of their incomes in cash to carry out transactions of goods and the Americans hold 10 per cent of their incomes in cash. The central banks of the two countries issue currencies worth Canadian dollars 2,000 and US dollars 3,000. Suppose wages and prices are fully flexible.
   (a) Determine the pre-trade price levels in the two countries.
   (b) Under PPP, determine the price level expressed in Canadian dollars and in US dollars at the global trade equilibrium after these countries trade with each other. Assume that 2 units of Canadian dollars exchange for one unit of the US dollar.
3. In the above example, suppose the Canadian central bank issues additional currencies worth Canadian dollars 1,000. What would be the trade balance position of the two countries and corresponding price level expressed in Canadian dollars at the short run equilibrium? During the adjustment towards the long run equilibrium, should this price level rise or fall?
4. In a monetarist world, automatic adjustment towards the long run BOP equilibrium under a flexible exchange rate is essentially a mechanism of demand adjustment whereas that under a pegged exchange rate regime is a mechanism of supply adjustment. Explain.
5. In a two-country monetarist world, if the central bank of a country issues new currencies, how does it affect the country's BOP in the short run and the domestic currency price in the long run?
6. Reformulate Mundell's income specie flow mechanism when the national incomes of India and the United States are inter-linked through trade.
7. In a closed economy government investment crowds out private investment. Does the same hold in an open economy with capital mobility? Explain.
8. Consider the following money market and BOP equilibrium conditions for India, with the exchange rate assumed to be fixed and normalized to one:

   $1000 = 5Y_i - r_i, \ 0 = 2000 - 2Y_i + 3(r_i - r_u)$

   (a) Starting from an initial BOP equilibrium, if government expenditure in India is raised by 10 units, what can you infer about the BOP position in the short run equilibrium?
   (b) Does your answer change if there is an increase in the money supply instead?
9. Why is it that a monetary expansion under a pegged exchange rate and perfect capital mobility cannot raise aggregate output and real income? Does imperfect capital mobility help?

10. Suppose wealth holders expect three units of rupees to exchange for one unit of the US dollar at a future date. In the current period, the money demand functions are given as:

    $L_i = Y_i - 100r_i$, $L_u = 0.5Y_u - 200r_u$

    RBI and the Federal Bank supply currencies worth Rs 2,000 and USD 3,000 respectively. If full employment prevails in both the countries such that Y_i = Rs 500 and Y_u = USD 800, find out the equilibrium rupee–dollar exchange rate.
11. Consider a rupee-denominated and a dollar-denominated asset that are certain to yield 10 and 5 per cent interest rates respectively at a future date. If the wealth holders are uncertain about the spot exchange rate at such a date and want to insure their expected returns through a forward contract, what will be the forward exchange rate that they will negotiate if the current exchange rate is 2?
12. Suppose the expected future spot rate rises by 20 per cent. Should the exchange rate depreciate or appreciate today? Explain your answer logically and check in terms of the example above.
13. Suppose effective demand for India's aggregate output is not sufficient to generate employment for all workers there. The effective demand relationship and the money market equilibrium condition are:

    $Y_i = 30 + M_u - eM_i$, $20 = Y_i - r_i$

    Determine India's real income and the current period rupee–dollar exchange rate given $M_u = 50$, $M_i = 0.4Y_i$, $r_u = 15$, and the expected future spot exchange rate being 8.
14. Suppose a German pharmaceutical MNC invents a new medicine and obtains an exclusive right of production and sale of this medicine across the globe. The demand functions for this medicine in India and Germany are estimated to be $x_i = 100 - 4P_i$ and $x_g = 150 - 2P_g$ respectively. If the production cost is $x_i + x_g$ and two units of rupees exchanges for one unit of the euro, does PPP or the Law of One Price hold?

SUGGESTED READING

Caves, R.E., J. Frankel, and R.W. Jones. (1995). *World Trade and Payments*. New York: HarperCollins College Publishers.

Dornbusch, R. (1980). *Open Economy Macroeconomics*. New York: Basic Books.

Krugman, P.R. and M. Obstfeld (2000). *International Economics: Theory and Policy*. Fifth Edition. Pearson Education Asia.

ADVANCED READING

Brander, James A. (1981). 'Intra-industry Trade in Identical Commodities', *Journal of International Economics,* 11: 1–14.

Dornbusch, R. (1987). 'Exchange Rate and Prices', *American Economic Review*, March: 93–106.

Flemming, J.M. (1962). 'Domestic Financial Policies under Fixed and Floating Exchange Rates', *IMF Staff Papers*, 9(3): 369–79.

Gopinath, G., O. Itskhoki, and R. Rigobon (2008). 'Currency Choice and Exchange Rate Pass-Through', *American Economic Review*, 100(1): 304–36.

Krugman, P.R. (1987). 'Pricing-to-Market When Exchange Rate Changes', in S.W. Arndt and J.D. Richardson (eds), *Real Financial Linkages in Open Economies*. Cambridge: MIT Press, pp. 49–70.

Lee, J.Y. (1997). 'Sterilizing Capital Inflows', Economic Issues No. 7, International Monetary Fund.

Mundell, R. (1961). 'International Disequilibrium System', *Kyklos* 14: 154–227.

——— (1963). 'Capital Mobility and Stabilization Policy under Fixed and Flexible Rates', *Canadian Journal of Economics and Political Science*, November: 475–85.

Obstfeld, Maurice. (1982). 'Can We Sterilize? Theory and Evidence', *American Economic Review*, 72(2): 45–50.

Obstfeld, M. and A. Taylor. (2004). *Global Capital Markets: Integration, Crisis, and Growth*. Cambridge, MA: Cambridge University Press.

Rogoff, K. (1996). 'Purchasing Power Parity Puzzle', *Journal of Economic Literature*, 34(2): 647–68.

25 Financial Crises in the Developing World

Financial crises have three different dimensions, which though may be intertwined and causing each other: external debt, balance-of-payments (or currency), and banking crises. While a few of the crises in the developing world have single dimensions, most crises have been a combination of these three dimensions: either, debt and balance-of-payments crises combining together ('dual' crises), or all three combining together ('triple' crises) as occurring mostly after the 1980s[1]. India's financial crisis culminating in 1991 is the typical example of having only the balance-of-payments dimension (the BOP Crisis), which has been discussed in Chapter 22. Asian Crisis in 1997 is the typical example of a dual crisis involving both balance-of-payments crisis and banking crisis. And, the financial crisis in Latin America and Africa in the early 1980s was essentially (private) external debt problems, though such debt problems eventually and inevitably triggered balance of payments crises as well. Altogether, the Debt Crisis in the early 1980s had turned into a major development crisis for these nations after the Great Depressions in 1930s. This Crisis, at the same time, can also be seen as a US banking crisis. Policies to manage the Latin American debt crisis eventually and effectively addressed and avoided a potential major banking crisis in the United States rather than lowering the debt burdens of the Latin American debtor countries and helping them return to path of growth and development (Ocampo, 2014). Compared to these examples of a Crisis originating in the developing world, the Great Depressions of the 1930s had multiple dimensions and originated in the United States after the collapse of Wall Street in October 1929. Recession was even stronger and widespread across the European countries and in many parts of the globe. The gold standard system collapsed resulting in a total disorder in the international financial system. There was also a sudden stop in external financing causing many countries including the Latin American countries to default on external debt obligations.

In this chapter, we will study about the 1980 Debt Crisis focusing on Latin America that led to a lost decade of development for these countries, and the policy issues involved in and management of the crises; and the financial (or dual banking and balance-of-payments) crisis in Asia during 1997–98, which spilled over to other parts of the globe as well, particularly Latin America and East Europe. There have been other crises in the world, the most notable being

[1] See Reinhart and Rogoff (2009) for different dimensions of crises including *domestic* debt crisis.

International Economics. Rajat Acharyya, Oxford University Press. © Oxford University Press 2022.
DOI: 10.1093/oso/9780192865144.003.0025

the Global financial crisis during 2007–08 — a combination of international banking crisis and housing bubble in the United States. But, here we limit our discussion on crises originating in the developing world, and most significantly, occurring under overvalued pegged (or crawling peg) exchange rate regimes with or without capital and exchange controls.[2]

25.1 LATIN AMERICAN DEBT CRISIS OF THE 1980S: NATURE, CAUSES AND CONSEQUENCES

As documented by Ocampo (2014), financial crises, in their different dimensions 'have been a recurrent phenomenon in Latin America's economic history'. But its debt crisis of the 1980s is unparallel and the severity and prolonged adverse consequences of the crisis have made it the most traumatic event in its economic history. Latin America faced strong *outside* pressures to avoid prolonged defaults and was forced to adopt contractionary macroeconomic policies (primarily in the form of public expenditure reduction). This helped avoid a banking crisis in the United States, but for Latin America this resulted in a lost decade of development.

During the first half of the 1980s, a rather large number of developing countries experienced external debt crises. They were in a situation where they could not fully service the *inherited* debts without further borrowing. The debt crisis reached a critical juncture when in August 1982 Mexico declared its inability to pay interests on external loans it had taken previously and pay back the principal on maturity. According to a World Bank Study report on 'Development and Debt Service: Dilemma of the 1980s' in 1986, 38 countries—mostly in Latin America and Africa—were almost on verge of defaulting on debt service and were engaged in multilateral debt re-negotiations (see Table 25.1 below). Figure 25.1 reports the growing external debt for a selected set of Latin American countries. Argentina, Brazil, Colombia, and Mexico are the largest countries in the region in terms of both their population sizes and gross domestic products. Venezuela is a medium-sized country. These countries, along with Chile, together account for almost 80 per cent of economic aggregates in Latin American region (Diaz-Alejandro, 1984). The dimension of the debt problem is evident from both jumps in external debt as a percentage of Gross National Income (GNI) and in debt servicing as a percentage of Gross National Income of these countries. The debt to GNI ratios doubled for Argentina, Brazil, and Mexico during 1980–83. Venezuela's debt ratio was almost stable before it increased steeply during 1982–84 (see Figure 25.1a). Colombia had a relatively

Box 25.1 Definitions of Different Dimensions of Crises

Reinhart and Rogoff (2009) defined different dimensions of financial crisis as follows. A currency crisis arises when under a pegged regime annual devaluation of 15 per cent or more is administered vis-à-vis US Dollar, or any other foreign currency of intervention. An external debt crisis occurs when a country defaults on payment of debt obligations including principal or interest. A banking crisis, on the other hand, is either a bank run that leads to the closure, merging, or takeover by the public sector of one or more financial institutions; or, large-scale government assistance to an important financial institution (or a group of institutions) that triggers similar outcomes for other financial institutions.

[2] There were, of course, a few other crises during the 1990s worth mentioning. First was the Mexican currency (or BOP) crisis in 1994 that started with sudden devaluation of peso against US Dollar and was ignited by the capital flight that it triggered. Similarly, the Russian currency crisis in 1998 occurred through devaluation of ruble and consequent default on its external debt.

Table 25.1 Highly Indebted Developing Countries in 1980s

Africa	Latin & Central America	Other
Central African Republic	Argentina	Jamaica
Equatorial Guinea	Bolivia	Philippines
Ivory Coast	Brazil	Romania
Liberia	Chile	Yugoslavia
Madagascar	Costa Rica	
Malawi	Dominican Republic	
Mauritania	Ecuador	
Morocco	Guyana	
Mozambique	Honduras	
Niger	Mexico	
Nigeria	Nicaragua	
Senegal	Panama	
Sierra Leone	Peru	
Somalia	Uruguay	
Sudan	Venezuela	
Togo		
Uganda		
Zaire		
Zambia		

Source: World Debt Tables: External Debt of Developing Countries, 1985–86 in World Bank report 'Development and Debt Service: Dilemma of the 1980s' (World Bank, 1986).

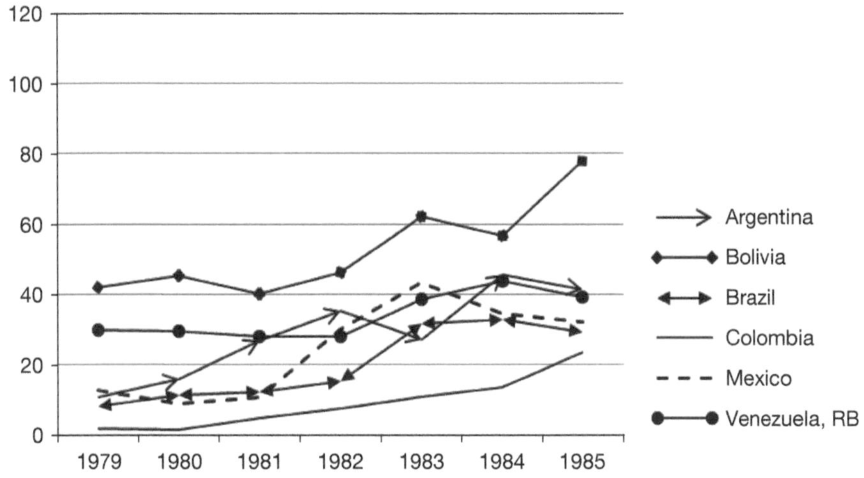

Figure 25.1a External Debt (% of Gross National Income)

Source: Author's compilation from World Development Indicator, World Bank https://databank.worldbank.org/).

slow growth in external debt as a percentage of her GNI, but it also doubled within a span of five years from a little over 20 per cent to more than 40 per cent. Bolivia, already having the largest stock of external debt among these countries, had experienced the largest and most prolonged increase in the debt ratio.

Figure 25.1b, on the other hand, shows the trends in debt service as a percentage of GNI for these countries. The steepest rise in the ratio can be observed for Bolivia and Mexico during 1981–82. Argentina experienced the most prolonged increase in the debt service ratio from below 4 per cent in 1979 to 8 per cent in 1984. On the other hand, Brazil's debt ratio peaked by 1981 and remained stable thereafter till falling off in 1984 to the 1979-level. The debt service to export ratio also had a similar trend.

From mid and late 1980s some of the Latin American debt-ridden countries began to restrict the amount of their debt servicing. Peru set the ball rolling by unilaterally declaring its debt servicing limit at 10 per cent of its value of exports. Soon internal political forces in Argentina, Bolivia, Brazil, and Mexico started pressurizing their governments to adopt similar policy limits on the amount of debt servicing.

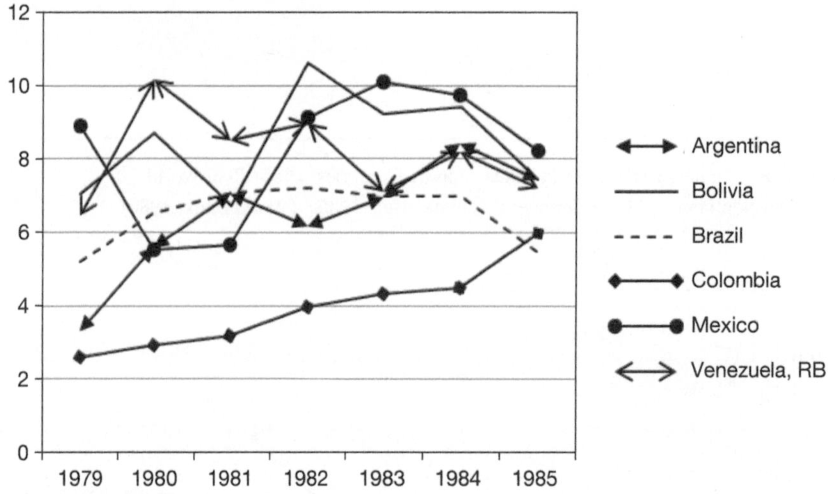

Figure 25.1b Total Debt Service (% of Gross National Income)

Source: Author's compilation from World Development Indicator, World Bank (https://databank.worldbank.org/).

To understand the plausible causes of the debt crisis, it will be helpful to look into the nature and dimension of the crisis. Investment projects undertaken by local firms in many Latin American countries were often financed by external loans and borrowing from abroad, mostly taken from the private banks in the United States and Europe[3]. The private local banks and financial intermediaries guaranteed those loans taken from abroad. The local banks and financial intermediaries, on the other hand, were de facto insured by governments. This, according to Diaz-Alejandro (1984), led to extravagant financial practices and massive

[3] In contrast, African countries borrowed largely from international institutions at subsidized rates. The nature of debt problem was thus different than in case of the Latin American (and some Asian) countries.

borrowing from foreign banks. There were also huge imbalances between private and public investments. The ability of the Latin American countries to repay back the principals and interest payments were adversely affected by the decline in the absolute dollar value of exports during 1981–83 for the major Latin American countries primarily due to the decline in the terms of trade (ToT), except for Brazil (see Figure 25.2). Changes in export destinations were also significant: with a few exceptions, exports to other Latin American countries and to OPEC declined quite significantly. This increased the debt to export ratio quite significantly for many Latin American countries.

Interestingly, until 1981–82, new bank loans were made available by the foreign banks even when the Latin American countries like Argentina, Brazil, Colombia, Chile, and Mexico defaulted on debt servicing of earlier bank loans. While this strategy of continued advancement of loans may apparently seem to be irrational on part of the creditors, economists like Krugman (1985) and Sachs (1984) quite convincingly demonstrated that such loans, being mostly *involuntary* in nature, are 'collectively rational'. We will return to their arguments in the following section. But, such loans collapsed dramatically during 1981–82, primarily for Argentina, Brazil, Chile, and Mexico. In most of the cases, dramatic fall in loans of 'involuntary' nature, that were collectively rational till a year ago, exceeded the fall in exports, and turned the export decline into the worst crisis for many Latin American countries since the early 1930s. Outflows due to interest payments far exceeded net new loans. Many private sector firms became bankrupt, which threatened local banks and financial intermediaries as the fear of acquisition of these firms by foreign banks and corporations loomed large. Such fears of acquisitions and takeover of domestic firms made the case for bailouts appealing and the governments stepped in to protect assets of the domestic firms and to maintain employment. By 1984 most of the private external debt had been socialized (Diaz-Alejandro, 1984). This had been largely the case in Chile. For all other countries, government bailout policies included subsidizing debt servicing through special exchange rates, scheduling of repayment of loans and tax concessions.

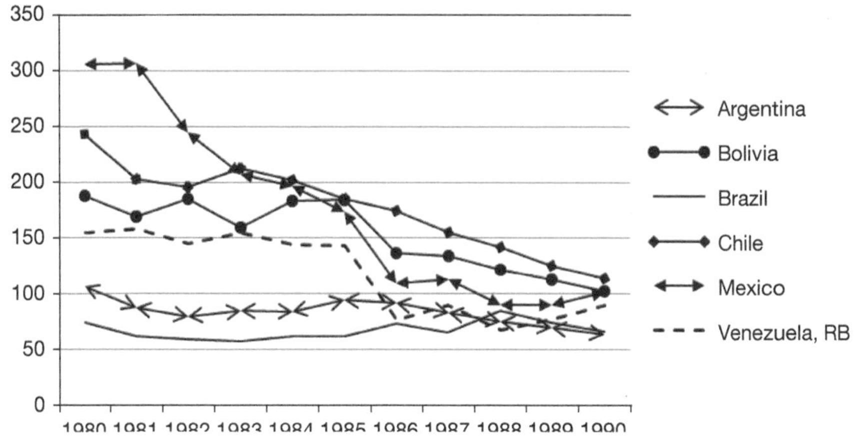

Figure 25.2 ToT deterioration for some indebted Latin American countries (Index Base Year: 2000)

Source: Author's compilation from UNCTAD data (https://unctadstat.unctad.org)

The crisis also reduced incentives to save and induced further capital outflows by domestic residents of these Latin American countries. Such capital flights worsened the crisis further. Due to political uncertainties, middle and upper classes in many Latin American countries had always diversified their portfolios, putting a significant part of their wealth in United States, UK, and Switzerland. Expectations that the overvalued pegged exchange rates could not be sustained for too long so that the domestic currency will depreciate significantly sooner or later causing capital losses on wealth held in domestic currency denominated assets created further incentives for such capital flight. On the other hand, unrestricted convertibility of currencies paved the way for capital flights.

Economists held different opinions regarding the cause of the debt crisis. Diaz-Alejandro (1984), Dornbusch (1985), and Ocampo (2014) emphasized upon external shocks as the primary cause, though they differed in respect of such external shocks. On the other hand, Branson, Krugman, Sachs, and others argued that domestic, trade and exchange rate policies pursued in many Latin American countries were no less important in putting the country in the trajectory of the crisis. For example, according to Diaz-Alejandro (1984), 'the breakdown of international financial markets and an abrupt change in conditions and rules for international lending' coupled with faulty domestic policies adopted by the Latin American countries spelt much of the debt crisis. The distribution of domestic income and wealth was also a contributing factor for many of them. He emphasized on the twin cause by commenting that the 'non-linear interactions between this unusual and persistent external shock and risky or faulty domestic policies led to a crisis of severe depth and length, one that neither shocks nor bad policy alone could have generated'. Krugman (1984), however, argued that the external shock of sudden and abrupt drying up of external loans to fund the investment projects and debt servicing was not something purely exogenous but was caused in part by the fundamentals like domestic economic management, the terms of trade, and interest rates. Worsening terms of trade and real appreciations of domestic currencies caused declines in exports and thus ability of countries to repay back.

There was also a purely exogenous shock causing the Crisis as the Federal Reserve Board of the United States decided to raise interest rates steeply after 1979 to mitigate its domestic inflation spiral (ECLAC, 1996). According to Ocampo (2014), this interest rate shock originating in USA, known as the 'Volcker shock' named after the then Chairman of the Federal Reserve Bank, had a 'direct impact on the debt service since much of Latin America's external debt had been contracted at floating interest rates'. These higher interest rates along with falling commodity prices resulted in steep increases in external debt ratios. Fall in GDP due to austerity measures in the form of expenditure reduction, and large devaluations to manage foreign exchange reserves compounded the problem. This triggered what Diaz-Alejandro said 'an abrupt change in conditions and rules for international lending'. Similar argument is put forward by Sachs (1986) for the debt crisis in Brazil. It suffered sharp terms of trade and interest rate shocks during 1979–81, and by 1982 it was burdened with the world's largest external debt. Suddenness and 'collective irrationality' of the lending cutoff that Diaz-Alejandro (1984) pointed out, also hit Brazil and worsened her crisis, like other Latin American countries.

Pegged (or crawling peg as in case of Brazil) overvalued domestic currencies vis-à-vis US Dollar by most of the Latin American countries prior to the 1980s—with the exception of Mexico which abandoned its fixed nominal exchange rate in 1976—did not help the situation either. This policy was primarily intended to keep inflation rates low. But, the international reserves of US Dollar that was needed to defend the pegged exchange rates were not sufficient. This had been more prominent for countries without exchange control, which essentially created incentives for capital flight in face of expectations of future depreciation of the domestic currency. As, Sachs (1986) pointed out, 'fixed exchange rates proved untenable in countries with high inherited inflation, large budget deficits, and weak financial sectors'. Furthermore, abrupt and massive devaluations of the early 1980s aggravated the crisis. External sector policies adopted in major Latin American countries had varied widely prior to their debt crises. Brazil and Mexico resorted to heavy external borrowing amongst them. While there were lesser restrictions on convertibility of domestic currency and capital movements in Mexico and Venezuela, these were severely restricted in Colombia and Brazil. Argentina and Chile were pursuing relatively freer trade policies along with dismantling of capital controls compared to the protectionist regime of Brazil.

An altogether different view of external shock causing the debt crisis was put forward by Dornbusch (1985): OECD macroeconomic performance shocks influencing the indebted Latin American countries through commodity prices, real interest rates, and quantity effects on exports. Branson (1985) and Cline (1985) held similar opinion. At the same time, Dornbusch argued that such performances had differential or asymmetric impacts on the debtor countries due to three main factors: differences in trade structure or initial indebtedness; differences in domestic policies; and, differences in ability to adapt to externals shocks. In general, indebted Latin American countries had much higher debt-export ratios than debt-GDP ratios compared to indebted countries in Africa or Asia, mainly because of their lower export-GDP ratios. The African countries, on the other hand, had low interest-export ratio, compared to their debt-export ratio because large part of their external loans were from international agencies at low concessional rates. Thus, according to Dornbusch (1985), 'the more closed economies in Latin America have less relative capacity for debt service than the more open Asian ones do, and so run into crisis conditions sooner.' However, as Branson (1985), had pointed out, these are intertwined: differential ability to adjust might be due to structural differences, which in turn are partly brought about by differences in domestic policies.

Box 25.2 Why Asian Countries did not experience the debt problem in 1980s?

Jeffery Sachs was of the opinion that the Asian economies like Korea, Malaysia, The Philippines, and Thailand managed their exchange rate regimes better by frequent devaluation of the exchange rates and allowing it to float downward. Such a policy helped prevent an overvaluation of the real exchange rate. There were capital account restrictions that did not allow free convertibility of domestic currencies in US Dollar. Inflation rates were much less in these economies compared to those in the Latin American countries. Thus, real depreciation and erosion of purchasing power of domestic currencies were much lower making the domestic-currency denominated assets adequate stores of value. As a consequence of all these, the Asian economies did not experience any significant degree of capital flight. Trade openness, export growth and consequent capacity to service debts also differed across Latin America and Asia. The Asian countries were relatively more open than many of the Latin American countries and thus had a relatively greater capacity for debt service, which helped them avoid the crisis.

25.1.1 Austerity measures and management of the Debt Crisis

There were several other policy changes that followed the crisis in the debtor countries. Import restrictions and exchange controls were put in force again in the crisis-laden Latin American countries, though in varying degrees. The policy prescription by the International Monetary Fund for handling or management of debt crisis by the debtor countries was the standard austerity measure: expenditure reducing through reduction of budget deficits. These resulted in significant declines in public investments, which had far-reaching adverse effects for these economies as it generated excess capacities (and unemployment) in the short run and constrained future growth. Sachs also endorsed this view that fiscal austerity measures of the IMF programmes for management of the debt resulted in contractionary real output effects. Accordingly, what was needed was a concomitant policy of depreciation of the real exchange rate (or increase in the price of traded goods relative to that of non-traded goods). This would have encouraged the production of traded goods which could compensate for the loss in output of non-traded goods.

At the same time, there was a remarkable movement of trade deficits (or small surpluses) leading to large surpluses. That by itself was an encouraging one as it signalled ability of the debtor countries to adjust their balances of payments, and might have been instrumental in restoring confidence of the creditors. However, economists differed in their opinions regarding which type of policies caused such a turnaround in trade surpluses. Was it due to IMF prescribed austerity measures causing expenditure reducing or real devaluations causing expenditure switching? Diaz-Alejandro (1984) was of the view that trade surpluses were achieved through expenditure reducing as a result of investment cuts and consequent fall in output and income in the debtor countries. If that be the case, then the gains emanating from large trade surpluses will evaporate when these economies expand by augmenting public investment. Krugman (1984), on the other hand, argued that trade surpluses were primarily brought about by large real devaluation and exchange controls that triggered expenditure switching effects: substitution of foreign goods (imports) by domestically produced goods in consumption. The view that IMF measures for indebted Latin American countries should focus more on the expenditure-switching policies than on the expenditure-reducing policies, was also shared by Rudiger Dornbusch.

Turning now to the management of the debt problem by the creditors, the post-1982 strategy of involuntary/concerted lending for financing debt was the popular and adopted view. In fact, creditors adopted a combination of debt rescheduling and concerted involuntary lending. This strategy, which is known as the financing of debt overhang, was intended to reduce the burden of the debtors in transfer of resources for debt servicing while allowing them to recover and thereby increase their ability of future payments and debt servicing (Krugman, 1989). Eventually, it served to protect interests of the creditors too. It was a concerted (or, collective) and involuntary lending strategy because in the face of the crisis, individual lenders—the banks in the creditor countries—would not have extended further loans or credits to the debt-ridden countries if they had acted independently and unilaterally. That is no voluntary individual lending would have taken place to finance the debt overhang.

Many economists have put forward rationality behind such concerted and involuntary lending. First, independent theoretical analyses by William Cline (1983), Paul Krugman (1985), and Jeffrey Sachs (1984) demonstrated that while for any individual lender continued lending is unprofitable because of the risks of future non-payment, lending to avoid an immediate default by the debtor countries (or their firms) is in the collective interest of creditors. This also called for official lending to mitigate the free rider problem (Krugman, 1989). Extending loans to debtor countries is also rationalized by stating that the indebted country is solvent but has a liquidity problem. But Krugman (1989) criticized this argument by pointing out that if a country is 'known to be solvent'—that is, is known to be able to repay its debt eventually—then she can find voluntary creditors and therefore should not have any liquidity problem. But, if the expected present value of repayment by the debtor-country is less than the outstanding debt it already has, then there is a liquidity problem. In such a case, Krugman (1989) argues that the creditors would still lend more to such a country precisely because 'while incomplete payment is possible, it is not certain'. Following his example, consider a country that may be able to make payments equal in present value to its outstanding debt eventually. But, there is a possibility of non-payment. Suppose this risk of default is sufficiently large so that no voluntary lender would extend further loans to this country. The country will then have to make repayments out of current resources. In case this is not possible, then the country will have no other option but to default immediately. If the country defaults, as many Latin American countries did in the 1930s, the creditors essentially lose all the money and foreclose the possibility of benefiting from later revival by the debtor country enabling it to pay back. Thus, creditors may actually like to postpone at least part of a country's obligations by giving it further loans and thereby preserving their future claims in the possibility of a turnaround. This is achieved through *concerted* lending—which is involuntary unilaterally—that covers at least a fraction of the current accumulated interest obligations. Note that for a heavily indebted country only a rescheduling of the principal is not enough since even the interest payments on accumulated debt may be beyond her current ability. Thus, deferring interest obligations is needed as well, and this is what the concerted lending does.

Second, as Sachs (1986) puts it, the strategy of financing the debt was rational on part of the governments in the creditor countries, like United States and Japan, as well since prospect of a major world financial crisis as a consequence of the debt crisis was looming large. World's largest commercial banks were holding huge claims on the debtor countries that often exceeded 100 per cent of bank capital. Given such a dimension of claims, any wholesale negation or disclaimer of debt by the debtor countries would have caused insolvency of these banks and would trigger a major financial crisis. Thus, continued servicing of debts or such bank claims by the debtor firms and governments in the Latin American countries was essential and this formed the basis and rationale for most of the policy initiatives by the creditor governments and the multilateral institutions. New loans were advanced by the official lenders to enable debtor countries to service their bank debts, often on conditions of policy reforms to be initiated by them.

The strategy of financing the debt worked to keep debts serviced as the debtors had paid back more than the new loans they received. This was evident from the observation that the (net) flow of new capital into the debtor countries less repayment of interest and profits on foreign investment had been negative since 1982 (Sachs, 1986). There was also a built-in asymmetry, what Sachs termed 'official creditors are indeed bailing out the banks'. This assertion came from his observation that during 1982–87 the debtor countries made large net transfers to the commercial banks in the creditor countries (the lenders) and received large net transfers from the creditor governments and the international agencies.

Box 25.3 Free-rider problem and gains from concerted lending

Gains from concerted lending to a heavily indebted country are nicely summarized in Krugman (1989). The study by Cline (1983) was first to argue strongly in favour of concerted lending and the potential gains there from. Such gains had been subsequently demonstrated formally by Sachs (1984) and Krugman (1985). By lending to the extent needed to avoid immediate default by debtors, creditors raise the value of their claims and the gains from concerted lending are *collective*. There is, however, a free rider problem. Since individually each new loan is made at a loss, so no creditor will have any unilateral incentive to lend. Thus, as Krugman (1989) puts it, 'lending may be in everyone's collective interest but fails to take place because no individual finds it in his or her interest'. Collective negotiations by the creditors and concerted lending under the pressure from the central banks in the creditor country (which in case of 1980 Debt problem was the Federal Reserve Bank) and international agencies overcome this free-rider problem.

But the strategy of financing of debt through concerted and involuntary lending did not seem to work and caused havoc for the Latin American countries. It did help USA, being the largest creditor country, to avoid its domestic banking crisis but at the cost of growth and development for the indebted Latin American countries. Ocampo (2014) was particularly critical as he observed: 'Thus, Latin America can rightly be seen as a victim of the way in which what was also a U.S. banking crisis was handled. Oddly enough, this is not fully recognized in the existing literature, which does not even include the Latin American debt crisis as the U.S. banking crisis that it actually was.'

On the other hand, the optimism regarding debtor countries reviving through austerity measures and other trade and exchange controls was short-lived. Debt rescheduling and continuous debt servicing of the (rescheduled) debt under strong international pressures and concerted lending together with the contractionary macroeconomic policies led to a prolonged fall in per capita GDP. The plight of most Latin American debtor countries, and the 'lost decade' of the 1980s, stretched into the 1990s. By the early 1990s per capita GDP was 9–10 per cent lower than it was in 1980 for the region as a whole, and was even below the 1970 levels for Argentina, Peru, and Uruguay. Unemployment increased significantly with a larger proportion of the workforce employed in the low-wage informal sectors. All these had far-reaching implications for poverty—which increased from 40.5 per cent in 1980 to 48.3 per cent in 1990—and inequality.

Realizing that the adopted policies were not working for the Latin American countries, James A. Baker III, the US Secretary of the Treasury, offered a new plan in 1985 to mitigate the continued crisis. But the Baker plan was not a significantly new policy as the commercial banks were to make new loans to the heavily indebted countries, while the multilateral lending institutions were to make new loans in return for policy adjustments in the debtor countries. Several alternative plans were also proposed. Foremost was the proposal of Kenen (1983) for a new public institution to repurchase debts at a discount from the commercial banks. Senator Bill Bradley of New Jersey in 1986, on the other hand, proposed for debt forgiveness by the commercial banks rather than debt rescheduling and full interest servicing. Again, the Bradley plan conditioned debt relief on economic policy reforms. As a modification to Senator Bradley's proposal, which seems to make debt relief available to all debtors, Sachs (1986) developed a selective debt relief plan based upon objective indicators, such as 'a country's decline in real per capita output over a period of several years'. The second Baker Plan was proposed in 1987 which added market-based schemes like debt buybacks, low-interest exit bonds, and debt swaps. Finally came the Brady Plan that helped create a market for Latin American bonds. But, it was very late as by that time Latin America had lost an entire decade of development. The main feature of the Brady Plan was introduction of bonds to allow the commercial banks in the creditor countries to convert their claims into tradable instruments. The debtor countries issued new bonds for the principal sum and also unpaid interest in some cases. Thus, the banks could get the debt off their balance sheets. Eight Latin and Central American countries—Argentina, Brazil, Costa Rica, Dominican Republic, Ecuador, Mexico, Uruguay, and Venezuela—participated in the initial round of issuing Brady bonds. Like all other earlier plans, issuing Brady Bonds by the participating debtor countries were conditional upon liberalizing their economies. Two main types of bonds were introduced in the Brady Plan. One was *Par bonds* equal to the value of the original loan, but the interest paid on the bonds is below market rate. The other was *Discount bonds* less than the value of the original loan but the interest paid on the bonds is at the market rate. For both types of instruments, principal and interest payments are usually guaranteed.

Box 25.4 Financing debt versus forgiving debt or debt relief

Debt relief is an arrangement that reduces the present value of debt obligations of the debtor country. Such reliefs may be interest rates on outstanding debt lowered below the market rate, forgiveness of principal, or repurchase of debts by the debtor country at below par. Debt financing, on the other hand, postpones debt repayment. While there can be potential collective gains for the creditors from financing the debt through concerted lending, the problem with such a strategy many argue is that it pushes the indebted countries into deeper debts. Accordingly, and arguably, debt financing rather than debt relief or debt forgiveness appears to be a strategy that was aimed at resolving the banking crisis in the United States rather than helping the cause of the debtor countries in Latin America. The creditor governments also endorsed debt rescheduling rather than debt relief or forgiveness in order to avoid the banking crisis and collapse of the international financial system that it could have triggered (Ocampo, 2014). Interestingly, the strategy of debt financing appeared self-defeating for the creditors since the Latin American countries grew much slowly during the debt crisis and this is partly due to the debt burden itself. Critics point out that the countries that rescheduled their debts in the past decade—in late 1970s in particular—and pursued IMF austerity measures and World Bank structural adjustments programmes did not succeed in pushing up economic growth and improving other macroeconomic indicators. This meant that by preserving their full claims on the debtors through concerted lending, creditors actually reduced expected repayment by debtors below that could have been achieved through reductions of debt burden of the countries. Thus, as Krugman (1989) emphasized, debt relief or forgiveness rather than debt financing, which signifies 'less may be more', may eventually be in everyone's advantage and this called for a 'replacement of the strategy of financing debt with forgiving it'.

25.2 FINANCIAL CRISIS IN ASIA IN LATE 1990S

25.2.1 Nature, Dimension and Cause of the crisis

The Asian financial crisis originated in Thailand in July 1997 as a balance-of-payments crisis, when it devalued its currency Baht significantly and subsequently allowed it to float against US Dollar after years of overvalued pegged regime became unsustainable in face of depleting foreign exchange reserves due to growing current account deficits. The situation was worsened further by sudden and massive capital flights and speculative attacks. There were a series of depreciations of the baht subsequent to the switch to float, and within six months the baht was down by more than 50 per cent in value. Equity, and property markets weakened as well, as a consequence and led to the dual crises—balance-of-payments and banking crisis. Soon four other economies in East Asia—Indonesia, Malaysia, South Korea, and the Philippines—were adversely hit through financial contagion. Similar capital flights took place in these economies, primarily through conversion of local-currency denominated assets (that reflected short-term debts) into dollar assets by foreign investors, and thereby setting off banking and currency crises. As we will elaborate later, such contagion took place through competitive devaluations and unpegging of local currencies in these four countries. Foreign exchange interventions were counterproductive as official foreign exchange reserves depleted quickly triggering even larger subsequent depreciations. Rupiah, the Indonesian currency, depreciated by almost 80 per cent at the end of 1996, the largest in the region, followed by the South Korean Won by 50 per cent and the Ringgit by approximately 45 per cent despite Malaysia's controls on short-term capital flows. The severity of the balance-of-payments crisis in South Korea caused it to almost default on its debts. Private investments were severely hit in these East Asian countries. Growth across East Asia slowed down quite significantly, and some countries entered into deep recessions. Soon, a significant number of financial institutions were bankrupt.

By 1998 the crisis also spilled over to other regions and countries such as Russia in Eastern Europe and Brazil in Latin America. Emerging markets in East Europe experienced declining capital flows. There was also sharp contraction of credit, which a World Bank study attributes to risk aversion in global financial markets due to outbreak of the Asian crisis (World Bank, 1999). In other parts of Asia, the crisis adversely hit the stock markets. There were also several speculative attacks on Hong Kong Dollar that was pegged to the US dollar, setting off short-term stock market sell-offs across the region. The already sluggish Japanese economy experienced a further shock with the failure of two of its largest brokers, Yamaichi Securities and Sanyo Securities in late 1997.

The economic crisis also triggered political crises in a few instances, most notable being the downfall of General Suharto, who had reined Indonesia as president for almost 31 years.

The Asian Financial Crisis surprised economists and policymakers alike since the affected East Asian countries were showcased as some of the most successful emerging market economies with rapid growth, much of which was export-led, and improving standard of livings for their populations. Fiscal and monetary policies were reasonably well designed, as recognized even by the IMF (1998). There was no evidence of fiscal profligacy either as all these five economies were running budget surpluses, and inflation rates were quite low as well. However, as the crisis unfolded, it became clear that the impressive growth records diverted attention away from the vulnerabilities in the financial system which was exposed by exchange rate shocks (Radelet and Sachs 1998a, 1998b). Rapid domestic credit expansion financed through short-term foreign borrowing exposed banks and financial institutions to potential exchange rate and funding risks. Huge short-term external borrowing was used to fund local currency-denominated assets. The resulting currency mismatches exposed banks and their clients to exchange rate shocks like devaluation of domestic currencies. Currency pegs with overvaluation had long insulated these entities from such risks. But once pegs became unsustainable and the currencies were devalued and subsequently allowed to float, currencies depreciated further. Consequently, the countries experienced sharp increases in value of their external debt and suffered significant losses from unhedged foreign currency borrowing putting many of them into insolvency.

There is more or less a general consensus by now that a sudden loss of confidence on part of the foreign investors and massive withdrawal of capital by them as well as by unhedged debtors aggravated the crisis in East Asia. For example, IMF (2000) study asserted that a change in market sentiment led to a vicious circle of currency depreciation, insolvency, and capital flight. There is, however, competing views regarding the cause of such herd-behaviour in sudden stop in investments in these countries, and, more devastating, withdrawal of capital from there. Current account deficit, appreciation of domestic currencies, too much of overvaluation due to strongly appreciating USD, reversal of declining asset returns in the West, all these may have combined together to cause such exodus. In fact, these factors were so much intertwined that it is difficult to single out one particular factor as the primary cause.

Growing current account deficits of these East Asian countries were caused primarily by appreciation of domestic currencies and loss of export competitiveness as a consequence. Domestic currencies in almost all the East Asian countries were pegged to the US Dollar. Since Asian exports were mostly concentrated in dollar-denominated markets, so in trade-weighted terms the value of domestic currencies increased or decreased in tandem with the US Dollar gaining or losing in value vis-à-vis the major currencies, most relevant being the yen. The yen-dollar exchange rate was extremely volatile in the 1990s. During 1994 and early 1995, the US dollar depreciated and so did the currencies of the East Asian countries in trade-weighted terms. This helped their net exports grow. But when the decline in the value of US dollar started recovering vis-à-vis the yen since mid-1995, the East Asian currencies started appreciating causing substantial losses in competitiveness, and consequent adverse effects on net exports and growth. The US dollar continued to appreciate till the end of 1997—appreciating by more than 50 per cent from the early 1995 level of 80 yen per US dollar—leading to not only growing current account deficits but also imbalances in the capital account (Eichengreen et al. 1998).

Growing pressure on currency peg due to current account deficits was further accentuated by capital flight after 1996. During the first half of the 1990s, most of these Asian countries experienced large capital inflows as declines in asset yields in industrial countries and impressive growth rates of these countries made them attractive destinations for investments. In face of recessions in the early 1990s, the major industrial countries, including Japan, lowered interest rates to boost investment. The United States, on the other hand, cut interest rates drastically in an effort to overcome debt deflation (Akyiiz, 2000).[4] As a World Bank (1998) study reports, by 1996 Thailand recorded a net private capital flows of 14.5 per cent of its GDP, the Philippines

[4] Debt deflation is a situation where falling price level raises the real value of the debt and causes loan defaults and bank insolvencies. These in turn lead to deflationary spirals and downturn in the economy.

12.7 per cent of its GDP, Malaysia 8.4 per cent of its GDP, Indonesia 6.1 per cent of its GDP, and South Korea 4.9 per cent of its GDP (which, however, was four times the share of GDP it had in 1994). Most of these capital inflows were, however, short-term in nature intended to make profits from the interest rate differentials, rather than looking for long-term returns on productive investment. However, such inflows took care of the pressure on the currency peg that growing current account deficits were putting. In fact, inflows were in excess of what was needed for financing current account deficits and resulted in rapid accumulation of reserves.[5] But in 1997, the inflows, the short-term arbitrage funds in particular, suddenly and abruptly reversed, with the magnitude of net outflow being approximately USD 12 billion. This was largely driven by increases in asset returns and yields in industrial countries including expectations of a rise in Japanese interest rate. Such capital flight put strong pressure on the Thai baht and compounded the problem of sustaining its peg in face of worsening current account mainly due to appreciating USD and consequent loss of export competitiveness. Switch to a floating exchange rate appeared inevitable, and expectation of such a policy change triggered speculative attacks and worsened the crisis further.

Soon the crisis spilled over to the other four East Asian countries through contagion effect. However, contagion did not operate through bilateral trade and investment amongst these countries because of low shares of such bilateral trade within the region. Rather, the contagion channels were financial. The major channel was exchange rates and what is termed as the competitive devaluation. As Thai baht depreciated significantly after the switch to the floating regime, the Philippine peso and the Malaysian ringgit came under pressure. These countries and the others in the region experienced further loss of competitiveness of their exports that worsened the current account deficits even further and made their currencies vulnerable to speculative attacks (Corsetti, Pesenti and Roubini, 1998). Soon a larger number of countries followed similar policies of undertaking large doses of devaluations and subsequently allowing their currencies to float (or move within a band as adopted by Malaysia). In anticipation of capital losses, not only the foreign exchange traders but also the domestic firms and financial institutions started selling domestic currencies. Contagious speculative attacks thus took place on other currencies in the region.

There was another channel of contagion. Immediately after the crisis in Thailand broke out exposing weaknesses in the financial system, international investors started reviewing financial systems and creditworthiness of other Asian countries. Soon they realized that several other East Asian economies had similar financial and structural weaknesses (Goldstein, 1998). There was a general lack of enforcement of prudential rules. Supervisions of financial systems were also inadequate in most of the countries. Lending to firms or individuals was often government-directed even if those may not be commercially viable. Competition among banks and financial institutions often led to bad loans. Asset values, rather than a firm's ability to debt service, were taken into account while granting loans. All these lending practices worsened the quality of banks' loan portfolios (IMF, 1998) and made the financial systems vulnerable to shocks. Realizing these vulnerabilities of financial systems in many East Asian countries, foreign creditors and investors pulled back from those countries as well thereby triggering a financial contagion (IMF, 2000; Carson and Clark, 2013).

[5] Interestingly, if the East Asian currencies were allowed to float during this period, capital inflows would have caused appreciations of the currencies, which in turn attracted further capital inflow while eroding export competitiveness further. That is, a vicious circle could have emerged between capital inflows, currency appreciation and current account deficits

25.2.2 Measures to manage the crisis

Financial support came from almost all the international agencies like the IMF, the World Bank, the Asian Development Bank, and also from the countries in the Asia-Pacific region, Europe, and the United States. Thailand, Indonesia, and South Korea—the three worst-hit countries in the region—received loans to the tune of USD 118 billion as part International support packages. This helped these countries rebuild official reserves, and gain time for policy adjustments to stabilize their economies and win back confidence of international investors. IMF was the major contributor to such international support packages as it provided USD 36 billion to support reform programmes in these three countries. Institutional loans and aids were conditional upon domestic economic reforms and austerity measures that IMF usually prescribes for any (and all) crisis-driven developing countries. The IMF was criticized for its 'one size fits all' approach as it applied the same set of policy prescriptions as designed for Latin America's debt problem. For example, despite the fact that neither did the East Asian countries indulge in fiscal profligacy prior to the outbreak of the Crisis, nor the Asian crisis could have been triggered by the fiscal profligacy, fiscal austerity measures were still put as conditions for support packages. To many, this did not help the countries to quickly recover from the recession and regain the growth trajectory they were onto before the crisis. On the contrary, while recognizing that its initial policy advice to these countries was not flawless, IMF claimed that required adjustments were made quickly, and 'the strategies adopted proved successful in restoring financial market confidence and stability, and in achieving a resumption of economic growth' (IMF, 2000).

At the same time, Federal Reserve Bank of United States played a pro-active role to make US banks that had given the largest loans to the South Korean banks voluntarily commit to restructure their short-term loans into medium-term loans (Carson and Clark, 2013). Similar efforts were initiated by the central banks of other industrialized nations, notably the G-10 countries. As a result, large number of foreign banks cooperated to restructure the debts of the East Asian countries. This policy response to the Asian Crisis through voluntary cooperation and commitment by private banks under the initiative of central banks of the creditor countries was same as the strategy of financing debts of the Latin American countries in the 1980s through the concerted (and involuntary) lending discussed earlier. Again the primary target was to avoid a potential banking crisis in the United States and also in Japan.

25.3 CURRENT SCENARIO: ANOTHER DEBT CRISIS ON THE CARD?

Currently, almost half of low-income countries fall under the category of heavily indebted countries with the growth of the indebtedness of sub-Saharan Africa, in particular, being a major concern. Debt stocks represent more than 25 per cent of GDP for all developing countries and debt servicing absorbs almost 14 per cent of export earnings on the average (UNCTAD, 2019). This is despite quite extensive debt reliefs received by most low-income countries between 2000 and 2012 under the Heavily Indebted Poor Countries (HIPC) Initiative and the Multilateral Debt Relief Initiative (MDRI) of the IMF and the World Bank. These initiatives were successful no doubt in reducing existing debt stocks and making debt servicing manageable. But, development needs and low tax revenues—due to low tax bases mostly—forced these countries to continue to rely on external borrowings and this caused their debts to

Box 25.5 Bailouts and moral-hazards problems

International support packages and bailout financial assistance to countries experiencing financial crises may lead to moral hazards problem by encouraging more reckless behaviour by borrowers, lenders, and investors. This is similar to insurance against a risk encouraging behaviours that makes the risk more likely to occur. Such moral hazards problems were not unlikely in the context of Asian countries since their banks were able to borrow funds from abroad without much caution and there was imprudent lending by them to local firms and investors, often for high risk investment such as speculations, as there was a general expectation of public guarantee of bank liabilities in case of crisis (Frankel, 1998; Krugman, 1998; Radelet and Sachs, 1998b).

Similar moral hazard problem may arise from IMF lending if policymakers care less about policy discipline and pursue more risky policies, knowing that the IMF would be bailing out if their policies fail (IMF, 1998). On the other hand, lenders would take excessive risks if they believe that debtor-country government or its banks would be able to pay their debts out of support packages offered by the IMF in case of a financial crisis. Thus, if a financial crisis is largely an outcome of policy indiscipline and irresponsible behaviour, then a bailout would encourage pursuance of more of such behaviour in the future (Krugman, 1984). To avoid such moral hazard problems in its lending and bailout policies, IMF policy advices in banking sector restructuring like closing of insolvent institutions. But, protection of the interests of depositors and foreign investors often limits the scope of such policy advices and makes it difficult to avoid the inherent moral hazard problem altogether.

grow again (UNCTAD, 2019). Moreover, unlike the previous cases like the 1980 debt crisis, the poor countries are now getting larger fractions of their loans at the market conditions from new lenders like China. The public debt at market conditions as a share of total debt stood at 46 per cent in 2017 for the low-income countries, which was almost double the share they had in 2007 (UNCTAD, 2019). These loans are short-term loans with higher interest rates compared to the concessional loans from the IMF and the World Bank. This makes the external debt unsustainable for most of the low-income and poor countries. Growing external debts of shorter maturities mean most of the current resources of these countries are spent in debt servicing and payment of principals rather than in investment. This constrains their growth and development.

Their problems have been further compounded by falling commodity prices since 2011, and structural problems like lack of export diversity—both in its commodity structure and in market destinations—that makes them vulnerable to such price declines and also to demand fluctuations in the world market.

Given the rising trends in global interest rates and the shorter maturities of loans provided to the low income countries, the debt sustainability of developing countries in the future remains a potential major problem for the developing world. Proper debt management is thus more than important now to avoid another debt crisis breaking out. In this context, mention may be made of measures implemented by international agencies like the Debt Management Facility of the World Bank and the Debt Management and Financial Analysis System Programme of UNCTAD. The scope of these programmes, however, needs to be further expanded and improved upon.

Box 25.6 HIPC Initiative and MDRI

These initiatives were launched by the IMF and the World Bank in 1996 to reduce the debt burden of 41 poor countries, out of which 33 were sub-Saharan African countries. The Heavily Indebted Poor Countries (HIPC) Initiative is intended to reduce multilateral debt of a poor nation to a sustainable level and overcome any debt overhang problem that may hinder the country's investment and growth. Under the MDRI, on the other hand, 100 per cent debt relief is provided by the IMF, the World Bank, and the African Development Fund (AfDF) for countries that have completed the HIPC Initiative process. There are three key preconditions for qualifying for HIPC Initiative and MDRI relief (IMF, 2019): a satisfactory track record of strong policy performance under the IMF and the World Bank supported programs; paying back earlier loans received from the IMF, the World Bank, and the African Development Bank (AfDB); and, preparing a document detailing civil society participation like Poverty Reduction Strategy Paper (PRSP).

SUMMARY POINTS

- Asian Crisis in 1997 is a dual crisis involving both balance-of-payments crisis and banking crisis. And, the financial crisis in Latin America and Africa in the early 1980s was essentially (private) external debt problems, which eventually triggered balance of payments crises as well. This Crisis, at the same time, can also be seen as a US banking crisis.
- Most of the crises originating in the developing world occurred under overvalued pegged (or crawling peg) exchange rate regimes with or without capital and exchange controls. Vulnerabilities of economies like weak financial systems were exposed once external shocks caused currency (or BOP) crisis and capital flights.
- Economists held different opinions regarding the cause of the Latin American debt crisis. Diaz-Alejandro (1984), Dornbusch (1985), and Ocampo (2014) emphasized upon external shocks as the primary cause, though they differed in respect of such external shocks. On the other hand, Branson, Krugman, Sachs, and others argued that domestic, trade and exchange rate policies pursued in many Latin American countries were no less important in putting the countries in the trajectory of the crisis.
- The policy prescription by the International Monetary Fund for management of 1980-debt crisis by the debtor countries was the standard austerity measure: expenditure reducing through reduction of budget deficits. These resulted in significant declines in public investments, which had far-reaching adverse effects for these economies as it generated excess capacities (and unemployment) in the short run and constrained future growth.
- Creditors adopted a combination of debt rescheduling and concerted involuntary lending. This strategy, which is known as the financing of debt overhang, was intended to reduce the burden of the debtors in transfer of resources for debt servicing while allowing them to recover and thereby increase their ability of future payments and debt servicing (Krugman, 1989). Eventually, it served to protect interests of the creditors.
- World's largest commercial banks were holding huge claims on the debtor countries so that any default by the debtor countries would have caused insolvency of these banks

and would trigger a major financial crisis. Thus, continued servicing of debts or such bank claims by the debtor firms and governments in the Latin American countries was essential and this formed the basis and rationale for most of the policy initiatives by the creditor governments and the multilateral institutions.

- The strategy of financing of debt through concerted and involuntary lending did not seem to work and caused havoc for the Latin American countries. It did help USA, being the largest creditor country, to avoid its domestic banking crisis but at the cost of growth and development for the indebted Latin American countries.
- The main feature of the Brady Plan was introduction of bonds to allow the commercial banks in the creditor countries to convert their claims into tradable instruments. The debtor countries issued new bonds for the principal sum and also unpaid interest in some cases. Two main types of bonds were introduced in the Brady Plan. One was *Par bonds* equal to the value of the original loan, but the interest paid on the bonds is below market rate. The other was *Discount bonds* less than the value of the original loan but the interest paid on the bonds is at the market rate.
- The Asian financial crisis originated in Thailand in July 1997 as a balance-of-payments crisis, when it devalued its currency significantly after years of overvalued pegged regime became unsustainable in face of depleting foreign exchange reserves. The situation was worsened further by sudden and massive capital flights and speculative attacks. There were a series of depreciations of the baht subsequent to the switch to float, and within six months the baht was down by more than 50 per cent in value. Equity, and property markets weakened as well as a consequence and led to the dual crises—balance-of-payments and banking crisis. Soon four other economies in East Asia—Indonesia, Malaysia, South Korea, and the Philippines—were adversely hit through financial contagion.
- As the crisis unfolded, the vulnerabilities in the financial system was exposed by exchange rate shocks (Radelet and Sachs 1998a, 1998b). Rapid domestic credit expansion financed through short-term foreign borrowing exposed banks and financial institutions to potential exchange rate and funding risks. Huge short-term external borrowing was used to fund local currency-denominated assets. The resulting currency mismatches exposed banks and their clients to exchange rate shocks like devaluation of domestic currencies.
- There is more or less a general consensus that a sudden loss of confidence on part of the foreign investors and massive withdrawal of capital by them as well as by unhedged debtors aggravated the crisis in East Asia. Current account deficit, appreciation of domestic currencies, too much of overvaluation due to strongly appreciating USD, reversal of declining asset returns in the West, all these may have combined together to cause such exodus.
- The major channel of contagion was the competitive devaluation. As Thai baht depreciated significantly after the switch to the floating regime, the other countries in the region experienced further loss of competitiveness of their exports. This worsened their current account deficits even further and made their currencies vulnerable to speculative attacks (Corsetti, Pesenti and Roubini, 1998). Soon a larger number of countries followed similar policies of undertaking large doses of devaluations and subsequently allowing their currencies to float.

- The policy response to the Asian Crisis through voluntary cooperation and commitment by private banks under the initiative of central banks of the creditor countries was the same as the strategy of financing debts of the Latin American countries in the 1980s through the concerted (and involuntary) lending discussed earlier. Again the primary target was to avoid a potential banking crisis in the United States—that had given the largest loans to the South Korean banks—and also in Japan.
- Moral hazard problem may arise from IMF lending if policymakers care less about policy discipline and pursue more risky policies, knowing that the IMF would be bailing out if their policies fail (IMF 1998). On the other hand, lenders would take excessive risks if they believe that debtor-country government or its banks would be able to pay their debts out of support packages offered by the IMF in case of a financial crisis. Thus, if a financial crisis is largely an outcome of policy indiscipline and irresponsible behaviour, then a bailout would encourage pursuance of more of such behaviour in the future (Krugman, 1984).

KEYWORDS

- **Financial crises** have three different dimensions, which though may be intertwined and causing each other: external debt, balance-of-payments (or currency), and banking crises.
- A **currency crisis** arises when annual devaluation of 15 per cent or more is administered vis-à-vis US Dollar, or any other foreign currency of intervention under a pegged regime.
- An **external debt crisis** occurs when a country defaults on payment of debt obligations including principal or interest.
- A **banking crisis** is either a bank run that lead to the closure, merging, or takeover by the public sector of one or more financial institutions; or, large-scale government assistance to important financial institutions (or a group of institutions) that triggers similar outcomes for other financial institutions.
- **Indebtedness** is usually measured by the ratio of debts to Gross National Product. Sometimes the ratio of debt to value of exports is taken as an alternative measure. The latter also indicates a country's ability to service and repay back the inherited debts.
- **Debt overhang** is the situation when inherited external debt is more than the expected present value of the future resource transfer to the creditors. Thus, creditors do not expect their loans to be repaid fully eventually.
- **Debt relief** is any arrangement that reduces the present value of debt obligations of the debtor country. Such reliefs may be interest rates on outstanding debt lowered below the market rate, forgiveness of principal, or repurchase of debts by the debtor country at below par.

- **Debt Financing** is extending further loans by the creditor to postpone debt repayment by the debtor.
- **Debt deflation** is a situation where the real value of the debt rises due to falling price level causing loan defaults and bank insolvencies, which in turn leads to deflationary spirals and downturn in the economy. There may, in fact, be a vicious cycle. Loan defaults may lead to a reduction in overall credit in the economy and consequently fall in investment, consumption and hence aggregate demand causing further price deflation and even larger debt inflation.
- A country is said to be **solvent** if it is expected to pay off its debt eventually.
- A country has a **liquidity problem** if it lacks the cash to service its debt on a current basis.
- **Brady Bonds** are new bonds for the principal debt amount and also unpaid interest in some cases. These bonds were created under the Brady Plan and were of two types. One was *Par bonds* equal to the value of the original loan, but the interest paid on the bonds is below market rate. The other was *Discount bonds* less than the value of the original loan but the interest paid on the bonds is at the market rate.
- International support packages and bailout financial assistance to countries experiencing financial crises may lead to **moral hazards problem** by encouraging more reckless behaviour by borrowers, lenders, and investors.
- The **Heavily Indebted Poor Countries (HIPC) Initiative** is intended to reduce multilateral debt of a poor nation to a sustainable level and overcome any debt overhang problem that may hinder the country's investment and growth.
- Under the **Multilateral Debt Relief Initiative (MDRI)** 100 per cent debt relief is provided by the IMF, the World Bank, and the African Development Fund (AfDF) for countries that have completed the HIPC Initiative process.

EXERCISES

1. To what extent do you think that the exchange rate policies of the developing countries had attributed to their financial crises?
2. What are the external shocks that economists talk about are responsible for the Latin American debt crisis during early 1980s?
3. Why do you think that the Asian Countries did not experience the similar debt problem in 1980s as the Latin American countries?
4. What was the rationality of financing debt of the Latin American countries? Was it ultimately worthwhile?
5. How does contagion explain Asian Crisis during 1997–98?
6. What arguments are often put forward against the nature of austerity measures and other policy prescriptions made by the IMF for crisis management while providing bailout loans to the indebted countries? Suggest some measures which you think should be prescribed.

SUGGESTED READING

Akyiiz, Y. (2000). 'Causes and Sources of the Asian Financial Crisis'. Paper presented at the UNCTAD Symposium on Economic and Financial Recovery in Asia (at the host country Bangkok), 17 February 2000.

Carson. M. and J. Clark (2013). 'Asian Financial Crisis'. Federal Reserve History. https://www.federalreservehistory.org/ essays/asian-financial-crisis

Diaz-Alejandro, C. F. (1984). 'Latin American Debt: I Don't Think We Are at Kansas Anymore'. Brookings Papers on Economic Activity, 2: 335–89.

Dornbusch, R. (1985). 'Policy and Performance Links between LDC Debtors and Industrial Nations'. Brookings Papers on Economic Activity, 2: 303–56.

Eichengreen, B., Mussa, M., Dell'Ariccia, G., Detragiache, E., Milessi-Feretti, E. and Tweediw, A. 1998, *Capital Account Liberalisation:Theoretical and Practical Aspects*, Occasional Paper no. 172, International Monetary Fund, Washington, DC.

Krugman, P.R. (1989). 'Market-Based Debt Reduction Schemes'. In: Frenkel, J., M.P. Dooley and P. Wickhan, eds., *Analytical Issues in Debt*. Washington: International Monetary Fund.

Sachs, J. (1986). 'Managing the LDC Debt Crisis'. Brookings Papers on Economic Activity, 2: 397–440.

UNCTAD (2019). 'Current Challenges to Developing Country Debt Sustainability'. Report prepared by Hawkins, P., S. Blankenburg and R. Kozul-Wright of the Division on Globalization and Development Strategies of UNCTAD. UNCTAD, Geneva.

ADVANCED READING

Branson, W. H. (1985). 'Comments and Discussion: Policy and Performance Links between LDC Debtors and Industrial Nations by R. Dornbusch'. Brookings Papers on Economic Activity, 2: 357–61.

Cabalu, H. (1999). 'A Review of the Asian Crisis: Causes, Consequences and Policy Responses'. The Australian Economic Review, vol. 32, no. 3, pp. 304–13.

Cline, W. R. (1983). International Debt and the Stability of the World Economy: Policy Analysis in International Economics, Washington: Institute for International Economics.

Cline, W. R. (1985). 'Comments and Discussion: Policy and Performance Links between LDC Debtors and Industrial Nations by R. Dornbusch'. Brookings Papers on Economic Activity, 2: 361–6.

Corsetti, G., Pesenti, P. and Roubini, N. (1998). 'What Caused the Asian Currency and Financial Crisis?' March. Available at http://www.econ.yale.edu/~corsetti/.

ECLAC (1996). The Economic Experience of the Last Fifteen Years. Latin America and the Caribbean, 1980–1995. Santiago: ECLAC.

Frankel, J. (1998). 'The Asian Model, the Miracle, the Crisis and the Fund'. Paper presented to US International Trade Commission, Washington, DC, 16 April.

Goldstein, M. (1998). 'The Asian Financial Crisis: Causes, Cures and Systemic Implications'. Policy Analyses in International Economics no. 55, Institute for International Economics, Washington, DC.

International Monetary Fund (1998). 'The Asian Crisis: Causes and Cures'. Finance and Development, 35(2).

International Monetary Fund. (2000). 'Recovery from the Asian Crisis and the Role of the IMF'. Report prepared by IMF Staff, June. International Monetary Fund: Washington DC.

International Monetary Fund. (2019). 'Heavily Indebted Poor Countries (HIPC) Initiative and Multilateral Debt Relief Initiative (MDRI)—Statistical Update'. IMF Policy Paper. International Monetary Fund: Washington DC.

Kenen, P.B. (1983). 'A Bailout Plan for the Banks', New York Times, March 6.

Krugman, P.R. (1984). 'Comments and Discussion: Latin American Debt: I Don't Think We Are at Kansas anymore by C.F. Diaz-Alejandro'. Brookings Papers on Economic Activity, 2: 390–3.

Krugman, P.R. (1985). 'International Debt Strategies in an Uncertain World'. In: J. Cuddington and G. Smith, eds., *International Debt and the Developing Countries*. Washington: World Bank.

Krugman, P.R. (1989). 'Market-Based Debt Reduction Schemes'. In: Frenkel, J., M.P. Dooley and P. Wickhan, eds., *Analytical Issues in Debt*. Washington: International Monetary Fund.

Krugman, P. 1998, 'What Happened to Asia?' MIT, January. Available at http://web.mit.edu/krugman

Ocampo, J. A. (2014). 'The Latin American Debt Crisis in Historical Perspective'. Paper prepared for the International Economic Association Project on 'Debt Crises and Resolution'.

Radelet, S. and Sachs, J. (1998a). 'The East Asian Financial Crisis: Diagnosis, Remedies, Prospects'. Unpublished manuscript. Harvard Institute for International Development, Massachusetts. Available at http://www.hiid.harvard.edu.

Radelet, S. and Sachs, J. (1998b). 'The Onset of the East Asian Currency Crisis'. Unpublished manuscript. Harvard Institute for International Development, Massachusetts. Available at http://www.hiid.harvard.edu.

Reinhart, C. and Rogoff, K. (2009). *This Time Is Different: Eight Centuries of Financial Folly*, Princeton: Princeton University Press, 2009.

Sachs, J. (1984). 'Comments and Discussion: Latin American Debt: I Don't Think We Are at Kansas anymore by C.F. Diaz-Alejandro'. Brookings Papers on Economic Activity, 2: 393–401.

Sachs, J. (1986). 'Managing the LDC Debt Crisis'. Brookings Papers on Economic Activity, 2: 397–440.

World Bank. (1998). *Global Development Finance 1998: Analysis and Summary Tables*. World Bank: Washington, DC.

26 Currency Regimes Revisited

As we have learnt in Chapter 22, by the end of the 1970s, many countries in the world switched to floating or flexible exchange rate regimes, marking the end of the Bretton Woods systems of pegged currency regime. But a clean float regime has rarely been adopted or practised by countries. Monetary authorities in countries have often intervened in the foreign exchange market to manage and stabilize exchange rate volatility. As discussed earlier, the nature of interventions varies widely across the countries, resulting in a wide range of currency regimes. Of late, even the idea of reviving the Bretton Woods system of international currency management has been floated in international forums by many economists and policymakers as the present system of flexible exchange rates has not been too successful in sustaining output growth and eliminating financial crises in the developed world.

This has also revived the debate over the relative efficacy of pegged and floating exchange rates in the developing world in promoting employment and growth and in stabilizing output and income fluctuations. The initial success and subsequent crisis in the Euro zone have also reopened the issue of an optimum currency area. Having learnt the implications of different exchange rate regimes and their relation to money supply and price levels, in this chapter we make a summary comparison between a pegged exchange rate regime, and broadly speaking, a flexible exchange rate regime. However, it is difficult to make a once for all choice in favour of a particular exchange rate regime. Neither the theory nor country experiences are very conclusive in this regard. Both regimes have their benefits and costs. Suitability of a particular regime, however, depends on the policy target of a country. Keeping this in mind, in the sections below the two exchange rate regimes are evaluated in terms of different policy targets.

26.1 POLICY TARGETS AND CHOICE OF EXCHANGE RATE REGIME

26.1.1 Targeting BOP Equilibrium

A major advantage of adopting a flexible exchange rate is the BOP equilibrium. Any BOP imbalance, deficit or surplus, is automatically and instantaneously corrected through exchange rate adjustment. As we have learnt in the earlier chapters, a BOP deficit means an excess demand for a foreign currency (or excess supply of the domestic currency) in foreign exchange or in the asset market. The exchange rate for the domestic currency being its price relative to

International Economics. Rajat Acharyya, Oxford University Press. © Oxford University Press 2022.
DOI: 10.1093/oso/9780192865144.003.0026

the foreign currency, such excess demand for the foreign currency depreciates the value of the domestic currency and restores the BOP equilibrium. Consequently, there is no impact of any BOP imbalance on a country's stock of foreign currency held in its central bank. That is, if in a particular year, a country's value of exports falls short of its value of imports of goods and services, or if there is any mismatch in asset trading, the country neither needs to adopt any corrective policy nor does it need to worry about losing its foreign currency reserves.

But, under a pegged exchange rate regime, the country runs the risk of losing its foreign currency reserves and eventually experiencing a BOP crisis. As explained in Chapter 22, an over-valued exchange rate creates a BOP deficit and consequently an excess demand for the foreign currency. Under the supply management policy, the central bank then must sell dollars from its reserves to meet this excess demand and prevent the exchange rate from moving away from the pegged rate. Thus, the central bank of a country needs to maintain foreign currency reserves to defend the pegged exchange rate regime. For a country for which trade deficit persists over a sufficiently long period of time, this supply management policy will mean a steady depletion of foreign currency reserves held by its central bank potentially leading to a situation of foreign exchange reserves drying up at some point of time in the future. The demand management policy in the form of exchange control is no solution to the problem either, as such a policy leads to a black market for foreign exchange and under-invoicing of exports. There will thus be a leakage of the scarce foreign currency from the official market so that the policy will be self-defeating. Official reserves of foreign currency now deplete not because the foreign currency is sold by the central bank to defend the pegged rate, but because foreign currency earners conceal part of their earnings and sell it in the black market at a premium over the officially pegged rate.

To sum up, if a country's target is maintaining an external balance or BOP equilibrium without worrying about its foreign currency reserves, it may like to adopt a flexible exchange rate regime. But, this target is achieved not without bearing any costs as the argument below indicates.

26.1.2 Insulating the Domestic Economy: Inflation and Output

An exchange rate adjustment that automatically corrects for any BOP imbalance under a flexible regime may not always be desirable since these changes have some far-reaching implications for the real sectors of the economy. A depreciation of the value of the domestic currency vis-à-vis the value of the foreign currency (or a depreciation of the exchange rate) in face of a BOP deficit may be inflationary. Recall from the discussion in Chapter 23 that an exchange rate depreciation raises the trade balance of the country under the elasticity condition $\frac{1}{\alpha}\varepsilon_u + \varepsilon_i > 1$, and consequently raises the effective demand for domestically produced goods. Under sticky wages and prices and with initial less-than-full-employment equilibrium, this increased demand will raise aggregate output and employment. But if the economy was already at full employment, the exchange rate depreciation will be inflationary. By similar reasoning, an appreciation of the exchange rate in the face of a BOP surplus lowers aggregate output and employment. Thus, external shocks such as change in tastes and preferences for goods consumed in the rest of the world, affect the real sector of the economy through changes in the exchange rate for its currency. Similarly, under flexible exchange rate regimes, monetary and fiscal policy changes are transmitted across the countries that are linked with each other through international trade. With falling barriers to international trade and increasing dependence of countries on each other in the present era of globalization, we can thus expect transmission effects to be much larger and pervasive, which are not always desirable. The severest of all is the transmission of inflation from one country to the other.

In fact, a flexible exchange rate regime may fuel inflationary pressure in an economy in more than one way. Consider, for example, a monetary expansion by our domestic economy under consideration. At near-full-employment, this will be inflationary. Further, by the argument of portfolio-choice approach or the Mundell-Flemming type monetary adjustment discussed in Chapter 24, the consequent decline in the domestic interest rate will cause the capital to flow out of the country and BOP to be in deficit. Excess demand for the foreign currency that such a BOP deficit (or capital outflow) implies will depreciate the exchange rate under clean float. The domestic-currency price of essential imported inputs (such as petroleum for oil-importing countries like India) thus rises and this causes further inflation. Moreover, if imports contain wage goods, exchange rate depreciation lowers the real wage of workers. Under unionized wage bargaining, there may thus be a demand for a higher money wage to compensate for this fall in real wage. This pushes the economy on to a path of wage-price inflation. Thus, a flexible exchange rate regime augments the inflationary pressure of a monetary (and similarly, a fiscal) expansion.

On this insulation property rests the major argument in favour of interventions in the foreign exchange market starting from a managed (or dirty) float to the extreme case of a pegged exchange rate regime. Under a pegged exchange rate regime any external shock changes only the reserve of the foreign currency held by the central bank of a country. Aggregate output now changes through the consequent change in the supply of domestic high-powered money (or the monetary base). But such real sector effects can be prevented through a policy of sterilization. Consider, for example, an exogenous decline in a country's exports due to a sudden change in tastes of foreigners away from their imported goods. If everything else remains the same, this causes a trade deficit and consequent excess demand for the foreign currency. The central bank now must sell foreign currency from its reserves in exchange for domestic currency to prevent the exchange rate from appreciating. The stock of high-powered money or domestic currency in circulation thus declines, which can be restored again at its initial level through an open market operation such as buying bonds issued to the public earlier. Thus, through sterilization of reserve flows, the economy can be insulated from external shocks under a pegged exchange rate regime.

Of course, there may be costs as well as practical limits of sterilization as we discuss later. But, the main point is that it is *feasible* to insulate the economy from adverse external shocks.

26.1.3 Uncertainty and Destabilizing Speculative Activity

Another case against a floating regime is the destabilizing speculative activity that the uncertainty regarding the movement of exchange rate may result in. If for some reasons, the domestic currency is depreciating and wealth holders expect that the domestic currency will depreciate further in the future, they will try to avoid future capital loss on holdings of the domestic currency assets. Foreign assets will thus be in demand in exchange for domestic assets. Alternatively, recalling the (uncovered) interest parity condition, a higher expected future depreciation of the domestic currency will raise the expected rate of return from foreign currency deposits over and above the rate of interest on domestic currency deposits. The portfolio of assets will thus shift in favour of foreign assets or foreign currency deposits. With all wealth holders acting similarly, the excess demand for foreign assets and the consequent excess demand for foreign currency will actually depreciate the exchange rate. Thus, wealth holders' expectations will be self-fulfilling. In the process, depreciation of the domestic currency accentuates. That is, speculation is destabilizing as it moves the exchange rate further away from its long run level.

Moreover, this destabilizing effect of speculation will add fuel to the price inflation that the exchange rate depreciation triggers for reasons spelled out above. Thus, an economy may find it difficult to contain price inflation when it adopts a flexible exchange rate regime and speculators actively engage in asset trading in expectation of future depreciation of the domestic currency.

26.1.4 Internal Balance and Effectiveness of Domestic Stabilizing Policies

When internal balance is the primary target of a country's government, benefits of a particular exchange rate regime depend on the policy instrument. As explained in the context of capital mobility in the Mundell-Flemming model, a pegged exchange rate regime makes a monetary policy totally ineffective. A monetary expansion is effective in raising aggregate output and employment in a less-than-full-employment situation only under a flexible exchange rate regime. A fiscal expansion, on the other hand, is effective under both exchange rate regimes, though its impact varies with the degree of capital mobility.

In cases of adverse internal shocks, a particular exchange rate regime may act as an automatic stabilizer for internal balance. However, which particular regime works better depends on the nature of the internal shock. The internal balance is more vulnerable to monetary shocks under a flexible exchange rate regime and to real shocks under a pegged regime. Consider, for example, a sudden increase in wealth holders' desire to hold real balances for any given domestic interest rate and income. The increased money demand, at the initial stock of money supply, raises the domestic interest rate above the world rate. This changes the portfolio of assets as wealth holders sell foreign currency assets in exchange for domestic currency to meet their increased desire to hold real balances. This, in turn, lowers the demand for foreign currency and appreciates the exchange rate. By the elasticity condition, trade balance worsens and consequently effective demand falls, which lowers aggregate output and employment. But under a pegged exchange rate regime, the central bank does not allow the exchange rate to appreciate by buying the foreign currency that the domestic wealth holders sell off. Thus, the stock of domestic currency in the economy rises, which restores the interest-parity condition and aggregate output and employment remain the same. That is, the adverse money market shock is absorbed through a monetary expansion.

On the other hand, an adverse real sector shock is partly absorbed in exchange rate changes under a clean float. The decline in aggregate output and employment can thus be minimized. But under a pegged regime such an adverse shock is realized entirely through a decline in aggregate output and employment. Figure 26.1 illustrates this case. Recall from the discussion in Chapter 24 that the *ee* curve represents the relationship between exchange rate and aggregate output (and income) that maintains equilibrium in the asset (or foreign exchange) market and in the money market. The Y_iY_i curve, on the other hand, represents the effective demand equilibrium. The initial equilibrium pair of exchange rate and income corresponds to point E_0 in both the panels. An adverse demand shock such as a change in tastes and preferences of domestic consumers towards foreign goods, lowers effective demand for domestically produced goods and consequently lowers aggregate output and income at the initial exchange rate. In both panels in Figure 26.1 this is shown by the leftward shift of the Y_iY_i curve. At the initial equilibrium exchange rate, aggregate output and (real) income falls by the amount aE_0. This lowers the (transactions) demand for money so that the desired holdings of money balance now fall short of the actual holdings. This induces people to buy bonds and assets, which in turn, serve to lower the domestic interest rate. This changes the portfolio choice and raises the demand for foreign currency. The exchange rate thus depreciates. Given the stability condition, such exchange rate depreciation raises income from its initially lower level. Therefore, exchange rate depreciation acts as a stabilizer as at the new equilibrium the income declines by a smaller magnitude than if there had been no change in the exchange rate.

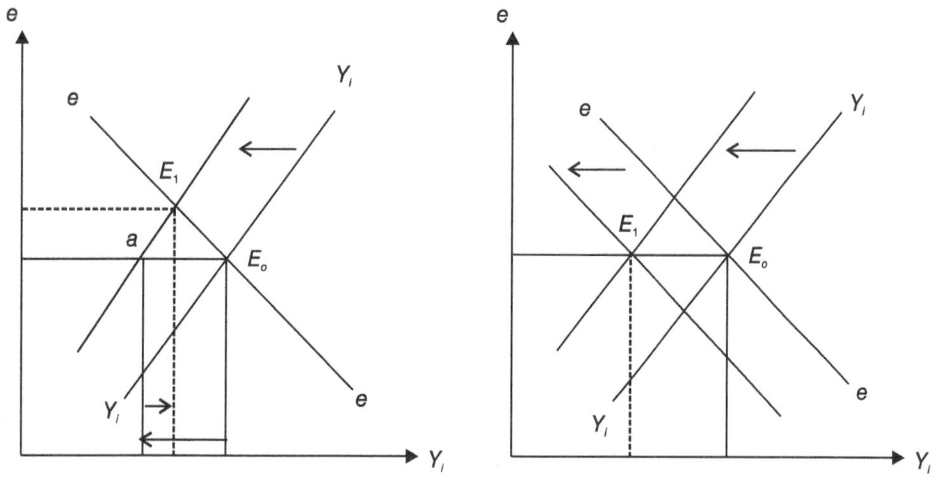

(a) Real Sector Shock under Clean Float (b) Real Sector Shock under Pegged Rate

Figure 26.1 Clean Float as Stabilizer of Real Sector Shocks

Under a pegged exchange rate, on the other hand, the adverse effect of the real shock will have been fully realized, as shown in panel (b). The logic is that when a decline in the domestic interest rate shifts the portfolio of assets towards foreign assets, and thereby raises the demand for foreign currency, the central bank intervenes in the foreign exchange market by selling dollars and thereby withdrawing real money supply to defend the pegged exchange rate. The *ee* curve thus shifts to the left as well, and the (real) income falls from E_0 to E_1.

26.1.5 Autonomy of Domestic Monetary Policy

The major argument in favour a flexible exchange rate regime is the autonomy of a country's central bank in pursuing monetary policy during periods of recession. Since exchange rate movements take care of the BOP problem, the central bank can use monetary policies in demand management. For example, when external shocks appreciate the exchange rate of a country's currency vis-à-vis foreign currencies and lowers aggregate output and employment, an expansionary monetary policy can be used to raise the effective demand for output at the initial level. To illustrate, suppose there is an exogenous adverse output shock and recession in the rest of the world. Under clean float, this transmits to the country under consideration as well. A plausible mechanism is through the interest parity condition and exchange rate appreciation. Recession in the rest of the world lowers the demand for money and thus lowers the rate of interest there. Domestic wealth holders then shift their portfolio of assets towards domestic assets by selling off foreign assets. Demand for foreign currency falls (or the demand for domestic currency rises) and the exchange rate appreciates. This, given the elasticity condition, lowers the effective demand for domestic output. In Figure 26.2, the *ee* curve shifts down along the Y_iY_i curve and aggregate output and employment in the country under consideration falls. In this case of recession in the outside world being transmitted to the domestic economy, the central bank has the *option* of pursuing an expansionary monetary policy to raise aggregate output at its initial level. An increase in domestic money supply now brings down the domestic interest rate to the level of the expected rate of interest on foreign assets to maintain the interest parity condition. The portfolio of assets thus remains the same as *before* the recession in the rest of the world, and so does exchange rate and output. In Figure 26.2, the increased money supply pushes up the *ee* curve to its original position. The point to remember is that the central bank is not obliged to pursue an expansionary monetary policy, but it may do so if it so wishes.

But under a pegged rate, this monetary expansion is no longer a policy option. During a recession in the rest of the world, the central bank of our domestic country *must* buy excess supply of dollars to prevent the exchange rate of its currency to appreciate. This raises domestic money supply, which at near-full-employment output level results in inflation. That is, under a pegged exchange rate regime, the central bank of the country cannot have the autonomy of an independent monetary policy.

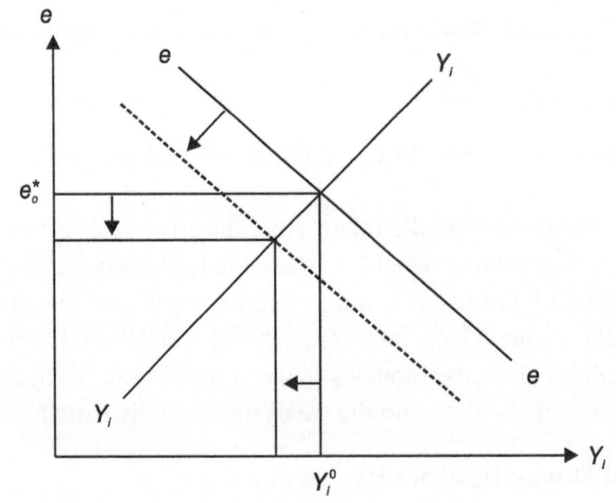

Figure 26.2 Autonomy of Monetary Policy under Clean Float

What is apparent from this discussion is a policy dilemma for a country that allows capital mobility. In the absence of direct capital controls, countries facing large capital inflows need to choose between nominal appreciation and inflation. We turn to this policy dilemma in the next section.

26.2 CAPITAL FLOWS, MONEY SUPPLY, AND EXCHANGE RATE: THE *IMPOSSIBLE TRINITY*

Countries that allow capital inflows potentially face a choice between a currency appreciation and domestic price inflation (Obstfeld and Taylor 2004). Large inflows of capital create an excess supply of foreign currency and thus appreciate the domestic currency. This currency appreciation erodes the country's export competitiveness and worsens its trade balance, which in turn lowers aggregate output and employment. That is, a large capital inflow, under clean float, is contractionary, when the aggregate output of an economy is effective demand determined. A policy response to this contractionary effect of a foreign capital inflow is to moderate the currency appreciation through buying of the excess supply of foreign currency by the central bank. But this means injecting more currency in the economy and thereby creating an inflationary pressure. India's experience has been similar since the mid-1990s. Large inflows of FDI and portfolio investments have forced RBI to moderate the consequent large appreciation of its currency vis-à-vis the US dollar and mitigate the adverse effect on aggregate output and employment through buying of dollars. This policy of managed float has been the primary feature of exchange rate management in India over almost the last two decades. The policy challenge now is to maintain a balance between currency appreciation and price inflation.

Thus, for countries that open up their capital account and experience large capital inflows a key policy decision is to what extent they must moderate the appreciation of their currencies by intervening in the foreign exchange market. The accumulation of foreign reserves required to keep the exchange rate from appreciating may lead to excessively loose monetary conditions, so that the real appreciation could occur through higher inflation, rather than through a decline in nominal exchange rates. This policy conflict is known as the *impossible trinity* paradigm of open economy macroeconomics: it is not possible to target the exchange rate, run an independent monetary policy, and allow full capital mobility simultaneously.

In practice, however, given that capital mobility is not perfect—even in the absence of direct capital controls—policymakers may have some scope to pursue intermediate options than this paradigm would suggest. Sterilization of reserve flows is such an option. Many countries have sought this sterilization of the monetary impact of intervention through open market operations and other measures in order to balance the monetary effects of capital inflows on the real sectors of their economies. But such sterilization may be difficult to execute and when assets are perfect substitutes so that the (uncovered) interest parity holds at the equilibrium, it will be self-defeating (see Box 24.4 in Chapter 24). Moreover, a successful sterilization may raise domestic interest rates and attract even larger capital inflows. On the other hand, imperfect asset substitutability is a necessary but not a sufficient condition for sterilized interventions to affect the exchange rate through changes in the portfolio of assets. There must be a stable relationship between government debt supplies and differential returns on domestic and foreign bonds.[1]

Moreover, it may be difficult for the monetary authority to *fully* offset the effects of a change in net foreign assets. In countries with less developed financial markets the ability to sterilize may be constrained by the development of the domestic bond market itself. There is also a fiscal burden of sterilization. As noted earlier, imperfect asset substitutability (and the corresponding interest rate differential) is a pre-requisite for sterilization to be successful. But in that case, when foreign capital flows in, sterilization requires that the central bank buys the low-yield foreign assets and sells the high-yield domestic assets. This is the fiscal cost of sterilization, and this depends on the interest differential between domestic and foreign assets. Furthermore, the accumulation of foreign assets consequent upon sterilization operations will expose the central bank to foreign exchange risk. If the domestic currency eventually appreciates, the country will experience a capital loss.

Because of these difficulties in sterilizing foreign reserve flows through open market operations, some countries have resorted to a *belts and braces* strategy, which combines indirect instruments of monetary policy with some capital controls.

Box 26.1 Foreign Exchange Reserves and Sterilization in China

In Chapter 22, we noted that in order to defend the pegged Renminbi in face of current account surpluses and large capital inflows, China has been buying foreign currencies and accumulating foreign exchange reserves. A large stock of foreign exchange reserves can be beneficial as well as a problem. A country can maintain a stable exchange rate in face of adverse BoP shocks and meet its foreign debt obligations if it has abundant foreign exchange reserves. But, an increase in foreign exchange reserves leads to an accumulation of foreign assets, which is a component of the money base. Thus, an increase in foreign exchange reserves causes a monetary expansion and puts inflationary pressures on the economy, resulting in an appreciation of the real exchange rate. Along with China, many East Asian countries like Indonesia, Korea, and Malaysia have experienced similar macroeconomic management problems induced by large private capital inflows during 1985–95. To offset the expansionary effect of the increasing foreign reserves, sterilization has been a common practice for monetary authorities of East Asian countries. China has also sterilized at least some of its rising foreign reserves, though the exact effectiveness of sterilization is unclear (Goodfriend and Prasad, 2006).

[1] If wealth holders recognize that they will have to pay higher taxes in the future, they will save the extra money in order to pay future taxes. Bonds issued under a sterilization operation cannot then be considered as net wealth. The extra saving by the public would exactly offset the extra spending by the government. Consequently, the overall demand will remain unchanged. This is known as the Ricardian equivalence. Sterilized intervention operations in such a case simply change the currency *composition*, and thus will have no effect on the foreign exchange market equilibrium.

26.3 OPTIMUM CURRENCY AREA

An optimum currency area is a geographical region, or a group of countries, that share a single currency. The theory of optimum currency area, pioneered by Robert Mundell (1961) and in an even earlier work by Abba P. Lerner, identifies criteria for a group of countries or regions to become a monetary or currency union, which is the final stage in economic integration that we discussed in Chapter 14. Note that a monetary union is the strongest form of a fixed exchange rate system as under a common and single currency the member countries effectively (and notionally) peg the value of their national currencies with each other.

Robert Mundell provides us three basic criteria for an optimum currency area or a successful monetary union. First, countries in the union should not be hit by highly asymmetric shocks so that while some countries experience deflation (or recession) the others experience inflation. Alternatively, countries must have similar business cycles. Recession (or boom) in one country in the currency union must be followed by recession (or boom) in all other countries. In either case, with symmetric shocks or similar business cycles, the optimal national monetary policies will be similar across countries in the monetary union. This makes the task easier for a supra-national monetary authority that manages the single currency: increase supply of the common currency in downturns (or in case of adverse output shocks) to promote growth and reduce it in booms (or expansionary output shocks) to mitigate inflationary pressure. But if countries in a monetary union have asymmetric or idiosyncratic business cycles, then optimal monetary policy for the countries diverges. Countries are, therefore, worse-off under a supra-national central bank and a single currency. Note that when a country joins a monetary or currency union, and accepts the common currency instead of its own national currency, its central bank loses the autonomy as well as the ability to respond to shocks through its own monetary policy.

Box 26.2 Monetary Cooperation, Monetary Integration and Monetary Union

International monetary cooperation can be defined to include exchange of information among monetary authorities and consultations among policymakers regarding the choice of monetary and exchange rate regimes. Cooperation is sometimes used interchangeably with the term coordination, which Frankel (1988) describes as 'the agreement by two or more countries to a cooperative set of policy changes, where neither would wish to undertake the policy change on its own'. Thus, monetary coordination is more specific than monetary cooperation. Coordination already involves the adoption of a mutually agreed policy stance, whereas monetary cooperation is a gradual process in which lower levels of monetary cooperation may provide the basis for an active coordination of monetary and exchange rate policies. A Monetary Union is defined as a Common Currency Area in which member countries use a common currency issued by a single central bank, instead of national currencies issued by the central banks of respective member countries. Monetary Integration, on the other hand, comprises all forms of coordinated currency stabilization including but not limited to a Monetary Union. Thus, Monetary Integration seems to be the highest form of policy coordination in the gradual process of monetary cooperation among a group of countries. That is, Monetary Integration is a much broader concept of cooperation and policy coordination than Monetary Union. It creates scope for not only a monetary union but also coordinated pegging to the same anchor currency or currency basket, and the establishment of a common exchange rate system.

This requirement of symmetric or not-too-asymmetric shocks in the union for an optimum currency area can be further explained by the following example. Suppose countries participating in the currency union have similar trade patterns with the rest of the world. If there is a sudden exogenous fall in demand in the rest of the world for goods exported by this group of countries, the countries will similarly be hit and the net exports of the entire union will fall. In each country, aggregate output and income will fall and accordingly people will have lower transaction demand for money. Thus, a part of their actual money holding will now be undesired holding. This will induce wealth holders across the union to buy assets and thereby lower national interest rates. With interest rates declining everywhere in the union, there will be capital outflow from the entire region to the rest of the world. This will worsen BOP of the union as a whole and depreciate the value of the common currency vis-à-vis the currencies in the rest of the world. This depreciation improves the trade balance and restores the BOP equilibrium in all countries alike in the union. The initial output shock in the entire region is also mitigated. But if instead, a country, small enough in the region, had a different export basket (say, Portugal in the European Union) and there had been a decline in demand for its exports in the rest of the world, we would have an asymmetric shock. This is because only Portugal's net exports would have fallen. Consequently, with only its own national interest rate declining for reasons similar to that spelled out above, there would have been a capital outflow to other countries in the union. Portugal having this asymmetric shock but being small in the union under our presumption, the net exports of the union as a whole would have remained unchanged and the exchange rate for the common currency would not have changed as well unlike in the case of a symmetric shock. In Figure 26.3, in a Mundell-Flemming setup, the IS curve for Portugal would have shifted left and its interest rate r_P would have declined below the (common) rate in the union r^* (as well as in the rest of the world, r_w). Thus the only effect would have been a contraction in the money supply in our small country (Portugal) which would have lowered output further. Note that the common currency would not have allowed Portugal to mitigate this secondary adverse effect on its aggregate output through policies like sterilization. Thus, in cases of asymmetric shocks like this, it is not optimal for a country to join the currency union and adopt the common single currency.

The second criterion for an optimum currency area is that there should be a high degree of labour mobility across the region or countries that adopt a common single currency. Mobility of labour or free movement of people requires physical and institutional arrangements such as visas and work permits, and lack of cultural barriers such as different languages and customs. To explain how important this labour mobility criterion is, suppose countries in a region are asymmetric in terms of their level of industrialization and export baskets. A bad monsoon adversely hits agricultural production and agricultural exports, but the magnitude of output and employment loss is felt non-uniformly across these countries. This is an example of an *asymmetric* shock. If unemployed workers in the worse hit country are able to migrate to other countries in the monetary union and find jobs, then the adverse impact of the asymmetric shock will be mitigated in that country. In isolation, or not being part of the monetary union, the country would have suffered because the unemployed could not move into the other countries for gainful employment. There is thus a clear benefit of forming a monetary union in cases of asymmetric shocks. Higher the ease with which people can move within the union, larger will be such benefits (or smaller will be the adverse asymmetric shock realized in one country). The alternative to labour mobility across countries in the union is wage flexibility. In such a case, those who lose jobs due to an asymmetric adverse shock in a country can be absorbed through lower wages. Lower wages will make outputs competitive, increase exports of the country and thereby provide gainful employment.

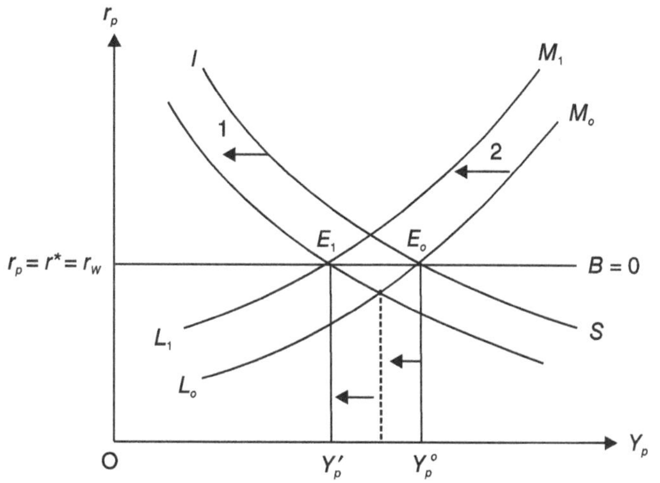

Figure 26.3 Asymmetric Shock in a Common Currency Area

The third criterion is that there must be a common fiscal policy rule based on a risk sharing system such as an automatic fiscal transfer mechanism to redistribute money and fiscal resources from the booming countries to those that are adversely affected by asymmetric shocks. Essentially this requires a tax-and-transfer policy agreed upon by all member countries according to certain norms for fiscal discipline and risk-sharing. Though theoretically this fiscal policy criterion makes sense, politically it is difficult to implement and is often not feasible since the better performing countries would be unwilling to forego a part of their revenues to finance recovery in other countries in periods of their recession.

The Euro-zone is often cited as the optimum currency area, but the criteria that the European countries defined in the Maastricht Treaty to determine membership in the European Monetary Union (EMU) are very different from the above set of Mundell-criteria. These criteria essentially required convergence in inflation rates, interest rates, fiscal deficits, debt, and exchange rate stability preceding the formation of the optimum currency area or EMU. Moreover, despite strong economic and trade linkages among countries in EU, asymmetries do exist in terms of the level of industrialization and dependence on agriculture. Thus, some countries are more vulnerable to certain shocks than others. On the other hand, though physical barriers to labour mobility within EU may have fallen significantly making it easier for people to move from one region to the other, and the cultural heterogeneity may be far less compared to what we observe between countries in Europe and America, language barriers are still quite dominant. Wage flexibility is also far from realized throughout Europe. Powerful trade unions

Box 26.3 Keynesian Critique of a Currency Area

The notion of a single currency in a monetary union without fiscal authority has been criticized by economists in the Keynesian and post-Keynesian tradition as a loss of monetary sovereignty of the countries. In the Keynesian effective demand theory, a fiscal expansion in the form of deficit spending is the only possible way out for an economy that finds itself in a liquidity trap. Such expansions will, however, not be possible if countries in a currency union are not allowed fiscal and monetary sovereignty to run sufficiently high budget and fiscal deficits. Moreover, a country's ability to print money is fundamental to its ability to monetize large fiscal deficits and thereby its ability to command the resources needed for raising aggregate output and employment. According to Keynesians and post-Keynesians, this loss of fiscal sovereignty far outweighs the transactional benefits of a common currency in a union.

have been instrumental in a high degree of wage regulations. Furthermore, concerned by fiscal indiscipline, Germany in particular took up a proactive role in including a provision of Growth and Stability Pact (GSP) in 1997, which required countries to limit their fiscal deficits within 3 per cent of their respective national GDPs. Countries overstepping this limit are to be fined whereas those having severe recession, measured by a contraction of GDP by 2 per cent or more, are allowed to spend more than the 3 per cent limit. But, GSP has a no-bailout clause, meaning that fiscal transfers across countries are not allowed. During the debt crisis in Europe in 2010, however, this no-bailout clause in GSP was abandoned. But on the whole, whether countries in EMU sharing the euro as a common currency form an optimum currency area is debatable.

SUMMARY POINTS

- It is difficult to make a once for all choice in favour of a particular exchange rate regime. The choice depends on a country's policy target.
- The major advantage of adopting a flexible exchange rate is BOP equilibrium. Any BOP imbalance, deficit or surplus, is automatically and instantaneously corrected through an exchange rate adjustment.
- But this target is achieved not without bearing any costs. A flexible exchange rate regime may fuel inflationary pressure in an economy in more than one ways.
- Containing price inflation is even harder under a flexible exchange rate regime when speculators actively engage in asset trading in expectation of future depreciation of the domestic currency.

(*contd*)

Summary Points (*contd*)

- A major argument in favour of interventions in foreign exchange rests on the insulation property. Under a pegged exchange rate regime any external shock changes only the reserves of the foreign currency held by the central bank of a country. Real sector effects can be mitigated through a policy of sterilization.
- When internal balance is the primary target of a country's government, benefits of a particular exchange rate regime depend on the policy instrument. A monetary expansion is effective in raising aggregate output and employment in a less-than-full-employment situation only under a flexible exchange rate regime. A fiscal expansion, on the other hand, is effective under both exchange rate regimes, though its impact varies with the degree of capital mobility.
- The internal balance is more vulnerable to monetary shocks under a flexible exchange rate regime and to real shocks under a pegged regime. An adverse real sector shock is partly absorbed in exchange rate changes under a clean float. The decline in aggregate output and employment can thus be minimized.
- Under a pegged exchange rate regime, the central bank of the country cannot have the autonomy of an independent monetary policy. It is not possible to target the exchange rate, run an independent monetary policy, and allow full capital mobility simultaneously.
- The Mundell criteria for an optimum currency area or a successful monetary union require that the member countries must have similar business cycles, there should be a high degree of labour mobility across the region or countries, and there must be a common fiscal policy rule based on a risk sharing system.

KEYWORDS

- **Impossible trinity** paradigm of an open economy macroeconomics states that it is not possible to target the exchange rate, run an independent monetary policy, and allow full capital mobility simultaneously.
- Buying low-yield foreign assets and selling off high-yield domestic assets (or the converse) is the **fiscal cost of sterilization** of reserves flows.
- **Belts and braces strategy** is a combination of indirect instruments of monetary policy and some degree of capital control.
- **Currency area** is a geographical region or a group of countries that share a single currency. It is an *optimum currency area* if the countries satisfy the three Mundell-criteria.
- **Growth and Stability Pact** is a fiscal provision in EMU that requires countries to limit their fiscal deficits within 3 per cent of their respective national GDPs.

EXERCISES

1. How is price inflation caused by domestic monetary expansion in a country accentuated under a clean float?
2. On what assumption is the insulation argument for a pegged exchange rate valid?
3. Suppose there is an oil-price shock. How does it affect the exchange rate and output for an oil-importing country like India? Can the adverse effects of this shock, if any, be avoided under a pegged exchange rate regime?
4. Why is it practically impossible to control the exchange rate and at the same time pursue an independent monetary policy when capital flows are allowed?
5. Define an optimum currency area. How relevant is the requirement that countries in the currency union be hit by symmetric shocks?

SUGGESTED READING

Krugman, P.R. and M. Obstfeld. (2000). *International Economics: Theory and Policy*, Fifth Edition. New Delhi: Pearson Education Asia.

ADVANCED READING

Frankel, J. (1988). 'Obstacles to International Macroeconomic Policy Coordination'. Journal of Public Policy: 353–74.

Goodfriend, Marvin and Prasad, Eswar. (2006). 'A Framework for Independent Monetary Policy in China'. *Economic Studies*, 53(1): 2–41.

Mundell, R.A. (1961). 'A Theory of Optimum Currency Areas', *American Economic Review*, 51(4): 657–65.

Obstfeld, M. and A. Taylor. (2004). *Global Capital Markets: Integration, Crisis, and Growth.* Cambridge, MA: Cambridge University Press.

Glossary of International Agencies

ASIAN DEVELOPMENT BANK (ADB)

www.adb.org

The ADB was founded in 1966 with an aim to free Asia and the Pacific region from poverty. Approximately 1.8 billion people in the region are estimated to be poor and unable to access essential goods, services, assets, and opportunities to which every human is entitled. The ADB aims at improving the livelihood of these people by investing in infrastructure, health care services, and financial and public administration systems. It also provides loans to the developing countries in the region.

FOOD AND AGRICULTURAL ORGANIZATION (FAO)

www. fao.org

FAO is an intergovernmental organization which has 191 member nations, two associate members, and one member organization—the European Union. Its headquarters is in Rome. As a knowledge organization, FAO creates and shares critical information about food, agriculture, and natural resources in the form of global public goods. FAO's mandate is to ensure food security for all, raise levels of nutrition, improve agricultural productivity, better the lives of rural populations, and contribute to the growth of the world economy.

GENERAL AGREEMENT ON TARIFFS AND TRADE (GATT)

The GATT is a multilateral agreement amongst countries for facilitating international trade. It was intended to achieve global free trade through substantial reduction of tariffs and other trade barriers based on a rule of reciprocation. GATT was signed in 1947 and in it was replaced by the World Trade Organization in 1995. The original GATT 1947 text is still in effect under the WTO framework, subject to the modifications of GATT 1994.

See also Keywords, Chapter 14.

INTERNATIONAL LABOUR ORGANIZATION (ILO)

www.ilo.org

The ILO is the international organization responsible for drawing up and overseeing international labour standards. It is the only tripartite United Nations agency that brings together representatives of governments, employers, and workers to jointly shape policies and promote decent work for all. The ILO was founded in 1919 and became the first specialized agency of the UN in 1946. The main aims of the ILO are to promote rights at work, encourage decent employment opportunities, enhance social protection, and strengthen dialogue on work-related issues.

INTERNATIONAL MONETARY FUND (IMF)

www.imf.org

The IMF promotes international monetary cooperation and exchange rate stability, facilitates the balanced growth of international trade, and provides resources to help members in balance of payments difficulties or to assist with poverty reduction. The IMF has 188 member countries. It is a specialized agency of the United Nations but has its own charter, governing structure, and finances. Its members are represented through a quota system broadly based on their relative size in the global economy.

UNITED NATIONS CONFERENCE ON TRADE AND DEVELOPMENT (UNCTAD)

www.unctad.org

Established in 1964, UNCTAD promotes the integration of developing countries into the world economy. UNCTAD has progressively evolved into an authoritative knowledge-based institution whose work aims to help shape current policy debates and thinking on development, with a particular focus on ensuring that domestic policies and international action are mutually supportive in bringing about sustainable development.

The organization works to fulfill this mandate by carrying out three key functions. First, it functions as a forum for intergovernmental deliberations, supported by discussions with experts and exchanges of experience, aimed at consensus building. Second, it undertakes research, policy analysis, and data collection for the debates of government representatives and experts. Third, it provides technical assistance to the specific requirements of the developing countries, the least developed countries, and economies in transition. UNCTAD also cooperates with other organizations and donor countries in providing such technical assistance.

The first UNCTAD was held in Geneva in 1964. Thereafter, the conference was institutionalized to meet every four years, with intergovernmental bodies meeting between sessions and a permanent secretariat providing the necessary substantive and logistical support.

WORLD BANK

www.worldbank .org

The World Bank is an international financial institution that provides loans to the developing countries for their capital programmes. The World Bank's official goal is to reduce poverty.

According to the World Bank's Articles of Agreement (as amended effective 16 February 1989), all of its decisions must be guided by a commitment to promote foreign investment, international trade, and facilitate capital investment.

The World Bank is one of the five institutions created at the Bretton Woods Conference in 1944. Although both are based in Washington, D.C., the World Bank is traditionally headed by a citizen of the United States.

In 2010, voting powers at the World Bank were revised to increase the voice of developing countries, notably China. The countries with most voting power are now the United States (15.85 per cent), Japan (6.84 per cent), China (4.42 per cent), Germany (4.00 per cent), the United Kingdom (3.75 per cent), France (3.75 per cent), India (2.91 per cent), Russia (2.77 per cent), Saudi Arabia (2.77 per cent), and Italy (2.64 per cent). Under the changes, the countries, other than China, that saw significant gains included South Korea, Turkey, Mexico, Singapore, Greece, Brazil, India, and Spain. Most developed countries' voting power was reduced, along with a few poor countries such as Nigeria. The voting powers of the United States, Russia, and Saudi Arabia were unchanged.

WORLD TRADE ORGANIZATION (WTO)

www.wto.org

For the purpose of establishing and monitoring rules for international trade in goods and services, the WTO was established through the Marrakech Agreement, and came into force on 1 January 1995. The WTO replaced the GATT and introduced new rules of trade policy that extends beyond the coverage of the GATT, and the multilateral and the plurilateral agreements. These new rules and agreements now govern the world trading system.

See Chapter 19 for a detailed discussion.

Index

About the Author

Rajat Acharyya is currently Professor of Economics, and Director (Additional Charge) of UGC-Human Resource Development Centre, Jadavpur University, Kolkata, India, and the former Dean, Faculty of Arts, Jadavpur University. He has published extensively in different areas of international economics, and is the editor of the e-journal *Trade and Development Review*. His current research interests include trade, export quality, and labour market implications. He is the author of *International Trade and Economic Development* (2014, co-authored with Saibal Kar), *Trade and Environment* (Oxford India Short Introductions Series, 2013), *Product Standards, Employment and Exports: An Analytical Study* (2005), and *International Trade, Wage Inequality and the Developing Countries: A General Equilibrium Approach* (2003, co-authored with Sugata Marjit). Volumes edited by him include *Research Methodology for Social Sciences* (2020, co-edited with Nandan Bhattacharya), *Trade, Globalization and Development: Essays in Honour of Kalyan K. Sanyal* (2013, co-edited with Sugata Marjit) and *Essays on International Trade: Theory and Policy for the Developing Economies* (2005). He was honoured with the EXIM Bank International Trade Research Award in 1997, the Global Development Network (Washington, D.C.) Research Medal in 2003, the Mahalanobis Memorial Medal Award in 2006 and the Shiksharatna (Best Teacher, University) award of the Government of West Bengal in 2016. Among his many assignments abroad, he was a Ford Foundation Research Fellow at Rochester University, USA (1997–98), Visiting Fellow at the University of Kent at Canterbury, UK (2008–10), and Visiting Professor at Utrecht University School of Economics, the Netherlands (2010).

9 780192 865144